Peony Pavilion *Onstage*

Four Centuries in the Career of a Chinese Drama

Catherine C. Swatek

CENTER FOR CHINESE STUDIES
THE UNIVERSITY OF MICHIGAN
ANN ARBOR

MICHIGAN MONOGRAPHS IN CHINESE STUDIES
SERIES ESTABLISHED 1968

Published by
Center for Chinese Studies
The University of Michigan
Ann Arbor, Michigan 48109-1106

First paperback edition 2012

Printed and bound by CPI Group (UK) Ltd, Croydon, CR0 4YY

Chapter 3 is a revised version of "Plum and Portrait: Feng Menglong's Revision of *The Peony Pavilion,* which first appeared in *Asia Major,* third series, vol. 4, part 1 (1993). Permission to reprint this material granted by *Asia Major.*

Library of Congress Cataloging-in-Publication Data

Swatek, Catherine Crutchfield.
Peony Pavilion onstage : four centuries in the career of a Chinese drama / Catherine C. Swatek.
p. cm. – (Michigan monographs in Chinese studies ; no. 88)
Includes bibliographical references and index.
ISBN 978-0-89264-136-9 (alk. paper)
1. Tang, Xianzu, 1550-1616. Mu dan ting. 2. Opera, Chinese – China – Kunshan Xian – History and criticism. 3. Chinese drama – History and criticism.
I. Title: Four centuries in the career of a Chinese drama. II. Title. III. Series.
PL2695.M83 S93 2002
895.1'246—dc 21

2001037225

ISBN 978-0-89264-908-2 (pbk. : alk. paper)

Contents

Illustrations

Acknowledgments

The books of C. T. Hsia made me want to study Chinese literature. He has been a generous mentor and an unsparing critic of my work, and I am proud to be counted among his students. David Roy, my cousin, has inspired me as well, as have his parents, Andrew T. and Margaret C. Roy. When in 1965 I formed the plan to study Chinese in Hong Kong, I never dreamed that our interests would converge on the same period and perhaps even the same author.

In 1978, Hu Wanchuan planted the seed when he suggested that I make the plays of Feng Menglong the subject of my dissertation. Feng Menglong's adaptations of *Mudan ting* and *Handan ji* led me to the originals, which captured my interest more. In 1982, Andrew Plaks made *Mudan ting* the focus of a seminar at Princeton, and chapter 3 grew out of ideas first presented there. The next year, I was able to read both *Mudan ting* and *Fengliu meng* with Lu Shulun of Fudan University, an authority on Feng Menglong and late Ming vernacular literature, who also introduced me to Kun opera. His patient and at times bemused responses to my questions reined in my tendency to overread Tang's erotic language and taught me a great deal about *chuanqi* drama. Lindy Mark suggested that I stop studying the arcane details of prosody and consider instead how *Mudan ting* has been performed. David Rolston continued to push me in this direction, suggesting that such a study could also sketch the outlines of Kun opera's history. He and his family provided a home away from home in 1994-95, and his steadfast support and careful reading and criticism of every draft have enabled me to complete the book. I am deeply indebted to him. The Center for Chinese Studies at the University of Michigan provided support in the form of a postdoctoral fellowship and offered to publish the manuscript at a critical moment in my career.

With additional support from the Committee on Scholarly Communication with China, I spent four months in Shanghai in the summer of 1995 gathering materials and deepening my understanding of Kun opera as it is currently performed. Through the good offices of Xie Boliang of the Shanghai Theatre Academy, I was made welcome at the Shanghai Kun Opera Troupe and the Shanghai Opera School. At the troupe Zhang Wanliang, the troupe's librarian, went out of his way to make me feel welcome, facilitated relations with members of the troupe, took me on excursions to Suzhou and Kunshan, and generously shared with me materials from his personal library. He often observed that you cannot write without materials, and I thank him for his help and his friendship. Cai Zhengren, head of the troupe, allowed me to observe rehearsals unimpeded and authorized my purchase of videotapes from the troupe's archive. Yue Meiti, a senior actor, graciously allowed me to observe rehearsals of "Wandering In the Garden, Startled by a Dream" she supervised and even offered at one point to teach me in how to sing the *xiaosheng* role. Isabel Wong smoothed my way at the troupe with introductions, shared her considerable knowledge of Kun opera, and offered her unique perspective on the controversies that plagued the Lincoln Center production. At the Shanghai Opera School, Zhang Xunpeng, a *guimendan* specialist, welcomed me to her classes, shared her thoughts about how to perform *Mudan ting*, and became an invaluable guide to the intricacies of performing *Mudan ting*. I was also welcomed to the weekly meeting of the Kun opera singing club, many of whose members invited me to their homes to share the pleasure of singing and performing *zhezixi*.

For access to materials I have many to thank. At Columbia Univesity, Ken Harlin and Charles Wu have offered help over the years, as have Linda Joe and Eleanor Yuen at the Asian Library of the University of British Columbia. Wu Ge gave timely access to reference materials at the Fudan University Library, shared with me his enthusiasm for Kun opera, and offered slices of watermelon during the dog days of August. At the Shanghai Library I received critical assistance from a man I knew only as Tang Xiansheng, who plucked me from obscurity in the third floor reading room and kept me supplied me with as many stacks of hand-copied scripts as I had time to peruse. Others who assisted along the way are Dr. Mi Chu of the Library of Congress, Jean Han at Berkeley's East Asian Library, and Dr. Y. C. Wan and Cheung Mo-ching at the Fung Ping Shan Library of the University of Hong Kong. Both the East Asian Library and the Fung Ping Shan Library sent photo reproductions of the woodblock illustration that appears on the dust jacket; the image supplied by Fung Ping Shan was used because of the exceptional quality of their imprint. I have also spent profitable hours at Princeton's Gest Library, the Harvard-Yenching Library, and the East Asian Library of the University of Chicago. Andrea Goldman, Jiang Jurong, Sheila Melvin, Oki Yasushi, David Rolston, David Roy, Kate Stevens, and Judith Zeitlin have shared materials with me and provided useful references.

Peter Sellars welcomed me to rehearsals of *Peony Pavilion* as the show toured in 1998-1999 and permitted unfettered access to his actors. Keven Higa, his assistant, was always responsive to my requests and kept me supplied with media coverage of the show. Susan Jain, translator and consultant for the production, also welcomed me to rehearsals and has become a good friend and colleague. Hua Wenyi, whom I first met in Shanghai in 1983, shared thoughts about the production on several occasions; it was a privilege to be able to observe her and Mr. Sellars at close hand. I was not able to attend rehearsals of the Lincoln Center production, but Chen Shi-Zheng, its director, gave me a lengthy interview in New York. I also profited from many long conversations with Sheila Melvin about the Lincoln Center production and the circumstances in Shanghai that contributed to the show's demise in 1998. Her friendship is another gain from my two years spent pursuing Peonies on three continents.

Judith Zeitlin read several drafts of the manuscript and offered suggestions about how to improve it. I thank her for her enthusiasm and support from the earliest stages of the project. Professors Cyril Birch and Robert Hegel also read the entire manuscript at a critical time and made helpful suggestions. David Roy read both dissertation and book manuscript, which are much the better for his erudition. Other friends and colleagues who have read portions of the manuscript and offered suggestions are Maggie Bickford, Chou Wan-yao, Katy Carlitz, Bryna Goodman, Howard Goodman, and two readers for *Asia Major.* In China Bu Jian, Gu Duhuang, JiangJurong, and Xu Fuming opened up new lines of inquiry. Charles Stone put his expertise about computers at my service in the late stages of editing and when compiling the index, as did Ken Takashima, my colleague at UBC. Naomi Sawada advised about technical details for reproducing the dustjacket image, and Christine Tan shared her knowledge about the print's history. Kwon Hyukchan and Lu Yipeng typed the Chinese characters for the book; Dai Lianbin assisted with the index, read the entire manuscript, and saved me from several embarrassing errors.

Writing and editing a book of this length and complexity has taxed me to the limit, and I am deeply indebted to my friends for their support along the way. In Vancouver, Alison Bailey, Alexia Bloch, Chen Jo-shui, Chou Wan-yao, Alexandra Diebel, Joy Dixon, Eli Franco, Tineke Hellwig, Hilary Mason, Sharlyn Orbaugh, Karin Preisendanz, and Linda Robbins have kept me sane. Among colleagues at UBC, I owe Ken Bryant a special debt for his efforts to win me the time needed to complete the manuscript. More distantly, Katy Carlitz, Margaret Decker, Bryna Goodman, JaHyun Kim Haboush, Kathryn Hansen, Laurel Kendall, Suzanne Lebsock, and Carla Petievich have been my friends, consultants, and in some cases my critics too. While still in New York I enjoyed reading *chuanqi* plays with Li Yao-tsung; in Princeton Diane Perushek provided working space in the Gest Library and living space in her home for a summer. Margaret Mirabelli expertly tightened my prose. Terre

Fisher, my editor, gave the manuscript two exhaustive readings, offering many suggestions about how to improve it and accommodated my efforts to wring errors out of the text. Those that remain are my responsibility.

I have been fortunate to have a large and close-knit family. My parents supported me always in my studies and encouraged me to explore the world, and my mother's family has had everything to do with my chosen career. I dedicate this book to my aunts Margaret and Harriet and my mother Catherine, who all encouraged me to go to China.

Note to Readers

When referring to Tang Xianzu's play, I use the original title, *Mudan ting*; when referring to Peter Sellars's production, I use *Peony Pavilion*, which is how it appeared in the stagebills. When referring to Chen Shi-Zheng's production of the play I use *The Peony Pavilion*, which was how that production was billed. And finally, when referring to Cyril Birch's translation of the play, I also use *The Peony Pavilion*, since that is the published title.

There is a shift in terminology that may be puzzling without a word of explanation: In chapter 6 where I discuss Sellars's production of the play in detail, the central "plum" image becomes "apricot," after Birch's translation.

With the exception of lyrics quoted in chapter 3 and items gathered in Appendix C, I have used romanized versions of Chinese titles, names, and terms in the main text and notes, and provide characters for them in a glossary. Characters provided in Appendix C and the bibliography are not repeated in the glossary.

Articles from the Chinese press cited in the notes to chapters 1 and 7 are not included in the bibliography, but Chinese characters for their authors, titles, and publications are given in the glossary.

With the exception of Sister Stone and Scabby Turtle, I use the Chinese version of characters' names in the main text and the notes. When referring to titles of scenes or *zhezixi*, I use the English translation in the main text and notes, and give a romanized version of the Chinese in Appendix B.

Part One

Peony Pavilion and Literati Playwrights

❀One

Mudan ting and the Theatrical Culture of Kun Opera

> As for *Mudan ting* [Peony Pavilion], you must perform it according to my original version; on no account can you follow the one revised by Lü. Although he has changed [only] a word or two to facilitate vulgar singing, still, his adaptation greatly differs from my original idea![1]

So wrote Tang Xianzu (1550–1616) to Luo Zhang'er, an actor he had directed in performances of his play, which was completed in the autumn of 1598. After his permanent retirement from office in that year Tang devoted much of his time to writing plays and directing performances of them in his native Linchuan (in modern Jiangxi Province).[2] He was well connected with other prominent dramatists—protégé of Xu Wei (1521–1593), friend of Ling Mengchu (1580–1644) and Zang Maoxun (1550–1620), and close friend of Pan Zhiheng (1556–1621), whose writings are an important window onto the world of late Ming theater. The impression gleaned from Tang's poetry and letters conforms to one we have of other literati who immersed themselves in the theater at this time. He enjoyed singing dramatic arias, but apparently did not take part himself in performances of fully staged plays. He did, however, work closely with professional actors, directing performances of his plays in a hall specially designed for that purpose inside the Tang lineage compound.

Perhaps the earliest mention of a performance of *Mudan ting* is a poem by Tang—the second of two "written in a tipsy condition" during a banquet:

> In White Camelia Hall we open the spring jade screens,
> The newly written lyrics of *Mudan ting* are being sung.
> It pains me that none can understand the placement of the beats,
> So I strike the clappers myself and teach the young actors.[3]

If this performance took place in 1599, as seems likely,[4] then 1999 marked the 400th anniversary of *Mudan ting*'s debut, and also the year of its second debut outside China, before audiences in Europe and North America. One aim of this study is to chart the course of its transmission and dissemination as a performed libretto over this four-hundred-year period. Another aim will be to explore the reasons for *Mudan ting*'s appeal to audiences from a broad social and cultural spectrum, in China and now outside China as well. In 1998 the American director Peter Sellars, working in collaboration with the Kun opera actress Hua Wenyi and the composer Tan Dun, staged an avant-garde version of *Mudan ting*. As this production toured in Europe and North America, an eighteen-hour version directed by Chen Shi-Zheng had its world premiere in New York in July 1999. These intercultural experiments got underway at a time when opera in China—especially classical Kun opera, the style in which *Mudan ting* is usually performed—is on the verge of extinction and creative talent is gravitating to centers outside China's mainland.[5]

I discuss these global productions in chapters 6 and 7, while the four other chapters examine what became of *Mudan ting* after it left the hands of its author. It achieved wide popularity and was subsequently disseminated in numerous editions, adaptations, and libretti, which were used for performances that ranged from "pure singing" at private gatherings to full stagings in commercial theaters. *Mudan ting*'s history, in print and onstage, replicates the history of Kun opera from the period of its greatest flourishing in the late Ming until the severe decline of the last one hundred or more years. It lends itself to a study of this kind because its popularity has been enduring, and its history richly documented as a result.

In what forms did *Mudan ting* circulate? How do the forms in which it circulated reflect changing interpretations of the play? A paradoxical aspect of *Mudan ting*'s appeal is that its linguistic texture, scene structure, character delineation, and plot development are hardly typical for a *chuanqi* romance, yet it has long been a sentimental hit with opera lovers.[6] Tang Xianzu's playwriting talents dazzled his highly literate peers, yet this most famous of his plays achieved iconic status in the repertoire of southern dramas that were popular on the "vulgar" stage. A good deal of what follows will consider *Mudan ting* as the crown jewel of the Kun opera repertoire. But this study also seeks to keep in sight the play that Tang wrote, which is one of the masterpieces of premodern Chinese literature. I examine the adaptations and revisions of *Mudan ting*, which constitute my primary sources, in their own right, but I also use them as lenses through which to examine the original play as Tang conceived it.

Earliest Performances of *Mudan ting*

The poem quoted above indicates that *Mudan ting* was performed shortly after Tang finished it, by actors with whom he worked closely. Tang referred to them either by name or as "the Yihuang actors." They were professional artists who performed at private gatherings in a new hall of the lineage residence, on a dais subsequently named Simengtai (Terrace of Four Dreams). Couplets, perhaps composed by Tang himself, but more likely written by one of his descendents, flanked this stage:

> Long have [actors on the stage] feigned loyalty, filiality, honesty, and chastity;
> If you take [their feigning] to be true, you are no different than a madman babbling about his dreams.[7]
> At times [characters in a play] are happy or sad, together or parted;
> If you consider their feelings to be false, you are like a deaf-mute watching a play.[8]

Yihuang, a district in Jiangxi, was also a local style of southern drama that grew out of the Haiyan regional musical style (*qiang*). This style remained popular in Jiangxi despite the rapidly growing prestige of Kun opera, another regional style of music centered around Suzhou to the north, in Zhejiang Province. In Linchuan, drama supported large numbers of people. A dedicatory inscription Tang wrote for a temple to the patron deity of the Yihuang actors mentions that upwards of a thousand were able to support themselves in this line of work. Having learned *Mudan ting* under Tang's direct supervision, some actors performed selected scenes in his home and the homes of his friends, but they also on occasion traveled and performed far from Linchuan, as the popularity of Tang's plays spread. Mei Dingzuo (1549–1618), a close friend of the playwright, recounts their visit to Xuancheng in Anhui:

> When the Yihuang actors came to our sparsely populated town, we could not offer them much. Still, the troupes that came from Wu and Yue were not as popular as yours. This is mainly owing to the fame of your *Mudan ting* and *Handan ji* [The Tale of Handan]. Nonetheless, the [Yihuang] actors were unable to perform more than three [scenes] out of ten. Among them,

> only Chen Shangzhi was good, and his disciple stuttered continuously—it was very funny. In our remote village, the Rites of Fortune are often held at the end of the winter. At that time we have a lot of plays performed. However, the Yihuang actors suddenly hurried home.[9]

The occasion Mei describes likely included public performances of *Mudan ting* as well as private ones. His account makes clear that the actors' success in this case depended more on the popularity of Tang's plays than their skill in performing them, despite the fact that Tang had worked closely with at least some of them and had made severe demands on them artistically. The dedicatory inscription Tang wrote for the actors' temple describes at length what makes a good actor:

> First concentrate your spirit, and maintain an upright bearing and an empty mind. Select a good teacher and fellow actors. Obtain a broad grasp of the language and ideas in the plays. When active, observe the transformations of Heaven and Earth, men and ghosts, the world and the objects in it; when still, bring your thoughts to bear on these transformations. Break free of the burdens of parents and family; give no thought to sleep or food. When young, maintain your purity and cultivate your looks; when grown, eat simple and bland food to cultivate your voice. Those who play the *dan* [female roles] should always think as if they were a woman; those who play the *sheng* [male roles] should always want to act as if they were that man. When you perform on stage, the notes should soar to the blue heavens, and dip back down like a thread of rippling silk; the sound should be round like a circlet of pearls, unceasing as a pure stream. At its subtlest and finest, it should reach the point where "one hears when there is no sound, and finds the Way in whatever meets the eye," so that the dancer does not know where his feelings come from, and the beholder does not know where his soul has gone. If you can be like this, then you can be disciples of Qingyuan Shi [Master Pure Source] and enter into the Way. All you *sheng* and *dan* apply yourselves to it![10]

Tang repeated the gist of these instructions in the letter to Luo Zhang'er cited at the beginning of this chapter.[11] His involvement with actors is revealed in poems addressed to them, in comments about performances, and in details concerned with sending them to entertain friends.[12] Whether or not Tang kept a private troupe, his relationship with professional actors was a close one.

Scattered references in Tang's extant writings suggest that early performances of *Mudan ting* were for the most part private affairs and that those performed in Linchuan were in the locally popular Yihuang style.[13] However, accounts by friends and contemporaries indicate that within a few years of its publication *Mudan ting* was also being performed in the Kunshan style (Kunshan *qiang*) then popular in Suzhou. Tang himself mentioned a performance by a household troupe belonging to Wang Xijue (1534–1611), a retired grand secretary. Wang's family was from Taicang, an early center of Kunshan singing, virtually assuring that the performance was in that style.[14] Zou Diguang (*jinshi* 1574), a close friend of the playwright, mentions directing his "boys" in performances of scenes from *Mudan ting* and *Zixiao ji* (The Purple-Jade Flute), Tang's incomplete first play. Zou's troupes were widely known for their artistry in the Kunshan style, and Zou was known as a stickler for technique, especially when it came to singing.[15]

The fullest contemporary account of a performance of *Mudan ting* in the Kunshan style was by Tang's friend Pan Zhiheng, who recorded his impressions of a performance by a female troupe belonging to his friend Wu Yueshi (born c. 1575). Pan describes Wu as a learned and cultivated man who recruited actresses in Suzhou and took great pains to elevate his performers' artistry.[16] In the case at hand, Wu Yueshi first invited a scholar to explain the meaning of Tang's text to the actors, then employed someone knowledgeable about prosody to match Tang's text to the Kun aria forms. Lastly, he invited another person knowledgeable about singing to clarify points of articulation and phrasing. Pan paid tribute to Wu's concern with technical artistry, but what impressed him especially was the ability of the actresses to capture the emotional intensity of the play's protagonists, Du Liniang ("Bridal" Du) and Liu Mengmei (Liu "Dreams of Plum").

In all of his plays Tang explored the place of the emotions in human experience, but his depiction of youthful passion is most intense in *Mudan ting*. The play falls into three segments, the first of which culminates, tragically, in Du Liniang's death from unrequited longing (scene 20). These early scenes center on Liniang's world, either her rooms or a garden behind the Du family residence in Nan'an. In the second segment of the play, the action focuses even more intensely on this closed world, into which Liniang's lover, Liu Mengmei, is drawn. Once come to the place where Liniang lies buried, Liu is visited by her ghost, set free by the underworld judge to wander in search of Liu in the human world. Her ghost takes him as her lover and in time persuades him to resurrect her corpse (scene 35). After scene 35, the action shifts to the world beyond the garden, as the lovers flee Nan'an and rebels press an invasion from the North. In these public scenes the pace of action quickens, becoming at times frenetic, as every important character is set in motion. Starting with scene 48, however, which depicts the reunion of the resurrected Liniang with her mother, the action moves towards resolution in the final scene, which depicts an obligatory happy reunion of family members (*tuanyuan*) at the emperor's court.[17]

It is for the earlier scenes that *Mudan ting* has been celebrated, in particular for the scene depicting Liniang's first experience of love in a dream (scene 10) and for the one showing her unsuccessful attempt to recapture that experience (scene 12). These are the scenes most frequently mentioned in contemporary accounts of *Mudan ting*, and it is likely that Pan Zhiheng's praise of Wu Yueshi's actresses was occasioned by watching a performance of one or both of them. In his accolade, Pan borrowed language from Tang's preface to *Mudan ting*:

> As for love's [*qing's*] course, we don't know where it begins or ends, where it departs to or where it comes from. It is as if at the margin between presence and absence, distance and proximity, existence and nonexistence; surely this is what love inevitably brings about, yet we do not know why it is so. We do not know why it is so, yet love becomes inexhaustible, and none should find it strange that it can cause the dead to live and the living to die. Only after being able to be obsessed [*chi*] [by love] can one experience it, and only after being able to experience it can he depict it [on the stage]. Du Liniang's love is obsessive and illusory [*huan*]; Liu Mengmei's is obsessive and abandoned [*dang*]. One seeks authenticity through dreams, the other in life. Only let their love be authentic, and there is no place where that love's illusoriness and abandon cannot go. The two actresses, Jiang Ru and Chang Ru, are both from Wuchang [Suzhou]. Each is "love obsessed" [*qingchi*], and in acting out Liniang's illusoriness and Liu Mengmei's abandon it is as if they don't know how they come about. . . . Notes purl from their throats, as if threaded on a string; their figures are as graceful as a fairy's.[18]

This account recalls Tang's instructions to the Yihuang actors, especially Pan's emphasis on the performer's ability to tap his or her own emotions—in his words, to "depict emotion by means of emotion" (*yi qing xie qing*). Pan was concerned about artistry and technique, but not at the expense of expression, and he emphasized that actors must understand the texts they performed and be able to convey the feelings that underlay the music: "They are able to create a complete performance that floats freely beyond what can be dimly discerned, and to convey a forlorn sadness beyond the notes of the music. Not one word has been left out; no subtlety has been left unexpressed."[19]

These accounts of early performances of *Mudan ting* give some idea of its impact on those who were able to savor the subtleties of the text in the intimate environment of household performances. But the play was not without critics, and several of the most prominent ones were natives of Suzhou. These men were ardent promoters of the Kunshan musical style as the most correct one for southern drama, and their remarks about Tang's plays reflect this partisanship. Zang Maoxun, a friend during years spent together in Nanking in the 1580s, was the most patronizing in his critique:

> Now Linchuan [Tang Xianzu] has never been in Wumen [Suzhou] in his life, and he has not made a study of prosodic rules. He embellishes the reputations of the wise men of former times and shows off in a wildly excessive style of writing. He has confined himself to the narrow horizons of his native country, and has composed according to a music whose rhythms are defunct. Would this not make him a laughingstock of the Yuan playwrights?[20]

Zang had made similar observations in the preface to his second edition of Yuan plays, where he complained that Tang achieved an admirable balance between elegant and rustic language in his plays, but often failed to match word tone to musical phrase. Such matching was extremely important as far as enjoyment of singing was concerned, especially in the Kunshan style. Zang, who claimed prosodic expertise in that style, took it upon himself to correct Tang's mistakes, and in 1618 he published an edition of Tang's four complete plays under the title *Yuming xinci, sizhong* (White Camelia [Hall]'s Four New Plays). Criticisms of Tang's prosody appear frequently in his commentary. Zang, however, was not the first who attempted to rein in Tang's wayward genius.

The Original Text and Subsequent Adaptations

The uncertain status of authors and the prerogatives of readers and audiences have been much debated by theorists of late, and never more than in the case of dramatic texts.[21] Although Tang Xianzu was active at a time when many literati playwrights exercised considerable control over how their works appeared in print—if they were published at all—that control was lost once the plays became popular with theatergoers as well as readers. Since it first won a following some four hundred years ago, *Mudan ting* has passed through the hands of contemporary publishers such as Zang Maoxun and Feng Menglong (1574–1646), professional actors, and now, foreign-based directors. The chapters that follow trace an ever-widening gap that opened between the complete written text of the play and the parts of it that became part of the performed repertoire. But these forays into the history of performances of *Mudan ting* will also be explorations of the original playtext and the author that can be discerned in that text.[22] What follows is thus premised on the notion that a clear cleavage exists between an "original" version of *Mudan ting* and subsequent theatrical adaptations of it.

By late Ming times, *chuanqi* playtexts were not scripts as we think of them. Many were written in the form of plays, but were read—almost like novels—and seldom, if ever, performed. These works circulated as manuscripts, and if printed, were published by the playwrights themselves or by persons known to them. In this respect they differed from Yuan *zaju* texts, which were far more likely to be written by men professionally connected to the theater and to remain within the ambit of commercial troupes. They differed as well from earlier southern plays (*nanxi*), many of which were collectively authored over a long process of transmission.[23]

No first edition of *Mudan ting* exists; even the date of its first printing is in doubt.[24] Despite the seriousness with which Tang Xianzu regarded his playwriting activities, none of his four complete plays was included in his collected works until 1636, and the text of *Mudan ting* preserved in that edition is not regarded as the most reliable one extant.[25] Xu Shuofang, the contemporary scholar most closely identified with Tang's *oeuvre*, feels that in the case of *Mudan ting*, collating extant editions in an effort to arrive at a definitive text is fruitless, because no filiation to an "original" edition can be traced. Differences between extant Ming editions are the result of deliberate changes that were introduced by adaptors and editors shortly after the play appeared in print, not mistakes committed by editors and copyists. Xu's solution has been to select the edition that he feels shows the fewest traces of revision, and keep collation notes to a minimum.[26] Even the edition of *Mudan ting* collated by Qian Nanyang documents a text that remained quite stable, in spite of several drastic adaptations that were made of it in the decades after it was published. Qian's notes turn up discrepancies at the level of the occasional word or phrase, but he has not encountered the problems that bedevil editors of Shakespeare's plays, who must select among markedly different versions that are all by the same hand.[27]

This stability of the complete text of *Mudan ting* was not achieved without a struggle, occurring only after friends and colleagues of the author, concerned that the integrity of the author's text had been compromised, undertook to publish an edition that was faithful to that text.[28] That edition was published in 1620, two years after Zang Maoxun had published his severely truncated version of the play using the title *Huanhun ji* (The Soul's Return). At least one other heavily edited adaptation had preceded Zang's, and another by Feng Menglong appeared sometime after 1623. These adaptations of the complete play were ostensibly undertaken to make *Mudan ting* performable in the Kunshan style, but more was at stake than the accommodation of Tang's lyrics to that repertoire of arias.[29]

With fifty-five scenes (and 403 arias), *Mudan ting* is one of the longest plays in the extant repertoire of complete southern dramas. It is written in language that ranges from elevated poetic diction to a vivid and often coarse vernacular. It has been observed that Tang brought the allusive complexity, imagistic vividness, and intellectual seriousness of the high tradition of *shi* poetry to the writing of dramatic arias (*qu*), which most of his peers regarded as vulgar entertainment. Tang persisted in writing plays in the face of criticism from his teacher, Luo Rufang, that he indulged himself with friends in impassioned song ("Does this have anything to do with the ultimate meaning of life?"), and despite the warning of another mentor, Grand Secretary Zhang Wei, that by consorting with actors he risked becoming a laughingstock, Tang responded that he preferred discussing emotions (*qing*) with actors to debating principle (*li*) with teachers, because few people were able to understand what the latter discussions were about. Interest in the emotions was intense at this time, and Tang's dramatic *oeuvre* can and has been read as an extended discourse on *qing*'s place in human life.[30]

For many, such intellectually serious use of drama amounted to a diversion of *qu* from its proper role as edifying and accessible public entertainment. This was the opinion of both Shen Jing (1553–1610) and Feng Menglong, who were ambitious promoters of Kunshan *qiang* as the only proper (hence orthodox) musical style for southern drama. Kunshan *qiang* had originated in Kunshan, a town that was part of the Suzhou hinterland. Commonly referred to as *Kunqu* (Kun opera), it was embraced by Suzhou's elite starting around 1550, first as a purely sung style of southern *qu*, but soon also as a style for musical drama. Both Shen and Feng had rigid views about how playtexts should be set to the fixed tunes (*qupai*) used for Kun opera and what kind of language was acceptable for use on the stage. Both men were interested in the practicalities of staging these long plays, and both claimed to be close to professional actors.

They found much to criticize in *Mudan ting* and did not hesitate to introduce the changes they felt were necessary if the play was to reach more than a handful of highly literate readers (that is, if it was to be more than an *antouju*, a "desktop play").[31] Tang vehemently denounced Shen Jing's adaptation, which was made shortly after the play began to circulate,[32] and probably for this reason Feng Menglong cloaked his critique in the arcane details of *qu* prosody. But the changes he made to Tang's text tell a plain tale of artistic appropriation. A debate over *Mudan ting*, which was ignited by these efforts to make it performable as a Kun opera, exposed sharp differences of opinion among literati about the proper uses of theatrical texts. Both the aesthetic and the ideological components of this debate will come up in chapters 2 and 3, where I discuss the adaptations published by Zang Maoxun and Feng Menglong. The recent furor over international productions of *Mudan ting* shows that these issues are still alive in China today. But now the debate pits Chinese cultural authorities against artists outside China and the cultural institutions backing them.

The contemporary adaptations were prescriptive in nature, and in this respect differ from the texts I will discuss in chapters 4 and 5.[33] Feng makes his intentions plain in prefaces he wrote for plays published under his studio name, and although the fineness of his editions puts into question his claim that they found favor with actors, their accessible format—printed in standard block characters with no illustrations—indicates his effort to influence performance practices and not simply reflect them. The differences between his editing decisions and Zang Maoxun's indicate that the two men published for distinct segments of the extensive late Ming readership for southern dramas.[34] Both men were successful publishers who extensively revised the works they printed. They knew the tastes of their readers, and we can learn a good deal about those tastes by observing what they chose to keep and what they rewrote or deleted from Tang's text.

The Practice of Performing Extracts

In Part Two (Actors and Performances), I turn my attention to textual versions of *Mudan ting* that are very different from those examined in Part One in that they reflect more directly how southern plays were commonly performed. Zang and Feng adapted *Mudan ting* with the whole play in mind, but while records of performances of complete *chuanqi* exist for the late Ming, none explicitly mention any for *Mudan ting*. Nonetheless, it is likely that *Fengliu meng* (A Romantic Dream) was performed complete, for it appears to have been used as a model for a similar adaptation of the monumentally long play *Changsheng dian* (The Palace of Lasting Life) more than half a century later.[35] By the time that *Changsheng dian* was published in 1688, severe truncations of *chuanqi* playtexts were commissioned by the playwrights themselves in an effort to insure that their plays were staged in acceptable ways.

The adaptation of *Changsheng dian* is not extant, perhaps because during the Ming–Qing transition creative agency in southern drama was increasingly exercised by actors rather than by playwrights. Historians of Kun opera suggest that the changeover occurred in the early Qing dynasty, as the Manchu rulers clamped strict controls on the theater and persecuted playwrights whose works offended them. The "second-stage creation" (*zaidu chuangzao*) of professional actors determined how plays reached the stage, and performances of extracted scenes from long works (*zhezixi*, sometimes referred to as "highlights") became the norm.[36] Whole plays continued to be published or else circulated as manuscripts, but these were intended for readers and no longer reflected, even prescriptively, thinking about how the works should be staged. Chapter 4 is a history of performances of *Mudan ting*, based on texts of *zhezixi* that I have been able to examine or about which others have written. It is a thinly stretched sample for a period reaching from the early 1600s to the 1990s, but a good deal of *Mudan ting*'s stage history can nonetheless be reconstructed from it.

Already in the early Wanli period (1573–1620), scenes had been extracted from *chuanqi* plays and published separately, either in literary miscellanies (*xuanben*) or household encyclopedias (*leishu*). Many extant Wanli encyclopedias predate *Mudan ting*, but even those that postdate it often lack highlights from it because their compilers favored plays written in styles more popular than Kun opera. For glimpses of how *Mudan ting* was being performed, one must look to the miscellanies.

The highlights from *Mudan ting* preserved in these collections are windows onto an operatic culture that was complex and quite different from that of European opera at roughly the same time. This culture was a fluid one, in which amateurs often consorted with professional actors across boundaries of class and status,[37] and it was not possible to sustain a "pure" form of Kun opera separate from common (*su*) forms of dialect opera such as Yiyang opera in the late Ming and clapper opera (*bangzi qiang*) in the Qing. We can distinguish texts designed for amateurs (for singing only) from those that catered to the user's enjoyment of full theatrical performances. But as we move into and through the Qing sources, we find that performed versions of *zhezixi* predominate in all the extant collections, including manuscript collections. We also find that the selections alter in response to the changing tastes of the Qing theater-going audience and as cross-fertilization occurred between the elegant and common styles.

As a result, the gap between complete texts of *chuanqi* plays, most of which had been written between 1550 and 1650, and highlights published in miscellanies widened. By the Qianlong period (1736–1795), the most extensive selection of *zhezixi* for *Mudan ting* was in *Zhui baiqiu* (A Patched Cloak of White Fur), a popular miscellany of Kun operas whose many editions I discuss in chapter 4. The *Mudan ting* documented in this collection is the iconic version created by actors, for by then Tang Xianzu's complete play was known to only a handful of highly literate readers. Even in this century, when the educational level of actors has risen and new adaptations of Kun operas have been undertaken with the help of amateurs and scholars, these efforts have rarely if ever entailed a return to the complete *chuanqi* versions for fresh material or fresh insights.

Revisiting the Complete Play: Two Contemporary Productions

It has fallen to directors working outside the Kun opera tradition to reexamine the complete *Mudan ting*, and their interpretations have encountered stiff resistance from Kun opera insiders. In Chen Shi-Zhen's case such resistance proved costly. Its world premiere set for July 1998 at Lincoln Center, the show rehearsed for eight months in Shanghai, giving its critics ample time to mount a campaign against it with local cultural authorities. One week after its dress rehearsal, the production was declared unfit for New York audiences, and visas were not issued to the actors.

But the idea of mounting a production of *Mudan ting* inspired by a fresh look at the complete play had taken hold. Additional funds were made available in China to mount a domestic production,[38] and the Lincoln Center initiative was revived with additional funding and a different cast. While Peter Sellars's production was inspired by the artistry of Hua Wenyi, known in China for her interpretation of the play's heroine, Du Liniang, Sellars combined Kun opera performance elements with other styles in a manner that was self-consciously eclectic. Chen Shi-Zheng's production, initially promoted as a re-creation of an "original staging" of *Mudan ting* in an authentic *Kunqu* style, was subsequently described simply as his personal interpretation.[39]

Both North American productions have in common directors who have been given a free hand at every stage of the artistic process. In this respect, Catherine Clément's observations about directors of Western opera in modern times are germane. She remarks that the most successful directors are those who:

> . . . reread the opera and who shape it; they pull from the words themselves, and from their surroundings, ideas that are capable of updating, or just plain bringing back to life, words that until then only served as a pretext for the song. This revival of opera through staging does not give the authors of the words and story back their words; but . . . [it] is first of all a work of reading.[40]

Readers familiar with Kun opera performances will immediately object that words are never merely a pretext for singing in that style, but are always the basis for elaborate and detailed movements that accompany the singing and convey the meaning of the text by means of formalized gestures and mime. These conventions have, however, at times obscured the meanings of the words rather than illuminated them, as will become evident when I discuss the views of Sellars and Chen, who have in some cases responded critically to the reticence of Kun opera's performance conventions. A similar observation can be made of the musical conventions of Kun opera, which have sometimes been used in ways that suppress the text. In chapter 3, for example, I show how Feng Menglong paid close attention to Tang Xianzu's text, ostensibly revising his arias musically, but in ways that obfuscated language either erotically explicit or crude.[41]

This distinguishes Feng fundamentally from Sellars, to whom another of Clément's observations usefully applies. Successful directors have come to the fore, she feels, because creative energies in opera have been exhausted. These directors "clarify" the works they revive, by returning to the text and to the "spirit of the times that gave rise to it":

> The direction, whether distanced, critical, poetic, dreamy or combative, develops the scenery, the gestures, and the objects, and gives the space a historical depth that it doubtless never had before.[42]

Sellars disavows any intent to revive in their classical forms the operas that he stages; he seeks to modernize them for contemporary audiences, and his staging of *Mudan ting* as *Peony Pavilion* has been aptly characterized as contemporary American theater, not updated Kun opera.[43] That said, he and his collaborators gave close attention to Tang Xianzu's complete playtext from a perspective that was both distanced and at times critical, as will become clear in chapter 6.

Extensive coverage in the Shanghai press during rehearsals of the Lincoln Center production suggests that Clément's observations about directors who bring historical depth to their staging of classic operas are also apt in Chen Shi-Zheng's case. His version has been described as an "export edition" (*chukouban*) that showcased many traditional performance arts, not just Kun opera.[44] As such, it sought to bring "historical depth" to the staging of the play by evoking for Western audiences the theatrical milieu of late Ming times. Chen's determination to restore the original play's sensuality and robust humor, which have been elided or suppressed in the *zhezixi*, also can be described as an effort to "clarify" the work he was reviving. I will consider some ways in which I feel Chen's interpretation respected the spirit of Tang's complete and some ways that it did not.[45]

Both of the new productions were iconoclastic. Sellars revised the central pairing of Du Liniang and Liu Mengmei. He was critical of performances he saw during a visit to China in 1997, which he felt portrayed the lovers too sweetly ("like two people on a wedding cake").[46] With his actors, he sought to bring out a dark strain in Du Liniang's character that he felt is present in the complete playtext, but elided in the Kun performance tradition. That side of her character comes out in scenes clustered at the play's midpoint (scenes 27–32), which are rarely if ever performed. Those scenes, set in a darkened garden, comprised the better part of Part Two in his production, and his staging was likened to an experience of dreamtime as a confusing and disorienting labyrinth.[47] Tan Dun's score for Part Two was melodically rich but also at times cacophonous, evoking emotions in the text more elemental, even primitive, than those conveyed by the soft and rather austere harmonies of Kun music. In these ways, both director and composer responded negatively to expressive forms in Kun opera that they identify with Confucian influence and rediscovered meanings in Tang's text that they feel can be attributed to Daoist and Buddhist forms of spirituality.

Chen Shi-Zheng's iconoclasm stemmed from his decision to scale back the use of the highly formalized gestures and movements for which Kun opera is especially known and to incorporate other popular performance arts in his staging, situating the actions of the characters more recognizably in everyday life. His restoration of the vulgarity and humor found in Tang's text meant that the characters were often presented in ways that were unfamiliar to the Kun actors and audiences in Shanghai.[48] Tang's humor was nonconformist, and Chen's decision to reinstate it worked against the grain of Kun opera traditions enshrined in *zhezixi*.

Then there is the sex. Sex in *Mudan ting* runs the gamut from sublime eroticism to farce, and has bedeviled performers both of *zhezixi* and of "complete" productions of the play constructed by stringing *zhezixi* together.[49] My discussion of traditional performance aesthetics in chapter 5 is indebted to the work of Chinese scholars who have been eager to document the existence of a popular style of Kun opera that developed alongside the more elegant Kun style and enriched it. These scholars have argued that within the Kun aesthetic there has always been room for common and vulgar elements (subsumed under the all-purpose Chinese word *su*), which complement and enhance the predominantly elegant forms for which Kun opera is prized. However, I argue that this aesthetic of combined elegance and vulgarity has never been able to accommodate the sort of provocative uses that Tang makes of vulgarity, if we judge by the textual evidence of *zhezixi* at any rate. Actors must have found ways to work crude humor into their performances, but in the texts earthiness was carefully circumscribed. In this regard I will frequently use one of

Tang's more intriguing creations, Shi Daogu (Sister Stone), as a touchstone for the vulgar in his aesthetic design. Sister Stone has rarely survived the amending process in anything like the form in which Tang conceived her. That Chen Shi-Zheng's reinstatement of her provoked strong criticism comes as no surprise.

Forms and Meanings of *Mudan ting*

Several recent studies have drawn attention to how the forms in which texts are made available to readers reveal a good deal about their historical and social significance. D. F. McKenzie has made subtle and convincing inferences about good readings and misreadings of Congreve's plays by paying attention to the expressive purposes underlying typographic signs and the "disposition of space"—a text's "nonverbal elements." He has suggested that modern ways of presenting texts efface such signs and at times obscure intentions that underline the manner in which texts were presented and received. Roger Chartier makes a related point when he observes that "[e]xamples abound of the ways in which transformations of material typography (in the broadest sense of the word) have profoundly changed the uses, circulation and understanding of the 'same' text."[50]

In an earlier book, Chartier also discusses the ephemeral nature of reading—an "infinity of singular acts"—and proposes that a proper history of books and reading practices must necessarily combine three kinds of work: textual criticism (analysis of texts to discern their structure, themes, and aims), bibliography (the history of books and other objects and forms that bear texts), and cultural history (study of the practices that seize on those objects and produce differentiated uses and meanings). In making his case for such a combined approach to the study of the circulation of printed matter, Chartier makes large claims for what such studies can reveal, asserting that they can suggest how forms of sociability were transformed, how new modes of thought came to be permitted, and how peoples' relationship to power changed.[51]

My goals are more modest. However, this study is more than a history of how *Mudan ting* has been performed or how Kun opera has evolved as a performance art. I am also interested in how the forms of texts, and appropriations of them over time, "invent, shift about and distort" meanings, depending on the competence and expectations of those who use them.[52] The means I use to this end are not unlike those proposed by Chartier here and in his more recent book, where he gives attention to how the forms and typography of books contribute to the creation of the meanings that readers (or audiences) find in them.[53] While I am not blessed with textual sources as diverse as those at Chartier's disposal, the material I have gathered has enabled me to give a quite full description of the different meanings that editor-publishers, actors, and directors have found in Tang Xianzu's text.

Only in chapter 3 do I engage in textual criticism of a more traditional kind. In it I discuss two important figures in *Mudan ting*, and use Feng Menglong's refashioning of them in *Fengliu meng* to explore the more inventive uses of them in Tang's playtext. In this chapter I am directly concerned with how Tang wrote, and with how his uses of language set him apart from other contemporary southern playwrights. Examples of his striking and original use of language appear in other chapters, but in chapter 3 this is the main subject.

In chapter 2 I am concerned with what Chartier would describe as the "prescriptive will" of editor-publishers. Publishing of all kinds of texts, by both individuals and commercial publishers, reached a high point as Tang Xianzu was completing *Mudan ting*, and both playtexts and novels were in demand. The late Ming also saw publication of the first great fiction commentaries for literati novels.[54] In both cases individuals other than the original authors were able to impose control on the meanings of the texts. This was easier to accomplish with novels, whose authors were shadowy figures, than with *chuanqi* plays because southern playwrights identified themselves as authors and took a proprietary interest in how their works appeared in print.[55]

Both Zang Maoxun and Feng Menglong were active editor-publishers. Zang published fine editions of both northern and southern *qu*; Feng published fiction, drama, and many other kinds of texts as well. Both men were inveterate revisers who made a good living publishing existing works in forms that they believed would appeal to the reading public they targeted. I believe their editions of *Mudan ting* were driven, at least in part, by an ideological agenda. Efforts to rein in Tang's keen wit (to "blunt the sharpness" of his writing) show up clearly in the adaptations discussed in chapter 2.[56] In addition, I suggest that the different editing strategies exemplified in these two editions of the complete play reveal that the readership for *chuanqi* plays already included highbrow readers who were able to enjoy the author's text, connoisseurs interested in owning an elegant text that presented the arias in the Kun style, and middlebrow readers who wanted playtexts that reflected the Kun style of theatrical practice. Soon after *Mudan ting* began to circulate, then, several distinct editions of the complete play were in print and were directed at specific segments of the late Ming reading public. They were meant to be read, and only secondarily might influence how the play was performed. We can use *Fengliu meng* to speculate about how *chuanqi* plays were performed in the 1620s and 1630s, but it does not reflect how *Mudan ting* was actually performed.

Sources that do reveal how *Mudan ting* was performed—other than the few poems and anecdotes written by Tang and his friends—are found in the drama miscellanies. I have discovered only nine that date from the early seventeenth century and contain scenes from *Mudan ting*, but even exclusion of this play reveals something about how it circulated, as do the contents and formatting of the *xuanben* that include it. In chapter 4 I discuss the miscellanies containing extracts from *Mudan ting* that date from the late Ming, from Qing collections, and from a few manuscript collections assembled in the late Qing and early Republican eras.[57] It is with such sources that Chartier's observations about how meaning follows form become especially relevant. My detailed analysis of *xuanben* focuses on the principles by which they were compiled, which are usually spelled out in prefatory comments (known as *fanli*). Editing entailed numerous decisions: whether or not to punctuate the text, what other kinds of notation to include (musical notation, rhythmic notation), whether or not to illustrate it, and how to distribute the extracted scenes through the volumes. I also compare the text of the extracts with the text of the scenes in the original complete playtext. These data are then the basis for my stage history of *Mudan ting* from roughly 1600 to 1900.

Forms of texts also suggest the uses that were made of them, and for *Mudan ting* our picture is a complex and changing one. As we move from the late Ming to the Qing miscellanies, the impact of actors comes into focus. Their modifications of the play become increasingly noticeable and increasingly varied. Lu Eting, whose history of Kun opera as a performance art has guided my research in many ways, gives prominence to the creativity of these actors. *Zhezixi* were their vehicle, and the popularity of performing southern plays as *zhezixi* coincided with decreased composition of new plays by literati.[58] Lu Eting and others attribute this change to repressive Manchu policies, but also to the emergence of new opera styles that challenged the hegemony of the Kun style and forced Kun actors to incorporate new techniques and material into the *zhezixi* that they performed. By the late Qing dynasty and Republican periods, it was routine for Kun actors to perform in other styles as well, especially Beijing opera style. The cross fertilization that took place shows up clearly in printed extracts from *Mudan ting*.[59]

It is registered most clearly in the widely popular miscellany *Zhui baiqiu*, whose contents underwent a rapid expansion in the 1760s and 1770s. The number of *zhezixi* for *Mudan ting* more than doubled, from four to ten, and the number and extent of actor-inspired changes increased correspondingly. Cross-fertilization continued throughout the Qing between professional actors and literati amateurs, many of whom enjoyed performing the plays, though they no longer wrote them. It is in the middle of the Qianlong reign that we get the first fully annotated libretti (*gongpu*) for *Mudan ting*, which were published by amateurs with the help of professional music masters. Henceforth, such *gongpu* become another important source on Kun opera and *Mudan ting*. Since I lack expertise in music, I have done little more than document the considerable variety of these texts. For persons trained in the highly embellished style of Kun singing, *gongpu* are another window on how users enjoyed and interpreted southern plays.[60]

I have little doubt that the printed *zhezixi* gathered in Qing miscellanies and in manuscript collections reflect how *Mudan ting* was performed at that time, but it is necessary to point out their limitations. These are not actor's scripts, and the few scripts that I have found are *shenduanpu*—*gongpu* that include detailed pointers made by and for actors. Where these exist I have made profitable use of them, but time did not permit a more wide-ranging search for them.

Performance Aesthetics

In chapter 5 I make use of a recent source, the actor's memoir, which consists largely of transcriptions of oral reminiscences. These memoirs date from the post-1949 period and because of the ideological climate in which they were produced, do not reliably reflect earlier performance practices. I have nonetheless found them useful, because they reveal how actors think about plays and how they envision the characters they impersonate. I also have benefited from contact with the current generation of Kun artists at the Kun Opera Troupe in Shanghai, most of whom were trained in the 1950s. Many of their teachers were from the "Chuan" generation of Kun actors ("*Chuan*" *zi bei*)—the last all-male troupe assembled. Through these artists, who were trained in the 1920s, the current performers retain an attenuated link to late Qing performance traditions. I have observed performances by actors who completed their training in 1961, attended rehearsals and classes taught by them, read their writings, and talked with some of them.[61] Though the audience for Kun opera in Shanghai now numbers in the hundreds only, it is an enthusiastic and close-knit group, and one can learn a lot from engaging its members. My discussion of the aesthetics of performance in *zhezixi* has been enriched by my ability to move beyond printed sources and talk with living performers, both amateur and professional.

Chapter 5 is relevant to the controversies that have overtaken recent international productions of *Mudan ting* because in it I discuss the place and role of common (or, at times, vulgar) elements in the Kun opera aesthetic. It is widely acknowledged that Kun opera is the most elegant, refined style of opera, and *zhezixi* are said to preserve only the "finest essence" (*jingcui*) of *chuanqi* plays. Yet it is also often said that *zhezixi* should ideally combine elegant and common forms (*ya su gong shang*). This aesthetic dictum, as it happens, reaches back to the time when Kun opera enjoyed its first golden age of popularity in the late Ming.[62] Tang Xianzu embraced it in his plays, and in this chapter I explore how actors' uses of commonness in their performances of *zhezixi* differ from Tang's uses of it in the original complete text.

This discussion leads naturally and inevitably to consideration of Kun opera's status as an elite national form of drama over its four-hundred-year history. As I have pointed out, Kun opera has never been socially or aesthetically pure, despite the efforts of dedicated amateurs who would prefer to believe that this is the case. Exposure to vulgar influences has never been more evident than in the present century, for both economic and ideological reasons.[63] But even before 1949, and at least since the Qianlong era, common touches have been added by performers—a process referred to as "added labor" (*jiagong*)—and undone much of the meaning in the complete text of the play.

The conclusion of chapter 5 discusses this longstanding interaction between "highbrow" and "lowbrow" Kun opera, making use of the work of Lawrence W. Levine to indulge in some comparisons between operatic cultures in nineteenth-century America and China.[64] Though suggestive, such cross-cultural comparisons can only go so far in shedding light on the complicated interactions between elite and popular culture in the case of this one play. One is struck by the slipperiness of the categories. Tang Xianzu's plays are *chuanqi* drama at its most "highbrow," yet his writing reveals an openness and receptivity to vulgar forms that far exceeds that found in the adaptations by Feng Menglong (a "middlebrow" playwright), or in *zhezixi* (also middlebrow). There is no gainsaying the fact that in the second half of the Qing dynasty Kun opera became a much more lowbrow form of opera, yet the uses made of common elements in printed texts of *zhezixi* reflect a conservative Confucian ideological bias.

In the conclusion of his book on illustrated fiction, Robert Hegel discusses how, in the Qing dynasty, the novel came to be linked with popular entertainments, customs, and superstitions as vulgar entertainment. Like other popular elements of culture, the novel was the Other against which the privileged high culture defined itself, hence it was despised by many of the elite.[65] It is more difficult to define the cultural status of drama. As a public art form it had an important place within the dominant culture, yet there was a strong antitheatrical bias among the elite. This was true even of Kun opera, despite its hegemonic status as "national theater" (*guoxi*) since the Wanli period. That it was performed by professional troupes vulgarized it in the eyes of many, and as it competed with and absorbed influences from dialect opera its aesthetic purity was further compromised. Art either written or performed in dialect was beyond the cultural pale in China, until this century in any case. Enthusiasts of Kun opera in late Ming times were disturbed by the disruptive presence of dialect in *chuanqi* playtexts performed in that style, and they sought to delimit the use of such language in the prescriptive treatises that they wrote.[66] The aesthetic of *zhezixi* presented in this study can be understood as the result of a centuries-long accommodation that Kun actors—and those who disseminated written representations of their artistry—reached with the forms of cultural Otherness subsumed under the rubric "*su*."

Pierre Bourdieu has proposed that of all cultural products, theater is the most conformist in its values, and he attributes this to the constraints of drama's bourgeois public in Europe. In the case of China, and Kun opera in particular, another of Bourdieu's formulations is even more pertinent. He notes that there is an especially close correspondence between categories of theater and divisions of the dominant class. Theater depends on the "connivance" of authors and their audiences, and we can extend this statement to include Kun actors, who usurped the creative role of authors once the practice of performing *zhezixi* took firm hold.[67] These actors, though utterly excluded from the dominant class, were nonetheless complicit with audiences drawn largely from that class, when it came to the strategies by which they incorporated popular theatrical forms into *zhezixi*. The values encoded in *zhezixi* for *Mudan ting* are conformist in Bourdieu's sense, far more so than the values expressed in the author's complete text.

Tang Xianzu's refusal to conform to the conventions of *chuanqi* drama can be correlated with the nonconformity of his thought, as I endeavor to demonstrate in several close readings of scenes. In short, Tang, who occupied a socially dominant cultural position, subjected the values implicit in *chuanqi* romantic drama to a searching reformulation in *Mudan ting*, while Kun actors, socially dominated, recreated scenes from the play in ways that drew the play back towards the mainstream, consistently blunting the subversive edge of the author's wit. The professional actors, operating in a field of large-scale theatrical production in the Qing dynasty, staged plays that supported dominant Confucian values. Tang Xianzu, working in a field of restricted cultural production at the end of the Ming dynasty, wrote plays that impress us even now as radical in their aesthetic and ideological design. He is an example of Pierre Bourdieu's autonomous producer, someone who creates art largely for other producers of art, according to his own criteria for production and evaluation. Kun actors, constrained by the market, appropriated fragments from *Mudan ting* in ways that were akin in spirit to methods of appropriation used by Feng Menglong, himself a producer working in the marketplace.[68] The performance histories of selected scenes that I present in chapters 4 and 5 thus will resonate with my discussion of *Fengliu meng* in chapters 2 and 3.

Chartier has urged the necessity to keep at the center of cultural history a notion of appropriation, by which he means "differentiated practices and contrasted uses of the same texts, codes or models." Concentrating on "concrete conditions and processes that construct meaning," he makes room for "experiences and interpretations that are historical, discontinuous and differentiated." Appropriations of "common cultural sets" are diverse, never the prerogatives of one social actor or group, and by recognizing this historians can move beyond existing models of cultural practice—and thinking about popular culture—which are simplistic because overly dichotomized. In place of these earlier models, which emphasize either popular culture's complete autonomy from the dominant culture or its complete subservience to it, Chartier urges the adoption of a reformulated model that "consider[s] for each epoch how complex relations were developed between forms imposed (more or less forcibly) and established practices (sometimes allowed to blossom and sometimes restrained)."[69]

Appropriation figures centrally in this history of *Mudan ting*, and although at times I indulge in textual interpretation of a more traditional kind, I have also made room for interpretations that are differentiated and discontinuous in the sense urged here. However, by calling attention to gaps that existed and widened between the author's design for *Mudan ting* and the designs of actors, and by suggesting that Tang Xianzu subverted dominant values in the complete playtext while the professional actors parroted them in *zhezixi*, I have, to a considerable degree, adhered to a dichotomized model of Kun theatrical culture.

To facilitate a more nuanced understanding of the kinds of relationships that can exist between cultural models on the one hand, and habits of receiving these models on the other, Chartier introduces another sense of "gap" into his discussion of appropriation:

> [W]e should assume that a gap existed between the norm and real-life experience, between injunction and practice, and between the sense intended and the sense constructed, a gap into which reformulations and procedures for avoidance could flow.[70]

He here refers to popular uses of books and texts, but the idea of a gap between injunction and practice is useful to keep in mind when thinking about performances of texts as well as readings of them. A published *zhezixi* (or even a videotaped performance of one) reveals little of the transactions between the actors on the stage and the members of the audience. Yet procedures for avoidance must have flowed into gaps opened during performances, even in a theater as bound by formalism and tradition as Kun opera came to be.

How a work has been received is difficult to get at. For *Mudan ting* one finds the occasional anecdotal account, fictional representation, or actor's description of a performance. But most of these sources date from quite recent times, when ideological constraints on those who have produced them have been severe. Such sources reveal little about the tactics actors may have used to perform *zhezixi* in ways that differed from the interpretations consecrated in the written versions that circulated in collections of plays. In my Conclusion, it will be necessary to revisit the intermingling of high and low forms, of conformist and nonconformist values in texts and performances of *Mudan ting*, lest readers be left with too simple an idea of Kun opera in any of its manifestations.

Role Categories

Finally, this is a history of performances, and in it I frequently refer to the system of role types common to all forms of premodern Chinese drama. The general contours of this system did not change much for southern drama; however, roles did become more specialized for Kun opera in the Qing dynasty than they had been for *chuanqi* drama in the Ming. Excellent discussions of the role categories for Beijing opera are available in English, and much of what is in them applies to Kun opera as well.[71] Rather than repeat them, I have provided an outline of this role system in Appendix A, which can serve as an aid for the more detailed discussions dispersed through the chapters of this book.

Two

The Musically Grounded Adaptations of Zang Maoxun and Feng Menglong

Zang Maoxun's adaptation of *Mudan ting* is likely the earliest extant.[1] Treating the entire play, it was published together with his adaptation of three other complete Tang plays in 1618, two years after his edition of one hundred northern dramas, *Yuanqu xuan* (Selection of Yuan Dramas), saw print.[2] Zang, like Feng Menglong after him, was active in the burgeoning field of publishing, and he turned his attention to drama in his sixties, near the end of his life. His first passion was *zaju* (otherwise known as northern *qu*), and it is for *Yuanqu xuan*, still the standard collection of *zaju* dramas, that he is remembered. His edition of Tang Xianzu's plays, *Yuming xinci, sizhong*, was a rare foray into the editing and publishing of southern *qu* and was among the most lavish of the editions of Tang's plays to appear in the wake of *Mudan ting*'s popularity.[3] It was produced for a different segment of the public than was *Fengliu meng*. Feng Menglong intended his editions for fellow playwrights and professional actors, while the quality of Zang Maoxun's edition and some of the features of the text suggest that he catered to connoisseurs like himself, who enjoyed drama in private settings.[4]

Another clue to likely users of Zang's editions is their lavish commentary. Zang was known for his expertise in prosody and singing technique, and he was an ardent proponent of the Kun singing style.[5] His over two hundred marginal comments (*meipi*) reveal that this expertise was one of his main contributions as editor; fifty-nine are concerned with prosody: aria structure, the matching of text to music, the use (or misuse) of rhymes, the suitability of an aria to the dramatic context, and its current popularity or lack thereof. Still other comments note, often approvingly, Tang's interpretation of a given aria, but the overall tenor of the remarks is critical. Although Zang had been Tang's friend and colleague, his statements about Tang's musical skills are condescending at best. In the most frequently quoted, Zang betrays narrowness in his conviction that only the Suzhou style of southern drama (that is, Kun opera) was worthy of mention. In this his views were similar to those of Shen Jing.[6] But unlike Shen, Zang did not assign overriding importance to prosody when evaluating a play. His commentary and manner of editing *Mudan ting* reflect broader concerns that associate him more closely with playwrights like Feng Menglong, though he moved in a more exclusive circle of opera aficionados than Feng did.[7]

Xu Shuofang enumerates these concerns under Zang's rubric for a good play and good playwriting—that it be *danghang* ("competent" in respecting the theatrical nature of the genre).[8] A competently written play should, first, proportion diction to feeling (*qingci wenchen*), such that "both elegance and commonness are present; seamlessly joined" (*ya su jian shou, chuanhe wuhen*). Second, the play should have a tightly constructed plot (*guanmu jincou*), such that each character speaks in his accustomed idiom, and each action exhibits its authentic color, with no overstepping of limits or false importations into the language. Third, the tones of the words and the music of the arias should fit together harmoniously (*yinlü xiexie*).[9]

Xu Shuofang feels that Zang's concerns progressed beyond Shen Jing's preoccupation with prosodic rules. For Shen, prosody was the hinge that joined the playtext to performances of it and the playwright to the performer. This is summed up in his dictum "let the playwright be competent, and the performer know the repertoire [of arias]" (*ciren danghang, geke shouqiang*).[10] Performability for Shen meant audibility, which in turn promoted comprehension. When it came to language he emphasized plainness, aligning his views with those of Xu Wei a generation earlier. Zang was closer in spirit to Wang Jide (d. 1623), the leading contemporary theorist for southern *qu*.[11]

Xu Shuofang thus believes that Zang's approach to drama and playwriting was more comprehensive than that of Shen Jing, who was myopically focused on the minutiae of prosodic rules and on how operas should sound.[12] Perhaps it is fairer to say that the two men catered to and spoke for different segments of the public. On that basis, Zang's compass was arguably narrower, since he produced luxury editions of plays for private reading and pure singing, while Shen's activities brought him into contact with commercial troupes and professional actors.[13]

Zang can be compared in turn to Feng Menglong, with respect to both the publishing of plays and the range of concerns each man brought to the editing and writing of critical commentary. Both favored revision and adaptation of existing plays over creation from scratch, and as redactors both addressed *chuanqi* drama's macrostructure—the arrangement of arias within sequences and of scenes within the whole play—as well as microstructure—the composition of text within the aria form, and the relationship of sung verse (*chang*) to dialogue (*bai*).[14] Both men were capable of rewriting extensively, in Zang's case, as much as sixty percent of the text in some plays.[15] While both cited prosodic reasons as the overarching rationale for changes made, careful examination of their handling of the text reveals that more was at stake for them than the arias' musicality.

This chapter will examine how both men approached the task of making *Mudan ting* singable and performable according to the standards they espoused, and will keep in view the impact of their changes on ideas and values expressed in the original playtext. As will become evident, I feel that the most interesting story emerges at the level of microstructure, in the ways that both men responded to Tang Xianzu's extraordinary uses of language.[16] Birch has noted that Tang wrote *Mudan ting* when colloquial Chinese was not yet in a settled state. Tang exploited this fluidity, such that "[n]eologisms and dialect words abound . . . [with] an extraordinary ease of movement between literary and colloquial diction."[17] It was this mobility of language, in which Tang so clearly delighted, that upset many other literati playwrights. This, as much as the vagaries of Tang's prosody, compelled them to wrestle with his text. When we pursue their changes, their efforts to rein in Tang's language, smooth out jarring shifts of diction, and tame the often exuberant idiom become painfully, but intriguingly, evident.

This is particularly true of Feng Menglong's close engagement with Tang's language, and because his "reading" of *Mudan ting* strikes me as more critically engaged than Zang's, I devote chapter 3 to that aspect of *Fengliu meng* alone. In this chapter I examine the methods Zang and Feng used to adapt the play for performances. While their methods are in some respects similar, it is the differences that impress us more.

The Need for Shorter Plays

Zang justified cutting *Mudan ting* to half its original text in his *Huanhun ji* by noting a recent trend towards shorter southern plays. In the preface to his adaptation of another of Tang's plays, *Zichai ji* (The Purple-Jade Hairpin) he wrote:

> Starting with works such as *Hongfu ji* by the Suzhou native Zhang Boqi [1527–1613], playwrights only used thirty scenes. Actors were happy with this, and plays became shorter and shorter. There are some that have only twenty scenes or so. What's more, when it isn't fast moving but rather is dull, the plot [of *Zichai ji*] drags and has many subplots that slow its progress. People find this rather tiresome.[18]

Zang here betrays impatience with the often languid pacing of southern drama, and in several marginal comments to Tang's plays, he discusses problems that extreme length and improper pacing pose for actors.[19] In addition Zang evidently preferred more brisk dramatic action than that found in the typical *chuanqi* romance, which is hardly surprising given his enthusiasm for *zaju*, a dramatic form notable for its brevity.[20]

Hirose Reiko has explored Zang's reworking of *Mudan ting*'s structure, examining changes he made at a number of levels: cutting secondary characters (notably Liu Mengmei's friend Han Zicai, his servant Camel Guo, and the Daoist priestess Sister Stone), eliminating scenes, and erasing extreme disparities in length by cutting long scenes and amalgamating short ones into longer units.[21] As a result, the play is flattened, having fewer scenes of approximately equal length, as opposed to having more scenes of greater variety and distinctiveness (see Table 2.1). Since all but the essential secondary characters are eliminated, Hirose suggests, the actions of the main characters become more self-initiated. At the same time, the plot becomes more focused on these main characters.[22]

Of more interest is how these structural changes affect plot development and the depiction of characters. Hirose observes that the characters are more rushed than in *Mudan ting*, where the action builds slowly. This sense of hurry results in part from Zang's telescoping of action that stretches over several scenes in the original play. The summoning of Liniang's tutor, Chen Zuiliang, for example, and his lesson on the *Shijing* (Book of Songs) for Liniang and her maid Chunxiang (Spring Fragrance), which set the plot in motion, take three scenes in *Mudan ting* (4, 5, and 7). Zang's

Mudan ting

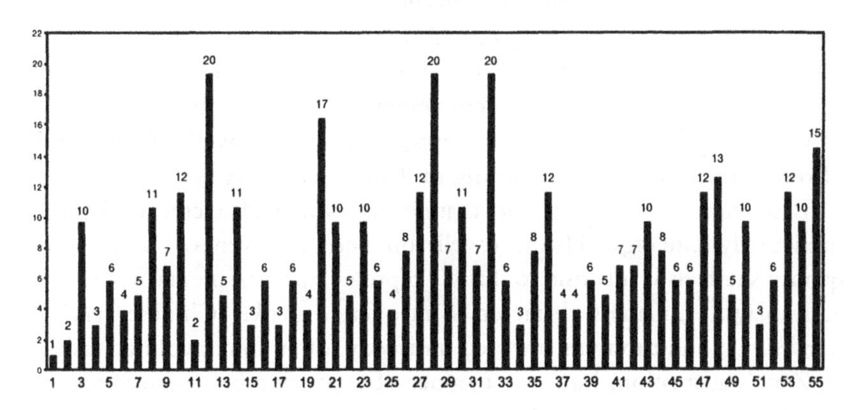

Huanhun ji

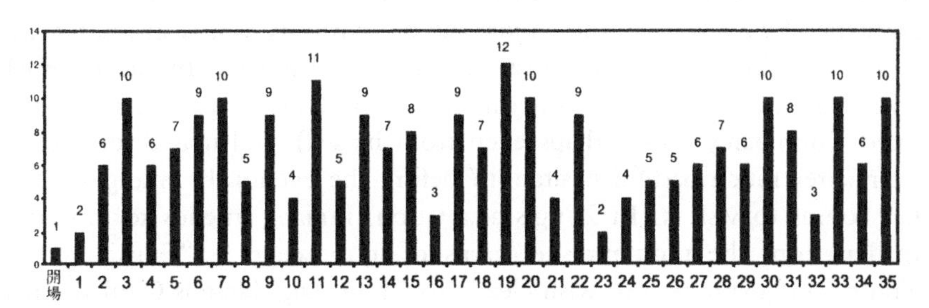

Fengliu meng

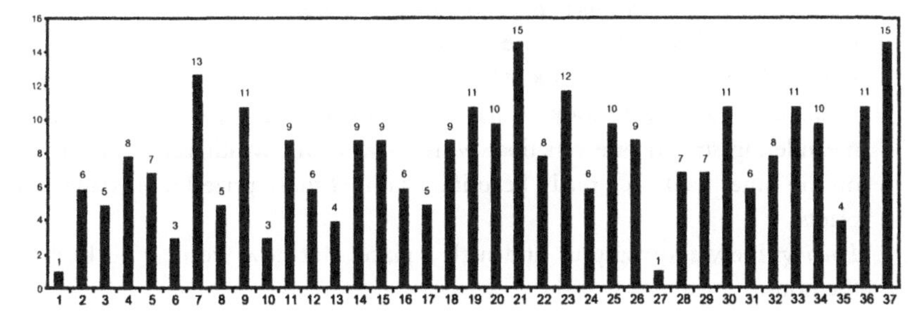

Table 2.1. Comparative scene breakdowns

version uses one (4, one of the longest scenes). The second example is Liniang's resurrection, which in *Mudan ting* requires three scenes (33–35), but in Zang's adaptation, only one (21).[23]

Zang's foreshortening of such actions and his tendency to change the order of scenes result in "inconveniences" in the time sequence. The play becomes jerky, its rhythm choppy rather than "swelling" (*moriagari*), Hirose's description for the pacing of Tang's scenes. A more far-reaching consequence, however, is the manner in which character is depicted, particularly Liniang's. Hirose dwells on her "pensiveness" (*monoomoi*) a quality she feels is intrinsic to Tang's representation of mental states in his early plays.[24] Liniang's character is introverted (*naikō*, Chinese *neixiang*), her feelings and thoughts revealed indirectly, often in convoluted fashion. In Zang's adaptation, Liniang's manner of expressing her feelings becomes direct, even purposeful, and as a result her character is more externalized.

The changed conception of Liniang emerges in the revision of the crucial early scenes, which reveal her incipient sexual desire as it is awakened by a lesson on the *Shijing* and her curiosity as it is stirred by the report of a beautiful garden just beyond her chambers. In the original schoolroom scene Liniang conceals her interest in the garden from her maid Chunxiang (and perhaps even from herself), and it is three scenes later (after much bashful hesitation) before she eventually emerges from her rooms to visit it. In Zang's adaptation, Liniang intends to visit the garden from the moment she learns of it in scene 3, "Engaging the Tutor," and expresses this wish clearly to Chunxiang. Here is Cyril Birch's translation of the original passage:

> *Liniang:* But tell me, where is this garden of yours? (*Chunxiang refuses to speak; Liniang gives an embarrassed laugh and asks again.*)
> *Chunxiang* (*pointing*): Over there, of course!
> *Liniang*: What is there to look at?
> *Chunxiang*: Oh, lots to look at, half a dozen pavilions, one or two swings, a meandering stream one can float wine cups down, weathered Taihu rocks on the other bank. It's really beautiful, with all those prize blooms and rare plants.
> *Liniang*: How surprising to find such a place. But now we may go back to the house.

Zang changes the last sentence of Liniang's response to, "When I can find the time, I'll go with you to have a look." The indirectness, even inscrutability, of her original response is clarified in the revision.[25]

Liniang's purposefulness is sustained in Zang's adaptation of the visit to the garden, scene 10 ("The Interrupted Dream") in the original play, scene 5 ("Wandering in the Garden") in *Huanhun ji*. In Tang's play two scenes intervene between Liniang's first hearing about the garden and her first visit there. In the first of these, scene 8 ("Speed the Plough"), the pageantry of which verges on burlesque, Liniang's father, magistrate Du Bao, visits the countryside to encourage the peasants in their planting; in the second, scene 9 ("Sweeping the Garden"), Chunxiang gives orders to prepare the garden for Liniang's visit. The account she gives the gardener of how her mistress selected the day for a visit again suggests bashful hesitation and indirection. Chunxiang begins by observing how jealously her mistress guards her reputation, but how study of the *Shijing* has made her pensive, so much so that Chunxiang has suggested she seek diversion in the garden:

> *Chunxiang*: So then I suggested, "Miss, you are tired from your studies, why don't you think of some way to amuse yourself?" She hesitated and thought for a moment. Then she got to her feet. "And how would you have me amuse myself, Chunxiang?" she asked me. So I said, "Why, miss, nothing special, just to take a walk in that garden behind the house." "Stupid creature," says the young mistress, "what would happen if my father found out?" But I said, "His Honor has been out visiting the country districts for several days now." Then for ages the young mistress walked up and down thinking, not saying a word, until at last she began to consult the calendar. She said tomorrow was a bad day, and the day after not very good, but the day after that is a propitious day because the God of Pleasure Trips is on duty for the day. I was to tell the gardener to sweep the paths ready for her visit.[26]

Zang abridged scene 8 and eliminated scene 9, but transposed this speech of Chunxiang's to the beginning of scene 5 of *Huanhun ji* (original scene 10):

> *Chunxiang*: Day and night I attend the young mistress. She has become very tired from her studies, and because His Honor lately has been out visiting the county districts and won't be back for several days, she wants to seize this chance and go on an excursion to the garden behind the house. I must order the gardener to sweep it out.[27]

Absent from this extremely condensed speech is any sense of Liniang's hesitation or pensiveness. As described by Chunxiang, her mistress's intention is simple and forthrightly expressed.

Lest it be thought that this directness is simply a by-product of textual condensation, we can note that Zang introduces changes immediately after this speech that reinforce the impression of eagerness, even urgency, underlying Liniang's desire to visit the garden. In order to avoid using the entrance aria, *Raochi you*, already used in his scene 2 ("Admonishing the Daughter"), Zang selected a different entrance aria for this scene, and rewrote lines originally sung by Chunxiang (ll. 3–4), assigning them to Liniang:

> *Liniang* (enters and sings to the tune *Shuangtian xiaojiao*):
> From dream returning, orioles coil their song
> Through all the brilliant riot of the new season.
> In my chamber unaccustomed to thoughts of love,
> What is it that causes me to cast aside needle and thread?[28]

With such an outburst of feeling, Hirose observes, the bashfulness and emotional subtlety exhibited by Tang's heroine are lost, as is her introversion (*naikōsei*, Chinese *neixiangxing*).[29]

The sense of Liniang's urgency is sustained in Zang's revision of the dialogue and aria immediately following. Liniang addresses Chunxiang, who comes onstage as her mistress finishes singing:

> *Liniang*: Chunxiang, have you given orders for the path to be swept?
> *Chunxiang*: Yes.
> *Liniang*: In that case, I'll go with you there. (She takes a few steps as she sings to *Bubu jiao*):
> The spring a rippling thread
> Of gossamer gleaming sinuous in the sun,
> Borne down into idle court.
> For a while I straighten the flower heads of hair ornaments,
> Perplexed to find that my mirror
> Steals its half-glance at my hair.
> *Liniang, Chunxiang*:
> These "gleaming clouds" are thrown into alarmed disarray;
> Walking here in the chamber, how can I let others see my form?

> *Chunxiang*: Without visiting this garden with you, how could I ever realize this splendor of spring![30]

Zang has sacrificed the logic of the original sequence, first by failing to mention Chunxiang's action of fetching Liniang's mirror case and gown so that she can prepare herself to go out, then by moving a direction in the text that indicates the moment when Liniang starts toward the garden. In the adapted text, Liniang is already on her way to the garden even before she begins to sing *Bubu jiao*. In his haste to propel the play forward, Zang throws the logic of performance to the wind, and his heroine's reserve with it.

Hirose highlights Zang's poor logic in eliminating Liniang's request that Chunxiang fetch her mirror and gown. These serve as props during the singing of *Bubu jiao*, whose lyrics, even as revised, describe Liniang performing her toilette in preparation to go out ("Having made such use of an aria originally sung inside the room, everything from 'For a while I straighten the flower heads of hair ornaments' onward is left hanging in mid-air"). The *dan* actress Fu Xueyi makes the same criticism, and adds that it defies common sense for a sheltered girl such as Liniang, fresh from her slumbers, to rush off to the garden in a disheveled state, with barely a look at her mirror.[31]

Other examples betray Zang's lack of common sense about his revisions, such as when he changes Liu Mengmei's response to Liniang's revelation that she is a ghost. The original playtext devotes one of the longest scenes to this moment (32, "Spectral Vows"). As conceived by Tang, Liniang reveals the truth about herself little by little, building tension to the moment when she tells Liu that she is "not yet mortal . . . a ghost." Liu's immediate response is fear ("Oh terror, oh terror!").[32] Zang rewrites the exchange as follows:

> *Liniang* (singing to the aria *Zhuo mu fan*):
>
> Master Liu,
> Don't be afraid
> It must be that I am kin to the sometime Prefect of
> Nan'an, Du Bao.
>
> *Liu*: Is that so? Where is it that His Excellency Du Bao was transferred to?
>
> *Liniang*:
>
> He was transferred to Yangzhou,

And left behind a daughter, Liniang.
Liu: So my darling is Du Liniang!
Liniang: But sir, not yet your mortal darling.
Liu: If not yet mortal, that doesn't mean you're a ghost?
Liniang: A ghost.
Liu (*startled*): How can that be! May I ask the years of your age?
Liniang:
Of years sixteen, fitted for matrimony,
In this life destined to fulfill my former life's debt.[33]

When revising this same passage, Feng Menglong insisted that Liu Mengmei momentarily betray terror when he first learns that he has been making love to a ghost. Commentary reveals that he regarded this moment as a high point, which required skill on the actor's part to modulate Liu Mengmei's feelings as he comes to grips with his lover's revelation: "In this scene, it cannot be that the *sheng* is not afraid. If he isn't afraid, then his feeling is not profound. For the most part, it is best to convey a mixture of stupefaction [*chidai*] and alarm [*jingya*]."[34]

In the opinion of his critics, then, Zang paid insufficient attention to how his modifications and cuts affected performances of what remained. This may have been the result of excessive haste and ruthlessness about the text,[35] but it also stemmed from a desire to present the characters in a different light, as more forthright and direct and, in Liniang's case, less complicated emotionally.

Two similar examples of cutting can be cited. Midway through "The Interrupted Dream," Liniang, having returned from the garden, is left alone. She sings a long aria (*Shanpo yang*), which expresses emotional turmoil occasioned by the spectacle of springtime in the garden. This aria caps the first half of the scene, expresses directly feelings only hinted at before in Liniang's garden-strolling arias, and sets the stage for the dream that immediately follows. Zang's decision to cut such a pivotal aria from the sequence demonstrates how ruthless his handling of subjectively rich moments could be.[36]

The second example concerns scene 12 ("Pursuing the Dream"), the most introspective scene in *Mudan ting* and one of the longest, consisting of twenty arias. Although Chunxiang and Liniang's mother, Madam Du, appear briefly, this is largely a solo scene for Liniang, who after a preliminary exchange with Chunxiang sings nine arias, uninterrupted, while alone on the stage.[37] Her singing is thus a monologue, an expression of thoughts not directed at any other party, only revelatory of her state of mind. Hirose Reiko uses *monoomoi* for scenes such as this one, and for the arias found in them. *Monoomoi* is the quality of a play's "atmosphere," created when objects (*mono*, Chinese *wu*) are given subjective coloration that speaks to a character's mental state (*omoi*, Chinese *si*). *Chuanqi* as a dramatic form differs from *zaju* in the propensity of its playwrights for using language that is subjectively colored, and Hirose discusses both dream scenes (10 and 12) in this regard.[38] If we accept this description of *Mudan ting*, it should come as no surprise that Zang responds quite consistently to this dimension of the text in his revisions.

The Pensive Atmosphere of "Pursuing the Dream"

Hirose singles out four arias in scene 12 that convey what is on Liniang's mind through the description of things rather than feelings expressed directly. Three are from the sequence of nine arias Liniang sings when she is left to herself and returns to the garden, drawn there in pursuit of her dream. Liniang sings the fourth as she first enters the garden, when Chunxiang has left her alone momentarily. Not one of these four arias was left intact. Zang eliminated the first, rewrote the second using a different tune, substantially rewrote the third to the original tune, and revised the fourth somewhat more lightly.[39]

To give some idea of how Zang worked with the text at the level of individual arias, I will examine how he treats three of the arias Hirose singled out. As originally written, the first is sung just as Liniang enters the garden through a gate that has been left ajar:

> *Liniang*: See how the ground is carpeted with fallen petals! (Sings to *Lan hua mei*):
>
> Never till now did spring so stir the heart.
> High and low over the plastered walls
> No place but springtime longings dance and fly.
> (*She stumbles*)
> Oh, the hawthorn catching at my skirt—
> Like my heart, it will not let me leave.[40]

This is the first of two arias to the tune *Lan hua mei* that Liniang sings, both of which contain emotionally packed language. Hirose singles out the hawthorns that pull at Liniang's skirt as the kind of closely observed detail (*komono*) that becomes a subjectively colored image of her thoughts. Just as Liniang's heart is drawn to the garden in search of her dream, so too the flowers in the garden, in her mind's eye, pull at her, as if unwilling to let her go.[41] Zang cut both arias, which serve as prelude to and prefigure the main sequence. As justification he states:

> Concerning Liniang's pursuit of the dream, there are things of which she cannot speak to others. All she can do is to enter the garden secretly and ponder the traces [of her dream]. And yet there are the warnings of her mother [to avoid the deserted garden] and the idle chatter [of her maid]. Is this good playwriting [*qi shi dangjia zhi zuo*]? Therefore I have cut all of the arias [sung when] Chunxiang summons Liniang to breakfast. Although they contain some fine lines, I dare not spare them.[42]

Instead, Zang sets the stage for Liniang's garden stroll with a rewritten aria and brief monologue newly conceived by him for the purpose. His aria evokes the image of a languid beauty suffering loneliness and ennui:

> Liniang (enters and sings to *Ye Jinmen*):
>
> Weary from springtime sleep
> Helpless, the bowels turn a thousand times.
> I am chagrined to see swallows nesting on painted beams;
> Tears streak the powder on my face.[43]

Having streamlined Tang's complicated opening, Zang rewrites the first aria of the main sequence (*Tete ling*, Hirose's second example). As Tang conceived the scene, Liniang is inside the garden at this point, where Chunxiang finds her when she comes a second time to call her to breakfast. Liniang sends the maid away a second time and resumes her search of the garden as soon as the maid has left:

> *Liniang*: Now that my maid is gone I can pursue my dream. (Sings to *Tete ling*):
>
> Rock garden above the pool,
> Path by tree-peony pavilion.
> Buds of peony inset along the balustrade,
> Strand by strand willows hover,
> String by string elm seeds dangle—
> Offerings of coins to mourn the spring![44]

Here, the closely observed details (peony buds, willow shoots, and elm seeds) are enigmatic, but Hirose is surely right when she suggests that they remind Liniang of the incremental passage of time and the season, something of which she has become acutely aware ever since her first garden stroll, when she identifies her fate, as one whose beauty has gone unappreciated, with that of the garden's profusely flowering plants. Hirose elsewhere points out that in the early scenes of *Mudan ting* this process of building up evocative details creates an intimate, even "closed" atmosphere, and she returns to this idea when discussing the next aria. Liniang has reached the place in the garden where, in her dream, Liu Mengmei made love to her:

> *Liniang*: How my longings stir to recall that moment! (Sings to *Pin ling*):
> Against the weathered rock
> He leaned my wilting body.
> Then as he laid my jade limbs down
> "Smoke issued from jade in warmth of sun."
> By balustrade, past swing
> There I spread the folds of my skirt,
> A covering for earth
> For fear of the eyes of Heaven.
> Then it was we knew
> Perfect mystery
> Of joy ineffable.[45]

Besides commenting on the allusion to a Li Shangyin poem that suffuses the aria with an erotic aura, Hirose focuses on the reference to Heaven in the eighth line, which, contrary to a feeling of expansiveness the word normally conveys, here "covers" the dense garden world and contains it. This reading is perhaps harder to see, but the image of overarching Heaven does seem to work by contrast, intensifying the darkness and intimacy of the garden world and of the dream.[46]

What happens to this accretion of evocative language—at once concretely objective and richly subjective—in the hands of Zang Maoxun? Here is my translation of his rendering of *Tete ling* to the tune *Jingu yuan*, which is, he claims, the one Tang should have used:

Liniang (*begins to walk*): Straightaway I am inside the garden. There is the peony pavilion, and the balustrade of tree-peonies. The scene is grand, but where is that student? (She sighs, and sings to *Jingu yuan*):

> Rock garden above the pool,
> Path by tree-peony pavilion.
> Spring's glory flowing everywhere.
> Strands of willow trail gracefully;
> Chatter of birds sheers the air.[47]

In this scene, as rewritten, Liniang's entry into the garden and progress through it have a hurried quality that precludes the slow build-up achieved in Tang's big scenes. In "Pursuing the Dream," there is a minor climax and decrescendo prior to the main sequence, which achieves the same effect more gradually, deflation coming both times with Chunxiang's return to the stage. Zang discards original language found in *Tete ling* just at the point where Hirose finds Tang's signature use of closely observed details to suggest Liniang's thoughts and build up a richly suggestive atmosphere. In Zang's hands details are not so resonant, but simply set the scene in a straightforward, typical way.

In the case of *Pin ling* Zang concentrates his changes in the second half of the aria:

Liniang: When I think of how I was embraced by that student beside the peony pavilion . . . (Sings to *Pin ling*):

> Coming to the Taihu rocks
> He leaned my wilting body.
> Then as he laid my jade limbs down
> "Smoke issued from jade in warmth of sun."
> Just as I prepared to spread my fragrant gold-threaded skirt,
> I became so bashful it was difficult to speak.
> How could I stop his blandishments?
> Then it was we tarried,
> Intimate thoughts, secret feelings were already conveyed.[48]

The image that Hirose finds most distinctive disappears entirely in the revision, which approximates the sense of the original in qualitatively different language.

Hirose suggests—and this brief analysis supports her—that Zang Maoxun sought to create a Du Liniang whose mental and emotional life is less complex and deep, and whose actions are correspondingly more transparent. In his version, Liniang's motives lie close to the surface, and Zang appears eager to portray her actions as clear and comprehensible to herself and to us. Hirose several times remarks on Liniang's purposefulness. By this, is she suggesting that Zang's brisk heroine is more capable of action than Tang's, more self-willed? She does not pursue the point, but I would add that Zang rewrote Liniang's character in the light of his project for *zaju*, which Stephen West has ably discussed in a recent article. When revising *zaju*, Zang sought to make earlier playtexts conform to an orthodox Confucian value system and world view. In an analysis of changes Zang made to Guan Hanqing's *Dou E yuan* (Injustice to Dou E), West demonstrates how Zang makes the action of that play conform to an idea of human relationships (and cosmic processes) that are ritually ordered and rationally just, a world view that West convincingly argues is absent from the earliest extant text of the play.[49] In other words, Zang appropriated the earlier play and rewrote it to conform to the values of his social group. When it came to *Mudan ting*, the situation was no different. What is interesting in this case, however, is how Zang accomplishes the transformation, because his methods often illuminate the ways Tang's play subverts the very world view to which Zang subscribed, or at the least pokes fun at it.

In *Huanhun ji* Liniang's filial devotion is emphasized, as is the devotion of her parents, especially Madam Du. This is easiest to demonstrate using Zang's revision of Liniang's death scene (20, "Keening"), which as Tang wrote it defies any simple understanding of the emotional bonds between parent and child. The scene, as Zang reconceived it, reveals the power of filial feelings, its high point reached as Liniang, dying, attempts to kowtow to her grief-stricken parents and collapses. Rather than describe his revision of that scene,[50] however, I will briefly consider Zang's handling of common (sometimes heterodox) elements, notably the Daoist priestess, Sister Stone. This permits us to consider another aspect of his editorial practice that Xu Shuofang singled out: the manner in which elegant and common elements are combined in the dramatic context.

Scene 48 of *Mudan ting* ("Mother and Daughter Reunited") depicts the reunion of Liniang, now resurrected, with her mother Madam Du, attended by Chunxiang. This scene has elements of Tang's elegant style—namely, subjectively dense language of the kind just analyzed—but it also contains an inelegant element in the person of Sister Stone, played by the *jing* role in the original play and the *fujing* role in the adaptation. Zang takes considerable pains to purge this character from his version of the play, and just how he contains her presence in this scene also speaks to another aspect of his editorial method—the ways song and dialogue are combined in the text.

"Cutting Away Ugly Bamboo" in "Mother and Daughter Reunited"

Scene 48 comes after a nearly unbroken sequence of military scenes devoted to Du Bao's tribulations as Pacification Commissioner and the raising of the siege of Huai'an (scenes 42–47; the one exception being scene 44, which is set in Hangzhou, where Liu Mengmei and Liniang settle after eloping). The military scenes proceed briskly, at times frenetically, and are filled with the dust of travel, the clamor and stench of war, and a great deal of humor besides. They exhibit the masculine atmosphere of the final third of the play (scenes 36–55), in which the action has moved beyond the close confinement of Liniang's world in Nan'an onto the public stage, where "everyone is on the move."[51] When mother and daughter meet in this scene, however, the action is momentarily thrust back into the feminine world of the first two parts (scenes 1–20 and 21–35). With this shift comes a return to the thick, lyrically freighted language often used in the earlier scenes.

From scene 20 forward Sister Stone replaces Chunxiang as Liniang's guardian, maid, and companion. As I will suggest elsewhere in this study, Tang's treatment of the old priestess, a comically grotesque figure, is not typical of that usually meted out to characters played by the *jing* role, who in *chuanqi* plays are either villains or clowns or some combination of both. In "Mother and Daughter Reunited" Stone participates in one of the most lovely moments in the play, when she returns with a freshly lit lamp to the darkened rooms that she and Liniang have occupied while Liu Mengmei is off in search of Du Bao. As the bearer of light, she performs a symbolically poignant action at a critical moment.

For a portion of the scene she is absent, having gone to find oil for the lamp. While she is gone Madam Du and Chunxiang come onstage. They have made their way on foot to Hangzhou and seek shelter on a moonlit night, with no idea that they have approached Liniang in their need. As the scene unfolds, much of the language in the arias has to do with darkness and light, suggesting that both mother and daughter are at a threshold. In Liniang's case, "clad all anew in fragrant flesh" (*rouxiang xin zhang*) and only just returned to the mortal world, she has yet to be recognized as daughter and wife by her parents. Madam Du, who is in flight from the chaos of rebel incursions and half dead of exhaustion, is also in the dark about her daughter's true condition. For both there is a movement in the scene from darkness towards light, and towards an understanding that comes with this transition.

Sister Stone's part in effecting this transition is a small but meaningful one. After an opening sequence of three arias that she sings together with Liniang, she leaves on her errand. She returns just as mother and daughter have recognized each other's voices, and when Madam Du and Chunxiang are most fearful and mistrustful of Liniang, whom they believe to be a ghost despite Liniang's pleas to the contrary. At that juncture—the women in darkness, Liniang weeping, mother and maid recoiling in fear—Stone reenters, lamp in hand. I give here Birch's translation of the first three arias from a sequence of four that Tang wrote to dramatize this moment. Madam Du and Chunxiang have just come onstage, and are standing outside the gate that leads to a room where Liniang is seated in darkness:

> *Madam Du* (*steps through the gate*): Oh, how empty and silent everywhere! Is anyone here?
> *Liniang*: Who is it?
> *Chunxiang*: A woman's voice. I'll ask her to open the inner gate.
> *Liniang* (startled, sings to *Bu shi lu*):
> As by sculptured balustrade I lean
> Whence come these gentle tones seeking admittance?
> *Madam Du*:
> Benighted on our journey
> Two ladies seek a moment's shelter
> *Liniang*:
> No man, indeed, from the voice.
> I'll open the gate to what the moonlight shows.
> (*They greet each other*)
> A lady visitor. Please come inside and sit for a while.
> *Madam Du*:
> I come in hope
> Of succor human or divine.
> *Liniang*:
> Excuse this rough reception,

Excuse this rough reception.

(*Each, for the first time, examines the other's face*)

Madam Du (*in surprise*): Lady (*sings to the same tune*):

In this tumbledown place

Why do you sit alone,

Your lamp unlighted?

Liniang:

Here in the paleness of this empty court

I watch and wait for the fullness of the moon.[52]

Madam Du (*aside to Chunxiang*): Chunxiang, who does this lady remind you of?

Chunxiang (*startled*): I daren't say it—the image of my young mistress!

Madam Du: Go quickly and look if there is anyone else here. If there is no one, I fear this must be a ghost. (*Chunxiang exits*)

Liniang (*aside*): This lady is the image of my mother, and that maid is surely Chunxiang! (*To Madam Du*) Where have you come from, Madam?

Madam Du (*sighs*):

From Huai'an,

Where my husband as Pacification Commissioner

Is beset by armed uprising.

I escaped with my life to reach this place of haven.

Liniang (*aside*): It is my mother! But how can I make myself known to her?

Chunxiang (*hastens back and whispers aside to Madam Du*): Empty house, no trace of anyone else. It's a ghost, it's a ghost! (*Madam Du trembles in fear*)

Liniang: This is indeed my mother and her story confirms it! (*She throws herself forward, in tears*) Mother! Mother!

Madam Du (*moves away from her*): Is this you, my child? Forgive me, I have neglected you, and now you are here as a revenant to accuse me. Chunxiang, take spirit money from our baggage and scatter it at once. (*Chunxiang does so*)

Liniang: I am your daughter, and no ghost!

Madam Du: If you are no ghost, I will call your name thrice and you must answer thrice, each time louder than before. (*She calls three times and Liniang answers three times, but each time weaker than the last.*) Yes, a ghost!

Liniang: Mother, let me tell my story.

Madam Du:

But first move back

For from your ghostly presence

An icy whirlwind blows.

Liniang:

No "ghostly presence" this!

Madam Du (*recoils in terror as Liniang clutches at her hand*): Child, your hand is cold!
Chunxiang (*kowtows*): Young mistress, please don't come and pinch me!
Madam Du: Child, we would have had a great mass said for your soul, but your father was set against it.
Liniang (*weeps*): Mother, however much you may fear me, nothing will make me leave you again!
Sister Stone (*reenters with lamp; sings to the same tune*):
Gate firmly barred,
What voices these in deserted court?
(*She lowers her lamp to light the path*)
And how did yellow spirit money
Light here on the green moss?
Chunxiang: Madam, isn't this Sister Stone?
Madam Du: It is indeed.
Sister Stone (*in surprise*): Ha, where can her ladyship and Chunxiang have come from, and everyone so confused and bewildered?
See them hover, hesitate.
Her ladyship
Recoiling in fear that the lacquer lamp is unlit.[53]
And the young mistress
In dim shades longing for light to let her draw near.
Liniang: Come quickly, aunt, to help my mother overcome her fear of me.
Chunxiang: Don't say Aunt Stone is a ghost too?
Sister Stone (*takes Madam Du by the arm and shines her lamp on Liniang*):
An end to fearful doubts!
Let lamplight aid the moon to show her features:
Surely this is the face of her we lost?
Madam Du, Chunxiang:
The face of her we lost!
Madam Du (*embraces Liniang and weeps*): My child, ghost or not I couldn't bear to give you up again![54]

Here is Zang's rendering of the same sequence, in scene 30 of *Huanhun ji*:

(*Madam Du steps through the gate*)
Chunxiang: Oh, how empty and silent everywhere! Is anyone here?
Liniang: Who is it?
Madam Du (sings to *Taiping ling*):[55]
We are come straight from Huai'an
Through all manner of humankind, our road has been a hard one.

Liniang: A lady visitor, who seeks lodging for the night. (*She goes out*) An old woman and a maidservant. Please come in and sit for awhile.

Madam Du (*gesturing her thanks*):

My thanks to you,
For looking kindly on us.
But why do you linger by yourself in the dark?

Liniang: There is a Daoist nun who keeps me company in this place. Because we had no oil for the lamp I told her to go next door to borrow some.

Madam Du (*examines Liniang closely and says in an aside to Chunxiang*): Chunxiang, who does this lady remind you of?

Chunxiang (*startled*): I daren't say—the image of my mistress!

Madam Du: Go quickly and look if there is anyone else here. If there is no one, I fear this must be a ghost. (*Chunxiang exits*)

Liniang (*aside*): This old lady is the image of my mother, and that maid is surely Chunxiang! (*Sings to the same tune*):

I look closely at her face,
How is it she is so like my mother?
The maid, too, resembles my companion of before.
Can it be we meet between dream and ghostly realm?

This lady surely is my mother! But how can I make myself known to her?

Chunxiang (*hastens back and whispers aside to Madam Du*): Empty house, no trace of anyone else. It's a ghost, it's a ghost! (*Madam Du trembles in fear*)

Liniang: That voice is even more familiar! It *must* be my mother! (*She goes towards Madam to make herself known*): Mother!

Madam Du (*moving away from her*): Is this you, child, who have shown yourself? Chunxiang, take the spirit money left over from yesterday and scatter it at once. (*Chunxiang does so*)

Liniang: Mother, I am your daughter, and no ghost!

Madam Du: If you are no ghost, I will call your name thrice and you must answer thrice, each time louder than before. (*She calls three times and Liniang answers three times, but each time weaker than the last*) Yes, a ghost, a ghost!

Liniang: Mother, let me tell my story.

Madam Du (*recoils again in terror as Liniang clutches at her hand*): Child, your hand is cold!

Chunxiang: You know, ghosts have cold hands.

Madam Du: Child, we would have had a great mass said for your soul, but it was your father was set against it.

Liniang (*weeps*): Mother, however much you may fear me, nothing will make me leave you again!

Sister Stone (*reenters with lamp; sings to the same tune*):

Gate deserted,

> Who is it has scattered paper money on the ground?
>
> *Chunxiang*: Madam, isn't this Sister Stone?
>
> *Madam*: It is indeed.
>
> *Sister Stone (in surprise)*: What are her ladyship and Chunxiang doing here?
>
> *Liniang*: Come quickly, aunt, to help my mother overcome her fear of me.
>
> *Chunxiang*: Don't say Aunt Stone is a ghost, too?
>
> *Sister Stone (takes Madam Du by the arm and shines her lamp on Liniang)*:
>
> Bring lamp up close to show her features,
>
> How can you take her for an importunate ghost?
>
> *Madam Du (embraces Liniang and weeps)*: My child, ghost or not I couldn't bear to give you up again!
>
> *Sister Stone*: Would a ghost be this beautiful?
>
> *Madam Du*: My child![56]

Zang, condensing, drains Stone's aria of its most resonant imagery, references to lamp and moonlight, and to Liniang's wish that light be shed on the darkness in which she dwells ("In dim shades longing for light to let her draw near"). In Tang's case language associated with the moon and moonlight pervades scenes devoted to Liniang's ghostly existence (27, 28, 30, and 32, all big scenes). In scene 48, at this moment, light of moon is augmented by light of lamp, in a gesture that brings Liniang out of her ghost-like state and marks another stage of her reintegration into the human world. The aria given to Stone dignifies her presence in the scene by the beauty of its language and meaning.

Zang does not eliminate either her action with the lamp or her aria, but the one he substitutes for Tang's contains only four sung lines (compared to nine originally), from which almost all of the original imagery is stripped. Even in the one line carried over from the original aria ("Let lamplight aid the moon to show her features"), Zang replaces *yue* (moon) with *jin* (close), which changes the line from one whose imagery is packed to one that approximates dialogue: "Bring lamp up close to show her features." As Zang conceives it, the aria amounts to dialogue put into the form of song; as rewritten, the entire sequence consists mostly of dialogue.

Dialogue is the medium of comic playacting in *chuanqi* drama, and Zang favors it in the case of Sister Stone and Liniang's tutor, Chen Zuiliang (played by the *mo* role), both of whom have a good measure of humor built into their characters, especially in the original play. I feel, however, that Tang's project for Sister Stone in *Mudan ting* is more ambitious than the role designation *jing* would suggest.[57] In the course of the play he employs her in a number of ways, many of them humorous, often outrageously so. But at times Stone also participates in lyrical moments, as here. Zang does not appear to be at all alive to the possibilities where Stone's character is concerned, and as commentator he frequently complains that her presence is either "pointless" (*wuwei*), "disgusting" (*keyan*), or in need of cutting, like "ugly bamboo" (*ezhu*).[58] The effort at containment is evident here when he strips her aria of its most evocative language and later in the same scene when he cuts an aria that Tang assigned to Stone, one of four sung to the same tune, in succession, by each of the women (Madam, Liniang, Sister Stone, and Chunxiang) to conclude the scene. In the original sequence Stone's aria (and Chunxiang's) are counterpoint, effecting a decrescendo from the emotionally intense singing of Madam Du and Liniang:

Madam Du (*turns back to Liniang, in tears*): My child! (Sings to *Fanshan hu*):
I had believed your pure spirit, risen to Heaven,
High placed on lotus throne in western paradise;
What thought had I of such reunion
After three years cut off in ghostly caverns?
I wept till limbs were numbed, bowels tormented,
Heart withered, moistened by nought but tears,
Dreams wracked with grief, and mind distracted.
One moment you were here on earth;
The next, your world and mine were not the same.
Fear grew that offerings of rice to your spirit
Were all cut off
And sheep and oxen grazed over your grave.

Madam, Liniang:[59]
What night is this?
What night is this?
Or do we meet now only in dream?

Liniang (*weeps; sings to the same tune*):
In shallow earth you laid your child
Where bones grew cold and sleep came slow;
The cold food you offered at the Feast of the Dead
There South of the River
Was more than I could eat.
Never dreaming of such a day as this
Now I find that past time

Impossible to relate.
Unfathomable riddle:
When, when will Heaven make all things clear?

Madam, Liniang:
What night is this?
What night is this?
Or do we meet now only in dream?

Madam Du: Aunt Stone, I am grateful to you for watching over my daughter.

Sister Stone (sings to the same tune):
Don't ask me to blurt out the story of what happened
For I go all of a cold sweat just to think of it.
In all good faith I performed the sacrifices every seventh day,
How did I know that she'd found herself a lover?
(*She sings in lowered voice, aside to Madam Du*)
There was I, out demon chasing—
How was I to know this shadow play was a real live show?

Stone, Chunxiang:
Miraculous destiny,
Miraculous destiny,
The wheel of karma comes full circle.

Chunxiang (sings to the same tune):
I've heard of maids like Qiannü
Who sent her spirit roaming
But here's the marvel of body and soul
Rejoined after three long years.
There I pitied her, encoffined
And never known a husband
And here she's dwelling, mistress of this court!

Truly, my young mistress,
Lovelorn spirit so determined
Now fulfilled in wifely devotion!
Never a day Chunxiang
Didn't set a meal for your departed spirit,
Never a festival her ladyship
Didn't offer sacrifices with her tears,
And all the time
You'd quit the halls of Hades
And joined him on that boat!

Stone, Chunxiang:
Miraculous destiny,

Miraculous destiny,
The wheel of karma comes full circle.[60]

Zang keeps the two arias sung by Madam Du and Liniang with minor changes only, but cuts the arias sung by Sister Stone and Chunxiang. In their place he writes the following exchange of dialogue, in which Stone recounts to Madam Du in the briefest of summaries what happened to Liniang:

Madam Du: Sister Stone, may I ask how it was that your mistress was able to come out from the grave?
Sister Stone: After your ladyship left, three years passed before we knew it. It seems that the young mistress's life span had not yet run its course. Then, too, there was a student from South of the Ridge, Liu Mengmei, who came to live at the shrine. He wandered into the garden behind the house, and with one kick opened the tomb and invited my mistress to come out.
Chunxiang: So there really is a Liu Mengmei! Strange, strange.
Madam Du: Where is this Liu Mengmei?
Sister Stone: He came here with my mistress to take the examinations. Because the lists have not yet been made public, and hearing that His Honor was besieged at Huai'an, my mistress asked him to go and find out what has happened.[61]

Hirose distinguishes *chuanqi* arias from those in *zaju*, in terms of the latter's greater tendency to take on the character of dialogue. Once the singing begins in a *chuanqi* play (in big scenes at least), the resulting expression of thought and feeling is not directed at any one person, but resembles a monologue.[62] In *zaju* the arias exhibit a greater heterogeneity, assuming more of the functions of speech, a fact that she attributes to the shortness of the plays, which necessitated that the arias advance the action.[63]

This is an interesting observation that has some bearing on the analyses just offered of Zang's revisions. Space does not permit a more thorough discussion of his methods, but the examples offered suggest that he was writing Kun arias in a more "northern" style. As will become evident, his handling of the arias' form and language differed not only from Tang Xianzu's, but also from that of Feng Menglong, who took singing in the direction of dialogue as well, but using very different methods.

The decision to curtail and contain Sister Stone's part in the play has an effect that goes beyond concentrating more attention on the main characters. Old, female, Daoist, and sterile, she is both a ridiculous and a percipient character, marginal socially, yet crucial to Liniang's eventually successful transit from death to rebirth. By giving her such an intriguing and diverting presence in his play, Tang was, I feel, making a statement about the proper and necessary relationship between what is orthodox and heterodox, central and marginal in life. The two positions are interdependent, each necessary to the other. At the same time, in aesthetic terms, what is elegant and exalted and what is common and base are also mutually implicated. A character such as Stone and the aesthetic qualities she brings to the play supply one key to *Mudan ting*'s uniqueness. Zang's disdain for her is a symptom of the conventionality of his thought and his aesthetic values.[64]

How to End a Scene: Zang Maoxun's Thoughts on Good Playwriting

Before leaving Zang Maoxun's adaptation, something more can be said about the performance-related concerns reflected in *Huanhun ji*. Here Zang fared no better with his critics than he did on purely literary grounds. In his commentary, in addition to discussing the musical interpretation of arias, he remarked from time to time, either directly or indirectly, on matters having to do with performance of the text. These comments—twenty-eight of them by rough count—refer to how the design of a scene or an action reflects good playwriting (*youzuo*)[65] and give some sense of how Zang envisioned the play as performed. Twelve are concerned with how a scene begins or ends; ten of these address endings. I will discuss two of the comments on endings because I feel they reflect Zang's thinking about dramatic action and illuminate how his approach to playwriting differed from Tang Xianzu's.

In this study I propose that Tang's portrayal of the relationship between Liniang and her maid Chunxiang is atypical, since Liniang often conceals her thoughts and feelings from Chunxiang, and Chunxiang tends, as the play progresses, to become isolated from her mistress and associated instead with Madam Du. In his drive to simplify the play, Zang cut through the ambiguities of the maid's role and restored to her the roles of Liniang's intimate and ally. Feng Menglong was to take this even further. Zang's conception of the relationship shows up in his revision of "Pursuing the Dream" (scene 7 in *Huanhun ji*), not only in how he begins the scene but also in how he changes the ending. For this scene and one or two others, Feng Menglong preferred Zang's conclusion to Tang's and incorporated it into *Fengliu meng*.

Both Zang and Feng took exception to Tang's decision to conclude most scenes with a pastiche of four lines culled from Tang poets. Both men discarded these and replaced them with quatrains written in a simple idiom, or occasionally in Feng's case, with proverbial couplets. Here is the conclusion Zang wrote to his scene 7. Chunxiang has come onstage just after Liniang has finished her long solo sequence and finds her mistress slumped at the base of the plum tree:

> *Chunxiang*: Aha! I've looked for my young mistress everywhere; why has she come alone to the garden and fallen asleep beneath this plum tree? (Sings to *Chuan bo zhao*):
>
> How has your garden roaming
> Brought you to rest against this plum's side?
>
> *Liniang*:
>
> I raised my eyes,
> Its branches filled my vision,
> And heartache overcame me.
>
> *Liniang, Chunxiang*:
>
> Why this dream, so sudden?
> Why this grief, so dark?
>
> *Chunxiang*: Let's go back now; her ladyship will be summoning you to breakfast. (*Liniang moves away, then pauses*)
>
> Chunxiang (sings to *Yi bujin*):[66]
>
> I help her, half in a swoon, to the painted railing's side,
> Announce breakfast in the hall with her ladyship.
>
> *Liniang*: Ah, Liniang,
>
> Abandoned you sleep alone, mocked by blossoming branch.
>
> *Chunxiang*: I see your spirits are unsettled. What can be the cause? (*Liniang sighs but doesn't speak*)
>
> Envoi:
>
> *Liniang*:
>
> Things there are in my heart,
> I find hard to speak of to another.
> (*Exits*)
>
> *Chunxiang*: Young mistress, why this concealment?
>
> Always have we been of one mind,
> What use is it to be guarded with me?[67]

Zang comments, "Liniang cannot conceal from her maid what she is thinking. For this reason, the exit verses are most stageworthy [*youzuo*]." This confirms the intent detectable in the revised ending, which suggests that Chunxiang is privy to her mistress's thoughts and feelings, even when Liniang is not fully forthcoming about them. Needless to say, Tang's conclusion to the scene suggests no such thing. In it Chunxiang, having discovered Liniang beneath the tree, asks Liniang what is troubling her, and gets only a riddling response when Liniang sings about what has happened (more to herself than to Chunxiang), without revealing that she is talking about a dream. Her response only baffles the maid even more, and she makes no effort to clarify matters. In the chorus Tang wrote for *Chuan bo zhao* there is no mention of the dream; one can only presume that Zang inserted it to diminish the enigmatic quality of Liniang's response, but the change makes no sense, since there is no basis for Chunxiang's having knowledge of it at this point. Here one idea of performance (having to do with how relationships between the characters are displayed) overrides another kind in which relationships are represented in the play of language. Zang is preoccupied with display at the dénouement of this scene, and is less concerned with ensuring that this display follows logically and organically from the sequence that leads up to it.[68]

Other examples of this kind of modification could be given. One concerns the representation of Du Bao at the end of scene 11, "Lamentation." This is Liniang's death scene, and, as Tang wrote it, it concludes with hurried preparations for the disposition and care of her body prior to the departure of parents and maid for Du Bao's new post. Zang softened this ending by having Du Bao remain onstage after all of the other principals have made their exits, to give careful instructions to the gardener about the care of Liniang's grave and the burial of her portrait. Compared with this, Du Bao's instructions in the original conclusion, which are directed at both Sister Stone and Chen Zuiliang, can seem perfunctory:

Du Bao (sings to *Yi bujin*):

> Our thoughts, like sunset clouds, rise not above the three-foot mound of our daughter's grave
> And this one task my wife and I bequeath you:
> We dare not ask that you should hour by hour watch over her,
> But at the Feast of the Tombs, on the day of Cold Food let her at least receive a bowl of rice.[69]

Zang's changes to *Yi bujin* are partially illegible, making a complete translation of it impossible. However, it is clear that his text is sung by both Du Bao and Madam Du, and addressed to Chen Zuiliang only. The last line of the Coda reads, simply, "Remember on the day of Cold Food and the Feast of Tombs to let her receive a bowl of rice"; the line of dialogue preceding, which colors the instructions Du Bao gives in the final sung line, has been removed. Zang then concludes the scene with Du Bao's more elaborate provisions for his daughter's welfare, set forth in his dialogue with the gardener.[70]

He draws his readers' attention to these modifications twice, first by noting that the rewritten Coda is "*danghang*," then by praising the scene-ending dialogue: "After the envoi there is more speech. Profound feeling lingers. This is good playwriting. [*chanmian buliao, ci shi zuofa*]." The comment makes explicit what the changes imply, that Zang wishes to put the feelings of Liniang's parents in the best light as Liniang's death scene concludes. This intent is consistent with his other revisions of the scene, which heighten the display of filial sentiment between Liniang and her parents at the deathbed. The rewritten conclusion gives point to the other revisions.

The care that Zang lavished on the beginnings and endings of scenes is indicative of his more externalized approach to the representation of character on the stage. Scene beginnings and endings, as well as the entrances and exits that mark them, are occasions in Chinese opera for displays of a kind that represent characters and relationships iconically, in the sense of ritualized show.[71] The fact that so many of Zang's comments related to performance are focused on these moments is a measure of the importance he attached to them. They also mark out an area of difference between his playwriting and Tang Xianzu's—and between Feng Menglong's and Tang's—since Feng emulated Zang in this respect.

"Beautiful on Both Desktop and Stage": Feng Menglong's *Romantic Dream*

Feng Menglong, who was twenty-three years younger than Tang Xianzu and Zang Maoxun (both of whom were born in 1550), is associated with his mentor Shen Jing and others who emphasized prosody over diction in *chuanqi* drama. However, his activities as playwright suggest that his approach was comprehensive and addressed the practical problems of performing in theatrical settings, not simply in the private households Zang Maoxun probably envisioned for performances of his new versions. Like Shen Jing and Wang Jide, Feng was eager to promote the Kun style, and to this end he was bent on establishing playwriting standards for others to emulate.[72] His adaptation of *Mudan ting* appears to owe little to Zang's earlier effort, or to Zang's expertise in Kun prosody. The fact that Feng produced yet another adaptation suggests that he felt it would meet a need not satisfied by the work of his predecessors.[73]

Gao Yu devotes two chapters of his history of directorial practice in Chinese drama (by which he means Kun opera) to Feng's contribution. He begins by noting that Feng sought to create a repertoire of performable plays that would reflect the norms for southern drama that he wished to promote. In Feng's words, he would "collect plays with noteworthy plots that don't betray the prosodic rules too much," and revise and publish them so that they would be available to both performers and other playwrights.[74] In emphasizing the repertoire of southern drama, Feng's concern anticipates that of Li Yu (1611–1680), who placed play selection at the head of items devoted to dramatic performance in *Xianqing ouji* (Casual Expressions of Idle Feeling).[75] Unlike Li, however, Feng did not create new plays but rewrote existing ones, selecting widely from among plays on folk themes,[76] by famous contemporaries,[77] and by younger protégés and friends.[78] At least seven of the nineteen (or so) plays attributed to him are historical plays, reflecting Feng's desire to expand the Kun opera repertoire beyond the romances favored by literati.[79] Although he claims to have revised the plays he selected only "slightly," in some cases his versions are recreations, often attested by changed titles, as in the case of *Fengliu meng*.[80] Nonetheless, this play has an umbilical relationship to *Mudan ting*, and many of Feng's comments in the text reflect, Gao feels, directorial thinking about the original play.[81]

As already noted, Feng published with two groups in mind: other playwrights, for whom the annotated playtexts could serve as models, and professional actors, for whom they could serve as a bridge from the original playtext to the stage. In rare cases (e.g., *Shagou ji*, Killing the Dog) Feng endeavored to elevate the quality of a crudely written folk play; more typically he revised in an effort to produce a stageable version of a desktop play.

Evidence that professional troupes made use of these adaptations is, at best, indirect;[82] that for Feng's influence on other literati playwrights is more immediate. Hong Sheng, in introductory comments to *Changsheng dian*, remarks on the difficulties actors encountered performing his original text, which led his friend Wu Wushan to adapt it modeled on Feng's play.[83] Original editions of Kong Shangren's *Taohua shan* (Peach Blossom Fan) contain the full array of directorial apparatus, in the form of prefatory comments, directions to actors, and marginal commentary, similar to, but even more extensive than that found in Feng's editions.[84]

Gao Yu emphasizes that Feng's published adaptations were not acting scripts (*wutai de chuanben*), such as were subsequently published in the Qing dynasty; nor did they resemble the manuals of prosody (*qupu*) edited by Shen Jing and others. They were "blueprints" (*lantu*), detailed reworkings for performance, carefully planned and at times based upon Feng's experience of having seen the plays performed. Gao challenges earlier assessments of Feng's plays that stress their literary nature and goes so far as to compare them to modern "shooting scripts" (*fenjingtou juben*) for cinema.[85] While agreed with Gao and Xu Shipi that Feng's revisions were directorial in intent (his prefaces and comments testify to that), I am also impressed with how his adaptation of *Mudan ting* engages Tang's text at a literary level, something that actor-inspired stage adaptations rarely do. In the degree to which it modifies Tang's language, *Fengliu meng* also stands apart from most of Feng's other adaptations, which do not modify the original language, especially of the arias, to nearly the same extent.[86] The changes that Feng made to *Mudan ting* reflect a "holistic" (*zhengti-xing*) approach to editing plays that was manifested at many levels: plot structure, characterization, and language as well as prosody. Both Gao and Xu point to these broader concerns as evidence of Feng's theatrical bias, and they see him as a forerunner of Li Yu, whose playwriting and drama criticism reveal many of the same concerns.[87] They may be correct in this view, but the evidence from *Fengliu meng* on this score can be interpreted in more than one way.

For example, Feng's concern with a well articulated plot and tightly organized sequence of scenes stripped of all "creepers" (*geteng*, needless side plots) is registered clearly in a reduction of both scenes and number of arias per scene. Twenty-four of eighty-four marginal comments, and two of five general critiques for *Fengliu meng*, address aspects of plotting and scene sequences, more than any other category, including prosody (nineteen comments). Much of his terminology is also found in commentary for vernacular novels, which is not surprising since both genres had features in common (i.e., great length and segmented structure) and were often written by the same individuals. The problem becomes one of deciding whether the concern with well-made, logically consistent plots served theatrical ends, or represents instead the imposition of a model from the novel onto the drama, for purposes that have more to do with reading than with enjoying a performance.[88]

With fifty-five scenes, several of which contain twenty arias, *Mudan ting* exhibits the overgrown structure that Feng Menglong deplored in southern drama. At the level of macrostructure (scene structure and plot), its excesses mirrored those that Feng and others deplored in Tang's arias, which often exceeded the formal limits deemed ideal at that time. The extreme length and resulting complexity of conception did more than tax actors' stamina and audiences' patience, according to this view; it could create confusion. For Feng this was particularly deplorable in drama, which should touch the listener's emotions directly.[89] By reducing the number of scenes to thirty-seven and arias to 286, Feng brought his adaptation closer to the length deemed appropriate for performances in his day.[90] So had Zang Maoxun, but with a different model of *chuanqi* drama in mind, and a different audience.

In the following discussion of *Fengliu meng* I accept the premise that it is a theatrically inspired "directorial" adaptation of *Mudan ting*, made for a broad, middlebrow, opera-loving public rather than for the highbrow audience of household performances. I examine briefly how Feng modified *Mudan ting*'s macrostructure before embarking on a more searching examination of his changes to the lyrically dense arias and to the dialogue (the microstructure). The changes he introduced, I believe, reflect a free-handed recreation of the earlier play, such as Catherine Clément finds to be common in our own "age of the director." In this respect, comparisons with Zang Maoxun's revision will be in order. Both men had a similar background, literary training, and familiarity with the theater. Feng appears to have been familiar with Zang's adaptation—or one now lost (perhaps Shen Jing's) that both men consulted—since his text agrees with Zang's rather than Tang's, or responds to features of Zang's version. However, as editors and revisers the two men's methods were quite different. I address how they differed, and the light these differences shed on the response to *Mudan ting* among literati playwrights, in the conclusion to this chapter.

Scene Structure and Plot

The first two of Feng's general critiques of *Mudan ting* reflect his concern with achieving a logically consistent, streamlined plot and with ridding the play of superfluous action and scenes. They also reveal terminology, used in his fiction criticism, having to do with how parts of a work are articulated into a whole. The first critique discusses a critical element of *Mudan ting*'s plot, the dream:

> With no prior arrangement, two dreams tally with each other—an extraordinary thing! In the original text, when Liu first appears, he divulges how, on account of a dream, he has changed his name. Only after three or four more scenes does Liniang first enter the dream. For the two dreams to be so disconnected is uninspired. Now, it is only by having Liu's change of name follow closely upon Liniang's dream that a sense of conjugal affinity is manifested. In the scene "[Husband and Wife] Match Dreams" [scene 26 of *Fengliu meng*] the two plot strands converge. Vulgar actors end the scene with Laitouyuan [Scabby Turtle]'s dialogue, and cut the two arias sung to the tune *Jiangtou jingui*—most regrettable![91]

Feng here refers to the fact that *Mudan ting* has two dreams and two dreamers instead of the more usual one.[92] What bothers him is the disconnectedness of the dreams, the fact that Liu Mengmei mentions his dream when we first meet him in scene 2, while Liniang's dream is not mentioned until scene 10. His solution is to delay Liu's account of his dream until after the scene devoted to Liniang's dream (7 in *Fengliu meng*). Liu's account comes in "The Lover Registers His Dream" (scene 8), whose title underscores the relatedness of the two dreams in Feng's design. Feng then solidifies the link at the end of "Husband and Wife Match Dreams" ("Elopement" in *Mudan ting* [scene 36]). He scraps an original sequence of four lyrically intense arias the lovers exchange, which Tang wrote to conclude his scene, and substitutes in their place two arias completely rewritten to a different aria pattern, the aforementioned *Jiangtou jingui*. These arias are written in a style that Feng favored, in which singing is frequently punctuated with dialogue.[93] They are preceded by a brief passage of dialogue spoken by Liu after he and Liniang have exchanged vows on board the boat bound for Hangzhou. Chunxiang has left them alone:

(*Liu Mengmei and Liniang sit side by side on a mat spread on the deck*)

Liu: Aboard this craft lit by moonlight and propelled by breeze, our nuptials newly solemnized, our joy can be imagined. My wife, it hasn't been easy for you and me to reach this point.

Liniang: "Beneath the branches of either willow or plum" was my heart's wish. May I ask how it was that you took the name "Dreams of Plum" [Mengmei]?

Liu: I had a dream.

Liniang: I'm listening—

Liu: (sings to *Jiangtou jingui*):

I remember how that day I took a nap when all was still,
And dreamt I saw a beautiful girl of sixteen.
She stood beneath a plum tree, her manner seemed inviting,
She opened her red lips, her breath redolent of orchid and musk—

She said, "Master Liu, Master Liu, I am the one you must meet to set foot on your road to love and to high office."

Her whispered words entreated me;
In my dream, I assented to them.
Awakening, they lingered in my ears;
On that day I changed my name.

As I was en route to Chang'an, in mid-journey I suddenly became ill.

I rested for a time at Plum Blossom Shrine, unable to continue my journey.

By chance I took a stroll in the garden. Beneath the Taihu rocks, I found a rosewood box, with a scroll depicting a beauty inside. When I unrolled and examined it, it was just like the girl I had seen in my dream.

I examined her pretty features, intoned her fine poem,

How infatuated I was then!

How was I to know that this would draw your pretty ghost to me? Truly,

The sun rises in the east, while in the west there is rain,
One thinks that feelings have gone when in fact they are there.

May I ask, wife, when you wrote your poem? How was it that the words "beneath the branches of either willow or plum" referred to my name?

Liniang (*smiling*): I also had a dream.

Liu: I'm listening—

Liniang: (*sings to the same tune*):

I recall that day when, eyes clouded with fatigue,
I dreamt of a clever young student.

Liu: That was me!

Liniang:

Holding a willow branch in his hand,
Smiling, he asked me to write new verses for him.

Liu: Did you oblige?

Liniang:

Embarrassed, not yet finished intoning my poem,
I awakened from my dream,
And contracted a spring sickness.
Without hope, I drew my portrait and inscribed a poem on it;
How, having left behind his name at my death, could I foresee
A time when I would meet my lord, so ardently loving?

Master Liu, have you brought that portrait with you?

Liu: It houses one portion of your spiritual parts; I would not be parted one inch from it. (*He produces the scroll, and they look at it; Liniang weeps*)

Liniang:

You examined the portrait,
And relied on it to be your go-between.
(*She points to the portrait*)

Master Liu, don't treat it carelessly!

This is the soul within the portrait,
Husband and wife because of a dream,
In death and in life—all for the sake of feeling.[94]

At the comparable moment in *Mudan ting* (scene 39, "Hangzhou") Liniang describes her dream to Liu, but there is no corresponding account from him concerning his dream, only a recollection of their "ghostly love-making" and fear that jealous minions from the underworld would keep them apart.[95] In *Mudan ting* Tang goes out of his way to confuse any perception that the dream in the Du family garden is one that the lovers share. He appears instead to suggest that it is a product of Liniang's uniquely powerful emotions, which have little if anything to do with those of the dream lover. Here and elsewhere he wrote against the norms for *chuanqi* romantic drama, which favored pairings, such that the representation of one character is part of a dialectic of similarity and difference with respect to the other character. Feng was sensitive to asymmetry in Tang's depiction of the central romantic pair, inasmuch as Liu Mengmei's character is inferior to Liniang's and more shallow. Here he labors to restore balance, by portraying Liniang and Liu as equal parties to the dream experience, and equally committed to it.[96]

The second of Feng's general critiques takes up the problem of splintering (*zhili*) in *Mudan ting*'s plot, with specific reference to another common pairing in romances, that of mistress and maid:

> In southern drama, what is most to be avoided is splintering. There is a *tie* [secondary female character] and a *dan*, but then he has written in a *xiaogugu* [little nun]. Isn't this exceedingly superfluous? Now I have changed it, so that it is Chunxiang who becomes a nun and have substituted her for the little nun. Moreover, this furnishes the ground [*zhangben*] for [Chunxiang's] recognition of the portrait, and gets rid of a number of creepers.[97]

The "little nun" is indeed a minor character, a young acolyte in the service of Sister Stone, a more formidable figure who in *Mudan ting* assumes many of Chunxiang's duties after Liniang has died and become a wandering ghost. The removal of the acolyte does little to change *Mudan ting*'s plot. However, by having Chunxiang take her place (in scene 20, Feng's version of the original scene 27), Feng restores to her the role of serving maid and confidant that is usurped in *Mudan ting* by the older and more worldly Stone. Here, as in the case of the dream, Feng's streamlining restores to its place of centrality a typical pairing in *chuanqi* romances—the *dan* and *tie* roles—while ridding the play of the anomalous pairing of Liniang and Stone (*dan* and *jing* roles).[98]

We can pursue one outcome of this enhanced role for Chunxiang by examining another aspect of Feng's adapting method, his frequent alteration of aria sequences, which goes beyond the simple cutting or piecemeal revision of specific arias typically undertaken by Zang Maoxun. I have already mentioned Feng's substitution of two arias written to a different tune for four original arias in his adaptation of scene 36.[99] A more interesting example of this occurs in "Mother and Daughter Reunited" (renamed "Mother and Daughter Meet" in *Fengliu meng*). The original scene brings together two pairings—Madam Du and Chunxiang, Liniang and Sister Stone—comprising two narrative lines that converge at this point, part of an incipient movement towards reunion, *tuanyuan*, that culminates in the final scene. Tang wrote a sequence of four arias (to the tune *Bu shi lu*), which are sung alternately by Madam Du and Liniang, with Stone singing the third aria and Chunxiang contributing an occasional line of dialogue. In his revision Feng collapsed the four arias into one long variant of the same basic aria type, *Zhuma'er zhuan*,[100] after which he wrote a shorter aria for Chunxiang (Sister Stone having dropped out of *Fengliu meng* after the lovers elope in scene 26).[101] My translation of Feng's text begins just after Chunxiang has gone out to buy oil for the lamps, leaving Liniang alone, sitting in the dark. No sooner does Chunxiang leave than Madam Du arrives, accompanied by an old serving woman:[102]

Madam Du (sings to *Zhuma'er zhuan*):

Flight in anger,
Has brought us almost to Hangzhou,
With no one to whom we can turn.

Old mother, since parting from my husband, our journey was uneventful until, nearing Hangzhou, a storm unexpectedly arose at Wuling and overturned our boat, casting servants and baggage into the water, all of whom perished, save you and me. Now, ten days later, we are at the gates of Hangzhou, but it is late, and we have no place to stay. What to do?[103]

Pitiable, we hesitate in the dark of night.

Old serving woman: For the time being we can seek lodging at the village inn, until we devise another plan.

Madam Du:

We cannot easily go to a village inn,
We would lose face.

Old serving woman: Things having reached this point, one cannot speak of losing face. I'll just knock on the gate. (*She knocks*) Is anyone there?

Liniang: Who is it?

Old serving woman: That's a woman's voice; I'll call again for her to open the gate.

Liniang:

Who is it that calls to me again and again,
Can you please say who you are?

Madam Du:

Because we have no place to rest,
Come to this place, we must bother you a while.
Two we are, women of good family.

Liniang: A lady. That voice is familiar, and as it happens, Master Liu is not here.

Their arrival is most opportune.

It is often said that, "To do others a favor is to favor yourself."

I'll ask them in and hear what they have to say.

Are you both women?

Madam Du: Truly, there is no man. (*Liniang opens the door*)

Madam Du (*in surprise*): Ah!
Sitting alone, lamp unlit;
How fearful the blackness, how can she endure it?
Liniang:
Please come inside
You can take your ease and listen while I explain.
Madam Du (*turning around and addressing the old serving woman*): Mother, that voice is very familiar.
Liniang (*in an aside*): Strange! That woman's voice resembles my mother's. (*Turning back*): May I ask where Madam is from?
Madam Du (*with a sigh*):
Fleeing the troops, we have come here—
Liniang: Of what family are you?
Madam Du: The Pacification Commissioner for Huai'an, my husband, Du Bao.
Liniang (*in surprise*): In that case, you are my mother!
Madam Du: Who is your mother?
Liniang: Mother, your daughter Liniang is here!
Madam Du (*in fear*): Aya! Aya!
My daughter died young,
And is buried in Nan'an.
How could her soul have wandered so far?
Liniang:
Please, don't be afraid;
Don't take me for a ghost and get upset.
Madam Du: If you aren't a ghost, you can't be human. Old mother, hurry! We must go.
Liniang: Where is mother going? (*Madam Du tries to go but cannot*)
Old serving woman: A ghost has come over the wall!
Liniang: Mother, please sit; I have something to say. (*She clutches at her hand*)
Madam Du (*very frightened*): Your hand is cold! A ghost; a ghost!
Liniang: I'm not a ghost—
Madam Du: Liniang, child, your father was stubborn and didn't have a mass said for you. Don't blame your mother.
Liniang (*weeps*): Mother, however much you may fear me, nothing will make me leave you again! (*The old maidservant performs a comic action; Chunxiang reenters with lamp*)
Chunxiang: (sings to *Manpai qian baochan*):
Restless and bored at the inn,
I went and begged fire with which to pass the night.
From where have come these cold night travelers?

And why all this chatter?

(*She enters and shines the lamp*)

Strange! She resembles her ladyship.

Liniang: Chunxiang, come quickly! Her ladyship is here!

Madam Du: How did Chunxiang get here? Don't tell me that she's a ghost too!

Chunxiang: It really is her ladyship. I must kowtow—

Happily, the young mistress was reborn,
I, as before, could not abandon her.

Madam Du: Child, if you really aren't a ghost, I will call your name thrice and you must answer thrice, each time louder than before. (*She clutches at Liniang, who begins to weep*) My dear child, ghost or not I couldn't bear to give you up again! (*She sits down. Liniang kneels down, clutching at her and weeping*)

Liniang: Dear mother!

Liniang, Madam Du:

By what good fortune do we meet at this difficult time?
Mother at sky's edge,
Child from the infernal realm.[104]

Immediately following the aria sung by Chunxiang, Feng creates an original passage of rhymed patter, in which Liniang, then Chunxiang, recount at length the history of Liniang's resurrection and marriage to Liu Mengmei.[105] The action then takes a new turn, since Feng chooses to have Madam Du meet her son-in-law at this juncture rather than in the final scene. In "Mother and Daughter Meet" Liu and Liniang are still together; Liu departs in search of Du Bao only after meeting his mother-in-law.

Tang follows up the *Bu shi lu* sequence with another consisting of four arias sung to the same tune (the aforementioned *Fanshan hu*). Madam, Liniang, Stone, and Chunxiang sing (in that order); each aria consists of sung lines only, and as a whole, the sequence balances lyricism (the arias of Madam Du and Liniang) with humor (those of Stone and Chunxiang), intense emotion with wry amazement, in a manner characteristic of Tang's compositional style.

Feng's handling reveals several of the methods he favored when rewriting Tang's text. Most obvious is his expanded use of dialogue: first, in the two arias he wrote in place of the *Bu shi lu* sequence, then in a long passage of dialogue, of which the rhymed patter comprises one part, which replaces the *Fanshan hu* sequence translated above (pp. 46–48). His greater reliance on dialogue flattens the tone, and shifts toward narrative exposition, a move reinforced by a singing that favors an exchange between two actors over solo singing by one actor. This is sometimes referred to as a "dialogue" (*wenda*, or *duida*) form, in which two actors alternate singing, or one actor sings and a second responds in dialogue.[106] Feng uses such patterns extensively in *Fengliu meng*. Tang favored solo singing much more than Feng did,[107] and as we have seen in "The Interrupted Dream" and "Pursuing the Dream" he often wrote in a dense, evocative idiom. To counter the effect of such emotionally "thick" arias, Tang would smuggle humor into adjoining arias rather than segregate it in dialogue. An example in the *Fanshan hu* sequence are arias sung by Stone and Chunxiang, which deflate the tensions of those sung by Madam Du and Liniang, bringing the emotions back down to earth with wry reflections.

Perhaps following Zang Maoxun's lead, Feng replaced the second pair of arias with a long section of jingly dialogue in which Liniang and Chunxiang recite the history of Liniang's romance with Liu and her resurrection. By so doing he removed complicated effects achieved by Tang Xianzu through pairing of characters, whose singing produces a rich interplay of sentiments.[108] Feng's motives when rewriting this scene were similar to Zang's, to preserve the essential action and remove elements he judged to be superfluous.

Responses to the Adaptations: Zang Maoxun vs. Feng Menglong

We can say with confidence that Zang Maoxun's methods of adapting *Mudan ting* were quite different from Feng Menglong's and that Feng took little from his predecessor's adaptation. Both men had similar agendas—they wanted to streamline the play and bring its arias into conformity with prosodic standards for Kun opera. Both wanted to simplify its structure and make its language easier to understand. The different methods for doing so reveal differences in taste and thinking about southern drama, as well as different senses of the public for it. Both men did more than simply adapt *Mudan ting* musically; each also stripped Tang's language of its distinctiveness and divested his heroine of her uniqueness.

Differences between Zang and Feng are clearest in the way they handled the relationship between dialogue and singing, and the way they approached the aria form. This is a highly technical subject, but some things can be said without getting drawn into the arcane details. Although each cut the original play quite ruthlessly, Zang was more likely than Feng to revise what remained of the musical score implied by the contextual, rhythmic, and tonal data of a *qupai* sequence.[109] That is, Zang rarely substituted different arias, preferring to tinker with the original ones, especially the tonal patterns of the text, where he kept some lines and revised others according to his knowledge of the Kun melodic repertoire, which was considerable if his own claims are to be credited.[110] Here, as well as at the level of larger structural units, scenes and scene sequences, Zang sought to streamline by removing padded syllables (Tang used far too many of them for Kun purists), and by excising dialogue from between sung lines within the aria. In general, he preferred to keep the sung and spoken portions of the text separate from and adjacent to each other rather than intermingle them.[111]

I have suggested that Zang was apt to put arias to dialogue-like uses, by the manner in which he rewrote them. He did not, however, favor the dialogue pattern in which singing and dialogue alternate frequently and passages of sustained singing are rare. Nor, as a rule, did he favor interactive singing patterns, in which two or more characters each sing a few lines, then yield to the other. Both of these, however, were patterns that Feng Menglong favored heavily.

I have also speculated that Zang's methods may have been influenced by the uses to which singing and dialogue were put in northern drama. Moreover, the form of Zang's text, in which the arias tend to stand apart from the surrounding dialogue, is compatible with a performance practice popular among literati opera lovers known as "pure singing" (*qingchang*). This consisted of singing only, without accompanying dialogue or stage action. The lack of notation in Zang's editions need not deter us from thinking that he intended them for such use. There is some evidence that literati connoisseurs disdained notational aids, at least in Zang's time.[112] In other words, we need not necessarily conclude that Zang meant his elegant edition of Tang's plays only for reading pleasure and aesthetic enjoyment.

Feng favored the *wenda* singing pattern that Zang avoided, quite heavily in the case of *Fengliu meng*. He freely substituted arias of his own devising for the originals, preserving more or less of the original language as he went. His approach to dialogue is almost the mirror image of Zang's. It is fairly rare to encounter passages of sustained singing in *Fengliu meng*, but very common to find short bursts of singing broken up with short passages of dialogue.[113] In this respect Feng's practice approximates that found in Qing dynasty texts of *Mudan ting*, which were modified by professional actors. The difference, a significant one, is that actors almost never tampered with Tang's language in the arias. They frequently cut arias, but almost never rewrote them.

Both methods of rewriting yielded a playtext whose language was less concentrated and lyrically dense than the original. The language was also less inwardly focused because in their different ways both Zang and Feng sought to naturalize Tang's diction by making it more closely approximate natural syntax and the conventional idiom used in vernacular genres. And where Tang Xianzu's representation of character is directed inward through the tensions created between character and setting of the action—Hirose Reiko's "objective details"—or antagonisms that arise between the characters as the action unfolds, the purposeful undoing of those tensions by other playwrights through simplification throws Tang's more intricate structures into relief.

The liberties Zang and Feng took with Tang's language elicited a sharp response from fellow connoisseurs that was directed especially at Zang's edition. Their defense of the original text resulted in the appearance, in 1620, of the "red ink" edition referred to in chapter 1.[114] This was the project of a man named Mao Ying, who asked his brother, Mao Yuanyi (fl. 1636), to contribute a preface. In that preface Mao Yuanyi leveled a scathing attack at Zang's adaptation:

> Zang Jinshu [Maoxun] of Zhiwei considered [*Mudan ting*] to be a desktop play, not one that could be performed on the stage. He deleted its brilliance and blunted its sharpness in order to make it suit [the tastes of] ordinary artisans and vulgar listeners. Reading the language, I find it painful that strange events are rendered in pedestrian lyrics, strange lyrics are put to pedestrian melodies, and strange melodies are given pedestrian rhythms. As far as the author's ideas are concerned, the obliteration is complete.[115]

These remarks suggest that Mao attributed Zang's treachery to a misguided attempt to popularize the play, i.e., to reach the same audience that Feng Menglong claimed to be writing for—"ordinary artisans" (*yong-gong*), who made their living in the theater and "vulgar listeners" (*su'er*).

I believe, however, that Zang produced his edition for the wealthy elite. No doubt one of his motives was commercial, and perhaps this was his chief motive. However, his intent as editor and publisher of southern plays, implied in the second preface to *Yuanqu xuan*, was more disinterested: to influence tastes by revising the southern plays of an admired contemporary, whose *oeuvre* epitomized the genre's baroque, even decadent excesses. Tang's complete plays, once rewritten in the straightforward and healthy manner of *zaju*, would be models for a new kind of southern drama. His collection bore the title *Yuming xin* ("new") *ci*. If this was Zang's project, it failed miserably. It is remarkable that one individual could cater so successfully to his audience in one dramatic genre (*zaju*) and fail to reach the same audience in the other (*chuanqi*).[116]

The response to *Fengliu meng* is more elusive. Collections of Feng's plays continued to be reprinted well into the Qing period, in groups of four, five, seven, and, most commonly, ten plays, but *Fengliu meng* never was included in them. This suggests that, in the whole play format at least, it did not command an audience, much less supplant Tang Xianzu's play, as happened in the case of some other plays Feng revised and many works of fiction that he published in substantially revised form.[117] Feng played a mediating role in his day between two publics for vernacular fiction and drama, one highbrow, the other middlebrow, and he was more successful when he revised crudely written popular works such as the vernacular novel *Pingyao zhuan* (Quashing the Demons' Revolt) and the early Ming play *Shagou ji* than he was when he chose to popularize highbrow works such as *Mudan ting*.[118]

There is scattered evidence that *Fengliu meng* had an impact on *Mudan ting*'s life on the stage. Traces of Feng's revisions crop up in Qing dynasty texts of *chuanqi* plays that were published in miscellanies. Unlike Ming collections such as Mao Jin's *Liushizhong qu* (Sixty Southern Dramas), Qing miscellanies were collections of scenes performed independent of the whole play. I take up this aspect of *Mudan ting*'s existence, both in textual form and on the stage, in Part 2 of this study.

In one other respect Feng Menglong's adaptation of *Mudan ting* is quite distinct from Zang Maoxun's, and that is the "readerly" way in which he revised Tang's language, especially the intricate imagery that is a distinctive feature of the play. Lu Shulun, in an article on Feng's playwriting methods, took his title from a comment made about Feng's plays by the noted critic and scholar Wu Mei (1884–1939), who praised them in these terms:

> For every aria he carefully indicated the rhythmic form [*banshi*], and expended no small amount of effort. . . . The workmanship of both arias and dialogue is marvelous, possessing beauty on both desktop and stage.[119]

Although Feng was as concerned as Zang with well-constructed plays that had clearly articulated plots, he also recognized that the plot should not be too straightforward, but should possess indirectness (*weiwan*) and "natural variation" (*bolan*). That is, it should not be too nakedly plain, or it would lose its audience.[120] In his commentary, he articulated ideas about "fine jointure" in the text that reflect concern about the articulation of parts into a well-conceived whole.[121] These concerns are also revealed in how Feng responded to the texture of Tang Xianzu's language, at a level that transcends the structural units (scene sequences, aria sequences, relationship of aria to dialogue) with which I have been concerned in this chapter. We might say that Feng unraveled Tang's linguistic fabric and rewove it according to his own design. It is to this "reading" of *Mudan ting*, the more strictly literary dimension of Feng's adaptation, that I turn in the next chapter.

Three

Containment of Imagery in *Fengliu meng*

In his studies of Renaissance art, Leo Steinberg has argued the usefulness for the critic of copies, even bad copies:

> That early copies may furnish evidence of damage accrued to the original, and of subsequent overpainting, is obvious and requires no argument. But copies have subtler uses. Where they depart from their models—provided these departures are patently willful and not due to incompetence—they constitute a body of criticism more telling than anything dreamt of in contemporaneous writing. The man who copies a painting looks harder, observes by the inch, and where he refuses to follow his model, follows an alternative, usually critical impulse. Few writers on art have the patience or the vocabulary to match the involvement of a recalcitrant copyist. His alterations reveal how a closely engaged contemporary regarded his model, what he admired or censured, or chose to omit.[1]

Steinberg goes on to point out that "in a strong design the detail is so integrated that it is hard to unthink," and that the "deviant renderings" of a copy can help us see the decisions that went into the original design. When we see what a copyist misses (or leaves out), it helps us to notice what we otherwise might not.[2]

This kind of critical technique, practiced brilliantly by Steinberg in two studies of Michelangelo,[3] is useful when considering Feng Menglong's adaptation of *Mudan ting*. In *Mudan ting*, Tang Xianzu's language is visual and marked by a conceptually bold use of imagery. Throughout *Fengliu meng* we see clearly that Feng Menglong was at pains to simplify and contain the effects of this language. His efforts may not have been "patently willful"—more likely his own ideas took hold in the process of rewriting—but he rewrote critically, with a different paradigm of romantic drama in mind. It is this aspect of his response to *Mudan ting* that I examine here.

Earlier I noted that the action of the first thirty-five scenes of *Mudan ting* takes place largely in Liniang's world, her private rooms and the garden that lies beyond them. While it is typical for romantic plays to be set in such a private space, Tang's treatment of Liniang's garden is unusually elaborate, suggesting the importance of the love theme in the play. One way to grasp this is through the intricacy of Tang's language, and this can be illustrated by isolating two key motifs in the play and examining their treatment over a number of scenes.

Both involve the use of figures that metaphorically represent one (or in some cases both) of the play's central characters. The first is a plum tree, which makes its appearance in scene 12, "Pursuing the Dream." From the moment it suddenly looms in Liniang's gaze, the plum clearly is no ordinary tree. The attention devoted to it at the end of one of the play's longest scenes alerts us to this fact. In some sense it represents Liniang's mysterious dream lover, but its attributes, considered in isolation, furnish few clues to the tree's other figurative possibilities.

The second figure is the self-portrait that Liniang paints in scene 14. This portrait, emblematic of the heroine (self-consciously so), can be readily seen as a conventional element of the southern drama.[4] Its use as a symbolic device is less remarkable than the introduction of the plum tree two scenes earlier. However, Tang's use of the portrait is original and warrants examination in conjunction with the plum. Because Tang represented both lovers with figures of this type rather than the usual single one, they are best considered together.

In both cases it will thus be necessary first to examine Feng's model—Tang's text—before taking up his reworking of it in *Fengliu meng*. The two plays must therefore be kept in view, and as I examine each figure, I will be asking how Feng's simplifications distorted Tang's conception and design. In the conclusion to this chapter, I will discuss how the differences between the two playwrights reflect on the late-Ming reception of *Mudan ting*.

The Plum Tree in *Mudan ting*

In scene 10 of *Mudan ting*, "The Interrupted Dream," Du Liniang takes a springtime stroll with her maid Chunxiang in the large, yet mysteriously empty, garden outside her bedchamber. Her ennui is perturbed by the burgeoning beauty of the place, and after returning to her room she falls asleep. She dreams of a young man who comes to her with a willow branch in his hand. He declares his love in an ardent song before carrying her behind a mound of weathered Taihu rocks. Their lovemaking, which takes place offstage, is described in an aria sung by a Huashen (Flower Spirit), who acts as both Liniang's protector and witness to the lovemaking. The lovers return, and the young man takes his leave. The scene concludes as Liniang is awakened by her mother, who chides her for napping in midday.

Two scenes later Liniang returns to the garden, drawn by the memory of her dream. She comes to a place very like the one she dreamed of: a Taihu rockery with an enclosed bed of peonies. She struggles with the power of her emotions and the apparent unreality of the experience that has stirred them. Who was her lover, and what is the nature of their bond? Is her experience of him to remain a dream? When, if ever, will he come to her? In this scene's climactic sequence Liniang struggles to reconcile the expectations aroused by her dream with the reality of her sheltered life. Highly susceptible to her dream's remembered pleasures, she soon surrenders to them, this time through the power of her imagination.

The rockery and enclosure of peonies, which figure prominently in both scenes, are a natural setting that reappears at key moments of the play. They are also a symbolic landscape, a topos associated with Liniang's initiation into love, her death, and her revival at Liu Mengmei's hands. In scene 10 the rockery is part of Liniang's dream—the place to which her mysterious lover carries her—while in scene 12 it is an actual place, a deserted corner of the family garden to which she is drawn, and where she recalls her experience of love.

It is at this moment, as her reverie ends, that Liniang notices a large tree that has appeared as if out of nowhere. The tree is remarkable both for the suddenness of its appearance and for Liniang's description of it:[5]

Liniang: Why! In a place where no one comes, suddenly I find a great plum tree, lovely with its thick clusters of fruit. (Sings to *Erfan yao ling*):

How can its hidden fragrance spread so clear,	偏則他暗香清遠
Its shade like a parasol reach full round?	傘兒般蓋的周全
Thriving,	他趁這
Thriving in this third month of spring "when rich rains swell the red to bursting,"	他趁這春三月紅綻雨肥天
Its leaves shine green,	葉兒青
Its full round fruit hide bitter heart.	偏迸著苦仁兒裡撒圓

Cherishing this daytime shade,	愛煞這書陰
Let me find again a dream of Lofu.[6]	便再得到羅浮夢邊

Isolated in a desolate corner of the garden, the tree elicits a complicated response from Liniang. Its sudden appearance as her dream fades suggests that it embodies the dream lover.[7] Its verdant foliage and ripening fruit, which contrast sharply in Liniang's mind with the cold loneliness of the garden setting, suggest vital and procreative forces of nature with which her lover has become identified, and the tree's shade associates it with the world of her dream. But the tree's imagery has more than one frame of reference. It evokes the male lover (real or imagined) and also reveals Liniang's state of mind about herself. In particular, the female associations of the plum are conveyed in the image of the bitter seed bursting from within the ripening fruit. The fruit suggests Liniang's sexual ripeness, and its "bitter heart" (*kuren*) her sadness at the passing of time and her youth.[8]

Subsequent references to the plum and recurrences of language first used in this scene carry this duality forward. In the song immediately following the one just quoted, Liniang commits herself to the plum tree, which has become identified in her mind with her absent lover:

Liniang: So be it: I am so drawn to this flowering plum, I should count it a great good fortune to be buried here beside it when I die. (Sings to *Jiang'er shui*):

My heart is drawn by chance,	偶然間心似繾
To this plum tree's side.	梅樹邊
Thus could we love which flower or herb we please,	這般花花草草 由人戀
Live and die according to our wishes,	生生死死隨人願
Then none would moan for bitter pain.	便酸酸楚楚無人怨
I will marshal my fragrant spirit,	待打併香魂一片
Through the dark rains of summer,	陰雨梅天
And keep company with this plum's roots.[9]	守的個梅根相見

Liniang's desire to remain beside the tree anticipates her later wish to be buried beneath it. In death she will "keep company with" the tree, as she kept company with her lover, briefly, in her dream. In the last line of this aria, the echoing of language from scene 10 establishes the link with him (in Liniang's mind, at least). The effect is to personify the tree; it is as if in death Liniang will leave her parents and go to her husband.[10] The tree's arching branches are several times associated with shelter and protection, suggestive of the roles of lover and husband.[11]

In *Mudan ting* references to the plum's blossoms—its most outstanding attribute for poets—are rare. Liniang's description evokes the tree's appearance at the height of spring, when the blossoms have long since faded and fallen. It is the third month, the season of "plum rains" that fatten the maturing fruit. Of interest here is Tang's allusion to a couplet by Du Fu:

Green hang wind-shorn bamboo,	綠垂風折筍
Red burst rain-fattened plums.	紅綻雨肥梅

In Du Fu's poem, the likely referent for *mei* is the plum's fruit, which "fattens" (*fei*) in the late spring rains.[12] Resituated in Liniang's aria, however, the reference to plum is elided, and the season (*tian*) of "plum rains" given instead, so that the referent for *hong zhan yufei* ("red burst rain-fattened") becomes vague. Is it other fruits that ripen red (in Chinese poetry, plum fruits are usually green or yellow), or is there retrospective reference to the plum's red blossoms, which have split (*zhan*) to form the fruit?[13] If the latter, Tang gives us in this aria a compressed cycle of imagery associated with the plum tree—from blossom to foliage to ripening fruit.[14] However understood, the colors associated with the plum here are green and red, colors also associated with vigorous youth.

Thus in *Erfan yao ling* the plum participates in the colorful fecundity of Liniang's garden at the height of spring. Green foliage, red bursting blossoms, and ripening fruit are its outstanding attributes. In subsequent contexts where the plum's blossoms are mentioned, they are also red, but now identified with Liniang dead. These references are suggestive and deserve a close look.

In scene 20 ("Keening"), Liniang, nearing death, asks her parents to bury her beneath the plum tree in the garden. When her mother asks why, she responds:

Liniang (singing *Yu ying'er*):

I can become no ailing Chang E	做不的病嬋娟
immortal in the moon's cassia grottoes,	桂窟裡長生
But am fated to be a pretty skeleton	則分的粉骷髏
in plum blossom's ancient cave.[15]	向梅花古洞

"Plum blossom's ancient cave" is the first of many references to tomb-like cavities, which appear in various guises through the middle part of the play.[16] Since cavities also suggest wombs, in a somewhat bizarre way the Liniang dead in her tomb hints at her rebirth. The second line contains two unusual juxtapositions: of beauty with death and of flowers with caves. Both images conflate categories usually kept distinct, and one effect is to dissolve (or weaken) the sense of indissoluble boundaries.[17]

In scene 27 ("Spirit Roaming"), the plum is used in a deliberately figurative manner, and here its blossoms are again identified with Liniang dead. The season is spring; three years have passed since Liniang's death, and the time has come for rituals to ensure that her spirit will be reborn in the Realm of Jade (Yujie). For this occasion Sister Stone, the priestess entrusted with the care of her grave, has put a flowering branch from the plum tree in a vase and placed it on the altar of Liniang's Plum Blossom Shrine.[18] In the eyes of the celebrants, the flowering branch represents Liniang herself, who was fated to die at the peak of youthful perfection:

> *Sister Stone*: I reflect that the young lady died of her passionate grieving for the flowers, and so today I have picked a sprig of flowering plum to present before her in a consecrated vase. (Sings to *Xiao nan ge*):
>
> In purified vase 瓶兒淨
> Under cold spring sun 春凍陽
> Set one last spray of plum, 殘梅半枝紅蠟裝
> its waxen blooms still red.
>
> Ah young mistress
>
> By whose side do you walk in fragrant dream 你香夢與誰行
> Spirit so determined? 精神忒孤往
>
> *Celebrants*: Tell us teacher, what is represented by the consecrated vase, and what by the sprig of plum?
>
> *Sister Stone:*
>
> Within the hollow of this vase 這瓶兒空像
> A world is concealed, 世界包藏
> While her body is like this faded spray of plum. 身似殘梅樣
> Watered but rootless, 有水無根
> It still brings a fragrance to our senses.[19] 尚作餘香想

The celebrants identify the plum branch with the dead girl in her tomb, an identification that Liniang herself makes when her wandering ghost visits the shrine after the ritual has been completed and the celebrants have withdrawn. Drawn by the sweetness of the incense, she reads the prayers and notices the fading blossoms in the vase:

> *Liniang*: Ha! A faded plum branch from atop my tomb. Plum blossoms, like Du Liniang, you faded in mid-bloom—how sad! (Sings to *Xia shan hu*):
>
> | | |
> |---|---|
> | These broken drumbeats, random striking of bells, intoning of gold-lettered scriptures | 則為這斷鼓零鐘金字經 |
> | Have broken in upon my yellow millet dream. | 叩動俺黃粱境 |
> | Thrusting its way past plum's roots in fissured earth | 俺向這地圻裡梅根迸幾程 |
> | My shade emerges forth. | 透出些兒影 |
>
> (*She weeps*): Unless I leave some trace of my presence, how can I show my appreciation for the devotion of these pious sisters? Then let me scatter petals of the plum here on the altar. (*She does so*)[20]

Liniang's song confirms the association of the plum with herself in respect to its fading red blooms and its rootlessness, cut off from the sources of life. In the immediate context the rootless stem symbolizes Liniang's morbid state, but as it emerges from the watery cavity of the vase its red blossoms, scattered on the shrine, take on other connotations.

Zang Maoxun, commenting on this passage, finds resonances between Liniang's gesture here and the Huashen's scattering of red blossoms on the lovers during the dream sequence in scene 10:

> The breaking off of a sprig of faded plum blossoms as an offering facilitates the ghost *dan*'s scattering of blossoms. [This act] reveals a trace of her presence. Moreover, it resonates with the matter of the Huashen.[21]

Overtly, Liniang's scattering of the faded blossoms suggests her grief over lost beauty and wasted youth.[22] But might there not be a covert meaning as well?

If there is resonance with the Huashen's gesture, another association linking fallen blossoms to Liniang's sexuality is also present. Ostensibly, the Huashen scatters the flowers to wake Liniang from her dream. But the profusion of red petals (*hongyu*) that rain down on the lovers at the moment of consummation also has erotic overtones, despite the fact that the consummation is only imagined, "fulfilled in the thought" (*xiangnei cheng*) but not yet in reality.[23] In scene 12 Liniang recalls the falling petals in her dream in language with clearly sexual overtones, as "red shadows, petals torn from heart of flower" (*yipian sahuaxin de hongying'er*).[24]

If such extended readings of Tang's imagery are permitted, then the faded blossoms scattered on Liniang's shrine are more than a pathetic image of wasted maidenhood; paradoxically they also have power as images of her sexuality. Liniang's description in the same aria of her ghost bursting from its root-encased tomb has similar force.

Aspects of Tang's imagery suggest that the procreative forces of nature are also on display in scene 28, "Union in the Shades." Liu Mengmei is gazing at Liniang's portrait, which he has found in its red sandalwood box among the rocks beside her tomb. Wondering who could have produced such a painting, and the poem written on it that seems to refer to him, he expresses his wonderment through fanciful allusion:

Liu (sings to *Huansha xi*):

These words she composed	拈詩話
For one who would understand	對會家
Predestined "willow" or "plum."	柳和梅有分兒些
Her spring longings burst from crevice in rock mound,	他春心迸出湖山罅
A Green Calyx soaring aloft to light on this painted silk.[25]	飛上煙綃萼綠華

Repetition of the strong word *beng* (to burst, or gush forth), used in several important passages in the play, creates suggestive linkages.[26] The lines echo Liniang's of the scene before ("My shade emerges forth"); both passages imply a regeneration in which Liu Mengmei has an important role to play but of which he is still unaware. Liniang *is* aware, and she intimates her knowledge on the occasion of her first encounter with Liu, after she has emerged from her tomb to wander as a ghost. Without revealing who (or what) she is, she offers herself to him and he joyfully accepts. In her grateful response Liniang cryptically refers to her return from death, with recourse again to the imagery of the plant world:

Liniang: Then my hopes in you are fulfilled. (Sings to *Shua Bao lao*):

In cold secluded vale	幽谷寒涯
You urge a flower to bloom through the night.[27]	你為俺催花連夜發

The resonance of these verses with others is conceptual rather than verbal. "Cold secluded vale" calls to mind other cavities that remind us of Liniang in her tomb: the watery hollow of the consecrated vase, the cavern beneath the tree, the crevice in the rock mound where her portrait lies hidden. The night-blooming flower requires no explanation, but Liu's part in urging it to bloom does.

The sexual nature of this urging is implicit in Tang Xianzu's elaboration of the plum as an image from nature. Virtually every one of its attributes, as described in this play, is suggestive of human sexuality, both masculine and feminine. The fact that human sexuality is so depicted underscores the fact that it is part of nature and the natural process of death and rebirth. For the most part, however, the sexual act is only obliquely suggested in contexts devoted to the plum. A similar obliqueness obtains in other passages devoted to Liniang in her tomb. Read alone, for example, a reference to a flower being urged to bloom in "cold secluded vale" would not seem a likely sexual metaphor, but when it is linked to other passages the case for a metaphorical meaning becomes stronger. In scene 32 ("Spectral Vows"), for example, the references become much more overtly sexual, when Liniang finally reveals to Liu Mengmei that he has been making love to a ghost and uses vivid language to tell him what he must do to revive her:

> *Liu*: Since you are to return to life from death, may I know the place of your untimely burial?
> *Liniang*: It is beneath the flowering plum tree that stands by the Taihu rocks. (Sings to *San duanzi*):
>
> | | |
> |---|---|
> | There at back of my beloved garden | 愛的是花園後節 |
> | Dreams were lonely | 夢孤清 |
> | In shade of plum's blossoms. | 梅花影斜 |
> | At the season of ripening plums, | 熟梅時節 |
> | Heart grew bitter as seed of fruit. | 為仁兒心酸那些 |
>
> *Liu*: So cold you must have been!
> *Liniang:*
>
> | | |
> |---|---|
> | Frozen body and soul, | 凍的俺七魄三魂 |
> | In coldest chastity. | 僵做了三貞七烈 |
>
> *Liu*: What if I should cause your soul to start in terror?
> Liniang (sings to *Dou shuangji*):
>
> | | |
> |---|---|
> | Beneath roots of flowering tree | 花根木節 |
> | Lies a cavern which leads to a mortal world. | 有一個透人間路穴 |

And my cold fragrant flesh you have already caressed half warm.	俺冷香肌早偎的半熱

. . .

Liu: Not knowing how deep you lie, I am afraid that we may not be able to open a way to you soon.

Liniang (sings to *Deng xiaolou*):

Ha,	咨嗟
A man shows his worth by "going through to the end."	你為人為徹
Full three feet of earth are piled atop my coffin;	俺砌籠棺勾有三尺疊
Take tempered spade and dig your way to me,	你點剛鍬和俺一謎掘
To where	就裡
Cold vapors disperse,	陰風瀉瀉
Some little way apart from sunlit world.[28]	則隔的陽世些些

Liu must penetrate to the cold moist world of Liniang's tomb and revive her. As Liniang implies, the process is already well under way ("And my cold fragrant flesh you have already caressed half warm").[29] When the actual revival takes place in scene 35, it is something of an anticlimax and is supplied with liberal doses of comedy. But in the scenes that lead up to that moment, the return of Liniang's soul to her body is the central drama. When depicting it Tang celebrates the creative force of passion with powerful images, unconventionally used. To understand better his treatment of this idea we must examine his elaboration of the other figure associated with his heroine—the portrait. But first let us examine Feng Menglong's response to Tang's images of the plum.

The Plum in *Fengliu meng*

In *Mudan ting* Tang singles out the tree for attention only at the moment when Liniang has returned to the garden in search of her dream. Its sudden and remarkable appearance then underscores its specialness, especially its natural vitality, which is further enhanced in the description given in Liniang's aria. Feng chose to eliminate that aria from his revision of scene 12, and in its place deployed only muted the natural imagery, focusing instead on Liniang's response to the tree:

Liniang: Look at that plum tree! (Sings to *Jin'e shen*):

From ancient trunk	老幹
Many branches curl	繁枝自卷
To form a cover pleasingly round.	圓如蓋可喜周全
Ai! Old plum, old plum,	
Before the beauty of spring has unfolded,	春色未舒
You are the first to bloom.	是他偏佔先
Just as you steal the march on spring,	
So Du Liniang found good fortune in a dream.[30]	似我杜麗娘夢兒裡可人方便

Feng has opted for a well-established meaning of the plum, as hardy precursor of spring,[31] and by resorting to the explicit mode of simile he muddles the metaphoric ambiguity that characterizes Tang's figure. As a result nothing about the tree hints at Liu's identity or future role; the only attribute that survives the rewriting is the reference to the tree's canopy, stripped of its most interesting qualities.

In other small ways Feng is not sensitive to the signs of the marvelous in the tree's appearance, and he appears to be intent on reducing the aura of mystery that attends its presence in the garden. When Liniang first meets her dream lover in scene 7 of *Fengliu meng* (the revised scene 10 of *Mudan ting*), careful mention is made of the plum tree as a feature of the garden topos:

Liniang (*in a low voice*): Where do you mean to go?
Liu: Over there, beneath the big plum tree, is a good place to talk. (Singing to *Shantao hong*):

Beyond the enclosed bed of peonies,	轉過這芍藥闌西
Up against the Taihu rocks.[32]	緊靠著湖山石邊

Mention of the tree in this scene prepares us for its reappearance in scene 9 of *Fengliu meng*, "Liniang Pursues the Dream." Feng aims for consistency in the arrangement of details, and in doing so sacrifices an element of surprise and wonder surrounding the tree that Tang preserved from his source.[33] In scene 12 of *Mudan ting* the tree's proximity to the rockery is noticed by Liniang only after she has emerged from her reverie. When it suddenly looms before her, its appearance is colored by the longings from her dream recollection. This gives the image a powerfully subjective cast. In Feng's scene, by contrast, the tree is always part of the rockery setting, and so when Liniang returns there she mentions it as one of the familiar elements of the place, even before she has her vision:

> *Liniang* (*walking*): Coming straightway, I am already inside the garden. I see the pavilion and the enclosed bed of peonies—just as I remember them! But where is that student? (Sings to *Tete ling*):
>
> Over there, the Taihu rocks, 那一搭可是湖山石邊
> Over here, the old plum's mossy green. 這一搭可有老梅蒼蘚
> See where the willow's branches bend low; 見柳枝低亞
> I think that the jade one is about to appear.[34] 疑是玉人出現

Willow is here mentioned together with plum in Liniang's aria. Tang also pairs the plum tree with the willow, but not to the same extent as Feng. This pairing occurs in the vernacular story upon which Tang drew, where willow (*liu*) and plum (*mei*) hint at Liu Mengmei's identity before he comes to the place of Liniang's burial. Both are mentioned in the story in connection with her self-portrait, and the representation is verbal as well as visual, in a poem that Liniang inscribes on the completed portrait:

> *Liniang* (*inscribing the poem, and reciting as she does so*):
>
> Viewed close up she is strikingly myself, 近睹分明似儼然
> Observed from afar she is as carefree as a fairy. 遠觀自在若飛仙
> Were she in some other year to join the man in the Toad Palace, 他年得傍蟾宮客
> Let it be by the side of either plum tree or willow.[35] 不在梅邊在柳邊

Until he appears, "willow" and "plum" represent the lover in the sense that they augur who he is. However, this form of representation is different from another also used in the source and unique to the plum, which relies on suggestive imagery (e.g., "a great plum tree lovely with its thick clusters of fruit," *da meishu yizhu, meizi leilei ke'ai*). Tang seems to have discerned this difference in the source-story, and he preserved it as two modes of representation, visual and verbal, in his play.

For example, in scene 14 of *Mudan ting*, Liniang depicts herself in her self-portrait as holding a branch of green plums in her hand (*nian qingmei*).[36] This visual detail is not in the source; here Tang includes a metaphoric representation of Liu Mengmei in the portrait in addition to the emblematic one of the poem. "Plum and willow" in Liniang's poem hint at Liu's social identity (his family name); "plum" alone (as fruit) suggests his attributes as lover.[37]

Feng favors the former mode of representation—the emblematic type—over the latter. Although his commentary does not distinguish between them, his manner of revising suggests that he sensed a difference.[38] As we have just seen, in scenes 7 and 9 of *Fengliu meng* he suppressed imagery that in Tang's text is unique to the plum and played up the association of "willow" with "plum" in his evocation of the garden setting. In the same vein, he suppressed the detail of the green plums in Liniang's self-portrait when revising scene 14. Liniang instead depicts herself standing against a backdrop of willow and plum. The visual representation matches the poetic one, simplifying Tang's more complicated representation.[39]

Vestiges of the plum as a motif remain in *Fengliu meng*, but they survive as pale versions of Tang's original ideas in heavily revised contexts. Feng's heroine, like Tang's, singles out the plum tree as resting place in her death scene (scene 15 in *Fengliu meng*), but her wish is expressed differently:

> *Liniang*: Should I die, it is my wish that you bury my body beneath that plum tree.
> *Madam Du*: Why do you ask this?
> *Liniang* (singing to *Huang ying'er*):
> My fragrant soul is already entrusted to plum blossom's cave.[40] 我香魂已托梅花洞

Here Feng eliminates an allusion and compresses two lines of verse into one, substituting "fragrant soul" for "pretty skeleton." Coming from the lips of a dying girl, the self-reference is more delicate, but the concreteness and expressiveness of the original language is lost. Tang's verses, written to the tune *Yu ying'er* (see p. 72), generate tension between the allusion to Chang E in her cassia grotto in line 1 and the image of Liniang's entombed corpse in line 2. Liniang in time will experience a reawakening more vital than the chaste immortality of the goddess. Feng's language is plain and one-dimensional. There is no play of ideas beneath the surface meaning of the words.

Feng also debases the plum as metaphor when he introduces a new reference to it (without willow) in his revision of Tang's scene 26 ("The Portrait Examined"). Liu Mengmei arrives in Nan'an destitute and ill after Liniang has died and her father has departed for a new post. While convalescing there, he discovers Liniang's portrait in the garden and takes it back to his study. He observes the willow and plum painted on it (in *Fengliu meng* only), reads the accompanying poem, and correctly interprets these as references to himself. The discovery excites him when he realizes that the beauty in the portrait must be his predestined mate:

> *Liu* (*infatuated*): Ah, young lady, come down! Beautiful lady, young lady, please! (Singing to *Cu yulin*):
>
> | | |
> |---|---|
> | Her wave-tripping feet move, | 動凌波 |
> | Slow and supple she is about to descend, | 盈盈慾下 |
> | But her image stays immobile. | 不見個影兒那 |
>
> Young lady, I, Liu Mengmei, am all alone in this place. (Sings to *Mao'er zhui*):
>
> | | |
> |---|---|
> | Like the old plum, single-trunked, | 似老梅孤幹 |
> | Through you I will make many branches.[41] | 借你做繁柯 |

Feng has here modified the last two lines of a coda Liu sings in *Mudan ting*:

> | | |
> |---|---|
> | Having found this lady, first rejoice: | 拾的個人兒先慶賀 |
> | Might this willow and plum have some entanglement?[42] | 敢柳和梅有些瓜葛 |

In both Feng's aria and Tang's coda, Liu's expresses a desire for social "entanglements" (e.g., marriage), but by using "plum" here alone, as simile, Feng mingles forms that in *Mudan ting* are distinct. As an image associated with the garden world, the plum tree in *Mudan ting* embodies the vitality of nature, with which both heroine and hero become identified: Liu through the image of the tree and its vigorous foliage and fruit, Liniang through the imagery of its fruit and especially its blossoms. This natural imagery mimics Liniang's death and rebirth, her physical and spiritual death and rebirth being the central action of the play. The drama of social death and rebirth—an important element of *chuanqi* romances with specific reference to the hero—is not absent from *Mudan ting*, but it is subsidiary to Liniang's story, which dominates the first thirty-five scenes of the play.

In scene 26 of *Mudan ting*, Liu's pairing of plum and willow is logical, since he has just read the poem on the painting and borrows its language to express his thought. Feng's reference to the "old plum, single-trunked," used in a manner so strikingly different from the form in *Mudan ting*, indicates his effort to direct more attention to the hero's plight as an orphaned and unmarried youth, and to the heroine's role in saving him by her love, which resurrects him from a kind of social death.[43] The change is a small one, but through it Feng sought to put a different spin on the scene, which in his version culminates in the spectacle of Liu feverishly appealing to the beauty in the portrait to descend and rescue him from loneliness. In *Mudan ting*, Liniang's initiation into the experience of passion, death, and resurrection constitute the subject of the play's middle scenes, with Liu Mengmei cast in the role of bearer of life, a role of which he only gradually becomes aware.[44]

Feng's appropriation of the figure of the plum in these scenes shows that he was determined to make *Mudan ting* conform more closely to his thematic expectations of romantic plays: never to allow the private play (the love story) to overwhelm the public play (the celebration of social values and harmonies). His different handling of willow and plum, and of natural imagery generally, reveals his effort to bring Tang's language into conformity with familiar usage.[45]

A final example of Feng's intentions can be found in his revision of scene 30 ("Disrupted Joy"). Tang's scene begins in the middle of the night, midway in the journey of Liniang's ghost from death to rebirth. She has taken Liu as her lover in scene 28, but has yet to reveal to him who and what she is—this will happen in scene 32. Liniang has made a gift of wine, green plums, and *meirenjiao* ("Lovely Lady" plantain flowers) to Liu, and as the couple share a loving cup the imagery of flowers and fruits is deployed in elaborate word-play to depict intimacy:

Liniang (sings to *Bailian xu*):

Into gold-leafed lotus cup,	金荷
Pour the sweet wine.	斟香糯

Liu:

Nectar you have brewed to stir hearts to spring:	你醞釀春心玉液波
Cheeks flush	拚微酡
As flower buds the east wind brings to reddest glow in leafy bower.	東風外翠香紅醱

Liniang:

Nor could I pluck a rarer flower or fruit,	也摘不下奇花果
For in these plantain flowers and green plums,	這一點蕉花和

	梅豆呵
You must know,	君知麼
Seed's charms are perfected,	愛的人全風韻
And flower acquires its root.[46]	花有根斜
Liu (sings to *Zui taiping*):	
To pursue:	細哦
As for these fruits and flowers,	這子兒花朶
The one is wilted like a lovelorn maid,	似美人憔悴
The other is as sour as an amorous swain,	酸子多情
Yet happily heart of plantain flower secretly unfolds,	喜蕉心暗展
Sullied for one night by plum's tip.	一夜梅犀點污
How comes this to be so?	如何
Tide of wine flushes cheeks dimpled by smiles.	酒潮微暈笑生渦
Soon lip drinks lip, wildly kissing.	待噉著臉恣情的嗚嘬
And then,	些兒個
Lids droop on loving eyes	翠偃了情波
Plantain is stained deeper red,	潤紅蕉點
Plum spits forth fragrance.[47]	香生梅唾

The language of this duet takes the form of an extended conceit, whereby the sexual act is thinly disguised as a session of wine drinking.[48] As paired gifts presented by Liniang to her lover, sour green plums suggest his condition; wilted plantain flowers her own. Liu's sourness (*suan*) is frustrated ambition, rechanneled as sexual desire ever since his discovery of Liniang's portrait; Liniang's faded state is the condition of her rootless existence as a wandering and lovelorn ghost, brought on by sexual neglect. Then, in the final lines of the duet, the tenor of Tang's language becomes unmistakably erotic: the fragrance emitted by plum's tip (*meixi*) can refer only to Liu, the plantain flower sullied (*dianwu*, *dian*) deeper red (*runhong*) only to Liniang.[49]

Why, in this most erotically charged passage of the play, has Tang elected to use the plantain as a metaphor for Liniang's sexuality rather than the plum? Elsewhere in the play, plum blossoms when identified with her are coded red (*hong*, closer to pink), but not here. I can only speculate that when Tang contextualizes the plum in overtly sexual contexts, he wishes to identify it with Liu Mengmei—more specifically, with Liu as a sexually potent male who "sullies" Liniang with his semen (*xiang*, fragrance) and by so doing sets in motion a process of regeneration that will eventuate in her rebirth. Tang's figurative use of plum imagery in *Mudan ting* is striking in the extent to which he uses it as a figure of male potency and vigor—traits not commonly associated with it in painting and poetry.[50]

The wine-drinking sequence in Tang's scene introduces several pivotal metaphors that bring a number of disparate thematic contexts into relation with one another. With respect to the natural world, it imitates the pollinating of the flower (the moistening of the plantain flower's petals by plum's fragrance); with respect to the human order, it imitates the sexual act (pouring "sweet wine" into a lotus-shaped cup); with respect to the world of art, it suggests, more indirectly, the moment of inspiration, when the artist breathes life into his work.

With regard to the first two contexts, my basic argument has been that Feng Menglong was unhappy with Tang Xianzu's unique uses of natural imagery. In *Mudan ting* the garden experience is eventually brought into harmony with a larger world of social relationships, but only belatedly so by the norms of the genre. Feng Menglong cuts the entire wine-drinking sequence, an indication of his determination to blunt Tang's language and achieve a different thematic emphasis. One effect of Feng's revisions is to constrain the lovers' experience of passion—in the dream world and especially in the ghostly realm—by their awareness of social duty and responsibilities.

Liniang's Portrait

In *Mudan ting*, Du Liniang's self-portrait, left as a testament to her beauty and early death, is the physical object most identified with her. In keeping with the conventions of southern drama, it is a material symbol that "threads the fabric of the play" like the shuttle of a loom, helping to create a sense of unity in the sprawling work.[51] It is introduced in scene 14 ("The Portrait"), buried with her in scene 20 ("Keening"), and discovered by Liu Mengmei in scene 24 ("The Portrait Recovered"). In the climactic mid-play scenes (scenes 28-32), the portrait represents Liniang's physical body, which has become separated from her soul in death. This is in keeping with its use in earlier stories and plays,[52] although Tang's treatment of the figure is characteristically rich with suggestion.

I cannot do justice to that richness here. Instead I propose to examine the portrait through the prism of Feng's changes, in conjunction with my earlier discussion of the plum figure.[53] There, Feng sought to contain and redirect a vital and erotic dimension of Tang's imagery. I believe that Feng responded to a similar dimension in Tang's treatment of Liniang's portrait, although in ways that are less immediately obvious.

In scene 14, Liniang paints her self-portrait as a testament to her fading beauty and as an encoded record of her dream, which she hopes will someday reach someone who will understand it.[54] The scene begins and concludes with allusions to the Goddess of Wushan, who made love to King Huai of Chu in a dream. Liniang's mention of the king's dream indicates her awareness of what happened in her own dream, even as that dream fades. In the scene's coda, her thoughts return to the Wushan goddess, this time in connection with the portrait she has just painted:

> *Chunxiang*: Young mistress, once the scroll is all complete, where shall I hang it?
>
> *Liniang* (*sings the coda*):
>
> None will come to the fragrant boudoir to enjoy its beauty, — 儘香閨賞玩無人到
>
> *Chunxiang:*
>
> This likeness is fit to hang in the temple on Wushan. — 這形模則合掛巫山廟
>
> *Liniang, Chunxiang:*
>
> Or might it take flight on account of clouds and rain?[55] — 又怕為雨為雲飛去了

Here Liniang expresses, with some ambivalence, the desire to expose her beauty to a lover. Of equal interest for the subsequent treatment of the portrait is Tang's manner of insinuating her act of self-portrayal into the scene. There is, first of all, Liniang's awareness of her ebbing vitality and life:

> *Liniang* (sings to *Shuazi xu fan*):
>
> So chill the spring's leave-taking — 春歸恁寒悄
>
> Daily my thoughts grow idler, — 都來幾日
>
> My will more feeble. — 意懶心喬
>
> My toilet made at last, I burn incense and sit alone, listless. — 意妝成燻香獨坐無聊
>
> Before I can find ease, — 逍遙
>
> How to root out the choking weeds that breed distress? — 怎剗盡助愁芳草
>
> By what means to bring to life the heart's tender shoots? — 甚法兒點活心苗

Whom to please if I mask my true feelings with smiles?	真情強笑為誰嬌
Tears gush forth as my dreaming soul drifts.[56]	淚花兒打迸著夢魂飄

The drifting of the soul foreshadows the moment of death, when the body is deprived of the spirit that animates it, yet Liniang clings to the hope that a way might be found to bring to life (*dianhuo*) her feelings ("heart's tender shoots") and restore her vitality. By painting her self-portrait she seeks to preserve her beauty against the ravages of illness, and once it is finished she identifies with it strongly, treating it as an extension of her person, especially her body. Fearing that it will fade with time, she orders that it be mounted:

Liniang (singing to *Bao lao cui*):

From burning of sun and buffeting of breeze, mount and line it well,	日炙風吹懸襯的好
For fear that "finest things are least enduring."	怕好物不堅牢
My portrait's pretty hues must not be sullied.[57]	把咱巧丹青休涴了

On their surface, these lines simply express Liniang's fear that her portrait will fade with exposure to the elements, but the use of the word *wo* to describe the destruction of "pretty hues" accomplishes far more. The same word refers to Liu Mengmei's semen at the beginning of scene 24, and in scene 28, after he has discovered Liniang's portrait he fears, in a context of sexual desire, that he may "soil the portrait's hues."[58] In this light, the above lines also suggest that Liniang fears her beauty may arouse impure thoughts in the beholder.

Liniang's desire to preserve her beauty inviolate, expressed through her efforts to mount and bury her portrait, is belied by other language suggesting that in her mind the portrait stands for her body, which awaits the coming of a lover who will reanimate it. At the moment of the portrait's creation, Liniang describes her act of self-portrayal as the conveying of her person into the painting:

Liniang (sings to *Yan guo sheng*):

With a silk cloth	輕綃
Lightly wipe the mirror.	把鏡兒擘掠
Hair tip lightly brushing, deftly limning;	筆花尖淡掃輕苗

Ah, mirror semblance,

You must be my close model	和你細評度
For cheeks with teasing smile	你腮門兒恁喜謔
And cherry mouth and willow leaf of brow.	則待註櫻桃染柳條
And now in washes of drifting mist,	渲雲鬟煙靄飄蕭
Before the black of eyebrow's tip is done,	眉梢青未了
My person is wholly captured in charm of "autumn's waves";	箇中人全在秋波妙
Just so do dainty ornaments bright with feathers and gems set off pale "spring hills."[59]	可可的淡春山鈿翠小

The eyes, the spiritual seat of a portrait, seem to contain Liniang's person (*gezhongren*). Elsewhere, she suggests that the portrait houses her spirit. At the moment of her death in scene 20 she speaks of it as the repository of her soul:

Liniang: One thing I have to tell you. That portrait on which I inscribed the poem, I do not care to expose it to the general view. When I am buried, put it in a red sandalwood box and hide it beneath the Taihu rocks.
Chunxiang: What is your purpose in this?
Liniang (singing to *Yu ying'er*):

That portrait and those brush strokes that possess my soul.	有心靈翰墨春容
May reach someday someone who understands.[60]	儻直那人知重

"Soul" (*xinling*) here retains concreteness through "heart" (*xin*), which has both a physical and a spiritual meaning and occurs repeatedly mid-play in both senses.[61]

At the comparable moment in *Fengliu meng* Liniang treats her portrait as a representation, and makes no mention of a lover:

Liniang: As for this picture of a spring outing (sings to *Cu yulin*):

It is I who painted it,	是俺親描畫
Close to willow and plum.	向柳梅叢
Next I indited a poem,	更題詩
And enclosed a riddle within.	將啞謎籠

I am fearful of exposing it to the general view. When I am buried, put it in a red sandalwood box and secrete it beneath the Taihu rocks.
Chunxiang: What is your purpose in this?

Liniang:

Were a spirit to appear, 敢精靈出現還如夢
it would still be like my dream.[62]

The portrait's physical and spiritual qualities are effaced; we are given instead a sense of it as a riddle awaiting a solution. Moreover, the referent of "spirit" (*jingling*), which in Feng's collapsed line replaces "soul" (*xinling*) in the original, is unclear. Is it Liniang's spirit or the spirit of her dream lover?[63] The ambiguity obscures Liniang's intentions; certainly there is no sense of a desire that her portrait (and the "soul" harbored within) might someday encounter an admirer.

Feng's particular sensitivity to Tang's handling of the portrait inspired a revision of two lines Chunxiang sings towards the end of scene 20 of *Mudan ting*, just after Liniang has died. In the midst of her keening Chunxiang recalls the portrait:

> *Chunxiang*: But that reminds me of the self-portrait she made. When it was seen by the master he ordered me to bury it with the corpse for fear that the sight of it would distress Madam Du. I think of my mistress' dying words (singing to *Hong na'ao*):
>
> As before she will lean against the Taihu rocks, 依舊向湖山石兒靠也
> But I fear that waiting for the garden-strolling youth will fade her portrait.[64] 怕等的箇拾翠人來把畫粉銷

Feng makes a revealing change, substituting *maizang* (to bury) for *kao* (to lean on) in the first line of the same aria pattern, so that Chunxiang instead sings:

> She is once again buried beneath the Taihu rocks, 依舊向湖山石兒埋葬也
> Waiting for the garden-strolling youth, 等得箇拾翠人兒來
> for fear her portrait will fade.[65] 怕畫粉銷

In *Mudan ting,* Chunxiang's wish to have her mistress "lean as before" by the rock mound recalls the moment in scene 10 when Liniang's dream lover leads her there to make love.[66] The repetition of *kao* has the effect of animating the portrait and underscoring its close identity with Liniang's person. Feng's *maizang* obliterates this effect (awkwardly, since he retains the phrase "as before") and identifies the portrait with Liniang's corpse.

His rearrangement of the second line removes the sense of agency conveyed in Tang's line by use of the word *ba*, which implies that the coming of the lover will entail, somehow, destruction (*fenxiao*) of the portrait.[67] Here, "fading" is a process of decay that takes place independent of any human action.[68] Feng's rewritten line is faithful to one element of the original context at the expense of a more provocative suggestion: that the coming of a lover will entail some violation of Liniang's person.

Exposure of the portrait occurs again in scene 26 of *Mudan ting*, "The Portrait Examined," when Liu Mengmei gazes at it and is overcome with passion. The first couplet of his entrance poem refers to "wind and rain" (suggestive of lovemaking); the second resorts to imagery of shadow and light to describe what Liu has found (in scene 24) in the garden where he is convalescing:

Hard for rain to linger on the plantain's leaves,	芭蕉葉上雨難留
In the tips of the peony's branches the wind subsides.	芍藥梢頭風慾收
Scrutinize the painting's obscure meaning,	畫意無明偏著眼
And look where gleam of spring light holds the clue.[69]	春光有路暗抬頭

To Liu, the portrait requires the illumination of his gaze. The "obscure meaning" is the painting's riddle, to be deciphered through the visual and verbal clues contained in it, which hint at his special connection to Liniang. Imagery of darkness and light concretizes this idea, so that the act of exposure is extended to the image itself. Shadow and darkness are associated with Liniang as ghost and image, and light with Liu Mengmei as lover and adorer of Liniang's portrait. Repeatedly characterized in this scene as shadow (*ying*), the portrait seems empty (*kong*) and insubstantial (*wuxing*) to Liu, yet it also seems to have a kind of life, or potential for life. Having unrolled the portrait and gazed at it, he expresses bewilderment over its origins by describing the beauty depicted in it as "light of moon born from brush's tip" (*pianyue yingguang sheng haomo*).[70] A feminine image, *yueying* (literally "moon's shadow"), is here endowed with masculine brilliance (*guang*, light), in a manner that evokes the male's part in procreation. Two scenes later, feminine agency in the portrait's creation is suggested when Liniang refers to it by using an allusion to the goddess Green Calyx "bursting from crevice in rock mound to light on painted silk."[71] By this logic, the portrait is created with a potential for life that can be actualized by some inspiriting action.

Feng shows little interest in such language. He eliminates Liu's opening poem, and when revising Liniang's painting aria in scene 14 he eliminates the line suggesting that the portrait's eyes somehow contain the subject's person (*gezhongren quan zai qiubo miao*). He is intent instead on reformulating Liniang's language to suggest a familiar idea: that eyes are the feature through which a subject's spirituality is captured for posterity:

Liniang (sings to *Yan guo sheng*):

Fine silk,	輕綃
"Bronze Bird" inkstone.	硯磨銅雀
This complete likeness of Du Liniang	
Entrust to "dragon's fragrance" and "rabbit's hair."	都付與龍香兔毫
(*Looks at herself in mirror and sighs*)	
I fear the mirror does not reflect how great is my sorrow,	怕青銅炤不出愁多少
Lightly daubing,	聊淡抹
Deftly limning,	試輕描
In painting, dotting the eyes is most difficult.[72]	論丹青只有點眼為高

When revising scene 26, Feng discarded the verse that describes the portrait as "image born from brush's tip" and returned to eyes as the portrait's spiritual seat when Liu Mengmei's attention is captured by them:

Liu: To speak of nothing else, these eyes alone are unearthly! (Sings to *Erlang shen*).

Perfect demeanor,	十分意態
Her soul conveyed in the eye's clear gaze.[73]	描神只在秋波

In a marginal comment, Feng explains: "The line about 'eye's clear gaze' recalls the earlier verse 'dotting the eyes is most difficult,' sung at the time of transmitting her soul into the painting."[74] His emphasis on the eye-dotting gesture comes at the expense of original formulation that links the actions surrounding creation of the portrait to procreation via language that has oblique but unmistakably sexual overtones—light streaming from brush's tip, goddess bursting from crevice in poolside mound. In Feng's hands, artistic creation is reduced to a formula ("In painting dotting the eyes is most difficult").[75]

When we pursue Tang's uses of inspiriting, we find that its sexual dimension is enhanced. In the central scenes of the play, the sexual dimension of the evolving relationship between the lovers is enacted via the portrait figure and a motif of inspiriting that is implicit in that figure. The reanimation of Liniang's corpse in scene 35 ("Resurrection") is anticipated through allusions to a well-known Tang story about a beauty in a portrait who is brought to life.[76] Tang borrows two actions from that story: the hero's calling out the beauty's name and his pouring wine on her portrait. By the time of Liniang's exhumation in scene 35, the infusion of her corpse with wine assumes rich significance as two constellations of language converge, one associated with the plum, the other with the portrait. The actual exhumation and revival scene is a lighthearted affair, but the manner in which Liniang is returned to life has been carefully anticipated.

As Liu contemplates Liniang's portrait in scene 26, he becomes excited by the green plums the beauty holds:

> *Liu*: Why is she holding a branch of green plums in her hand, just as if she were holding me? (Sings to *Ying ti xu*):
>
> | | |
> |---|---|
> | Green plums in hand, she softly intones her verse, | 他青梅在手詩細哦 |
> | Luring my heart to stumbling thoughts of love. | 逗春心一點蹉跎 |
> | Just as I "sketch a cake to appease my hunger" | 小生待畫餅充饑 |
> | So she "gazes at plums to slake her thirst." | 小姐似望梅止渴 |
>
> Ah, my young lady, my young lady!
>
> | | |
> |---|---|
> | A lotus bud, not yet open, | 未曾開半點么荷 |
> | Red lips lightly daubed harbor a smile. | 含笑處朱脣淡抹 |
> | Full of charm and passion, | 韻情多 |
> | Sadly she longs to speak, | 如愁慾語 |
> | But lacks breath.[77] | 只少口汽兒呵 |

Hunger and thirst refer here to sexual desire and mark the culmination of erotic tensions that have built through the scene. In the aria immediately preceding, the word *chun* (spring) occurs four times, indicative of Liu's mounting excitement. Given this tension, mention of the beauty's closed lips that "lack breath" is suggestive, especially in the light of what is to follow.

Liu will breathe life into those lips, and the literal means by which he does this is to pour wine mixed with a life-giving potion down the throat of Liniang's corpse. Prior to this (scene 30), as already noted, he has shared a loving cup of wine with Liniang's ghost. Both moments are memorable, the former because of the erotic boldness of the language, the latter because it is part of the exhumation and revival of Liniang's inert body, graphically enacted. Read beyond their literal meaning, both actions involving the drinking of wine can be understood as inspiriting and inseminating gestures.[78]

I believe the links between this moment in scene 35 and the wine-drinking sequence in scene 30 are established through shared language. Wine is poured into a lotus-shaped cup (*jinhe*), a gesture that in turn calls to mind Liu's erotically charged description of Liniang's portrait in scene 26, in particular her tightly closed mouth "like lotus bud" (*yaohe*), which "lacks breath" (*zhi shao kou qi'er*). The sullying (*dianwu*) of the plantain flower and staining (*runhong*) of its petals as "plum's fragrance fills the mouth" call to mind Liniang's fears that her portrait might be sullied (*woliao*)—an association with sexual intimacy and with Liu's role as Liniang's lover and savior. The unfolding of the "flower's heart" in the release of passion may even find a counterpart in the references to the heart-soul contained within Liniang's portrait, waiting to be touched to life.[79] The return of Liniang's soul to her body (*huanhun*) is inextricably bound up with sexual awakening in these scenes.[80] The same holds true for her physical resurrection, which soon follows.

Wine disappears from Feng's revision. In scene 22 of *Fengliu meng* ("Sister Stone Obstructs Joy," revising scene 30 of *Mudan ting*) he confines Liu's and Liniang's intimacy to a brief and decorous duet:

Liu: Mistress, (sings to *Chenzui dongfeng*):

In twilight gloom I hoped for your early coming,	我坐黃昏盼伊早過
Why did you stop and dawdle so?	為甚鎮消停恁般延惰

Liniang:

It isn't that I kept my darling waiting.	非是我慢歡哥
I waited until parents were fast asleep	候雙親堅臥
Then gathered up my flower-embroidered quilt.	又收拾起繡床花朵

Liu, Liniang:

Two pairs of eyes gazing,	四目共睃
Our feelings one,	兩情正和
Why at this hour of bliss this urge to words?[81]	偏則是幽期處話多

In his version of the exhumation Liniang is revived with ginger tea, and the trouser-patch potion and the scene devoted to its concoction (34, "Consultation") are eliminated.

Feng retains one aspect of the inspiriting motif, however, which provides a clue to his use of the portrait in *Fengliu meng*. In scene 33 of *Mudan ting* ("Confidential Plans"), Liu Mengmei presents himself at Liniang's shrine as her husband and offers to prove his claim to a dubious Sister Stone by inscribing Liniang's spirit tablet with a dot, a ritual normally performed by a person of distinction. We are told that Liniang's father, Du Bao, neglected to perform it in his haste to depart for a new post. When Liu inscribes the dot the tablet moves. This convinces Sister Stone of his claim, and she decides to assist him in the exhumation and revival of Liniang's corpse.

The significance of this action appears to be essentially social, marking the passage of authority from Du Bao (as father) to Liu Mengmei (as husband).[82] In *Mudan ting* the tablet-dotting gesture, which anticipates Liu's role in Liniang's exhumation, also assumes an inspiriting quality.[83] This dimension, together with its implication about the sources of Liu Mengmei's power, is lost in Feng's revision, but the social meaning is retained.

Feng passes over his revisions of erotic language in silence, but he does comment several times about the portrait, an indication of the importance he assigned to it.[84] That importance can be summed up as "recognition." The portrait doesn't simply represent Liniang, it also represents Liu and holds the clue to his future relationship with her. It contains an encoded message that he must decipher. In scene 26 of *Mudan ting*, Liu reads the poem on the portrait and recognizes that he has some connection to the lady depicted there, but he subsequently fails to act on this knowledge. He fails to link the beauty in the portrait to the "lovely girl" in his dream (scene 2, "Declaring Ambition"), and likewise fails to see that the maiden with whom he has formed a liaison (Liniang's ghost) is the beauty depicted in the portrait. Indeed, after making love to Liniang's ghost, he appears to forget the portrait altogether. In Feng's view, this makes him fickle (*boxing*),[85] his sexual infatuation exposing a lack of good faith and weakness of character unbefitting a hero.

Feng is at pains to point out these defects in Tang's hero and to indicate how he has rectified them in *Fengliu meng*. When revising scene 26 of *Mudan ting*, in which Liu first examines the portrait, Feng depicts

Liu as instantly recognizing the lady depicted in it as the girl of his earlier dream. In light of this recognition, his growing infatuation with the portrait is firmly rooted in a conviction that this lady (he does not yet know her name) is his destined mate. In other words, desire is grounded in loyalty—to the lady and to the alliance with her that the portrait represents.[86]

By contrast, *Mudan ting* has Liniang point out the connection between herself and the portrait after she and Liu exchange vows in scene 32. Liu's forgetfulness is puzzling, and Feng was among the first to condemn it. One clear aim of his revision of *Mudan ting* is the rehabilitation of its hero. When we examine his treatment of these motifs, we can see that it is part of a deliberate effort to change the thematic emphasis of the play, to portray the love affair between Liniang and Liu Mengmei in a different light, and especially to redefine Liu's character.

Feng Menglong's Recalcitrant Reading of *Mudan ting*

This comparison of *Mudan ting* and *Fengliu meng* highlights aspects of revision that go unmentioned in Feng Menglong's "critiques" and commentary. I have used his commentary, but have based my understanding of his methods and intentions largely on evidence furnished by a close reading of both texts. This has enabled me to go beyond Feng's own account of what he was doing. Reading *Mudan ting* in the light of *Fengliu meng* shows that Tang Xianzu's unconventional language, as well as his idiosyncratic prosody, made Feng's engagement with the play "recalcitrant" in Leo Steinberg's sense.

Written before the Kunshan musical style became preeminent, *Mudan ting* was created not in ignorance of prosodic requirements for *chuanqi* drama, as Tang's critics alleged, but in a different musical style and according to less rigid notions of how linguistic and musical text should be fit together. Tang was comfortable with varying song-forms to fit the requirements of his text. His critics were not, and when they began to rewrite his plays according to the fixed forms prescribed in their manuals, a struggle to define the play's text was engaged, which lasted for several decades.[87] In the end Tang's original libretto emerged from this struggle unscathed, and revisions such as Feng's were largely forgotten, especially in "pure singing" performances of the play. Once the forms of Kun arias were well defined, Tang's libretti posed difficulties, but no insurmountable obstacles, to adaptation for singing in that style. Once the necessary musical accommodations were made, three of his plays went on to become staples of the Kun opera repertoire.[88]

What divided Tang and his critics at least as sharply as their differences over musical form were their differences over dramatic language. Tang favored an unconstrained literary style that made no concessions to the reader, viewer, or performer, while revisers such as Zang Maoxun and Feng Menglong favored language more familiar and accessible. Translating *Mudan ting* into simpler language inevitably changed the ideas conveyed, and I have suggested that Feng's choices contain a thematic critique of the play that may not have been fully conscious. His criticisms of Tang's prosody appear to have reflected a largely unacknowledged discomfort with Tang's elaborate, and at times obscure, depiction of romantic passion in a text destined for the stage.

In his treatment of the plum, Feng eschewed the openness of Tang's metaphors and reverted to simile. Feng identifies the tree primarily with Liu Mengmei, his plight as orphan, and his search for social connections. In his passage where Liniang compares herself with the tree,[89] it reminds her of her desire to find a mate and blossom, a canonically familiar association for a young girl to make. The plum's other attributes—red blossoms, green fruit, verdant foliage, and (soul-restoring) fragrance—go unremarked. The attributes that Feng singles out are roots and branches, suggestive of Liu Mengmei's desire and need for social ties.

In striking contrast, Tang exploited the plum's "metaphoric mutability" in terms of gender and its wealth of associations.[90] As tree, the plum is identified with Liu as lover and eventual savior of Liniang. In this respect Tang may have wished to underscore Liu's role as "Lord of Spring" and restorer of Liniang's soul; this was one dimension of the plum's meaning in poetry. The plum tree's powers of renewal, even into old age, made it a symbol of vitality and vigor,[91] and although references to sexual vigor by way of this image were muted in poetry and painting, in *Mudan ting* this dimension is vividly in evidence, with reference to both Liu Mengmei and Liniang. With respect to the plum's blossoms, I have suggested that they refer to Liniang's emerging sexuality, and here Tang's preference for red blossoms rather than the white ones favored by poets may have to do with well-established associations of falling red blossoms with lost maidenhood. Even the fruit, the most canonical image of the plum by virtue of its mention in the *Shijing*, is transmuted in *Mudan ting* from an image suggestive of the desire to marry and procreate into something more complex, partaking of both bitterness and desire.

It is tempting to find in Tang's elaborate use of the plum a deliberate subversion of its orthodox symbolism, in particular its close identification with such Confucian values as chastity and moral rectitude, which, in their extreme form, are caricatured in *Mudan ting*'s important males: Chen Zuiliang, Du Bao, and Liu Mengmei.[92] But one cannot carry such a reading too far. What can be said is that the plum as figure pertains to the garden, and thus to the realm of human emotions (*qing*), not the world of principle (*li*). Once Liniang and Liu Mengmei flee the garden and depart from Nan'an in scene 36, the plum is no longer an important figure.

Feng likewise reduced the complexity of Tang's figurative use of the portrait. In *Mudan ting* it embodies beauty for both Liniang and Liu Mengmei, and their responses to it reveal more about their own subjectivity than anything else.[93] Liu's infatuation with it is based solely on sensual attraction, which causes him to forget all else. In this respect his experience matches that of Liniang with her dream: each becomes obsessed with passions aroused by the imagined presence of the sought-for loved one, so much so that the illusory is confused with the real.[94] In *Fengliu meng*, the portrait is the device that brings Liu to Liniang. Its messages furnish him with necessary clues to his destiny, and in his treatment of it he is shown to be an attentive and devoted lover. His steadfast devotion to Liniang's portrait demonstrates how his sensual impulses are domesticated and his infatuation (*qingchi*) is governed by his reason. The distortion of Tang's idea is particularly striking in this case. Feng's rational bias is evident not only in these efforts to redefine Liu Mengmei's character, but also in his concern for a logically consistent plot and a harmonious prosody free of jarring improvisations.[95]

Tang Xianzu, on the other hand, praised writing that was unconstrained by conventional notions of form and plausibility. A preface he wrote for a friend's collection of marvels reveals contempt for the excessively literal imagination:

> In this world, the only people with whom one cannot discuss literary art are narrow-minded pedants and fusty scholars. There is much that they have not heard and more that they have not seen, and yet they make a show of their superficial and limited knowledge. Looking over writing in the world today, one wonders, will there ever be writing again after this? I think that what is miraculous in writing does not consist in a slavish adherence to

> appearances. Spiritual inspiration comes naturally in a flash, in the absence of conscious thought [*ziran lingqi, huanghu er lai, bu si er zhi*]. Uncanny and amazing, this is a state to which none can give a name, not anything with which one ordinarily can manage to identify. When Su Zizhan [Su Shi, 1037–1101] painted withered trunks, bamboo, and rocks, he broke completely with painters of both the past and his present, and the style of his paintings became all the more marvelous. If one were to assess his paintings in terms of painting style, it is almost as if they do not have one.[96]

Tang was fond of invoking the example of great painters in his own defense,[97] and his disdain for models is well illustrated in *Mudan ting*, at both the musical and the linguistic level. His aesthetic and Feng's agenda were diametrically opposed, and we can assume that had Tang read *Fengliu meng*, he would have been as outraged by it as he was by Shen Jing's *Tongmeng ji*. Although both men are identified with the late-Ming cult of *qing*, and both shared a love of vernacular literature, when it came to the writing of plays the differences between them were very great.

In this chapter my manner of describing two strands of figurative language in *Mudan ting* and *Fengliu meng* is similar to a reading technique that has been fruitfully applied to the great full-length Ming novels. It assumes that figural patterning is a feature of the text that is self-consciously designed to guide the reader's responses, beautifying language and also adumbrating important themes.[98] The examples in this chapter demonstrate Feng's sensitivity to the figurative resonances of language in *Mudan ting*, a sensitivity I did not find nearly as acute in the adaptation undertaken by Zang Maoxun. It is in this sense that I feel, with Lu Eting, that *Fengliu meng* is the most "literary" of the extant adaptations of *Mudan ting*.

Feng's revisions of these figures reveal something akin to anxiety over Tang Xianzu's expansive treatment of the emotions, particularly in their extreme forms of passion and rage. By lavishing attention on the causal scheme for the play (the dreams, poems and other signs of Heaven's intentions), he labored to restrict the compass of actions and impulses falling outside the bounds of reason (*li*) and decorum (*li*). In comprehensive fashion he set out to restore a basis of rationality to the play's action, something Tang had subverted.[99] Tang Xianzu also refused to respect the stylistic and ideological boundaries separating genres and addressed personal concerns in his plays in a distinctive and linguistically challenging idiom. His use of drama as a personal vehicle became an issue, and by rewriting his plays Feng and others reappropriated them for public poetry, asserting control over the ideas expressed in them in the name of performability.[100]

Although *Fengliu meng* did not enjoy the same success as Feng's revised novels and short stories, it did not suffer the obloquy and oblivion that overtook *Huanhun ji. Fengliu meng* did have some impact on how *Mudan ting* was performed, and in this respect Feng Menglong does appear to have been in tune with the theatrical culture of his time and subsequently. Some of the ways his thinking coincided with that of actors will become apparent in Part Two.

Part Two

Actors and Performances

❁Four

Mudan ting in an Actor-centered Environment

In the sixteenth and seventeenth centuries plays were published not just as whole plays, but as extracts (*zhezixi*) in compendia. Over time the variety of such collections proliferated, reflecting various uses and different publics. In this chapter we focus on several questions: Which scenes from *Mudan ting* were selected for inclusion, and were these replicated from collection to collection? How did the compilers organize and present the extracts? Do the texts agree with versions found in the complete play? If not, how do they differ? What kinds of notation and comments are added to the texts, and what do these suggest about how the extracts were used?

The compendia fall into three categories and span a period from the early 1600s to the late Qing period.[1] Taken together, they reflect parallel contexts in which Kun opera texts were transmitted—one refined and elite, the other more popular and theatrically based.[2] They also reveal a gradual shift from a theatrical literature controlled by playwrights to one that registered the creative efforts of performers. I first document this shift in the case of *Mudan ting*, after which I examine the two most important printed collections that reflect theatrically based practices, *Zhui baiqiu* and *Shenyin jiangu lu*, in an effort to reconstruct how the play was performed during the period when actors modified playtexts.

Miscellanies

Miscellanies (*xuanben*) containing play extracts began to be published in the mid-sixteenth century, peaked in popularity in the final decades of the Ming, and were often reprinted in the early Qing dynasty. Several of the earliest editions extant reflect the diversity of styles popular before Kun opera became preeminent. These included Qingyang opera and a style of opera popular in Anhui province, in which vernacular phrases recited in "rapid recitative" (*gundiao*) made the arias more intelligible.[3] Although several of these miscellanies date from the early seventeenth century, it is not surprising that they do not contain extracts from *Mudan ting*, given their popular orientation.[4]

The first that do contain *Mudan ting* extracts date from the late Wanli period (i.e., after 1600), from about the time that Feng Menglong and Zang Maoxun were producing their whole-play adaptations of *Mudan ting*. One of these, *Shanshan ji* (A Collocation of Corals, preface dated 1616) advertises itself as favoring new and hitherto unanthologized operas; the other, *Yue lu yin* (Sounds Drenched in Moonlight, Wanli edition), also stresses a preponderance of new plays in its selection.[5] Perhaps because it is a continuation of an earlier miscellany, *Shanshan ji* is the smaller of the two, with seventy-three extracts taken from forty-one plays.[6] One extract is from *Mudan ting*, scene 2, "Declaring Ambition," consisting of two arias that are Liu Mengmei's self-introduction. By contrast, *Yue lu yin* contains eight scenes: scene 10, "The Interrupted Dream"; 12, "Pursuing the Dream"; 14, "The Portrait"; 20, "Keening"; 26, "The Portrait Examined"; 27, "Spirit Roaming"; 28, "Union in the Shades"; and 53, "Interrogation Under the Rod."[7]

Seven of these eight extracts are placed at the head of two of the work's four collections (*ji*) and given pride of place in acknowledgement of *Mudan ting*'s popularity.[8] *Yue lu yin*'s extracts are grouped under broad rubrics: "grandly correct" (*zhuang*), "freely unhampered" (*sao*), "intensely sorrowful" (*fen*), and "happily expansive" (*le*). Each extract is designated by a two-word title that presumes the reader knows the play from which it comes. All dramatic paraphernalia have been removed. There is no indication of who sings the arias, all dialogue and stage directions have been removed, and the arias are unpunctuated, with no indication of line breaks or rhythmic notation (*dianban*). The format is identical to that used for nondramatic *qu* (*sanqu*) in miscellanies that date from this period, including *Shanshan ji*. That work devotes two collections to *sanqu* and two to dramatic *qu*, and for both its compiler does provide rhythmic notation. But for all but a fraction of the dramatic *qu* other features indicative of theatricality are omitted.[9] The contrast between these miscellanies and the early, more diverse Wanli miscellanies is striking, for those texts preserved and often enhanced dramatic features.[10]

Shanshan ji's presentation minimizes differences between dramatic and nondramatic *qu*. *Yue lu yin*'s grouping of extracts according to mood also tends to downplay their specifically dramatic character, and through its distribution of extracts among four collections, presents them out of sequence. Its cutting of the scenes themselves is additionally fragmenting. In all but one of the *Mudan ting* extracts, introductory arias that bring characters onstage and set the scene have been omitted, and in scenes where several roles appear, arias extraneous to the dominant mood are cut, particularly if they are sung by a secondary character. For example, in Liniang's death scene ("Keening," 20), the core sequence in which six of ten arias are sung by Liniang, the *dan* role, is kept, while seven other arias—three sung by Chunxiang (*tie*), two by Du Bao (*wai*), and one each by Sister Stone (*jing*) and Madam Du (*laodan*)—are cut.[11] In "Spirit Roaming" (27) a sequence of six arias sung by Liniang's ghost when she visits her shrine is kept intact, but only one of five arias sung by the *jing* role (Sister Stone) and her attendants remains. In other words, *Yue lu yin* directs the reader's attention to singing by the *sheng* and the *dan*, the roles favored in household performances of *Mudan ting*.[12]

In his discussion of *Yuefu hongshan* (preface dated 1602), Patrick Hanan notes that its hundred extracts are arranged according to themes more numerous than the fifteen categories in *Yue lu yin* and more specific to occasions where dramas might be performed.[13] Hanan does not speculate about the intent that underlies these thematic groupings, but he does observe that some of the "general rules" for the collection "have a practical air about them which befits an anthology of pieces intended to be performed."[14] Many extracts in this collection differ substantially from the scenes that survive in complete editions, evidence, Hanan feels, of successive adaptations made by professional actors.[15] But this is not at all the case with the earliest preserved *Mudan ting* extracts. To the extent that the *Yue lu yin* extracts suggest a performance, it is the intimacy of a household performance or the most private performance of all, in which the reader sings the text while striking out the beats with his or her fan.

Two miscellanies from the Chongzhen era (1628–1644) continue to favor scenes from *Mudan ting* that feature the *dan* and *sheng* roles:[16]

Yichun jin (Brocade of Spring Delights): "The Interrupted Dream" (10), "Pursuing the Dream" (12), "Meeting in the Shades" (28, renamed "Youhui").

Xuanxuepu (Dark Snow Collection): "Declaring Ambition" (2), "The Interrupted Dream" (10), "Pursuing the Dream" (12), "Joy in the Shades" (28, renamed "Youhuan"), "Interrogation Upside-down" (53, renamed "Diao da").

Nothing is cut from the scenes in these collections, and what is added (punctuation and commentary) does not substantially alter the text. The compiler of *Xuanxuepu* displays many of the same scruples as do Mao Yuanyi and his associates, who sought to rescue *Mudan ting* from adaptors such as Zang Maoxun and Feng Menglong. In his general rules the *Xuanxuepu* compiler distinguishes his collection from those that include extracts modified by actors (*youpai*) or that cater to amateur singers and feature only arias.[17] He is something of a textual purist, eschewing inclusion even of *dianban* notation for the arias, which by this time had become a regular feature in collections that favored newer (Kun) plays. For him, discerning readers need not be bound by the vulgar prescriptions found in manuals of prosody (*qupu*); they can take a flexible approach and adapt their singing to the particular environment of each aria.[18] *Xuanxuepu* caters instead to the reader's literary sensibilities, by providing notation that evaluates each extract according to the beauty of its diction (*ci*) and sentiment (*qing*),[19] and by including marginal comments that point out especially fine passages of verse and dialogue.[20]

The contents of *Yichun jin* are more diverse than those in *Xuanxuepu*. It includes extracts in the more popular Yiyang style, but they are sequestered in their own collection (the last of six) rather than interspersed among extracts from plays of other styles, as is the case for the earliest Wanli collections. In four other collections (a fifth is devoted to nondramatic *qu* by Ming authors), the extracts are again grouped under various rubrics.[21] The most thematically consistent collection is the first, devoted to "Portrayals of Secret Meetings." Reading through it, one suspects that readers took pleasure from the variety of approaches taken to a familiar dramatic moment—when an ardent lover attempts to overcome the sexual resistance of the heroine.[22] These are written in language that exhibits a lot of erotic play and depicts an ever-shifting balance of conflicting impulses, whose resolution depends on the playwright's scruples about how to handle such material in a performance. This method of presentation also enabled readers to see how later playwrights worked variations on well-known scenes. "Portrayals of Secret Meetings" concludes with an extract from a now-lost play, "Meng yuan" (A Dream Perfected), which gives a new twist to the plot of "The Interrupted

Dream" from *Mudan ting* (no. 13 of the seventeen extracts in this collection). In it a sympathetic deity leads the *dan* into the *sheng*'s dream rather than the other way around.[23]

The inclusion of *dianban* notation distinguishes many Chongzhen and early Qing miscellanies from early Wanli ones. This is true for *Yichun jin*, which provides it for all but the Yiyang plays. Use of such notation coincides with the increased popularity of the Kun style of singing. *Shanshan ji* (1616) provides it,[24] and so does *Cilin yixiang* (Unconstrained Music from a Forest of Verse, 1623), whose compiler assures the reader that when assigning beats he follows the "orthodox" school (*zhengpai*), correcting numerous errors found in commercial editions of plays (*fangke*).[25]

Mudan ting extracts appear in those Ming miscellanies whose compilers are anxious to distinguish their collections from ones more popular in orientation and eclectic in content. Respect for the integrity of the arias is the hallmark of these late Ming miscellanies. Some strip the texts of other features, but none add things to the text, other than punctuation, illustrations, and commentary. This chaste approach to editing distinguishes the *Mudan ting* extracts from those preserved in early Wanli miscellanies, where selections frequently differ from the same scene in complete versions of the play or else are from lost plays based on the same subject matter.[26] The *Mudan ting* extracts lack any trace of influence from the more popular performance-based styles.[27] To find such traces we must turn to the Qing miscellanies, *Zuiyi qing*, a popular and influential collection, and *Zhui baiqiu*, the most widely circulated miscellany of all.

Mudan ting in Qing Dynasty Miscellanies

Both *Zuiyi qing* and *Zhui baiqiu* were first published in the late Ming, and both went through several reprintings.[28] The Qing editions reflect the situation of opera, Kun opera especially, at the time when it flourished as both a stage art and as a form of social entertainment.[29] In places the collections cover practically the same items, and the intended public for both was broader than for the Ming miscellanies.[30] The first place we find evidence of the impact of staged interpretations of *Mudan ting* turns out to be a Kangxi edition of *Zuiyi qing*.

For most plays represented in it (thirty-nine of forty-four) four extracts are given; for *Mudan ting* these appear in the following sequence: "Entering the Dream" (10, "Ru meng," original title "Jingmeng"), "Pursuing the Dream" (12), "The Portrait Recovered" (24), and "Infernal Judgment" (23). Altered titles sometimes indicate that a scene has been reworked, and this is the case for scene 10, which exhibits modifications hitherto not seen. The most interesting of them is a full-blown version of an interlude now known as "Heaped Blossoms" ("Duihua"), which became a fixed feature of performances of this scene and thus can be traced back to early Qing times by way of this miscellany. The interlude consists of five arias sung in "Entering the Dream" by the Huashen and his attendants after Liu Mengmei forcibly embraces Du Liniang and exits the stage. The "Heaped Blossoms" additions are given here in italics:[31]

(*Liu embraces Liniang and exits. Enter xiaosheng as Huashen, accompanied by attendants*)

Huashen (*sings to Chu duizi*):

Tender crimson, soft white,
Vie to open to Spring's breezes.
I would that the Lord of Heaven protect each root and tendril,
Lest in profusion they litter the green moss.
Let this marriage in a dream go to the young graduate.

Commissioner of the Flowers' Blooming, come with the new season
From Heaven of Blossom Guard to fulfill the springtime's labors.
Drenched in red petal rain the beholder, heartsore,
Anchors his yearnings amid the clouds of blossom.

In my charge as Huashen is this garden in the rear of the prefectural residence at Nan'an. Between Liniang, daughter of Prefect Du, and the young graduate Liu Mengmei, there exists a marriage affinity that must someday be fulfilled, and now Miss Du's heart has been so deeply moved by her spring strolling that she has summoned the graduate Liu into her dream.[32] I am here to watch over her and to ensure that the play of clouds and rain will be a joyous experience for her. *Attendant huashen, escort my carriage and proceed with me to the vicinity of the Taihu rockery.*

Attendant huashen: We do. We of myriad crimsons and purples should cherish in compassion the jade-like incense ones even more. (*They sing to Hua mei xu*):

Beauteous scene bedazzles Yang terrace,
Myriad crimson and purple are abloom everywhere.
Filling the carved railings,
Their roseate freshness clusters on gemmed staircases.
We oversee Spring's tasks,
Ensuring that fragrance emitted by night,
Not be made to tremble at dawn's wind.

Attentive to the happiness of "beauty and genius,"
Their happiness in dream is complete.
(They sing to Diliuzi):
By lakeside mound,
By lakeside mound.
Clouds coil while rain falls soft as down.
Beyond carved rail,
Beyond carved rail,
Crimson tosses, green burrows in.
Don't make the oriole grieve, the butterfly lament.
Destiny by Rock of Rebirth,
No figment of a dream.
In this pillow land of Huaxu
A joyful awakening for both.
. . . by the Taihu rockery.[33]

Huashen: See how the two of them are just in the sweet spell of their dream. (Sings to Bao lao cui):

Ah, how the male force surges and leaps,
As in the way of a wanton bee he stirs
The gale of her desire
While her soul trembles
At the dewy brink of a sweet, shaded vale.
A mating of shadows, this,
Consummation within the mind,
No fruitful Effect
But an apparition within the Cause.

Ha, but now my flower palace is sullied by lust. Let me throw fallen petals to awaken them. (Scatters petals in the entrance to the stage)

Loath she may be to loose herself
From the sweet spellbound dream of spring's delight,
But petals flutter down like crimson snow.

So, graduate Liu, the dream is but half-complete. When it is over, be sure to see Miss Du safely back to her chamber. I leave you now, and return to my palace. (*Sings to Shuangshengzi*):

Liu Mengmei, Liu Mengmei,
Your marriage is fulfilled in a dream.
Du Liniang, Du Liniang,
Your fragrant soul has been perturbed enough.
This marriage affinity of yours is not one of chance,
Lucky you were to meet in a dream, and to share happiness there.
(Exit. Enter Liu, leading Liniang by the hand)[34]

Some interlude is called for, to fill the period of offstage lovemaking, and performers plainly felt that the single aria that Tang Xianzu wrote for the Huashen (*Bao lao cui*) was insufficient. Until relatively recent times musical interludes were not used in Kun opera,[35] so the only way to prolong the lovemaking was to write additional arias. In his adaptation of *Mudan ting* Feng Menglong discarded *Bao lao cui*, with its jarringly abstract language, and substituted one of his own devising (titled *Wuban yi*). But he neither prolonged the singing with more arias, nor filled the stage with additional actors.

The *Zuiyi qing* extract does both, contributing an element of spectacle to a scene that as Tang wrote it is subdued in tone and atmosphere. A source for this amplification may have been a scene from the early Qing play *Yuanyang meng* ("Matched Dreams" ["Hemeng"]), in which a Mengshen (God of Dreams) brings lovers together and six *huaxian* (flower immortals) sing and dance in celebration.[36] By the Yongzheng era (1723–1735), one performance of "The Interrupted Dream," perhaps inspired by "Matched Dreams," included twelve attendant *huashen*, elaborately costumed. The additions documented in *Zuiyi qing* preserve a version of the scene similar to the one performed on that occasion.[37]

The *Zuiyi qing* cuts of this scene also differ from those documented in late Ming extracts. There arias cut almost always fall outside the core sequence and are assigned to secondary roles. Here the two arias cut are sung by Liniang when she is alone onstage. Both follow long soliloquies, which are left undisturbed. But their removal seems prompted by more than a desire to tighten the scene. Taken together with the addition of the sentimental "Heaped Blossoms" sequence, these changes reflect an aesthetic of performance that both permits substantial changes to the written playtext and also reinterprets freely the action of the play and character of its central figure.[38]

Zuiyi qing registers the early stages of a shift from a text-based drama to one that was performance-based. Lu Eting has suggested that the practice of performing extracts, which he feels began in the late Wanli period, became an obstacle to the performing of whole plays. As the new format took hold, plays were "renewed" (*wei zhi yixin*) in thought and appearance. The older the play, the more likely it was to undergo repeated modification by actors, which is registered in the published extracts. Lu sees the onset of actor-inspired revision as a positive development and speaks of how it enriched the old plays' content by paring away parts that had gradually been lost on audiences and building up "positive features" (*jiji yinsu*).[39]

We see the early stages of the enrichment of scenes from *Mudan ting* in *Zuiyi qing* and can pursue it into other Qing collections of later date, *Zhui baiqiu* and *Shenyin jiangu lu*. The fourth collection of *Zhui baiqiu xinji*, published in 1767, preserves a performance-based version of scene 10 that exhibits some but not all of the features found in the *Zuiyi qing* extract.[40] The scene has split into two, reflecting a tendency to perform Liniang's garden-strolling sequence ("Wandering in the Garden" ["Youyuan"]) and dream sequence ("Startled by a Dream" ["Jingmeng"]) separately.[41] The lovemaking interlude consists of two arias only, but the added aria, *Shuangshengzi*, is also found in *Zuiyi qing*. Contrasts between the language of *Bao lao cui* and *Shuangshengzi* are as jarring here as in the longer version of the "Heaped Blossoms" sequence, but there is no choral singing by attendant *huashen*. Instead, the Huashen is attended by a Mengshen whose *raison d'être* is to stage manage Liu Mengmei and Du Liniang's entry into the dream.

Shenyin jiangu lu reproduces a version of scene 10 that incorporates features found in both the *Zuiyi qing* extract and the one preserved in *Zhui baiqiu xinji*. Here, too, the scene is split, but at a different point, and the segment performed by the Mengshen (renamed the Shuimoshen [God of Sleep]) restores stage directions from Tang's text that are cut in *Zhui baiqiu xinji*.[42] In the following passage, original text and stage directions from *Mudan ting* found in all versions of the scene appears in roman type, added text common to *Zhui baiqiu xinji* and *Shenyin jiangu lu* is italicized, that unique to *Shenyin jiangu lu* is bolded, and text cut from *Zhui baiqiu xinji* and restored in *Shenyin jiangu lu* is in bold italics.

(A fumo actor enters as the Shuimoshen and speaks as if in a dream):[43]

Shuimo, Shuimo. Confused and fragrant, whenever has one sorrowful dream been savored to the full? I am the **Shuimoshen** *and have received orders from the Huashen, who says that Liu Mengmei and Du Liniang are later to be united in wedlock. He has sent me to lead the two of them to enter a dream. (He leads Liu Mengmei onstage, bearing a branch of willow in his hand; he again leads Liniang to face Liu.* **Liniang mimes surprise and the Shuimoshen exits.**)

Liu: "Sister, so this is where you were—I was looking for you everywhere. (Liniang glances shyly at him, but does not speak.) I just chanced to break off this branch from the weeping willow in the garden. Sister, you are so deeply versed in works of literature, I should like you to compose a poem to honor it.

Liniang* (*starts in surprised delight and opens her lips to speak, but checks herself*): *I have never seen this young man in my life—what is he doing here?

***Liu* (*smiles at her*):** Sister, I am dying of love for you!" (Sings to Shantao hong):

With the flowering of your beauty
As the river of years rolls past,
Everywhere I have searched for you
Pining secluded in your chamber.

Lady, come with me just over there where we can talk. (***She gives him a shy smile, but refuses to move.***) **Ai!** (***He tries to draw her by her sleeve.***)

Liniang* (*in a low voice*): *Where do you mean?

Liu:

There, just beyond this railing peony-lined
Against the mound of weathered Taihu rocks.

Liniang* (*in a low voice*): *But sir, what do you mean to do?

***Liu* (*sings softly*):**

I will open the fastening at your neck
Loose the girdle at your waist,
While you
Screening your eyes with your sleeve,
White teeth clenched on the fabric as if against pain,
Bear with me patiently a while
Then drift into gentle slumber.

(***He approaches her, and she pushes him away, blushing.***)[44]

Liu, Liniang:

Somewhere at some past time you and I met.
Now we behold each other in solemn awe.

But do not say

In this lovely place we should meet and speak no word.

(Liu again approaches. Liniang pushes him away, smiling, and hurries away. Liu, lifting the hem of his robe, gives chase. Liniang stands at some distance, looking at him intently. She turns and exits first, Liu following closely after.)[45]

"Startled by a Dream" begins with the entry of attendant *huashen* in pairs, who form opposing ranks, after which the Huashen comes onstage and stations himself in their midst, flanked by a subordinate (Runyue huashen, Flower Spirit of the Intercalary Month). The first three arias of "Heaped Blossoms" are sung chorally, then the Huashen sings the concluding two as solo arias, after which the deities exit the stage and Liu Mengmei and Liniang enter hand in hand. The correspondence between this sequence and the one in *Zuiyi qing* is very close; only the Huashen's concluding aria, *Shuangshengzi*, is missing, its place taken by *Wuban yi*, which Feng Menglong wrote for his adaptation:

> Liu Mengmei, Liu Mengmei,
> Your marriage is fulfilled in a dream.
> Du Liniang, Du Liniang,
> Your fragant soul has been perturbed enough.
> This marriage affinity of yours is not one of chance,
> Lucky you were to meet in a dream, and to share happiness there.[46]

An illustration in *Shenyin jiangu lu* depicts twelve figures who observe the lovers as the Huashen prepares to rain blossoms down on them (Fig. 4.1). By the time this edition appeared in the early nineteenth century, the practice of having twelve actors perform "Heaped Blossoms" had taken hold.

These Qing miscellanies document a performance tradition for scene 10 of *Mudan ting* that was cumulative. Innovations, once made, were likely to persist in later versions that have come down to us, even when there is no direct textual link between these versions, as is the case for the extracts preserved in *Zuiyi qing* (published ca. 1700) and *Zhui baiqiu xinji* (completed in 1767). In all likelihood a 1740 work entitled *Zhui baiqiu quanji* reproduced the version of scene 10 found in *Zuiyi qing*, but the editors of the expanded edition of *Zhui baiqiu* that came out in the 1760s included play versions popular in their time, not earlier.[47] The compiler of *Shenyin jiangu lu* (1834) set out to produce a volume that combined the strengths of earlier collections, and his extracts may be composites assembled from versions found in other collections. The link to performance is thus less direct than for *Zhui baiqiu xinji*, but like that work *Shenyin jiangu lu* registers the shift from a dramatic form focused on the voice to one focused on the actor as a physical presence on a stage.[48]

Five other extracts from *Mudan ting* appear for the first time in the edition of *Zhui baiqiu xinji* completed in 1767: "The School Hall" (scene 7, "Xuetang," original title "Guishu"), "Speed the Plough" (8), "Calling to the Portrait" (26, "Jiao hua," original title "Wan zhen"), and "Reunion at

Fig. 4.1. Huashen and attendants watch over the lovers. *Source: Shenyin jiangu lu*

Court" (55).[49] Another three were included in the twelfth and final collection that rounded out the combined edition (*hebian*) of 1774: "The Soul's Departure" (20, "Li hun," original title "Nao shang"), "Asking the Way" (40, "Wen lu," original title "Pu zhen"), and "Interrogation Upside-down" (53, "Diao da," original title "Ying kao" 53).[50] Several of these added extracts feature roles other than the *dan/sheng* pairing overwhelmingly favored in earlier selections. Scene 7 features Liniang's maid Chunxiang (played by the *tie*); it also offers a juicy role for the actor of *laosheng* (aging scholar) roles, with its comical portrayal of Liniang's tutor. Scene 8 takes Du Bao as the central figure (played by the *wai*, an older male role); scene 40 features two *chou* actors, one of whom plays Liu Mengmei's hunchbacked servant, Camel Guo, the other Sister Stone's scabies-afflicted nephew, Scabby Turtle. Scene 53, in which Liu Mengmei confronts Du Bao and is strung up and beaten, gives the *xiaosheng* actor an opportunity to develop the comical side of Liu Mengmei's character, as does the newly added extract, "Calling to the Portrait." "Infernal Judgment," (23, earlier included in *Zuiyi qing*) features the painted face or *jing* role. The increased selection of scenes from the play expands the number of featured roles for *Mudan ting* extracts from three in earlier Qing collections (*dan, xiaosheng,* and *jing*) to seven in *Zhui baiqiu xinji* (*xiaosheng, laosheng, wai, jing, chou, dan,* and *tie*).[51]

The twelve extracts preserved in *Zhui baiqiu xinji hebian*, and nine collected in *Shenyin jiangu lu*,[52] reveal how *Mudan ting* was performed in the Qianlong era. The scenes that were added confirm the essential function of *zhezixi* as a form of social entertainment. Whether the audience was the Manchu court, wealthy merchants, or patrons at teahouses and urban theaters, the taste in Kun opera was for lively plays full of humor and spectacle as well as for romantic scenes that had been the staple of the Kun repertoire in the late Ming. Four of the added scenes are humorous, two others ("Speed the Plough" and "Reunion at Court") offer pageantry in countryside and at court, and the last ("The Soul's Departure") the spectacle of Liniang's death, which in the staged version becomes the occasion for an elaborate display of filial piety.

Some historians of Kun performance see the development towards *zhezixi* as beneficial, since it gave Kun opera a new face and brought to life stilted literati plays with refreshingly theatrical productions.[53] Others, however, deplore the chasm that opened between those who wrote plays and those who produced them. In their view the elaborations and refinements of *zhezixi* register Kun opera's creative decline, which they attribute in large part to the policies of Manchu rulers, who were remarkably successful in stifling the writing of new plays. The failure to produce new plays that made a successful transition to the stage left the public presentation of opera almost entirely in the hands of actors, whose interest in the expressive side of the texts (especially the arias) was often superficial and whose aesthetic approach to performance often took their interpretation in new directions.[54] Tensions involved in this process can be illustrated using three scenes from *Mudan ting* that typify actor-inspired revising strategies frequently found in *zhezixi*.[55] These three scenes were seldom anthologized prior to the appearance of *Zhui baiqiu xinji*.

Supplementation

Scene 10 offers a rare example of actors expanding a scene by adding arias. A more typical example of supplementation involves dialogue, as in scene 40, "Asking the Way."[56] Merely a brief transitional scene in *Mudan ting*, "Asking the Way" as *zhezixi* offers a virtuoso part to the *chou* actor. The scene Tang Xianzu wrote consists largely of dialogue, but more was needed for the scene to stand alone. This was accomplished by exploiting the dialogue already provided for its comic potential and thickening it with a stage form of Suzhou dialect.[57] The segment below presents the most interesting part of the scene from the actor's perspective, a play within a play that features Sister Stone's nephew, Scabby Turtle. In it he recounts how he tangled with the local magistrate after his aunt decamped with Liu Mengmei to avoid arrest. A translation of Tang's text comes first, followed by the one found in *Zhui baiqiu xinji hebian*:

Scabby Turtle (enters, laughing and wearing Liu Mengmei's jacket; sings to *Jinqian hua*)

Scabs all over, ugly from a kid,
Ugly from a kid,
Nabbed for what my auntie did
What my auntie did.
Up before his nibs,
Bang, wallop, thud,
Only saved my skin by
Selling up for good;
Now I run court errands
Round the neighborhood.

"Deeds you wish unknown,
best were never done!"

There's no one around just now, so let me tell you what happened to me, Scabby Turtle, at your service. A fine thing they did, my auntie Sister Stone and that Liu Mengmei, and a fine escape they made too. Then along comes that old cuss Tutor Chen and reports it all to Nan'an prefecture, and I get arrested. They beat me, then "Where's your auntie gone? How come Miss Du's grave got robbed?" Say I'm not so sharp, I sure was smart then. I just hung my head and never made a sound. "Beat a horse to make it strong, squeeze a man to make him talk," shouts the damn judge, "put the hoop around this scoundrel's head and squeeze it for me!" Ai-yo, ai-yo, that hurt! Now those torturers, they'd already beaten gold bells and jade chimes out of me, so now they did me a favor, they said, "This little devil's brains are oozing out!" "Get a bit on your finger and show me," shouts the judge. Takes a look, wipes it under his big nose and says, "It's true, you've squeezed the little devil's brains out!" Never struck him it was pus from the scabs on my head! So they loosen the hoop and let me go, but I've got to stay within call as a witness. Well, I got out of there in one piece, so here I come swaggering along in the jacket Master Liu gave me. (He chants):

Sway and swagger, swagger and sway
No one around, I'll swagger all day.[58]

In the *Zhui baiqiu xinji hebian* text Scabby Turtle sings the same entrance aria; the translation below begins after that aria. Language common to both versions is in bold type, approximations of Tang's language in dialect are italicized, and additions in dialect are in plain type:[59]

There's a saying:

"Deeds you wish unknown,
best were never done!"

Scholars are petty sorts the world over. **Scabby Turtle at your service.** *There's no one around just now, so I'll tell you what happened to me. My auntie Sister Stone and that Liu Mengmei did something. Having done it, they hid it, and having run off, they got away clean. Where to begin? That old sonofabitch Tutor Chen visits Miss Du's grave, and when he sees what happened, he up and reports it all to Nan'an prefecture.* They want to seize my aunt and His Honor Liu and send people to make the arrest, and I say I haven't seen them. They say, "We hear that there's a Scabby Turtle who's Sister Stone's nephew, lives at Little West Gate. We'll arrest him and take him to see the magistrate; that way we'll have something to go on." I was just on my way to the privy, when I see those officers. They say, "That scabby head there is him; let's nab him!" When I hear that, I'm all set to get away, but those two guys shout "Grab him, grab him!" Once they have me, they say, "So, are you Scabby Turtle?" I say, "I am. What do you want?" They take a rope and put it around my neck, and one of them pushes at my back and says "Go, go!" So, we go to the yamen, and court's in session. I hear one of the guys say, "Request permission to enter," and from inside someone says "Enter." "Your Honor, Sister Stone and graduate Liu have run away. We've brought Stone's nephew, Scabby Turtle, instead." The magistrate says, "Bring him in." "Hey! Bring him in!" They haul me off to the front of the bench. That magistrate looks me over and says, "*Where did your aunt and that graduate go?" When I don't answer, that judge pulls a face and says,* "**Beat a horse to make it strong; squeeze a man to make him talk. Put the hoop around this**

scoundrel's head and squeeze it for me!" You're thinking, what's that? It's a round band so big, with two knots on it as big as walnuts. No sooner did they fit it on my head, than two attendants stand on either side of me and say, "Confess!" But I don't say a thing, so the judge says, "Squeeze!" and no sooner were those bands squeezed than, *ai-yo, that hurt! I nearly died! Those attendants had already gotten gold bells and jade chimes out of me.* You're thinking, where did the gold bells and jade chimes come from? From out of a mine, that's where. *Once they get what they want, they do me a favor, and say, "Your Honor, this little devil's brains are oozing out!" That judge says, "I don't believe it, get some and show it to me." Once he sees that it's the stinking rotten pus from the scabs on my head, then it's "Ugh, ugh, take it away!" He tells his attendants to get me to stay within call as a witness and sends me off.* I take to my heels, and when I get to where no one is about, I say, "Did they really squeeze my brains out?" When I put my hand to my head and feel it, I see that it's blood and pus from the scabs on my head. Under the circumstances, it's lucky for me that my scabs got me out of there in one piece. Now that I've suffered this harsh treatment, all I have left is the clothes on my back. Didn't graduate Liu give me something of his? Now is the time to put it on and cheer myself up. *Now I'll just saunter about a bit—Eee, it's a perfect fit! I'll sing a song and make merry. (Sings a mountain song):*

Sway and swagger, swagger and sway
No one around, I'll swagger all day.[60]

Scabby Turtle's character is the more lively of the two *chou* roles featured in this scene, the second being Liu Mengmei's servant Camel Guo, who is old and hunchbacked, hence slow of movement and speech. The *zhezixi* plays up the contrast between the young nephew and old servant, and in the process Scabby's part is augmented, especially when he reenacts his encounter with the law. This requires him to play in quick succession a number of different parts (the yamen runners sent to arrest him, the attendants at the court, and the judge, in addition to himself), repeatedly kneeling down and getting up as appropriate.[61] Such a sustained segment would be out of place in the complete play, but in the *zhezixi* it is the *pièce de résistance.*[62]

Consolidation

Two scenes in *Mudan ting* that feature Liu Mengmei—"The Portrait Recovered" (24) and "The Portrait Examined" (26)—offer an example of how several scenes could be consolidated into a single *zhezixi.* This method is sometimes also used in adaptations of complete plays. Both Zang Maoxun and Feng Menglong collapsed these two scenes into one, but it wasn't until 1767 that this strategy crops up in published extracts. *Zhui baiqiu xinji* gives shortened versions of both scenes, entitled "Shi hua" ("Recovering the Portrait") and "Jiao hua" ("Calling to the Portrait"). Although listed separately in the collection, in practice the two extracts were usually performed together.[63] In scenes that Liu shares with Liniang, his is the subsidiary role, and extracts in Ming and early Qing miscellanies that feature him are rare.[64] In "Recovering the Portrait and Calling to It" ("Shi hua Jiao hua," often called "Jiao hua"), however, his role is featured, just as a revised version of Liniang's scene with her tutor ("The School Hall") features the *huadan* role playing the maid Chunxiang. In the Qing repertoire of *zhezixi* "Calling to the Portrait" is the counterpart for Liu of Liniang's solo scene ("Pursuing the Dream"),[65] and as a *zhezixi* it better satisfies the aesthetic requirements of the *xiaosheng* role as these were refined by actor-specialists. For this reason the interpretation of the scenes in combination is quite different from their meaning in the original context.

Tang Xianzu gave Liu Mengmei solo sequences in three noncontiguous but closely linked scenes (24, 26, and the first half of 28, "Union in the Shades"). All are focused on the portrait Liniang painted before she died, which is hidden where she lies buried. Like the solos written for Liniang in "The Interrupted Dream" and "Pursuing the Dream," Liu's solos reveal the urgency and quality of his feelings (*qing*) as his imagination is carried away by the contemplation of feminine beauty. But these sequences did not excite the enthusiasm that Liniang's did.[66] This likely is because Liu Mengmei is not the central figure of the play, and also because at moments of high feeling his behavior fails to satisfy expectations for the *xiaosheng* role.

Most disturbing is his inability to keep in mind the girl he met in his dream, and the confusion this produces when he encounters her later, first as portrait, then as ghost. In Tang's hands "The Portrait Examined," in which Liu examines Liniang's portrait, tries to guess her identity, and fails to recall who she is even as he becomes entranced with her, becomes a mildly comical display of the vagaries of male ardor. Liu's reactions to Liniang are based on sensual attraction.[67] His failure to associate the portrait with the girl to whom he made love in the dream *and* his subsequent failure to connect the painted image to whom he swears devotion with the ghost he takes as lover have occasioned much puzzled comment. Feng Menglong's disenchantment with Liu's character caused him to revise these scenes,[68] and as recently as 1982, Yue Meiti, a star performer of *xiaosheng* roles in the Shanghai Kun Opera Troupe, had this to say about "Calling to the Portrait":

> The idea of "Calling to the Portrait" is to depict Liu's sincerity of feeling and total commitment to love [*chiqing*]. The unfolding of the scene is clear and detailed, but in the original *zhezixi*, it is not clear who is the object of Liu's pursuit. The revised scene underscores the fact that once Liu's scrutiny of the portrait reveals it to be the woman he met in his dream, his feelings rush out in a torrent. His repeatedly calling to the portrait is for the purpose of proclaiming his thoughts to the woman in the dream and the true feelings that both of them seek.[69]

To achieve this, Yue devised a sequence of mimed actions that Liu performs early in the scene, at the point when he first comes upon the garden where Liniang's portrait lies hidden. She labels this sequence "Remembering the Dream" ("Yi meng") and describes it as follows:

> Confronted with the garden scene, and feeling that it is very familiar, he picks up a willow branch without thinking and this suddenly brings back his dream. When the two first met, he was holding a willow branch in his hand, and they fell in love. Now he repeats the movements of "Startled by a Dream"—how they bumped shoulders, turned to look at each other, and how he asked her to write her poem in praise of the willow. This enables the audience to recollect the circumstances of their dream meeting. These mimed actions bring out Liu's pursuit of happiness and through it his love, "growing ever deeper," is expressed.[70]

Such a moment of recollection never comes in the scene Tang Xianzu conceived. In the second aria of "The Portrait Examined" Liu experiences fleetingly a sense of *déjà vu* as he tries to guess the identity of the lady depicted on the scroll:

> But if this is neither Guanyin nor Chang E, how could it be some mortal girl? (Sings to *Erlang shen man*):
>
> Bewildered,
> Seeming to recognize her
> I search my heart.[71]

But memory fails and the moment passes. Soon his excitement is aroused by the portrait's physical charms (*Huang ying'er, Ying ti xu*), and these effusions continue in scene 28. Yet no sooner does Liniang's *ghost* appear at the door to his study than the portrait is forgotten as Liu shifts his attentions to her. In *Mudan ting*, male displays of ardor are extravagant (scene 26), at times impassioned (several arias in scene 28), but also always indiscriminate. Tang doubtless intended the inchoateness of Liu Mengmei's *qing*, but some readers and actors find this depiction of him too callous (*boxing*).[72]

The first adaptation of these scenes that attempts to rehabilitate Liu on the stage is in *Zhui baiqiu xinji*.[73] Interestingly, the inspiration for the adaptation is the sequence Feng Menglong wrote for *Fengliu meng*—direct evidence that actors used his text when adapting some scenes from the play.[74] The following translation of "Calling to the Portrait" can be compared to Birch's translation of the original scene. Here rewritten arias and changed arias taken from *Fengliu meng* are in italics; other actor-inspired changes (added dialogue, exclamations, and occasional revisions of Feng's arias) are in bold:

Liu: **I have already come to my study. Let me close the door and unroll the painting. Oh, how majestic!** (*Sings to Erlang shen*):

All complete,

Her gentle visage only fit to grace lotus's jewelled pedestal.

My, my—

Why does she stand gracefully alone by the side of plum and willow

No purple bamboo planted there,

No parrot at her side?

So it turns out that it isn't Guanyin

I see two golden lotuses from underneath her skirt.

Where would Guanyin get two tiny feet? If it isn't Guanyin, it must be Chang E. Hmh, it's Chang E

I don't really see her faery cloud,

It isn't Chang E either.

So! Since it's neither Guanyin nor Chang E. Could it be a portrait of a mortal girl?
Where in the world could one find such extraordinary beauty!

This portrait's strangeness causes me to examine my own mind.[75]

Wait a minute, *I'm in a muddle, making wild guesses,* when here at the top of the picture, I see an inscription of small characters. *Let me take a look.* **Ha, ha, ha!**

"However close the likeness viewed from near at hand,

From farther off one would say this was some airborne sprite.
Union in some year to come with the 'courtier of the moon'
Will be beneath the branches either of willow or plum."

So, this is a self-portrait by some mortal girl. But why does she say "beneath the branches either of willow or plum"? Most mysterious! (Sings to Ji xianbin):

How to draw near her in her Toad Palace?
I fear that the River of Heaven cuts us off.

Aiya! *Lovely lady, Lovely lady, Can it be that beauty such as yours lacks for a mate?*

What outcome do you seek by willow and plum?

There is no lack of plums and willows in this world, but as my name is "Willow Dreams of Plum," then "beneath plum" must refer to me, and as for "beneath willow" (**he smiles**), *it must refer to me too,*

Happily she waits beneath plum and willow.

Oh! *There is something very familiar about this beauty.* **Where have I met her before? Yes, for a moment I couldn't think of it! Hah!**

Doubts not dispelled,
It seems that she met me somewhere before.

Ah (makes a clucking noise), last year, in the late spring, I had a dream. In the dream I was in a garden, and there was a beautiful girl standing underneath a flowering plum tree—it was she! She said to me. "Master Liu, I am the one you must meet to set foot on your road to love and to high office." **Aiya! If it is you, speak!** *Lovely lady, tell me that it's true,*

Don't be difficult,
Can that already perceived in dream be true?

Let me take in the portrait's features more closely. Why does she bear a sprig of green plums in her hand? **Hm, hm!** Just as if she were holding me in her arms! (Sings to Tiying xu):[76]

Green plum in hand, she softly intones her verse,
Luring my heart to stumbling thoughts of love.
Just as I "sketch a cake to appease my hunger"
So she "gazes at plums to slake her thirst."
A lotus bud, not yet open,
Red lips lightly daubed harbor a smile.

Lovely lady, I see how your pretty eyes keep gazing at me. I stand here, with her looking at me. I go over here—Na, na, na! She's still looking at me! Aya! Lady, ya! Lady, why do you keep looking at me? Why don't I call to her to descend? Ah, Lovely lady, lovely lady, please—Ai! Liu Mengmei, Liu Mengmei! How can you be so infatuated with her?

Full of charm and passion,
Sadly she longs to speak,
But lacks breath.

So! The young lady rivals in her skill the painting of Cui Hui, the poetry of Su Hui, the calligraphy of the Lady Wei. Though I have cultivated my own talents, how could I ever hope to match this girl, my chances one in ten-thousand. Brought suddenly face to face with her like this, I shall try a verse in corresponding meter (he writes):

"The excellence of the painting is nature's inspiration,
A sprite either of heaven or of earth below;
The 'moon-palace union' may be near at hand or far
But hopes of spring are lodged in willow and plum.
Liu Mengmei from South of the Ridge, having burnt incense and bathed himself, respectfully has matched verses."

Hai! *Young miss,* **young miss, this, this, this is my** ***clumsy verse*****! I want,** I want you to *give me instruction.* (Sings to Cu yulin):[77]

I indite my verses,
Match tones and rhymes,
Suddenly stricken with love, my cheeks flush.

Let me call her as earnestly as I can. **Ai! Young miss, young miss**. Lovely lady, **lovely lady!** Gracious mistress. **My own very dearest mistress!**

Till my throat bleeds I cry for Zhenzhen, but does she hear?
The proverb says
One whose name is spoken will sneeze in response:

Oh! come down, come down!

Her wave-tripping feet move,
Slow and supple she is about to descend,

Yo! Cui!

But her image stays immobile.

So, as I stay on, solitary in this place, I shall spend my days before this portrait, to admire her and present my obeisances, to call her and sing her praises. (Sings to coda):

Having found this lady, first rejoice:
Might this willow and plum form a closer union yet?

Young miss! Young miss! **I fear that**

Image without form, your gaze will destroy me!

So, there is a breeze here. Will the young lady please go inside? Young lady, please, I will follow after. How dare I presume, you are the guest. How dare I be so bold? Please, you first, that way, we will not go in side by side. (He exits)[78]

According to Yue Meiti, this *zhezixi* encompasses three actions on Liu's part: examining the portrait (*xiang hua*), guessing who the portrait is (*cai hua*) and calling to the portrait (*jiao hua*).[79] In Feng Menglong's revision, Liu's moment of recollection comes after he has read Liniang's poem and realizes that it contains veiled references to himself. This triggers the memory of his dream and the girl in it, which is then recounted in a passage of dialogue inserted into the aria *Ji xianbin*.[80] Feng's rehabilitation of Liu's character met with acceptance, and *Ji xianbin* is one of two arias from his adaptation that made their way into the text collected in *Zhui baiqiu xinji*. Despite its clarification of "the object of Liu's pursuit," Yue Meiti elected to enhance Liu's powers of recollection (and those of the audience) even further, by inserting a mimed sequence at this point as well.[81]

Ji xianbin is the only aria that substantially alters the depiction of Liu's character in this scene. A passage of dialogue inserted in *Ying ti xu* becomes the occasion for Liu to move about the stage as the portrait's eyes follow him. This performance-inspired interpolation is not found in the original text or in Feng's revision. It becomes part of a prolonged effort on Liu's part to "engage" the portrait, first by exchanging glances with it, then by calling out to it and pleading with it to come to life.[82] Such mimed elaboration of dialogue (what Yue Meiti refers to as "dumb show," *ya dongzuo*), performed at intervals between the lines of the arias, is often found in *zhezixi* preserved in the late Qing collections and is evidence of a more popular style. We will see a more elaborate use of it in Liniang's death scene, the last to be discussed in this chapter.

The modern scholar Zhao Jingshen has praised "Calling to the Portrait" as an artistic gem perfected by generations of actors. He has analyzed the revisions introduced into the *zhezixi* from Feng's adaptation and feels that they are narrow in scope and do not change the spirit of the scene as Tang Xianzu envisioned it.[83] But by confining his analysis to how Feng's changes condense the language in Tang's arias and solve prosodic problems, Zhao overlooks how the passages of added dialogue simplify and exaggerate Liu Mengmei's character in the *zhezixi*. The essentializing techniques fundamental to the aesthetics of *zhezixi* run counter to the complex aesthetics of southern plays, which have been compared to the novels of the same era.[84] The autonomy of the extracted scene, brought about by a changed context of performance, led to a very different treatment of the actions portrayed in it.[85] This is an underlying cause of *zhezixis*' tendency to take on a life of their own apart from the plays that spawned them. In the case at hand, the process of simplifying Liu's scenes, already begun in Feng Menglong's adaptation, was taken even further in the *zhezixi*.

Enrichment

Scenes in *chuanqi* also exhibit internal complexities of structure and presentation that are at odds with the aesthetics of *zhezixi*. This is especially true of major scenes in *Mudan ting*, which sometimes reach a length of twenty arias. Liniang's death scene ("Keening," 20) is complex not only because many characters appear and participate in the singing (four in addition to Liniang: Chunxiang, Madam Du, Du Bao, and Sister Stone), but also because their responses to Liniang's dying and death run the gamut from pathos to humor.[86] Here I will focus on how Liniang's death is staged and how the emotions surrounding the event are condensed and heightened in *zhezixi* preserved in *Zhui baiqiu xinji hebian* and *Shenyin jiangu lu*.

Once it gets under way at the third aria (after Chunxiang has escorted the dying Liniang onstage), the scene as Tang Xianzu wrote it builds in intensity through three segments that Liniang sings with Chunxiang (arias 3–5), with her mother (6–9), and finally with Chunxiang, her mother, and her father, who comes onstage after the tenth aria. Prior to Madam Du's entry at the sixth aria, the singing pattern is subdued, in keeping with the somber opening mood—Liniang dies on a rain-darkened night of the Mid-autumn Festival. Both Liniang and Chunxiang sing their solo arias to the same tune, *Ji xianbin*, but after Madam Du sings her first aria (6), the singing gradually becomes more interactive. The next five arias (7–11) have choral refrains, and in arias 9 through 11 exchanges of sung lines reach a crescendo in the eleventh and penultimate aria, in which Du Bao, Madam Du, and Chunxiang all sing. Liniang then sings a brief coda as death is imminent (aria 12), and all leave the stage.

The death itself is not staged, and Liniang's exit marks a break at which the scene logically can conclude. Tang prolongs it, however, by having Chunxiang immediately return to announce her mistress's death and sing a keening aria. This break in the illusion, as Chunxiang addresses the audience directly, could have served to introduce a display of grieving by those present at the death.[87] Instead, a new element is introduced with the entry of Sister Stone, enlisted by Du Bao to pray for Liniang's recovery. She sings next:

> *Stone*: Now that your young mistress is gone you will find things a lot easier.
> *Chunxiang*: How is that?
> *Stone*: (Sings to *Hong na'ao*)
> She won't be needing you
>   To chitter-chatter over what to wear in weather cold or hot.
> She won't be making you
>   Stay awake late at night, get up with the dawn.
> *Chunxiang*: Well, I'm used to that.
> *Stone*: And there are other ways you'll be saved a lot of trouble.
>   You won't have to pull a wry mouth when you pick her corns
>   Stop your nose when you empty the chamber pot.
>   (*Chunxiang spits in disgust*)
> There's another thing too: a young mistress in the bloom of youth,
>   No telling when she might have been at it
>   And Madam her mother would have
>   Broken your back there in that garden.
> *Chunxiang*: Stop your nonsense! Here's the mistress. (*Madam Du enters weeping.*)[88]

Stone is soon to take Chunxiang's place (as caretaker of Liniang's tomb), and a mild rivalry is expressed here, in her jibing response to Chunxiang's grief.[89] Nor is the sadness that attends the parents' grieving sustained for long. After each has come back on stage and sung a keening aria, the mood is again broken with the arrival of a messenger, who brings news of Du Bao's promotion to the post of Pacification Commissioner. This announcement sets in motion hurried measures to entrust the care of Liniang's tomb to Stone and Liniang's tutor, Chen Zuiliang, after which Du Bao, Madam Du, and Chunxiang depart, and the scene concludes. Tang's dramatization of Liniang's death thus works against prolongation of one emotional key. No histrionics attend the death, and in its aftermath the shift to humor, with the unedifying spectacle of priestess and tutor squabbling over their respective privileges as appointed guardians of Liniang's tomb, is accompanied by a change from singing to dialogue. By scene's end, Liniang is almost forgotten.[90]

All adaptations of "Keening" make radical changes that simplify its action and eliminate the unsettling shifts of mood. Zang Maoxun focused attention exclusively on the parent-child relationship—Liniang's expression of filial piety on her deathbed, and her parent's prostration after she has died.[91] Feng Menglong enhanced Chunxiang's role, retaining four arias sung by herself and Liniang at the beginning of the scene and reducing those exchanged between mother and daughter from four to two. These changes draw attention to the closeness between mistress and maid.[92] Chunxiang's loyalty is played up, and Stone's role as a comic foil is greatly reduced. Neither adaptor is comfortable with the comic elements of the scene. Zang Maoxun emphasizes filial piety; Feng foregrounds devotion (*yi*).[93] Neither is highlighted in the original scene.

The reduction of "Keening" to a few dramatic high points was carried much farther in the *zhezixi*. In these the first high point comes when Madam Du is called to her daughter's bedside. The contrast with Tang's treatment can be seen by juxtaposing Birch's translation of the two arias that he wrote for this encounter with the corresponding passage from the *zhezixi* in *Zhui baiqiu xinji hebian*:

> *Chunxiang* (*in alarm*): The chill in my young mistress' body has numbed her limbs—I must ask Madam to come.
> *Madam Du* (*enters, declaims*):
> My husband eminent, in old age hale and strong;
> So delicate my daughter, her short life filled with pain.
> How is your sickness progressing, my child?
> *Chunxiang*: She is worse, Madam.
> *Madam Du*: How can this be? (Sings to *Ji xianbin*):
> Unforeseen a dream in the garden,
> But how to explain this continued failure to wake?
> Her heavy head droops in deep slumber.
> (*She weeps*)
> Oh, why did we not have you long ago "mount the dragon" of a successful match!
> Nightly the lone wild goose
> Strips the soft feather sheen from this my "fledgling phoenix."
> All becomes void
> And time now also for your mother's life to pass.
> *Liniang* (revives; sings to *Zhuanlin ying*):
> Now my spirit stirs like the air of a mirage,
> As the breeze sets to tinkling the pendants below the eaves.
> Mother, I make obeisance to express my gratitude—(*stumbles to her knees in prostration*)

From my first years you have prized me as your "thousand gold pieces"
But I, unfilial, cannot serve you to the end of your days.
Mother, this is Heaven's decree. In this life
A flower no sooner red . . .
Ah, let me only serve anew these parents, lily and cedar, in the lifetime to come.
Liniang, Madam Du, Chunxiang (*weeping*):
O cruel west wind,
So sudden, so callous to scatter green leaf and red petal.[94]

In the *Zhui baiqiu xinji hebian* extract, Madam Du's aria is eliminated, and Liniang's aria is interrupted by long passages of dialogue:

Chunxiang: Ah! Young mistress—What happened? Mistress, wake up! Wake up! Oh dear!
Madam Du (*enters, declaims*):
My husband eminent in old age hale and strong;
So delicate my daughter, her short life filled with pain.
Chunxiang: Madam, My young mistress' body has broken into a cold sweat, and she has lost consciousness.
Madam Du: Ah! Is that so? Child, wake up! Wake up!
Liniang (revives; sings to *Zhuanlin ying*):
Now like the air of a mirage my spirit stirs.
As the breeze sets to tinkling the pendants below the eaves.
Chunxiang: Young mistress, your mother is here.
Madam Du: Mother is here.
Liniang: Ah, Mother, where are you?
Madam Du: Child! I am here.
Liniang: Mother, I want to make obeisance to express my gratitude.
Madam Du: Child! Why say such mournful things?
Liniang: Chunxiang, help me to get up.
Chunxiang: Young mistress, you are ill and musn't move.
Madam Du: Just so, you musn't move. Don't get up.
Liniang (*in irritation*): It doesn't matter, help me to get up.
Madam Du, Chunxiang: Ah, we'll help you up. (*They help her to get up; she sits again and falls down*)
Madam Du: Better that you don't move.
Liniang: It doesn't matter (*she gets up*).
Madam Du: Chunxiang, support her.
Liniang: Chunxiang, let go.

Chunxiang: If you let me support you, it will be easier to walk.
Liniang (in anger): Aiya! Let me go!
Madam Du: Let her go. Why are you watching her? Stand back from her a little.
Chunxiang: Yes M'am.
Liniang: Mother, where are you?
Madam Du: Child, I am here.
Liniang: Stand a little farther away.
Madam Du: All right.
Liniang: Farther still.
Madam Du: All right.
Liniang: Mother, I want to make obeisance to express my gratitude.
Madam Du: It's not necessary!
Liniang (sings):

From my first years you have prized me as your "thousand gold pieces"

(*She makes her obeisance and stumbles to the ground*)

Madam Du: Aiya, my child! Aiya, child!
Chunxiang: Young mistress, young mistress!
Madam Du: Ha—wretch! Why didn't you help her?
Chunxiang: I am helping her. (*Both call*): Wake up, wake up!
Liniang (coming to): Ah, Mother!
Madam Du: Quick! Help her inside.
Liniang (sings):

I, unfilial, cannot serve you to the end of your days.

Madam Du: Ai, seeing you like this, what can I do?
Liniang: Ai, It's finished.
Chunxiang: What are you saying?
Liniang: It's finished. This is Heaven's decree.
Madam Du, Chunxiang: What can be done?
Liniang (sings):

In this life, a flower no sooner red . . .

Aiya, Mother! (*She clasps Madam Du around the neck*) Let me only serve anew these parents, lily and cedar, in the lifetime to come.
Madam Du, Chunxiang (sing)

O cruel west wind.
So sudden, so callous, to scatter green leaf and red petal.[95]

Spoken exchanges between mother, daughter, and maid and accompanying actions dramatize Liniang's attempt to kowtow to her mother in her extremely weakened state. In Tang's text, a stage direction mentions that she "stumbles to her knees in prostration," but there is no indication that Madam Du acknowledges this gesture. Instead, in her following aria she is absorbed in her own thoughts.[96]

Madam Du (sings to the same tune):

Lacking sons
What pains we took with this child all fragrant charm
To smile her joy about us.
Grown not to womanhood,
She was to care for us, her revered elders, to our end;
But now, alas, childless and lost shall we remain at rim of sky.

My child, very soon

From clash of moon and year a void of time
Shall quench your troubled spirit.

Liniang, Madam Du, Chunxiang:

O cruel west wind,
So sudden, so callous to scatter green leaf and red petal.[97]

This aria is cut in *Zhui baiqiu xinji hebian,*[98] which focuses instead on Liniang's attempt to make her kowtow, and her mother's and maid's dismayed response to her efforts. An acting style had developed, built upon uses of dialogue that complemented (and here supplanted) a style organized around the singing of arias. The two texts of this scene reflect an evolution from the literary style of Kun opera in the late Ming, in which arias were the expressive core of the singing, to the theatrical style of the mid-Qing, in which singing was reduced to allow for an expansive and varied use of dialogue and accompanying dance-acting and action.[99]

The stylized dance-acting of Kun opera is movement devoted to exterior display, but because it is linked to language that correlates descriptions of external scenes with feelings, it can express, indirectly, the character's interior mental states. In the hands of a playwright like Tang, the depiction of these interior states is often complex and unexpected. In "Keening," for example, each character responds to Liniang in a way that is unique to his or her situation and emotional makeup (*qing*). One effect of this depiction of character when reading the scene (and likely when seeing it performed) is to isolate Liniang emotionally at the moment of death.[100] In the *zhezixi*, action becomes more externalized, and takes on a ritualized quality as histrionic displays of emotion come to the fore.

The following translation of Liniang's "kowtowing" aria, as preserved in *Shenyin jiangu lu*, conveys the effect of histrionic display in "The Soul's

Departure." It is based on the version of this aria in *Zhui baiqiu xinji hebian*, but the directions about movements and gestures unique to it (here given in bold italics to distinguish them from those common to both versions) are far more detailed.

Chunxiang: Aiya! Oh dear, Madam, come quickly!
Madam Du (***enters in haste, declaims***):
My husband eminent, in old age hale and strong;
So delicate my daughter, her short life filled with pain.
How is the young mistress's illness progressing?
Chunxiang: Madam, my young mistress's body has broken into a cold sweat, and she has lost consciousness.
Madam Du: Ah! Is that so? Child, wake up! Wake up!
Chunxiang: Young mistress, wake up, wake up! (***Madam Du and Chunxiang should call out in an urgent, high-pitched voice***)
Liniang (***after faintly answering***, sings *Zhuanlin ying*):
Now like the air of a mirage
Madam Du, Chunxiang: Good!
Liniang:
My spirit stirs.
Chunxiang: Young mistress, your mother is here.
Liniang: Aiya! (*sings*)
The breeze sets to tinkling the pendants below the eaves.
Madam Du (***The laodan's chair seems to be set beside the xiaodan***): Child, mother is here.
Marginal comment: At this point, the mother is as if in a daze.
Chunxiang: Young mistress, Madam is here.
Liniang (***struggles on both hands to left and right; her hand tremblingly touches Madam Du's hand***): Aiya, Mother! I want to express my gratitude for the final time.
Madam Du: Dear child; seeing you like this, what can I do?
Liniang (***coughs, then presses down with both hands and faces forward***): Chunxiang—
Chunxiang: What is it?
Liniang: Help me to get up. (***She first struggles herself to rise***)
Chunxiang: Aiya, You're ill; you musn't move!
Liniang (***shakes her head and struggles until she is half-standing***): It doesn't matter; help me to get up.

Chunxiang: Yes. (***As soon as she is on her feet, Liniang immediately sits back down and hurriedly coughs to her right***)

Chunxiang: Aiya! I said you were ill. You had better sit a while.

Madam Du: You needn't get up.

Liniang (***shakes her head and struggles to stand, hands pressed down on the table***): It doesn't matter.

Chunxiang: Please be careful.

Liniang (***struggles out from behind the right side of the table***): Chunxiang, let me go.

Madam Du: Let her help you.

Chunxiang: Wait for me to help you.

Liniang (***frowns; her body leans heavily on her right arm***): Aiya, Let go!

Chunxiang: You're standing.

Liniang (***supporting herself on the table, moves to one corner of it***): Mother—

Chunxiang: Madam—

Madam Du: Child.

Liniang: I want to make obeisance to express my gratitude for your loving care. (***Madam Du chokes back sobs and tears and with her hand gestures no***)

Chunxiang: Young mistress, Madam has said that you musn't make obeisance.

Liniang: Aiya, Dear Mother!

Madam Du: Aiya, Child!

Liniang: Aiya, Mother!

Madam Du: Aiya, Child! (***weeps***)

Chunxiang (***covers her face with both hands and weeps***): Ah!

Liniang (*sings*):

From my first years you have prized me as your "thousand gold pieces."

(***As she sings, she comes from behind the table while supporting herself on it and with both hands clasped takes several steps as if to kneel***, *then stumbles to the floor*)

Madam Du (***this dialogue is also spoken as Liniang is singing***): Chunxiang, help her.

Chunxiang: I'm here. (***Aside to herself***): What to do? (***Sees Liniang fall down and hurriedly helps her. Vulgar actors mistakenly embrace the laodan; this is very wrong***):[101] Aiya, young mistress!

Madam Du: Aiya, child! (***Castigates the maid***): You little wretch, how could you let her fall?

Chunxiang: Aiya, I'm helping her!

Liniang: Ah, Mother—

Madam Du: Child, is it any better? (***She helps Liniang to sit on the ground; Liniang leans against Chunxiang's left knee. Madam Du sits facing her and supports her with both hands***)

Liniang (*sings*):

I, unfilial, cannot serve you to the end of your days.

Madam Du: Ai, seeing you like this, what can I do?

Liniang: Ai, Mother—

Madam Du: Child!

Liniang (***looking at Madam Du, says***): This is Heaven's desire.

Madam Du: Ah, bitter!

Liniang: In this life (*sings*):

A flower no sooner red . . .

(*She places both hands, **trembling**, on Madam Du's shoulders*)

Ah, let me only serve anew these parents, lily and cedar, in the lifetime to come.

(***Madam Du and Chunxiang help Liniang to rise, and from front and behind assist her to the table***)

Madam Du, Chunxiang:

O cruel west wind,

So sudden, so callous, to scatter green leaf and red petal.[102]

Explanatory notes in *Shenyin jiangu lu* far exceed those in Ming *chuanqi* texts, which in turn are far more abundant than those in Yuan *zaju*. They offer highly specific guidance to performers, describe the attitude and demeanor their actions and movements should convey, comment about how characters should be portrayed, and criticize performances of some actors by name.[103] In the case of *Mudan ting*, the compiler worked from the extracts preserved in *Zhui baiqiu hebian* and his familiarity with performances based on them. Although he sometimes finds fault,[104] he praises the compilers for including dialogue and stage directions and criticizes those who include only arias in their collections.[105] He also caters to the theatrically oriented reader.

It seems unlikely that professional actors, who learned their art orally, would consult works such as these. However, the claim is made that with successive printings, these compilations turned into "guide-books arranged at the hands of people from within the theaters" (*juchang-*

zhong renshou yibian de shuomingshu).[106] Which is to say that even though actors neither produced printed texts of *zhezixi* nor read them, extracts preserved in *Zhui baiqiu xinji hebian* and *Shenyin jiangu lu* are close to the theater and reflect actors' interpretations. This distinguishes them from the adaptations of whole plays discussed in chapter 2, which were blueprints for performance that furnish no evidence about the uses eventually made of them.[107] In Chinese opera, and Kun opera especially, there was constant contact between amateurs and professionals. Opera aficionados were active in their appreciation: most knew how to sing the arias, and many loved to perform them as well. Given the amount of contact between the two groups, these miscellanies influenced professional actors indirectly by way of the amateurs who read them, and amateurs because each successive printing introduced them to more changes made by the professionals.[108] *Zhui baiqiu xinji hebian* thus registers clearly the impact of popular styles of opera on Kun opera, and is the first edition to add several new extracts for *Mudan ting*. Scenes with the greatest theatrical appeal are favored,[109] and some old favorites ("The Interrupted Dream" and "Calling to the Portrait") are more substantially revised than heretofore. For the first time since the early Wanli period when drama miscellanies began to circulate, Kun opera by the 1760s no longer was in a position of dominance, even with the opera-going elite.[110] This is surely why the contents of this collection differed substantially from earlier ones published under that title.[111]

Not only does the selection of *zhezixi* differ in kind from that found in earlier collections, but the texts are more extensively revised. Was this the cumulative effect of a tradition of performing *zhezixi* that by the mid-eighteenth century spanned more than 150 years? It is often claimed that the *zhezixi* collected in this "popular" edition of *Zhui baiqiu* reflect performance practices in the early years of the Qing dynasty (and perhaps even earlier).[112] Similar claims have been made for *Shenyin jiangu lu*, which contains a disproportionate number of extracts from "old" plays—more than one third (twenty-four of sixty-five) are from the early Ming plays *Pipa ji* and *Jingchai ji*. That the oldest plays included have the greatest number of extracts has prompted one scholar to describe this collection as a testament to the accretive nature of performance traditions, as generations of artists built on the legacy of foundational plays, taking the contributions of earlier masters as their starting point.[113] The older the play (the argument goes), the greater the number of extracts preserved from it, indicating the amount of talent that had been lavished on performing it.

With nine extracts (from eight scenes), *Mudan ting* ranks third in terms of representation in *Shenyin jiangu lu*, but the artistic legacy recorded in this miscellany can be traced textually no earlier than *Zhui baiqiu xinji*.[114] Discontinuities between extant editions of *Zhui baiqiu* testify to the existence of disparate traditions of performing and transmitting *zhezixi*. While the extracts in *Shenyin jiangu lu* build upon those in *Zhui baiqiu xinji hebian*, the same relationship does not hold for the latter collection and extant Qing miscellanies earlier in date (i.e., *Zuiyi qing* and *Zhui baiqiu quanji*). Based on the evidence furnished by this one play, the compilers of *Zhui baiqiu xinji* seem to have started afresh, using new sources for their selection of materials as well as new criteria for what to include.[115]

This kind of sea change in the nature and contents of drama miscellanies had happened before. In the earliest Ming *xuanben*, extracts ostensibly from the same play differed from one edition to the next and often bore little or no resemblance to "orthodox" (Kun) versions. These earliest miscellanies are a window on a period when operatic culture was both more lively and more fluid. Once Kun opera became dominant, its texts stabilized, registering very little influence from popular operas or from popular styles of performance until well into the Qing period. The popular editions of *Zhui baiqiu* (*tongxingben*) are evidence that this stability was eroding, though there were already signs of this trend with the publication of *Zuiyi qing*.[116] In a sense, the situation had come full circle in the two hundred years from 1550 to 1750. Kun opera once again found itself in competition with popular styles of opera, and this competition was registered in its playtexts. But to say that the changes registered in the mid-Qing texts are the fruit of an unbroken performance tradition is an assertion difficult to demonstrate.

One thesis of Lu Eting's history of Kun opera is that a popular theatrical style always existed alongside the elite tradition of pure singing and armchair enjoyment of drama.[117] If Lu is right, it is possible that the "new" scenes from *Mudan ting* published as *zhezixi* only in the 1760s had been perfected over many generations by professional actors, transmitted orally, and finally written down for the enjoyment of the opera-going public.[118] However, it is also possible that these heavily revised *zhezixi* reflect belated efforts to popularize Kun opera. As clapper operas became popular, *zhezixi* in the Kun repertoire were adapted for performance in that style, and the reverse was also likely true.[119] Kun actors absorbed the techniques and style of clapper opera, and that influence was then registered in the published extracts. It therefore seems likely that the collections published in the 1760s and after reflect trends specific to the time when they were compiled and tell us little about the earlier state of affairs.

Gongpu: Musically Annotated Texts for *Mudan ting*[120]

In none of the printed miscellanies, even those such as *Yue lu yin* and *Shanshan ji* that are not theatrical in orientation, is there indication of how the arias should be sung, beyond the provision of *dianban* notation. The first works that do this were compiled at roughly the same time as *Zhui baiqiu xinji hebian* and *Shenyin jiangu lu*. The most important of them is *Nashuying qupu* (A Collection of Arias for the Bookshelf), a collection of Kun dramatic arias that was the work of a master of the pure singing form, Ye Tang (ca. 1722–ca. 1795). Ye published, in installments, musical scores for all arias from five southern dramas and a collection of extracts under this title. The second of these installments, published in 1791, is devoted to Tang's four complete plays, and for all but one of them (*Zichai ji*) Ye had access to old musical scores, which he edited to ensure that the musical interpretation of the arias conformed to the taste and singing practice of Kun opera connoisseurs as he understood it.[121] Subsequent musical interpretations of Kun operas have built on his work.[122]

Why did a work of this kind appear only at this comparatively late date? Two reasons suggest themselves, both related to the pressure on Kun opera starting about this time. In the late eighteenth century, Kun opera was in decline, despite continued enthusiasm for it at the Qianlong emperor's court.[123] Ye Tang was a private citizen and a wealthy one, and he may have wished to document and preserve a tradition that was threatened with both corruption and loss. His marginalia are addressed to three groups of readers: connoisseurs of music (*zhiyinzhe*), stage performers (*banyanjia*), and beginners (*chuxuezhe*). In them Ye and his collaborator, Wang Wenzhi (1730–1802), warn against practices of "common actors" (*suling*) that were becoming popular, perhaps the very same actors whose interpretations are documented in *Zhui baiqiu xinji hebian*.[124]

A second reason why traditions transmitted orally among performers were now written down may have to do with the Qing passion for evidentiary research (*kaozheng*), the desire to construct an authentic record based on a meticulous investigation of sources. Several compilations made at this time, some under imperial auspices and others (such as Ye Tang's) undertaken privately, suggest that these methods were being used to document and transmit dramatic texts.[125] But Ye was not interested in documenting Kun opera music as it was being performed in the theaters. His musical notation of the arias was not descriptive in that sense, but rather "prescriptive and exclusive," intended for intellectual singer-composers (i.e., amateurs), who could be expected to chart a course independent from that of common actors.[126]

Ye's interest was focused entirely on the arias, and since his editions were intended as handbooks for performances not staged, dialogue and stage directions are omitted. He is firmly within the tradition of pure singing, and many who have called themselves his disciples have held themselves aloof from the theatrical tradition of Kun performance.[127] However, Ye himself acknowledged and occasionally made use of popular theatrical texts; the contents of his collections correspond closely to that of the most popular edition of *Zhui baiqiu*. He knew the theater and its actors; his selection of texts was influenced by the taste for "lively" (*huabu*) plays in Suzhou. Based on both written and oral sources for Kun opera, his works address both amateur purists and stage actors (the *banyanjia* of the commentary).[128]

The earliest printed collections of dramatic *qu* that contained musically annotated playtexts complete with dialogue were *Yinxiangtang qupu* (Fragrance-Humming Hall's Register of Songs, 1789) and *Eyunge qupu* (Cloud-Stopping Pavilion's Dramatic Scores, 1870).[129] The compiler of *Eyunge gupu*, Wang Xichun (fl. late Qing), converted texts for singing (*qinggong*) into texts for performance (*xigong*) by combining the musical features of Ye Tang's *qupu* with the theatrically based texts of *Zhui baiqiu*. *Zhezixi* for *Mudan ting* include nine of the twelve in *Zhui baiqiu xinji hebian*, but the respective versions occasionally differ significantly.[130] Wang kept a household troupe, and his collection caters to the taste for private performances. Its orientation is intermediate, between that of *Zhui baiqiu xinji hebian* and *Shenyin jiangu lu* on the one hand and the *Nashuying* collections on the other.[131]

Many of these Qing collections, though directed at distinct groups of opera lovers, exhibit a common tendency: Their compilers make use of both written and oral sources when assembling them and thus work within a loose and somewhat eclectic "tradition" consisting of two distinct streams, one elite and literary, the other popular and theatrical. What is impossible to ascertain is the contribution of each stream to the final product.[132] However, it is fair to say that most theatrically based texts of drama that made their way into print in the nineteenth century drew on the work of Ye Tang and the popular editions of *Zhui baiqiu*, with emphasis either on singing the arias or performing them.[133]

Hand-copied *Gongpu*

Printed collections such as Ye Tang's were expensive, and many opera lovers copied favorite plays for personal use. *Zhezixi* transcripts that date from the latter half of the nineteenth century survive in great quantities, and these were likely the chief medium in which *zhezixi* circulated. The distinction between printed *gongpu* for *zhezixi* and manuscript copies was not as significant, for example, as that between printed folios and "foul papers" in Shakespeare's time. These are not necessarily scripts as we think of them; in most cases comparison of the handwritten text of a *zhezixi* with a printed version from a collection such as *Eyunge qupu* shows that the copyist worked from the printed text or, more likely, from another handwritten copy of it.

Nonetheless, the variety of their formats and ways in which their users personalized them, convey some sense of how *zhezixi* were enjoyed in the late nineteenth century. Their covers often bear the name of the person who fashioned the text, and a few of them furnish clues to how they were used. A large collection of Kun opera extracts assembled over fifty years by members of the Wu lineage consists of fifty-three volumes, each containing a half dozen or more *zhezixi*. The cover of one volume is inscribed with the motto "Practices Diligently" ("Yongxin xixue"), and another volume contains a slip of paper respectfully soliciting a friend or teacher's criticisms; this would appear to be a collection belonging to a family whose members enjoyed Kun opera as amateurs.[134] Title pages of volumes in some collections also have mottos, "Contemplation and Study" ("Jingxin xuexi"), "Gay With Joyous Cries" ("Shangxin leshi"), "Momentary Diversions" ("Liao yi zi yu"), which evoke an atmosphere of refined enjoyment and study.[135]

That the texts were more than simply copies is suggested by the ways in which their makers identify themselves. One, who identifies himself by his sobriquet "The Layman whose Pleasures are Ordinary"

(Changle jushi), describes himself as the "maker" of the register (*zhipu*), a term that suggests it has been put together and not simply copied. Some describe themselves as "setters" (*ding*) of texts; others use *zhi* to describe their recording activities, a term that implies active engagement with the text and not merely passive copying.[136]

The nameless compiler of one collection meticulously documents at least nine collections he has consulted when making his personal collection of eighty-one *zhezixi*. Seven of the collections contained musical notation; at least two of the nine (*Nashuying qupu* and *Zhui baiqiu*) and perhaps more were published collections.[137] But the majority appear to be collections that circulated privately. For the first several volumes he appears to have used Ye Tang's interpretation of the arias as the basis for his notation, supplementing this with information gleaned from his other sources as well as his own knowledge. Often he inserts more than one interpretation in the text. In the case of four *zhezixi* from *Mudan ting*, for example, Ye Tang's notation is written to the right of the text, as was customary, but occasionally it is supplemented with information taken from a collection belonging to one Shen Yunfei, written to the left. For other extracts he drew on sources other than Ye Tang; one volume of nine extracts, for example, is based on a *gongpu* belonging to someone surnamed Tan, from Jiangxi.[138]

The method employed resembles that of Ye Tang. The collection is based on an exhaustive examination of available sources and informed by the compiler's personal knowledge of the prosody of Kun arias. The overriding interest is in the musical interpretation. Dialogue, when included, does not receive the same degree of attention, though there are exceptions.[139] In cases such as the one at hand the text reflects the copyist's personal interpretations; one senses that the detailed musical notation is both a summation of the writer's experience listening to opera and a reflection of his own performance of it.[140]

A few collections betray no hint of their creator's contributions, one example being an elegant text that reproduces only arias for each scene, in a manner that effaces any features that would identify them as *qu*, much less dramatic *qu*. The text of each aria is written on a grid of five characters per column, the only other markings being *gongche* notation, with downbeats marked in red (see Fig. 4.2). The fastidious layout of text and pristine condition of the manuscript suggest that it was enjoyed visually but not used as a script.[141]

At the other extreme are texts written in a hasty cursive script that are grimy with use, likely in performances. Not only is dialogue included, but notation relevant to performance (entrances and exits, who sings and

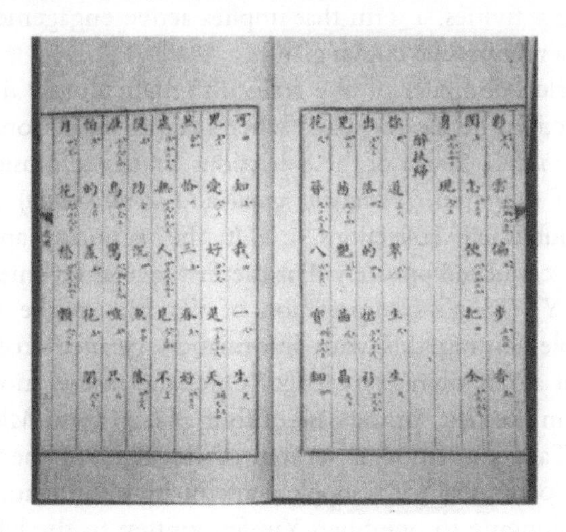

Fig.4.2. Shanghai Library MS 781943

when, passages where gongs and drums are used, exclamations and other gestures) is quite detailed (see Fig. 4.3). In some collections, often accumulated over several decades by more than one individual, dramatic extracts are interspersed with musical scores for which there are no texts, perhaps for use as interludes. It is in these editions that one is liable to encounter emendations (corrections or substitutions) made after the text had been copied.[142] The calligraphy is often poor, and the text gives every appearance of being a working script.[143]

These manuscripts have been gathered centrally in the Shanghai Library, and once uprooted it is difficult to surmise precisely how they were used, and by whom. However, a work that sheds a good deal of light on them is a two-volume mimeographed collection of source materials compiled under the direction of Xu Chongjia of Kunshan. It devotes three chapters to the history of Kun opera in the locale of its origin, subsequent to the earliest historical mentions of the Kunshan musical style, most of which date from early Ming times.

Fig. 4.3. Shanghai Library MS 485587

The second of these chapters is largely devoted to the activities of professional artists known as *tangming*. These men, most of whom were either illiterate or barely literate, sang operas for a living but did not stage them. They performed in and around Kunshan, at weddings, funerals, or on other important occasions, and were paid for their services. They did not wear costumes or make-up, but did perform dialogue and other comic business as well as sing, seated at a table and accompanying themselves on an array of instruments (see Fig. 4.4). They usually learned their craft orally, but many possessed handwritten copies of *zhezixi*, which were treasured and closely guarded possessions. The typical *tangming* artist commanded a repertoire of two to three hundred *zhezixi*. He was able to sing more than one kind of role and play several instruments. Versatility was a job requirement; a good grasp of the plays, as literature, was not.[144]

These men performed during the agricultural off-season, coming together into "halls" (*tang*), which usually consisted of eight members, one of whom was largely responsible for finding engagements and organizing their activities. Some of the most musically gifted *tangming* also made money as singing masters and teachers (*paishou*), or as accompanists on the flute (*dishi*). This work brought them into contact with the amateurs who

Fig. 4.4. *Tangming* gathered at Suzhou in 1983

enjoyed singing the operas in clubs (*qushe*). But as a group *tangming* should be distinguished from *piaoyou*, based on different levels of education and economic background. The typical *tangming* professional had little formal education and came from a poor or very modest background. The earliest manuscripts collected from them date no earlier than the final years of the Qing dynasty (ca. 1860 and later), beyond which it is not possible to date this kind of performance. "Halls" might specialize in Kun operas, or Beijing operas, and perform other popular styles as well. Perhaps unique to the Suzhou hinterland, this is one tradition of Kun performance that goes unmentioned in Lu Eting's history.[145]

This information about performances in the hinterland where Kun opera originated fits well with the data from these manuscript collections. Some of the more elegant of them were almost certainly created by *piaoyou*; the rougher copies, which often form large sets whose contents are diverse, were almost certainly the possessions of *tangming*. Taken together, these manuscript collections are the residue of a rural tradition of performing opera. Here, too, we find the intersection of professionals and amateurs, whose activities were carried on at some distance from the large, urban-based troupes.

Of the *Mudan ting* scenes, that found most often—in eight of the thirty-two handcopied texts I examined—is "Speed the Plough," which depicts Du Bao's ceremonial visit to the countryside to celebrate the arrival of spring and spur the peasants on to their labors. This extract is rivaled in number only by Liu Mengmei's scene with Liniang's portrait ("Recovering the Portrait and Calling to It," ten examples). Liniang's dream scene crops up in four collections, two of which give only the garden-strolling sequence ("Wandering in the Garden").[146] Assembled in the twilight of Kun opera's existence as a living operatic tradition, these collections reflect the shift in repertoire also detectable in the expanded Qianlong editions of *Zhui baiqiu*, towards livelier plays and away from the romances that had entranced elite audiences during the golden age of Kun opera. "Speed the Plough," which in the original borders on a burlesque of a district magistrate's ceremonial visit to his "folk," was likely played straight as a *zhezixi*. In records of performances at the Qing court, it is the most frequently performed scene from *Mudan ting* and almost always was used as the grand finale of a program of several *zhezixi*.[147] Judging from this small sample of manuscripts from a comparable period, the scene was also a favorite beyond the court. Performed as a ritualized display of harmony and well-being enjoyed by ruler and ruled alike, "Speed the Plough" had universal appeal.

The most interesting *zhezixi* from *Mudan ting* in manuscript form are the two written for Liu Mengmei, sometimes referred to by the abbreviated title "Recovering and Calling" ("Shi Jiao"). Some of these manuscript versions expose, even more clearly than the version in *Zhui baiqiu*, the different conception of Liu's character in the popular repertoire of Kun opera. I will briefly revisit the scene and consider how it represents masculine sexual desire, using a small but revealing number of revisions that show up in the manuscripts.

One collection in the Shanghai Library that contains a text of "Shi Jiao" (MS 506238) stands out as documenting Kun operas in a popular milieu. Its forty-seven volumes of *zhezixi* date from the late nineteenth century and seem the most likely of any examined to have been used by professional artists. The collection includes scores for percussion and music in several of its volumes, which I take to be an indicator of use by professionals. Also striking is the presence of miswritten characters, as well as condensation and simplification of the texts beyond that found in *Zhui baiqiu*.[148] There are also occasional mangled allusions inconceivable in a text produced by a highly literate individual, as well as aria titles not part of the regular repertoire of Kun operatic tunes.[149]

倩眼精只管看着小生⋯⋯走到這边他又看着小
生待我走那边去哪⋯⋯他又看着小生美人你不
必這般看我何不走下来相叫一声便好
請吓吓柳梦梅吓你好痴也
美人吓看你畫
多如愁欲語只少一口氣兒呵 字推挥詩如
蘇蕙行詩畫真術夫人小生雖則典雅怎到得
小娘子萬分之一驀地相逢不免賀詩一首丹
青妙處却天然不是天仙即地仙欲傍蟾宮人
近遠恰然春在柳梅边嶺南居士柳梦梅薰
沐敬和小娘子這是小生的 簽 鄉林 題詩句牌
据足早晚还要請教哩 待我叫他一
韻和題可的害想思顔自金 吓小娘子
阿呀䁖䁖的
姐姐吓 向真真啼血你知应 我叫

Fig. 4.5. Shanghai Library MS 506238

These texts have the appearance of working scripts. They are not written in fine calligraphy, nor is their format regular. This is most evident in the way dialogue is treated. It tends to fill the available space on a page and is not arranged to distinguish it clearly from the texts of the arias. These, of course, are distinguishable by the *gongche* symbols that slant off to the right in a "raincoat" style of notation. Dialogue that follows an aria or is inserted between sung lines is written to the right of the aria's text and may also be marked *bai* ("speaks"). But whenever it continues into a new column of text, it is written in characters as large as those used for the arias (Figs. 4.3 and 4.5). This calligraphically equal treatment of arias and dialogue is very different from that found in printed texts.[150] We can only presume that the reason for the difference is practical, a desire for a clear and readable text. Numerous terse directions in cursive script also seem put in the text to direct the user most efficiently. Little effort is made to beautify the text or include unnecessary information, such as titles that in printed texts and polished manuscripts set off declaimed verse passages from surrounding dialogue.[151]

The kind and number of changes made in these texts are the most interesting things about them. In many manuscripts produced by amateurs interest is focused on the arias and the creation of a visually pleasing text (Figs. 4.2 and 4.6). The compilers sometimes cut arias or selectively rewrote dialogue, and these changes, though modest in scope, can affect the interpretation of the scene.

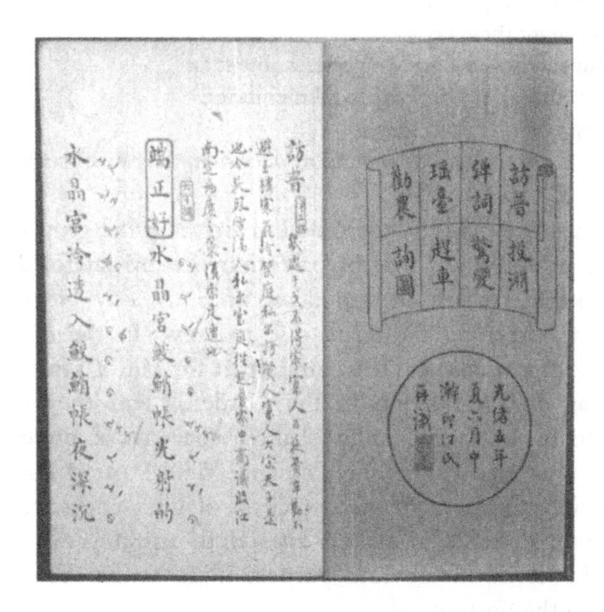

Fig. 4.6. Shanghai Library MS 500725

In "Shi Jiao," for example, the originator of MS 506238 is ruthlessly efficient in propelling Liu Mengmei to his fateful discovery of Liniang's portrait, hidden among the rocks of the garden grotto. In the original scene, the build-up is gradual and comes only after Liu has absorbed the full impact of the garden's desolate beauty. Tang Xianzu weaves an atmosphere of mystery about the garden, beginning early in the scene with Sister Stone's cryptic warning to Liu to "while away some time there, but be careful to avoid grieving" (*ze liu san men, buxu shang xin*). Liu's wonder at this remark is further aroused by the sight of the garden's decayed splendor, evoked in two lovely but disorienting arias (*Haoshi jin* and *Jinchan dao*), which describe it as the haunt of persons long departed, who have left mysterious traces of their presence. By the time he draws near the grotto where Liniang's portrait lies hidden, these sights have made a deep impression on him:

Liu (sings to *Jinchan dao*):
Amid drifts of mist lakeside pavilion leans askew,
Painted boat lies on its side,
Girl's sash dangles from motionless swing.
No pillaging of armed men
Wrought these ravages
But surely some grieving owner absent far
Fills this place with sorrowful memories;
Try as you may to forget,
Each turn of path by mound or pool captures your thought again.[152]

We can even suggest that by the time Liu arrives at the grotto, he is in an altered state of awareness that prepares him for his fateful discovery of Liniang's portrait, which comes in an uncanny way when the rocks suddenly shift, exposing the scroll case to view. In the original scene, *Haoshi jin* and *Jinchan dao* are the counterpart for Liu of Liniang's garden-strolling arias in "Wandering in the Garden," and they lend a new dimension to his brash and rather shallow character as presented in the play's opening scenes.[153] In Tang's design, "The Portrait Recovered" is therefore quite important in the depiction of Liu's character, but when combined with scene 26 to make a *zhezixi*, its arresting evocation of the garden world served no obvious purpose in an action focused on Liu's dalliance with the portrait.

In *Zhui baiqiu xinji*, both of Liu's arias are retained, and thus some of the aura of mystery surrounding his visit to the garden is preserved. But two of the manuscripts further curtail his entry into the garden by eliminating *Jinchan dao* and Sister Stone's admonition as well. As a result, there is little in the depiction of Liu's excursion to distinguish it from a typical spring outing. In what follows from MS 506238, italicized passages of dialogue differ from their counterparts in *Zhui baiqiu xinji*, which are given in the notes:

Liu (*enters and sings the lead-in aria*):
Never did spring torment man so:
Through all my journeying
No other thought.
Pear blossom fills the court with gentle fragrance,
Useless to dwell on the past year's discontents.
How much spring longing can this "willow" bear

Before his waist grows thinner than Master Shen's?

I am Liu Mengmei. Sickness has detained me in this Plum Blossom Shrine. By good fortune my new friend Chen Zuiliang is skilled in medicine and has restored me to health. But for some days past I have been suffering an ennui born of springtime longings and I can find nowhere to divert myself. Some time ago Sister Stone said that there was a large garden in these precincts *that was very beautiful. Wending my way, I am already come to the western gallery.*[154] What a fine wicker gate, green and imposing, but half fallen from its frame. I'll just go on in. Marvelous!

"Still leaning on this marble balustrade
My sad gaze shuns the walls on every side.
Such moons, such breezes, nights of long ago!
Willows once lush as mist now sere and dry."

What a fine garden it is![155] (Sings to *Haoshi jin*):

How silently the splendor has eroded.
One stretch of painted wall still stands,
The next stands all awry.[156]
Slipping on mosses,
Stumbling by broken banks
To a gate shaped as butterfly wings
Bolted for no good reason.

There must have been many visitors in times gone by, to judge from the names cut into the bamboo stems.

Guests came
And as months and years drew on
A thousand emerald tablets bore inscriptions.

But already

Wildflowers invade the steps
And weeds form thickets.[157]

What a handsome Taihu rockery, but sadly fallen down. Ai! See—what is that underneath the rock? I will fetch it out. *It's a small scroll, but what can be depicted on it? Let me unroll it and look. Marvelous! A portrait of Guanyin.*[158] Wonderful! Rather than leave it buried here, I shall take it back to my study, there to *make formal obeisances before it.*[159]

The extreme condensation of the original sequence (only one of four original arias, *Haoshi jin*, is preserved intact) means that up to the moment of his discovery, Liu's character is undeveloped. What development there is occurs during his examination of the portrait. For that sequence, portions of Feng Menglong's adaptation had been widely adopted in *zhezixi*, as has been shown above. Those modifications simplified Tang's paradoxical treatment of a familiar dramatic moment, in which the hero, confronted with the portrait of the absent beloved, is called upon to recognize who she is. Having earlier discussed Feng's "clarification" of this moment of recognition and the consequences for the presentation of Liu's character, I will here briefly consider another aspect of the scene, the portrayal of Liu's erotic response to the portrait.

In the original scene that response remains below the level of conscious thought and is only betrayed in language Liu Mengmei uses in two arias he sings after he first feels the portrait's gaze. In the first of these (*Huang ying'er*) the repetition of the word "spring" signals Liu's rising passion; in the second of them (*Tiying xu*) erotic feelings continue to be betrayed indirectly, in Liu's description of the portrait's mouth and the associations he makes with it:

> *Liu*: See how she gazes back at me! (Sings to *Huang ying'er*):
>
> Image of slender grace trailing her silken robe
> Where leaves of spring plantain seem to sway:
> Love's longings locked between her brows,
> Which curve, gentle as spring hills to soft mist of hair.
> We meet each other's eyes—
> How can gaze of either lightly move?
> Ah, flashing rays transfixing me again and again!
>
> Why is she holding a branch of green plums in her hand, just as if she were holding me? (Sings to *Tiying xu*):
>
> Green plums in hand, she softly intones her verse,
> Luring my heart to stumbling thoughts of love.
> Just as I "sketch a cake to appease my hunger"
> So she "gazes at plums to slake her thirst."
>
> Ah, my young lady, my young lady!
>
> A lotus bud, not yet open,
> Red lips lightly daubed harbor a smile.
> Full of charm and passion,
> Sadly she longs to speak,
> But lacks breath.[160]

Very little of this indirect expression of erotic feeling finds its way into the performed version of the scene. In *zhezixi*, attention focuses instead on the exchange of glances between Liu and the portrait. *Huang ying'er* is discarded, and in its place dialogue inserted midway through *Tiying xu* becomes the occasion for Liu to move about the stage as he grows increasingly excited by the portrait's following gaze. That excitement is registered in part by inarticulate cries:

> Lovely lady, I see your pair of eyes gazing at me. I stand here, with her looking at me. I go over here—na, na, na! She's still looking at me! Aya! Lady, ya! Lady, why do you keep looking at me? Why don't I call to her to descend? Ha! Lovely lady, lovely lady, please—ai! Liu Mengmei, Liu Mengmei! How can you be so infatuated with her?

Then, in a rising crescendo of blandishments, Liu calls out to the portrait:

> Ha, I'll call to her ardently. Hai! Young mistress, young mistress! Lovely lady, lovely lady! Sister, my own sister![161]

Such broad gestures indicative of Liu's feelings are minimized in the original text. Feng Menglong, who was close to the popular theater of his time, chose to play up the physical dimension of Liu's ardor in rewritten text for *Huang ying'er*:

> Image of slender grace,
> She examines a spring branch,
> And softly intones her verse.
>
> Young mistress, you lean your body against the plum tree, as if you were leaning against me. You hold a sprig of willow in your hand, as if you were holding me in your arms. Young mistress! Lovely lady! What are you thinking?
>
> Will you take up with this young "Dreamer of Plum"?
>
> One thing—you are like one who "gazes at plums to slake her thirst"; I am like one who "sketches a cake to appease my hunger."
>
> With cold eye I gaze, while my hot bowels churn.
>
> I want nothing but
>
> To tarry awhile in a dream
> Walking and sitting at your side.
>
> Oh! When I look closely, it no longer looks like a painting, but like a living person,
>
> Full of charm and passion,
> Sadly she longs to speak
> But lacks breath.[162]

This aria didn't find favor, most likely because it was *too* explicit.[163] Instead a more coy image—the man grown excited by the woman's gaze—became the preferred representation for the stage.

Turning again to our two manuscripts, we find that they enhance a vaguely sexual familiarity in Liu's overtures to the portrait, which is already evident in the *Zhui baiqiu xinji* adaptation. In MS 506238, this is accomplished by the insertion of familiar speech into a line of dialogue that Liu speaks just before singing the concluding coda. The tone of the original dialogue is almost formal at this point, a decrescendo from the emotionally charged language of the arias:

> So, as I stay on, solitary in this place, I shall spend my days before this portrait, to admire her and present my obeisances, to call her and sing her praises.[164]

The emended version of this dialogue in the manuscript is:

> So as I stay on, solitary in this place, I must make the young lady's portrait my companion, and admire her, praise her, and present my obeisances.

"Companion" (*banlü'er*), although inoffensive in English, in the Chinese context introduces common diction into Liu's pious declarations and subtly coarsens his expression of devotion in the scene's concluding lines.[165] The change, though small, is symptomatic of the direction that interpretation of the scene took in the theatrical tradition of Kun opera.

A comparable example crops up in MS 485587,[166] in small but telling emendations of dialogue connected with the aria which, in *Zhui baiqiu*, furnishes the occasion for Liu to call to the portrait and grow excited as he paces back and forth in front of it:

> *Liu* (sings to *Tiying xu*):
> Green plum in hand, she softly intones her verse,
> Luring my heart to stumbling thoughts of love.
> Just as I "sketch a cake to appease my hunger"
> So she "gazes at plums to slake her thirst."
> A lotus bud, not yet open,
> Red lips lightly daubed harbor a smile.
> Lovely lady, *I see how your pretty eyes keep gazing at me.*

For the highlighted text, our copyist has "I see how her two pretty *thirsty* eyes *love to* go on gazing" (*kan ta zheshuang qiaokeyan zhi ai gupan a*).[167] To the extent that dialogue in opera is used to comment on and support language that is sung ("So she 'gazes at plums to slake her thirst'"), these emendations strike a blow for explicitness.

Two other handcopied versions of these scenes that differ from the two just described show up among the manuscript collections in the Shanghai Library. One (MS 781944), a pristine manuscript already described above, preserves arias only in a rigid format of five characters per line. This compiler also follows *Zhui baiqiu xinji*'s version of the scene, but preserves intact the garden arias from "The Portrait Recovered," which are severely curtailed in the manuscripts just described. The same is true of another elegantly written manuscript (MS 14689), which differs from 781946 only in its arrangement of the text on the page and restoration of the scene's original title, "The Portrait Examined."[168] Both eliminate Liu's brief lead-in aria for "The Portrait Recovered," so their version of the *zhezixi* begins with and preserves whole its garden-strolling sequence.

Manuscripts, though often made from printed copies of *zhezixi*, thus reflect the aesthetic and interpretive preferences of those who made them. In the case of "Recovering the Portrait" and "Calling to the Portrait," the cruder manuscripts that I identify with professional use, and especially MS 506238, exhibit a preference for the latter sequence, which offers possibilities for mimed actions and a style of performance I would venture to call "camp."[169] The elegant manuscripts ignore the dialogue that enables such a performance and instead preserve the arias, and with them more of the scene's original ambiance. Reading their text of these two scenes, we are restored to a more interiorized experience of Liu's character, stripped of staginess.[170]

The "Actors' Take-over" of Kun Opera

The collections of *zhezixi* described in this chapter represent a fraction of the total number produced,[171] but they are intriguingly diverse in their contents and arrangements and offer glimpses of how *Mudan ting* was enjoyed as both closet drama and theatrical art. In some respects they confirm our expectations; in others they surprise us. One surprise is the relatively late date at which several of the most popular *zhezixi* ("The School Hall," "Speed the Plough," and "Calling to the Portrait") made their way into print. Another has been the manuscript collections, which are more than simply handwritten counterparts of printed *gongpu*.

Ming miscellanies show two approaches to the text, one that reproduces only the arias (*Shanshan ji* and *Yue lu yin*) and, at a later date, one that preserves the text of the scene intact (*Yichun jin* and *Xuanxuepu*). This suggests that where Kun opera was concerned the readership for miscellanies was expanding, taking in readers who were interested in plays in their specifically dramatic dimension. But one has to be careful. Both *Yichun jin* and *Xuanxuepu* were compiled at the same time that Feng Menglong and other Suzhou-identified playwrights were energetically endeavoring to enhance Kun opera's theatrical appeal. None of their efforts are reflected in the extracts from *Mudan ting* reproduced in these collections, which suggests that their compilers held public theatricals at arm's length.[172] Moreover, the approach of the abovementioned Chongzhen miscellanies is distinctly "highbrow." The compiler of *Yichun jin* persists in grouping his extracts under broad thematic rubrics, an arrangement favored for nondramatic *qu*. When adopted for dramatic *qu*, this method detaches each extract from its uniquely dramatic setting and obscures its link with its source.[173] The compiler of *Xuanxuepu* broke with this arrangement, dispensing with categories and placing the extracts for each play together. He condemned the practice of mingling dramatic *qu* (*juqu*) and nondramatic *qu* (*qingqu*) in the same collection and favored the former in his selection; five of the six collections that make up *Xuanxuepu* are devoted to *juqu*. Even so, he is so selective that his extracts probably did not call to mind the whole play for the reader.[174] Moreover, the selections are rated solely in terms of their literary qualities.

At this still early period in the history of publishing *chuanqi* texts as *zhezixi*, the example of *Mudan ting* suggests that scenes extracted from Kun operas did not depart significantly from the text of the scene in the complete play. This distinguishes Chongzhen miscellanies, which tend to favor plays from the Kun opera repertoire, from many popular Wanli miscellanies that preserve *zhezixi* performed in other styles. Texts of the latter often differ substantially from comparable scenes in extant versions of whole plays. This different treatment of the Kun repertoire suggests that however they were performed (sung only or fully staged), those performances did not entail substantial revisions of the text. This is consistent with what we know about how *Mudan ting* was usually performed at this time, by household troupes, in intimate gatherings that reduced the distance between actor and audience and circumscribed the actor's interpretive freedom.[175]

Historians of Kun opera mark the beginning of the shift from a playwright-dominated drama centered in household troupes to an actor-dominated one centered in professional troupes based in urban areas as taking place during the Kangxi and Yongzheng reigns (1662–1735). At this time a number of measures were enacted that prohibited members of the official bureaucracy from enjoying theatricals either in public or in private, and the practice of maintaining household troupes declined. Though the effects of these measures were felt only gradually, they precipitated the shift of creative energy away from the privately owned troupes, whose activities reflected the tastes and resources of their owners, to troupes managed by professional actors. The Manchu rulers continued to enjoy theatricals at court and did not prohibit public performance in teahouses and theaters,[176] but the shift in the social base of Kun opera's audience and emergence of the professional actor is reflected, belatedly, in the miscellanies. The extracts from *Mudan ting* collected in *Zuiyi qing*, and perhaps duplicated in the edition of *Zhui baiqiu* reprinted in 1740, differ textually from those in the original play for the first time, because of extensive cutting of arias and dialogue. But there is little alteration of the remaining text, nor are there many actor-inspired additions, with the notable exception of the "Heaped Blossoms" sequence in "Entering the Dream." Nor did the selection of scenes change, either to accommodate the tastes of different audiences or the artistic requirements of professional troupes.[177]

The tendency to shorten scenes without adding new material is consistent with a situation in which performances were light entertainment that did not significantly engage audience with actor. In the case of "Infernal Judgment," set in the court of the underworld judge Hu Panguan, a dazzling and outrageous sequence of erotic puns on the names of flowers is cut from the text preserved in *Yichun jin*. In "Entering the Dream," the "Heaped Blossoms" sequence is reported to have been inspired by a wealthy merchant's penchant for conspicuous display. "The Portrait Recovered," not a particularly long scene in the original, lacks its most striking aria, *Jinchan dao*, in the *Zuiyi qing* extract.[178] The two early Qing collections appear to document a low point, aesthetically speaking, in the dissemination of Kun operas as *zhezixi*, inasmuch as the revisions delete material that might have proved offensive or difficult to appreciate, without adding much.[179] Given the political control of drama by Manchu rulers and the repression of cultural life generally, this state of affairs is not surprising.[180]

The pronounced shift in orientation comes in the second Qianlong edition of *Zhui baiqiu*, the so-called popular edition that appears in the 1760s, issued in four collections as *Zhui baiqiu xinji*, then expanded to twelve collections and issued in a "combined edition," *Zhui baiqiu xinji hebian*, in 1774. This compilation broke decisively with earlier collections published under this title. The *Mudan ting* scenes listed for *Zhui baiqiu quanji* (1740) appear in this edition in distinct versions,[181] and the number of *zhezixi* more than doubles (to twelve). Six of the added extracts are furnished with new titles and extensively adapted in ways intended to enhance their performability and show to advantage the talents of the actors, who by this time have creative control of the texts.[182] The state of affairs recalls that of Yiyang opera extracts preserved in the late Ming popular miscellanies.

The appearance in print of Kun extracts written in a more popular key may have had something to do with the Qianlong emperor's court, where enthusiasm for elaborate theatricals fostered contact between Kun actors, by this time under imperial patronage, and actors proficient in styles popular in the population at large but subject to sometimes oppressive official control. I have been unable to detect the influence of these popular styles on *Mudan ting* earlier than Qianlong's reign, though it may be possible to do so for other plays that lent themselves more readily to popularization. The fact that *Mudan ting*, written in notoriously difficult language, is so well represented in this new performance milieu testifies to the theatrical appeal of the original text and the ingenuity of actors in mining existing plays for new material.[183]

In the popular edition of *Zhui baiqiu* that appeared midway through the Qianlong reign, a few plays were represented using extracts adapted to more than one style of performance. By the 1780s hybrid styles of opera appeared, which combined the singing techniques for Kun opera with those of other styles, such as Qin *qiang* and clapper opera, both northern in origin. Different styles of opera, distinguished in Qing sources as "elegant" (*yabu*) and "popular" (*huabu*), were now often performed within the same troupe, a situation that encouraged cross fertilization.[184] Although there is no indication in either *Zhui baiqiu xinji* or *Zhui baiqiu xinji hebian* that extracts from *Mudan ting* were being performed in these hybrid styles, the extracts that were last to be added (in the 1760s and especially the 1770s) register the influence of such styles. "Asking the Way" (1774), an extract for the *chou* role that features dialogue and miming skills, is one example; "The Soul's Departure" (1774) and "Calling to the Portrait" (1764) reflect the adaptation of Kun opera texts to a popular style in which the singing of the arias is broken up with dialogue. Feng Menglong had favored this technique over a century earlier, but it shows up in miscellanies only at this time.[185] The addition of "Interrogation Upside-down" (1774) reflects the popularity of beating scenes; "Speed the Plough" and "Infernal Judgment" offer pageantry and spectacle of the kind also supplied by the "Heaped Blossoms" sequence discussed earlier.[186]

By this time there is also scattered evidence that material written by actors was circulating in written form. A very few manuscript copies of *zhezixi* exist that date from the Qianlong and Jiaqing reigns (1736–1820); these contain musical notation and detailed notes about costumes and stage movements (*shenduan*) that rival those found in *Shenyin jiangu lu* for completeness.[187] Such efforts to document performance techniques, and interpretations that had been transmitted orally, are rare for this period. *Shenyin jiangu lu* is the single extant printed collection that attempts to do the same thing.[188] Its sixty-six extracts document the performance artistry, by now highly developed, of the Qianlong and Jiaqing periods. This collection was assembled at the end of an exceptionally fluid period in the history of Chinese opera, when much interaction occurred between *yabu* and *huabu* actors and also between professionals and amateurs (*chuanke*), some of whom formed troupes and performed on stage for money.[189] By the 1820s Kun opera had lost its audience in many parts of the country; *Shenyin jiangu lu* and the three editions of *Nashuying qupu* were attempts to document an orally transmitted tradition now threatened with loss.

The small sample of manuscripts of *zhezixi* described here do not contradict this picture. By the late nineteenth century, the extracts most often collected from *Mudan ting* were those that lent themselves to the popular style of performance now dominant: "Speed the Plough," "Recovering the Portrait," "Calling to the Portrait," and "Infernal Judgment," which account for twenty of the thirty-two extracts located. The manuscripts alone do not reveal much about the circumstances of their use. Stage directions in some suggest they were used in performances; others lack these features and dialogue as well, and were likely used for singing only. Almost all derive from the late eighteenth-century printed miscellanies; only one of ten collections containing extracts for *Mudan ting* uses the original version of the scene rather than the one in the popular edition of *Zhui baiqiu.*[190] It is probable that many of these manuscripts were kept by *tangming,* rurally based professionals who performed the plays, occasionally, in the restricted way described above.

The remaining manuscripts were made by amateurs, although by this time "amateur" encompassed at one extreme devotees of pure singing whose antitheatrical bias was strong and semiprofessional *chuanke* at the other. Texts used by both are found among the collections surveyed here. None contain the kind of detailed notes found in the Qianlong era manuscripts that circulated among professional actors. But there is enough detail in some to indicate that they were used by people performing at an artistic level well below that documented in a work such as *Shenyin jiangu lu.*

A striking feature of some handcopied *zhezixi* is their assembled nature; their compilers worked not only from memory, but also by consulting more than one written version of the scene.[191] In these cases the compilers were not working in an exclusively oral tradition, but neither did they work exclusively with written texts, as indicated by the phonetic nature of some of the changes made. In these cases, what we appear to have are scripts made by moderately literate individuals who were interested in performing plays, not just singing them. But whether they performed to make a living, full time or part time and for whom, cannot be determined. Distinctions between professional and amateur use become hard to make, based on the texts alone.[192]

In a pioneering article on drama miscellanies, Zheng Zhenduo suggested that such compendia enabled readers and theatergoers alike to read highlights from their favorite plays without having to wade through the many dull intervening scenes in the complete playtext.[193] This view is misleading if it implies that the extracted scenes maintained an umbilical relation to the mother play. Such may have been the case in late Ming times, when *zhezixi* were sometimes performed in sequences that preserved a sense of continuity with the whole. However, as the practice of performing them became popular outside private households, with their highly literate audiences, this tie attenuated. The manuscript collections attest to the dissociation of *zhezixi* from the complete play by very late Qing times; even when the person who wrote out the manuscript consulted the original playtext, he or she rarely did more than restore odd bits of dialogue to the established version of the *zhezixi*. The two textual forms of the play had become almost entirely distinct from each other.

For the first 150 years of the period when drama miscellanies were a favored way of disseminating playtexts, *Mudan ting* was represented in them by only a few extracts, taken from the subjectively rich scenes that best fit Zheng Zhenduo's description of "highlights" as signature pieces of exceptional literary quality. For the next 150 years (1740–1890) the selection favored theatrically rich scenes of a kind hardly ever mentioned in late Ming accounts of performances written by literati.[194] In the popular edition of *Zhui baiqiu* both kinds of scene are represented, but this diversity creates an impression of fragmentation as far as the relation of performed scenes to original play and to each other is concerned.[195]

Once detached from its parent play, a scene entered contextual fields that attenuated or even removed its links to the original dramatic action. I have not investigated the effects of such attenuation, but they are worth pursuing since formats in the miscellanies are so diverse. A parallel investigation of how *zhezixi* were grouped together in performances is also in order. What effect did such recontextualizing have on a reader's or a viewer's appreciation of the *zhezixi*? Some methods of presentation in miscellanies encouraged readers to make comparisons between the extracts on literary grounds and perhaps on performance grounds as well. In the latter case, both the occasion of a performance and the kind of audience present would affect how a scene was received.[196]

Another contextualizing issue concerns the plays selected for inclusion and the scenes chosen to represent them. In the case of the manuscript collections especially, the grouping of extracts in each volume might throw light on how they were performed. At the least, the selection of plays reveals the owner's tastes, in terms of both subject matter and style (*ya* versus *hua*).[197] Such determinations require a knowledge of the operatic repertoire that few now possess, but was second nature to the users of these texts. *Zhui baiqiu* illustrates how drastically the selection of plays and extracts could change in a few decades, and a knowledge of these shifts is invaluable for gauging the tastes of any segment of the opera-loving public.

The texts themselves exhibit the process by which a scene took on an identity apart, revealing the shift of interest from arias to dialogue, and the change from singing to performance in a broader sense.[198] The importance of dialogue is visually most evident in those manuscripts where arias and dialogue are written similarly. The blurring of the boundary between arias, dialogue, and declaimed verse in the handwritten text also distinguishes it from the printed *zhezixi* and *chuanqi* playtext, in which the arias are almost always given pride of place by being printed in large type, often in single as opposed to double columns of characters, and sometimes embellished with *dianban* notation.

I alluded earlier to the argument of Lu Eting's widely praised study of Kun opera as a performance tradition: Lu acknowledges the "abyss" (*honggou*) of class that divided devotees of pure singing from those who enjoyed Kun opera on the stage, but he insists that Kun opera has had a rich tradition of performance by professional artists and that without this tradition it could not have endured for so long. He also maintains that despite the barriers separating the two kinds of performance and the two segments of Kun opera's public, there was contact and exchange between them, with the more popular style emerging as the main current.[199]

This study of *Mudan ting*'s existence as *zhezixi* supports Lu's claims in ways that need not be elaborated here. The earliest scenes extracted from the play reflect an aesthetic of "stasis," identified in the West with hostility to the public theatre and that theater's delight in spectacle and action.[200] Descriptions of performances of *Mudan ting* written by literati in the late Ming reflect such a taste for quiet and poetically evocative scenes, to which the miscellanies from that period cater.[201] This aesthetic bias changed only slowly in the case of *Mudan ting*, but change it did. By the middle of the eighteenth century, the older stratum of *zhezixi* was overlaid with a new stratum of theatrically lively and vivid scenes. Whether this change was precipitated from above by the court or from below by the resurgence of popular styles, the effects on Kun opera were pervasive.

Although I suggest that the barrier between "high" opera and "middlebrow" was permeable, it is important to keep the barrier in mind, especially when considering how the plays were understood by those who performed them and by those who saw them performed (or else read the texts that were derived from such performances). I have drawn attention to the reconceptualization sometimes evident as a scene became a *zhezixi*, and at times I have betrayed some antitheatrical bias in my choice of language. I have drawn attention to the chasm that separates *zhezixi* from *chuanqi* and suggested reasons why this must be so.

In the next chapter I will look beyond the texts to examine how actors conceptualized their performances and how the actors' training and their relationship to audiences influenced their understanding of the text in ways that a reading would not. This is a difficult undertaking, since until very recent times such information was almost never written down. By the time it was, the transmission of the acting traditions had suffered, because the stylistic schools (*liupai*) had dwindled, from dozens in each major center to the present five troupes for the entire mainland. Given the staying power of the forms, however, we can glean some information from accounts produced in this century and some by consulting artists who are still active. I will, of course, use earlier sources when I can identify them.

Five

"Elegance and Commonness Combined"

In a recent article Lu Eting, the foremost historian of Kun opera as a performance art, renews his defense of the tradition of performing Kun operas as extracts. He singles out the combination in *zhezixi* of both elegant (*ya*) and common (*su*) elements as an important factor in Kun opera's success at winning a larger audience, surviving as living theater, and exerting influence on other performance-based arts that emerged after it had achieved its dominant position.[1] In the first period of its glory, from the late Ming period to the early Qing, Kun opera was a quintessentially "*ya*" form of theater, which prized elegant and allusive language and made prosodic exactness the *sine qua non* of musical interpretation. Movement was another cornerstone of this high aesthetic, and its standards were as exacting as those for singing arias. Just as every syllable had to have a head, belly, and tail when sung, even at the expense of intelligibility, so too the performer had to bend the waist so many inches, the hands so many, and place the feet just so. Movement that was precise (*you chicun*) created the aura of cultivated refinement (*shujuanqi*) prized by connoisseurs as the essence of the Kun style (*Kunwei*).[2] These qualities were nurtured in the environment of household performances that brought playwright, actor, and audience into close proximity. In this milieu the cultural level of all the participants was high, and there was little divergence between playwright and actors when it came to interpreting the playtext.[3]

However, as performances of Kun opera moved to other venues and urban-based professional troupes entered the picture, the situation became more confused aesthetically. Troupes sought to inject "liveliness" (*re'nao*) into their performances and to create a stage reality that more closely approximated the mentality of an audience no longer limited to scholar officials, wealthy merchants, and their household members. While they did not abandon elegance, professional actors sought to achieve "commonness in elegance" (*yazhongsu*), and this amalgamation of hitherto antithetical qualities became the dominant aesthetic standard for performances of Kun opera in the post-Kangxi period.[4] But this came at a cost—the gradual alienation of the intelligentsia from the theater, summed up by the Qing critic Gong Zizhen, who lamented in verse that "when actors get their hands on a text, elegant poets are sorely vexed."[5]

Lu suggests that the best *zhezixi*, those that have enjoyed the greatest success on the stage, exhibit this amalgamation of *ya* and *su* elements, the result of their rich tradition of interpretation on stage. He cites "Wandering in the Garden, Startled by a Dream" as a classic example:

> In performance texts there are two additions: one of these is the Shuimoshen. In the original text, when the dream commences, there are only the brief directions "mimes sleeping" and "mimes dreaming of the *sheng*." In the performance version, the Shuimoshen, bronze "sun and moon" mirrors in hand, leads Liu Mengmei onstage, willow sprig held high above his head. This is Liu's beautiful "mode of entry." . . . Using the Mengshen to usher in the dream world is a very old theatrical form, and its history is a long one. The second addition is "Heaped Blossoms." In the original play, while Du [Liniang] and Liu [Mengmei] are making love, "the *mo* actor enters as the Huashen in red cloak strewn with petals and ornamental headdress on his piled-up hair." He sings one aria, *Bao lao cui,* and "scatters petals in the entrance of the stage." [The action] is rather monotonous. In the performance version, the sequence of arias beginning with *Chu duizi* entails, in addition to the Huashen, the appearance of the whole troupe onstage as twelve [attendant] *huashen* . . . who sing in chorus onstage and arrange themselves in various formations. . . . These kinds of insertions into the performance text impart to an otherwise elegant and quiet scene a fervent and lively atmosphere that excites much more interest in the audience and does this in an appropriate and clever way that is very effective. Even Ye Tang, in his *Nashuying qupu,* could not help but acknowledge this, although when he included it he added a note stating that this was a "vulgar addition." Actors understand best the entertainment value of additions such as "Heaped Blossoms," and to varying degrees they find ways to introduce them into the plays. But this kind of sensibility is precisely what playwrights lack.[6]

Lu thinks that it is worthwhile to identify the "common" elements that professional artists contributed to the original playtext, which constitute the second stage of creativity (*zaidu chuangzao*) in the transmission of Kun opera.

In the previous chapter, I compared certain extracts from *Mudan ting* with the corresponding scenes from the whole play and suggested how they took the interpretation of the scenes in new directions. Lu speaks of a divergence (*fenqi*) between playwright and actor that accompanied this second creative stage, and uses the word *maodun* (conflict, tension) to describe both the audience's response to the play in performance and the relationship between *ya* and *su* elements in performance-based texts.[7] Perhaps influenced by Marxist aesthetics, Lu's analysis of the *ya/su* dichotomy posits mutual antagonism, followed by a synthesis in which each element enhances the effect of the other on the audience. It is essential, therefore, in appreciating Kun opera as the quintessentially *ya* form of traditional opera to understand the complex nature of this elegance over the full span of its history.[8]

It is not easy to illuminate the performer's perspective prior to the modern period. Even literate professional actors rarely documented their art.[9] *Shenduanpu*—scripts with notes about movements and facial expressions to be used in performance—are rare and largely inaccessible.[10] The richest sources on stage interpretations of Kun operas date from very recent times, when some of the aging generation of Kun performers recounted their stage careers, often orally.[11] Published memoirs contain detailed discussions of how plays were staged. Other materials that occasionally yield insights are works that discuss particular formal elements (*chengshi*) of a performance style—for example, the use of sleeves or fan.

It is also possible to talk to modern Kun actors, observe how they learn plays, and attend rehearsals. First-hand contact with artists, access to scripts, and tapes of performances illuminate how contemporaries create performances, but we must remember that modern artists operate at a considerable remove from practices current when Kun troupes were sufficiently numerous to sustain different artistic lineages (*liupai*). Despite their waning influence, the performance traditions of the most popular *zhezixi* from *Mudan ting* ensure substantial continuity between present and late Qing practices. This is especially true when the extracts are performed separately and are not linked together in a "whole play" format.[12]

By far the most richly documented scene is "Wandering in the Garden, Startled by a Dream." Several actors who specialized in either the *guimendan* ("boudoir" *dan*) role (Du Liniang) or the role of *xiaosheng* (Liu Mengmei) have left detailed accounts. Because this play, and this scene in particular, is considered foundational not only in the Kun opera repertoire but also for the *guimendan* role, it is often taught to actors being trained in non-Kun styles of opera; it is also one of the first *zhezixi* that newly fledged Kun actors perform publicly. In the summer of 1995 I was able to observe two groups of *guimendan* actresses at the Shanghai School of Traditional Opera (Shanghai shi xiqu xuexiao) as they learned the first three arias from "Wandering in the Garden."[13] I also attended rehearsals and performances of "Wandering in the Garden, Startled by a Dream" by Kun actors recently graduated from the school who are now assigned to the Shanghai Kun Opera Troupe.

What follows is not a systematic account of Kun performance theory and how it is applied. Rather, it draws on materials at hand, supported by my observations of and conversations with Kun artists, and presents thinking about *Mudan ting* that mere reading of the texts does not stimulate.[14]

Role Categories and the Depiction of Du Liniang in "Wandering in the Garden"

Of the scenes from *Mudan ting* that maintained a life on the stage, "Wandering in the Garden, Startled by a Dream" underwent the least textual alteration. The most significant changes performers introduced were additions designed to enliven the presentation, and most versions retained all eleven arias that Tang Xianzu wrote for the scene. Reluctance to cut arias can be attributed to the importance of the dream scene[15] and to the occasional practice of performing "Wandering in the Garden" and "Startled by a Dream" separately. The six arias of the former and the seven of the latter bring both segments within the length preferred by actors.[16]

"Wandering in the Garden" attracted interest from the start, beginning with accounts of the whole scene in Tang Xianzu's time and continuing to the present, when discussion concentrates on the garden-strolling sequence.[17] Its six arias are written in obscure but evocative language that works both as pure description of Liniang's surroundings (important in a theater that lacks physical scenery) and as objective correlatives of her feelings, in the best tradition of writing for the *dan* role. Although the male romantic lead also sings in "Startled by a Dream," his is a minor part, and attention remains focused throughout on Du Liniang.[18] As a scene that features the female lead, aesthetic interest is concentrated on singing accompanied by dance-acting and on the actor's skill in depicting the character's emotions, as delineated in the poetic language of the arias.[19]

The most engrossing aspect of "Wandering in the Garden" for both reader and viewer is its portrayal of a young girl's state of mind prior to an erotic dream. Once the dream is underway in "Startled by a Dream," the *dan* actress sings very little;[20] her performance opposite the *xiaosheng* consists almost entirely of dance movements and gestures—the use of face and eyes and of her highly expressive long "water sleeves" (*shuixiu*).[21] The discussion that follows concerns the segments the *dan* actress performs prior to the *xiaosheng*'s entrance.

Although scene 10 is a vehicle for the *dan* actress (*danjuexi*), she is paired in it with the *huadan* (Liniang's maid Chunxiang) in the "Wandering in the Garden" sequence and with the *xiaosheng* (Liu Mengmei) in "Startled by a Dream." In her solo pieces, a soliloquy and long aria (*Shanpo yang*), Liniang expresses her feelings openly—and alone—for the only time in the scene.[22] Up to this point in the play she has betrayed her feelings indirectly, in her manner of responding to her physical surroundings and to her maid.[23]

In Tang's version of the garden-strolling sequence, Chunxiang's presence is unobtrusive, but in performances of the *zhezixi* this is not the case. Her onstage presence is lively, and she is given more lines to sing. The interplay of the two roles (*guimendan* and *huadan*) has prompted many of the changes to this scene. Even though Tang Xianzu's language has been only mildly disturbed, the changes introduced into "Wandering in the Garden" over time have been consequential to Du Liniang's character and suggest how the theatrical character necessarily differs from the written one.

Guimendan and *Huadan*

In most discussions of Chinese opera role categories, the major categories are defined opposite each other, as pairings. The *dan* actor, who plays the most important female character, is paired with a *sheng* actor, who plays the most important male character, and so on for other subcategories within these two groupings: *laodan* with *laosheng*, *xiaodan* with *xiaosheng*.[24] However, within the *dan* category, a pairing that offers interesting dramatic and aesthetic possibilities is that of the "boudoir" *dan* role with the "flower" *dan* role. This became evident when I observed "Wandering in the Garden" being taught and read descriptions of it by actors.

When Tang Xianzu wrote *Mudan ting*, *dan* roles were distinguished according to the importance of the character represented. The *dan* (sometimes *zhengdan*) portrayed the lead female character, while the term *tie* (or *tiedan*) was used for the actor who performed another female character (of any age) who accompanied the female lead in what we would call the supporting role. Other subcategories found in late Ming *chuanqi* playtexts are *xiaodan* (a role that was age specific, reserved typically for vivacious young women other than the female lead), *xiaotie* (used for minor characters other than the *tie*), and *laodan* (who played women of advanced years). Late Ming texts of *Mudan ting* indicate that Du Liniang is to be played by an actor specializing in the *dan* role, while Chunxiang is played by the *tiedan*.

With the rise of Kun opera, role categories were further differentiated, and the designations became associated with specific types of characters and performing techniques associated with these types.[25] In the Qianlong era, the *xiaodan* role no longer performed a wide range of youthful female characters other than the leading lady, but was restricted to a particular kind of young woman whose sheltered existence is suggested by the other designation commonly used for the role, "*guimendan*," described in one source as depicting young unmarried girls who are "chaste and quiet, reserved and elegant in appearance, correct and dignified in bearing, with a voice that is graceful and subdued, and a manner of expression that is detailed and complete." By the same token, the *tiedan* role came to be known as the "romantic (*fengyue*) *dan*" or *huadan*, described in the same source as "alert in all facets [of her actions]. In her singing, acting, and expression, she must possess an open and ingenuous spirit. Moreover, her sole means of expressing feelings is through the eyes. She must be pretty and petite, her conduct informed by an air of childishness."[26]

These descriptions of key female roles come from Wang Jilie (1873-1952), an ardent promoter of Kun opera in the 1920s and 1930s. They reflect ideas of these roles (hence, implicitly, of the characters they represent) still current among performers of Kun operas and those who enjoy listening to them. Although those who write about performance in the Chinese context stress that the role is the vehicle through which the actor realizes a particular character,[27] nonetheless the interplay between role and character is ever present in performances and can have interesting consequences for how a character is interpreted on the stage. When I observed actresses being taught "Wandering in the Garden," I became intrigued with how aesthetic requirements associated with the *guimendan* and *huadan* roles may at times work at cross purposes to the written portrayal of Liniang's character.

The pairing of unmarried girl of good family with her more vivacious and audacious maid is of long standing in literary drama. It is exemplified in the Yuan drama *Xixiang ji*, where the maid Hongniang acts as Yingying's alter ego, teasing out her mistress's feelings and inciting her to act.[28] In the written play and doubtless in performances, this interplay helps represent the reticent main character, who by status and temperament is constrained in what she may say and do. These contrasts, a basic element of Chinese romantic drama, are reflected in the iconography of the *guimendan* and *huadan* roles as these evolved in Kun opera. They are also reflected in a dialectic of similarity and contrast that became a feature of their interplay on the stage.

Actors' descriptions of "Wandering in the Garden" often touch on these points. When portraying Du Liniang and Chunxiang, one aim should be to suggest "differences within similarity"; although the two young women are close in age and emotionally attuned to each other, the maidservant acts "like a bird set free from a cage," while her mistress's demeanor reflects more complicated feelings: of pleasure at the garden's natural beauty mingled with sadness at the realization that just like the garden flowers, her beauty is destined to fade unappreciated.[29] Actors also speak of the need to exploit the dynamic of this pairing to suggest "similarities within difference," especially when choreographing the dance-acting sequences the actors perform together.[30] These acting points suggest that Chunxiang's presence reflects on Liniang's character not only through contrasts in behavior and demeanor, but also through basic affinities of age and impulse.

We can examine how these effects are created in the staging of "Wandering in the Garden," concentrating on the opening arias and then considering the two arias of the garden-strolling sequence, especially the stylized movements performed to them. The first three arias are important for establishing Liniang's character and anticipate what transpires after mistress and maid emerge from Liniang's chamber for their garden excursion. I will conclude by discussing *Shanpo yang*, the first aria in "Startled by a Dream" and the last that Liniang sings before her dream commences. It is when performing *Shanpo yang* that ideas of decorum associated with the *guimendan* role become most apparent and the actor's choices about how to realize the character within the constraints of the role are most strikingly differentiated.

The Opening Sequence

The centerpiece of the opening sequence is *Bubu jiao*, the first aria sung to a regular beat and thus the first in which dance-acting accompanies the singing. This aria and the next one, *Zui fu gui*, are sung with no intervening dialogue, and Tang assigned both entirely to Liniang. After *Zui fu gui*, Chunxiang declaims four lines of verse as she accompanies Liniang out from her chamber and into the garden. The next aria, *Zaoluopao*, is sung inside the garden and forms a unit with *Haojiejie*. Liniang sings the first several lines of each of these arias, and Chunxiang joins in the singing of the concluding lines. Thus as Tang Xianzu conceived the opening sequence, Liniang does most of the singing.

The exception is the introductory aria, *Raochi you*, for which she sings the first three lines and Chunxiang the concluding three. Entrances establish a character in the audience's eyes, and here Chunxiang acts as a foil to suggest the inward turn of Liniang's feelings. Liniang enters enveloped in a long cloak (*doupeng*), her hair confined by a cloth cap. The cloak inhibits the use of stylized movements (*shenduan*) as the actress sings the opening lines just inside the stage entrance:

> From dream returning, orioles coil their song
> Through all the brilliant riot of the new season
> To listener in tiny leaf-locked court.[31]

The *doupeng*'s color (solid, usually pale) suggests highborn status. It conceals the body almost completely and works effectively with these opening verses to suggest Liniang's confinement before she emerges from her chambers to experience the springtime spectacle in the garden.[32] At her entrance the *guimendan* actress's movements are slow, almost languid, and her singing to *Raochi you*'s irregular beat is slow. After singing the third line she moves to the center of the stage, gathers her cloak around her, turns her back to the audience, and walks slowly to stage rear, seating herself on a chair placed there.

While her back is to the audience, Chunxiang enters dressed in the gaily colored costume of the *huadan* role, and the pace quickens. Moving to stage center, she mimes gathering up threads, an action suggested by the lines she sings:

> Burnt to ashes the aloes wood
> Cast aside the embroidering thread,
> No longer able as in past years to quiet stirrings of the spring's passions.

Her briskness contrasts with Liniang's languor, which suggests the lingering effects of a dream and "spring ennui." The symbolism of the maid's gestures, as she picks up and untangles threads that hang loose from her mistress's embroidery frame, establishes a more subtle contrast—between the tangled complexity of Liniang's emotions and Chunxiang's cheerful simplicity. The staging of *Raochi you* thus establishes a clear impression of Liniang at the outset, largely by means of a contrast between her actions and those of her maid.[33] These contrasts are sustained in the next two arias, during which Chunxiang performs many actions while Liniang, who does all the singing (in the original version at least), remains focused inward (*neihan*). However, the way their movements are choreographed also suggests affinities between the two young women, though it does so more in some performances than in others.

Before discussing how *Bubu jiao* and *Zui fu gui* are staged, something should be said about them, as written. Six of *Bubu jiao*'s eight lines describe Liniang's actions and reactions as she gazes at her mirror. The most striking of these comes when she imagines her mirror to be someone stealing a look at her. In her imagination the mirror is personified as an admiring lover, and she becomes self-conscious about her beauty's effect on others.[34] She becomes aware that she is both beautiful and desirable, and her confused response to this awareness is captured in the ambiguity of the aria's concluding line:

> Walking in my chamber, how can I reveal myself?[35]

These preoccupations continue in *Zui fu gui*, as Liniang sings of how she has made herself beautiful for her excursion out of doors and worries that her beauty will find no human admirer. She identifies "spring's glories" with her beauty and laments that both remain "hidden from man."[36]

Some have remarked on Liniang's self-absorption (*zishang*) in this scene, and point to *Bubu jiao* and *Zui fu gui* as examples of Tang Xianzu's unusual treatment of his heroine's subjectivity. Liniang's dream, and the lover in it, are products of intensely self-conscious feelings, which are triggered when she sees herself from the viewpoint of the desiring other.[37] Longing for a lover awakened by her reading of the *Shijing* causes Liniang to imagine a lover's response to her as she looks into her mirror. Having thus imagined him, it is only a matter of time until she dreams him up. Liniang's awakening feelings intensify during the excursion to the garden, where she finds both beauty and decay and realizes that her beauty too may not find one who will appreciate it.

In *chuanqi* romances, however, a male perspective is usually privileged over a female one when depicting the intensity of erotic passion. Moreover, to portray in a *zhezixi* Liniang's subjective intensity as Tang did risked subverting the decorum exemplified in the *guimendan* role. When we consider the performance tradition of this scene, it becomes evident that actors resisted some aspects of Liniang's portrayal in the written text and strove to make her character conform more closely to the *guimendan* role. This is evident in the manner in which the two boudoir arias have long been staged.

Two ideas underlie performances of *Bubu jiao*: Liniang's contemplation of her reflection in her mirror and her hesitancy about emerging from the seclusion of her chamber. Directions in Tang's text call for her to change her robe and make herself up during this aria, but almost all performance versions of the scene omit mention of the robe.[38] Logically speaking a costume change is called for, but when Liniang removes the *doupeng* (an indoor garment) she is dressed in the robe she wears for her garden stroll. This outdoor robe is then removed at the end of "Wandering in the Garden," after Liniang returns to her rooms.[39]

The action of removing the *doupeng* is effective staging, since it frees Liniang to perform elaborately choreographed dance movements in front of her mirror, together with Chunxiang. First she rises from the chair at the rear of the stage, moves forward and to her left, and seats herself at her make-up table. She primps before the mirror, admires what she sees there, then rises and turns away as she unties the strings of the *doupeng*. She does this while singing the first of several lines for which the mirror is the focal object:

> A long while I pause
> To arrange my hair ornaments;

> Who would have known?—the mirror
> Slyly peeping at my face,
> Throws all my curls again into confusion.
> Yet can I conceal myself when I walk out from my chamber?[40]

At the last line, Liniang steals a final admiring glance at the mirror and moves away from the table back to stage center, where Chunxiang proffers her fan. She takes it and starts across the imaginary threshold that marks a boundary between her chamber and the world beyond, only to shrink back. As she does so, she turns to look at Chunxiang, her arms circling her body in a gesture of self-embrace.

It is difficult to capture Liniang's personification of the mirror in gestures. Instead, the closely synchronized dance movements in front of the mirror cast Chunxiang in the role of admiring observer, a role she continues to play in her performance of *Zui fu gui.* This diffuses admiration of Liniang's beauty between the two women, moderating the impression of self-enchantment given by the arias as written. Some *huadan* performers take this logic further, by having Chunxiang admire her own reflection in a hand mirror that she ought to be holding so as to enable Liniang to examine her coiffure from behind.[41] This is an amusing aside constructed along the principle of "similarity within difference," which distracts attention from Du Liniang only momentarily. But by linking mistress and maid in acts of delighted self-discovery, such performances further dilute this aria's impact. When reading *Bubu jiao,* one's attention is exclusively on Liniang.

Performances of *Zui fu gui* also diffuse the written text's intense focus on Liniang. As Tang conceived it, the aria is sung entirely by her, in response to dialogue from Chunxiang: "How beautifully you are dressed and adorned today!"

> You would say
> The emerald skirt shows up the madder crimson gown, 1
> Matched with a glittering gem-studded floral hairpin. 2
> Know, then:
> Love of the beautiful was ingrained in me from birth. 3
> But the glories of spring are here hidden from man; 4
> Only the birds flutter at the sight of beauty 5
> And the flowers in their pride grieve at their own eclipse.[42] 6

In performances, Chunxiang's admiring remark, which introduces the aria, is cut, and all lines except the third are reassigned. Chunxiang sings the first two lines while she puts the finishing touches on her mistress's garments and hair. Liniang sings the third line, with its reference to her love of beauty, but the last three lines, with their implied comparison of Liniang to outstanding beauties of antiquity, are also reassigned. Either Chunxiang sings alone (*Zhui baiqiu*), or else an offstage chorus sings while Chunxiang and Liniang perform closely matched dance movements.[43] Symmetrical movements performed to ensemble singing enhance an impression of affinity between the two and subdue disquiet over Liniang's immodesty were she alone to sing the aria.[44]

As Chunxiang sings the first two lines of *Zui fu gui* Liniang receives her attentions poised at the threshold of her chamber. She turns to her maid as she sings the third line and gestures to indicate that the beauty she admires is that of the natural world just beyond.[45] At "glories of spring" she finally steps over the threshold, moving to stage left while Chunxiang performs a similar movement to stage right. At "hidden from man," Liniang covers her face with her fan, using a movement Mei Lanfang describes as "thrice bashful" (*sanxiu*).[46] Depending on how this gesture is performed, the link between nature's beauty and Liniang's, implicit in the aria's text, is given different emphasis. Hua Wenyi, former star of the Shanghai Kun Opera Troupe, performs it three times in the prescribed manner, peeking out each time from behind the fan, her eyes registering curiosity and wonder at what she sees. Zhang Jiqing, head of the Nanjing troupe, whose performances reflect a more traditional interpretation of Liniang's character, performs the movement only once with eyes cast down so as to suggest Liniang's lingering bashfulness about exposing herself to view. Hua's more externalized performance, which suggests eagerness to see (and be seen), is bolder than Zhang's inwardly focused one. In both, however, the rearrangement of the singing pattern keeps Liniang's "self love" within the limits of decorum, by putting the most extravagant references to her beauty in the mouths of others.

Yu Pingbo finds these long-standing changes inappropriate, all resulting from logical inconsistencies occasioned by the omission of dialogue and reassignment of singing parts. But he accepts the rationale for them—a need to give the *huadan* actress more lines to sing as well as more things to do in a scene that, as written, is too quiet for the stage—and expresses the *piaoyou*'s deference to actor-inspired revisions. This is an interesting reversal of the late Ming relationship between the amateur who espouses *ya* reverence for the author's text and the professional actor who interprets it according to *su* canons of theatricality.[47] Nowhere does Yu suggest that a changed singing pattern might affect the interpretation of the aria, but it is certainly the case that the original language, though kept, is reinterpreted in the performance environment. Liniang's feelings about herself conform better to the *guimendan* stereotype; as a result they lose their most interesting edges.

In a book on theatrical presentation, Bernard Beckerman describes the actor-to-actor relationship as the foundation of drama and devotes a chapter to such pairings. The most common and efficacious of these is one of contrasting characters. Writing about Western representational drama, Beckerman discusses how these contrasts "set off sparks in each other," create suspense, and impel the resolution of some unresolved impulse. He allows, however, for another kind of performance, in which behavior is externalized and artistically shaped, and speech and gestures are precisely defined. In these "iconic" performances, action is defined spatially more than temporally, and the viewer experiences awe or revelation rather then release of tension and catharsis.[48] Performances of "Wandering in the Garden" are iconic in this sense; its action is organized spatially, and its contrasts between characters exist to reveal Liniang's character. Even when other actors are onstage, they are there to concentrate attention on her.[49]

The Garden Sequence

In the garden sequence, contrasts between Liniang's complicated responses and Chunxiang's unalloyed excitement are a prominent element of the dance-acting movements performed to the arias *Zaoluopao* and *Haojiejie*. Mei Lanfang describes *Zaoluopao* as expressing Liniang's feelings of melancholy (*shanggan*) as she tours the garden; these are betrayed by the manner in which she describes what she sees. His line-by-line commentary further modulates her responses.[50] Having just entered the garden, Liniang says to Chunxiang, "Away from gardens and groves, how should one learn of spring's delights?" She thereby expresses feelings of regret (*gankai*) awakened by her first sight of the garden, but her regret over pleasures foregone turns to happiness as she sings *Zaoluopao*'s opening line, which describes:

Gay purple and exquisite red abloom everywhere,

By the second line, however, grief returns as she notices crumbling walls and a broken-down well amidst the splendor:

But all abandoned to a dried-up well and crumbled walls,

She realizes that like the garden flowers, her beauty is likely to fade, unappreciated by a lover. Mingling of joy and sadness is even more condensed in the next two lines, each of which refer to good things (*haoshi*) that come to nothing (*luoliao kong*):

That glorious moments amidst this splendid scene
  should enshroud despair!
In whose courtyard do hearts still rejoice in the present?

Mei notes elsewhere that the *guimendan* actress's use of her face and eyes are especially important in bringing out Liniang's complicated response to the garden,[51] and her dance-acting also supports this in subtle ways. In addition, the fan is instrumental, not only in differentiating Liniang's responses from Chunxiang's, but also in delineating the succession of emotions she experiences. The folding fan the *guimendan* actress uses is much more expressive than the round fan used by the *huadan*, and for *Zaoluopao* its deployment is especially intricate. As Liniang sings the first line, she tosses her sleeves twice; then, at "exquisite red" (*yanhong*) opens and holds her fan horizontal at waist level, while Chunxiang gestures with her round fan in a mirrored sequence of movements. At "abloom everywhere" (*kaibian*) mistress and maid both sink down, fluttering their fans in a sweeping movement that suggests the expanse of gaily colored blossoms and also emotional excitement at the sight of them. They exchange glances, rise, and move away from each other for the next line, during which Liniang's expression again becomes focused inward and her movements contained. She moves forward to a position at stage right and directs her gaze downward at the dried-up well, then upward as she gestures towards crumbled walls in the distance. In the meantime Chunxiang remains active and animated, her movements describing an arc behind Liniang until she finishes at stage front to Liniang's right, also gazing at the distant walls. The performance of these two lines illustrates beautifully the dialectic of similarity and difference that is fundamental to the pairing of *guimendan* and *huadan*. In this case, Chunxiang's unmodulated response to the garden foregrounds Liniang's more complicated one.[52]

The fan continues its role in this dialectic during the singing of the next two lines. For "glorious moments amidst this splendid scene" (*liangchen meijing*) Liniang continues to hold it open, but at "enshroud despair" (*naihe tian*) she closes it and keeps it closed as she sings the next line. For the two lines after that she again opens it and uses it for certain mimetic effects that accompany language describing various scenes within the garden:

> Streaks of rain borne by a stray breeze;
> A painted boat on the rippling waves:
> The cloistered maiden holds cheap sweet springtime.[53]

At "streaks of rain borne by a stray breeze," the "*sanxiu*" gesture is redeployed to suggest warding off nature's elements rather than hiding from a lover's gaze. The "painted boat on the rippling waves" is evoked by a paddling gesture, another of the basic movements for the folding fan. Beyond their obvious aesthetic appeal, these movements also have subliminal effects on the viewer. The fan is usually open when Liniang is happy and closed when her mood becomes subdued.[54]

Lu Eting also finds uses of the fan in "Wandering in the Garden" to be especially important, since these differentiate the two young women by status, personality, and demeanor. Although he doesn't say so explicitly, the *huadan* actress's round fan is *su*, in that its use strikes a single note and correlates with the naïveté of the typical *huadan* character; the folding fan is *ya*, its uses are varied and subtle, and they correlate with the complex make-up of the *guimendan* character.[55]

By the conclusion of the garden-strolling sequence the contrast between Chunxiang's excitement and Liniang's quiet despair is fully drawn and captured in the following brief exchange of dialogue at the conclusion of *Haojiejie*:

> *Liniang*: Let us go.
> *Chunxiang*: One can never see enough of this garden!
> *Liniang*: Why speak of it again?[56]

Recent scripts and videotapes that I have seen, all of which follow the text of the *zhezixi* in *Zhui baiqiu*, modify this exchange in a way that diminishes the contrast between Liniang and Chunxiang so carefully built up in the preceding sequence:

> *Chunxiang*: One can never see enough of this garden!
> *Liniang*: Why speak of it again?
> *Chunxiang*: Why not save some of our excitement and come again tomorrow to play?
> *Liniang*: A good suggestion.[57]

Yu Pingbo deplores the decision to have Chunxiang initiate the departure from the garden, an action he finds to be both out of keeping with her character and inappropriate to her station (*shenfen*). He finds unconventionality in Tang's handling of the garden sequence, particularly the predominance in it of melancholy over joy in Liniang's experience. The revisions are unsatisfying because they are commonplace (conventionality being another dimension of *su*). However, because they diminish a feeling of coldness (*lengdan*) that has crept into Liniang's treatment of her maid, Yu sees why actors have introduced them and concedes that they have been well received.[58]

Twice, as *Haojiejie* concludes, the actresses strike a pose (*liangxiang*). These moments of stasis are iconic in Beckerman's sense. The relationship of the two actresses is captured visually and spatially in such a way as to create a beautiful effect and project the essential quality of the action—here, of difference within similarity and distance in proximity. Throughout "Wandering in the Garden" and especially in the garden-strolling sequence, Liniang and Chunxiang dance in close formation,[59] but the effect of their proximity ultimately is to isolate Liniang in her feelings. The stage is set, so to speak, for the moment of revelation, which comes as Liniang sings her long solo aria after Chunxiang has made her exit.

Shanpo yang

The aria *Shanpo yang* marks a high point in "Startled by a Dream" aesthetically and expressively, and because it is unsupported by a second actor, it makes special demands on the *guimendan* actress. As noted earlier, in this aria the expression of emotion becomes direct, no longer veiled in the obscure language of scenic description, and the danger of overly explicit acting (*su* in a pejorative sense) increases correspondingly.[60] Moreover, the emotions expressed in *Shanpo yang* touch on Liniang's awakening sexual feelings, a particularly sensitive area for the performer of the *guimendan* role. For this reason conventional expectations of this role are likely to affect the interpretation of the character as written.

In the opening lines of *Shanpo yang*, Liniang expresses her "secret discontent," which comes from frustration at her parents' failure to find a husband "of equal eminence" for her. As her longings for such a husband surface in the second half of the aria, so do her repressed desires:

> What eyes may light upon my sleeping form?
> My only course this coy delaying
> But in secret dreams by whose side do I lie?
> Shadowed against spring's glory I twist and turn.
> Lingering
> Where to reveal my true desires!
> Suffering
> This wasting,
> Where but to Heaven shall my lament be made![61]

Mei Lanfang, who published at least four accounts of his performances of this *zhezixi* observed that the movements the actor performs to *Shanpo yang* are particularly detailed, necessitating that he or she first become calm (*jing*) after the excitement of the garden sequence. Otherwise the performance will fail to convey feelings that Liniang expresses "unconsciously" in this aria. That is, the expression of feelings will become too direct, and directness is inappropriate for the boudoir *dan* role. Mei's concern about the manner of presentation appropriate to the boudoir *dan* role comes out in the following remarks:

> At "Shadowed against spring's glory I twist and turn," the actor must lean against the table. From its side he turns his body to the center, at which point he slowly sinks down, then rises, sinking down a second time. This sinking down and rising up, performed two or three times, is the movement that depicts [Liniang's feelings] in the most pointed way [*kehuade zui jianrui de yige shenduan*]. It is an old movement common to both the northern and the southern Kun traditions. I used to perform it this way, but lately I have decided to change it for the following reasons: First, I'm getting older every day, and if I continue to perform this kind of action, I feel that it is too extreme [*guohuo*]. I gave some thought simply to not singing the

> scene. But because it is so full of meaning [I decided against this]. It expresses the frustration and constraints young girls suffer because of their families and the old Confucian morality. The thirst for freedom in love is a feeling that is no different, then or now. And, from an artistic standpoint, this is a scene that was often performed and that underwent countless refinements by generations of performers before coming down to us. Then, too, I had expended no small amount of effort on it, and to stop singing it simply because of my age seemed a pity. Second, according to my understanding, Du Liniang is very much a sheltered and cosseted girl in the old society. Although she has her encounter with Liu Mengmei, she is after all a young girl who has been constrained by the old morality. Besides, everything that takes place is a perfectly natural desire on the part of a young girl. All we can do is to think of it as the product of Liniang's imagination [*huanxiang*]; in no respect is this the behavior of a woman who is licentious and without morals. These are a young girl's "spring sorrows," which should be distinguished from her "thoughts of love." I didn't necessarily want to depict them in too exposed [*lugu*] a way, and so I decided to keep the language but tone down the movements.[62]

These concerns, particularly Mei's caution about "exposed" (that is, erotically exposed) performances, are echoed by Bai Yunsheng, a *xiaosheng* actor who was active in Beijing from about 1920 onward:

> In the traditional repertoire for Kun opera there are many scholar-beauty plays, and though their diction is very beautiful, it is never sexually passionate [*bu seqing*]. As for the actions and demeanor of the lovers, although they are [depicted in a way that is] detailed and full of sentiment, it does no harm to elegant forms [*bu shang yadao*], so that when people see the play, they feel sympathy and liking without disgust.[63]

Both actors wrote these comments under a puritanical communist government, and Mei's motivation for toning down his performances had something to do with his age.[64] Whether they should be taken at full face value is therefore open to question. However, Mei's comments are valuable because they acknowledge a sexual undercurrent in both the language of *Shanpo yang* and the manner of performing that language—something rare in the voluminous literature about this scene.[65]

Anyone who has seen *Shanpo yang* performed cannot fail to be impressed. Effective use is made of a table, around which the actress performs the prescribed movements for the more than five minutes it takes to sing this aria. In particular, the sinking movement in front of this table certainly fits Mei Lanfang's description of it, and some modern actresses draw attention to this movement by dipping the body low, then holding the position before repeating it. This is how the movement is performed by Hua Wenyi, who also makes very active use of her eyes as she carries out the movement frontally, her back to the table, looking straight into the audience.[66] Zhang Jiqing, on the other hand, performs the aria, and the sinking movement in particular, in a subdued (*jing*) style for which she and her teacher Yao Chuanxiang are known.[67] At "Shadowed against spring's glory I twist and turn," she stands away from and oblique to the front of the table; as she sings "Lingering," she performs a slight sagging movement, which she then repeats at "Where to reveal my true desires?" This time she faces forward, her back to the table in the manner described by Mei Lanfang, but without engaging the audience with her eyes. The sinking motion is attenuated. Zhang's performance is understated physically, in keeping with the "high intrinsic dignity" of the *guimendan* role.[68]

Zhang Jiqing, who heads the conservative Nanjing troupe, is known for her singing; her dance-acting style, as noted, is "quiet." It is more in keeping with the traditional concept of the *guimendan* role than that of Hua Wenyi, whose concept of Liniang's character is more "up to date" and whose style of performing is more provocative, though within the limits of decorum for this role.[69] The Shanghai troupe is known for its willingness to innovate, and after Hua's departure in 1989, it mounted a new production of *Mudan ting*, the first since 1982, casting its star *huadan* actress, Liang Guyin, in the lead role. This experiment in cross-casting (not of gender, but of role category) has received mixed reviews, almost certainly in part because Liang's performance was even more explicit in its depiction of Liniang's feelings than Hua's. While I cannot speak to her singing,[70] her performance of *Shanpo yang*, on tape at least, was more explicit physically than performances that adhere more closely to the *shenduan* outlined by Mei Lanfang. In the case of movements flagged by him as potentially "extreme," she departed from the established approach (*luxian*) and prolonged and elaborated them, by performing them first frontally (over a railing behind a bench that was used in lieu of the traditional table), then with her back to the audience at "Suffering, this wasting" (*yanjian, pocansheng*). Those with whom I discussed her performance felt that a style of acting associated with the *huadan* role was too vulgar (*su*) when used to depict a "boudoir" heroine.[71]

In Lu Eting's dichotomy, *ya* in this scene can be associated with the rich but obscure classical language of the arias and the complicated inner life of the high-born heroine, *su* with the conventions of the stage, and especially the somewhat exaggerated, emotionally transparent actions of the *huadan* actress, who acts as foil to the *guimendan*. Chunxiang's liveliness supplies most of the action that the written scene lacks, and when the requirements of such action change the meaning of the text, theatrical gains offset liberties taken with the playwright's design.[72] Chunxiang's behavior, crossing and recrossing the boundary between *ya* and *su* as her actions suggest affinity with or difference from Liniang, foregrounds the intrinsically elegant quality of Liniang's character. By the time that Liniang is alone onstage, the ground of this interplay shifts to Liniang herself, as she struggles with feelings of melancholy (a state of *ya* passivity) and desire (an insurgent *su* condition). Modern performances of *Shanpo yang* reveal how different actors strike a balance between these two qualities and how the paradigms of the role categories delimit their choices.

Ya and *Su* Dialectics

Lu's idea of a clash (*pengzhuang*) of *ya* and *su* elements in the performance tradition of Kun opera calls to mind Bakhtin's theory concerning the dialogic structure of the European novel, in which hitherto exclusive genres and languages coexist and "talk" to one another, taking on altered meanings in the new linguistic environment. These ideas have been applied to the Chinese vernacular novel,[73] but Lu's is the first discussion I have read that pursues a related line of thinking for drama, and Kun drama at that, the most elite style. Lu's juxtaposition of *ya* and *su* are most Bakhtinian when he discusses "Startled by a Dream," where a figure from popular opera (the Mengshen) and an interlude of pure dance ("Heaped Blossoms") have been incorporated to enliven the scene.[74] Do these importations do more than simply enhance the scene's theatricality? Do they establish a "dialogue" between incorporated elements and existing ones? Before attempting to answer these questions, I will cite one actor's thoughts about "Heaped Blossoms":

> After the two exit the stage, the *huashen* enter, and there is a segment of singing and dance-acting known as "Heaped Blossoms." The sung lyrics and dance forms of the *huashen* are all for the purpose of manifesting the circumstance of the love tryst between Du [Liniang] and Liu [Mengmei]. Its

> use is to reveal that the love between man and woman does no harm to elegant forms and moreover is beautiful to contemplate. This is an excellent feature of performance technique in the heritage of traditional Chinese opera.[75]

Bai Yunsheng here betrays the professional actor's unease with the gorgeous diction of the high Kun style.[76] He finds *su* implications in the elegant language Liu Mengmei sings as he disrobes Liniang and prepares to make love to her (in *Shantao hong*). The beautiful movements and ensemble singing of the *huashen* run parallel to the lovemaking and draw a veil over what is taking place offstage. This line of thinking reverses Lu Eting's. Lu feels that "Heaped Blossoms" contributes a much-needed element of lively entertainment to an overly quiet scene, but does not mention the love tryst. The singing and dancing of the *huashen* (*re'nao*, hence *su*) coincide with the lovemaking of the *sheng* and *dan* (*jing*, hence *ya*), and a more pleasing, varied atmosphere is created.

Neither description of "Heaped Blossoms" suggests that the relationship between the original and added elements is mutually transforming, as Lu's "amalgamation of *ya* and *su*" seems to imply. Both he and Bai Yunsheng refer to incorporated elements that either enhance a pre-existing element through contrast or suppress it through containment, depending on which analysis one finds persuasive. In Lu Eting's view the interweaving of lively and quiet segments is mutually enhancing, but he does not address what is lost in the process—an original, even "dialogic" use of another figure in the scene—the Huashen.

Wai-yee Li's discussion of this figure is incisive. She speaks of Tang's treatment of sensuality in *Mudan ting* as something both uplifting and comical:

> There is an interesting example of this [treatment] in scene 10, where we have the juxtaposition of two languages: the elevated tone of sentimental professions of love and the crude language describing the sexual act. In the quasi-mystical tone of the lines sung by Liu and Du, there is a sense of destiny fulfilled and contemplated with awe and wonder:
>
> Somewhere at some past time you and I met.
> Now we behold each other in solemn awe
> But do not say
> In this lovely place we should meet and speak no word.

But the Flower Spirit [Huashen] watching over their lovemaking uses rather more detached and cruder language:

> Ah, how the male force surges and leaps
> As in the way of a wanton bee he stirs
> The gale of her desire
> While her soul trembles
> At the dewy brink of a sweet, shaded vale.
> A mating of shadows, this,
> Consummation within the mind,
> No fruitful Effect
> But an apparition within the Cause.
> Ha, but now my flower palace is sullied by lust.
> I must use a falling petal to wake her.[77]

She then suggests that in these two arias the register of language shifts three times, from ardent lovemaking in the opening lines of *Shantao hong*, sung by Liu Mengmei, to "quasi-mystical" sentiments in the duet, the concluding three lines of *Shantao hong*, to graphic description of lovemaking in the first five lines of *Bao lao cui*, to abstract language laced with Buddhist terminology in the concluding five lines. The effect of these abrupt shifts, Li argues, is to create a "double perspective of ardent longing and amused detachment," represented by Liniang and the Huashen, respectively. This double perspective prevents both reader and listener from becoming committed to a position that identifies fully with either the ardent passion of the lovers or the amused detachment of the Huashen. This strategy informs the entire play and depends for its effects on the manipulation of two perspectives: lyrical and comic.[78]

In the *zhezixi*, the strategy exemplified by the inclusion of "Heaped Blossoms" is quite different. Arias borrowed from other operas are introduced either before *Bao lao cui* or after or both. All are written in the conventional language of romantic opera, their portability in and out of the sequence testifying to their generic nature.[79] Whether intended or accidental, the effect is to dilute or obliterate the abrupt shifts of the original sequence (*Shantao hong* and *Bao lao cui* only). An approach originating with actors, in which "ready-made" popular arias are combined with the original elegant ones, replaces that of the playwright, who had compressed different languages together for deliberate effect. The playwright's method is dialogic in that each language assumes meaning different than it would have if used exclusively.[80] In the actors' method, each element, vulgar or elegant, is enjoyed on its own terms.[81] Lu Eting's ideal of an "amalgamation" of *ya* and *su* in the drama is not dialogic in Bahktin's sense.

However, that ideal does entail a significant recontextualization of the original sequence, in this *zhezixi* and doubtless in others. The examples of the "second-stage creativity" discussed in this chapter substantiate Lu's idea of the divergence between playwright and actor, text and performance, in the post-Kangxi phase of Kun opera's history. Performances realize the implications of a script and they also depart from them. This is a given for theatrically based literature,[82] but the special circumstances of the Chinese theater aggravated the tendency when the practice of performing extracts supplanted that of performing whole plays, and the venues for performance were so various. This is especially apparent in the case of importations into "Wandering in the Garden, Startled by a Dream" that alter the original progression of the action, but it is also true of subtler alterations that do not entail cutting or changing the text.

An example of such an importation is the Mengshen, who effects the encounter between the lovers in the staging of the dream sequence. Tang indicated the commencement of Liniang's dream by a brief direction ("She sleeps and begins to dream of Liu Mengmei, who enters bearing a branch of willow in his hand"). But during a performance, how will the audience know, when Liu comes on stage, whether he is real or part of Liniang's dream?[83] Bai Yunsheng discusses problems that arose in productions that dispensed with the Mengshen, deemed a vestige of superstition in post-Liberation China:

> Liu Mengmei comes onstage by himself; his face is not obscured, nor are his eyes closed; he looks as if he is looking for someone. At the same time, Du Liniang comes out from behind the table, and she looks as if she is seeking someone as well. Suddenly the two meet, and immediately the dialogue and singing begin.[84]

When Liu's entrance was staged in this way, audiences failed to grasp that the lovers' meeting takes place in a dream. Bai concludes that it is necessary to have the Mengshen stage-manage the entrance to avoid this confusion. He also feels that the god's presence has a beautifying effect.

Wai-yee Li situates her discussion of *Mudan ting* in the context of a late Ming fascination with dreams and the intense feelings that produce them. The feelings awakened during Liniang's visit to the garden produce both her dream and the lover who comes to her in it. Quoting from Tang's preface ("Love in a dream: why can't it be real?"), Li observes:

> In a philosophy of radical subjectivity, the margin between dreaming and the wakeful state is immaterial, insofar as the affective power of dream images is no less than that of images from waking life. There is an implicit claim here that love in a dream is more absolute: it is self-generated, independent of any real-life counterpart.[85]

In "The Interrupted Dream," Tang Xianzu portrays Liu Mengmei as someone Liniang dreams up, not as himself a dreaming subject present in Liniang's dream as she is in his. Li's observations offer grounds for believing that Tang would not want either his reader or his audience to discriminate clearly Liniang's wakeful and dreaming states. Leaving the boundary vague enhances the "affective power" of Liniang's dream and undermines certainty that her experiences when awake and when dreaming differ qualitatively.[86]

The introduction of the Mengshen sets Liniang's dream off clearly from her wakeful experience and weakens the impression that Liu Mengmei's appearance is occasioned by her longing (since the god acts as go-between). Liu's manner of entry as Tang conceives it conduces to an impression that he appears because of the "willful autonomy" of Liniang's desire.[87] This idea is no easier to suggest in a performance than is that proposed earlier for Liniang's mirror sequence, but staging Liu Mengmei's entrance as Tang wrote it does at least sew confusion in the audience's mind, which is conceivably what the playwright intended.

Bai Yunsheng gives the actor's view of the dream and of the Mengshen, and in doing so provides more evidence of the divergence between actor and playwright to which Lu Eting refers:

> "Startled by a Dream" is not the same as dreams in other plays. These other dreams are ones in which only one person has the dream; apart from the dreamer, all other personages are illusory [*huanxiang*]. However, in this play, both parties are in the same dream and so, in performance, the dreamworld is completely different from others. The exchange of feelings between the two parties must be very detailed, because later, in "Calling to the Portrait," Liu must remember that the portrait is the image of the beautiful girl he met then in his dream. When in "Union in the Shades" Liniang sees Liu Mengmei in his study whispering and calling to the portrait, she too

> recognizes that he is the student she met then in her dream. Southern plays are very long; even when one performs only one scene, still, with respect to the subjective feelings [of the characters] and the performance, one must grasp the resonances back and forth in the plot of the whole play.[88]

This explication is based on actors' adaptations, which have treated the dream as shared since the play first seized the imagination of the theater-going public, so that Liu Mengmei's experience of the dream is given equal standing with Liniang's. Despite the comment cited above about the whole play, Bai betrays no familiarity with the original scene, and thus it is not surprising that he defends the Mengshen as a vital element of the performance and of the play's design. With the original version in view, however, the divergence between the actors' conception and the playwright's becomes apparent and turns out to be very significant, as far as the representation of Du Liniang is concerned.[89]

Writing about the relationship of script to performance, Richard Hornby proposes that, ideally, actors continue the creative work of the playwright, but in a reactive rather than an active way. Governed by an interpretation of the playtext, they strive to realize that idea in their performance, much as a sculptor tries to realize an idea embedded in a piece of marble. The text is embedded in a performance and, equally important, the performance is not something added to the text: "The audience should be unable to tell which parts of the production were in the original text, and which came from the director, designer, or actors, because performance is not something added to a text."[90]

This idea about the relation of texts to performances does not fit the case of Kun opera, because of the cultural and social gap that separated the authors of playtexts from the actors who performed them and because in Qing times the audience for opera had become so diverse. Lu Eting acknowledges "tensions" that persisted between playwrights and actors on the one hand and between actors and their public on the other,[91] which promoted the enrichment of the original legacy of plays and emboldened actors to introduce elements extrinsic to the original playtext. Such "second-stage creation" went well beyond Hornby's model. Hornby maintains that when elements are added in a performance, it is no longer possible to speak of that performance as a realization of the original text. Instead, one has a new text, because the integrity of the original play (its "commanding form") has been lost.[92] But in the case of *zhezixi*, one finds a performance practice that sanctioned piecemeal alteration of texts. This attitude was pervasive; it also underlies Lu Eting's model for *zhezixi*, in which both the original and the added elements have aesthetic validity.

The analysis of "Wandering in the Garden, Startled by a Dream" just offered reveals how changes introduced by actors over time work at cross purposes to the design of the original sequence in ways that Hornby suggests such extrinsic elements must. Chapter four suggested reasons why this happened, chief among them being the fragmentation that occurred when scenes were detached from whole plays and performed separately. Despite the alienation of the *zhezixi* from the *chuanqi* text, for some segment of the Kun opera public a sense of the original play remained important to their experience of any one scene from it when performed. This would be even more likely when several scenes from a *chuanqi* were linked together in a performance, as sometimes happened. For this reason, the issues Hornby raises about the relationship between playtexts and performances of them have also surfaced in the Chinese context.

There have always been voices that criticize adaptations for disrupting the design of the original text. This was true when *Mudan ting* first appeared, and it remains true today. A case in point is an article by Chen Duo that presents examples of serious distortions in performed versions of "The Interrupted Dream," "The Schoolroom" (scene 7) and "Reunion at Court" (scene 55). Chen does not write as one hostile to performance, but rather as one protective of the text, and hence he differs from Lu Eting. His discussion of the original and added elements in "The Schoolroom" (renamed "The School Hall" ["Xuetang"] when performed as *zhezixi*) is far more critical than Lu's analysis of "The Interrupted Dream" as a *zhezixi*.

Actor-inspired Additions in "Xuetang"

Three characters appear in "The School Hall": Chen Zuiliang (Liniang's tutor), Liniang, and Chunxiang. Its main sequence consists of three arias written for the tune *Diao jiao'er*, which are sung by the tutor, Chunxiang, and Liniang in that order. For Chen Duo, the governing idea of "The Schoolroom" (i.e., "Guishu")—its "commanding form"—is to establish a clear contrast between Liniang and Chunxiang. This is accomplished by depicting how they respond differently to the tutor and his lesson and to the garden outside the classroom. Chen feels that the contrast between the two established in this scene runs through the whole play, decisively influencing the representation of Liniang's character.[93]

He uses two examples to illustrate this point—an entrance aria that establishes temperamental differences between the two, in much the same way as in scene 10, and dialogue at the end of the scene, after Chen Zuiliang has ended the disrupted lesson and left the stage. No sooner does he leave than Liniang begins to question Chunxiang about the garden from which she has just returned brimming with excitement:

> *Liniang*: Let me ask you now; where is that garden? (*Chunxiang does not speak. Liniang smiles to placate her and again asks the question*)
> *Chunxiang* (*pointing with her finger*) Look! Isn't it there?
> *Liniang*: Has it got any interesting vistas?
> *Chunxiang*: Vistas? There are six or seven pavilions, a swing or two, and a gentle, winding stream in front of a Taihu rockery. The place is full of the rarest herbs and flowers and is really gorgeous.
> *Liniang*: So indeed there is such a place!—However, we must return to the house.[94]

Chen Duo's analysis of this brief exchange is worth quoting at length:

> That Du Liniang, who has just finished reprimanding Chunxiang with "Your feet shall not tread on the garden path," should now ask her about the garden with a placating smile makes it clear that she, like her maid, is moved and excited by it. However, we must be clear that after "So indeed there is such a place!" there follows the non sequitur "However, we must return to the house." . . . With respect to this non sequitur, people can make their own interpretations. For example, from her inquiry about the garden, one might suppose that on an impulse Liniang conceives the thought of a garden stroll. However, whether it is because her thought, conceived in a moment's feeling [*qing*], is then curbed by decorum [*li*], or because she worries "at what father might hear," or because she already has a dim premonition that "[w]e can never see enough of it—so let longing be! Better to return content and while away our time within," she breaks off her thought and says, "However, we must return to the house."[95]

Citing the Qing critic Huang Zhen, who praised just such a use of non sequitur in another play, Chen observes that however the reader or viewer interprets this break in Liniang's thought, it effectively establishes how different she is from her maid when it comes to the garden and venturing into it.[96]

Chen deplores changes introduced into this exchange in various stage adaptations, but he attributes them to careless reading of the text rather than deliberate intent. He is particularly severe about the following version of "The School Hall," because it "makes chaos of the logic of [Liniang's] thinking":

> *Liniang*: Tell me truthfully; where is the garden? I want to play there too.
> *Chunxiang*: Young mistress, do you really want to?
> *Liniang*: Yes, really.
> *Chunxiang*: Young mistress, come! Come! Isn't the garden there? Isn't it here?
> *Liniang*: Has it got interesting vistas?
> *Chunxiang*: It has. There are six or seven pavilions, a swing or two, and a gentle, winding stream in front of a Taihu rockery. The place is full of the rarest herbs and flowers and is truly and utterly gorgeous.
> *Liniang*: So indeed there is such a nice place!
> *Chunxiang*: When would you like to go?
> *Liniang*: Ah, ah—tomorrow is no good, and the day after that isn't propitious. Yes! It will have to be the day after that, when father goes to the countryside to hasten the spring planting. Tell the garden lad to sweep clean the pavilions and terraces, so that I can make an outing with you. Go quickly and tell him to tidy up the place; we will certainly go on that day.[97]

The altered depiction of Liniang's thoughts obliterates the distinction between the two young women in their thinking about the garden, and this change "distorts completely the 'roundabout method' [*quyi*] found in the original text, such that the author's profound thinking is buried."[98]

Chen makes Hornby's point, that there are key concepts that are part of a play's design, the distortion of which must alter completely its meaning. A difference in quality of thought and feeling between Liniang and Chunxiang, the result of differences in status and upbringing, is one such governing concept for *Mudan ting*.[99] Chen's understanding of the pairing differs from that offered by actors, which proceeds according to a dialectic of difference and affinity rooted in thinking about role categories, hence extrinsic to any particular text.

Such thinking about roles also underlies the other major alteration Chen (and many others) cite, which is that in the performed repertoire the scene has become a vehicle for the *huadan* actress. Besides turning Liniang into a "living prop"—for long stretches she does little but sit at her desk—this actor-inspired change gives Chunxiang a large role as the agent of Liniang's decision to visit the garden and all that follows from that, a change that Chen also condemns for distorting the original play's key concept.[100]

Even as Tang conceived the scene, "The Schoolroom" is a vehicle for the comedic talents of the *tie* (later *huadan*) role. Chunxiang's mischievous provocation of the pedantic tutor runs through the scene and contrasts with Liniang's demure and respectful demeanor. At least since mid-Qing times the onstage humor was quite broad, taking on a slapstick quality in places. In the modern era it has become broader still, as the conflict between maid and tutor has turned into farce with a sharply satirical edge.

Chunxiang's provocation comes to a head at the second of the main arias, which she sings. Up to that point, her behavior is mischievous but not openly disrespectful. But during a segment of dialogue that leads into her aria, she grows bored with the lesson and asks to be excused.[101] Here and below, changes and additions introduced into the dialogue by actors are italicized:

> *Chunxiang (assuming a vacant expression): Mistress, I need to be excused.*
> *Liniang: Ask Tutor.*
> *Chunxiang:* Tutor, this pupil begs to be excused.[102]
> *Chen: Ah? How long has it been, that you now want to be excused?*
> *Chunxiang: A long time!*
> *Chen: Permission denied!*
> *Chunxiang: Aiyo! It's urgent!*
> *Chen (making a "tsk" of disapproval): Go and return at once.*
> *Chunxiang: Ah, with your permission—*
> *Chen: At once!*
> *Chunxiang: I know. Pshh! What's this about "begging to be excused?" I'll go have some fun and then come back (runs off).*
> *Liniang:* May I ask how old my Tutor's lady is?
> *Chen:* She is just sixty.
> *Liniang: Oh, in that case,* I wish to embroider a pair of slippers for her birthday. I beg for a pattern.
> *Chen:* How kind of you! Simply follow the pattern in Mencius, and make sandals without knowing the size of the feet.[103]
> *Liniang: All right.*

Chen: Ah, Chunxiang has been gone for a long time. Why isn't she back?[104] *Chunxiang, Chunxiang!*
Chunxiang (entering): Aiyo! You do nothing but study here! There's a large garden, red with peaches and green with willow trees, very pleasant to sport in.
Chen (calls again): Chunxiang! Chunxiang!
Chunxiang: I'm coming![105] *That old fleabag is still calling me. Ha! I'll just go in pretending that I haven't quite finished my business.*

(Puts the tally in her mouth and mimes tying the sashes of her skirt)

Chen: Chunxiang—
Chunxiang: Oh—I couldn't finish my business, but I'll just hand in the tally.
Liniang: Why did you have to go?
Chunxiang: Aiya! Young mistress,[106] you do nothing but study here, when out there is a large garden, *red with peaches* and green with willow trees, very pleasant to sport in.
Chen: Ha! Ha! You fail to attend your mistress in her studies and on top of that go to the garden to play? If it were just you, that would be one thing, but now you're enticing your mistress? Fetch the thornstick, I'm going to beat you.[107]
Chunxiang: Tutor—who are you going to beat?
Chen: Who else but you!
Chunxiang: Me? Why not make some allowances?
Chen: Why did you entice your mistress?
Chunxiang: Aiyo—that again! (Sings to *Diao jiao'er*):

> *I am*[108]
> A young lady,
> Do I aspire to examination honors or magisterial eminence?
> Need I do more than read, or write crow-like characters?

Chen: When the ancients applied themselves to books, some kept fireflies in a bag, others read by moonlight.
Chunxiang:

> Dazzled by the silvery light,
> Poor, moonstruck Toad had giddy fits.[109]
> What? They stuffed fireflies in a bag
> And smothered harmless insects?

Chen: Were there not those who, to stay awake, tied their hair to the beam and pricked their thigh with an awl?
Chunxiang:

> Tied to the beam
> Your hair will thin;
> Pricking the thigh
> But adds to your scars and blotches.

And this is glory!

(*From within, the cry of someone selling flowers*)

Chunxiang: Eee, young mistress, (*sings*)

Hear the flower-seller's cry

Breaking in upon the sound of reading.

Chen: Again trying to entice your mistress from her books! I really will strike you. (*He beats her; Chunxiang mimes grabbing the stick*)

Chunxiang: Let me go! Let me go! (sings)

I'm a tender child,

How can I endure such a harsh beating?[110]

(*Snatches stick from Tutor and throws it on the floor*)

Chen: Aiyo—Can this be? You're infuriating me! Tomorrow I'll report this to His Honor. Such conduct as this will force me to resign my position.

An interesting aspect of Tang Xianzu's handling of this aria is the reversal of the usual relationship between sung verse (allusive, elevated in diction and tone) and dialogue (plain, often used to comment on the verse, sometimes humorously). Here Chen Zuiliang's allusions to scholarly exemplars of antiquity come in the dialogue and are then mocked by Chunxiang in the verse. This aria is largely preserved as written in the *zhezixi*, but dialogue about the garden is much more prominent, first with the business surrounding Chunxiang's request to be excused, then with Chen Zuiliang's outraged response at her efforts to distract Liniang after she returns to the schoolroom.

Xu Lingyun remarks that the sound of the flower vendor's cry midway through Chunxiang's aria ushers in the most tumultuous (*da'nao*) part of the scene, during which Chen Zuiliang attempts in earnest to beat Chunxiang, and she responds by grabbing his thornstick and engaging him in a tug of war. As Xu describes the ensuing melée, the struggle continues to the final syllable of Chunxiang's aria, at which point she gives a final tug and Chen lets go, the thornstick clattering to the floor. Chen then performs a hopping dance of indignation as Chunxiang lies on the floor crying noisily, kicking her legs, and screwing the backs of her hands into her eyes.[111]

Xu goes on to point out that in performances of this scene as a Beijing opera, the comedy becomes even more broad (*hua*): as the tutor comes out from behind his desk to beat Chunxiang, he places his chair to his right (at stage right), so that at the end of Chunxiang's aria, when he lets go of the thornstick, he falls backward and trips over the chair, tumbling to the ground. Liniang orders Chunxiang to submit to Chen's chastisement; the tumble is then repeated when Chunxiang jerks her hands away just as he strikes, causing him to fall down again.[112] These and other farcical details were not used in Kun performances until the 1950s, when efforts were made to increase Kun opera's appeal and enhance its content ideologically. Many of the elements that Xu Lingyun identifies as unique to Beijing opera performances crop up in a detailed account written by Bai Yunsheng, a Kun actor, who refers to the *zhezixi* using its more popular name, "Chunxiang nao xue" (Chunxiang Disrupts the Lesson).[113] Performances during the Cultural Revolution were probably in the style of Beijing opera and have since been condemned as distortions. Even in the nineteenth century one encounters criticisms of performances that lack proportion because they carried Chunxiang's provocation of the tutor too far:

> Recently there is an actress whose voice and looks are quite delicate and whose body is well rounded. When performing Chunxiang she looks the part, but during the confrontation with Zuiliang, she is utterly without scruples, too ready with her rebukes. During the beating sequence, she whirls and turns, feet flying, skirts swirling. At the end, she gives Zuiliang a push and he nearly falls down. This really defies credibility, causing one to laugh out loud.[114]

In "The Schoolroom" the use of the three actors is proportioned, a quality that the author of this comment also expected of performances. Tang assigned one aria to each actor. The maid's cheeky (*huopo*) interaction with Chen Zuiliang alternates with Liniang's demure (*jing*) response to him, and the antics are sufficiently restrained that Liniang's character remains the focal point, even though her performance is understated, limited for long stretches to the expressive use of only the face and eyes.[115] Actors apparently found her inactivity to be a problem, no doubt because in a large theater such subtleties were lost on the audience, so the logical solution was to play up the comedy between the maid and the tutor. With time "The School Hall" became a scene for the *huadan* actress, and the original balance was sacrificed, with Liniang's role reduced to little more than a bit part.[116]

Actors also catered to the tastes of a more diverse audience than the one that Tang Xianzu envisioned. The tastes of this audience were shaped in good part by popular (*huabu*) dramas. "The School Hall" is one of only two scenes from *Mudan ting* that became part of the Beijing opera repertoire ("Wandering in the Garden, Startled by a Dream" was the other). This version portrays the relationship between maid and mistress in terms of affinity rather than the differences that Chen Duo feels are part of Tang's design. Chunxiang acts out impulses that Liniang represses, but which begin to emerge after Liniang performs a mock chastisement of Chunxiang to appease Chen Zuiliang. After Chen leaves the two young women alone, Liniang immediately questions Chunxiang about the garden, betraying her inclinations by her curiosity and her eagerness to visit it.

A star system, which had developed in tandem with the elaboration of role categories in Kun opera, motivated the reconceiving of relationships in "The School Hall" so that it could become a showcase for the *huadan* actress. The acting style of the *huadan* actress catered to the audience's love of lively, even rowdy plays, which in turn encouraged interpretations that brought out Chunxiang's anarchic streak, an implicit but undeveloped dimension of her character in the original.

There is the potential for Liniang to be implicated in Chunxiang's antics as well, because of the ambiguity in the gravity (*wenzhong*) she displays throughout the scene. Bai Yunsheng, whose manner of performing "The School Hall" was influenced by Beijing opera, acknowledges this possibility while describing how to perform the opening lines of Liniang's aria, the last to be sung to *Diao jiao'er*. At this point, Liniang is chastising Chunxiang for her treatment of Chen Zuiliang. While she sings, Chen, who has reseated himself at his desk, discovers that he has lost a shoe. This leads to a dumb show between him and Chunxiang that is carried on while Liniang sings. I give a translation of this aria starting from where my translation of Chunxiang's aria stopped, as found in *Zhui baiqiu xinji.*[117] I then give Bai's discussion of how to perform it:

> *Liniang: Huh!—wretch! Carrying on like this. Tutor, don't be angry.*[118] *Forgive this first offense, and allow your pupil to punish her this time.*
> *Chen: She should be punished! She should be punished!*
> *Liniang: That such a thing could have happened! Wretch! Pick it up.*
> *(Chunxiang picks up the thornstick)*
> *Liniang: Bring it here.*
> *Chunxiang: Ah! Young mistress, shall I give it to the tutor?*
> *Liniang: Nonsense!* Bring it here!
> *Chunxiang: Ah—*

Liniang: Come and kneel down.
Chunxiang: What do you want me to kneel for?
Liniang: Huh! Still won't kneel?
Chunxiang: I'm kneeling!
Liniang: Kneel facing Tutor.
Chunxiang: Let me kneel before you.
Liniang: Nonsense!
Chunxiang: I'm kneeling before Tutor!
(Kneels. Liniang commences beating her.)
Chunxiang: Aiyo! Aiyo!
Liniang: A fine maid you are, carrying on like that. In the past it was said "Tutor for a day, father for life." Tutor couldn't beat you, and you are rude to him anyway?
Chunxiang: I wasn't rude to him!
Liniang: You still talk nonsense! (Beats her again)
Chunxiang: Aiya! Aiya!
Liniang: From now on (sings to the same tune),
Your hands shall not touch the ropes of the swing,
Your feet shall not tread on the garden path.
Chunxiang: Can I talk about it?[119]
Liniang: This incontinent mouth—we'll burn holes around it with a smoking incense stick!
Chunxiang: Can my eyes look on?
Liniang: Those roving eyes—we'll stab them with embroidery needles till they go blind.
Chunxiang: Blinded, what use should I be?
Liniang: Wretch! Why would I want you?
I can then have you tied to the inkslab, chained to the desk,
Chanting after me "The Poem says—"
"The Master said—"
Without default.
Chunxiang: Default is best.
Liniang: Nonsense! (sings to the same tune)[120]
We'll count the number of hairs on your head
And give you the same number of stripes on your back!
Some lingering fears you may have
For my lady mother's household rules.
(*Commences beating*)
Chunxiang: Aiya! Young mistress, I dare not offend again. Hey! Tutor, Please intercede for me! Please intercede for me![121]

Bai Yunsheng's discussion focuses on the dumb show and its effect on how the audience receives the *guimendan* actress's performance.

> As Liniang sings "Your hands shall not touch the ropes of the swing," her raised hands describe the shape of a swing; as she continues "Your feet shall not tread on the garden path," her left hand depicts the garden path by means of an undulating gesture. At "This incontinent mouth—we'll burn holes around it with a smoking incense stick" she points at Chunxiang with the thornstick, and continues to sing "Those roving eyes—we'll stab them with embroidery needles till they go blind." During the singing, Chunxiang fidgets nonstop where she lies prostrate, picking at things and fiddling with her handkerchief—the actor is free to improvise. At "till they go blind" Liniang hits Chunxiang once with the thornstick, and as she sings "I can then have you tied to the inkslab, chained to the desk," she points at the tutor's desk. During the singing of these lines, Chen is searching around his desk for his shoe; not finding it, he turns both palms up and makes a gesture at Chunxiang. When Chunxiang looks at him, he indicates what he means by raising his shoeless foot. Chunxiang, who has seated herself on the lost shoe during the pushing match with Chen, pretends not to know where it is and points to the stage entrance. While Chen turns to look for it there, she pulls out the shoe. When Chen turns around and see this, he points a finger at Chunxiang. The actors playing the parts of Chunxiang and the tutor must pay attention that the use of mime here in place of speech is both refined and clear; they musn't generate so much activity that it impacts on [*yingxiang*] Liniang's singing.[122]

Bai may simply mean that the dumb show shouldn't distract from the *guimendan*'s performance, but the humor at this point has the potential to cut more than one way, depending on how the actress portrays Liniang during the singing of her aria. If her demeanor is one of mock sternness (implied by the hyperbole of the language), then she is allied with Chunxiang. If she sustains the seriousness, however, she becomes the butt of Chunxiang's pranks along with the tutor, precisely because of the onstage antics. Reading Bai's description, one can see how both performances are possible, depending on the inclinations of the actors.

Actors' descriptions of "The School Hall" reveal how much interpretation expressed through mimed actions never shows up in printed versions of the text.[123] This is especially the case for comic scenes, where dialogue that facilitates such action predominates. Most additions to "The School Hall" take this form; many are made in the spirit of the scene as Tang wrote it, but cumulatively they change it, by making Chunxiang the center of attention. This alters the rhythm of the scene: once the lesson becomes a confrontation between Chunxiang and Chen Zuiliang, the counterpoint of responses between Liniang and Chunxiang is sacrificed. Once Liniang becomes ancillary to the action, a kind of performance that aligns her more closely with the tutor—making both embodiments of the authority that Chunxiang mocks—becomes at least a possibility. That said, I have yet to encounter a description of such a performance, even in the ideologically charged climate of the Cultural Revolution, when "Chunxiang Disrupts the Lesson" became a play that ridiculed Confucian moral teachings about sexuality.

Highbrow/Lowbrow in America and China

In his study of public culture in America, Lawrence Levine examines the popularity of Shakespeare among Americans from all walks of life in the nineteenth century. Among the factors contributing to this were a love of oratory, a liking for plays with clear heroes and villains that lent themselves to a melodramatic style of performance, and allegiance to an ideology of individual responsibility that was congenial to the forceful characters found in Shakespeare's plays (Hamlet, Macbeth, Richard III). After church, the theater was the most important cultural institution in America, having penetrated to the frontier town as well as the city. It was, Levine argues, "a kaleidoscopic, democratic institution presenting a widely varying bill of fare to all classes and socioeconomic groups." As such, it was the crucible of a vigorous public culture that emerged at this time, with Shakespeare as one of its mainstays, but a Shakespeare "swallowed, digested, and part of the cultural body." This nineteenth-century Shakespeare is no longer familiar to us, because America's public culture has since fragmented into a number of categories, high and low, pop and mass. Shakespeare's plays have now become "highbrow" art, regarded by the average person as "theatrical spinach," something learned at school that is good for you but not much fun to consume.[124]

With the transformation of America's public culture from something eclectic and democratically shared—above all in the theater—to something stratified and exclusive to certain segments of the population, art that appeals to a large audience has come to be regarded as popular in a pejorative sense, "lowbrow" because banal, crude, or poorly written. Levine maintains that it has become difficult for those living in the late twentieth century to envision how art now considered "highbrow" could have been popular in the more neutral sense of entertainment widely shared. If Shakespeare's plays were broadspread, it must have been because they were performed in an overly simplified or vulgarized way that failed to do justice to their complexity and subtlety.

Levine is critical of those who use "popular" in this pejorative sense and believes such aesthetic judgment tells us more about the writer than about the reasons for a work's popularity at a particular historical moment:

> Certainly, the relationship of an audience to the object of its focus—be it sermon, political speech, newspaper, musical composition, or play—is a complex one and constitutes a problem for the historian who would reconstruct it. But the problem cannot be resolved through the use of such ahistorical devices as dividing both the audience and the object into crude categories and then coming to conclusions that have more to do with the culture of the writer than that of the subject.[125]

In applying the categories *ya* and *su* to the language and performances of the Kun opera I have employed terms used by Chinese scholars as both aesthetic and descriptive categories. *Ya* can refer both to literature written in elegant and allusive language and to works that have restricted ("highbrow") appeal, *su* to literature written in simple and often crude language and to works that have wide appeal (in the case of opera, works widely performed in public as well as in private). These categories have been part of the aesthetic vocabulary of drama criticism from at least the late Ming, especially in the former sense.[126] In adopting them to discuss the transformations that *Mudan ting* underwent, do I clarify the nature of its appeal or only betray my own aesthetic biases?

In his consideration of the *su* side of Kun opera, Lu Eting reminds the modern reader habituated to think of Kun opera as "highbrow" that at one time it was more truly popular because it had a wide audience. By focusing on performances of *zhezixi*, Lu clarifies the transformation of the Kun repertoire that took place in the theatrical setting and shows how this happened in response to a number of factors: the changed composition of the audience, the shift of artistic control from literati playwrights to professional actors based in commercial troupes, and the fact that *huabu* and *yabu* operas were sometimes performed together, enabling cross-fertilization to take place.

The fact that *hua* and *ya* styles of opera were not strictly separated, that plays of both styles were often performed together, contributed to the popularization of Kun operas. This evolution, discussed by both Lu Eting and Hu Ji, is not unlike that described by Levine for Shakespeare in nineteenth-century America. Levine notes that Shakespeare was so familiar to audiences at that time that it was a common practice to perform an evening of acts taken from different plays, much like a performance of *zhezixi*. Or a play might be the centerpiece of an evening of entertainments that included a farce or musical interludes as between-act specialties. In such a setting, Levine insists, "Shakespeare was performed not merely alongside popular entertainment as an elite supplement to it; Shakespeare was performed as an integral part of it."[127] Coming to the defense of the widespread practice of adapting Shakespeare's plays, Levine comments:

> Much has been made of the adaptations of Shakespeare as instruments that made him somehow more understandable to American audiences. Certainly, the adaptations did work this way—not primarily, as has been so widely claimed, by vulgarizing or simplifying him to the point of utter distortion but rather by heightening those qualities in Shakespeare that American audiences were particularly drawn to. . . . Thus many small changes were made for practical and moral reasons without much fanfare or fuss: minor roles were consolidated to create richer acting parts; speeches and scenes, considered overly long or extraneous, were shortened or omitted, sexual references were rendered more palatable by shifting such words as "whores" to "wenches," having Othello refer to "stolen hours of unfaithfulness" rather than "stolen hours of lust," and changing the phrase "happiness to their sheets" to "happiness be theirs" . . . . Some of the alterations bordered on the spectacular, such as the flying, singing witches in *Macbeth* and the elaborate funeral procession that accompanied Juliet's body to the tomb of the Capulets in *Romeo and Juliet*. On the whole, such limited changes were made with respect for—and sensitivity to—Shakespeare's purposes.[128]

In the Chinese case, however, it becomes difficult to follow Levine's lead, even though conditions for such an analysis are tantalizingly similar. Commercial theaters in Qing times, though hardly democratic in Levine's sense,[129] brought together people from all classes, and entertainments in them combined highbrow and lowbrow operas. Lu Eting's description of how Kun operas were combined with clapper and Beijing operas on a single bill resonates with Levine's description of how Shakespeare's plays were made to fit into the eclectic entertainments of American theaters. The *zhezixi* from *Mudan ting* examined here and in chapter four illustrate the transformation that scenes from *Mudan ting* could undergo in the theatrical culture of the Qing period (Kangxi to Qianlong reigns). Although all were theatrically successful, it is not possible to conclude, as Levine does for Shakespeare, that they were adapted in ways that were sensitive to the playwright's purposes.

In the tradition of *zhezixi*, actors endeavored to accommodate Tang's text to the tastes of the mainstream theater-going public. In the process they consistently modified unconventional uses of languages in different registers, both elegant and crude. I have already mentioned several instances of such modification. The Huashen's aria in "The Interrupted Dream" (*Bao lao cui*) is one example, since the actors' expansion of the "Heaped Blossoms" interlude changed the impact of the deity's arrival from that in the original scene, where it introduces a distinct perspective, expressed in distinct language. Once his aria is incorporated into that musical interlude, the sentimental lyrics of the other arias neutralize its incongruities so that a very different effect is produced.

In "The School Hall" and "Asking the Way," we find the most familiar form of actor-inspired adaptation: dialogue that prolongs humor in a "low" vein. In the case of "The School Hall," the change disrupts interplay between Liniang's *ya* (because demure and understated) responses to Chen Zuiliang and Chunxiang's *su* (because active and provocative) ones. As Tang conceived the scene, both positions are sustained, but in the *zhezixi* the interplay is sacrificed to broad (monologic) humor. Changes to Chunxiang's aria in the *zhezixi* exemplify the difference: dialogue and funny business that attend her departure to and return from the garden in the *zhezixi* divert attention from her aria, in which the usual relationship between song and dialogue is inverted, such that the maid's singing pokes fun at the tutor's dialogue. Both forms of humor are at the tutor's expense, but one is achieved broadly, with liberal amounts of action, while the other is delivered subtly, via manipulation of expectations of how language will be used in the aria form.

Changes introduced by actors into "The Soul's Departure" ("Lihun") have a similar effect, since extensive cutting of arias accompanied by equally extensive introduction of dialogue result in a deathbed scene that is consistent in its depiction of melancholy and grief. In chapter 4 I discussed the arrival of Sister Stone at the moment of Liniang's death and her exchange with Chunxiang during the "keening" sequence, both humorous intrusions that break the intensity of a preceding sequence and use crude language to deflate elegant language. In performed versions of "The Soul's Departure" *su* elements are deployed differently. A lengthy dialogue between mother and daughter draws attention away from their sung exchange, which is severely cut, and becomes the occasion for an elaborate demonstration of maternal concern and filial response. Such displays can be thought of as *su* in yet another sense, of being spectacles whose meaning is transparent. In Tang's dramatization, the feelings of mother and daughter are presented in a manner that can be thought of as *ya*, since their sequence of arias focuses feelings inward to private concerns and fears, as much as outward in solicitude for each other, complicating the representation of grief.[130]

Tang wrote *Mudan ting* at a time when literati playwrights were self-consciously experimenting with dialect and humor, both inelegant elements rarely found in the high poetic tradition. His contemporaries remarked, not with unqualified approval, on the degree to which his plays betray his enthusiasm for popular forms, especially dialect opera. This enthusiasm went together with his perceived disregard for formal harmony, which remained an aesthetic *sine qua non* for contemporary playwrights such as Wang Jide and Lü Tiancheng.[131] Tang's genius was acknowledged, but he was also criticized as wild. Outstanding examples of such wildness in *Mudan ting* are "Sorceress of the Dao" (scene 17) and "Infernal Judgment" (scene 23). In the former, a text written in archaic language that was both a calligraphic model and a moral primer for beginning students becomes a vehicle for Sister Stone's outrageously explicit sexual autobiography. In the latter a catalogue of flower names sung by the Huashen furnishes the opportunity for the infernal Judge Hu, like Sister Stone played by a *jing* actor, to indulge his flair for erotic puns. Common to both scenes is sexually charged humor achieved by mingling elegant and crude language. Neither sequence made its way into the performed repertoire for *Mudan ting*, though "Infernal Judgment" was popular as a *zhezixi*.[132]

Tang's treatment of the mistress-maid relationship also took unorthodox turns. In several key scenes Chunxiang's presence more often than not draws attention to the uniqueness of Liniang's feelings and experiences; the two young women are rarely associated as kindred spirits, as was commonly the case with the *guimendan-huadan* pair. After Liniang dies, Sister Stone takes Chunxiang's place, first as attendant at the garden shrine, then as attendant to the living woman. The substitution of the earthy and worldly wise Stone for the childish and ingenuous Chunxiang pairs a *jing*-style maid with a *guimen*-style mistress. Both Stone and Chunxiang are *su* with respect to Liniang (who is *ya* by virtue of status and breeding), but Stone's advent supplies a different dynamic to this pairing, since the humor associated with her character creates distance from the emotionally "thick" feelings of the complex and cryptically reserved heroine. Distance in this case differs from that effected by Chunxiang's presence at key moments. Stone's comic perspective distances us from Liniang in a manner that Wai-yee Li associates with irony, but without sacrificing our sympathetic engagement with her. As a result, the audience sustains both attachment and detachment. In the case of Chunxiang, however, the effects of isolation sometimes created by her presence intensify audience engagement with Liniang's experiences and feelings by calling attention to qualitative differences between the two young women. The drastically curtailed comic presence of Sister Stone returns the onstage humor to familiar and safe channels in most stage adaptations of *Mudan ting*—safe because the sentiments and experiences of the heroine are no longer subjected to the corrosive effects of such a character's perspective.[133]

Many of Tang's *ya/su* juxtapositions are best experienced over several scenes or from familiarity with the entire play, as was suggested by Chen Duo's analysis of the mistress/maid pairing in "The School Hall." There are no documented performances of *Mudan ting* in its entirety,[134] and by the Qianlong era a good portion of the public for Kun opera, especially the theater-going audience, likely knew only those scenes from the play that were performed as *zhezixi*, and then only in their adapted form. As for Kun actors, it is rare even today for professional actors to consult the text of the original scene on which a *zhezixi* is based, much less to read the entire play from which it has been extracted. Actors such as Mei Lanfang, who made it a point to consult scholars about the original playtext,[135] are the exception.

For these reasons, scholarly and critical studies of Kun opera often refer to "contradictions" that have persisted between playwrights and their public on the one hand and playwrights and actors on the other. These schisms became pronounced by the mid-eighteenth century, when literati playwrights no longer were keenly involved in writing operas and when interpretations of them on the stage were largely in the hands of actors.

Unlike the situation Levine describes for nineteenth-century America, the opera-loving public was as vertically stratified when Kun opera was performed most widely as it was in late Ming times, probably more so. A Kun opera might be enjoyed purely as armchair drama and read much as long novels were read; it might be sung only, or performed before a select audience in an intimately private setting; it might be staged in a commercial establishment before a much larger audience, or it might be part of a theatrical program performed before a huge gathering at a temple. It could be enjoyed in its entirety (most likely when read), in a sequence of linked *zhezixi* from the same play, or in combination with *zhezixi* from other operas. Although *zhezixi* were performed before mixed audiences in commercial theaters and some professional troupes performed Kun operas together with clapper and later Beijing style operas, the tendency for "highbrow" and "lowbrow" operas to be performed separately before distinct audiences was, and remained, more likely in China than was ever the case in America, even after the public culture that Levine celebrates began to erode in the mid-nineteenth century. The one truly "democratic" venue for opera in China in Levine's sense was the religious festival, during which operas were performed for the benefit of the entire community. Performances of Kun operas before large outdoor gatherings are mentioned in late Ming sources, when enthusiasm for all kinds of opera was widespread.[136] By the time that Tang Xianzu wrote *Mudan ting*, however, such a public culture for opera in China was about to be severely curtailed, for the Manchus regarded the theater as an institution in need of strict control. That public was not reconstituted subsequently.

Even though a lively theatrical culture did arise under the Manchus, and even though Kun opera (including *ya* operas such as *Mudan ting*) did have a presence in this theatrical culture, these operas did not become "part of the cultural body" in the sense that Levine claims was true for the plays of Shakespeare in America.[137] As we have found to be the case with *Mudan ting*, the absorption was piecemeal and partial and was effected by strategies of adaptation that so transformed the scenes in question that the playwright's purposes were no longer recognizable.

Responses by Literati: The Case of Wang Jide

Tang Xianzu's contemporaries had found his manner of writing plays unique, by which they meant, in part, his manner of mingling language associated with popular forms of (dialect) opera with embellished language that was favored in *chuanqi* texts authored by literati. However, even when praising Tang's style they expressed reservations about it, as can be seen in the following comment by Wang Jide:

> He studs his plays with down-to-earth [*bense*] [language] and intermingles this with beautiful diction [*liyu*]. As one enters the world [of his plays], it comes to life; so cleverly is the language fitted together that one finds another route to the Yuan playwrights. Such skill comes from Heaven and is not a human gift. . . . There were none like him in the past, and there will be few after him of such outstanding ability. In the last two hundred years, there is only this one man.[138]

Wang's praise is tempered by his feeling that Tang's style could not be imitated and also by a feeling that it should not be imitated because it was wild (*kuang*).[139] Wang, who abhorred extremes of any kind in *qu*, had this to say about the proper balance between elegant and common forms in dramatic *qu*:

> In general, if one uses purely down-to-earth language, it is easy to feel desolate; if one uses a purely literary language, the style is marred by ornateness. [The style of] *Baiyue ting* [Moon Prayer Pavilion] is extremely plain, while in *Pipa ji* [The Lute] one finds that both are used together: The language of the short *qu* is down to earth, while that of the long *qu* and introductory pieces . . . feasts the eye with beautiful brocades. For this reason it is the correct form. . . . The defect of language that is down-to-earth is that it easily becomes common [*lifu*], and the ill of literary language is that it becomes too literary. Subtle are the distinctions of elegant and common, shallow and deep! It rests with those who are good at using their talents to determine these.[140]

Wang welcomed plain language in dramatic *qu*, so long as its use was kept within proper bounds and did not produce awkward juxtapositions. As an example of the latter, he cited two short arias from *Pipa ji*, where a single elegant line intrudes incongruously into a passage otherwise written in a plain style. He preferred that the languages be kept separate:

> There are two forms of main arias [*guoqu*]: for long arias, one should use language that is embellished [*wenzao*], but avoid becoming too deep; for short *qu* one should use language that is down to earth, but avoid becoming too vulgar [*li*]. The language must be performable, such that all can

> comprehend it, village boys and elders as well as scholars and ladies; only then can the technique be said to be proficient.[141]

Wang defines language appropriate for each kind of aria, but doesn't envision mingling these languages in a single aria; the two languages can and should coexist, but should not encroach too closely on each other. Likewise, when discussing the use of stage business in dramatic *qu* (another element that can be identified as *su*), he describes its function as diversion, lest the action of the play become too "cold":

> Generally speaking, in places where the *qu* are cold and [the action] is quiet [*bu nao*], if one inserts some stage business between the *jing* and *chou*, it will get a rise out of the audience. This, too, is one crux [*yanmu*] in [the writing of] drama.[142]

Humorous language must strike a balance between overrefinement and crudity, such that the common element in it does not subvert the effect of elegance that remains the overriding desideratum:

> One must not use any words that are too literary, nor can one write a single sentence of peddler's language. One must employ what is common [*su*] to make something elegant [*ya*], so that once the words are spoken the audience is immediately seized with laughter.[143]

Running through these remarks is an attitude both receptive to the use in drama of common elements to ensure accessibility to the widest possible audience and cautious lest these elements destroy the decorum intrinsic to drama as a form of public poetry. Wang was especially concerned about the use of dialect in southern drama and worried often about the corrupting influence of regional styles of opera that he found both crude and lewd.[144] In short, drama's "elegance" was bound up in its modes of expression, and these were inseparable from its role as public poetry, which Wang identified with the poems in the "Daya" ("Greater Elegantia") section of the *Shijing*. For this reason it must accommodate folk idiom, but appropriate it to a higher use.

In these respects his vision of opera, by which he meant Kun opera, was to achieve a style reminiscent of one that had prevailed in the Yuan dynasty as he envisioned that time—when official and commoner playwrights labored side by side and scholars did not disdain trying their hand at writing operas. Wang viewed this past nostalgically, as a time when culture was not divided into high and low,[145] and expressed dissatisfaction with the state of opera in his own time. But when it came to emulating the example of Yuan playwrights, he did not look upon Tang Xianzu's practice as a model for other playwrights.

Tang's style was often compared by his contemporaries to that of Yuan playwrights, and a likely reason for this was his readiness to draw on the full expressive range of the language. In doing this he allowed common, even crude and lewd, language to encroach freely on elegant forms that were the norm for *chuanqi* drama in his day. There can be no question that he did this deliberately, to achieve effects that we, from our modern perspective, identify with irony and parody—forms of expression that exclude some segments of a work's public.[146]

A larger irony, then, is that Tang's operas, written for an audience that could be presumed to appreciate the playwright's linguistic pyrotechnics, became as popular as they did. As this happened, however, the blend of common and elegant forms that he had achieved was modified, and many of its effects were neutralized. As demonstrated in these chapters, efforts to contain Tang's language were made at first by Tang's contemporaries in an attempt to influence the practice of actors and subsequently by the actors themselves. In the process, parts of the play were absorbed into mainstream public culture, first in popularized Kun form, then more selectively in other popular styles of opera and performed genres such as *zidishu* ("young men's books") and *tanci* ("plucking rhymes").[147] Du Liniang and Liu Mengmei became romantic icons in this public culture, but as icons they lost their original identity.

The manner in which *Mudan ting* was transmitted in Qing theatrical culture is indicative of gaps that persisted between different styles of opera and their respective publics—one exclusive, the other popular and eclectic in some of the ways discussed by Levine for a very different cultural context. To the extent that *Mudan ting* negotiated this gap, it was transformed, and the transformation in this case changed it into something no longer the work of its creator.

Six

Peter Sellars's Efforts to Reawaken Kun Opera

In the spring of 1997 I learned of a collaborative effort underway in the United States to reawaken Chinese classical drama.[1] This effort brought together the American director Peter Sellars, Hua Wenyi, a *Kunqu* actress and former head of the Shanghai Kun Opera Troupe, and Tan Dun, a Chinese-born composer now residing in New York. That spring, plans were well underway for an "avant-garde" production of *Mudan ting*, to be co-produced by underwriters in both Europe and North America. It would open in Vienna in May of 1998 and travel to London in September, Rome in October, Paris in December, and Berkeley in March of 1999.

The idea for this production was conceived in 1990, when Sellars was artistic director for the Los Angeles Festival and invited Hua Wenyi to participate. Together with several other professional Kun opera actors who were also residing in the United States, she performed a program of *zhezixi* that included "Wandering in the Garden, Startled by a Dream." Sellars was so moved by her performance that he began to think about staging his own production of the play, which would feature Hua and Shi Jiehua, a *huadan* specialist who performed the part of Chunxiang at the festival. Over the next several years, he taught the play in classes at UCLA, and in workshops with Hua Wenyi at UCLA, Princeton, and Berkeley.[2]

Sellars's idea initially was to create a version of *Mudan ting* that would include scenes rarely or never performed in China. Dismayed by what he feels has been the emasculation of Liu Mengmei's character in the Kun opera performance tradition, he was determined to make Liu's a powerful onstage presence by devoting more scenes to him. To this end, portions of three scenes—"Declaring Ambition," "Despairing Hopes," and "In Search of Patronage"—were included in the rehearsal script; in them Liu declares his ambition to pass the imperial examinations and delivers a ringing denunciation of the imperial court. By reinvigorating the romantic male lead, Sellars set out to give his *Peony Pavilion* a more overtly political dimension: Liu Mengmei speaks to "the frustrated hopes of a younger generation" both in and outside China.[3]

Equally dissatisfied with traditional Kun opera depictions of Du Liniang, which he finds overly "cute," Sellars was determined to bring out a dark, erotic side of her character that emerges powerfully in three long scenes at the heart of the play: "Union in the Shades" (28), "Disrupted Joy" (30) and "Spectral Vows" (32). In them Liniang's ghost seeks out her lover, seduces him, and secures his promise to revive her corpse—behavior scarcely befitting the sort of highborn young woman typically portrayed by the *guimendan* actor. Unconstrained by traditional role categories, Sellars made these hitherto neglected scenes the centerpiece of Part Two of his production, "Three Nights of Making Love to a Ghost."[4] He also flirted with the idea of including some of the late scenes (36–55), which are devoted to the misadventures of Liu Mengmei after he parts from Liniang to seek recognition in the larger world, and of Du Bao as he repels a barbarian invader. Comedy—much of it farce, some laced with satire—predominates in the late scenes, few of which have ever been performed.[5]

By the time *Peony Pavilion* had its world premiere in Vienna, two developments caused Sellars to modify these plans. Foremost of these was the decision of John Rockwell, then artistic director of the Lincoln Center Festival, to commission a new production of *Mudan ting* in six episodes, an eighteen-hour-long "Ming Ring." Rockwell envisioned that this staging of the play in its entirety would take place in conjunction with performances of Sellars's version and offer contrasting interpretations, traditional and modern. A few months after he made this decision and selected Chen Shi-Zheng, a Chinese-born, America-based actor, to direct it, Sellars and Hua decided to withdraw their production from the festival. Committed to staging classic operas in a manner that addresses the concerns of modern audiences and challenged by Hua Wenyi to revitalize Kun opera by making *Mudan ting* new, Sellars was loathe to participate in a "battle of the bands" that would pit his vision of the work against that of a director who claimed to be resurrecting *Mudan ting* in an historically authentic form.[6] He also decided to scale back his version of the play to the length of an evening's entertainment.

The second development had to do with the reinstated scenes of ghostly lovemaking. Only a skeletal musical score in the Kun opera style existed for two of them,[7] and so Sellars invited Tan Dun to compose a new score for all of Part Two. Tan responded with an opera for soprano and tenor voices, sung in English, which runs for more than two hours. To accommodate this length, ten pages were cut from the script for Part One two days before the world premiere. In its present form Part One, which is built around Hua Wenyi's performance in the Kun opera style, is a prelude to Tan Dun's opera.[8] Accordingly, the political interpretation centered on Liu Mengmei has given way to Sellars's goal of heightening Du Liniang's erotic life and giving her character more edges. Plans to include some late scenes were also abandoned.

In September of 1998, the script included the following:[9]

Part One: "The Interrupted Dream"
- *Scene 1:* Prologue: Recited in English
- *Scene 2:* "Declaring Ambition" (2): Spoken in English
- *Scenes 3–6:* "The Interrupted Dream" (10): Spoken English and Kun opera
- *Scene 7:* "Pursuing the Dream" (12): Spoken English and Kun opera
- *Scene 8:* "In Search of Patronage" (13): Spoken English
- *Scene 9:* Portions of "The Portrait" (14), "The Invalid" (18), "Keening" (20), and "Traveler's Rest" (22): Spoken English and Kun opera

Part Two: "Three Nights of Making Love to a Ghost"
- *Scene 1:* "Infernal Judgement" (23): Spoken English and opera, with some Kun opera
- *Scene 2:* Portions of "The Portrait Recovered" (24), "The Portrait Examined" (26), "Spirit Roaming" (27), and "Union in the Shades" (28). Spoken English and opera; "Spirit Roaming" combines opera and Kun opera
- *Scene 3:* "Disrupted Joy" (30): Spoken English and opera, with one segment of Kun opera
- *Scene 4:* "Spectral Vows" (32): Spoken English and opera
- *Scene 5:* Parts of "Resurrection" (35) and "Elopement" (36): Spoken English, opera, and Kun opera

This script stayed within parameters observed in other modern Kun opera productions, which have focused on the love story, restricted humor to one or two scenes, and suppressed off-color comedy scattered liberally through Tang's complete text.[10] Like them, Sellars's *Peony* was intensely romantic, its comedy confined largely to one scene in Part Two.[11] Joel de la Fuente's portrayal of Liu Mengmei's frustration and anger was eventually so scaled back that audiences were hard put to hear Sellars's political message. One British critic, averse to Sellars's earlier work, praised *Peony Pavilion* for being free of "political fatuousness."[12]

More than his refashioning of the script, Sellars's staging took *Mudan ting* in new directions, as did Tan Dun's music. In what follows I attempt to understand what Sellars was up to conceptually in this staging and to examine how his direction brought out hitherto neglected dimensions of Tang Xianzu's masterpiece. These observations are based on attendance at rehearsals and performances in Vienna, London, and Berkeley, and supported by conversations with cast members and published reviews. Over a period of eleven months (April 1998 to March 1999), I was able to see firsthand how Sellars's directing evolved and how any performance by his cast was "just another rehearsal in an ongoing process of discovery."[13]

Linear Melodies and Dialogic Staging

A major innovation was Sellars's casting of three pairs of actors in the lead roles. In Part One, Lauren Tom and Joel de la Fuente spoke in English, while Hua Wenyi and Shi Jiehua spoke and sang in Chinese. Jason Ma, an off-Broadway actor, partnered Hua Wenyi in Vienna, London, and Rome. Stylistically speaking his was the most fluid performance, since with Joel he spoke English, while opposite Hua Wenyi he performed movements but never spoke. After Rome, Ma was replaced by Michael Schumacher, a dancer, the better to enable Sellars and Hua to choreograph movements, especially in Part Two.[14]

Regardless of whether she was paired with an actor or a dancer, Hua Wenyi's stylized acting contrasted with the uninhibited naturalism of the English-speaking pair. Sometimes, however, the actions of Lauren Tom and Joel de la Fuente paralleled those of Hua and Schumacher, and when they did, the performances resonated. Through the resulting dialogue between actors from different traditions and different cultures, Sellars crafted an aesthetic of similarity within difference, but the inspiration for this kind of directing owed nothing to traditional Kun opera performance aesthetics discussed in chapter 5.[15]

In Part Two, three pairs of actors shared the stage. The dominant presences were the soprano Ying Huang, the tenor Lin Qiang Xu, and the English-speaking pair; Hua Wenyi and Michael Schumacher hovered at the margins and rear of the stage and occasionally performed choreographed sequences together that combined the stylized movements of Kun opera with hand gestures and modern dance (Fig. 6.1). As in Part One, singing was interwoven with speaking, but English predominated. Shi Jiehua portrayed Sister Stone in Chinese, but a shamanic ritual she conducted at Liniang's tomb was called forth by Tan Dun's music and had no precedent in stagings of the work as Kun opera. In Part Two the main conversation, stylistically speaking, was between contemporary European-style opera and spoken North American drama. Hua Wenyi's performance was no longer anchored by the tradition in which she was trained; both she and Shi Jiehua had to invent movements for scenes they had never before performed.

Fig. 6.1. Reprise of *Shantao hong* in Part Two

Tan Dun's score breaks with the Kun musical style of Part One.[16] A stringed instrument (*pipa*), rather than the horizontal flute (*dizi*), supports the singer, and a rock-style drum set replaces the bamboo clapper that marks beats for the Kun opera performer. The Kun opera drum is kept, but augmented by assorted other drums, bells, and gongs. A Korean *piri* (Sister Stone's signature instrument) is used for the ritual dance at Liniang's tomb, and the breathy notes of a *xun* (a bowl-shaped wind instrument) simulate winter's cold. Electronic Midi horns, synthesizer, and sampler complete the musical ensemble.

Despite breaking completely with traditional Kun opera instrumentation, Tan claims continuity with its music in several respects: (1) use of musical patterns that repeat with variations, (2) improvisation between performers and musicians, (3) vocalizing that relies heavily on melisma, and (4) linear melodies as opposed to polyphony. Concerning the first of these points, he has this to say:

> [T]here are several kinds of traditions in [K]un theater. They have orally passed down these patterns through history that aren't written down but the musicians know how to play them. They have thousands of patterns, patterns from 'floating' to something for chasing, or for happy moments, or for a ceremony.[17]

By "patterns" Tan has in mind the *qupai* aria structure of Kun opera. His *qupai* are prerecorded motifs that repeat and create musical links between Parts One and Two. Associated with specific themes or emotions, they were sung by him as prerecorded vocalizations, which were played at various points of the performance. Otherwise the organization and embellishment of melodic patterns in the score was the task of his singers and musicians, and this is where improvisation came in:

> But how are these elements organized? How are they put together? The musicians working together on the improvisational patterns require a high artistic level. Everyone has their own interpretations. For example the patterns that I designed will work in a similar way to the traditional [K]un opera patterns because when different people play along with my prerecorded vocal improvisations of each pattern the results will be totally different.[18]

Vocal technique furnished other links to Kun opera. The melodies in Tan's score climbed high and descended low, varying in intensity from very loud to barely above a whisper.[19] Kun opera makes similar demands of the singer, who must modulate the voice from loud and resonant to soft and low. Tan's setting of text to music also used melisma, Kun opera's most distinctive vocal technique, where one syllable of text is sustained for several bars of music. Strong melodic lines, melisma, and absence of harmony (through composing) all linked Tan's score to Kun opera music on a conceptual level,[20] but the uninitiated listener would be hard put to hear any similarity. Hua Wenyi worried that the break with traditional musical patterns was too sharp[21] and urged Tan to find ways to link the two parts more clearly. His prerecorded vocalizations responded to this concern.

In a conversation reproduced in the stagebill ("One Stroke and a Thousand Colors"), both Peter Sellars and Tan Dun spoke of a common thread that must run through the performances of the actors and musicians. In Tan Dun's words, actions and lines were to be performed such that each led forward to the next. For him, linearity suggested continuity (in time, between traditions) and connection (across cultures and life experiences, between individuals). His modern *qupai* linked different parts of his composition and the opera together, creating "a chain that puts all the performers/participators in touch spiritually"; they also perpetuated a practice in Chinese opera of relying on improvisational patterns. Ying Huang and Lin Qiang Xu used melisma like *Kunqu* performers do, but for Tan Dun melisma also calls to mind Monteverdi, who stands at the watershed of opera in Europe. Monteverdi and Tang Xianzu were contemporaries, and melisma became a bridge that linked his score for *Peony Pavilion* to both European and Kun opera. Reaching back one finds a way forward,[22] and if one goes back far enough, one comes in touch with music of the same character regardless of the culture that produced it.[23] Different styles, different languages, and different theatrical traditions can be blended into something new that can "communicate with anybody":

> It's an older generation and young generation; it's Monteverdi and Tang Xianzu. It's *kun* opera and a contemporary development of western opera; medieval and rock 'n'roll; traditions of the *kun* opera, Peking opera, *Kabuki*. Everything is a parallel, a circle, a mosaic image: out of many, but as one!

Tan compares his score for *Peony Pavilion* to a mosaic, its melodic patterns to Chinese calligraphy: "one stroke and thousands of counterpoints are there." With some reluctance, he likens his practice to "crossover," which "allows for a bigger choice of resources, but meanwhile also makes 'personality' more and more difficult." Sellars responds, " . . . for you, it's not crossover because you are not going from anywhere to anywhere—you live there." Tan agrees that he has drawn on childhood memories and experiences of rituals that "link the current life and the beyond life, the other world."[24] He suggests that Sellars's staging also has created a new kind of language that runs parallel with his music.

Sellars's staging juxtaposed different traditions of opera onstage, but where Tan conceived of his score as a mosaic in which particularities are subsumed, Sellars relied on the particularities of his performers' artistry to create a dialogue between different styles of theater and different onstage embodiments of Du Liniang. This was especially evident in Part One, in which Lauren Tom's physically energetic portrayal of Liniang was counterpoint to Hua Wenyi's restrained one. A case in point is a solo aria in scene 10 (*Shanpo yang*), which expresses Liniang's longing for a lover. While singing this aria, the Kun opera actress circles a table while turning and dipping her body. For this production Hua Wenyi adapted the prescribed movements to the new setting and performed them in a manner more physically explicit than I had ever seen her do before.[25] Audiences in Europe and North America likely would not have found these movements particularly erotic in and of themselves, but since Sellars directed Lauren Tom to recite the same aria moments earlier, twisting and turning her body while lying on the stage, the juxtaposition illuminated by contrast. In Vienna Mark Swed found that "all that is physically extravagant in Tom's Bridal Du is implied in Hua's performance."[26]

Stylistically, contrasts were less sharp in Part Two. Here Tan's image of a mosaic seems better to describe what one saw and heard. In the words of one critic, Part One was "a fusion of Western spoken theatre and Chinese opera," whereas Part Two was "a mélange in which West and East, ancient and modern, are not polar opposites, but contiguous points."[27] "Fusion" suggests merging, but in Part One especially Sellars preserved what is distinctive in the Chinese and North American styles. "Dialogic" better describes this technique than "fusion."[28]

On two occasions in Part One, the two Du Liniangs acknowledged each other's presence with gestures. The first of them came at the beginning of "The Interrupted Dream." As Lauren Tom recited the lyrics of *Bubu jiao*, Hua Wenyi entered from stage left and moved to the far side of the panel that was both Liniang's mirror and window on the world beyond her secluded rooms. From there she gazed at Lauren as she completed her recitation, after which the roles were reversed. Hua Wenyi sang *Bubu jiao* in Chinese using the stylized gestures prescribed in the Kun operatic tradition, while Lauren made herself up, thumbed through teen magazines, then observed her counterpart appreciatively (Fig. 6.2).

Fig. 6.2. Lauren Tom and Hua Wenyi perform *Bubu jiao*

A second, more deliberately self-conscious gesture came when Liniang painted her self-portrait in scene 9. Lauren was seated at the mirror/ window assembly with her back to Hua Wenyi, who was seated to her left. As she trained the lens of a camcorder over her features, she recited the lyrics for *Putian le*:

> Now to damp down the burning
> Of desire in the soul's brief resting place of flesh,
> Take brush and paper, ink and inkstone,
> The "four jewels of the study,"
> . . .
> And render eyebrows to rival the Western Maid's.[29]

As she finished this recitation both actresses turned and looked at each other. Lauren then resumed her self-scrutiny in the camera lens, but at the first line of the next aria ("With silk cloth lightly wipe the mirror") she turned a second time to gaze at Hua Wenyi; this time the actresses touched hands (Fig. 6.3).

Fig. 6.3. *Putian le* (from "The Portrait")

In its nontechnical sense, "dialogic" suggests a recognition that springs up between these Du Liniangs from different cultures and distinct historical moments (late sixteenth-century China, late twentieth-century America).[30] Sellars's video-assisted multiplication of Tang's heroine was inspired in part by Dorothy Ko's book on women's lives in seventeenth-century China, specifically her chapter on "The Enchantment of Love in *The Peony Pavilion.*" He was captivated to learn that ever since it began to circulate in print, young women in China have read the play, looked at portraits of Liniang reproduced in woodblock illustrations, and found themselves reflected in Tang's heroine. Some of these women wrote poems about Liniang and commentaries on the play, and they in turn became the subjects of plays, poems, and illustrations.[31] Over time a cult grew, comprised of women who identified intensely with Du Liniang and with other female readers of *Mudan ting.* As a result, literary images and meanings associated with Liniang proliferated. Sellars sees in all of this an empowerment of women in premodern China; with exchanges of looks and touching of hands he sought to convey a sense of sisterhood that transcended social, physical, and temporal barriers in China and now has transcended cultural barriers as well.[32]

Set Design: Video Elements

George Tsypin's set facilitated a proliferation of Du Liniang's image and the meanings associated with it, by incorporating television monitors into four large perspex panels and a platform that functioned as both Taihu rockery (in Part One) and tomb (in Part Two).[33] Displayed on these monitors, Lauren Tom's image was sometimes live, at other times frozen in a snapshot. Frozen, it was a video variant of Liniang's self-portrait and was put to many of the same uses as the portrait in the original play. In scene 2 of Part Two, Liniang's video portrait captivated Liu Mengmei as he convalesced in a room adjacent to her tomb; in scene 3 Hua Wenyi hid behind Lauren's video snapshot while Sister Stone conducted her search of Liu's room. (Fig. 6.4).[34]

Fig. 6.4. "Disrupted Joy"

In Part Two, Sellars responded to the eclecticism of Tan's music by setting three pairs of actors in motion onstage who were occasionally joined by a fourth pair onscreen. He has said that "theatre is always playing against the edges," and Part Two exemplified this idea. No one pair held the viewers' attention, and no one viewer could take in everything that was happening. An attendee at Berkeley remarked that

> I am the sort of person whose eye at any performance is drawn towards the periphery; . . . Sellars' production of *Peony Pavilion* therefore proved a kind of puzzle, because everything before me was in some sense peripheral: the

> video screens, the musicians, the glass bowl illuminated by a lamp in the dimness of the wings. Du Liniang and Liu Mengmei themselves provided no fixed focal point, since they were played by first two, then three sets of performers, all of them on stage at the same time. When the lights came up, there was a buzz; you could hear people asking each other what they were focusing on, what element of the production held their interest. The production seemed to be as much about the act of visual selection as it was about desire, or love, or even the revival of *Kunqu*. . . . Patterns in *Peony Pavilion*, whether musical or dramatic, rarely reached a traditional conclusion; they either changed or spun themselves out without resolution, which gave the whole production a kind of wildness that was both frustrating and peculiarly lovely.[35]

As in previous productions, Sellars here sought to capture the texture of life in the contemporary world, which is one of simultaneity and contradiction. "There are no single gestures anymore, every gesture is multifaceted or surrounded by enough other gestures that it no longer means the same thing, and has to be considered in an interdependent mode." His staging requires that the viewer make choices about what to focus on, and the writer of this comment appears to have got the idea.[36]

The Portrait

In London Fiona Maddox found the uses of video narcissistic, and Paul Taylor noted that Lauren Tom and Joel de la Fuente "are always ready for their close-up, Mr. De Mille."[37] One comment refers to the director, the other to the lovers, and both unwittingly put their finger on a dimension of the original play: Liniang's narcissism.[38] Lauren Tom's poses before mirror and camera suggested as much and were in keeping with Tang Xianzu's portrayal of Du Liniang's self-enchantment in the complete play.

That said, playful mystification seems to have been another intended effect of Sellars's uses of video. In the late sixteenth century China's literati became fascinated with illusion and the manipulation of illusions, and *Mudan ting* is a product of this time. Liniang's self-emancipation begins when she realizes that she is an object of desire to others; this realization excites her imagination, and causes her to dream up a lover (since her parents don't find her a real one). Pining for him after she wakes, she paints her self-portrait, dies, and returns as ghost to woo him when he materializes in human form. Confusion of reality with illusion, of substance with shadow, drives the action of Tang's play, and in this production video technology was repeatedly put at the service of this idea.

As an example, the substitution of video snapshot for scroll painting was more than simply a clever updating of Tang Xianzu's figure. Video images supported Sellars's Buddhist interpretation of the love theme, which complemented Tan Dun's Daoist take on the play. When I first began to attend rehearsals in New York, Sellars handed me a book by the art historian Wu Hung, one of two that had a big influence on his thinking about how to stage the play. Wu's book is a study of double screens—panels that divided interior and exterior spaces in Chinese dwellings. Paintings often were mounted or painted onto these screens, and special visual effects could be created by exploiting a technique of doubling in them. In his final chapter ("The Emperor's Choice"), Wu discusses *portraits* painted on screens that contained a second portrait of the same subject. When the owner of the screen was also the person whose portrait was doubled in this way, he became a participant in a game of mystification initiated by the portraitist. Wu translates an inscription written by the Qianlong emperor (r. 1736–1795), which speaks of the effect one such double screen had on him:

> One or Two?
> —My two faces never come together yet are never separate.
> One can be Confucian, one can be Mohist.
> Why should I worry or even think?

Of the emperor's self-mystification Wu comments, "According to Qianlong, his two (mirror) images in *One or Two?* could represent his two different political identities or strategies, one following the Confucian path, the other honoring Mohist doctrines. But these were only 'faces'; and the emperor's true identity remained beyond comprehension." In the inscription's signature, the emperor referred to himself as Narayana, a Buddhist deity with three faces.[39]

The perspex panels of Tsypsin's set, like Chinese screens, divided spaces on the stage, especially in Part Two. When Liniang's video image appeared in triplicate on each of them, her presence was multiplied yet again. Even as portrayed by Tom, the faces that Liniang presented to her lover and to us were many. In Part One, she was high-strung and restless, in Part Two, sexy and at times wild until she resumed her human form.

Hua Wenyi's Du Liniang was demure but passionate in Part One, restlessly seeking in Part Two; Ying Huang's Liniang was seductive and eerily spooky.[40]

Imagery

Another *raison d'être* for the video cameras was Tang's imagery (discussed in chapter 3). A good deal of the visual experience of a Kun opera performance is via poetry whose imagery is conveyed by the elaborate and colorful costumes, formalized gestures, dance, and mime. In Sellars's production costumes were simple and the set spare. This was particularly the case in Vienna, where the panels were unadorned, but for the monitors embedded in them (Fig. 6.5).[41]

Fig. 6.5. Perspex panels at the world premiere in Vienna

Sellars did not limit his use of the monitors to generating images of Lauren Tom and Joel de la Fuente. He projected other images on them as well, in a process that became more elaborately layered as the show toured. His attentiveness to Tang's language by means of images, colors, and gestural detail was in keeping with the elaborately detailed aesthetics of a performance of Kun opera, but the means he employed were from outside that tradition. Images and colors appeared onscreen throughout the performance, but the palette of colors was most vibrant in Part One, especially during the dream sequences; and the imagery was most elaborate in Part Two when the stage was dimly lit. Those who paid attention to the language of the arias were confronted with accompanying images that were suggestive but obscure, even to the actors.

Examples are images Sellars generated for three arias sung by Du Liniang and Liu Mengmei in scene 3 of Part Two, in which lovemaking is simulated by means of an elaborate conceit. In the first of them, *Bailian xu*, Liniang pours "sweet wine" into a lotus-shaped cup and Liu Mengmei observes how "cheeks flush as flowers buds [are brought] to reddest glow." Liniang responded that "this fair plantain flower flowers for you alone,"[42] and at Lauren Tom's recitation of this line, red blossoms appeared in the monitors—an image Sellars used earlier in Part One, at the moment when the Huashen interrupts lovemaking with a shower of red petals in "The Interrupted Dream." Here, water on which the petals float was then agitated, causing the image onscreen to pulsate. This image remained there for the first of two vocal improvisations by Ying Huang and Lin Qiang Xu. Inserted between the first and second arias of the original sequence, the vocalizing "mimicked the oohs and aahs of energetic sex" and expressed graphically what is only implicit in the conceit of drinking wine.[43]

At the conclusion of the vocal improvisation, Joel de la Fuente recited the opening lines of *Zui taiping*:

> Fruit's taste sours tongue as thwarted hope of amorous swain,
> Yet joy is born as heart of plantain flower secretly unfolds
> Moistened by apricot fragrance in the night.[44]

The image of red petals on the monitors gave way to one of the exterior of a shell, which at "moistened" gave way in turn to a more obscure image that glistened, darkly iridescent. Those who did not grasp that this was the interior surface of the shell may have been hard put to divine how the image was related to the words that Joel was reciting.[45] The vocalizing resumed after this recitation, and the glistening image gave way to one of red blossoms and fruits. It then reappeared, as Joel and Lauren recited, alternatingly, the remaining lines of the second aria:

> When dimpled smile appears
> On cheeks dizzied by tide of wine
> Then lip drinks lip in eager draught

And soon
Lids droop on loving eyes
Plantain petals stain deeper red
Apricot fragrance fills the mouth.[46]

It remained on the monitors for the rest of the sequence, except for a brief moment in the third aria (*Bailian xu*), when Joel told Lauren to "Sleep now, my sweet," at which the red blossoms and fruits reappeared. Only when Sister Stone interrupted the lovers did Lauren's snapshot appear on the screens to become the portrait that shielded Hua Wenyi's Liniang from Stone's prying eyes (Fig. 6.4).

Most of Sellars's images were fairly readable. At the beginning of scene 4 (in Part Two), an entrance verse mentioned a cloud that "steals light from the moon," and onscreen an orb shone through some kind of webbing. Moments later this image switched to negative, when Liniang reveals to Liu that she is a ghost (images in negative having been linked to ghostliness in scene 1 of Part Two). Her true nature revealed, Liniang tells Liu that her body "already . . . caressed to warmth" lies in a tomb that he must reach "[t]hrough caverns dug by spreading roots." At this the orb reverted to its positive form, and webbing now clearly suggested roots. Even when Sellars's images were obscure they appeared in suggestive contexts. In the case of the petals and shell, alternation of a glistening, dark image with a pulsating crimson one evoked visual language in the "high erotic" mode. In Part Two Lauren Tom's beringed hand appeared in a close-up shot, gesturing (to Joel?) as she lay atop the perspex tomb. At the exhumation, a feather undulated as she emerged from the tomb, water-soaked.[47]

Sellars also used images as visual counterpoint to music, another instance of his fondness for setting up dualities in his staging of opera. In this case the duality was between things seen and things heard; as with the multiple casting, one was confronted with "two or more entities operating in tandem or against each other."[48] Marcia Citron finds models for these techniques in soap operas and camera work on MTV, where there is no sustained focus of representation and the eye is constantly moving. The video imagery in *Peony Pavilion* pulled the viewer, momentarily, away from involvement in the illusion. In this respect it reminded me of an effect of Tang's humor, which creates distance and invites reflection.[49]

Colors

Not everyone is as favorably disposed as Citron is to Sellars's uses of video. After the London opening Andrew Clements wondered whether he had put together a production that was "texturally and textually over-rich" and asked audiences to work too hard, before concluding that "in the end, the means are justified."[50] Fiona Maddox, as we have seen, found Sellars's realization of the text "florid and narcissistic" and capped her largely dismissive review with the observation that "there was much of beauty. If only there had been less of it."[51] Both comments responded to the video imagery and lighting of the set—the latter yet another layer of visual enhancement supplied by Sellars and his frequent collaborator James Ingalls. The TV monitors often glowed with color, and "[had] the look of an enchanted swarm of tropical fish."[52] Shades varied from gold to lime green to Merthiolate pink and bright blue and combined with softer pastels (peach, apricot orange, icy blue) that were projected onto a back-curtain. Thus illuminated, the set was austere but chromatically vibrant.

In Part One color was most vibrant for the garden scenes, the warmest uses of it associated with Liniang's dreamings and imaginings. At the onset of her dream, the backcurtain was suffused with a pastel peach color as Joel de la Fuente's entrance verse alluded to the garden as the "Peach Blossom Source of my desire." Sellars here seized on a familiar allusion (for Chinese audiences), which associates Liniang's garden world with a hidden paradise discovered by a fisherman who followed a stream strewn with peach blossoms to its source. This peach color often flooded the backcurtain in Part One, as did apricot orange, identified with Liu Mengmei, and buttercup yellow, associated with the dream.[53] On the monitors hot colors predominated, but when Liniang awakened from her dream (in "The Interrupted Dream") and came out of her reverie (in "Pursuing the Dream"), the monitors went blank, bathing the stage in white light. This lighting was also used for other affectively cold moments, as when Liniang accused her mother of "[using] food against one who truly starves" in scene 7 of Part One.

Some colors, like some images, had no obvious significance. Why did bright blue appear on the monitors during lovemaking mimed by Jason Ma and Hua Wenyi in "The Interrupted Dream"? Their movements, more explicit than those performed by Kun opera actors, enacted the words of *Shantao hong*, which Liu Mengmei sings as he disrobes Liniang and asks her to "bear with me patiently for a while." Blue had no obvious connection to the actions being performed,[54] and when I caught up with the show in Berkeley, lilac appeared instead as Michael Schumacher and Hua Wenyi performed that *pas de deux*. Even when the color symbolism was clear, its meaning probably escaped all but the most alert viewer, or else worked subliminally. Subliminal touches are not out of place in Kun opera, especially when it comes to the complicated feelings that are depicted in *Mudan ting*.[55] In this respect as well, Sellars's aesthetic goals were congruent with those of Kun opera, although the means used to achieve them differed.[56]

Fig. 6.6. *Zaoluopao* (from "The Interrupted Dream")

Bodies

The uses to which Sellars put the actors' bodies were of his own devising, but some of them were in keeping with Chinese stage practice, in which actors can serve as props, or, with a movement of one part of the body, represent an object. In Vienna Lauren Tom circled her arms and became a well, then stood and became a wall while Hua Wenyi sang *Zaoluopao*, whose words describe the garden Liniang is seeing for the first time (Fig. 6.6). Jason Ma knelt and became the table on which Liniang's portrait was painted and inscribed in Sellars's staging of "The Portrait." By Berkeley, these details had disappeared, and in the meantime Sellars had been busy with the play's governing image, the plum tree (*mei*), rendered "apricot" in this production because Sellars found Birch's translation more evocative than the standard "plum." In Vienna, Joel de la Fuente and Jason Ma had stood with arms raised overhead to represent the apricot as tree, but with the arrival of Michael Schumacher, Sellars's representation of it became more elaborate.

Originally, embodying the tree onstage was part of Sellars's project to reinvigorate Liu Mengmei's character and enhance the play's political meaning.[57] Both peony and apricot are symbols of regeneration,[58] but the apricot in particular suited Sellars's political subtext, since it "makes its own spring" by blooming while snow still falls. For Sellars, Liu Mengmei is an agent of regeneration not only as lover but also as a student determined to make himself heard (e.g., to Deng Xiaoping, Li Peng, and their kind in the capital). This use of Liu as mouthpiece for the outrage of the students who demonstrated in Tian'anmen Square—and that of youth the world over[59]—will startle those who are familiar with his buffoonery in the original play. By means of a break in the actors' otherwise naturalistic acting, Liu as tree became an iconic figure in Sellars's staging.

Some interesting effects resulted. In "Pursuing the Dream," at the moment when Liniang discovers the tree in the family garden, Joel entered and raised his arms as Lauren Tom recited the lyrics of *Erfan yao ling*:

> How can its hidden fragrance spread so clear,
> Its shade like a parasol reach full round?
> Thriving,
> Thriving in this third month of spring "when rich rain
> swells the red to bursting,"
> Its leaves shine green,
> Its full round fruit hide bitter heart
> Cherishing this daytime shade,
> Let me find again a dream of Luofu.[60]

As the recitation began, Lauren's Liniang lay on the ground, prostrated by grief at the fading of her dream and the desolation she finds in the garden to which she has returned. But the tree has an invigorating effect, and to convey this Sellars instructed Lauren to cling to Joel's body as she struggles to her feet ("Make this very physical, really hold onto him!"). While reciting *Jiang'er shui*, Lauren was to nestle close to him, so that his upraised arms appeared to embrace her (Fig. 6.7):

> My heart is strangely drawn
> To this apricot's side.
> Just as we please ourselves which flower or herb we most love,
> Ah, could we only live or die at will,
> Then who would moan for bitter pain?
> Let me commit my fragrant spirit,
> Though rains be dank and drear,
> To keep company with this apricot's roots.[61]

As this recitation concludes, she was to sink down at Joel's feet, while he bent down, briefly, then resumed his tree pose.

Fig. 6.7. Lauren Tom and Joel de la Fuente perform *Jiang'er shui*

For the remainder of Part One, both Joel and Jason often assumed their tree pose, especially when partnering their respective Du Liniangs. For "The Portrait" they were stationed behind the assembly of panels on which Lauren Tom and Hua Wenyi were seated, and remained there after that scene concluded. The backcurtain then was lit a pale blue, and as the *xun* piped a shivering melody, winter arrived. Liniang lies near death, as Liu Mengmei sets out on the northward journey that brings him, ill, to the garden where she is buried. Joel and Jason held their poses stiffly, as if frozen, while Lauren, wracked with fever, recited arias that build to the moment of death (Fig. 6.5).[62] Hua Wenyi then sang *Jiang'er shui* a second time using the traditional Kun opera movements. Part One concluded as she too sank to the ground.

At the London rehearsals, Sellars stressed to Joel and Jason that their affect during the death scene must not be completely rigid. They must make small movements because:

> You're alive and moving. So, sometimes there can be a giant move to hang things on, but otherwise do little things. He's trying to survive—that's what Liu Mengmei's about. She's dying but he's trying to endure; someone has to get through the winter.

"Little things" were gestures that responded to Liniang's actions. In London, parallel gestures used by both actors gave "The Portrait" a highly formalized look. As the scene began, Lauren trained a video camera over her face as she recited *Yan guo sheng* (Fig. 6.8).[63] Hua Wenyi then intoned the poem that Liniang inscribes on the portrait, which predicts "Union in the year to come with the courtier of the moon / will be beneath the branches of either willow or apricot."

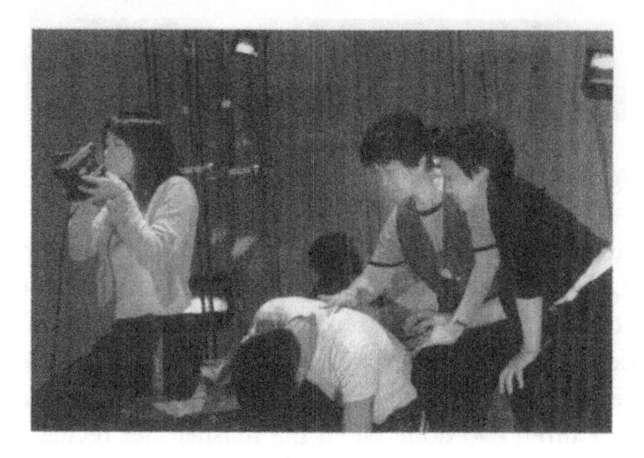

Fig. 6.8. *Yan guo sheng* (from "The Portrait")

As she sang, Joel and Jason entered and assumed their tree poses behind the panels at which the two women were seated. When Hua Wenyi's

Liniang recounted to Chunxiang how in a dream she had met a man, "willow branch in hand," Jason reached from behind his panel to stroke her cheek; Joel did the same as Lauren Tom studied the finished portrait and recited:

> My own self, captured in likeness,
> Bearing in hand a green sprig of apricot,
> As I recall my lover.

Their movements were synchronized, as they were in "Pursuing the Dream," when both moved their "limbs" to embrace Liniang as she nestled up to the tree.

Fig. 6.9. Hua Wenyi reprises *Jiang'er shui* (in "Keening")

Other gestures resonated more distantly. With Liniang near death in "Keening," Lauren Tom spoke her dying request that she be buried in the garden near the apricot tree. Hua Wenyi then sang *Jiang'er shui* as a reprise; at "Let me commit my fragrant spirit / though rains be dank and drear / to keep company with this apricot's roots," she sank down at Jason's feet, as Lauren had done when she finished her recital of *Erfan yao ling*. Jason, echoing Joel's gesture, bent down in response to these movements before resuming his tree-pose (Fig. 6.9). Through such "little things" Sellars sought to suggest Liu Mengmei's staying power, which is essential both to his survival and to Liniang's.

The parallel movements were much more evident in the London performances than they were in Vienna—an example of the accretive layering a Sellars's production undergoes. However, Sellars found that his two Liu Mengmeis were "too joined at the hip," and at Berkeley the parallelism was largely gone. For Hua Wenyi's performance of *Jiang'er shui*, Joel and Michael were positioned behind the panels as before, but now their bodies were pressed against them, Michael Schumacher's face so compressed that his distorted features conveyed the brute fact of separation (Fig. 6.10). His sinuous representation of the tree (Fig. 6.11) offered a contrast to Joel's stiffly iconic one; this was one big reason why the parallel movements so evident in London had faded.[64]

Fig. 6.10. Staging of *Jiang'er shui* at Berkeley

Fig. 6.11. "The Interrupted Dream"

A Buddhist "Take" on *Mudan ting*

Both Sellars and Tan Dun use language congenial to a Buddhist outlook when talking about this opera. Tan's embrace of diverse musical forms is allied with a vision—of future time as a return to time past—that can seem more Indian than Chinese; Sellars is struck by simultaneity in artistic creation, in which barriers of culture, distance, and time collapse.[65] Tan Dun is attracted to music that puts the listener in touch with experiences and feelings that elude "personality"—by which he means

Western individualism; Sellars exhorts his cast to act in such a way that "one feeling runs through all and you are not the center of attention. . . . As you come together, there are no individual performances."

Unity in multiplicity has informed Sellars's interpretation of Tang Xianzu's heroine. Hua Wenyi's shy yet bold young woman, Lauren Tom's restless teenager, and Ying Huang's seductive goddess were different embodiments of Liniang that, in Sellars's words, "are simultaneous yet always manifesting." Occasional passages in Tang's text support this idea, and Sellars has seized on them. For example, there is reference in the prologue to "the history of this longing / on the road that led through three incarnations to *Peony Pavilion*." This is the playwright's personal statement; the synopsis in the stagebill had it refer to Du Liniang.[66]

After the world premiere in Vienna, Sellars's most significant modification was to add segments designed to make a Buddhist meaning more prominent. Beginning in London these were performed during scene changes in Part Two and were accompanied by a prerecorded chorus sung to a single melody that runs like a thread through Tan's opera. In each of the four segments Hua Wenyi took up a position inside the assembly of panels that served in Part One as mirror, window, and writing table. Here the four panels marked the enclosure of Liniang's tomb and were pushed in a circle by other members of the cast (one per panel). Hua turned and bent down at the circle's center, her movements suggesting restless life within the tomb's confines that seeks release (Fig. 6.12).[67] There were no overt indications that this represented a "dharma wheel," but the choral chanting imparted a Buddhist flavor.[68]

At the conclusion of Part Two, after Hua Wenyi emerged from the tomb, she joined her counterparts at the front of the stage. The three Liniangs formed a circle and touched hands before each turned to join her partner.[69] As they performed these movements, voices chanted the chorus a final time:

> Secretly departing beneath the shifting moon
> Fair breezes blow to escort the nuptial pair.
> No onlooker understands the mystery of this barge
> Only the happy bride knows all there is to know.[70]

This touching of hands repeated gestures exchanged between the two Liniangs in Part One. Repeated, they seemed intended to suggest sisterhood, an idea that Sellars imported into his production in acknowledgment of *Peony Pavilion*'s appeal to women.[71] His dharma wheel was another repetition, in this case linked to ideas of multiplicity and simultaneity that run through Sellars's operas.[72] For many viewers these actions must have been enigmatic, but Sellars is comfortable with the possibility that some in the audience will be baffled by what they see:

> Some of the most important things the audience can't even see. You [the actors] don't know some of the things that happen, so even when you're in the dark, don't think that nothing is happening. There's no "on" and "off." There's one continuous unbroken thread. Some of the most important insights come when you're waiting in line at the post office; sometimes the still movements are the most important ones.[73]

Fig. 6.12. "Resurrection"

Peony Pavilion received mixed reviews from critics who were not familiar with Kun opera, much less with Tang's play either as written or as commonly performed. For those who were, Sellars's interpretive decisions provoked feelings pro and con, as was evident in lively discussions at the symposia held at Berkeley, where for the first time the audience included significant numbers of people knowledgeable about Kun opera and Chinese culture.

Writing from the standpoint of familiarity with the play and its performance history, I have found Sellars's strategies for staging always interesting, at times inspired, very engaged with Tang's text, and based on an impressive amount of research. I have derived much pleasure from the many details of his staging that respond to Tang Xianzu's language and have discussed some of these details in this chapter. But I have also wondered how this richly textured staging struck those who were not familiar with the play and saw only one performance of it. Did they experience sensory overload (as some critics have)? Might they have found that the staging called too much attention to itself, inhibiting their ability to respond spontaneously to the performances?[74]

The interweaving of different performance styles is a case in point. Sellars's juxtapositions enabled the viewer both to get some idea of how the play is performed in the original language and also to experience it in a manner familiarized by translation into an American performance idiom. A naturalized style illuminated the formalized style of Kun opera, and the use of three actresses facilitated a multifaceted interpretation of Du Liniang's character that broke free of the rigid prescriptions of the *guimen-dan* role.[75] But there were costs associated with this trisection of the role ("[l]ike a Cubist painting come to life").[76] In Part One key scenes were performed twice, slowing the pace even though the performances of Lauren Tom and Hua Wenyi did not duplicate each other exactly.[77] That the three pairs of actors did not interact onstage in Part Two also made the pacing of Tan Dun's opera static at times. Complaints about the slow pace were not limited to the English language media. Liao Ben wrote of "slowness verging on blockage" (*chihuan shenzhi tingzhi*) in an article published in the Chinese newspaper *Wenyi bao*.[78]

My greatest quarrel has been with Sellars's determination to idealize the lovers and elicit performances that are beautiful and never crass.[79] This aim was of a piece with his desire to give Liu Mengmei's character more weight and with his different handling of political content as well. Both aims were departures from Tang's play. There are flashes of politically inspired satire in scenes devoted to Liu Mengmei that depict him advancing his career with the backing of a powerful patron, but hard-edged satire does not predominate, as it does in Tang's late plays. Sellars's productions of European opera often are laced with humor directed at the protagonists, but he avoided satire here because it got in the way of the message he wanted to convey, especially to younger members of the audience. This message didn't pack much punch for audiences in Europe and North America, however, and even had the opera made it to China, I doubt that it would have been heard in its present form.

The boldness of Sellars's Du Liniang would have been noticed, and this alone would prevent the show from ever reaching China, especially after all the furor over the Lincoln Center "Peony." Sellars was disappointed in the "cute" young women portrayed in the *Kunqu* tradition, and one idea he got during his visit to Kun opera companies in China came to him when he saw a *huadan* actress, Liang Guyin, cross over to perform the character. Liang's portrayal of Liniang in "Infernal Judgment" brought out dark facets of the character that Sellars took even farther in the ghost scenes that were featured in Part Two of his production. By the same token, passages of harshly dissonant music that Tan Dun composed for Part Two conveyed Liniang's sexuality in ways that are unthinkable on the Chinese stage, as did his unorthodox vocal improvisations. Hua Wenyi did not resist these innovations, but neither was she comfortable with them. At rehearsals in New York I heard her complain to Tan Dun, jokingly, that to her, Ying Huang and Liu Qiang Xu's "Hey, Ho!" duet "seemed like working hard, not like making love" (*bu xiang zuo ai, xiang laodong*).[80] She was also puzzled by Lauren Tom's sudden metamorphosis into a wild woman, at just the moment when her lover discovers that she is a ghost. I was hard put to explain to her what I thought Sellars had in mind and asked Lauren Tom. She didn't know either and asked Sellars about it at a rehearsal. He mentioned the performance he had seen by Liang Guyin.

Sellars feels that love in *Mudan ting* has been portrayed as "a nice candy bar" when it is not. When rehearsing "The Interrupted Dream," he asked, "Who has the courage to deal with the fact that love is not perfect, that no one is perfect?" Love is "scary, a bitter fruit." While rehearsing "Pursuing the Dream," he asked Joel de la Fuente what it meant to have a beautiful woman die at his feet. "Are you going to let her die, or are you going to go to her grave and dig her up?" His questions anticipated Part Two, where Liniang was more than just a seductive goddess or a passing physical attraction for Joel's character. Even when she turned scary, Liu didn't lose heart. Love has turned his heart from other goals; "It's not just the sex part."[81]

This rehabilitation of Liu Mengmei reminded me of earlier efforts by Kun opera actors to transform him into a more worthy object of Liniang's love—efforts I have documented elsewhere in this book. C. T. Hsia long ago pointed out that Liu Mengmei is partly an object of satire and that Liniang is the only serious character in Tang's play.[82] For those of us who are accustomed to Tang's ungentle depictions of young scholars, Sellars's conception of Liu's character has been a tough sell. But when I raised objections, he brushed them off.

Sellars has described this *Peony Pavilion* as part reconstruction of Chinese classical drama, part reinterpretation:

> One thing doesn't have to die that another thing can live. Authenticity is a very Western notion. It was Hua herself who insisted that everything must be new, every gesture questioned.[83]

Over weeks and months spent watching this *Peony* take shape, I came to realize that Sellars had no interest in recuperating the sly comedy and subtle ironies of Tang Xianzu's text. His reinterpretation was part of a self-described utopian project that "sees art as a source of spiritual strength and a counterweight to the gross materialism of our times."[84] Sellars is impatient with critics who are so fettered by ideas of what is intrinsic or original to a work that they are unable to see it afresh. Four hundred years after Tang wrote *Mudan ting*, its rebirth at his hands has been every bit as remarkable as that of its heroine.

Seven

"To Perform '*Chuanqi*' We Will Recreate a *Chuanqi*"

> Speaking of the complete *Mudan ting*, I have gathered in as treasures all the "dregs" that had been cast aside. . . . In fact, it is precisely the so-called "dregs" that are the most intelligent things in Chinese dramas.
>
> Traditional drama goes too much after beauty and casts aside many things that are essential to life.
>
> Chen Shi-Zheng[1]

Comments such as these, culled from articles that appeared in Shanghai newspapers in April of 1998, reflect the thinking that underlay Chen Shi-Zheng's staging of a "complete" version of *Mudan ting*. The production, a much-anticipated part of Lincoln Center's "Festival 98," was prevented from traveling to New York for its world premiere, and much of the controversy over it centered on the fact that Chen claimed to be recreating an authentic Ming dynasty performance of the play when in fact, it was alleged, he was offering the foreign audience a "hodgepodge" (*zahui*) of traditional art forms. After two dress rehearsals in Shanghai, Chen's critics noted that he had asked Kun opera stars to share the stage with the likes of puppeteers, stilt-walkers, and an amateur *pingtan* story-teller.[2] The refined and beautiful parts in *The Peony Pavilion* comingled with parts that were anything but beautiful. In one scene, it was noted, prostitutes ogled audience members as they emptied chamber pots (real wooden ones) into a fish pond that fronted the stage; in another, a Daoist nun recounted her sexual history in a disconcertingly comprehensible Sichuan dialect, and for one evening's finale,[3] a funeral ritual complete with paper money and firecrackers was taken into the audience and out to the streets. Using such unorthodox staging ideas, Chen had turned one of China's finest Kun opera companies into an "itinerant troupe" (*caotai banzi*). To allow that company to depart on its world tour would be to give foreign audiences a distorted idea of traditional Chinese culture and classical Chinese drama.

The culture wars that have erupted over Chen's fifty-five scene, eighteen-hour production, both inside China and between Shanghai cultural authorities and the show's Western co-producers, deserve consideration in and of themselves. They replay controversies that have dogged *Mudan ting* ever since it first became popular and expose sensitivities about what properly belongs on the public stage. Chen has challenged the dogma that a performance of *xiqu* drama must above all be beautiful and has added insult to injury by defending the artistic merit of the very "dregs" (*zaopo*) that others have excluded from their performances of this play. An outsider to the Kun opera establishment, he shared his unorthodox views with the media while working on Kun opera's home turf. It is not surprising that both his methods and his comments about them ruffled feathers, but the ferocity of the backlash when it came caught many by surprise.

By the summer of 2000, Chen's show had had its world premiere (a year late, with only two members of the original cast)[4] and was enthusiastically received by audiences on three continents (North America, Europe, and Australia). He has triumphed over his critics and won over many of them (myself included), but it will take time to sort through the issues that this international collaboration ignited and assess the aesthetic contributions of this iconoclastic staging of Tang Xianzu's play. While in Shanghai, Chen remarked that *The Peony Pavilion* should amuse audiences as well as move them, and in the early excitement generated by the dress rehearsals at least one reviewer agreed, crediting him with a performance of the work that was both scholarly (*xueshuxing*) and entertaining (*yulexing*).[5] Peter Sellars's *Peony Pavilion* was experimental and conceptually challenging; Chen's eighteen-hour marathon was middlebrow and accessible, deliberately so. The two works were positioned very differently in the current field of cross-cultural production.

In this chapter I will concern myself with some of the ways that Chen's production broke with the tradition of performing *Mudan ting* that I have documented elsewhere in this book.

Breaking the Traditional Frame

After negotiations with the authorities in Shanghai failed and Chen had returned to New York, he released a statement in Chinese in which he outlined the conceptual underpinnings of his staging and answered his critics both in Shanghai and in North America. In particular, his statement spoke to the charge that the dress rehearsal had revealed a "confused artistic project" (*fuzade yishu gongcheng*), which had "failed to embody the fundamental artistic spirit of traditional *xiqu* drama."[6] In the first paragraph Chen wrote that for him a tradition is always evolving, such that a particular staging of a work doesn't simply imitate tradition, but matches a certain content with a certain form.[7]

He had made the same point earlier, in a long interview that appeared in several Shanghai papers in April. Responding to a question that solicited his opinion about *Mudan ting* as it is currently performed in China, Chen replied:

> It's canonical [*jingdian*], but it has nothing to do with me. I want to stage my interpretation of *Mudan ting* and perform my way of thinking about it. The only normal state of affairs is when every person has their different understanding and interpretation of so famous a play and audiences are able to see performances of different versions of it. If stagings of *Mudan ting* by all the Kun opera troupes are the same, what interest can there be? Let me emphasize that creativity isn't hostile to tradition, exactly the opposite is true. The quantity of research I have done is precisely so that the tradition can reach a higher stage of development. . . . What I oppose is blind imitation of tradition without going through any independent thinking. Beyond that, another point I would like to emphasize is that I have no interest in perpetuating traditional stylized movements [*chengshi*]; what I *am* interested in are the creative principles [that underlie] them.[8]

Chen here took aim at the tradition of performing *Mudan ting* piecemeal, as *zhezixi*. In the statement released in New York, he noted that Chinese drama has always undergone change and pointed to the retreat of literati from active involvement in the theater and the rise of a star system as reasons why *xiqu* drama today differs so greatly from what must have obtained in Ming times.[9] Even within a tradition-bound star system, Chen pointed out, a star like Mei Lanfang went beyond his teacher Wang Yaoqing and innovated. He then asked: What is the tradition? What is the genuine (*zhenzheng*) tradition? What is the genuinely worthwhile tradition? The order of the questions implied the answer: that a tradition, if it is alive, winnows out forms that no longer have meaning for artists and audiences.

In the case of Kun opera and *xiqu* drama generally, Chen feels that the tradition has become a straightjacket.[10] At an early stage of the rehearsals in Shanghai, it was reported that he was startled to learn that no member of his cast had ever read the complete text of a work they regularly performed, and that he intended to break with the current conventions of Kun opera and recapture a liveliness (*linghuoxing*) and innovativeness (*jiadingxing*) that prevailed in *xiqu* formerly. A few weeks later, another article reported that "[i]n the course of his research, Mr. Chen has come to feel that so many vivid things as Tang Xianzu wrote them are gone from the present stage; all that remains are prescribed movements such as ways of pointing or of [tossing] the water sleeves."[11]

Overrefinement and preoccupation with beautiful forms squeezed performances of Kun opera into a narrower and narrower mold, and with this production Chen sought to break out of that mold and recapture the expansiveness of social and cultural life captured in the complete text of Tang's play. He has likened this production to *Qingming shanghe tu* (Qingming Festival on the River), a Song dynasty scroll that depicts commercial and cultural life in the capital city of Kaifeng in its variety and dailiness. Like the scroll, *Mudan ting* depicts people from all conditions and walks of life: court officials, scholars, women of good family, Daoist nuns, bandits, an underworld judge and his minions, and wandering ghosts.[12]

Sister Stone is a prime example of Chen's more expansive staging. He finds her to be one of the most interesting of the "dregs" that have been distilled out in performances of *zhezixi*, and his statement offered the following assessment:

> The mid-Ming era in which Tang lived was a time in China's feudal society when the development of Cheng-Zhu orthodoxy had reached a high point. [The injunction to] "preserve Heavenly Principle and obliterate human desires" created many crippled people, and almost all of the characters in *Mudan ting* are crippled to varying degrees, either biologically, or psychologically, or both together. Sister Stone is a classic instance. . . .
>
> Actually, even when looked at today, the vivid depiction of sexuality in "Sorceress of the Dao" [Stone's solo scene] is extraordinarily bold; it isn't going too far to say that it is extraordinarily licentious. The reason for this, from Tang Xianzu's perspective, is probably that anything less extreme would not have sufficed to challenge Cheng-Zhu orthodoxy, nor would it have sufficed to make the playwright's attitude clear.

Chen also has singled out his treatment of Du Liniang as contributing something new to the tradition of performing *Mudan ting*: his Liniang is a more fearsome (*mohuan*) heroine than the traditional one, and some of her behavior is more strange (*liqi*).[13] Chen also feels that Chen Zuiliang has been misrepresented in *zhezixi*. The complete *Mudan ting* is laced with satire of officials. Accordingly, Chen depicts the tutor, who longs to be one, with broad and not always gentle humor. When we first meet him in "Pedant's Lament," he is in his medicine shop plying his pestle, and upon hearing that he is to become Liniang's tutor, the pace of the pounding quickens. In "Engaging the Tutor," he cringes and fawns before Du Bao and falls down as he makes his exit, not for the last time. He takes another tumble in "Traveler's Rest," when he comes upon Liu Mengmei, who himself has tumbled into an icy stream. Having disdained at first to offer help ("How disagreeable to run across a drowning fool"), he sees an opportunity for a good deed, but lands on top of Liu when he reaches down to lend a hand.[14]

Liu Mengmei is also often a butt of humor. Chen Shi-Zheng points out, rightly, that Liu's character is more complex than the lovable and pure-hearted young student portrayed in *zhezixi*. Careerism is comically evident in his scenes with Miao Shunbin, and Liu's penurious life as an expectant student is made light of in "Despairing Hopes," as is Chen Zuiliang's poverty in "Pedant's Lament." When an offering of rice balls arrives at the temple where he is residing, Liu and fellow-student Han Zicai scuffle over them, and Liu ends up speaking some of his lines through a mouthful of food. In his first scene ("Declaring Ambition"), a stage attendant removes a table at which Liu is seated, then a chair out from under him. He is even strung up on a frame in "Interrogation Under the Rod"—a first in the history of performing *Mudan ting*. Yue Meiti, a senior *xiaosheng* actor at the Shanghai troupe, was grateful to be spared this ordeal. For Zhang Jun, her junior counterpart, Chen's interpretation of Liu's character came as a revelation.[15]

Having documented in this book the heavy hand of orthodoxy in stage interpretations of *Mudan ting*, I am very receptive to these arguments and largely in agreement with these interpretations. In the case of Sister Stone, I can see how the outrageous humor of the character exposes the unnatural repressiveness of orthodox moral teachings. What I missed in this production is the character's essential humanity. Caught up in his cross-dressed performance, Lin Sen's portrayal—for me—drew on a stock comic type (the sexually repressed Daoist nun) and failed to capture Sister Stone's lyrical side, which shines from beneath the grotesque surface.[16] I was less troubled by the lampooning of the tutor, and when it came to Wen Yuhang's Liu Mengmei, I felt the performance struck a nice balance between the calculating career worm and the more admirable fellow who comes through at key moments.

However, some who saw the dress rehearsals in Shanghai were not at all sympathetic to Chen's approach. Early signs of trouble came in April when the troupe rehearsed two scenes for local reporters, many of whom are seasoned observers of *xiqu*. In the question period afterward, these reporters challenged Chen's qualifications to direct and wondered how he could claim to have captured the original flavor of Tang's play.[17] The "hodgepodge" label cropped up in the coverage of this event, as did questions about Chen's decision to discard the style of "old Kun opera" in favor of a more open one that incorporated other arts forms such as puppetry and oral storytelling.[18] One reporter wrote that the *Mudan ting* long familiar to everyone had been rendered "completely unrecognizable" (*mianmu quanfei*). Novelty began with the set, which confronted the audience with a new environment for each of the six episodes and incorporated real elements. There is a real peony pavilion with a real fish pond and real peasant games in the first episode, and a real funeral ritual in the second one. Real instruments of underworld torture appear in the third and fourth episodes, and the audience sees an actual bridge that dead souls cross to the underworld. "In short, from what one sees to what one hears and what one tastes, everything seems 'real.'" Without criticizing these innovations directly, the reporter suggested that *The Peony Pavilion* will amaze those who see it, but cause them to avert their gaze.[19]

The relative naturalness of the performances and realism of the set were often noted in the Chinese press coverage. Prior to the dress rehearsals in early June they were presented matter of factly, as elements of Chen's overall concept. It was reported that a more natural style is consistent with Chen's feeling that the performance style for *xiqu* (Kun opera especially) is overrefined and overly formalized. Moreover, Chen and his company had no tradition to fall back on for the bulk of the scenes, all of which had to be blocked out and memorized in eight months.[20] In such a circumstance a style that used fewer prescribed gestures was a practical necessity, but it was to become a point of contention after the whole play was unveiled.

Greater realism in the set design aroused curiosity and interest at first, but was subsequently seized on by the show's critics. One of Chen's aims has been to open up the stage visually, by abandoning the "picture frame" stage (a Western import) and making use of a traditional three-sided stage as well as two smaller wing stages, one for the musicians, another for actors engaged in activities normally hidden from view backstage, such as applying make-up and donning costumes. The backstage was left uncurtained and open to view, and wing curtains were not used. The boundary between the front and back of the stage was removed, the announced goal of this transparent (*touming*) staging being to recreate the old-style setting of Chinese *xiqu* theatricals, whether held in rural villages or in the gardens of the urban elite.[21] By removing the barriers that separate actors from audiences in modern Chinese theaters, Chen sought to recreate the leisured atmosphere in which a Ming dynasty audience would have taken in a performance of *xiqu*.

In Shanghai, Chen's determination to open up the staging appears to have produced an effect opposite to the one intended, in some cases at least. Instead of feeling relaxed, some who saw the dress rehearsals found the more open staging unsettling, never more so than during the enactment of the grand and starkly shrill funeral ceremony that concludes the death scene. Conducted by the entire cast, who are dressed in the traditional hemp garments, it began on the stage, moved out into the audience, and concluded with the burning of paper money and lighting of firecrackers in the street outside the theater. Other paper objects (horses, carriages, even an opera troupe) were burned, as they would be at a real funeral.[22] The staging in this instance combined expressive (*xieyi*) elements that are typical of *xiqu* drama and realistic elements that are alien to it (here, the paraphernalia of actual funeral rituals).[23] Chen explained that use of real objects onstage enhanced the *xieyi* expressionism through contrast; at the same time these objects served to bring Chinese customs before Western audiences.

Articles that appeared after the dress rehearsals asked whether Chen had crossed a line that shouldn't be crossed. An otherwise enthusiastic review in *Renmin ribao* asked whether the funeral ceremony went too far, and Ye Changhai, a professor at the Shanghai Theater Academy sympathetic to the project, was reported to say that the funeral should not have been carried beyond the stage. These comments saw print before Cheng Ji's article appeared on June 20, which found the show to be "freely colored by feudal, superstitious, and pornographic dregs."[24] Cheng Ji refuted Chen's approach on general principles and made only passing mention of the funeral as one of several innovations that "did harm to the character of traditional Kun opera." On the same day Jia Fang addressed the audience's response, writing in *Jiefang ribao* that people in the theater were so unsettled when the ceremony was carried into the street that they spat to get rid of the bad luck. From then on, attacks on the funeral and other forays into realism escalated.[25]

How to account for such vehement resistance to Chen's breaking of the traditional frame? One reporter suggested that theatergoers accustomed to the squeaky clean post-Liberation stage were hard put to accept the crude elements that Chen was determined to include. Cheng Ji complained that by including all manner of folk displays, the essential color of Kun opera had been thinned, leaving only an "empty shell" (*kongke*) of culture. He concluded that "great vulgarity doesn't compare with great elegance" (*dasu daya bu ji*). In New York Ben Wang, who was excited by Chen's concept, had mixed feelings about the use of real props, because "having a real flower onstage would only compete with the magical illusion."[26] Inability to see how realistic and expressionistic techniques can be combined was one root of the resistance;[27] allegiance to traditional stage aesthetics focused on beauty was another.

Western audiences, unencumbered by tradition, have embraced the "dregs" along with the "essence" (*jinghua*). Reviewers in the English language press invariably cited the funeral as a high point, and the brothel scene worked precisely because it got the audience involved. In New York the "girls" bantered with the audience and drew laughter when they splashed the front rows as they emptied their pots into the fish pond—a touch that aroused indignation in Shanghai.[28] Chen has acknowledged that this production is conceived for a foreign audience, and in Shanghai it was tagged a "foreign model" (*waixiangxing*).[29] But Chen also wants to see it performed in Beijing, and there is reason to believe that there would be a receptive audience for it there, only not, perhaps, among the community of Kun opera experts and fans.

My own response to Chen's additions is mixed. In the case of the funeral, when I first heard about it after the show was cancelled, I wondered what such an elaborate ritual had to do with the spirit of the original play. For example, in chapter 4 I have suggested that in "Keening" Tang uses humor to undercut sustained grieving at the moment of Liniang's death. Du Bao, Madam Du, and Chunxiang do lament, briefly, but they are upstaged by Sister Stone and Chen Zuiliang, who bicker over who is to tend Liniang's grave. I take "nao" in the original scene title to refer to mundane distractions of this kind, which intrude while Liniang's corpse is still warm. In Chen's production this is the only scene to get a new title ("Nao sang," "Loud Keening"), and I understand "nao" here as referring to the cacophanous wailing found in Chinese mourning rituals. The funeral mass was impressively shrill, and it was also an impressively solemn conclusion to the second segment I was finally able to see in New York. But in my opinion it had little to do with *Mudan ting* as Tang Xianzu wrote it, and much more to do with Chen's need to capture and hold the interest of Western theatergoers.

Authenticity vs. "The Tradition"

In fairness, the funeral ceremony also exemplified Chen's love of forms of drama embedded in rural life that have strong religious roots. In an interview for *Shenjiang fuwu daobao* that appeared on April 1, 1998, he talked about childhood memories of *nuoxi*, an indigenous form of Hunan ritual drama whose wild extremes of emotion can overwhelm those present at performances. For Chen, such performances cannot be mentioned in the same breath with the ones given by state-subsidized urban-based troupes.[30] One of the things that he clearly has in mind when recreating an old style of performance is this kind of rural play.

However, recreating the original look (*yuanmao*) of a Ming-era performance isn't simply a matter of returning to the spontaneous and unscripted style of rural drama. Chen also speaks of how *The Peony Pavilion* became for him the ideal vehicle for displaying both the style of *chuanqi* drama and the variety of traditional culture. It is a *chuanqi*—that most expansive of dramatic forms—and among *chuanqi* it presents life in premodern times most expansively. For Chen, it is a latter-day example of the variety show (*zaju*) from which all Chinese drama has evolved. For this reason he wants his audience to see every facet of the staging; they are not simply to be caught up in a performance, but also to be aware that they are participating in a reenactment of Chinese drama as it once was:

> By means of the reality and illusion [created] in front of the curtain and behind it, . . . and by showing the performance process without hiding anything [from the audience], what we want to emphasize, simply, is that

> "we are performing a play." By means of the human environment [created] both inside and outside the theater and the amusing atmosphere [centered on] real feelings and true emotions, what we want to emphasize, simply, is that "you are watching a play." *Mudan ting* is a *chuanqi*. If we were to recreate a *chuanqi* [milieu of performance] around a *chuanqi* play and let the performance explain what a *chuanqi* is [to the audience], wouldn't that be fun?[31]

By using *Mudan ting* to simulate a late Ming theatrical experience for the audience, Chen will explain what a performance of *chuanqi* must have been like. This was an essential part of his mandate from Lincoln Center, since John Rockwell envisioned this production as a "creative reinterpretation of the past," along lines envisioned in the Early Music Movement.[32]

Chen has used the term *chuanqi* rather than *Kunqu* to show his eagerness to distance this production from Kun opera. In Shanghai he was collaborating with a Kun opera troupe, his actors were singing in the Kun musical style, and the two leads in particular drew on their training in Kun opera. But he emphasized early on that his undertaking was in the style of a *chuanqi* drama, not a Kun one. In an interview with Yang Haipeng he pointed out that *Mudan ting* was not originally performed in the Kun style, and the next day he told a reporter for *Yangzi wanbao* that "I haven't the least interest in stylized movement. As far as I'm concerned, it isn't important whether [this production] is Kun opera or not; what is key is whether or not it is *Mudan ting*."[33] He restated these views after returning to New York and added that *Mudan ting* can never be encompassed by one style or one performance tradition because it lends itself to many different interpretations.[34]

In his review of this production, David Rolston notes the "three ring circus" aspects of the staging, many of which he feels were likely intended to keep the audience from becoming bored.[35] Chen doesn't deny that this is also a motive for the additions, but throughout the long rehearsal period in Shanghai he defended his decision to break with traditional Kun performance techniques on artistic grounds as well. Like Rolston, I initially was skeptical of Chen's motives and felt protective of the tradition that he has criticized so openly. But after reading dozens of articles and interviews that appeared in the Chinese media between October 1997 and July 1998, I find myself more sympathetic to his goals and overall approach. Rolston wonders if there is anything that can be emulated in this production and whether there is much in it that is innovative. I agree that it is very unlikely that another mounting of a complete *chuanqi* play will be undertaken, and add that Chen's defiance of his critics in Shanghai was gutsy but also imprudent, considering where the rehearsals were being conducted.

Reading the press coverage I also found myself confronted—once again—with the centuries-long debate between partisans of "elegant" drama and performers of "common" styles. Influenced by rural performances of drama since childhood and trained in *huaguxi*, Chen can be placed at the "*su*" end of the *ya/su* spectrum I discussed in chapter 5. But he resists such placement and bristled when I suggested it, telling me that unscripted dialect dramas have as much artistic value as the most elaborately scripted national styles. He also told me that in his opinion *piaoyou* have had an unhealthy influence on *xiqu* drama and the practice of amateurs and professional actors performing together has been demeaning to the professionals. Small wonder, then, that his foray into the last bastion of Kun opera in China ended as it did.

Conclusion

"Highbrow/Lowbrow" in Kun Opera

> The *dan*, having already left the stage, returns. This, simply, is the epitome of feeling. Vulgar opinion has it that Linchuan is not a man of feeling, but I dare not give credence to it.[1]
>
> Zang Maoxun, marginal comment

This aside, observing Du Liniang's manner of exiting the stage after her longest scene with Liu Mengmei (scene 32, "Spectral Vows"), is intriguing for its mention of those who dissented from the view that *Mudan ting*'s heroine, and her creator, are quintessentially motivated by their feelings. *Mudan ting*'s immediate popularity can be attributed, in part, to a preoccupation with the role of the emotions in human life. In the late Ming cult of *qing*, Liniang became an icon of one who is "possessed by feeling" (*chiqing*), and her creator was admired as one of the cult's high priests.[2]

Zang's comment seems disingenuous, given the extent to which he recontextualized Liniang's actions in his adaptation of the play. By the end of this scene in *Huanhun ji*, Liniang has shown her willingness both to die for love and to seek to be reborn for that love, but this commitment rarely entails the sort of angst that Tang Xianzu's heroine repeatedly suffers as she struggles to come to terms with her *qing*. In the case at hand, characteristically, Zang drains "Spectral Vows" of undercurrents of uncertainty and fear that accompany the lovers' conventional pledging of troth. As a result, that convention becomes the governing idea of his scene. Secure in his knowledge of Liniang's social background, Liu Mengmei is unfazed when she reveals that she is a ghost; having extracted Liu's promise to restore her corpse to life, Liniang assures him that such a course of action has the approval of underworld bureaucrats who have issued her a "return-to-life permit" (*huisheng tie*).[3] One change (Liu's lack of fear) is major, the other (the matter of the permit) trivial, but both exemplify an intentness on having the lovers' actions unfold within a context of values and motives that are supernaturally sanctioned and reassuringly familiar.

Several times I have remarked Tang Xianzu's complex handling of the structures and conventions of *chuanqi* drama, among which must be counted his orchestration of the aria sequences that comprise each scene.[4] My analysis of some of them has suggested that they serve to portray Liniang's uniqueness; her *qing*, it seems, is of a different kind from that of the other characters in the play. It is risky to suggest that Tang envisioned a heroine who emerges as an individual in the course of the play, given the associations of "individual" with Western modes of thought, but it does seem that time and again, at key moments, Liniang's experiences and emotions individuate her, setting her apart.

Theodore de Bary has explored the thought of several late Ming Confucians of the Wang Yangming school, in terms of a concern with the self and with the subjectivizing and internalizing of sagehood.[5] The key term here is "subjectivity," an interest in the workings of the mind and distrust of external standards (fame and profit, success in the examinations). Tang Xianzu was identified intellectually with these men, so it should not surprise us that these concerns surface in his plays. Why he chose to explore selfhood through a central female character is something I have not considered heretofore. I can only speculate that using a female character appealed to him because it enabled him to explore ideas of great personal importance—the role of creativity and spontaneity in human experience and relationships, for one—while maintaining a distance from his play's central figure. As previously noted, Tang made no distinction between drama and other forms of poetry as vehicles for self-expression. This set him apart from playwrights such as Shen Jing, Zang Maoxun, and Feng Menglong, who did not recognize such a *raison d'être* for *qu*, at least not for dramatic *qu*.[6]

In Part Two, while pondering how actors performed *Mudan ting*, I have demonstrated how their staging of extracted scenes repeatedly diverged from the original scene design, subverting Tang's subversions of convention. I have also proposed that the formalized conventions of stage depiction and highly elaborated aesthetics of the role categories have compelled a reinterpretation of Liniang's character. The public nature of a performance, and the imperative that characters act within the limits of decorum prescribed for their roles, sat uncomfortably with a play whose central figure is strongly individuated. It comes as no surprise that Liniang's character loses much of its definition and edge in its transition to the stage.

In chapter 5 I speculated about how the long history of *Mudan ting*'s life on the stage exposes enduring cleavages between "highbrow" and "lowbrow" audiences for plays in China, which persist to this day. That said, this study has also revealed how a literati playwright of Feng Menglong's ilk had more in common with actors than he did with a playwright from his own social class, namely, Tang Xianzu. Often enough, we have seen how actors have performed *Mudan ting* in ways first adumbrated in *Fengliu meng*. On a few occasions they have adopted Feng's version of the text; more often, the numerous adjustments made to a scene over time turn out to be in keeping with the spirit of Feng's changes, as when actors have striven to rehabilitate Liu Mengmei's character, enhance Chunxiang's role, and downplay the autonomy of Liniang's dream.

In my first chapter I borrowed the theoretical formulation of Pierre Bourdieu to describe Tang Xianzu as an autonomous producer of plays. While recognizing such autonomous producers, Bourdieu debunks notions of artistic creativity as "pure," that is, as unconstrained by the marketplace or by the institutions and agents who assign economic and symbolic value to cultural works—a process he refers to as "consecration." Artists, even those who produce for a select coterie of fellow artists, operate in a "field" of cultural production that is hierarchically structured and socially institutionalized. Like all cultural producers, they are governed by habits of thinking inculcated at birth and nurtured by circumstances, and although they may see themselves as operating apart from prevailing cultural values, they are nonetheless affected within this field, and the works they produce are subjected to its processes and pressures. In the case of a work that becomes consecrated in turn, this subjection continues long after its author has died. Having demystified the artist as disinterested genius, Bourdieu nonetheless distinguishes artists who disdain commercial success from those who produce within the cultural mainstream. Artists in general "have an interest in disinterestedness," but the disinterest of artists who disdain commercial success takes the form of a "heretical break with the prevailing artistic tradition." They make a bid for autonomy and the authentic experience that comes with nonconformity.[7]

Although the field of cultural production in late Ming China differed in significant ways from the one that Bourdieu has in mind (that of

European bourgeois society in the nineteenth century), his formulations about cultural production usefully apply to an artist like Tang Xianzu, who wrote plays first and foremost for his own pleasure and that of his friends, and who would never have dreamed of profiting commercially from them. Tang did not disdain a larger public's enjoyment of them, but he did disdain those who attempted to set the standards by which they should be appreciated in the greater (unrestricted) cultural field. These were men such as Shen Jing, who had published a manual of model arias for the Kun style of drama, and Zang Maoxun and Feng Menglong, who sought to influence *Mudan ting*'s public meaning as they put their editions of it before the public. Almost certainly with Shen Jing in mind, Tang complained to a friend, "What do they know of the meaning of *qu*? To them the writing of *ci* is only a matter of the nine modes and the four tones."[8]

He compared writing plays to painting landscapes, and advocated a style in which "expansive and unrestrained feelings play beyond brush and ink" (*taidang yinyi zhuan zai bimo zhi wai*).[9] A gifted amateur writing in a culture that honored amateurism, Tang endorsed its ideal of disinterested artistry, and contemporaries saw him in this light, praising his gifts as inimitable and unique.[10]

First commodified in the printed editions of Zang Maoxun and Feng Menglong, *Mudan ting* was subjected to no small amount of "legitimate symbolic violence" at their hands and then as it circulated in the late Ming cultural market and beyond. The forms in which its text have come down to us reflect the tastes of the different markets in which it was reproduced and enjoyed, and its changing meaning must be understood in relation to those markets. Bourdieu exhorts those who work with texts to abandon the arbitrary formalism of strictly internal interpretation and explore instead the "systems of social relations" in which artistic works are produced and used.[11] I have not attempted in this study to situate the many texts of *Mudan ting* within the social setting of Chinese opera and Kun opera in particular. I have not, for example, given much attention to the troupes that performed the play, the venues in which they operated, or the audiences that patronized them.[12] In my readiness to lavish attention on the texts themselves, I have thus presumed a great deal—undoubtedly too much—on my readers' knowledge of the Chinese theatrical scene. But I have not indulged in the kind of strictly internal interpretations that Bourdieu finds subjective and arbitrary. In this regard I hope that this study will contribute, modestly, to a history of Chinese traditional opera that is more attentive to the social circumstances and pressures that influenced both the production of plays and the reception of them.

Bourdieu also remarks that the dynamic of cultural production is driven by struggles that are often expressed as conflicts between the orthodoxy of established traditions and the heretical challenges of new modes of cultural practice. At both the beginning and the end points of this history, I have situated *Mudan ting* in the midst of such conflicting positions. The first of these were being articulated when the play began to circulate. Tang's disdain for rules was unacceptable to playwrights in Suzhou, who were busy codifying Kun opera's prosodic practice and eager to subject his new play to its strictures. One goal of chapters 2 and 3 has been to demonstrate how these critics were bent, no doubt less consciously, on reclaiming the play for the values of orthodox culture, as they understood those values. These two chapters analyze *Mudan ting* in relation not to other plays but to other playwrights; what emerges is a sense of vigorous position-taking, at a time when interest in the theater was high and standards for southern drama were less fixed.

Like Tang Xianzu, Zang Maoxun worked within a restricted field of production, but his position was at the opposite extreme, since he published editions of plays for wealthy connoisseurs and was very much occupied with questions of orthodoxy—what Bourdieu refers to as "the question of the criteria defining the legitimate exercise of a certain type of cultural practice."[13] This was true of Shen Jing and Feng Menglong as well. All three men felt strongly that the Kunshan style of southern drama was the only correct one (the *zhengti*), and all of them held other playwrights to the standards they were instrumental in explicitly defining. Bourdieu's theory suggests that a good deal of the dynamism of cultural production—what leads to the creation and consecration of new "classic" works over time—emanates from the restricted field of production, what others would label "elite" culture, as a result of tensions generated when standards become set and some producers resist them. The late Ming was a dynamic period in the history of *chuanqi* drama, and the reception of *Mudan ting* exposes the taking of positions that was part of that dynamism.

At the other end of this history, I have situated the recent North American productions of *Mudan ting* amidst other positions that are in dynamic tension. Peter Sellars's avant-garde staging, and Chen Shi-Zheng's historically self-conscious recreation of a Ming performance are motivated by distinct ideas of what modern theater can be in a global culture. Their interpretations have provoked position-taking in turn by those who have seen them in China and in "the West." This is a subject for another book, and I will make only a few observations here. Sellars is a committed internationalist when it comes to cultural production. At the "Critics Circle" symposium in Berkeley, a questioner asked him to explain what he thought he had kept of the traditional way of performing Kun opera. He responded by first noting that tradition is larger than one person or point of view and that any production of a work is one step in a process of making the tradition new. In this century theatrical traditions, in this case Kun opera, have lost their dynamism and become frozen, particularly within their constituted fields (here, China). In Sellars's view, cultural perspectives can no longer be confined within national boundaries; culture is created by intersection and interaction. He and his collaborators—one a master interpreter within the Kun opera tradition living in Los Angeles, the other a composer classically trained in China and based in New York—are "having a discussion across cultural and generational lines, and trying to have it at a level where the intersection is one of mutual respect."

Chen Shi-Zheng, like Tan Dun trained in China but now based in New York, is also a cultural producer working in a global environment, and like Sellars he is interested in intercultural productions of classical works. But his staging of *Mudan ting* made use of a variety of traditional Chinese performance arts, eschewed intercultural eclecticism in favor of intracultural borrowings, and avoided the contemporary touches that are the hallmark of Peter Sellars's directing style.[14] As one critic has noted, his production "attempts to feel authentic rather than be authentic," by recreating the complete play "in a manner both true to its origins, yet meaningful to a modern audience."[15]

What these two directors share, on the other hand, are critics from within the relatively closed world of Kun opera who defend the traditional way in which the play has been staged and regard both North American productions as unacceptable—for audiences in China at least, and in Chen Shi-Zheng's case for audiences outside China as well. According to their public rhetoric, these latter-day guardians of orthodoxy have been deeply dismayed at the innovations of directors working outside their tradition, and their response has been, on the whole, defensive. It remains to be seen what impact these productions will ultimately have, but it seems safe to say that the traditional way of performing Kun operas in China has come unstuck as a result of them, in the case of *Mudan ting* at least. This is evident from the decision of the Chinese cultural authorities to commission a new production of the play by the Shanghai troupe. It is unlikely that this would have happened but for the challenges thrown out by Sellars and Chen.[16]

The pairings of Zang Maoxun and Feng Menglong and of Peter Sellars and Chen Shi-Zheng reflect other positionings within their respective cultural fields. Zang and Sellars, in their very different ways, have produced within a restricted field, and presume both sophistication and knowledge in their audiences. Feng and Chen operate within a more expansive field, attempting to make a complex and difficult play accessible by borrowing techniques from popular performed genres. Zang and Sellars fall on the elite/highbrow side of the cultural divide; Feng and Chen belong on the popular/middlebrow side—as far as directorial styles are concerned.[17] If we take interpretations into account, positions become more difficult to encapsulate neatly. From our vantage point and in retrospect, Sellars has broken less decisively with traditional interpretations of the play, since he has emphasized the love theme and kept Tang's crudity and humor largely off the stage. Chen Shi-Zheng, by contrast, has embraced the comedy in the text, exaggerating it at times with techniques of slapstick humor and farce, and has darkened the play's lyricism by giving full attention to Tang's sometimes biting social and political commentary. Sellars's interpretation also breaks new ground, darkening the depiction of the love story by bringing out a spooky and wild side of Liniang's character in the scenes where she wanders as a ghost in Part Two. Chinese officials who have seen his production have doubted that it can be performed in China in its present form, and Chen is regarded as a heretic in Shanghai, paradoxically for recapturing the full range of the original play.[18]

Occupying the long middle stretch of Kun opera's history as a fully theatrical art are the professional actors. Their impact on *Mudan ting*'s onstage history is registered in the texts of *zhezixi*, beginning with the late Ming miscellany *Zuiyi qing*, which was printed in Suzhou in the Chongzhen period, and culminating in the Qianlong collections *Zhui baiqiu* and *Shenyin jiangu lu*.[19] In chapters 4 and 5 I have paid fleeting attention to the different settings in which these professional artists operated—private households, tea and winehouses, urban theaters, native place associations. I have also stressed their agency as "second-stage creators," facilitated by the dwindling involvement of literati as playwrights in the production of theatrical culture after the Manchu conquest. What I would like to consider here, however, is the lingering cultural agency of literati in their role as *piaoyou,* and to ask to what extent their tastes and values have shaped interpretations of *zhezixi* from *Mudan ting.*

I have been struck with the degree of conformity to dominant Confucian values found in these texts and the censoring of nonconformist elements from the original playtext. Such a response is already evident in Zang Maoxun and Feng Menglong's adaptations of the whole play, and it was carried further, incrementally, by actors in the *zhezixi* extracted from the play. On its surface, this seems counterintuitive. Would not actors, positioned differently in the Qing social world than were the literati, find meanings in the play that differed from those found by the likes of Zang and Feng? Bourdieu exhorts us to consider systems of social relations when working with texts[20]—how is this to be done in the case at hand?

First, it should be noted that my survey of miscellanies in chapters 4 and 5 does indicate that shifts in subject matter took place in the tradition of performing *zhezixi*: from scenes that featured lyricism, singing, and dance ("The Interrupted Dream," "Pursuing the Dream," "The Portrait," "The Portrait Recovered," "Union in the Shades") to scenes that offered spectacle ("Infernal Judgment," "Interrogation Under the Rod," "Reunion at Court"), possibilities for comedy ("In Search of the Master," "The Schoolroom," even "The Portrait Examined") and ritual display ("Speed the Plough," "Keening"). Several *zhezixi* from the last two groups appear only in the Qianlong era collections, and crop up more and more frequently in subsequent collections. As I proposed in chapter 4, this shift in taste reflects a response by actors to pressures from more popular styles of opera. The newly favored extracts also reflect the impact of the increasingly specialized role system in Qing dynasty troupes. The twelve *zhezixi* from *Mudan ting* in *Zhui baiqiu xinji hebian* are vehicles for all of the major role categories (*sheng, dan, jing, chou*), not just the *sheng* and *dan* roles favored in late Ming *zhezixi*. This amounts to a diversification of the play's social tapestry, presumably in response to the interests of the more socially diverse Qing audience.

Bourdieu himself notes that drama, as an artistic genre, differs from poetry and the novel in the time scale of its transformations. Because of drama's tendency to remain "ever green" (i.e., ever popular with the public even when its subject matter has become dated), aesthetic revolutions take place only slowly, at least prior to the development of avant-garde theater. Bourdieu attributes theater's relative imperviousness to innovation to a "closed network" of critics and consecrated authors who are deployed to frustrate "pretentious *parvenus*." He also finds complicity in the theatrical world—between producers and clients, playwrights and audiences—such that the fundamental values of mainstream culture are affirmed. Theater, in Europe at least, "most directly experiences the sanctions of the bourgeois public, with its values and conformisms."[21]

His case for the ideological conservatism of classical drama can be made for China as well, especially when, as here, we are concerned with a national style as opposed to a regional one. In the hierarchy of styles specific to drama, Kun opera is at the apex, and as the "crown jewel" of its repertoire, *Mudan ting* has canonical status. Moreover, drama in China has always been valued by the ruling elite—and not just by government authorities—for its educational and socializing functions. Inculcation of fundamental Confucian values clearly was one of Feng Menglong's aims as an editor and publisher of plays, and that aim is clearly reflected in his adaptation of *Mudan ting*.[22] In contemporary China such thinking about the theater's *raison d'être* is slowly giving ground, but only in experimental forms such as spoken drama and in regional styles that are popular but have relatively low prestige, such as Subei opera in Shanghai. In the case of Kun opera, as the experience of the Lincoln Center production makes clear, actors and troupes are hardly free agents when it comes to producing new versions of classic plays.[23]

But what about the period extending back in time, from 1949 into the late Qing period and earlier? In the absence of playwrights to connive with audiences,[24] what was the relationship of Kun actors with their public? This is impossible to determine from texts alone, and my reliance on textual evidence, much of which cannot be adequately contextualized, seriously limits me. I will confine myself to general observations about the creative environment in the culture of Kun opera and consider factors that I feel go some way towards explaining the ideological conformism evident in the *zhezixi* from *Mudan ting*.

Chapters 4 and 5 have documented an actors' takeover of *Mudan ting*, and when suggesting reasons for this shift in creativity from playwrights to actors, I have relied on the work of Chinese historians of Kun opera. Since writing these chapters, I have come across observations made with respect to other arts (notably painting), which suggest parallels with respect to the creative environment of the theater. Writing about the culture of painting, Robert Hegel notes that there was a great deal of social integration in the visual arts, especially during the Wanli period of the Ming dynasty. Literati amateurs and professional painters collaborated across boundaries of status, and common use was made by them of styles, motifs, and composition techniques, such that it was not always possible to draw clear distinctions between the work of the two groups. Both kinds of artist recycled and skillfully varied the same "motivic vocabulary," and they made common use of a single set of conventional elements.[25]

Hegel's observations about the culture of painting resonate with the culture of the theater during the transition from the Ming to the Qing dynasties, especially when it comes to performances of *zhezixi*. Professional actors worked with a motivic vocabulary that they had inherited from *chuanqi* plays written by the literati, and their performances were appreciated for the skill with which they executed and manipulated this vocabulary. Like painters, actors drew on a repository of common subjects and techniques and worked collaboratively. The guild system of commercial troupes can be compared to that for professional painters, especially journeymen painters who had little formal education. Like the literati amateur, the professional painter copied models handed down to him through masters, "re-creating the same sanctioned images endlessly" and parroting the ideology that had been assigned to the consecrated models.[26] Hegel finds the critical distinction between amateur and professional to be their respective levels of education. When the painter's educational level was low, his adherence to convention was high. Iconoclasm and unrestrained representation were the prerogatives of the literati amateur; the professional's relationship to the authority inherent in his models was acquiescent.[27]

This notion of the ideological conformism may help to explain the interpretations of Tang's play that are encoded in *zhezixi*. As my discussion demonstrates, the polishing and embellishing they underwent reveals how actors seized on what was conventionally familiar in Tang's text and ignored or erased what was not.[28] Second-stage creativity opened up a gap between the extracted scenes and the text that Tang had authored because the actors imitated the type-forms of drama obediently, where Tang had done so iconoclastically. The gap was more significant here than for the landscape painters that Hegel discusses because differences in educational level between Ming literati playwrights and

Qing professional actors were great, whereas differences in the cultural level of amateur and professional painters were often not as clear. In the case of Kun opera, these differences become more and more significant as we move through the Qing dynasty and into the present century, when they begin again to recede. In the late Ming, when *chuanqi* plays by the literati were written for performance in private households, the creative environment for Kun opera more closely approximated the one that Hegel has described for painting, and collaborations between the playwright and his actors were more often possible.[29]

Another factor in the equation are the *piaoyou*, who have ever been more than simply fans of Kun opera. They are its self-appointed conservators, and their impact on its traditions—as least the textual dissemination of them—has been considerable. Inasmuch as the late Ming adaptors of *Mudan ting* were motivated, at least in part, by commercial concerns, they should not be counted as *piaoyou*. But they were positioned between the amateur lovers of pure singing and the professional actors who brought plays to the stage, so they catered to the needs and interests of both groups. In the early reigns of the Qing dynasty, Kun opera's *piaoyou* recede from view, but many of the extant miscellanies of *zhezixi* that date from this period reveal their tastes and interests. With the publication of popular editions of *Zhui baiqiu* during the Qianlong reign, the combined influence of actors and *piaoyou* is evident, both in printed editions of *zhezixi* and in manuscript copies. By the final years of the Qing period, enjoyment of *zhezixi* by both amateurs and professionals had converged. Regardless of who produced them, few manuscripts of *zhezixi* from *Mudan ting* diverge significantly from the versions disseminated in *Zhui baiqiu*. There was little turning back to the original author's text.

When interest in the original full text of the play was revived by directors working outside the tradition, reaction among *piaoyou* both in Shanghai and abroad was largely critical. At the "Critics Circle" panel convened in Berkeley during performances of the Sellars production in March of 1999, audience members familiar with Kun opera complained that the traditional forms were insufficiently highlighted. Mark Swed, a Los Angeles-based music critic, found it necessary to point out that the production was not a revival of a Kun opera, but an example of contemporary American theater. In the case of the Lincoln Center production, I suspect that *piaoyou* discontent played a part in the demise of the original production. Many of them are retired cadres who maintain close ties to the officials in the Bureau of Culture in Shanghai who stopped the show. As the months of open rehearsals went by, and Chen Shi-Zheng's ideas became clearer, might not dissatisfactions expressed by them have alarmed those officials?[30]

Since the turn of the twentieth century, it has been *piaoyou*, in their capacity as club members and academic experts, who have been active at every stage of efforts to maintain Kun opera's economic viability. In the 1920s *piaoyou* bankrolled the training of the "Chuan" generation of Kun opera actors, each of whom was given a stage name that began with that character, since it was hoped that through them the tradition would be preserved and transmitted. Since that time *piaoyou* have published numerous collections of *zhezixi* in forms that are easier to learn than those that use *gongche* notation. In the 1950s and 1960s *piaoyou* sometimes had a hand in writing scripts or consulted on productions of new plays. Professional Kun opera actors regularly sang together with them in singing clubs (*qushe*) and the practice of performing together outside the clubs is reviving. The influence of amateurs has always been a factor in Kun opera's history, and in the past century it has been large.[31]

Chen Shi-Zheng, for one, does not find this situation to be a healthy one, artistically speaking. He feels that in such an environment actors become subservient to the tastes and interests of their patrons. He personally finds this demeaning for the actor, and his distaste for *piaoyou*, and for the practice of performing plays as *zhezixi*, must have been obvious during the extended rehearsal period in Shanghai. Like Sellars, Chen feels that this way of staging Kun operas is moribund, and he attributes to lingering *piaoyou* influence the rigid adherence to formalized movements in this tradition. That influence has made it very difficult for actors to attempt something new that might capture the interest of a wider audience.[32]

Chen voices these opinions as an outsider to Kun opera, but as one familiar with the artistic environment for traditional theater in China. Two actors from an earlier generation, to whom I have occasionally referred, are Mei Lanfang and Yu Zhenfei. Both men made their living as Beijing opera actors, but had a large presence in the Kun opera world as well. Mei learned approximately thirty *zhezixi* for Kun opera and is credited with introducing many new ideas and techniques when performing them that subsequently have been adoped by Kun opera actors. Yu Zhenfei began as an amateur performer of Kun opera and made the difficult, and rare, transition to professional status as a Beijing opera actor. Neither Mei's memoirs nor accounts of Yu Zhenfei's career by Yu himself and others suggest that either man felt constrained in his dealings with *piaoyou*. What the memoirs and biographies richly reveal is a great deal of give and take between them. Since late Qing times at least, the boundary between professional performers and *piaoyou* has been porous, and complicity between them, in Bourdieu's sense, most likely considerable.

It would not invariably have been this way. Actors surely have found ways to resist the ideological tug of *zhezixi* in ways that were complicit with the tastes of other segments of their audience. One glimpses moments of such complicity in novels,[33] in anecdotal accounts of performances,[34] and, occasionally, in stage memoirs. Tang Baoxiang's biography of Yu Zhenfei, based on the actor's reminiscences about his long career, recounts a performance of "Duanqiao" ("Broken Bridge," from the early Qing opera *Leifeng ta* [Thunder Peak Pagoda]), which Yu gave just after he had returned to China in 1955 after a prolonged sojourn in Hong Kong. He found himself sharply criticized for his "overly explicit [*lu*], overly slick [*you*]" depiction of the male lead, and his critics attributed these shortcomings to the years he had spent catering to the tastes of Hong Kong audiences. In this passing mention of postwar Hong Kong's unhealthy environment for actors, one glimpses a theatrical culture that must have also flourished in pre-Liberation China.[35] In his reminiscences to Tang Baoxiang, Yu credited the "wholesome environment" (*lianghao de huanjing*) of post-Liberation China with elevating his artistry as a performer, but we should remember that it is on the pre-Liberation career that his fame rests. While Yu himself began as a *piaoyou*, his entry into the ranks of professional actors after his father's death appears to have influenced his acting in ways that required correction in the puritanical artistic environment of post-Liberation China.[36]

Accounts such as this one remind us that an actor's interpretation of a text can go with a scene's apparent ideological thrust or against it. The analysis of the schoolroom scene from *Mudan ting* given in chapter 5 suggested how an actor's portrayal of Chunxiang could take mischief to the point of insurgency. In "Broken Bridge," Yu's portrayal of Xu Xian's efforts to win back his wife's affections apparently brought out a seductive (*fengliu*) urbanity implicit in the character and in the scene, which was deemed unsuitable for performances in revolutionary China. On the other hand Yue Meiti, Yu's disciple, has written of her distaste for such salacious portrayals of young male leads and has described her efforts to correct this in her own performances.[37] Her choices doubtless have much to do with the ideological climate of post-Liberation China, as well as with her own temperament and gender. Yu Zhenfei, a ladies' man offstage, brought out the erotically provocative side of the characters he played onstage, when opportunity offered.[38]

Roger Chartier has proposed that it is useful, when thinking about cultural practices, to consider the complex relations between cultural models that have been imposed more or less forcibly and practices that are sometimes restrained but at other times permitted to blossom. Influenced by the work of both de Certeau and Bourdieu, and addressing current thinking about popular culture in Europe, he suggests that

> [W]e should assume that a gap existed between the norm and real-life experience, between injunction and practice, and between the sense intended and the sense constructed—a gap into which reformulations and procedures for avoidance could flow.[39]

This leads him to a critique of Lawrence Levine's model of American culture, which as we have seen opposes an earlier period of exuberant assimilation to more recent times, when culture has become bifurcated and elites have retreated, rejecting much of the public culture as beyond the pale of serious forms. Chartier feels that this model oversimplifies because it finds too much homogeneity in the shared public culture and makes distinctions between legitimate and disqualified culture that are too watertight.[40]

Criticisms such as these make me uncomfortably aware of the degree to which I have relied on Lu Eting's formulation of the relationship between elite and popular forms in Kun opera. I have found this formulation to be a useful one from which to begin thinking about the strategies that adaptors and performers used when they appropriated Tang's text. When I mentioned Lu Eting's formulation to Chen Shi-Zheng, however, he dismissed Lu's distinctions as less then useful. For him, all cultural forms are equally legitimate; therefore why employ such labels? While I understand Chen's point, I stand by my use of them here, because attention to how different forms of language and different staging techniques have been used to interpret this one play has illuminated Tang Xianzu's distinctiveness. That distinctiveness has often been misunderstood, as the various appropriations of *Mudan ting* examined here make clear. More than once, I have been astonished at the interpretive chasm that opened over the centuries between Tang's *Mudan ting* and the play now canonized in "the tradition."

Tang Xianzu's uniqueness, recognized in his own time, is thus confirmed by the fate of his most famous play. The theater absorbed *Mudan ting* and in so doing altered its chemistry and composition. As a result, the play was not only simplified but also divested of a good portion of its mystery. That said, I must in closing distinguish Kun and other actors from the "directorial" Ming adapters in one vital respect. Feng Menglong and Zang Maoxun, when reworking the *text* of the play, sought not only to "fix" its prosody but also to rationalize its plot. In Feng's case especially, he did this so thoroughly that his Du Liniang has little about her that perplexes and hence enchants. Such is not the case for the actor, who can bring his or her mystique to bear on the performance of the character. My discussion of performances of Du Liniang by modern actors has suggested how they have kept faith with the beauty and complexity ("involutions") of Liniang's finely tuned emotions as portrayed in the original text. One reason for this is that actors have generally respected the lyrics Tang wrote for the arias, which is where the play's subjective intensity is generated. In the late Ming adaptations, much of the denaturing of Tang's text takes place in the rewritten arias.

In dwelling on the complexity of *Mudan ting*'s design and the paradox of its popularity, I have paid too little attention to the simple fact of the play's appeal when performed. Lovers of Kun opera in China frequently speak of its special charm, a charm I felt upon first seeing a performance of the "whole play" in 1983, starring Hua Wenyi and Yue Meiti.[41] In 1995 I returned to Shanghai and saw a performance of "Wandering in the Garden, Startled by a Dream" by Qian Yi, who at eighteen was the right age for the part and impressed me then as having a lovely voice. Seated to my left were two girls of about twelve, who sang along to Liniang's garden-strolling arias. How much they understood of what they were singing I cannot say; most likely they were simply caught up in the "fog" of the music. But seeing them absorbed in their enjoyment of Qian Yi's performance, I witnessed the play working its magic at first hand.

Appendix A

System of Roles for *Chuanqi* Drama and Kun Opera[1]

Sheng: Dignified male characters

1. *Chuanqi* drama

   A. ***Sheng***: Liu Mengmei (*MDT, HHJ, FLM*).[2] Plays the leading male character, typically young, kind, and refined, or handsome and urbane; paired with the *dan*.

   B. ***Xiaosheng***: Miao Shunbin (*HHJ, FLM*); military official (*FLM*); interpreter (*HHJ, FLM*). Plays the secondary male character; can be either young or old; when young, paired with the *xiaodan*.

2. Kun opera

   A. ***Laosheng***: Chen Zuiliang (*SYJGL*).[3] Plays older male characters; wears a beard and typically plays a character of high (official) status. By late Qing times the *wai* role (part of the *mo* category in Ming times) was absorbed as a subdivision of the *laosheng* role.

   B. ***Xiaosheng***: Liu Mengmei (*ZBQ, SYJGL*), Chen Zuiliang (*ZBQ*).[4] Plays young male characters; by the Republican period, further divided by actors into four subcategories: 1) ***jinsheng*** ("turbaned" *sheng*), also known as ***shanzisheng*** ("fan-carrying" *sheng*); 2) ***shamaosheng*** ("gauze-capped" *sheng*); 3) ***guansheng*** ("official-capped" *sheng*); 4) ***zhiweisheng*** ("pheasant-tailed" *sheng*).

   C. ***Sheng***: Chen Zuiliang (*ZBQ, SYJGL*).[5] Sometimes designated *zhengsheng*; also depicts older male characters of dignified status.

Dan: Female characters

1. *Chuanqi* drama

   A. ***Dan***: Du Liniang (*MDT, HHJ, FLM, ZBQ*).[6] Principal female character. An educated, nobly bred, and chaste woman, who is paired with the *sheng*. Should excel in looks, singing, and dancing skills. The character need not be young but often is.

   B. ***Tiedan***, or simply ***tie***: Chunxiang (*MDT, HHJ, FLM*); Yang Po (*HHJ*); Daoist nun (*MDT, FLM*); civil official (*MDT, HHJ*); interpreter (*MDT*);

Big Sister Wang (*MDT*). The next most important female character. Paired with the *xiaosheng*, but also supports the principal female character. Often youthful, but the *tie* actor also depicts older women in some plays.

C. ***Xiaodan*** or ***zhengdan***: Not used in *MDT*, *HHJ*, and *FLM*. Both portray youthful characters; the *zhengdan* excels in looks, acting skills and singing, while the *xiaodan* portrays vivacious and lively characters younger than those portrayed by the *zhengdan*, including sometimes young boys.

D. ***Laodan***: Madam Du (*MDT*, *HHJ*, *FLM*); military official (*MDT*); rebel sentry (*MDT*); Jin envoy (*MDT*). Older women other than the principal and secondary female characters; in some plays ugly male characters are also assigned to this role (here, the Jin envoy).

E. ***Hundan***: Du Liniang's ghost (*MDT*, *HHJ*). The *hundan* is costumed and moves in ways that suggest ghostliness.

2. Kun opera

A. ***Xiaodan***: Du Liniang (*SYJGL*). The principal female character; referred to by actors as the ***guimendan*** ("boudoir" *dan*). Portrays chaste, elegant, and "quiet" (*jing*) young women of good family and dignified bearing. Must have a good singing voice and expressive acting skills. Unlike her counterpart in Beijing opera, the *xiaodan* in Kun opera can wear colorful costumes, but not as brightly colorful as those for the *tiedan*.

B. ***Tiedan***, or simply ***tie***: Chunxiang (*ZBQ*, *SYJGL*). Sometimes referred to by actors as the ***huadan*** ("flower" *dan*) or ***fengyuedan*** ("wind and moon" *dan*). Depicts lively young women of a naive and romantic type, cute and immature compared to the *xiaodan*.

C. ***Laodan***: Madam Du (*ZBQ*, *SYJGL*); soldier (*ZBQ*). Same as for *chuanqi* drama.

Jing: A miscellaneous category, largely but not exclusively male.

1. *Chuanqi* drama

A. ***Jing***: Hu Panguan (*MDT*, *HHJ*, *FLM*); military official (*MDT*, *HHJ*, *FLM*); Camel Guo (*MDT*, *FLM*); jailer (*MDT*, *HHJ*); colonel (*MDT*, *HHJ*); Li Quan (*MDT*, *FLM*); Miao Shunbin (*MDT*); Sister Stone (*MDT*); Jin Emperor (*MDT*); Jin envoy (*HHJ*); boatman (*HHJ*); privy councilor (*HHJ*); rebel sentry (*HHJ*); gatekeeper at Du Bao's court in Huai'an (*FLM*). This role typically plays the principal villain, but also other minor characters,

B. ***Fujing***, also ***xiaojing***: Zang assigns Sister Stone and the Huashen to the *fujing*; Feng assigns several characters to the *xiaojing*: Scabby Turtle, military official, boatman, old female servant, Jin envoy. Second in importance after the *jing*; this actor plays other male characters and, in some plays, old female characters of menial status.

2, Kun opera

A. ***Jing***: Camel Guo (*ZBQ*, *SYJGL*); Hu Panguan (*ZBQ*, *SYJGL*); palace guard (*ZBQ*). More positive characters are assigned in some plays to the ***zhengjing***, whose voice must be high and strong. Villains and traitors are assigned to the ***baijing***, who wears distinctive white make-up.

B. ***Fujing***, or simply ***fu***: Sister Stone (*SYJGL*). Similar to *chuanqi*'s *fujing*.

Mo: Another miscellaneous category

1. *Chuanqi* drama

Chuanqi playwrights used five designations, two of which occur in these texts:

A. ***Mo***: Chen Zuiliang (*MDT*, *HHJ*, *FLM*); Huashen (*MDT*, *FLM*); civil official (*HHJ*); privy councilor (*HHJ*, *FLM*). Reciting the prologue is a specialty of this role, but other characters (eunuchs, young scholars, officials, immortals, etc.) are played by this actor.

B. ***Wai***: Du Bao (*MDT*, *HHJ*, *FLM*); privy councilor (*MDT*); boatman (*MDT*); rebel sentry (*MDT*, *HHJ*). Tends to portray older males, but younger characters are also sometimes assigned to this role.

2. Kun opera

Same as for *chuanqi*:

A. ***Mo***: Miao Shunbin (*ZBQ*, *SYJGL*); Chen Zuiliang (*ZBQ*);[7] Huashen (*ZBQ*, *SYJGL*).

B. ***Wai***: Du Bao (*ZBQ*, *SYJGL*).

Chou: Humorous characters

1. *Chuanqi* drama

A. ***Chou***: Han Zicai (*MDT*, *FLM*); herdboy (*MDT*, *HHJ*); gardener's lad (*MDT*, *FLM*); Yang Po (*MDT*, *FLM*); Sister Stone (*HHJ*, *FLM*); military official (*MDT*, *FLM*); innkeeper at Huai'an (*MDT*); gatekeeper at Du Bao's court in Huai'an (*MDT*, *HHJ*); turnkey in jail at Huai'an (*MDT*, *HHJ*); Scabby Turtle (*MDT*); colonel (*MDT*); Lali (*HHJ*); Li Quan (*HHJ*). Portrays a wide range of characters; if villainous, neither the chief villain nor the most treacherous and evil character in the play.

2. Kun opera

A. ***Chou***: Scabby Turtle (*ZBQ*); herdboy (*ZBQ*, *SYJGL*); palace guard (*ZBQ*, *SYJGL*); soldier (*ZBQ*, *SYJGL*).

Kun opera playtexts use one designation, "*chou*," but distinctions are made between civil and military types.

Appendix B

Scene Summaries for Complete Texts of *Mudan ting*

Translations of *Mudan ting* (*MDT*) scene titles follow Cyril Birch (*PP*); for Zang's (*HHJ*) and Feng's (*FLM*) versions of the scenes, the scene number and number of arias are separated by a slash. When the *HHJ* and/or *FLM* scene titles are the same or functionally the same, I do not repeat the Chinese. An asterisk after a scene number for *HHJ* or *FLM* indicates that the scene either does not occur in *MDT* or occurs "out of order" with reference to its place in *MDT*.

Scene 1

"Legend" (Biaomu), 1 aria; *HHJ* 0/1:[1] "Opening" (Kaichang); *FLM* 1/1: "Prologue Overview" (Jiamen dayi).

The *mo*[2] actor assumes the voice of the author, then rehearses briefly the events of the play. *HHJ* adds dialogue between the *mo* and an actor offstage after the aria.

Scene 2

"Declaring Ambition" (Yanhuai), 2 arias; *HHJ* 1/2: "Declaring Ambition"; *FLM* 2/6: "Two Friends Declare Ambition" (Eryou yanhuai).

Liu Mengmei (*sheng*), courtesy name Chunqing (Spring Lord), at twenty has not yet made a name for himself and lives on the sale of fruit from the family orchard. He once dreamt of a girl standing beneath a plum tree who told him, "I am the one you must meet to set foot on your road to love and high office." After waking from this dream he changed his name to Mengmei (Dreams of Plum). He hopes both to succeed in the imperial examinations and meet the girl of his dream. First he will visit his friend and fellow student, Han Zicai.

HHJ omits Liu's mention of his servant, Camel Guo (Guo Tuo), and friend Han Zicai. *FLM* eliminates reference to Liu's dream and shifts the change of name to after Liniang has had her dream. Feng augments the scene by folding in portions of Tang's scene 6, retaining the gist of the interview between Liu and Han Zicai depicted there, but suppressing Han's account of Han Yu's amorous escapades after he was banished to Guangzhou and the Emperor Gaozu's contemptuous treatment of scholars at the Han court.

Scene 3

"Admonishing the Daughter" (Xun nü), 10 arias; *HHJ* 2/6: "Admonishing the Daughter"; *FLM* 3/5: "Du Bao Admonishes his Daughter" (Du Gong xun nü).

Liniang (*dan*) wishes blessings on her parents. Du Bao (*wai*) laments the lack of a son and is displeased when he learns that his daughter naps during the day. He and Madam Du (*laodan*) desire that Liniang gain some knowledge of the *Book of Rites*, and the decision is made to engage a tutor.

FLM has Du Bao insist on finding a tutor for his daughter; Madam Du's priority is to find her a husband.

Scene 4

"Pedant's Lament" (Fu tan), 3 arias; *HHJ* and *FLM*: see under scene 5.

Chen Zuiliang (*mo*) has failed the imperial examination fifteen times in forty-five years, and his stipend has been cut off. His name means "Chen So Good," but he has come to be known as "Chen No Food." He gets by working in an herb shop started by his grandfather. But his luck is about to change: he has been summoned to an interview with Du Bao, who is seeking a tutor for his daughter.

Scene 5

"Engaging the Tutor" (Yan shi), 6 arias; *HHJ* 3/10: "Engaging the Tutor"; *FLM* 4/8: "Engaging the Tutor in the Official Residence" (Guanshe yan shi).

Court having adjourned for the day, Du Bao receives Chen Zuiliang. He summons his daughter, who enters obedient and demure, accompanied by her maid Chunxiang (Spring Fragrance, *tie*). Du Bao cautions Tutor Chen to watch Chunxiang, lest she misbehave.

HHJ, combining portions of scenes 4, 5, and 7, suppresses Chen's pedantry and failed ambitions and moves briskly to the schoolroom scene after an abbreviated interview with Du Bao. Zang suppresses funny business between the tutor and Chunxiang, and at the end of the scene Liniang indicates that she will visit the garden at the first opportunity. The flower vendor's cry at scene's end is cut since scene 9 ("Sweeping the Garden"), which it anticipates, is cut. *FLM*, combining and abridging scenes 4 and 5, presents Chen's failed ambitions more sympathetically and amplifies his interview with Du Bao, presenting both men in a warm light (Du Bao is more sensitive to nature, Chen less blind to his inadequacies). Feng adds dialogue between the lines of arias that Liniang and Du Bao sing as she is introduced to the tutor.

Scene 6

"Despairing Hopes" (Chang tiao), 4 arias; *HHJ*: cut; *FLM*: cut.

Liu Mengmei visits Han Zicai (*chou*) at the temple of his illustrious ancestor, Han Yu. He complains that their talents have gone unrecognized. Han suggests that Liu seek the patronage of Miao Shunbin, Imperial Commissioner for the Examination of Gems.

Scene 7

"The Schoolroom" (Guishu), 5 arias; *HHJ*: see under scene 5; *FLM* 5/7: "Teaching the Classic and Practicing Calligraphy" (Chuanjing xizi).

As Chen Zuiliang conducts a lesson on the *Shijing*, Chunxiang is mischievous, then bored, and asks to be excused. After she relieves herself in the family's garden, she continues to provoke the tutor and snatches his bramble switch when he tries to beat her. Liniang reproves her, but after the tutor leaves them, she asks Chunxiang about the garden.

FLM gives Chunxiang a higher profile in this scene, by having her come onstage first.[3] Chen's pedantry is toned down, and the tutor and Liniang share an aria that expresses orthodox views ("Only when a correct mind guides the brush / is one then a true calligrapher").

Scene 8

"Speed the Plough" (Quan nong), 11 arias; *HHJ* 4/6: "Speed the Plough"; *FLM*: cut.

Du Bao visits the village of Qingle (Pure Joy) and is greeted by processions of singing villagers (elders, farmers, a herdboy, and women presenting mulberry and tea leaves). He praises the "rich and muddy" plots and urges the peasants on in their labors. After dispensing flower garlands and wine to all, he departs.

HHJ cuts one aria sung by the elders and one by the tea pickers. Zang adds dialogue and joking by the elders to end the scene.

Scene 9

"Sweeping the Garden" (Su yuan), 7 arias; *HHJ*: cut; *FLM* 6/3: "Chunxiang Sweeps the Garden" (Chunxiang su yuan).

Chunxiang reports that her mistress at first indignantly rejected her suggestion that she amuse herself in the garden, but changed her mind when she learned that her father is out in his district. Enroute to order the garden swept Chunxiang runs into the tutor, who disapproves of the garden visit but does nothing to stop it; instead, he cancels classes. She next engages a drunken gardener's lad (Xiaohualang, *chou*) in dialogue laced with sexual innuendo, before delivering her mistress's order to sweep the garden.

FLM eliminates the tutor and begins with the gardener's lad. He describes a beautiful garden, which the Prefect Du Bao seldom visits. Chunxiang's entrance aria and dialogue are kept, but her dialogue with the gardener's lad is cleaned up. When he suggests that they take "a little tumble," she indignantly rebuffs him.

Scene 10

"The Interrupted Dream" (Jingmeng), 12 arias; *HHJ* 5/7: "Wandering in the Garden" (Youyuan); *FLM* 7/13: "Spring Feelings Perceived in a Dream" (Meng gan chunqing).

Liniang makes herself up before her mirror, then emerges from her chamber with Chunxiang to visit the garden, bashful that others might glimpse her beauty. Confronted with the garden's decaying splendor, she hopes that she herself may bloom, and laments that the flowers are buried in a deserted place that no one visits. Back in her rooms she frets that her life is passing unfulfilled and asks "where to reveal my true desires?" Falling asleep, she meets a handsome young scholar, whose spirit has been drawn into her dream. He makes love to her in a rock grotto, until they are interrupted by the Huashen (Flower Spirit, *mo*), who witnesses their lovemaking. Madam Du comes to Liniang's room, wakes her, and scolds her for napping. After Madam leaves Liniang recalls the dream and weeps because of longings left unfulfilled.

HHJ begins with dialogue by Chunxiang taken from scene 9. Zang cuts five arias from this scene, including *Zui fu gui* (in which Liniang boasts of her beauty) and *Shanpo yang* and *Bao lao cui* (which contain erotically exposed language). He reassigns the Huashen to the *fujing* role, and eliminates the mid-scene Coda. He cuts Madam Du, concluding with Liniang's ruminations about her dream. *FLM* replaces key arias *(Haojiejie, Bao lao cui)* with others written in simpler language (*Yipen hua*) or in language less exposed erotically (*Wuban yi*). Liu and Liniang make love beneath the plum tree rather than in the grotto; after Liu departs the scene ends quickly, with a rewritten speech and a rewritten aria for Liniang, in which she ponders the handsome lover of her dream and their connection from a former life. Feng rewrites more extensively the scene's second half. As with *HHJ*, Madam Du does not appear.

Scene 11

"Well-Meant Warning" (Cijie), 2 arias; *HHJ*: cut; *FLM*: cut.

Madam Du, alarmed by her daughter's listlessness and learning that it has been caused by a visit to the garden, interrogates Chunxiang, then issues orders that Liniang is to remain indoors at her embroidery or her books. The garden is too vast and deserted a place for a young girl to visit.

(*HHJ* 6*: see scene 21.)

(*FLM* 8*/5: "The Lover Registers His Dream" [Qinglang yin meng]).

Created using arias from scenes 2, 6, and 13. In this composite scene the dream lover introduces himself as Liu Chunqing, a student stranded in Guangzhou. Once while taking a nap he met a beauty in a dream who predicted that their meeting will set him on the road to high office. He has since changed his name to Mengmei, and hopes to claim both success in the examinations and the beauty as wife. He entrusts care of his orchards to Camel Guo and departs in search of patronage.)

Scene 12

"Pursuing the Dream" (Xun meng), 20 arias; *HHJ* 7/10: "Pursuing the Dream"; *FLM* 9/11: "Liniang Pursues the Dream" (Liniang xun meng).

Chunxiang serves breakfast, but Liniang refuses the food and sends her maid away. She re-enters the garden; Chunxiang returns to discover her standing alone beneath a plum tree and is again sent away. Liniang pursues her dream in earnest; coming to the grotto, she recalls her lover and their lovemaking. As her dream fades she looks up and catches sight of a magnificent plum tree. She is drawn to it and wishes to be buried beneath it when she dies. Chunxiang discovers Liniang drowsing beneath the tree and escorts her reluctant mistress back to her rooms.

HHJ has Liniang return to the garden secretly; Chunxiang appears only at scene's end. Zang rewrites the core sequence in which Liniang recalls her dream; erotically suggestive language is reduced, and Liniang's description of the garden is less subjectively thick. The tree becomes her emblem, chaste and firm. After Chunxiang finds Liniang sleeping beneath the tree, the scene rapidly concludes. *FLM* begins with both Liniang and Chunxiang onstage. In Liniang's core sequence, Feng substitutes conventional language for Tang's erotically suggestive variety. Liniang must search for the plum tree, and when at last she finds it, she responds as in *MDT*. After Chunxiang returns Feng gives her a rewritten aria, in which she urges Liniang to return to her rooms without delay.

Scene 13

"In Search of Patronage" (Jue ye), 5 arias; *HHJ*: cut; *FLM*: see *FLM* 8* above.

Liu recalls Han Zicai's advice and informs Camel Guo (*jing*) that he will go in search of a patron. He gives the garden to his servant, "to provide for your needs."

(*HHJ* 8*: see scene 16.)

(*FLM* 10*: see scene 19.)

Scene 14

"The Portrait" (Xie zhen), 11 arias; *HHJ* 9/9: "The Portrait"; *FLM* 11/9: "In Brocade Chamber A Portrait is Painted" (Xiuge chuan zhen).

As spring departs, a deeper ennui afflicts Liniang. Chunxiang observes how changed she is; looking in her mirror Liniang decides to paint her self-portrait as her testament. She inscribes a verse on it that refers to her lover, summons the gardener's lad, and tells him to have the portrait mounted.

HHJ combines scenes 14 and 18. After Liniang completes her portrait she falls asleep, and Chen Zuiliang arrives to discuss remedies with Chunxiang. Zang leaves most of the sexual innuendo in Chen's diagnoses intact. After he leaves, Sister Stone (Shi Daogu, *fujing*) presents herself, offers charms and prayers on Liniang's behalf, and departs. Liniang expresses doubts about Sister Stone's cures and places more faith in her tutor's remedies. *FLM* follows *MDT* closely but rewrites some arias, making the singing more interactive and interweaving the maid's dialogue and Liniang's singing. Chunxiang divines the reasons for Liniang's illness (she too is affected by the garden and wishes that Liniang had taken her along in her dream). After a compressed painting sequence, it is Chunxiang who suggests that the painting be mounted (but the gardener's lad is cut). Feng adds dialogue after the envoi.

Scene 15

"A Spy for the Tartars" (Lu die), 3 arias; *HHJ*: cut; *FLM*: cut.

We meet the emperor of the Jin dynasty (*jing*). He is eager to seize Hangzhou and has commissioned a portrait of himself on horseback on a mountain crest overlooking West Lake. He intends to engage the help of the Huaiyang bandit Li Quan.

Scene 16

"The Invalid" (Jie bing), 6 arias; *HHJ* 8*/5: "The Invalid"; *FLM* 12/6: "A Mother's Solicitude" (Cimu qi fu).

Madam Du frets that she will be left childless and summons Chunxiang. She becomes enraged when she hears that Liniang has been out among the "flowers and willows." She beats Chunxiang, then asks for more details and summons Du Bao. He attributes Liniang's sickness to a cold and sends for Sister Stone.

HHJ moves this scene earlier, since it makes more sense for Madam Du to learn how gravely ill Liniang is before Liniang paints her self-portrait, not after. Chunxiang makes no mention of the dream when Madam Du interrogates her about her daughter's illness. Zang cuts the aria Madam sings as she beats the maid. After Du Bao arrives, Madam suggests that a shaman be called; Du Bao suggests that Sister Stone, a Daoist nun, be summoned instead. *FLM* has Du Bao dismiss as witchcraft (*xieshu*) a plan of Madam's to have Sister Stone write charms and orders that she not be admitted to see their daughter. After he departs the scene is prolonged: Sister Stone (*chou*) is announced. Madam sees her, but tells her that she needn't see the patient. Instead, she requests that Sister Stone offer prayers for Liniang's recovery.[4]

Scene 17

"Sorceress of the Dao" (Daoxi), 3 arias; *HHJ*: cut; *FLM*: cut.

Sister Stone (*jing*) introduces herself through a long and bawdy parody of the *Qianzi wen* (Thousand-character text).

Scene 18

"Diagnosis" (Zhen sui), 6 arias; *HHJ*: see scene 14; *FLM* 13/4: "Zuiliang Diagnoses the Illness" (Zuiliang zhen bing).

With autumn's arrival Liniang's illness deepens; Chunxiang is unable to persuade her to cease thinking of her dream. Chen Zuiliang's arrival lightens the scene as he prescribes cures in language laced with sexual innuendo; he predicts that if Liniang can get past the Mid-autumn Festival, she will live. Sister Stone calls, but her charms have no effect. Liniang asks to be left alone, "to seek by incantation to renew my dream."

FLM has Madam Du call on her daughter and angrily reject Chunxiang's suggestion that a husband might cure her. Some of the innuendo in the tutor's dialogue is toned down and the scene ends with his departure. Sister Stone does not appear.

(*FLM* 14*: see scene 21.)

Scene 19

"The Brigandess" (Pinzei), 4 arias; *HHJ* 10/4: "The Brigandess"; *FLM* 10*/3: "Li Quan Martials Troops" (Li Quan qi bing).

The bandit chief Li Quan (*jing*) has defected to the Jin. Under orders from his ally, he and wife Yang Po (Dame Li, *chou*) will provision their troops, march south, raise havoc in the Huaiyang region, then attack the Southern Song.

HHJ assigns Li Quan to the *chou* actor and Yang Po to the *tie* role. [*FLM* virtually rewrites the scene, but Li Quan is still in awe of his spear-carrying wife, and basic plot details are unchanged.]

Scene 20

"Keening" (Nao shang), 17 arias; *HHJ* 11/11 "Lamentation" (Dao shang); *FLM* breaks the scene into 15/9: "Weeping at Night in Mid-autumn" (Zhongqiu qi ye) and 16/6: "Plans for Burying the Deceased Daughter" (Mou cuo shangnü).

At mid-autumn Liniang gazes on the moon and faints from weakness. Madam Du is summoned and weeps as Liniang stumbles when greeting her. She laments—again—the childless future that beckons and promises Liniang a proper burial. Liniang asks that she be buried beneath the plum tree in the garden. Her mother gone to fetch Du Bao, she tells Chunxiang to hide her portrait in the grotto, then faints again. Her parents hasten to the bedside to make their farewells. All exit; Chunxiang re-enters, announces Liniang's death, and sings a dirge; Sister Stone enters and sings a dirge that disgusts Chunxiang with its crude banter. Madam Du and then Du Bao enter, each singing to the same aria used for Chunxiang and Stone's grieving. As Du Bao finishes, word comes of his promotion to the post of pacification commissioner. He entrusts care of his daughter's shrine to Chen Zuiliang and Sister Stone.

In *HHJ* subjective intensity is reduced by cutting two of Liniang's opening arias and reassigning a third to Chunxiang. Zang eliminates Liniang's kowtowing aria (and the kowtow), and also the aria in which Madam laments a childless future. Du Bao enters dressed for travel, and most of his affecting exchange with Liniang is cut, perhaps because such a show of emotion on the father's part is inappropriate. The death is differently staged: Liniang attempts the kowtow here and collapses, then exits with Chunxiang. Chunxiang returns but makes no announcement, since Madam Du (still onstage) has begun her grieving. Du Bao then sings, but neither Chunxiang nor Sister Stone do. The squabbling between Chen Zuiliang and Sister Stone is cut, along with other funniness at scene's end. After the envoi, Du Bao lingers to instruct the gardener's lad (Hualang, *jing*) to bury Liniang's portrait in the grotto. *FLM* also truncates the exchanges between mother and maid and mother and daughter; the sequence at Liniang's bedside is also shortened as the scene quickly concludes. *FLM* starts a new scene with Chunxiang's announcement, no longer addressed to the audience. The entire keening sequence is kept, with the arias by Chunxiang and Sister Stone done in the interactive pattern (singing and dialogue interwoven) that Feng favors, but Sister Stone's comic side is expressed as greedy demand for payment rather than crude banter directed at Chunxiang. As in *HHJ*, Feng tones down the humor directed at the tutor at scene's end, and in a major change has Chunxiang become a nun so that both she and Sister Stone will tend Liniang's shrine. After Chen Zuiliang departs, two arias, exchanged between Chunxiang and Liniang's parents, are added to highlight the maid's sacrifice.

Scene 21

"The Interview" (Ye yu), 10 arias; *HHJ* 6*/9: "The Interview"; *FLM* 14*/9: "Interview at Many-Jewelled Temple" (Baosi ganye).

At Many-jewelled Temple Imperial Commissioner Miao Shunbin (*jing*) offers jewels to the Tathagata as he completes his tour of duty in Guangzhou. Liu

Mengmei requests an interview and proposes to Miao that he is a "living pearl." Miao, impressed, offers to pay the expenses for Liu's journey to the capital. He is certain that Liu will pass the examinations; Liu is grateful for Miao's patronage.

HHJ cuts one aria, reduces dialogue, and tones down Liu's boastfulness, while playing up his respectful gratitude to Miao Shunbin (*xiaosheng*). *FLM* also has Miao played as a *xiaosheng* but makes only light revisions.

Scene 22

"Traveler's Rest" (Lü ji), 5 arias; *HHJ* 12/5: "Traveler's Rest"; *FLM* 17/5: "A Sick Traveler Takes Refuge at the Shrine" (Bingke yi an).

Liu falls ill while traveling north. Attempting to ford an icy stream he tumbles in and calls for help. Chen Zuiliang happens by and offers to shelter Liu at Liniang's shrine.

HHJ appears to revise only lightly, but a page is missing from my edition. *FLM* simplifies, and cuts funny business that has Chen Zuiliang topple into the stream on top of Liu Mengmei.

Scene 23

"Infernal Judgement" (Mingpan), 10 arias; *HHJ* 13/9: "Infernal Judgement"; *FLM* 18/9: "The Infernal Judge Takes Love's Part" (Mingpan lianqing).

Three years have passed. Hu Panguan (Judge Hu, *jing*) presides at an underworld tribunal and sentences malefactors to rebirth as oriole, swallow, butterfly, and bee. Liniang is brought before him, and Hu Panguan summons for questioning the Huashen, who enumerates the flowers in his bag of tricks. Hu Panguan blames him for Liniang's premature death. Learning that she is the daughter of Du Bao, he checks the Register of Marriages and grants her a passport to wander as a ghost in search of her destined lover, the "Coffin Breaker." The Huashen must guard her body from corruption.

HHJ cuts Hu Panguan's long aria, *Hunjiang long*, and also the most outrageous erotic puns in *Houting hua*. Otherwise Zang revises lightly. *FLM* also cuts outrageous puns on flower names. Otherwise the long scene is little changed. With it, the first half of *FLM* concludes.

Scene 24

"The Portrait Recovered" (Shi hua), 6 arias; *HHJ* and *FLM*: see scene 26.

Restored to health, Liu grows restless as spring nears and is directed to the garden by Sister Stone, who warns him to "avoid grieving." Once inside, he discovers a magnificent but decaying garden, whose pavilions lean askew; from a motionless swing a girl's sash eerily dangles. Liu discovers a box in the rock grotto and the portrait scroll within. Taking it to be a picture of the goddess Guanyin, he decides to install it in the shrine and burn incense to it.

Scene 25

"Maternal Remembrance" (Yi nü), 4 arias; *HHJ* 16*/3: "Maternal Libation" (Dian nü); *FLM*: cut.

On Liniang's birthday, almost three years after her death, Madam Du faces towards Nan'an and tearfully offers prayers, tea and rice for the deceased. She is attended by Chunxiang, who calls Liniang's name out loud, as Madam Du instructs her to do. Chunxiang advises Madam Du to install a concubine who might bear Du Bao a son.

HHJ changes the title (to emphasize the ritual?), cuts one aria assigned to the maid, rewrites another because it is "throat wrenching" and has Chunxiang rather than Madam Du weep as tea and rice are offered. The scene is moved "because the *dan*'s appearances onstage are too many."

Scene 26

"The Portrait Examined" (Wan zhen), 8 arias; *HHJ* 14/7: "The Portrait Examined"; *FLM* 19/11: "The Portrait Discovered" (Chu shi zhenrong).

Back in his study, Liu unrolls the painting to inspect his find. His first guess, that it depicts the goddess Guanyin, is belied when he spies tiny feet peeking from beneath her skirt; nor can it be the goddess of the moon (no cloud). His suspicion that some mortal girl has painted her own portrait is confirmed by the poem inscribed on it, which he answers with one of his own. Excited by verses that appear to refer to him as the lady's future mate, he examines the painting more closely, finding in every detail confirmation of his hopes. Transfixed by her gaze and desires fully aroused, Liu calls to the lady to descend from the painting and join him.

HHJ suppresses some details (reference to "stains of a passionate dream' on Liu's bedclothes; Liu's comment that Sister Stone has "seen through his scholar's poses"). The content of scene 24 is summarized in speech; Liu then inspects the portrait. His guessing game is preserved but shortened, leaving out erotic details (the feet) and cutting the most suggestive aria, which conveys sexual excitement via references to Liu's thirst and Liniang's mouth. The conclusion is unchanged. *FLM* incorporates language from scene 24, but eliminates Liu's encounter with Sister Stone and sharply telescopes his tour of the garden; here Liu sees the garden as a world of care that distracts him from his ambition. After he discovers the portrait, however, Liu's infatuation (*chiqing*) and sexual frustration are even more exaggerated. In a major change, Liu recognizes that the portrait depicts the beautiful girl in his dream.

Scene 27

"Spirit Roaming" (Hunyou), 12 arias; *HHJ* 15/8: "Spirit Roaming"; *FLM* 20/10: "Feelings Experienced While Spirit Roaming" (Hunyou qinggan).

On the third anniversary of Liniang's death Sister Stone, accompanied by a young Daoist nun (*tie*) and novice (*chou*), prays for the release of Liniang's soul and offers a plum sprig at her Plum Blossom Shrine. After the celebrants withdraw, Liniang's ghost (*hundan*) enters, drawn by the sound of their prayers. Companionless, she prays that she may be reborn; noticing the plum sprig, she scatters its blossoms as a sign. Liu's cries arouse longings, but she cannot stay. Her departure is marked by the novice; she informs Sister Stone, who offers a final prayer.

HHJ has only Sister Stone pray at Liniang's shrine. Language associated with the plum sprig as emblem is cut but the sprig itself is retained as an offering (and useful staging device). More detailed stage directions about Liniang's costume as ghost are given (she is mentioned as wearing a headcloth [*mo*] used by the "ghostly *dan*" [*hundan*]). Liniang's exit is changed: she collides with Sister Stone, who notices the blossoms scattered on the shrine and is terrified. Other revisions address prosodic concerns (too many padding words [*chenzi*]). *FLM* has only one year pass, not three. Sister Stone and Chunxiang make offerings at the shrine; Chunxiang's first aria is modified (to offer a plum sprig is seasonally wrong, since *FLM* has the season as autumn). Liniang's ghost (*dan*) is "beautifully costumed" (*yanzhuang*) when she makes her entrance. She prays at the shrine, notices Chunxiang's written prayer, and is touched; overhearing Liu's cries in his sleep, she finds his spirit "pure" (*qing*). After her ghost exits, Sister Stone jokes with Chunxiang that were her mistress to live again she would make trouble for her again, and is rebuked.

(*HHJ* 16*: see scene 25.)

Scene 28

"Union in the Shades" (Yougou), 20 arias; *HHJ* 17/9: "Union in the Shades"; *FLM* 21/15: "A Secret Tryst in Plum Blossom Shrine" (Mei'an yougou).

Liu unrolls the portrait; its radiance soon "makes clamorous chaos of my thoughts." He lights incense, scrutinizes Liniang's verse, and wonders how to bring about a rendezvous. When the wind stirs, he douses his candle lest it harm the portrait, and sleeps. Liniang's ghost enters. She has heard Liu's cries and seen her portrait with his verse inscribed on it, and now taps at his window. A guessing game ensues, as Liu tries to learn who the lady is and she gives cryptic replies. Liniang offers herself ("a flower you bring to bloom in dark of night") and Liu joyfully accepts, but still he cannot learn her name.

HHJ makes deep cuts, eliminating seven arias Liu sings as he gazes at the portrait. The entrance aria sung by Liniang's ghost, which conveys distracted emotion, is also cut, reflecting a relative lack of interest in subjective emotions. Once the teasing, sexy guessing game begins, puzzling or troubling details (Liniang's reminder to Liu that he has "strayed in a butterfly dream" and an aside by Liu that betrays unbecoming concern over Liniang's social status) are omitted, while Liniang's direct invitation and Liu's ardent acceptance of it are curtailed. In *FLM*, Liu's arousal at sight of the portrait is blunt, with little or no bemused yearning (the beauty in the portrait is "good enough to eat"). He falls asleep hugging it, in hopes that "while I dream of her she dreams of me." Once Liniang's ghost gains entry to Liu's room, the guessing game is toned down and Liniang's offer of herself becomes coy: she has come to his door by mistake, but "the hungry and thirsty student is so handsome" that she will stay. Liu assures Liniang that "were there another she wouldn't be my wife."

Scene 29

"Gossip" (Pang yi), 7 arias; *HHJ*: cut; *FLM*: cut.

Sister Stone hears voices in Liu's study at night and accuses the young nun of wandering into his rooms. Chen Zuiliang breaks up their quarrel and defends Liu's reputation, but the women decide to investigate.

Scene 30

"Disrupted Joy" (Huan nao), 11 arias; *HHJ*: cut; *FLM* 22/8: "Sister Stone Obstructs Joy" (Shi gu zu huan).

Meeting Liniang has turned Liu's heart from other goals. It is night, and he refreshes himself with a nap as he awaits her arrival. She comes bringing wine and fruit. Drinking, they sing an impassioned duet. As passion subsides, they are rudely interrupted by Sister Stone and her accomplice. Liniang conceals herself in the portrait's shade and makes her escape. The women find only the portrait, which Liu tells them he carries on his travels.

FLM has Sister Stone suspect Chunxiang of breaking her vows with Liu; the women quarrel and decide to investigate. Feng removes Liu's comment that love has turned him from other goals, and adds dialogue in which he regrets having neglected the painting.[5] He chides the lady in the portrait ("It isn't as if you couldn't have descended"); his nocturnal visitor is as pretty as she is—in fact, they are very alike! Once Liniang's ghost arrives, no wine is drunk or duet sung. Instead Liniang explains that she had to wait for her parents to retire and so is late. When Sister Stone and Chunxiang intrude Liniang slips away, but not before Sister Stone thinks the portrait is bewitched. Chunxiang accuses Liu of having stolen the portrait and seizes it from him.

Scene 31

"Defensive Works" (Shan bei), 7 arias; *HHJ* 18/7: "Defensive Works"; *FLM*: cut.

Du Bao and his officials civil (*tie*) and military (*jing*) survey Yangzhou's defenses and stocks of salt for the merchants who will supply his troops. He greets the merchants (*zhong* [extras]), and all rejoice that the city is well fortified against Li Quan's armies.

HHJ leaves out the merchants. The civil official is reassigned to the *mo* actor. This scene concludes Part One of *HHJ*.

Scene 32

"Spectral Vows" (Mingshi), 20 arias; *HHJ* 19/12: "Spectral Vows"; *FLM* 23/12: "Swearing Vows and Baring Hearts" (Sheshi mingxin).

Liu calls on Sister Stone to allay her suspicion. Liniang's ghost arrives, fearful because this is the night when she must reveal to Liu who she is. Liu returns and inquires if she is betrothed; she answers that she fears she will be his concubine, not wife. He offers to present himself to her parents; tension builds as she still withholds her identity. After they exchange vows, Liniang weeps, tells Liu to remain calm, then points out the resemblance between herself and the portrait. Liu trims the lamp, and Liniang tells him that she is at the midpoint between ghost and living woman. Momentarily terror-stricken, Liu quickly recovers and asks how to secure her return. Liniang tells him to dig his way to her grave beneath the plum tree. At cock-crow she departs, but returns with a warning: "Do not make me hate you from the yellow springs below."

HHJ begins the scene with the *hundan*. After Liu returns, their conversation immediately turns to Liniang's betrothal. Arias that refer to Stone's intrusion and Liu's background are cut. In the revised sequence, the gradualness of Liniang's revelation to Liu is lost and, implausibly, Liu shows no fear. After the revelation *HHJ* does not depart substantially from *MDT*, but at scene's end Liniang's ghost again wears the *mo* (ghostly headcloth) when she returns, alarming Liu. *FLM* also has the *dan* as the first onstage. She is concerned lest Chunxiang find her with her lover, but more confident of success with him than Tang's hesitant ghost. But when Liu brings up her betrothal, she expresses fear that people will think her dissolute. He presses for details about her family; when she remains evasive he asks himself if she is "a demon who bedazzles by moonlight." *FLM* builds gradually to the revelation using an interactive singing pattern (Feng comments that her confession must be slow and indirect; "one must not dislike the fact that there are so many arias"). Liniang broaches who she is by way of the portrait (which Liu must recollect, since Chunxiang has taken it). Liu shows fear when he learns the truth (Feng comments: "If Liu is not afraid, then his *qing* is not profound"), recovers, but becomes frightened again when he learns that Liniang's return to life is not yet complete. Liniang directs him to Chunxiang for help, exits, then returns to tell him to inscribe a dot on her spirit tablet to complete the character for "host" (*zhu*) written thereon; doing so will convince Chunxiang to help him.

Scene 33

"Confidential Plans" (Mi yi), 6 arias; *HHJ*: see scene 35; *FLM* 24/6: "Conceiving a Plan to Open the Tomb" (Xie mou fa mu).

Liu calls on Sister Stone and asks to see Liniang's shrine. He tells her that Liniang is his wife, and when she tells him he's possessed, he inks a dot on Liniang's tablet. When the tablet moves, Sister Stone is convinced and agrees to help him.

FLM has Chunxiang learn in a dream that her mistress has a husband and will soon visit her. She hangs Liniang's portrait in the shrine and is joined there by Sister Stone and by Liu, who sees the spirit tablet and tearfully confesses that Liniang is his wife. He inscribes the dot and the tablet moves. (He has caused her tablet to move and wants to move her body too!) Recalling her dream, Chunxiang believes him. Liu assures her that she will be reunited with her mistress. They will exhume the body the next day, and Sister Stone will seek the help of her nephew, Scabby Turtle (Laitouyuan).

Scene 34

"Consultation" (Xiong yao), 3 arias; *HHJ*: cut; *FLM*: cut.

Sister Stone visits Chen Zuiliang in his shop. She pretends that a nun at the convent has been possessed. To revive her, Chen prescribes wine mixed with ashes obtained from burning a he-man's pants.

Scene 35

"Resurrection" (Hui sheng), 8 arias; *HHJ* 20/10: "Resurrection"; *FLM* 25/10: "Miss Du is Resurrected" (Du nü hui sheng).

When Scabby Turtle (*chou*), Sister Stone, and Liu arrive at Liniang's grave, Liu weeps, prostrates himself, and prays. Scabby is all business, burning paper money and commencing the dig. They reach the coffin and open it, and Liniang emerges, giving off a heavenly fragrance. They pour the wine mixture down her throat. She revives and is too dazed at first to speak, but recognizes Liu; all hastily depart after throwing the coffin boards into the pond.

HHJ enfolds scene 33. Stone is persuaded to help without Liu's having to ink the dot on Liniang's tablet, and she enlists the aid of her nephew, Lali (*chou*). Zang gives detailed instructions about how to stage the resurrection.[6] Wine is administered (*sans* ashes), and Stone and Liniang exit. Left alone, Liu plans to ask Stone to raise the subject of marriage after Liniang is restored to health. *FLM* has Chunxiang also present at the graveside and she prays with Liu while Stone and Scabby Turtle (*xiaojing*) dig. They find a passageway (Scabby wonders if the soul is in residence or "off making clouds and rain"). Reaching the coffin, Liu and Chunxiang lead Liniang forth.[7] Liu rewards Scabby with his jacket, but refuses his other requests for reward.[8] After she is revived with ginger tea, Liniang addresses

Chunxiang first ("Reliant on each other in life and death / feelings were not shallow"), thanks Stone next, and only then expresses blushing gratitude to Liu for bestowing life. Chunxiang and Stone caution Liu to allow Liniang time to recover before talking of marriage.

(*HHJ* 21*: see scene 42.)

Scene 36

"Elopement" (Hunzou), 12 arias; *HHJ* 22/9: "Elopement"; *FLM* 26/9: "Husband and Wife Match Dreams" (Fuqi he meng).

Liniang ("tender infant you must raise anew") tells Sister Stone details of her past and insists to Liu that he find a matchmaker and grant her a spell of rest. She and Stone withdraw when Chen Zuiliang arrives at Liu's gate. The tutor is puzzled to hear female voices, but Stone's return allays suspicion. He proposes a picnic at Liniang's grave. Threatened with exposure, Liniang agrees to exchange marriage vows, with Stone as go-between. No sooner are the vows sworn than she informs Liu that she is still a virgin. Scabby Turtle hails a boatman (*wai*). Stone agrees to accompany the couple to Hangzhou if Liu rewards her nephew. Liu gives Scabby his jacket but refuses to part with the mercury Liniang has vomited. Once onboard, the couple celebrate their joy with impassioned singing.

In *HHJ* Stone is Liu's ally more than Liniang's confidant (Zang feels that confidences Liniang shares with Sister Stone in *MDT* are not "true to life" [*yukuo*]). She offers to act as go-between and remains with him to confront the tutor after Liniang withdraws. Liniang is reluctant to elope, preferring to have Stone cover up her deeds (Zang reassigns all mention of their lovemaking from her to Liu). Once she agrees to elope, Zang plays up the arrival of the boatman (*jing*), and there is no passionate celebrating after the couple set sail. In *FLM*, Chunxiang acts as go-between and together with Stone accompanies the couple to Hangzhou. Feng accentuates the *ya/su* divide, by removing Liniang's indecorous mention of lovemaking and rewriting the boatman's (*xiaojing*) song in Wu dialect. Onboard the boat, Liu and Liniang match dreams in a long exchange after the Coda;[9] Liu assures Liniang that her portrait is ever with him; she enjoins him never to treat it lightly.

Scene 37

"The Alarm" (Hai bian), 4 arias; *HHJ* 23/2: "The Alarm"; *FLM* 27/1: "Zuiliang Investigates the Tomb" (Zuiliang xing mu).

Chen Zuiliang finds the shrine deserted and Liniang's tomb leveled; he concludes that Liu Mengmei is a grave robber. He will first notify the authorities in Nan'an, then travel to Yangzhou to inform Du Bao.

HHJ and *FLM* both incorporate more dialogue for the tutor into this short scene, and Feng softens Chen's indictment of Liu as grave robber.

Scene 38

"The Scourge of the Huai" (Huai jing), 4 arias; *HHJ*: cut; *FLM*: cut.

Li Quan has ravaged the Huaiyang region for three years and now receives orders to spearhead a great southern expedition. Yang Po proposes that he draw Du Bao away from Yangzhou by attacking Huai'an. Her armies will then attack Yangzhou and cut off his supply lines.

Scene 39

"Hangzhou" (Ru Hang), 6 arias; *HHJ* 24/4: "Hangzhou"; *FLM*: cut.

In Hangzhou, at the time of the tidal bore, Liu is studying for the examinations. He asks how Liniang came to write his name into her poem, and she tells him about her dream. He in turn recalls how love overcame his fear, so that he was able to revive her corpse and bring her to the imperial city. Sister Stone returns with wine and reports that scholars are flocking to the examination halls. Liniang hurries Liu on his way, reminding him of the prophecy in his dream.

HHJ replaces the couple's arias of parting, which contain elaborate wordplay, with a shorter and simpler aria.

Scene 40

"In Search of the Master" (Pu zhen), 5 arias; *HHJ*: cut; *FLM*: cut.

The trees in the Liu family's orchard no longer fruit, and Camel Guo has left Guangzhou in search of his master. Arriving in Nan'an, he seeks word of Liu's whereabouts from Scabby Turtle, recognizes Liu's jacket, and presses him about it. Scabby gives a highly embroidered and lurid reply, but does reveal that Liu and Liniang have gone to Hangzhou, accompanied by his aunt.

(*HHJ* 25*: see scene 45.)

Scene 41

"Delayed Examination" (Dan shi), 7 arias; *HHJ* 26/5: "Delayed Examination"; *FLM* 28/7: "Holding Examinations and Recruiting Talent" (Gaokao xuancai).

Rebel incursions have postponed the examinations; once held, questions on military policy are set. But Miao Shunbin finds grading gems easier than grading examinations. He ranks the three top answers just as Liu arrives, late. Liu requests a make-up exam, is refused, and bursts into tears. Hearing his weeping, Miao orders that Liu be admitted. He recognizes his protégé, administers a make-up examination, and judges Liu's paper to be the best. At the imperial court, discussion of the urgent frontier situation delays Miao's announcement of the examination results. The emperor (from offstage) orders that Du Bao repel Li

Quan at Huaiyang; publication of the examination lists must await the outcome of this campaign.

HHJ moderates Tang's satire of the examination system (Miao's aria denouncing the candidates as "blockheads" is cut, as is Liu's *sotto voce* reminder to Miao of who he is). Zang abridges by cutting dialogue and an aria assigned to the privy councilor (*mo*) concerning the military emergency.[10] Only after Miao has been to court does Liu recognize him, and even then he dares not identify himself. Miao does, however, inform Liu that his paper has been ranked first, and Liu's modest deflection of Miao's high praise concludes Zang's scene. *FLM* also ameliorates Tang's satire by presenting Miao as an impartial arbiter, who attributes the decline of scholarly brilliance to the corruption of the examination system under the traitor Qin Gui.[11] The encounter between Liu and Miao is substantially the same, but here Miao says to the emperor that the court has failed to attract brave men (*haohan*) such as Li Quan. The emperor's response to Miao concludes his scene.

(*HHJ* 27*: see scene 46.)

Scene 42

"Troop Transfer" (Yi zhen), 7 arias; *HHJ* 21*/4: "Troop Transfer"; *FLM*: cut.[12]

Du Bao and Madam Du are accompanied by Chunxiang. They have been three years in Yangzhou. Du Bao is sorrowful as he gazes towards the lost north; Madam's thoughts are of her daughter to the south. Concerned about the rebels, Du Bao wonders at his wife's incessant grieving. Madam urges her husband to take a concubine, a suggestion he dismisses. Orders arrive to proceed by boat to Huai'an to counter the rebel attacks. They survey the Huai River at dusk and sing of autumn's approach. A second messenger arrives with orders that Du Bao proceed by land to Huai'an; Madam and Chunxiang will go by boat to Hangzhou. Du Bao and Madam part; each must look to messages or to dreams "to know if the other lives."

HHJ compresses by cutting arias and substituting dialogue, including dialogue for Du Bao and Madam after the Coda and before the envoi. The scene is moved before "Resurrection" rather than after to give the *sheng* and *dan* a rest.

Scene 43

"The Seige of Huai'an" (Yu Huai), 10 arias; *HHJ*: cut; *FLM* 29/7: "Du Bao Transfers Troops" (Du Bao yi zhen).

Du Bao advances towards Huai'an, which is under siege. After a skirmish with Li Quan's forces, his troops break through enemy lines, enter the city, and are received by anxious civil (*laodan, mo*) and military (*jing, chou*) officials. Du Bao learns that Huai'an is well provisioned and gives orders to bide time and await reinforcements. If the Jin main force attacks, they will fight for their lives.

FLM cuts "Troop Transfer," which portrays Du Bao's more tender emotions. In this scene Feng enhances Du's heroic side by removing Tang's touches of humor (a local civil and military official plan how best to flee the besieged city) and playing up the ceremonies of officialdom (two local officials, one civil [*xiaosheng*] and one military [*xiaojing*], receive Du Bao as he enters the city). He simplifies in order to make the expression of feelings more direct. Du Bao is all business, and an already fast-paced scene moves even more briskly, following Tang's text closely.

Scene 44

"Concern for the Besieged" (Ji nan), 8 arias; *HHJ* 28*/7: "Concern for the Besieged"; *FLM*: cut.

Autumn in Hangzhou finds Liniang anticipating good news. Liu returns and tells what happened at the examinations. Liniang asks him to travel to Huai'an for news of her parents. Liu finds it difficult to leave Liniang before the lists are published. What can he say to her parents? Liniang fears her father will be enraged by Liu's claims and gives him her portrait; seeing it, Du Bao will hear him out. At scene's close, Liu anticipates the joy his news will bring to his in-laws; Liniang tells him not to distract himself with the pleasures of Yangzhou.

(*FLM* 30*: see scene 48.)

Scene 45

"A Spy for the Rebels" (Koujian), 6 arias; *HHJ* 25*/5: "A Spy for the Rebels"[13]; *FLM* 31/6: "Zuiliang Meets the Rebels" (Zuiliang yu kou).

Li Quan's sentries (*laodan, wai*) are on the lookout for someone to take a message to Du Bao. Chen Zuiliang enters in travel gear. Aware of danger as he makes his way through rebel territory, he takes a short-cut and is immediately captured. Back in the rebel camp Yang Po concocts a plan to fool the tutor into believing that Du Bao's womenfolk are dead so that he will take this news to Du Bao and demoralize him. Her trick works, and Chen begs to be allowed to intercede with Du Bao in an effort to get him to surrender the city. After they send him on his way, Chen castigates his erstwhile captors as "plain thieves and robbers."

HHJ has the tutor less comical, but his garbled discourse on the art of war is kept. Chen's denunciation of the rebels at scene's end is cut; he leaves the stage to Yang Po, who issues orders to her troops. *FLM* simplifies the language, but otherwise follows Tang's text. Li Quan's sentries are played by extras (*za*).

Scene 46

"The Rebels Countered" (Zhe kou), 6 arias; *HHJ* 27/6: "The Rebels Countered"; *FLM* 32/8: "Surrounding the City, Dispatching a Spy" (Wei cheng qian jian).

Du Bao and his troops, besieged, await relief. Du questions Heaven's purpose in permitting "rank stench of sheep and goat" to invade the central lands. A messenger brings word of an old friend who has broken through the lines. Chen Zuiliang enters and breaks the news of Madam Du's death. Du Bao weeps, but dries his tears lest the news weaken his will. Chen delivers Li Quan's ultimatum, but when Du Bao learns that Yang Po "sits side by side" with Li Quan he is confident that he can raise the siege. Learning that his daughter's tomb has been rifled, he is again saddened, but gathers himself and entrusts the reluctant tutor with a return errand to the rebel camp.

HHJ introduces small changes that make the tutor less comical and Du Bao less emotional. *FLM* suppresses an unflattering detail concerning the tutor[14] and directs more contempt at the rebels. Otherwise, changes are largely formal.[15]

(*HHJ* 28*: see scene 44.)

Scene 47

"Raising the Siege" (Wei shi), 12 arias; *HHJ* 29/6: "Raising the Siege"; *FLM* 33/11: "The Prince-Errant Raises the Siege" (Liu Jin jie wei).

Caught between northern ally and southern foe, Li Quan has worries and summons Yang Po, but before they can consult together a Jin envoy (*laodan*) arrives and must be humored with koumiss and mutton. He takes a fancy to Yang Po, who performs for him her spear dance. He propositions her, enraging Li Quan. They fight, and no sooner does the envoy flee than Chen Zuiliang arrives, with letters from Du Bao offering titles for both if they will "return to the light." The rebels accept Du's proposals. After Chen leaves them, they decide to become pirates and take to their boats.

HHJ writes elaborate stage directions for the Jin envoy (*jing*), but truncates his encounter with Yang Po by cutting three arias, including her spear dance. Nevertheless, the lewd proposition remains. After the envoy exits and Chen Zuiliang enters, he is seized and bound under protest.[16] Li Quan, barely literate, asks Chen to read Du's letters. He, not Yang Po, makes the final decision to surrender, and the decision to become pirates is made before Li Quan gives Chen a formal document of surrender (rather than after Chen has left them, as in *MDT*). Li and Yang exit first,[17] leaving Chen to envision the reward he likely will obtain from the court. *FLM* is lightly revised. Feng's changes exaggerate the outrageous humor, as when Yang Po demands that the Song empress personally make her new wardrobe. The lecherous envoy is assigned to the *xiaojing* role.

Scene 48

"Mother and Daughter Reunited" (Yu mu), 13 arias; *HHJ* 30/10: "Mother and Daughter Reunited"; *FLM* 30*/11: "Mother and Daughter Meet" (Zimu xiangfeng).

Liniang and Sister Stone wait for word from Liu, having sought refuge at an inn by the Qiantang River. At nightfall Stone goes to fetch oil for the lamp. Madam Du and Chunxiang arrive seeking shelter, and Liniang admits them to her darkened court. Each recognizes the other; Liniang identifies herself first, but Madam has concluded that she is a ghost and cowers in fear. Only when Stone returns, lamp in hand, is an end put to doubt. Mother and daughter embrace, and Madam Du learns that she has a son-in-law. She recalls her grief at Liniang's death, Liniang recalls her existence in the grave, and Stone recalls how she tended Liniang's shrine; Chunxiang marvels that her Liniang had found a lover even as she and Madam tearfully offered prayers for her soul's deliverance. At scene's end, Liniang assures her mother that Liu will seek Du Bao out.

HHJ changes include having Madam Du and Chunxiang arrive after their boat has capsized.[18] Zang truncates an intricate ensemble sequence of four arias, rewriting it to a different tune pattern because he finds Tang's sequence "slow" (*lengchang*). He curtails another sequence of four arias, cutting two that are assigned to Sister Stone and Chunxiang and writing dialogue instead.[19] He leaves the conclusion unchanged. *FLM* has Liu gone into the city for word of Liniang's parents, while Liniang is eager for news of his success in the examinations. Chunxiang fetches oil for the lamp, and while she is gone Liniang takes in Madam Du and an old female servant (*xiaojing*), who were cast ashore enroute to Hangzhou when their boat capsized in a storm.[20] In the dark the women recognize each other's voices; Madam is afraid until Chunxiang's lamp's light furnishes proof that Liniang is human. Madam accepts her daughter and meets her son-in-law for the first time. Liu brings news of the urgent situation in Huai'an. Liniang asks him to seek out Du Bao. Her portrait will support his claims, but her father is by nature unyielding, and Liu must be careful.

Scene 49

"Moored before Huai'an" (Huai bo), 5 arias; *HHJ*: cut; *FLM*: cut.

Autumn. In travel gear, Liu arrives penniless in Huai'an, wondering how to announce himself to Du Bao. He has nothing of value to exchange for food and lodging, and when he tells an innkeeper (*chou*) that he is Du Bao's son-in-law, the man shows him a warrant for his arrest as an imposter. After the innkeeper leaves to report him to the authorities, Liu prays at a local shrine honoring the woman who aided a Han dynasty hero, Han Xin, in his time of great need.

Scene 50

"Uproar at the Banquet" (Nao yan), 10 arias; *HHJ* 31/8: "Uproar at the Banquet"; *FLM* 34/10: "Scholar Liu Creates an Uproar at the Banquet" (Liu sheng nao yan).

Li Quan has withdrawn his armies and peace is restored, but Du Bao finds victory bittersweet as he mourns the loss of his wife. Liu Mengmei presents himself at Du's gate and is rebuffed. He learns from the gatekeeper (*chou*) that a banquet to celebrate the peace is about to begin. As Du Bao fetes his officials and they congratulate him, word arrives of his promotion to chief minister. Just as he is overcome with emotion and nostalgia Liu is announced, and no sooner is Liu announced than Du Bao orders him taken away and beaten. When Liu returns and forces his way into the banquet, he is trussed up and hauled off to jail.

In *HHJ*, Zang's changes are dictated, in part, by his cutting of scene 49, and by a desire to condense, cutting some arias and eliminating entrance verses and couplets. But the scene is preserved largely intact. *FLM* preserves most of the dialogue, but rewrites some arias to different song titles. The effect of the changes is that Du Bao's arias are a little less emotion filled, and Liu's one aria a little more comically blunt. The place of the gatekeeper is taken by a military official (*jing*).

Scene 51

"The Lists Proclaimed" (Bangxia), 3 arias; *HHJ* 32/3: "The Lists Proclaimed"; *FLM*: cut.

Now that peace is restored, the examination lists can be announced. At court, Miao's petition is preceded by Chen Zuiliang's submission of Li Quan's letter of surrender. Liu Mengmei is decreed prize candidate, and for skill in negotiation Chen Zuiliang is appointed grand chamberlain within the palace.

HHJ's revisions reflect concern over ritual: Miao and Chen do not address the throne directly, but through the privy councilor (*jing*). Zang cuts a stage direction that indicates that Chen wears a tattered gown and cap when he arrives at court, and also cuts comments by the privy councilor at the tutor's expense.

Scene 52

"The Search for the Candidate" (Suo yuan), 6 arias; *HHJ*: cut; *FLM* 35/4: "Going in Search of the Candidate" (Xing fang zhuangyuan).

As Camel Guo arrives in Hangzhou, two colonels (*laodan, chou*) are combing the city for the prize candidate, who is nowhere to be found. They are directed to Big Sister Wang's (*tie*) house in the pleasure quarter, but she has never heard of him. Guo also can find no trace of his master. He collides with the soldiers, and is amazed and delighted to learn that Liu is the prize candidate.

FLM's substantial change is to cut the soldiers' search of the pleasure quarters, and with it Big Sister Wang.

Scene 53

"Interrogation Under the Rod" (Ying kao), 12 arias; *HHJ* 33/10: "Interrogation Under the Rod"; *FLM* 36/11: "Interrogating the Son-in-law Upside-down" (Diao da dongchuang).

In jail, Liu is indignant at Du Bao's treatment of him and must also endure ill treatment from the jailer (*jing*) and his turnkey (*chou*). Brought before Du Bao, he cannot bring himself to bow and scrape before one so proud and stiff. When he repeats his claim, Du Bao orders his baggage searched, and Liniang's portrait is uncovered. Du orders Liu to confess to plundering Liniang's tomb. Liu refuses and recounts at length how he opened the tomb and warmed Liniang's flesh. Convinced that Liu is possessed, Du orders him strung up and beaten. Camel Guo arrives with guards (*zhong*) as the beating is in progress. He identifies his master, and Liu is cut down. However, the beating resumes as soon as Camel Guo's party has left to report, and it continues until Miao Shunbin arrives and orders Liu cut down a second time. Liu dons his robes of honor over Du's violent protests, and leaves for his banquet. Chen Zuiliang tries to intercede, and Du consents to have him submit the matter to the emperor.

HHJ makes numerous, rather minor changes. Zang omits stage instructions that give details of the stringing up,[21] and rewrites some erotically charged lines in the aria that catalogues Liu's efforts on Liniang's behalf. Miao Shunbin's jocular chiding of Du Bao is toned down, as are two of Liu's more insolent arias.[22] Camel Guo does not appear. *FLM* begins the scene with Du Bao, cutting portions that depict Liu with the jailer and turnkey. In Feng's scene Liu is, if anything, more confrontational before Du Bao. Some revisions are similar in nature to Zang's: Feng reduces erotic language in Liu's aria cataloguing efforts on Liniang's behalf, cuts stage directions that detail the stringing up, and reduces somewhat Miao Shunbin's amused detachment from the conflict. Miao is a bit more respectful of Du's dignity and a bit more critical of Liu's mistakes. Camel Guo is not cut from the scene.

Scene 54

"Glad News" (Wen xi), 10 arias; *HHJ* 34/6: "Glad News"; *FLM*: cut.

Autumn deepens and Liniang has no news. Impatient, she sews a robe in expectation of her husband's success and recounts to Chunxiang the experience of her dream and resurrection. But when the maid asks about the intimate details, she is brushed aside. First Madam Du, then Sister Stone rush in with news that Liu is the prize candidate! Colonels (*wai*, *chou*) also rush in and confirm that Liu is *zhuangyuan*, then recount all that transpired at Du Bao's court. Madam is relieved that her husband is well. Du has petitioned the throne to deprive Liu of his prize, and Liu has answered his petition with one of his own. The emperor is perplexed and summons all parties to court. Despite her trepidation, Liniang realizes she must recount in detail her experience of life and death. As Madam Du reassures her, Camel Guo arrives and informs the ladies that it was he who secured Liu's release at the chief minister's mansion.

HHJ follows closely, but Zang cuts a long transitional aria sung by the colonels who come with news of Liu's success because it is too long to sing easily. At scene's end, he also cuts Madam Du's aria wondering why Du Bao has acted harshly and caused the emperor distress. Neither Sister Stone nor Camel Guo appear.

Scene 55

"Reunion" (Yuan jia), 15 arias; *HHJ* 35/10: "Reunion"; *FLM* 37/15: "Celebration by Imperial Grace" (Huang'en ci qing).

Chen Zuiliang has summoned all parties to appear at court so that the emperor can separate truth from falsehood and reach a verdict. Du Bao and Liu arrive first and almost come to blows. Liu continues to provoke and directs some of his barbs at Chen Zuiliang, who deflects them with laughter. Liniang arrives, and student and former tutor again meet. She passes her first test, by casting a shadow and leaving footprints. The emperor next gathers her testimony and Liu's concerning their respective histories; there is a lot of recapitulation in this scene. Liniang must defend herself for negotiating her own betrothal. When Du Bao challenges her account, she finds his disbelief "bitter as wolfsbane." Madam Du arrives to back her daughter's claims, and Du Bao is convinced that *she* too is a malicious sprite. However, the emperor finds the mother's testimony convincing and pronounces Liniang mortal. He questions Liniang about the underworld. She responds with a lurid account of how traitors are punished there, which all save Du Bao are agog to hear. Liniang then accuses her father of equally harsh measures. The emperor orders all to resume their proper relationships. Du Bao remains intransigent, but relents when Liniang, overcome with emotion, faints. All that remains is for the other players (Chunxiang, Sister Stone, Han Zicai) each to make a brief appearance onstage. Han Zicai reads the emperor's final proclamation, which bestows honors on each member of the family. There is no final reconciliation between Du Bao and Liu, however.

HHJ has Chen Zuiliang, as chamberlain, speak the emperor's lines rather than an actor offstage. Liu's personal history and Liniang's defense of her actions are cut, as is Liniang's lurid account of punishments in the underworld, and the emperor's question concerning them. After Madam Du gives her testimony, the family is ordered to retire to the prime minister's residence and resume their proper relationships.[23] Zang reassigns Du Bao's cry from the heart when Liniang faints: "Liniang, my daughter!" to Madam Du, and as the play concludes Miao Shunbin reads the emperor's final edict (Han Zicai's character having been cut). *FLM* rewrites some arias and some dialogue, but little of significance is changed.

Liniang's account of the underworld is less long and less lurid; Chen Zuiliang finds fault with all three parties when he attempts to mediate. Most interesting is Feng's handling of the moment of recognition between father and daughter. Where Zang reassigned this gesture to Madam Du, Feng makes Du Bao's action more explicit: "Daughter, your father recognizes you." After Han Zicai reads the emperor's edict, Feng deploys two short, rewritten concluding arias that mention key elements in the play's design: the two dreams and the portrait. The final envoi (of two) mentions Feng as reviser of Tang's play.

Appendix C

Extracts from *Mudan ting*

Three kinds of collections of extracts from *Mudan ting* are listed below in the order used in chapter 4. Commas separate items arranged in sequence in the source; semi-colons separate extracts not in sequence. If an extract has been given a new title, the original title is given in parentheses (for items listed under "Miscellanies"); for the rest, both new and original titles will be given only at the first occurrence.

Miscellanies (選本, with no musical notation)[1]

1. *Shanshan ji* 珊珊集 (1616; *SBXQCK* 14): 言懷 (2).
   Four volumes. An augmented reprint of an earlier work of the same name, containing seventy-three extracts from forty-one plays. The plays are not equally represented. *Pipa ji*, *Xixiang ji* and *Jingchai ji* have five extracts each; other early Ming plays: *Baiyue ting* (four), *Huansha ji* (three), *Mingzhu ji*, and *Fenxiang ji* (three). The remainder are allotted either one extract or two. Very little dialogue is included.
2. *Yuefu xianchun* 樂府先春 (Wanli): 驚夢 (10).
   Not seen. Full title: *Jingxuan dianban Kundiao shibuji Yuefu xianchun* 精選點板崑調十部集樂府先春 (Select dramas in the Kun style, 'Early spring at the Music Bureau,' ten collections, with rhythmic notation). Compiled by Chen Jiru 陳繼儒 (1558–1639). Copy in Beijing Library.[2]
3. *Yue lu yin* 樂露音 (late Wanli; *SBXQCK* 15–16): 硬拷 (53); 驚夢 (10), 尋夢 (12), 玩真 (26), 幽媾 (28); 寫真 (14), 鬧殤 (20), 魂遊 (27).
   Four volumes. Dramatic *qu* only. Two hundred and twenty-two extracts from eighty-eight plays (sources for nine extracts not identified).
4. *Cilin yixiang* 詞林逸響 (1623; *SBXQCK* 17–18): 驚夢 (10), 尋夢 (12).
   Four volumes: two collections are devoted to *sanqu*; two others to dramatic *qu*. Early Ming *chuanqi* make up one collection with seventy-four extracts from eight plays. *Pipa ji* (thirty-three extracts) and *Xixiang ji* (fifteen) are best represented. In the other collection of dramatic *qu*, sixty-seven extracts from thirty-six of the "most popular" plays are given. Arias only.
5. *Yuefu eyun bian* 樂府遏雲編 (Ming, post Wanli): "還魂記."
   Not seen. Three volumes. Compiled by Huai Ding 槐鼎 and Wu Zhijun 吳之俊. Extracts from fifty-five *chuanqi* plays. Those from *Huanhun ji* are in vol. 1, with extracts from ten other plays. This fine illustrated edition preserves arias but no dialogue. Copy in Nanjing Library.[3]
6. *Wanhuo qingyin* 萬壑清音 (1624; *SBXQCK* 48–49): 冥判還魂 (23).

Eight volumes. Sixty-eight extracts from thirty-seven northern and southern plays. Northern *qu* only, with *dianban* notation. Original in Kyoto University Library.

7. *Yichun jin* 怡春錦 (ca. 1628–1644; *SBXQCK* 19–20): 驚夢 (10); 尋夢 (12), 幽會 (28, 幽媾).
Six volumes. Reissue of an earlier collection entitled *Xinjuan chuxiang dianban Chantou bailian* 新鐫出像點板纏頭百練 Newly engraved, illustrated 'One hundred silks for wrapping the head,' with rhythmic notation. Sixty-one extracts from forty-seven plays, in four collections organized by category. A fifth collection contains *sanqu* by Ming authors, a sixth, fifteen extracts from fifteen plays adapted for the "elegant" Yiyang style. The Kun extracts are faithful to the versions in the complete playtext.[4]

8. *Chantou bailian, erji* 纏頭百練二集 (ca. 1628–1644): 存真 (14, 寫真), 冥誓(32), 硬拷 (53).
Six volumes. Not seen. Compiler same as for *Yichun jin* (Chonghe jushi). Seventy-six extracts from fifty-one *chuanqi*, topically arranged. With three extracts, *Mudan ting* is outnumbered only by *Yougui ji* (幽閨記), with four. Five other plays are represented by three extracts. Copy in National Library of Beijing.[5]

9. *Xuanxuepu* 玄雪譜 (ca. 1628–1644; *SBXQCK* 50): 自敘 (2, 言懷), 驚夢 (10), 尋夢 (12), 幽歡 (28, 幽媾), 吊打 (53, 硬拷).
Four volumes. Eighty-two extracts from thirty-nine plays. The texts follow the versions in the complete plays. The compiler boasts that he has corrected the mistakes and emendations made by actors that mar the text.[6]

10. *Zuiyu qing* 最娛情 (ca 1647; 1661 rpt): 驚夢 (10), 尋夢 (12), 幽媾 (28).
Not seen. Alternate title: *Laifengguan jingxuan gujin chuanqi* 來鳳館精選古今傳奇 (Returning Phoenix Lodge's select southern dramas, old and new). 1661 reprint of ca. 1647 edition. Compiled by Qingyaoyue zhuren 清邀月主人. Extracts from some forty *chuanqi* have both arias and dialogue. Copy in National Library of Beijing.[7]

11. *Zuiyi qing* 醉怡情 (ca. 1700; *SBXQCK* 54–55): 入夢 (10, 驚夢), 尋夢 (12), 拾畫 (24), 冥判 (23).
Eight volumes. One hundred sixty-five extracts from forty-four *zaju* and *chuanqi*; most (thirty-nine) are represented by four extracts, printed sequentially. A single extract is from a Yiyang opera. Arias, dialogue, and verse are included; the extracts differ in some places from the scene in the original play.[8]

12. *Xinjuan Zhui baiqiu hexuan* 新鐫綴白裘合選 (1688): no extracts fr. *Mudan ting*.
Four volumes. Update by Yishengtang 翼聖堂 of a Ming miscellany titled 白裘. Eighty-five extracts from thirty-nine plays. Copy in National Library of Beijing.[9]

13. *Zhui baiqiu* 綴白裘 (1724): contents not examined.
Not seen. Eighty extracts from fifty-three plays; eighteen extracts from fifteen plays are identified as from Kun operas. Copy in Beijing University Library.[10]

14. *Zhui baiqiu quanji* 綴白裘全集 (1694, 1740): 入夢 (10, 驚夢), 尋夢 (12), 拾畫(24), 冥判 (23).
Four volumes. Not seen. Full title: *Xinke jiaozheng dianban Kun qiang zaju Zhui baiqiu quanji* 新刻較正點板崑腔雜劇綴白裘全集 (Newly carved and corrected 'Complete patched cloak of white fur,' variety plays in the Kun style). Preface dated 1739; reprint of a Kangxi 33 (1694) edition, by Wenzhengtang

聞正堂. Compiled by Chen Erqiu 陳二球 and Wanyulou zhuren 萬玉樓主人. One hundred and twenty extracts from thirty-six plays. Collection of Lu Gong 路工.[11]

15. *Zhui baiqiu xinji* 綴白裘新集 (four collections, 1764–1767; *SBXQCK* 72 [1764 collection only]): first collection (1764): 冥判 (23); third collection (1766): 勸農 (8), 拾畫 (24), 叫畫 (26, 玩真); fourth collection (1767): 學堂 (7, 閨塾), 遊園驚夢 (10, 驚夢), 尋夢 (12), 圓駕 (55).
Sixteen volumes. Only the 1764 collection seen. Full title: *Shixing yadiao Zhui baiqiu xinji hebian* 時興雅調綴白裘新集合編 (A new collection from 'A patched cloak of white fur,' currently popular Kun operas), published by Baorentang 寶仁堂. Two hundred and thirty-two items from sixty-nine plays, distributed as follows: first collection: seventy extracts from thirty-one Kun plays, plus two opening pieces and two clapper plays; second collection: sixty-seven extracts from thirty-three plays (twenty-one first included in this collection), plus two opening pieces, one clapper play, and one occasional piece; third collection: thirty-eight extracts from nineteen Kun plays (twelve new), plus four opening pieces, two extracts for Qin *qiang*, and one clapper play; fourth collection: thirty-seven extracts from fourteen plays (five new), plus three opening pieces and two clapper plays.[12]

16. *Zhui baiqiu* 綴白裘 (1770, combined edition of six collections): first collection: 冥判 (23), 拾畫 (24), 叫畫 (26, 玩真); fourth collection: 學堂 (7, 閨塾), 遊園驚夢(10, 驚夢), 尋夢 (12), 圓駕 (55); fifth collection: 勸農 (8).
Six volumes. Not seen. Published by Baorentang. Full title for the first five collections: *Xinding shidiao Kunqiang Zhui baiqiu* 新訂時調崑腔綴白裘 (Newly revised 'Patched cloak of white fur,' current Kun operas); for the sixth collection: *Xinding Zhui baiqiu liubian wenwu shuangban heji* 新訂綴白裘六編文武雙班合集 (Newly revised 'Patched cloak of white fur,' sixth collection, combined collection [of plays from] civil and military troupes). Preface by Cheng Daheng 陳大衡 dated 1770, with additional prefaces by Shen Yingzuo 沈瀛作 (fifth collection, dated 1768) and Ye Zongbao 葉宗寶 (sixth collection, 1770). First five collections: 203 extracts from sixty Kun operas, plus twelve opening pieces and two occasional pieces; sixth collection: thirty-four extracts from thirteen Kun plays (eight new; two new plays, *Hudie meng* 蝴蝶夢 and *Feicui yuan* 翡翠園, account for twenty-one extracts), plus twenty-two clapper operas and three opening pieces. A 1770 reprint of this edition by Hongwentang 鴻文堂 is in the Capital Library of Beijing.[13]

17. *Zhui baiqiu xinji hebian* 綴白裘新集合編 (1777; *SBXQCK* 58–71): Contents for *Mudan ting* for first five collections as for 1770 combined edition. Twelfth collection: 離魂 (20, 鬧殤), 問路 (40, 僕偵), 吊打 (53, 硬拷).
Published by Hongwentang; reprint of the Baorentang combined edition of twelve collections published in 1774 under the title *Zhui baiqiu shishang Kunqiang bubian shier ji* 綴白裘時尚崑腔補編十二集 (Supplemented twelve collections of currently popular Kun operas from 'A patched cloak of white fur'). This was itself a continuation of the 1770 Baorentang edition (see preceding item). The twelve collections contain altogether 429 extracts from eighty-six Kun operas, sixty-four clapper operas, and forty opening pieces. The seventh and eighth collections appeared in 1771, the ninth and tenth in 1772. A combined edition of ten collections came out in 1773, an augmented combined edition of twelve collections in 1774. The eleventh collection, *Zhui baiqiu bangziqiang shiyi ji waibian* 綴白裘

梆子腔十一集外編 (Eleventh outer collection of clapper operas from 'A patched cloak of white fur'), contains fifty-one clapper operas; the twelfth and final collection adds thirty-seven extracts from twenty Kun operas (five new), including three new extracts for *Mudan ting*. This is the so-called "popular edition" (*tongxingben* 通行本) of *Zhui baiqiu*, from which subsequent editions derive. It was supplanted by an edition published by Sijiaotang 四教堂 also published in 1777, whose arrangement and contents differ slightly.[14]

18. *Shenyin jiangu lu* 審音鑒古錄 (1834; *SBXQCK* 73–74): first collection: 勸農 (8), 學堂 (7, 閨塾), 遊園驚夢 (10, 驚夢), 尋夢 (12), 離魂 (20, 鬧殤), 冥判 (23); continuation: 吊打 (53, 硬拷), 圓駕 (55).
    Sixty-five extracts from nine plays. Extracts from *Pipa ji* (sixteen) and *Jingchai ji* (eight) account for more than one third of the total. The last two scenes named for *Mudan ting* are part of a continuation of the collection (*xuxuan* 續選). An edition (also dated 1834) published by Huaidetang 懷德堂 under the title *Qizhong qu* 七種曲 (Seven dramas) appears to be identical with this one, but lacks the continuation.[15]

Printed *gongpu* (宮譜, with musical notation)[16]

1. *Eyunge qupu* 遏雲閣曲譜 (Preface dated 1870): 學堂 (7), 勸農 (8), 遊園驚夢 (10), 尋夢 (12), 冥判 (23), 拾畫 (24), 叫畫 (26), 問路 (40).
   The first collection to use the "raincoat style" (*suoyi* 簑衣) of notation. Both arias and dialogue are included. With the exception of "Jing meng," all other extracts are the same as those in *Shenyin jiangu lu*.[17]
2. *Kunqu zhuijin* 崑曲綴錦 (1881): 遊園 (10, but no 驚夢).
   Shanghai Library 361723. Twelve extracts (many abbreviated), from nine plays; arias only, no dialogue. Preface includes eight items on singing technique; personal entries (in red ink) by the head of the Tianyunshe 天韻社, Wu Wanxiang 吳畹鄉.
3. *Mudan ting qupu* 牡丹亭曲譜 (1921): 學堂 (7), 勸農 (8), 遊園驚夢 (10), 尋夢 (12), 離魂 (20), 冥判 (23), 拾畫 (24), 叫畫 (26), 道場魂遊 (27, 魂遊), 前媾後媾 (28, 幽媾), 問路 (40), 硬拷 (53), 圓駕 (55).
   Shanghai Library 36149–36152. Arias and extensive dialogue. Part of a set of five plays that also includes *Pipa ji*, *Baiyue ting*, *Xixiang ji* and *Chunxuege sanji* 春雪閣三記 (Three plays from Spring Snow Hall). Published by two celebrated Suzhou singing clubs. Unique to this edition, scene 27 ("Spirit Roaming") is divided in two. The first part, "The Funeral" (Dao chang 道場) consists of three arias sung by Sister Stone and celebrants, after which a lengthy Daoist liturgy has been added.[18]
4. *Jicheng qupu* 集成曲譜 (1924): 訓女 (3), 學堂 (7), 勸農 (8), 遊園驚夢 (10), 尋夢 (12), 寫真 (14), 離魂 (20), 冥判 (23), 拾畫 (24), 叫畫 (26), 魂遊 (27), 前媾後媾 (28), 回生 (35), 婚走 (36), 問路 (40), 急難 (44), 硬拷 (53), 圓駕 (55).[19]
5. *Kunqu daquan* 崑曲大全 (1925): 學堂 (7), 遊園驚夢 (10), 尋夢 (12).
6. *Kunqu xindao* 崑曲新導 (1928): 學堂 (7), 勸農 (8), 遊園驚夢 (10), 冥判 (23), 拾畫 (24), 叫畫 (26), 硬拷 (53).[20]
   This and *Kunqu xinpu* were intended as textbooks for high school students.

7. *Kunqu xinpu* 崑曲新譜 (1930): 拾畫 (24), 叫畫 (26).
8. *Mengyuan qupu* 夢園曲譜 (1933): 春香鬧學 (7, 閨塾) 遊園驚夢 (10).
   Not seen.[21]
9. *Kunqupu* 崑曲譜 (n. d.): 勸農 (8), 遊園驚夢 (10).
   Fudan University Library 994092; forty-five extracts from twenty-five plays; most plays (fourteen) given two extracts; *Changsheng dian* has the most (five). Arias and dialogue. In "Jing meng" the Huashen is played by the *chou*, and is given only a few lines of dialogue.
10. *Kunqu jijing* 崑曲集淨 (n. d.): 冥判 (23).
    Two volumes. Fudan University Library. Extensive introductory material; large sized format. Eighty extracts feature the *jing* role.
11. *Yuzhong qupu* 與衆曲譜 (1947): 學堂 (7), 勸農 (8), 遊園驚夢 (10), 花判 (23, 冥判), 拾畫 (24), 叫畫 (26).
12. *Sulu qupu* 粟廬曲譜 (1953): 遊園驚夢 (10), 尋夢 (12), 叫畫 (26).[22]
13. *Pengying qupu* 蓬瀛曲集 (1972): 學堂 (7), 遊園驚夢 (10), 拾畫 (24).
14. *Renzi qupu* 壬子曲譜 (1972, 1980): 學堂 (7), 遊園驚夢 (10), 尋夢 (12), 拾畫 (24).
    Not seen.[23]
15. *Zhenfei qupu* 振飛曲譜 (1982): 遊園驚夢 (10), 尋夢 (12), 拾畫, 叫畫 (24–26), 拾畫 (24, 錦纏道 only), 硬拷 (53, 折桂令 only).
16. *Cunxin shuwu qupu* 寸心書屋曲譜 (1993): 學堂 (7), 遊園驚夢 (10), 尋夢 (12), 離魂 (20), 冥判 (23), 拾畫 (24), 硬拷 (53).
17. *Hou Yushan Kunqupu* 侯玉山崑曲譜 (1994): 冥判 (23).
    This collection is by an actor who has specialized in the *jing* role.

Handwritten *gongpu*

These are collections containing anywhere from two to hundreds of extracts: ten of the seventeen collections examined had scenes from *Mudan ting*. There were also three extracts copied in the *zhejing* (folding text) style. I have supplied numbers for the Shanghai Library and Fudan University Library items, and where possible, have indicated dates.

1. *Zhongyang yanjiuyuan lishi yuyan yanjiusuo suocang suqu* 中央研究院歷史語言研究所所藏俗曲 (Popular songs stored at the Academia Sinica Institute of History and Philology, late Qing–Republican periods): reel 227 has three items: 遊園驚夢 (10, undated); 堆花 (scene 10 addition, 1893); 拾畫 (24).
   "Youyuan jingmeng" is written in a fine hand and follows closely the version in *Zhui baiqiu*, but with some truncation of dialogue and augmentation of stage directions. It gives *dianban*, but no *gongche* notation. The extract is referred to on the

cover as a "combined text" (*zongben* 總本) meaning that all roles are recorded rather than a single role only. "Duihua" recorded by "Wang of Fortune Fount Hall" 祿泉堂王 in a clear hand, gives *dianban*, but no *gongche* notation. This appears to be a more elaborately scripted version of "Heaped Blossoms," with dialogue for the female and male flower gods (twelve, divided into two groups according to which month they represent) and the addition of a thirteenth flower goddess for the intercalary month. "Shi hua" written in a much poorer hand. The date is based on a notation at the end of the volume in which this extract is recorded.[24]

2. *Qupu, ershiwuce* 曲譜二十五冊 (Dramatic scores in twenty-five volumes). Shanghai Library nos. 485583–485607 (ca. 1851–1908): 485584 (undated): 勸農 (8); 485587 (1868): 拾叫 (24–26); 485605 (1867): 勸農 (8); 485607 (likely date 1885–1895): 冥判 (23).

   Twenty-five volumes. Collection of the Wu lineage; *zhezixi* mingled with occasional pieces (for birthdays and auspicious occasions). Contents noted for fifteen volumes only. Nineteen plays identified; seventy-two extracts, many not identified by play.

3. *Yuchilou qupu* 玉尺樓曲譜 (Dramatic scores from the Jade Rule Studio). Shanghai Library nos. 781943–781955 (Qing, n. d.): 781944: 勸農 (8), 遊園 (10, no "驚夢"), 尋夢 (12), 魂遊 (27), 冥判 (23), 拾畫 (24), 叫畫 (26); 781945: 問路 (40), 圓駕 (55).

   Twelve volumes. Compiled by Lu Jianceng 盧見曾 (1690–1768) from Dezhou 德州 County, Shandong Province. Rare book; sixty extracts, no plays identified. Arias only, no dialogue, with *gongche* notation written vertically below each character. Elegant calligraphy, written inside red frames, on a grid of eight lines, four characters per line; no title page or prefatory material. In "Ming pan" a short aria replaces the erotic original aria *Houting hua gun*.

4. *Qupu* 曲譜 (Dramatic scores). Shanghai Library no. 14689 (Qing, n. d.): 拾畫, 玩真 (24–26).

   One volume. Forty-five extracts (plays not identified). Neat format; good calligraphy (four to five lines per page; sixteen to seventeen characters per line). Arias only; this extract follows "Shi hua Jiao hua" as found in *Zhui baiqiu*, but restores the original title for "Jiao hua."

5. *Yangchun yazou* 陽春雅奏 (Elegant renditions for the spring season). Shanghai Library nos. 500725–500728 (1875–1879); 500725: 勸農 (8).

   Four volumes. Thirty extracts, not identified by play. Elegant edition, bearing owner's seals. Arias spaced three lines per page; twelve characters per line. Both arias and dialogue included; punctuation, *dianban* notation in red; role designations outlined in red.

6. *Qupu, shiqizhong* 曲譜十七種 (Seventeen dramatic scores). Shanghai Library nos. 505309–505312 (n. d.): 505310: 勸農 (8); 505311: 駭變 (37).

   Four volumes. Thirty-three extracts from fifteen plays; arias and dialogue, all Kun operas. Nine are from plays by Tang Xianzu (two from *Mudan ting*, three from *Nanke ji*; four from *Handan ji*). For each character in dialogue tones are indicated by using a red circle at one of its four corners.

7. *Qupu, sishiqice* 曲譜四十七冊 (Dramatic scores in forty-seven volumes). Shanghai Library nos. 506229–506275 (ca. 1877–1911): 506238 (1897): 拾叫 (24–26); 506274 (1898): 勸農 (8), 506275 (1898): 勸農 (8).
   Forty-seven volumes. Approximately 130 extracts, about thirty-one plays mentioned. Some may not be Kun operas. Musical scores for gong, drums and flute are in some volumes. Many extracts (twenty-six) are not identified by play.
8. *Qupu zhi shiyizhong* 曲譜之十一種 (Eleven dramatic scores). Shanghai Library nos. 530613–530621 (n. d.); 530615: 吊打 (53); 530616: 遊園驚夢 (10), 學堂 (7).
   Nine volumes. Eighty-one extracts, forty-four plays. All appear to be Kun operas. One volume is devoted to *sanqu* and occasional pieces, and one self-authored *sanqu*, a "boudoir lament" 閨怨. Uniformly good calligraphy; the compiler has consulted several sources while assembling this collection: "Ye's scores" 業譜, "Shen Yunfei's scores" 沈雲飛譜, "Feng Xiaoru's Henan scores" 馮小如河南譜, "Zhu Minhuai's Suzhou scores" 祝民懷蘇州譜, "Zhao Yichun's scores" 趙亦純譜, "Scores of the Tan lineage from west of the river" 江右譚氏之譜, 'A patched cloak of white fur' 綴白裘, and other unspecified "old" 舊 or "borrowed" 借 scores. The title may refer to them.
9. *Qupu* 曲譜 (Dramatic scores). Shanghai Library no. 533474 (n. d.): 遊園 (10, no "驚夢").
   Nineteen extracts, seven plays (but four extracts unidentified). Neatly inscribed in notebook ruled for *gongche* notation; titles outlined in red cartouches. Arias only; no introductory aria or dialogue; *dianban* notation in red ink.
10. *Mudan ting 'Quan nong'* 牡丹亭勸農 ("Speed the Plough" from 'Peony pavilion'). Fudan University Library (late Qing, n. d.)
    A single volume of two extracts, the other being "Fragrant Hall" 馥堂, no play identified. Annotated by Feng Qisu 馮起夙. Neatly written; *dianban* notation in red ink.

Folding pocket size:

11. Fudan University Library no. 99104 (no date): 拾畫叫畫 (24–26), 尋夢 (12).
12. Collection of Zhang Wanliang 張萬良: 堆花 (scene 10 addition), 硬拷 (53).

Other listings not seen

1. Manchu court playlist for *kunqu*: plays in active repertoire ca. 1850–1875: For *Mudan ting*: Twenty-two scenes listed:[25] 言懷 (2), 請先生 (4, 腐歎?), 拜先生 (5, 延師?), 勸農 (8), 學堂 (7) 遊園, 驚夢 (10), 別駝 (13, 訣謁), 尋夢 (12), 起兵(19, 牝賊?), 寫真 (14), 拷春 (11, 慈戒), 離魂 (20), 冥判 (23), 拾畫叫畫 (24, 26), 幽媾 (28), 掘墳 (35, 回生), 問路 (40), 尋元 (52, 索元), 吊打 (53, 硬拷), 圓駕 (55).
2. Manuscript *gongpu* from the collection of the Shengpingshu, now in the library of the Chinese Drama Academy in Beijing (Zhongguo xiju yanjiuyuan tushuguan):[26] 言懷 (2), 悵眺曲譜 (6), 勸農曲譜 (8), 遊園驚夢

(10), 遊園驚夢 (10), 慈戒, 尋夢曲譜 (11–12), 訣謁曲譜 (13), 寫真曲譜 (14), 鬧殤曲譜 (20), 吊打, 硬拷曲譜 (53).

3. Other Qing manuscripts of single scenes in the collection of the Chinese Drama Academy:[27] 遊園驚夢 (10), 尋夢 (12), 尋夢曲譜 (12), 拾畫叫畫 (24–26),[28] 硬拷曲譜 (53), 吊打曲譜 (53), 硬拷, 圓駕曲譜 (53, 55),[29] 吊打, 圓駕曲譜 (53, 55).
4. Manuscript *gongpu* from the collection of the Shengpingshu in the Palace Library, Beijing (Gugong bowuyuan tushuguan):[30] 閨塾曲譜 (7), 勸農 (8), 遊園驚夢曲譜 (10), 尋夢曲譜 (12), 拾畫, 叫畫曲譜 (24, 26).[31]
5. Other: 遊園驚夢 (10).[32]

Notes

List of Abbreviations

Full citations for these works appear in the bibliography under either the author's name or the title of the work.

FLM	*Fengliu meng*	Feng Menglong
GBXQ	*Guben xiqu congkan*	*See under title*
HHJ	*Huanhun ji*	Zang Maoxun
MDT	*Tang Xianzu xiqu ji*	Tang Xianzu
MDTZL	*Mudan ting yanjiu ziliao kaoshi*	Xu Fuming
PP	*The Peony Pavilion*	Cyril Birch
SBXQCK	*Shanben xiqu congkan*	*See under title*
SWJ	*Tang Xianzu shiwen ji*	Tang Xianzu
TXZZL	*Tang Xianzu yanjiu ziliao huibian*	*See under title*
XBHB	*Zhongguo gudian xiqu xuba huibian*	Cai Yi
ZBQXJ	*Zhui baiqiu xinji hebian*	*See under title*
ZGCD	*Zhongguo gudian xiqu lunzhu jicheng*	*See under title*

Notes to Chapter One

[1] "Yu Yi ling Luo Zhang'er," in *Tang Xianzu shiwen ji*, comp. Xu Shuofang (Shanghai: Shanghai guji chubanshe, 1982), 1426 (hereafter cited as *SWJ*).

[2] Gao Yu, *Gudian xiqu daoyanxue lunji*, (Beijing: Zhongguo xiju chubanshe, 1985), 172. Tang wrote two more plays: *Nanke ji* (The tale of the southern bough), completed in 1600, and *Handan ji* (The tale of Handan), 1601. For the date of completion of *Mudan ting*, see *Wan Ming qujia nianpu*, comp. Xu Shuofang (Hangzhou: Zhejiang guji chubanshe, 1993), vol. 3, 379, 484.

[3] *SWJ*, 735. The poem is dated the seventh day of the seventh lunar month, but no year is given; nor do we know whether the lyrics were sung only, or also staged.

[4] Huang Zhigang believes that *Mudan ting* was first performed during a ten-day celebration of Tang's fiftieth birthday, in the eighth month of Wanli 27 (1599). See *Tang Xianzu biannian pingzhuan*, (Beijing: Zhongguo xiju chubanshe, 1992), 225–26. It is possible that the complete play was performed (see n. 35 below).

[5] Over two hundred professional opera and martial artists now live in the New York area. Peter Sellars, director of the avant-garde version, *Peony Pavilion*, observed recently that the future of Chinese culture is being made outside of China, because "[t]his big question of

tradition/innovation, of generations looking for expression, is very difficult to arrive at in China." See Bob Graham, "The Tent Where Harmony Lives," Datebook, *San Francisco Examiner and Chronicle*, February 28–March 6, 1999, p. 34.

[6] *Chuanqi* designates a form of drama that originated in the south of China (hence the translation "southern drama") and was distinct from *zaju* drama, which became popular in the Yuan dynasty and was often referred to as "northern drama." Southern drama's origins can be traced to before Yuan times, but plays for which the term *chuanqi* is reserved date from the late Yuan or early Ming period. By the mid-sixteenth century *zaju* were no longer performed. Kun opera was becoming the dominant style of southern drama and would remain the major dramatic form in China until the emergence of Beijing opera in the mid-Qing dynasty.

[7] I.e., the viewer thinks the illusions are real.

[8] I.e., the viewer has no idea what is going on. The stage and couplets are mentioned in a description of the residence of the Tang lineage reprinted in *Tang Xianzu yanjiu ziliao huibian*, comp. Mao Xiaotong (Shanghai: Shanghai guji chubanshe, 1986), 1384 (hereafter cited as *TXZZL*).

[9] Mei Dingzuo, "Da Tang Yireng [Xianzu]," in his *Luqiu shishi ji* (1623 Chunxuanbaitang edition), vol. 63, 23a–b. This is a slightly modified version of a translation in Yung Saishing, "A Critical Study of *Han-tan chi*." Ph.D. diss. (Princeton University, 1992), 120–21. Yung (p. 122) concludes from the context of Mei's remarks that at least some of these performances were public and commercial in nature. Zhou Yude also discusses this letter in "Tang Xianzu shidai 'Simeng' de yanchu," in *Tang Xianzu lungao* (Beijing: Wenhua yishu chubanshe, 1991), 228–29.

[10] *SWJ*, 1127–28. Xu Shuofang dates this inscription between 1598 and 1606. Qingyuan Shi (Master Pure Source) was the patron deity of actors for whose temple Tang wrote this inscription. *Sheng* and *dan* refer to performers of lead male and female characters. A somewhat truncated translation of the inscription appears in Faye Chunfang Fei, ed. and trans., *Chinese Theories of Theater and Performance from Confucius to the Present* (Ann Arbor: The University of Michigan Press, 1999), 54–57.

[11] "When you are sent to someone's household to perform, you must at all times observe your proper station. Don't presume on people's love of my plays and demand too much wine and food, or money and gifts. Nowadays, in human affairs, the maintenance of sincerity is always difficult; how much more is this so in the theater! If one is sincere, then such things as wine and food, money and gifts cannot be enduring. All my life I have tried to be sincere, and so I have been a failure in my conduct as an official and as the head of a household." See also Tang's reply to Gan Yilu, in which he complains of actors who "learn acting only for the sake of money," *SWJ*, 1367.

[12] *SWJ*, 740, 769, 784, and 798 (for poems addressed to actors or describing performances by them); 757, 799 (prefaces that refer to performances). See also Gao Yu, *Daoyanxue*, 69–71.

[13] This according to Xu Shuofang. See *SWJ*, 1129.

[14] Wei Liangfu (fl. sixteenth century), credited with refining the technique for singing Kunshan fixed tunes (*qupai*), lived in Taicang. One of his disciples was a member of Wang's troupe. Tang learned of the performance by Wang's troupe from Vice Censor-in-chief

Zhou Mingxing, and recorded it in a preface to a poem he wrote mourning the death of a young woman from Wang Xijue's home town of Loujiang. The girl had died of anguish after reading *Mudan ting* and writing a commentary on it. For this poem, see *SWJ*, 654–55; see also Zhao Shanlin, *Zhongguo xiqu guanzhongxue* (Shanghai: Huadong shifan daxue, 1990), 31–32 (for Taicang), 65–66 (for Wang Xijue's troupe). Huang Zhigang dates these performances to 1606 or slightly later in his *Biannian pingzhuan*, 317.

[15] Pan Zhiheng gives an account of Zou's methods in "Yuan jin," in his *Luanxiao xiaopin* (Informal Essays by Whistling Pheonix), vol. 2. In poems addressed to Zou's actors Pan is highly complimentary, but his description of Zou's directing methods is not. Zou "devotes himself to ordering the rules and arranging the patterns; he draws on the ground to direct their movements and counts out grains to prescribe the rhythms." As a result, "the actors tremble with fear, their only concern to excel." Zou stressed well-rounded performances, but "under this double constraint his actors are not at ease; the higher they sing, the more scattered the notes become." See Pan Zhiheng, *Pan Zhiheng quhua*, comp. Wang Xiaoyi (Beijing: Zhongguo xiju chubanshe, 1988), 23–25.

[16] In his essay Pan mentions that he and Wu were members of the same club (*she*), perhaps one of the singing clubs that were popular among the gentry at this time. What is known of him is given in Pan Zhiheng, *Pan Zhiheng quhua*, 18 n. Pan was from Anhui and on a friendly footing with scholar officials, but did not hold a degree. For singing clubs, see Luo Di, *Xiqu yu Zhejiang*, (Hangzhou: Zhejiang renmin chubanshe, 1991), 313–14.

[17] An outline of the scenes from the play appears in Appendix B.

[18] "Qing chi," in *Luanxiao xiaopin*, vol. 4; see *Pan Zhiheng quhua*, 72–73. This description is partially translated in Fei, *Chinese Theories of Theater and Performance*, 58–59. My translation draws on one by Wai-yee Li, in *Enchantment and Disenchantment: Love and Illusion in Chinese Literature* (Princeton: Princeton University Press, 1993), 52.

[19] Fei, *Chinese Theories of Theater and Performance*, 72.

[20] These comments are from Zang's preface to his edition of Tang's four complete plays, dated 1618. The preface is included in *TXZZL*, 776–77.

[21] For Elizabethan playwrights see Stephen Orgel, "What is a Text?" *Research Opportunities in Renaissance Drama* 24 (1981): 3–6, and "The Authentic Shakespeare," *Representations* 21 (1988): 1–25. Robert E. Hegel discusses the highly differentiated audience for fiction in premodern China and reading practices associated with the various forms in which novels circulated in *Reading Illustrated Fiction in Late Imperial China* (Stanford: Stanford University Press, 1998).

[22] For the "author in the text," see Roger Chartier, "Figures of the Author," in *The Order of Books: Readers, Authors, and Libraries in Europe Between the Fourteenth and Eighteenth Centuries*, trans. Lydia G. Cochrane (Stanford: Stanford University Press, 1994), 25–59. Following the lead of Michel Foucault, Chartier discusses the emergence in Europe of an idea of the radical autonomy of a work of art and the unfettered creative power associated with it. Texts acquire an identity that is referable to the subjectivity of an author (an "author-function," defined as "the principle of a certain unity of writing").

[23] For the authorship of *nanxi* in writing clubs, see Wilt Idema and Stephen H. West, *Chinese Theater 1100–1450: A Source Book* (Wiesbaden: Franz Steiner Verlag, 1982), 127–31.

Cyril Birch notes that complete *chuanqi* playtexts were often read like novels; see his *Scenes for Mandarins: The Elite Theater of the Ming* (New York: Columbia University Press, 1995), 41. See also Hegel, *Reading Illustrated Fiction*, 12.

[24] Huang Zhigang thinks that the play was already in print in 1599, but Xu Shuofang, basing himself on the same source, is uncertain whether it references a printed or manuscript copy. He feels that the first reliable reference to a printed edition is datable to 1605 and places the printing at some time near that date. See Huang, *Biannian pingzhuan*, 245; Xu, *Wan Ming qujia nianpu*, vol. 3, 401, 485.

[25] Xu Shuofang, *Wan Ming qujia nianpu*, 3: 479. The full title is *Dushenju dianding Yumingtang ji* (Selected works from White Camelia Hall, punctuated and set by Dushenju). Dushenju was a sobriquet of Shen Jifei (fl. 1636).

[26] That edition was published by Huaidetang, which he dates to the Wanli period (1573–1620); see Tang Xianzu, *Tang Xianzu quanji*, comp. Xu Shuofang (Beijing: Beijing guji chubanshe, 1999), vol. 3, 2067–70. Xu's approach differs from that of Qian Nanyang, whose edited edition of Tang's plays was published in 1978. Qian selected a different basic text and collated it using six other editions of the complete play (five Ming, one Qing), plus two that reflect musical concerns: one compiled by the Kun opera master Niu Shaoya (c. 1560–c. 1650) and published in 1694, another with musical notation by Ye Tang (c. 1722–c. 1795), published in 1792. Xu's collation notes largely address musical rather than textual emendations.

[27] Shakespeare's habit of revising his plays, and the resulting difficulties for modern editors, is the subject of a study by Grace Ioppollo, *Revising Shakespeare* (Cambridge: Harvard University Press, 1991).

[28] This "red ink edition" (*zhumoben*) is discussed in chapter 2.

[29] One by Shen Jing (1553–1610), never printed and no longer extant, was given a new title, *Tongmeng ji* (The shared dream), as was the adaptation by Feng Menglong, retitled *Fengliu meng* (A romantic dream). Another heavily cut stage adaptation of the complete text by a man named Xu Rixi (*jinshi* 1622), was included in *Liushizhong qu* (Sixty southern dramas), a collection of popular plays published by Mao Jin (1599–1659). It was given the title *Shuoyuan shanding Mudan ting* (Shuoyuan's abridged 'Peony pavilion'), to distinguish it from a largely uncut text edited by Mao Jin, and published under Tang's name in the same collection. Xu, a native of Xi'an in Zhejiang Province, cut ruthlessly but did not rewrite. I have not discussed his redaction in chapter 2, which focuses on the adapting strategies of prominent editor-publishers and promoters of the Kunshan style.

[30] For the anecdote about Tang's teacher Luo Rufang (1515–1588), see *SWJ*, 1166, "Xiucai shuo"; for Tang's exchange with Zhang Wei (grand secretary, 1592–1598), see *TXZZL*, 855 or *SWJ*, 1544–45 (Chen Jiru's [1558–1639] preface to *Mudan ting*). For Tang's elevation of *qu* to the status of *shi*, see Cheng Pei-kai's discussion of his inscription for the temple honoring Qingyuan Shi cited above, in "Reality and Imagination: Li Chih and T'ang Hsien-tsu in Search of Authenticity" (Ph.D. diss., Yale University, 1980), 300–2. C. T. Hsia discusses Tang's dramatic *oeuvre* as an extended meditation on the place of *qing* in human experience in "Time and the Human Condition in the Plays of T'ang Hsien-tsu," in *Self and Society in Ming Thought*, ed. Wm. Theodore de Bary (New York:

Columbia University Press, 1970, 249–70, as does Wai-yee Li in *Enchantment and Disenchantment*, 50–77. Lu Shulun of Fudan University likewise discussed Tang's drama in the context of late Ming discourse on *qing*, in a lecture course on Ming drama that I attended in 1983.

[31] *Antouju* was a pejorative label used for plays written for coteries of highly literate readers, which seldom if ever were publicly performed.

[32] Xu Shuofang feels that Shen Jing wrote *Tongmeng ji* shortly after 1607. See *Wan Ming qujia nianpu*, vol. 1, 315–17. In letters to friends Tang derided Shen and those like him for their obsession with rules, and in letters to actors he insisted that they use his text. See *SWJ*, 1299, 1337, 1345, 1426.

[33] *Fengliu meng* has been described as a "directorial playtext" (*daoyan juben*) in Gao Yu, *Daoyanxue*, 91. In his preface to *Shuangxiong ji* (A pair of heroes), Feng announced that he planned to issue several dozen revised *chuanqi* plays one by one "to instruct the specialist" (*yi shou zhiyin*). Patrick Hanan, however, feels that many of the marginal comments in Feng's editions critique performances by "vulgar" (i.e., professional) actors and were directed at them in an effort to influence their performances; see *The Chinese Vernacular Story* (Cambridge: Harvard University Press, 1981), 93. In *Reading Illustrated Fiction* (p. 272) Robert Hegel suggests that models were used in the traditional arts in China, in particular where professional artists were concerned, in ways that entailed "parroting" ideology assigned by authority and inscribed in the model. Such parroting is consistent with Feng's project to create and publish model *chuanqi* plays.

[34] Feng's dialogue is punctuated and rhythmic notation is provided for the arias. Extensive marginal commentary is devoted largely to stagecraft, but no illustrations are included. Zang's text lacks notation of any kind—a mark of connoisseurship—and his commentary is devoted largely to fine points of Kun opera singing technique. Tang's preface is reproduced in elegant cursive script, with high-quality illustrations for thirty-seven of fifty-five scenes placed at the beginning of the first of two volumes. Feng's prefaces—his own and Tang's—are produced in standard block forms. For standard formats as aids to reading, see Hegel, *Reading Illustrated Fiction*, 110–27; for the practical bent of Feng's drama commentaries, see Hanan, *Vernacular Story*, 91.

[35] See chapter 5 for evidence supporting this inference. As already noted, Huang Zhigang feels that *Mudan ting* was performed entire for Tang's fiftieth birthday, based on the fact that the celebrations went on for ten days, a likely interval for performance of a complete *chuanqi* play. Jiang Jurong feels that the entire play has been performed several times, using adaptations such as *Fengliu meng* on most occasions; see "*Mudan ting* yanchu xiaoshi," *Shanghai xiju*, no. 6 (June 1998): 1–4. Lu Eting presents evidence that the play was performed complete (but sanitized) at the Qianlong emperor's court in "Qingdai quanbenxi yanchu shulun," in *Ming Qing xiqu guoji yantaohui lunwen ji*, ed. Hua Wei and Wang Ailing (Taibei: Zhongyang yanjiuyuan Zhongguo wenzhe yanjiusuo choubeibu, 1998), vol. 1, 336–38.

[36] Hu Ji and others coined the term "*zaidu chuangzao*" for the work of actors who reworked *chuanqi* as *zhezixi*; see Hu Ji and Liu Zhizong, *Kunju fazhan shi* (Beijing: Zhongguo xiju chubanshe, 1989), 401. Yan Changke traces the practice of performing

extracted scenes to the Jiajing and Longqing reigns of the Ming dynasty (1522–1572), and suggests that the term itself derives from the designation for scene divisions used in Yuan *zaju*; see "Tantan zhezixi," *Zhonghua xiqu*, no. 6 (August 1988), 243–44.

[37] Amateurs typically came from the social elite, professional actors from the social margins.

[38] Three million *yuan* (approximately $365,000 U.S.) was given to the troupe by the government, and it is rumored that then-Party Secretary Jiang Zemin, a fan of Kun opera, ordered the support.

[39] James R. Oestreich, "Lincoln Center to Revive Opera Thwarted by China," *The New York Times*, March 16, 1999. For the original claim, see Ann Haskell, "Dream Lovers," *Stagebill*, July 1998, 7, and publicity by the Lincoln Center Festival, which described Chen's production as "the most extensive presentation of Kunju opera in the world." Mr. Sellars expresses "deep interest" in tradition, and describes himself as "in dialogue" with it, but he also feels that traditions have become frozen in the twentieth century, and that in this transition period he is endeavoring to "make it [tradition] new." These comments were made at a "Critic's Circle" panel convened on March 7, 1999, in conjunction with performances of his *Peony Pavilion* at Zellerbach Hall, on the campus of the University of California at Berkeley.

[40] Catherine Clément, *Opera, or the Undoing of Women*, trans. Betsy Wing (Minneapolis: University of Minnesota Press, 1988), 18–19.

[41] Clément speaks of Western operatic music as a "fog" that obscures the words. But libidinal pleasure is not occluded, since music taps directly into the unconscious, circumventing the rationality of language, so that "the less one hears the words, the greater the pleasure." *Opera*, 21.

[42] Clément, *Opera*, 21. She refers to this recent development as "something like the latent return of the opera text."

[43] By *Los Angeles Times* music critic Mark Swed, at the "Critics Circle" panel in Berkeley.

[44] The person who described it to me in this way liked the production. Others with whom I spoke in Shanghai a year after the show was blocked from leaving disparaged it as a "traveling museum" of traditional Chinese performance arts that catered to foreigners' curiosity.

[45] An informative account of the production's genesis and fortunes, by the man who came up with the idea for it, is John Rockwell, "Love, Death and Resurrection, in and of *The Peony Pavilion*," *Kaikodo Journal* 15 (spring 2000): 10–24. A critical assessment by David L. Rolston is "Tradition and Innovation in Chen Shi-Zheng's *Peony Pavilion*," part of a symposium on this production and that by Peter Sellars in *Asian Theatre Journal* 19, no. 1 (spring 2002).

[46] I recorded this comment during rehearsals in Vienna in the spring of 1998. I am very grateful to Mr. Sellars and the members of his cast and crew for welcoming me to rehearsals there and in New York, London, and Berkeley.

[47] This comment by Meiling Cheng, of the School of Theater at the University of Southern California, was made at the "Critic's Circle" panel.

[48] This was pointed out by the performers themselves during rehearsals in the spring of 1998. The *xiaosheng* actor Zhang Jun remarked to a reporter that he had always conceived the character he played as a handsome, urbane, and pure youth, but "only after having read the complete playtext did I know that he [Liu Mengmei] is a common sort of man [*suren*] intent on becoming an official and getting rich." See Cai Ying, "Shang Kun xiaozibei jiqing tiao daliang" (The young generation of Shanghai Kun opera [actors] enthusiastically shoulder the main beam), *Qingnian bao*, April 1, 1998. The *raison d'être* for *zhezixi* is to preserve the "essence" of the old *chuanqi* plays, while getting rid of the "dregs." This view was expressed in a preface to a combined edition of the popular drama miscellany *Zhui baiqiu*, first published in 1774: "suck the essence and spit out the dregs; get rid of the trite and replace it with what is new" (*ju jinghua er tu zaopo, qu chenfu er geng xinying*). For this quote, see Yan Changke, "Tantan zhezixi," 251.

[49] "Complete" here refers to productions consisting of several scenes linked together to make up an evening's entertainment. Most of the scenes are revised *zhezixi*. One such production by the Shanghai troupe in 1982, which removed or rewrote sexually sensitive language, set off a debate in the press about how best to handle the erotic language of the original text.

[50] McKenzie, *Bibliography and the Sociology of Texts* (London: The British Library, 1986), 8–16; Chartier, *Forms and Meanings: Texts, Performances, and Audiences from Codex to Computer* (Philadelphia: University of Pennsylvania Press, 1995), 21.

[51] Chartier, *Order of Books*, 2–3. He bases these observations on Michel de Certeau's assertion that "the text has a meaning only through its readers; it changes along with them; it is ordered in accord with codes of perception that it does not control"; see *The Practice of Everyday Life*, trans. Steven Rendall (Berkeley: University of California Press, 1988), 170.

[52] Chartier, *Order of Books*, viii–xi.

[53] Chartier, *Forms and Meanings*. One case study in this book concerns a comedy by Molière that was performed both at Court and for commoner (bourgeoise) audiences in Paris. Relying on a rich array of sources, Chartier speculates about different social meanings the two audiences would find in the play, which presents the spectacle of a rich peasant who marries above his station.

[54] For Ming publishing and the respect accorded fiction and drama in the late Ming period, see Hegel, *Reading Illustrated Fiction*, 154–62; see also Lin Heyi, "Wan Ming xiqu kanxing gaikuang," *Hanxue yanjiu* 9, no. 1 (June 1991): 287–328. For commentaries and fiction, see David L. Rolston, *Traditional Chinese Fiction and Fiction Commentary: Reading and Writing Between the Lines* (Stanford: Stanford University Press, 1997).

[55] That Tang Xianzu took such interest is attested in the letter to Luo Zhang'er quoted at the head of this chapter. See also his "Da Ling Chucheng," *SWJ*, 1344–45. Proprietary interest did not insure control, however. Tang did not personally oversee the printing of his plays; nor did Shen Jing, many of whose works were printed with the assistance of his friend Lü Tiancheng (1575–c.1624). See Wang Jide's *Qulü*, "Zalun," item no. 92. I have consulted Chen Duo and Ye Changhai's annotated volume, *Wang Jide Qulü* (Changsha: Hunan renmin chubanshe, 1983) and follow the continuous numbering of Wang's "Zalun" there. For this item, see page 246; see also *Zhongguo gudian xiqu lunzhu jicheng*, comp. Zhongguo

xiju yanjiuyuan (Beijing: Zhongguo xiju chubanshe, 1959), vol. 4, 172 (hereafter cited as *ZGCD*). Rolston notes the practice whereby *chuanqi* playwrights claimed authorship of their work in prefaces or prologues in *Traditional Chinese Fiction and Fiction Commentary,* 243 n. 86. Tang Xianzu, for example, identified himself and injected a strongly subjective tone into the first aria of *Mudan ting*'s prologue.

[56] The quoted phrase is from Mao Yuanyi's preface to the "red ink" edition of *Mudan ting* published in 1620, which sharply criticizes Zang's adapting strategy.

[57] See Appendix C. Wu Shuyin names thirty-five collections he has seen, but notes that there are many others he has not yet examined; see "Ming chuanqi qumu gouchen," in *Xiqu yanjiu* 40 (1992): 157–74. Many of these are reprinted in the series edited by Wang Qiugui, listed in the bibliography. Li Ping numbers late Ming drama miscellanies in the hundreds, but doesn't specify how inclusive his designation is. See his "Liuluo Ouzhou de sanzhong wan Ming xiju sanchu xuanji de faxian," in *Haiwai guben wan Ming xiju xuanji sanzhong*, ed. Li Fuqing (Boris Riftin) and Li Ping (Shanghai: Shanghai guji chubanshe, 1993), 9.

[58] Hong Sheng (1605–1704) and Kong Shangren (1648–1718) were the last of the great literati playwrights of southern drama.

[59] It is also illustrated by the careers of Yu Zhenfei (1902–1993) and Mei Lanfang (1894–1961). The former, one of the major Kun artists in the twentieth century, supported himself as a performer of *xiaosheng* roles in Beijing opera. Mei Lanfang, the century's most famous female impersonator in Beijing opera, was also known for his performances of several *zhezixi* in the Kun opera repertoire. He introduced many innovations still used by Kun actors when performing these extracts. For Yu Zhenfei's life and career, see Tang Baoxiang, *Yu Zhenfei zhuan* (Shanghai: Shanghai wenyi chubanshe, 1997).

[60] In Beijing in 1995 I met Shen Huazhong, who exemplified the passion for musical annotation of libretti that is unique to Kun opera. Shen, then retired, explained that revision of *gongpu* had to be undertaken in every generation, not only because the tonality of the language was constantly changing, but also because interpretation of the texts also changed. As an example he cited a phrase from scene 10 of *Mudan ting*—"*xian tingyuan*" (untrodden court)—for which musical notation in the late Qing *gongpu Eyunge qupu* is highly embellished, hence inappropriate, in his opinion, for a sheltered young woman such as Du Liniang to sing. For reasons such as this, he feels it is impossible to reconstruct how arias from *Mudan ting* sounded when they were first performed.

[61] In 1995 I became acquainted with some of the next generation of Kun actors, who completed their school training in 1992. But the complicated circumstances in which the troupe was enmeshed as they rehearsed a seven-hour production of *Mudan ting* that was to premiere in October 1999 prevented me from renewing the contact during a visit to Shanghai in May of that year. For the "Chuan" generation of Kun actors, see Hu Shanyuan, "Xianni she zhi qianhou," *Zhongguo kunju yanjiuhui huikan* 3 (October 1987): 30–39.

[62] In poetry this aesthetic reaches back to the Song dynasty. See Murakami Tetsumi, "Gazoku kō," in *Chukoku ni okeru ningensei no tankyū*, ed. Osamu Kanaya (Tokyo: Sōbunsha, 1983), 455–77.

[63] Contemporary actors turn to dialect opera for new ideas about how to stage *Mudan ting*, and scholars in Suzhou and Kunshan have documented traditions of rural *Kunqu* sustained by itinerant professional artists (*tangming*) into the 1950s. Generally speaking, few *zhezixi* from *Mudan ting* have been performed in these forms. I discuss a few of these sources in chapter 4, but lack adequate material to write about *Mudan ting* as dialect opera.

[64] Lawrence W. Levine, *Highbrow/Lowbrow: The Emergence of Cultural Hierarchy in America*. Cambridge: Harvard University Press, 1994.

[65] Hegel, *Reading Illustrated Fiction*, 333.

[66] See chapter 5.

[67] Pierre Bourdieu, *The Field of Cultural Production: Essays on Art and Literature*, ed. Randal Johnson (New York: Columbia University Press, 1993), 51, 93, 96.

[68] For restricted and large-scale fields of cultural production and Bourdieu's concept of autonomous cultural production, see his *Field of Cultural Production*, 115–31, 37–41.

[69] Chartier, *Forms and Meanings*, 86, and 83–90 more generally, especially 89, where Chartier explains how his idea of appropriation differs from existing definitions: "I propose a reformulation of the concept of appropriation that accentuates plural uses and diverse understandings and diverges from the meaning Michel Foucault gives appropriation when he holds 'the social appropriation of discourse' to be one of the primary procedures for gaining control of discourses and putting them beyond the reach of those who were denied access to them. It also parts company with the meaning hermeneutics gives to appropriation, which is identified with the process of (postulated as universal) interpretation."

[70] Chartier, *Forms and Meanings*, 86, 93, for the difficulties of describing such popular uses of texts.

[71] See Elizabeth Wichmann, *Listening to Theater* (Honolulu: University of Hawaii Press, 1991), 7–12; A. C. Scott, *The Classical Theatre of China* (London: George Allen and Unwin Ltd., 1957), 58–78.

Notes to Chapter Two

[1] Feng Menglong's *Fengliu meng* appeared sometime after 1623, Xu Rixi's redaction of *Mudan ting* sometime in the Chongzhen era (1628–1644), in Mao Jin's anthology *Liushizhong qu*. Zang Maoxun titled his adaptation *Huanhun ji* (hereafter cited as *HHJ*).

[2] This edition was published in 1616. *Yuanqu xuan* was published in two parts of fifty plays each in 1615 and 1616. See Xu Shuofang, *Yuanqu xuanjia Zang Maoxun* (Beijing: Zhongguo xiju chubanshe, 1985), 48; see also Xu's chronological biography for Zang in *Wan Ming qujia nianpu*, vol. 2, 479–80.

[3] Xu Shuofang notes that the illustrations for Zang's edition were the finest of any made for the play; see *Yuanqu xuanjia*, 37. They appear in the edition of Tang's plays edited by Qian Nanyang, *Tang Xianzu xiqu ji* (Shanghai: Shanghai guji chubanshe, 1978; hereafter cited as *MDT*). Yung Sai-shing concludes that Zang's editions were intended for members of his own social circle (official-literati); see his "Critical Study," 168. Other southern dramas

with which Zang is associated are *Tanhua ji* (Night-blooming cereus), by his friend Tu Long (1542–1605), and the early Ming play *Jingchai ji* (The thorn hairpin).

[4] Yung, "Critical Study," 156–58, 167–68. Illustrations aside, other evidence of Zang's intended audience is the form in which the text is printed. Nothing indicates how the arias should be sung. *Chenzi* (padded words) are not printed in lighter type, and marks are not provided that indicate beat placement (Feng Menglong provided both). For this format as an indication of connoisseurship, see chapter 4.

[5] Yung, "Critical Study," 164.

[6] For this preface, see the edition of *Yuanqu xuan* published in 1958 by Zhonghua shuju (vol. 1, 3–4), reprinted in *Zhongguo gudian xiqu xuba huibian*, comp. Cai Yi (Beijing: Qi Lu shushe, 1989), vol. 1, 339–40 (hereafter cited as *XBHB*). James Crump translates Zang's prefaces to the first and second collections in "Giants in the Earth: Yuan Drama as Seen by Ming Critics," in *Chinese and Japanese Music-Dramas*, ed. J. I. Crump and William P. Malm (Ann Arbor: Center for Chinese Studies, 1975); for the passage concerning Tang in the second preface, see p. 15. See also Zang's preface to his edition of Tang's plays, "Yumingtang chuanqi yin," reprinted in *TXZZL*, 776. Xu Shuofang remarks on the superiority complex of Zang, Shen Jing, and Feng Menglong, for whom those who did not write in the Kun style were, in Xu's words, "self-taught outsiders" (*pangmen waidao*). He points out that Tang Xianzu wrote *Mudan ting* before Kun opera had achieved hegemonic status (*Yuanqu xuanjia*, 10). Wu Mei (1884–1939) likewise had found it unreasonable to criticize Tang for failing to conform to a later standard. See his *Zhongguo xiqu gailun* (General outline of Chinese drama), in *Wu Mei xiqu lunwen ji*, ed. Wang Weimin (Beijing: Zhonghua xiju chubanshe, 1983), 158; also *SWJ*, 1574.

[7] For the exalted circles (social and literary) in which Zang moved, see Yung, "Critical Study," 157–68.

[8] *Danghang* refers to the work of a theatrically oriented playwright (*hangjia*) as opposed to one known for literary brilliance (*mingjia*); see Xu Shuofang, *Yuanqu xuanjia*, 5.

[9] Xu, *Yuanqu xuanjia* 6, from the preface to the second (combined) edition of *Yuanqu xuan* (1616); see *XBHB*, vol. 2, 439, and Crump, "Giants in the Earth," 13–15.

[10] "Repertoire" in the sense of each aria's musical form and the styles of singing appropriate to each. The phrase is from a song suite "On Qu," which originally appeared at the beginning of Shen's play *Boxiao ji* (Occasions for laughter). It is reprinted in *Shen Jing ji*, comp. Xu Shuofang (Shanghai: Shanghai guji chubanshe, 1991), 849–50.

[11] Xu Wei had written that "rather than making an aria literary and obscure, why not leave it crude, [even if it runs the risk of] being despised for being too easy to understand?" See item 12 in his *Nanci xulu*, in *ZGGD*, vol. 3, 243. I have used the translation by K. C. Leung, *Hsu Wei as Drama Critic: An Annotated Translation of the Nan-tz'u hsü-lu* (Eugene: University of Oregon Press, 1988), 72. Xu Wei's bias favored northern drama. Shen Jing and Wang Jide were friends, but Wang criticized Shen because he thought his language was not sufficiently embellished; Wang himself favored a balance of elegant and plain language in southern drama. I return to this aesthetic of balance in chapter 5.

[12] *Wan Ming qujia nianpu*, 6; see also Edmond Yee's entry on Shen in *The Indiana Companion to Traditional Chinese Literature*, ed. and comp. William H. Nienhauser, Jr. (Bloomington:

Indiana University Press, 1986), 675. For a different appraisal of Shen's dramatic *oeuvre*, see the next note.

[13] Zhu Wanshu draws attention to Shen's practical interest in performance and contact with popular troupes, in "Changshang zhi qu de changdaozhe yu shijianzhe—Chongping Shen Jing de xiqu lilun ji chuangzuo," *Xiqu yanjiu* 27, no. 9 (1988): 185–207. He feels that Shen's tendency to string together playlets of three to five scenes, in a format of thirty to thirty-five scenes altogether, was "actor friendly" (p. 199). I discuss the practice of pure singing in chapter 4.

[14] Zhou Yude surveys each man's methods for editing plays in "'Linchuan simeng' de Ming Qing gaiben," *Tang Xianzu lungao*, 239–52. He offers a more detailed discussion of Zang's methods in "Hua shuo Zang Jinshu gaiben Simeng," *Jiangxi xiju*, no. 3 (1982): 14–18.

[15] Zang's versions of some *zaju* preserve less than half of the original text and in others perhaps sixty percent; see Xu Shuofang, *Yuanqu xuanjia*, 43. Zhou Yude notes that Zang cut more than half of the arias from *Mudan ting*, keeping 195 of the original 403, exclusive of codas. Many of these were extensively rewritten. See Zhou Yude, "Hua shuo Zang Jinshu," 16. Yung Sai-shing discusses Zang's revision of *Handan ji*, but not how he rewrote text. See "Critical Study," 179–87.

[16] Yung Sai-shing feels that Zang's most significant changes to *Handan ji* are at the level of individual arias. See "Critical Study," 179.

[17] Birch, *Scenes for Mandarins*, 152.

[18] From Zang Jinshu [Maoxun], "*Zichai ji* zongpi," in *Yuming xinci, sizhong*, 1618 woodblock edition in the National Central Library, Taiwan; microfilm, University of Michigan, vol. 2, 36.57a–b. Jinshu is Zang's courtesy name. At the end of his adaptation of *Mudan ting*, Zang wrote that actors lacked the stamina to perform such a long play, and "for this reason I joke that Linchuan [Tang Xianzu] never came to Suzhou to see plays." Both passages are cited in Zhou Yude, *Tang Xianzu lungao*, 242.

[19] Zang several times transposes scenes in *Mudan ting* to enable actors (i.e., the *dan* and *sheng*) to conserve energy. See commentary for his scene 21 (scene 42 of *Mudan ting*, "Troop Transfer"), transposed and inserted between the scene that depicts Liniang's resurrection (35) and the one that depicts her elopement with Liu (36). In a comment written for scene 25 (45, "A Spy for the Rebels"), Zang notes that southern dramas lack the interludes of music and dance found in *zaju*, which give actors time to rest. Another comment about sparing the *dan* and *sheng* can be found for his 16th scene (25, "Maternal Remembrance"). See Appendix B for a scene synopsis of *Huanhun ji*.

[20] In his preface to the combined edition of 1616, Zang suggests that his selection of *zaju* can serve as models for writers of southern *qu*. See *Yuanqu xuan*, "Zixu er," reprinted in *XBHB*, 440.

[21] Hirose Reiko, "Zō Mojun ni yoru *Botan tei Kankon ki* no kaihen ni tsuite," *Tōhōgaku* 81 (1991): 73–76.

[22] Hirose, "*Kankon ki* no kaihen," 73 (for secondary characters), and 74 (for scenes of similar length). Twenty-six of the thirty-five scenes in Zang's adaptation (exclusive of the

prologue) contain from five to ten arias, compared to twenty-eight of the fifty-five scenes in *Mudan ting* (see Table 2.1).

[23] Hirose, "*Kankon ki* no kaihen," 74–75, 76 for the "swelling" rhythm of *Mudan ting*.

[24] Hirose Reiko, "Mindai denki no bungaku: Tō Kenso no gikyoku ni okeru shinri hyōgen o chūshin to shite," *Tōyō Bunka* 71 (December 1990): 63–80.

[25] When citing passages from *Mudan ting*, I use the collated text in volume 1 of *Tang Xianzu xiqu ji* (*MDT*). References are to scene number and page number in this edition. For this passage, see 7.257. Unless otherwise indicated, I use the translation by Cyril Birch, *The Peony Pavilion* (Bloomington: Indiana University Press, 1980; hereafter cited as *PP*); this segment can be found on p. 30. The passage from scene 3 of *HHJ* is in *Yuming xinci, sizhong*, 1.13.12b. Here the first number indicates the part of the play (1 or 2), the second the scene number, followed by the page number. This scene is an amalgam of three from *Mudan ting*, including scene 7 ("The Schoolroom"), from which this passage is quoted. I discuss how actors subsequently have handled this segment in chapter 5.

[26] *MDT*, 9.263; *PP*, 39.

[27] *HHJ*, 1.5.16b.

[28] *HHJ*, 1.5.16b; cf. *MDT*, 10.267; *PP*, 42.

[29] Hirose Reiko, "*Kankon ki* no kaihen," 78. The Kun opera actress Fu Xueyi comprehends Zang's changes even less: how can Liniang be afflicted with lovesickness when she has yet to meet Liu Mengmei? Such venting of feeling on her part, without a hint of reserve, is completely out of character and also unbefitting her status. See Fu Xueyi, "Yi, qu, shen, se: zhengli *Mudan ting* qianshi, jian tan Zang Jinshu gaiben," *Xiju xuexi*, no. 2 (1982): 20; Zhou Yude is similarly critical of Zang's change, in "Hua shuo Zang Jinshu," 17. I discuss the original entrance aria shared by Liniang and Chunxiang in chapter 5.

[30] *HHJ*, 1.5.16b–17a; cf. *MDT*, 10.267; *PP*, 43.

[31] Hirose Reiko, "*Kankon ki* no kaihen," 79; Fu Xueyi, "Zang Jinshu gaiben," 20. For modern stage interpretations of the original aria, see chapter 4.

[32] *PP*, 180–91; for a brief introduction and commentary about this scene, see Birch, *Scenes for Mandarins*, 167–81.

[33] *HHJ*, 2.19.4a; cf. *MDT*, 32.369; *PP*, 187.

[34] See the facsimile reproduction of *Fengliu meng* in volume 3 of Feng Menglong's *Mohanzhai dingben chuanqi* (Beijing: Xinhua shudian, 1960); subsequently reprinted, with supplements, in *Feng Menglong chuanji*, ed. Wei Tongxian (Shanghai: Shanghai guji chubanshe, 1993), vol. 3 (hereafter cited as *FLM*). Citations from this play follow the method used for *Huanhun ji*. For this passage, see *FLM*, 2.23.18b–19a. At the end of Liniang's aria (*San duanzi*, which replaces *Zhuo mu fan*), Feng comments: "After this, the *sheng* need not show fear; an air of confusion [*huanghu*] will do." Earlier in the same scene he says of the portrayal of Liniang: "The most difficult thing is for a ghost in love to tell the truth [about who she is]. The performance must be hesitant and indirect. The actor mustn't criticize the arias as too many." Although he nowhere mentions Zang's adaptation, Feng probably knew of it and is likely here reacting to it.

[35] A comment by Mao Ying in his red ink edition of *Mudan ting*, published in 1620, chides Zang for "planning for the actors and giving no thought to the author's effort." See marginal comments from that edition for scenes 6 and 28, reprinted in Xu Fuming, comp., *Mudan ting yanjiu ziliao kaoshi* (Shanghai: Shanghai guji chubanshe, 1987), 116, 126–27 (hereafter cited as *MDTZL*). In his commentary, Zang states as an imperative that one must not spare even beautiful arias if they are "not good playwriting" (*fei dangjia zhi zuo*). See *HHJ*, 1.7.24a.

[36] I discuss how this sequence is now performed in chapter 5.

[37] Liniang sings two other solo arias in addition to the nine that make up the main sequence. If one excludes from the count four arias sung in irregular meter (one introductory aria, two mid-scene interludes, and the coda), Liniang sings eleven of the sixteen main arias in the scene with no other actors present.

[38] Hirose Reiko, "Shinri hyōgen," 63–68.

[39] In view of the number and kind of changes made to these and to other arias in "Pursuing the Dream," it is curious that Zang expresses concern that he might be "converting gold into iron" (*dian jin cheng tie*) only with respect to a trivial change in the fourth aria here mentioned (*Yu jiao zhi*), where he reverses two characters in one line to achieve a more felicitous rhyme. See *HHJ*, 1.7.25b.

[40] *MDT*, 12.277; *PP*, 57.

[41] Hirose Reiko, "Shinri hyōgen," 67.

[42] *HHJ*, 1.7.24a–b. At the beginning of the original scene, Chunxiang enters and exits three times, twice to summon Liniang to breakfast, and the third time (just before Liniang's long solo sequence) to convey injunctions and warnings from Madam Du concerning the garden. These annoy Liniang ("How they bully me, / Turning a simple garden / Into a forbidden paradise"). This is an example of how Tang conceives of the maid as both Liniang's intimate and Madam Du's ally. Her presence in this scene serves to increase Liniang's sense of isolation. As such, it intensifies the "pensive" quality of her interior monologue in the main sequence. Zang's comment betrays no awareness of this possible use of the maid in the scene. For another scene where the presence of maid and mother onstage draws attention to Liniang's isolation, see my discussion of Liniang's death scene in chapter 4.

[43] *HHJ*, 1.7.24a. *Ye Jinmen* replaces the introductory aria *Ye you gong* found in the original scene.

[44] *MDT*, 12.278; *PP*, 58–59.

[45] *MDT*, 12.280; *PP*, 59. The allusion in l. 4 of *Pin ling* is to a poem by Li Shangyin, "Jinse" (The patterned lute).

[46] It works that way in the last aria that Hirose discusses (*Yu jiao zhi*, sixth in this subsequence, *Pin ling* being the fourth): "So wild a place, no other hut or kiosk near, / So hard to seek, eyes misty with love / Under clear white sun and bright blue sky [*tian*], / How can I grasp what happened in a dream?" *MDT*, 12.280; *PP*, 60. Hirose feels that references to Heaven in these two arias are mutually reinforcing, "Shinri hyōgen," 67.

[47] *HHJ*, 1.7.24b. As is often the case in revisions of this kind, three new lines have been cobbled together using language from discarded arias: *Shanpo yang* in scene 10 (for l. 3), and *Haojiejie* in the same scene (for l. 5).

[48] *HHJ*, 1.7.25a.

[49] Stephen H. West, "A Study in Appropriation: Zang Maoxun's Injustice to Dou E," *Journal of the American Oriental Society* 111, no. 2 (1991): 283–302, esp. 300–2. Zang's editing of *zaju* is discussed in Patricia Sieber, "Rhetoric, Romance, and Intertextuality: The Making and Remaking of Guan Hanqing in Yuan and Ming China," Ph.D. diss., University of California at Berkeley, 1994.

[50] Hirose briefly discusses the scene in "*Kankon ki* no kaihen," 82–83; I examine Qing dynasty performance versions of it in chapter 4.

[51] C. T. Hsia, "Plays of T'ang Hsien-tsu," 271.

[52] The full rounding of the moon is a metaphor for human reunion.

[53] Shen Bin asked to be buried beneath a tree in his garden. When he died, a tomb was discovered containing an unlit lacquerware lamp and tablet bearing his name.

[54] *MDT*, 48.452–54; *PP*, 275–78.

[55] Zang complains that the use of *Bu shi lu* here four times in succession is "deadening" (*lengchang*); he substitutes *Taiping ling*. Another reason why he consistently removed *Bu shi lu* from Tang's plays is that, according to him, it is sung in a high pitch in the Haiyan style, and thus is presumably out of place in a sequence of Kun opera tunes. See his comment to *Zichai ji*, 1.6.16a, and discussion of this point in Yung, "Critical Study," 186.

[56] *HHJ*, 2.30.45a–47a.

[57] *Jing* actors in *zaju* usually portray either treacherous or low comical types; in *chuanqi* they typically portray villains or minor secondary characters. See Zeng Yongyi, "Zhongguo gudian xiju juese gaishuo," in *Shuosu wenxue* (Taibei: Lianjing chuban shiye gongsi, 1980), 275–76. Hirose ("*Kankon ki* no kaihen," 76) notes that Zang reassigns Stone to the *fujing* role, and attributes this decision to his desire to redistribute parts among a larger number of roles (ten as opposed to Tang's eight); it may also indicate a desire to relegate Stone's character to a more marginal status.

[58] *HHJ*, 1.9.34b: Stone's travesty of the *Thousand-Character Text* in "The Invalid" is "particularly disgusting"; 1.11.41a: her insertion into the mourning sequence in "Keening" is "pointless"; 2.20.8b: he has cut Tang's scene 34 ("Consultation"), in which Liu Mengmei and Stone plan for the exhumation of Liniang's corpse. Although Zang does not say why he cuts "Consultation," the motive is clearly to "cut away ugly bamboo" (*zhan ezhu*), a phrase used elsewhere in his commentary for cuts that rid the text of salacious comedy (*ehun*). See Zhou Yude, *Tang Xianzu lungao*, 244–45.

[59] Birch indicates that "all" sing. Influenced by Xu Shuofang (see n. 108 below), I think it likely that this chorus is sung by Madam Du and Liniang only.

[60] *MDT*, 48.454–55; *PP*, 279–81 (modified). In the Yuan *zaju* "The Soul of Qiannü Leaves her Body" (*Qiannü li hun*) the heroine wanders as a spirit and joins her lover, leaving behind her apparently lifeless body, which revives when her spirit returns together with the lover.

[61] *HHJ*, 2.30.47b.

[62] "Even in contexts where one character is having an exchange with another, once the singing commences we can say that it is as if the other person cannot hear the words." See "Shinri hyōgen," 63. Hirose suggests that this is the case even for arias in "The Interrupted Dream," where Liniang sings while Chunxiang interjects comments in dialogue.

[63] She cites Yoshikawa Kōjirō's discussion of singing and dialogue in *zaju*, in his *Gen zatsugeki kenkyū* (Tokyo: Iwanami shoten, 1948), 201–3, 215–16; trans. Zheng Qingmao, *Yuan zaju yanjiu* (Taibei: Yiwen yinshuguan, 1960), 191, 200–5.

[64] Elegant and common elements in drama are discussed in chapter 5. For two studies of Zang's *zaju* plays that underscore his commitment to order and reproduction of the values of his class, see the works by Kimberly Besio listed in the bibliography.

[65] Zhou Yude defines *youzuo*, as used by Zang, to mean "theatrical, suited to performance." See "Hua shuo Zang Jinshu," 16. Nine comments use this terminology; others do not, but reflect similar concerns.

[66] The scene ending coda, sung in the original by Liniang, here is shared (in slightly modified form) by maid and mistress.

[67] *HHJ*, 1.7.26a–27a. Where Zang retains Tang's language, my translation draws on that of Birch, *PP*, 61–62. For Feng's ending, which is clearly based on this one, see *FLM*, 1.9.22b–23a.

[68] Kimberly Besio, however, finds Zang's editorial interventions in *zaju* to be motivated by a desire to impose logic and order. See "From Stage to Page: Moments in the Textual Reproduction of Two Yuan Plays" (paper presented at the annual meeting of the Association for Asian Studies, Chicago, Illinois, March 1997).

[69] *MDT*, 20.317; *PP*, 109. After this coda, the scene closes with the usual pastiche, whose lines are parceled out among Du Bao, Madam Du, and the tutor Chen Zuiliang.

[70] *HHJ*, 1.11.42b–43b. Birch imparts this color by including "at least" in the last line, language not overtly indicated in the Chinese text. Zang several times concludes scenes with dialogue, another aspect of "stageworthy" writing.

[71] For iconic display in drama, see Bernard Beckerman, "Iconic Presentation," in *Theatrical Presentation* (New York: Routledge, 1990), 43–55. For ritualized comedy in Ming recensions of *zaju*, as opposed to the more unruly comedy of Yuan editions, see Besio, "From Stage to Page."

[72] Gao Yu links him as much to Wang Jide as to Shen Jing in this concern for the standardization (*guifanhua*) of southern drama, that is, Kun opera. See *Daoyanxue*, 79.

[73] Zang adapted *Mudan ting* by cutting text and rewriting arias to make them conform to the musical forms used in Kun opera; Feng also revised with Kun opera's musical structure in mind, but the scope of his changes was broader. I prefer "adaptation" to "revision," because it suggests both a process of bringing a playtext into conformity with the Kun musical style (by this time well defined prescriptively) and a process of making a literary playtext performable. In Feng's case, performability also meant accessibility both to actors and to a public that was potentially quite broad, even for this most "elite" of styles.

[74] Preface to *Shuangxiong ji* in *Mohanzhai dingben chuanqi*, vol. 1. Gao Yu notes that for this and other plays Feng rewrote and published under his studio name, he set forth many examples directed at performers, in comments placed at the beginning of his editions as well as in the upper margins. See Gao's discussion of this preface in *Daoyanxue*, 88–91.

[75] Excepting observations on the selection and training of actresses, Li Yu organized items devoted to drama under two broad headings: *ciqu* (plays) and *yanxi* (dramatic training and performance). See his *Li Liweng quhua*, ed. Chen Duo (Changsha: Hunan renmin chubanshe, 1980).

[76] *Shuangxiong ji*, *Shagou ji* (Killing the dog), and at least three plays by Li Yu (Xuanyu, c. 1591–c. 1671): *Renshou guan* (Between man and animal), *Yong tuanyuan* (Forever together) and *Zhanhua kui* (The oil peddler and the queen of the flowers; no longer extant).

[77] *Mudan ting* and *Handan meng* by Tang Xianzu, and two plays by Zhang Fengyi (1527–1613): *Hongfu ji* (Red whisk) and *Guanyuan ji* (The gardener).

[78] *Xilou ji* (The western bower), by Yuan Yuling (1592–1674), the above-mentioned plays by Li Yu, and *Sanbao en* (Thrice-requited kindness) by Bi Wei (fl. 1640s). Plays by friends or contemporaries include *Liangjiang ji* (Measuring the river) and *Saxue tang* (Snow-sprinkled hall).

[79] In addition to the two by Zhang Fengyi: *Jiujia yong* (Servant in a wine shop) and *Jingzhong qi* (Flag of perfect loyalty), *Liangjiang ji*, *Menglei ji* (A dream of rocks) and *Yipeng xue* (A handful of snow, another Li Yu play). An excellent survey of Feng's extant dramatic *oeuvre* is in Lu Shulun, *Feng Menglong yanjiu* (Shanghai: Fudan daxue chubanshe, 1987), 114–29. See also Hanan, *Vernacular Story*, 90–95 and Gao Yu, *Daoyanxue*, 85–88.

[80] Gao Yu, *Daoyanxue*, 83. In the case of Yuan Yuling's *Xilou ji*, Feng first made modest changes and substitutions in his *Xilou meng* (The western bower dream, copy in Naikaku Bunko), and subsequently revised more extensively, giving the resulting work the title *Xilou Chujiang qing* (The western bower Chu River romance). Another play that went through successive editions was *Jiujia yong*. Six of the nineteen extant plays have new titles. Hanan distinguishes plays that Feng himself wrote from those he adapted or "merely edited," in *Vernacular Story*, 91–92; for *Xilou meng*, see 121 n.

[81] Gao Yu, *Daoyanxue*, 92–117, where Gao examines "general critiques" (*zongping*) that Feng wrote for many of his plays. With eighty-four marginal comments (*meipi*), *Fengliu meng* is second only to *Chujiang qing*'s 102 in that category. See Xu Shipi, "Feng Menglong xiqu chuangzuo lilun jianlun," *Xiqu yanjiu* 31 (1989): 39. Xu numbers such comments in Feng's extant dramatic *oeuvre* (seventeen plays) as in excess of six hundred items. Feng's "general critiques" and prefaces to his and others' plays are the main sources for the studies by both Xu and Gao. Xu makes the point that Feng's comments are practical in nature, and not primarily concerned with prosodic technicalities, as were many of Zang Maoxun's. Nor are there many comments of a literary nature to be found among them. Another article that discusses Feng's comments related to performance is Lu Shulun and Li Ping, "Feng Menglong lun xiqu biaoyan yishu," *Xiju bao*, no. 13 (July 15, 1961): 32–35.

[82] Comments in some of Feng's prefaces (e.g., to *Yong tuanyuan*) would have us believe that actors used his adapted playtexts even before he completed the revisions. For changes by him that crop up in Qing performance-based versions of *Mudan ting*, see chapters 4 and 5.

[83] Hong's introductory notes to *Changsheng dian* are reprinted in *XBHB*, vol. 4, 1579–80; see also Gao Yu, *Daoyanxue*, 160–61. The difference, of course, was that Wu Wushan (1647–still living 1704) was Hong Sheng's close friend and intellectual companion. His adaptation, which reduced the number of scenes from fifty to twenty-eight, is no longer extant; his commentary to the full-length text of *Changsheng dian*, and its debt to earlier drama commentary, is discussed in Liu Hui, "Lun Wu Shufu," *Xiju yishu* 37, no. 1 (1987): 113–17.

[84] Lu Shulun believes that all first editions of Feng's plays contained a preface, general critiques, and marginal comments. See his note on editions of Feng's plays in *Feng Menglong yanjiu*, 129. Kong Shangren's comments are reprinted in *XBHB*, vol. 3, 1601–7.

[85] Gao Yu, *Daoyanxue*, 85 (for "blueprints"), 91 (for "shooting scripts"), and 118 (for earlier assessments).

[86] Alteration of original language is greatest for plays by Tang Xianzu and Zhang Fengyi—the most literary of the playwrights that Feng revised.

[87] Gao Yu, *Daoyanxue*, 88; Xu Shipi, "Xiqu chuangzuo lilun," 51. Hanan also makes this point in *Vernacular Story*, 91.

[88] In an article on Feng's methods of editing plays, Lu Shulun takes the position that Feng sought to create playtexts that would be enjoyable whether read or performed, "Xiqu bixu antou changshang liang shan qi mei," in his *Feng Menglong sanlun* (Shanghai: Shanghai guji chubanshe, 1993), 23–46. On the practice of reading southern plays as if they were novels, see Birch, *Scenes for Mandarins*, 41.

[89] See Xu Shipi, "Xiqu chuangzuo lilun," 55; also my "Feng Menglong's *Romantic Dream*: Strategies of Containment in his Revision of *The Peony Pavilion*" (Ph.D. diss., Columbia University, 1990), 7–15, where I discuss Feng's ideas about *qu*, drawing on prefaces he wrote for his own plays and for those of other playwrights.

[90] According to Yung Sai-shing, in the late Ming plays of thirty to thirty-five scenes could be performed in one day. "Critical Study," 177–78. By Hong Sheng's time, they took two days to perform.

[91] *FLM*, "General Critiques." A summary of the scenes in *Fengliu meng* can be found in Appendix B.

[92] Bai Yunsheng, a Kun opera actor active in this century, like Feng, is eager to interpret the dream in *Mudan ting* as one that the lovers share. He notes how scene 10 differs from other dream scenes, since two characters are party to the same dream: "For this reason, it is very different from other dreamscapes as far as performance is concerned. The interchange of feeling between the two parties [Liu and Liniang] must be very detailed because later in "Calling to the Portrait" ["Jiao hua," scene 26 of *Mudan ting*], Liu must recall that the portrait is the likeness of the beauty he met in his dream. Liniang, upon seeing Liu in his study calling to the portrait in "Union in the Shades" [28 of *Mudan ting*], also realizes that this is the student she met in her dream. *Chuanqi* narratives are very long; although one performs a single scene, with respect to inner feelings and performance, one seeks to grasp the interrelatedness [*qianhou huying*] of the whole play's plot." *TXZZL*, 1234.

[93] Note that Feng's remark about actors implies that it is his version of the scene that they have mangled, not Tang's, for Tang did not use *Jiangtou jingui* in this scene.

[94] *FLM*, 2.26.29a–b.

[95] *MDT*, 39.409; *PP*, 221.

[96] For the pairing of roles and dialectic of similarity and difference in *chuanqi* drama, see Zhang Jing, "Chuanqi juese zhi peida ji changmian zhi anpai," in *Hanxue yanjiu* 6, no. 1 (June 1988). See also chapter 5. For an extremely illuminating discussion of Du Liniang's and Liu Mengmei's dreams, see "The Lover's Dream," in Tina Lu, *Persons, Roles, and Minds: Identity in Peony Pavilion and Peach Blossom Fan* (Stanford: Stanford University Press, 2001).

[97] *FLM*, "General Critiques." Feng elaborates further on this critique in a marginal comment to scene 16 of *Fengliu meng* ("Plans for Burying the Deceased Daughter"): "As for Chunxiang's becoming a nun, this can be said to be [the action of] a loyal maidservant. It lays the groundwork for [her later appearance as] the little nun [scene 20, "Feelings Experienced While Spirit Roaming"], and for her recognition of Liniang's portrait [22, "Sister Stone Obstructs Joy"]. Later, after her mistress returns to life, Chunxiang becomes her companion as before. The original draft [*yuangao*] had many creepers, which I have gotten rid of with one stroke of my brush." See *FLM*, 1.16.40a. Feng's use of *gao* (a rough copy or draft) to refer to Tang's play both here and on the first page of *Fengliu meng* implies (to me) that he regarded Tang's play as a "work in progress" that he was free to improve upon. He uses similar terms, *chuanggao* (draft manuscript) and *caochuang* (rough draft), for many plays he revised heavily.

[98] In *Fengliu meng* Stone's role is reduced to one of providing occasional comic relief, indicated by a change of role assignment from *jing* to *chou* (clown). Huang Derong's assessment of her differs from mine, in "*Mudan ting* zhong Shi Daogu xingxiang lüe bian," *Jiangxi shehui kexue* nos. 5–6 (1981): 135. Shen Min's resembles mine; she proposes that "Sister Stone's function and significance are not easy to overlook," in "*Mudan ting* Shi Daogu xingxiang jianlun" (paper presented at a conference commemorating the 450th anniversary of Tang Xianzu's birth, Dalian, August 2000).

[99] The arias eliminated are two to the tune *Jiban ling*, one to the tune *Yicuo zhao*, and the coda (*Weisheng*).

[100] Tune titles that conclude with the character *zhuan* are sung to a slow, uncadenced melody and typically mark transitions between subsequences in a scene. *Bu shi lu* has similar melodic characteristics and uses. Feng thus adopts a song pattern similar to the one used in *Mudan ting* but having a different form, and rewrites the lyrics and dialogue. For *zhuan* see Wang Shoutai, ed., *Kunqu qupai ji taoshu fanli ji* (Shanghai: Shanghai guji chubanshe, 1994), vol. 1, 169–71. *Bu shi lu* is used to effect transitions between parts of a sequence with differing emotional coloration. See Zhang Jing, "Nanqu liantao shulie," *Wen shi zhe xuebao* 14–15 (1965–66): 385. Zhang elsewhere observes that Tang's use of four *Bu shi lu* aria patterns in a row in this scene is "unprosodic" (*guailü*), "Tang Ruoshi *Mudan ting Huanhun ji* qingjie peitao zhi fenxi," *Dong Wu wenshi xuebao* 1 (1976): 20.

[101] The aria Chunxiang sings, *Manpai qian baochan*, typically marks the end of a sequence or subsequence. See Wang Shoutai, *Kunqu qupai*, vol. 2, 1451.

[102] Compare the original sequence and Zang's modified version above.

[103] This dialogue matches Zang's revision, not dialogue in the original text.

[104] *FLM*, 2.30.7b–39a. Compare *MDT*, 48.451–52 (beginning with the aria *Yue'er gao*), and *PP*, 275–78.

[105] An approximation of Chunxiang's patter in English goes:

> Once she took a stroll in the garden,
> Playing with a plum sprig she became very tired.
> She dreamt of a student with a broken willow branch,
> And the two of them felt a love inspired.
> Because of this by sickness beset,
> She left behind her portrait inscribed with a lament.
> Buried it was 'neath the Taihu rocks;
> Who would have thought that Heaven would relent?
> Came a young student from South of the Ridge;
> At Plum Blossom Shrine he had to stay.
> Chancing upon her portrait there,
> He reverently called to it night and day.
> His sincerity moved her infernal soul,
> And one fine night came love's consummation.
> The Infernal Judge had permitted her rebirth,
> All that remained was the coffin's exhumation.
> That student undertook the task all alone,
> And bored his way right into her tomb.
> Gently he bore her from the nether world,
> And restored to her cheeks their peachy bloom.

FLM, 2.30.39a. In Zang's adaptation this account is accomplished in four sentences spoken by Sister Stone; in the original, Liniang sketches her experience in the underworld and resurrection in the final aria of the *Bu shi lu* sequence (*PP*, 78).

[106] So described to me by Lu Shulun of Fudan University, with whom I discussed Feng's adaptation at length.

[107] Tang sometimes used the *wenda* pattern (as in the *Bu shi lu* sequence here), but did so selectively.

[108] Tang used a similar strategy in Liniang's death scene (scene 20, "Keening"). Xu Shuofang's analysis of Shen Jing's revision of the *Fanshan hu* sequence in *Mudan ting* (one of only two fragments preserved from his adaptation) is relevant to this discussion: "In scene 48, Madam is in flight with Chunxiang from Yangzhou to Hangzhou, and unexpectedly meets with the resurrected Liniang and Sister Stone on a moonlit night. The playwright wrote an aria to the tune *Fanshan hu* for each actor. 'What night is this? / What night is this? / Or do we meet now only in dream?' This is the chorus shared by mother and daughter. When happiness is at its limit, there is doubt, which delineates most fittingly the depth of feeling between kin. The chorus sung by Chunxiang and Stone is 'Miraculous destiny, / Miraculous destiny, / The wheel of karma comes full circle.' Compared with mother and daughter, their relationship is more distant, and the emphasis here is on their feeling of amazement. Madam Du and Liniang's choral lyrics cannot be shifted to

Chunxiang and Sister Stone, and Chunxiang and Stone's choral lyrics cannot be shifted to Madam and Liniang. This is precisely the fineness of the [original] author's psychological delineation [of his characters]. Shen Jing combines Chunxiang and Sister Stone's arias into one, and has the four characters sing the same chorus. This is to force the personalities and relationships among the characters into one mold; artistically speaking, it is a retreat from the original." See "Tang Xianzu he Shen Jing," in *Lun Tang Xianzu ji qita*, 115, 114, for Shen Jing's version of Chunxiang's aria (rewritten to the tune *Manshan yi*).

[109] Marjorie Bang-ray Liu, "Tradition and Change in Kunqu Opera" (Ph.D. diss., University of California at Los Angeles, 1976), 131.

[110] Zang's approach suggests that adjusting Tang's text to suit the Kun opera musical style need not have entailed wholesale translation between two distinct repertoires of tunes, but rather local adjustments within individual tune patterns, the majority of which were part of a common repertoire for southern drama that had evolved over time. Zang himself, when commenting on a mistaken tonal pattern in an aria Liu Mengmei sings in scene 53 ("Interrogation Under the Rod") to the tune *Yan'er luo dai Desheng ling*, acknowledged that actors can simply "bend" their singing to the words as Tang wrote them (*wei qu jiu zhi*). See *HHJ*, 2.33.60a. Subsequent to the adaptations of Zang, Feng, et al. that freely revised Tang's text (and in Feng's case also changed the aria blueprint), surgical solutions were found for problems posed by Tang's text. These left the original language intact while adjusting the musical blueprint, and it was these adaptations that prevailed. For them, see my "Strategies of Containment," 65–77.

[111] This is a tendency, not a blanket rule. Some Kun opera tune patterns require that dialogue be used between the sung lines, and Zang preserved such features in his revision.

[112] For example, some editors of drama miscellanies published at the same time as Zang's edition catered to the taste for pure singing. They eschewed the use of rhythmic notation and the setting off of extrametrical words in smaller or lighter print (see chapter 4). Zang did neither; Feng did both, and he also provided information in the text about the musical structure of the tunes, including their modal category, and the constituent parts of composites (*jiqu*), which were pieced together using segments from existing tunes.

[113] Feng's preference for this manner of combining singing and dialogue likely accounts for his frequent reliance on composites. For example, both tunes he used in place of the *Fanshan hu* sequence in scene 48 of *Mudan ting* are composites.

[114] The "red ink" edition of *Mudan ting* is reproduced in *Guben xiqu congkan, chuji* (Shanghai: Shangwu yinshu guan 1954; hereafter cited as *GBXQ*). In it, some of Zang's upper margin comments, so identified, appear in red ink. Yagisawa Hajime discusses the relationship of this edition to Zang's in "*Botan tei* no hampon ni kansuru ikkōsatsu: Zō Mojun kaiteihon to Bō shi shubokuhon to no kankei ni tsuite," *Shibun* 19, no. 11 (1937): 61–65.

[115] Both Mao Yuanyi and Mao Ying's prefaces are reprinted in *TXZZL*, 852–55. A text of Mao Yuanyi's preface with annotation and explication appears in Li Ping, Jiang Jurong, and Huang Qiang, annots., "*Pidian Mudan ting ji* xu," *Yitan* no. 3 (December, 1980): 32–33.

[116] A useful study and critique of Zang's redacting methods for both *chuanqi* and *zaju* is Yagisawa Hajime, "Zang Maoxun de xiqu yanjiu," in *Mingdai juzuojia kaolüe*, trans. Luo Jintang (Hong Kong: Longmen, 1977), 449–74.

[117] Luo Jintang lists collections of four, five, seven, and ten plays, all with Feng's studio name, "Ink-Crazy Studio," in their titles. None of them include *Fengliu meng*. See his *Zhongguo xiqu zongmu huibian* (Hong Kong: Wanyou tushu gongsi, 1966), 109–10. Aoki Masaru lists a collection of seven plays (Ming edition) and one of ten plays (Qianlong period reprint of a Ming edition) in *Zhongguo jinshi xiqu shi*, trans. Wang Gulu (Hong Kong: Zhonghua shuju, 1975), 730; originally published as *Shina kinsei gikyoku shi*, in volume 3 of *Aoki Masaru zenshu* (Tokyo: Shunjūsha, 1969). A Ming edition of four plays and a collection of five plays of uncertain date are in the Naikaku Bunko in Japan. The most often mentioned and presumably most widely disseminated collection contained ten plays. According to Zhang Jing, collections of *chuanqi* plays by individual Ming playwrights were the exception, general collections (*zongji*) such as *Liushizhong qu* the rule; see *Ming Qing chuanqi daolun* (Taibei: Dongfang shudian, 1961), 98. Lu Shulun believes that the edition of *Fengliu meng* reproduced in the first series of *GBXQ* is the original one, published as a *danxingben* (single edition); see his *Feng Menglong yanjiu*, 129. It is one of only three of Feng's extant plays that enjoy this distinction. Some of Feng's revisions and adaptations went through several editions, but *Fengliu meng* was not one of them.

[118] In the preface to his collection of art songs, *Taixia xinzou*, Feng states that the role of connoisseurs of *qu* such as himself is to protect the genre from both the over-refinements of highly literate writers and the crudities of professional artisans. Lu Shulun has reproduced this preface in *Feng Menglong yanjiu*, 132–33. Feng's *Shagou ji* supplanted earlier versions of the play, and his revision and expansion of the vernacular novel *Pingyao zhuan* superceded the original work, which survives in only two copies. In the case of *Mudan ting*, it is his adaptation that has become rare.

[119] Wu Mei, *Guqu zhutan* (Leisurely talks about reading drama), in *Wu Mei xiqu lunwen ji*, 107. Lu's article is entitled "Xiqu bixu antou changshang liang shan qi mei" (The play must have beauty on both desktop and stage).

[120] Xu Shipi cites a comment by Feng to the effect that when it comes to plot in drama, audiences "hate directness and like indirection" (*wu qi zhi, xi weiwan*). I have yet to locate this comment, quoted in "Xiqu chuangzuo lilun," 54.

[121] Xu Shipi ably lays out these concerns in "Xiqu chuangzuo lilun," 51–56. For "fine jointure" (*xijie*), see page 53.

Notes to Chapter Three

[1] Leo Steinberg, "The Line of Fate in Michelangelo's Painting," in *The Language of Images*, ed. W. T. J. Mitchell (Chicago: University of Chicago Press, 1980), 85.

[2] Steinberg, "Line of Fate," 85 and 86.

[3] In addition to "Line of Fate," see his "The Metaphors of Love and Birth in Michelangelo's Pietas," in *Studies in Erotic Art*, eds. Theodore Bowie and C. Christenson (New York and London: Basic Books, 1970), 231–335.

[4] See my discussion of this convention on p. 84.

[5] In this chapter Chinese characters are provided for cited portions of sung text, but for reasons of space I am unable to differentiate metrical and extrametrical words in this chapter in most cases. I have modified Birch's translations in some places to reflect the syntax of the original verse, in other places to bring out aspects of Tang's language that serve my argument. Translations of *Fengliu meng* are my own. I am grateful to Chou Wan-yao of the Institute of Taiwan History, Academia Sinica, for assistance with these translations.

[6] *MDT*, 12.280–81; *PP*, 60. There is a pun on *ren* (seed), whose homophone *ren* (man) refers to Liniang. Xu Shuofang and Yang Xiaomei paraphrase l. 6: "I lament that the plums form their round fruit in the face of my bitterness." See their annotated edition, *Mudan ting* (Beijing: Renmin wenxue chubanshe, 1982), 64 n. My adaptation from Birch suggests correspondence between the plum's bitter seed and Liniang. In a discussion of this passage, Lu Shulun proposed that bitter seed, or bitter heart (*kuren*), intimates Liniang's death, for which see also the passage cited on p. 76. For plum's bitter fruit as a figure connoting masculine acerbity (which would link the image to Liu Mengmei), see Maggie Bickford, ed., *Ink Plum: The Making of a Chinese Scholar Painting Genre* (Cambridge and New York: Cambridge University Press, 1996), 45. The allusion is to the story of a man who encountered a beauty on Mount Lofu and drank wine with her. He fell asleep, and awoke to find himself beneath a flowering plum tree. See Hans H. Frankel, "The Plum Tree in Chinese Poetry" *Asiatische Studien* 6 (1952): 107–10.

[7] This is its sense in the vernacular story "Du Liniang muse huanhun" (Enamoured of love, Du Liniang returns to life), discussed in Hsia, "Plays of T'ang Hsien-tsu," 286 n. One of two extant versions is in *MDTZL*, 12–19.

[8] In *Shijing* 20 ("Biao you mei," "Plop Fall the Plums"), ripening plums are an image of a girl's approaching maturity; as they fall, they express the passing of time and the transience of beauty. See Hans Frankel's note to this poem, at the head of a section devoted to poems about the flowering plum, which are translated by him in Maggie Bickford, ed., *Bones of Jade, Soul of Ice: The Flowering Plum in Chinese Art* (New Haven: Yale University Art Gallery, 1985), 151–91.

[9] *MDT*, 12.281; *PP*, 61.

[10] At their first meeting, Liniang and her dream lover sing: "Somewhere at some past time you and I met [*xiangjian*] / Now we behold each other in solemn awe." *MDT*, 10.270; *PP*, 48. For earlier personifications of the plum tree in poetry and prose, and associations of plum with refined but neglected beauties, see Bickford, *Flowering Plum*, 18–22, *Ink Plum*, 54–56.

[11] In scene 12, Chunxiang discovers Liniang "Standing beneath the trailing branches of the flowering plum [*xiao li zai chuichui huashu bian*]"; in scene 22, Liu Mengmei is directed to seek shelter at Liniang's Meihuaguan (Plum Blossom Shrine), "Where snow-laden branches smile a welcome [*kan yishu xue chuichui ru xiao*]"; in scene 27 prayers are offered in the hope that Liniang might return to life and dwell beneath the canopy of the plum's flowering branches (*meihua zhang*). *MDT*, 12.277, 22.326, 27.350; *PP*, 57 (modified), 119, 150.

[12] This is how it is understood by Negeyama Tōru; see "*Kankon ki* ni okeru To shi no juyō," *Chūkoku bungaku ronshū* 20, no. 12 (1991): 50.

[13] For the allusion to Du Fu (712–770), see the annotated edition of *Mudan ting*. Birch's translation, which I keep, leaves vague what "red" refers to (blossom or fruit? If fruit, what kind?). The strong verb "*zhan*" can mean "to split," "to break open," as when a blossom splits open to form fruit. See *Hanyu da cidian*, comp. Luo Zhufeng et al. (Shanghai: Hanyu dacidian chubanshe, 1992), vol. 9, 912. For Du Fu's poem, see *Du shi xiangzhu*, comp. Chou Zhao'ao (Beijing: Zhonghua shuju, 1979), vol. 1, 151.

[14] Maggie Bickford has pointed out in a personal communication to me that "*hong zhan yufei tian*" refers to the season of "plum rains"; thus *hong zhan* cannot refer to plum blossoms, "unless he [Tang] is giving us a compressed cycle." I incline towards just such a conflation of meanings, in both Du Fu's poem and Tang Xianzu's manner of alluding to that poem.

[15] *MDT*, 20.313; *PP*, 101–2.

[16] I document these in "Strategies of Containment," 198 n. 17.

[17] *Fen kulou* (powdered skeleton) is usually a disparaging reference to a beautiful woman (*Hanyu da cidian*, vol. 9, 202–3), but that cannot be the sense here. However, I retain the sense of *fen* as "powdered" (i.e., made up). Birch translates so as to convey, delicately, a sense of decay ("Yet I should wish my bones to powder white / The caverns at the ancient apricot's roots"). Such a sense is not out of place with the readings I propose here. Caverns suggest wombs, and in this context an image of decay also conveys an impression of death as part of an ongoing process of sexuality and fertility. For caves as wombs, see Rolf Stein, *The World in Miniature: Container Gardens and Dwellings in Far Eastern Religious Thought* (Stanford: Stanford University Press, 1990), 71, 111, 291 n, 305 n. In scene 23 ("Infernal Judgment") this idea is resumed on a grand scale, when Hu Panguan (Judge Hu) makes erotic puns on a long list of flower names recited by the Huashen.

[18] Meihua anguan, also referred to in scenes 23 and 33 as "Red Plum Shrine" (Hongmeiguan).

[19] *MDT*, 27.350; *PP*, 150. The conceit of the universe contained in a plum blossom is a common one in Neo-Confucian writing of the Song and Yuan dynasties. For plum worlds as small as a flowering branch in a crystal vase, see Bickford, *Ink Plum*, 30.

[20] *MDT*, 27.352; *PP*, 152–53.

[21] *HHJ*, 1.15.56a. A comment in the "Three Wives" edition makes the same point: "Making an offering of faded plum blossoms is instrumental to Liniang's scattering of the blossoms. Before, there were only the plum tree and plum fruits; now [the author] adds plum blossoms. Moreover, [this gesture] reflects subtly on the Huashen['s action] in "The Interrupted Dream." See *MDTZL*, 126.

[22] The association of faded blossoms with lost youth is well established. See Frankel, "Plum Tree," 95–96. See also Bickford, *Ink Plum*, 53–60, and two more comments in the "Three Wives" edition (cited in *MDTZL*, 126) that comment on this trope.

[23] *MDT*, 10.271 (*Bao lao cui*); *PP*, 49. In *Xixiang ji* (The western wing), both chantefable and play, red blossoms raining in profusion (*hongyu*) mark the season of love; see Wang Shifu, *Xixiang ji*, annot. Wang Jisi (Shanghai: Shanghai guji chubanshe, 1978), 164. See also *The*

Moon and the Zither: The Story of the Western Wing, trans. Stephen H. West and Wilt L. Idema (Berkeley: University of California Press, 1991), 368. Reference to Yingying's hymenal blood in the play is delicate, but suggestive with respect to the language Tang will use with reference to Liniang: "Its spring silk [Yingying's handkerchief] was at first sparkling white / But now I see a red fragrance has sprinkled [*dian*] its tender color." See Wang Shifu, *Xixiang ji*, 138; Idema and West, *The Western Wing*, 334. For the word "*dian*," see below.

[24] *MDT*, 12.280 (*Douye huang*); *PP*, 60. The blossoms "torn from flower's heart" that she scatters on her shrine would then adumbrate shedding of hymenal blood, "flower's heart" being a euphemism for the vagina.

[25] *MDT*, 28.357; *PP*, 157. In a fourth century legend, the goddess Green Calyx achieves liberation of soul from body after 900 years of discipline. One plum species is known as "Green Calyx" (*lü emei*); Bickford, *Flowering Plum*, 247.

[26] See my "Strategies of Containment," 211–14.

[27] *MDT*, 28.361; *PP*, 163. For the association of plum with seclusion (*you*) and secluded places, see Iwaki Hideo, "Baika to hankon: Soshoku ni okeru saiki no higan," *Nippon Chūgoku Gakkai hō* 30 (1979), 135, 138, 145, 146, 148. I am grateful to Professor Ōki Yasushi of Tokyo University for bringing this article to my attention.

[28] *MDT*, 32.380–81; *PP*, 188–89.

[29] "Cold fragrance" (*lengxiang*) commonly describes plum blossoms, an attribute of their elegant chasteness that is here eroticized. See translations of poems in Bickford, *Flowering Plum*, 161, 187.

[30] *FLM*, 1.9.21b–22a.

[31] See Bickford, *Flowering Plum*, ("The Flowering Plum Recluse," 22–25); also her *Ink Plum*, ("The Flowering Plum and the Seasonal Round"), 50–53.

[32] *FLM*, 1.7.16a.

[33] Feng's garden is less remarkable than Tang's. Compare Liu Mengmei's first visit in *Mudan ting* (scene 24) with the comparable visit in *Fengliu meng* (scene 19). In both the garden is wild and deserted, but Feng omits several of Tang's arresting details (e.g., an empty swing from which dangles a girl's sash). See *MDT*, 24.338–39 (*Haoshi jin*, *Jinchan dao*); *PP*, 137; *FLM*, 2.19.1b (*Yanzi le*).

[34] *FLM*, 1.9.20b.

[35] *MDT*, 14.290; *PP*, 70. For Tang's source, see *MDTZL*, 14, This translation follows closely an unpublished version by C. T. Hsia, which he kindly made available to me. Toad Palace (*changong*) refers to the moon, while the phrase "to break off a cassia bough in the Toad Palace" (*changong zhe gui*) describes the fabulous accomplishment of success in the imperial examinations.

[36] *MDT*, 14.289 (*Qingbei xu*); *PP*, 69. In "Meifei zhuan" (Biography of the flowering plum consort, c. 12th c.), the neglected palace lady, before she dies, depicts herself standing between a pine and plum tree (emblems, presumably, of her steadfast love for the fickle emperor Xuanzong). A postface to this anonymous biography notes that a typical portrait of a court lady would depict her holding a plum branch (whether of flowers or fruits is

unclear). This story and the related tradition of court portraiture appears to be the indirect inspiration, via Tang's vernacular source, for Liniang's self-portrait. A complete translation of the biography and postface is in Howard Levy, *Harem Favorites of an Illustrious Celestial* (Taichung: Chungtai Printing Co., Ltd. 1958), 134–42. My thanks once again to Professor Bickford for supplying this reference.

[37] When Liniang's ghost gives Liu green plums in scene 30, he compares their acidity (*suan*) to his unfulfilled desire. In the same passage (and in scene 2) *suan* also refers to Liu's frustrated scholarly ambition; *MDT*, 2.235 (*Jiuhui chang*), 30.369 (l. 4 and *Zui taiping*); *PP*, 172. For the political implications of plum's sour taste (frank counsel as opposed to sycophantic speech), see Bickford, *Ink Plum*, 67. I translate portions of the passage from scene 30 below.

[38] In *Mudan ting*, the plum is mentioned exclusively in forty-five passages (nineteen in dialogue, three in poems, twenty-three in arias), and in four scenes it is especially prominent. In *Fengliu meng* there are twenty-five references (fifteen in dialogue, two in poetry and only eight in arias), with prominent mention in only one scene. *Mudan ting* contains eleven places that refer to willow and plum either in the same line of verse or in adjacent lines (three in poetry, eight in arias), while in *Fengliu meng* there are nineteen (two in dialogue and seventeen in arias). This excludes references to "willow and plum" in Liniang's poem, which are common to both plays.

[39] Feng removes all references to the plum's fruit, including a rare deletion in scene 18 ("Diagnosis") of verses declaimed by Du Liniang that refer to her dream affair as "my joy in sprig of plum" (*zan nong mei xinshi*); *MDT*, 18.303; *PP*, 88.

[40] *FLM*, 1.15.36b.

[41] *FLM*, 2.19.4a.

[42] *MDT*, 26.348, *PP*, 146–47.

[43] References to Liu Mengmei as a "bare stick" (*guanggun*), "wandering stick" (*yougun*), or simply "stick" (*gun, guntu*) are concentrated in part 2. See *FLM*, 2.32.45a.1 (l. 3 of *Liang xiuxiu*); 34.53b.3 (dialogue); 36.56a.4, 8 (both dialogue), 56b (l. 8 of *Bubu jiao*) and 58b.7 (dialogue). Tina Lu's book, which I read as this book is going to press, complicates the question of social identity for both hero and heroine in this play.

[44] Wu Mei remarked upon the fact that Tang broke with convention by assigning the principal role to a female character in two of his four plays; see *TXZZL*, 711–12.

[45] Similar concerns surface in his revisions of other Ming plays, notably *Hongfu ji* and *Guanyuan ji* by Zhang Fengyi. Feng's revisions can be found in *Mohanzhai dingben chuanqi*, vol. 1; Zhang's plays are included in *GBXQ*.

[46] There is again a pun on *ren* (man) and *ren* (seed).

[47] *MDT*, 30.369; *PP*, 172–73 (modified). See also n. 79 below regarding plantains.

[48] An anonymous commentator singles out this passage and one in scene 28 for erotic language "exceptionally subtle and obscure, outstanding from antiquity to the present." See the Bingsiguan (Ice Silk House) edition presented to the throne in 1791, which is the basis

for Liu Shiheng's edition, *Nuanhongshi huike Linchuan simeng* (1919; reprint, Yangzhou: Jiangsu Guangling guji keyinshe, 1990).

[49] Tang here borrows language spoken by Zhang Gong to Yingying in the chantefable that is the precursor to *Xixiang ji*: "Would I have deflowered you casually [*zhe ba meixi dianwu*]?" Ling Jingyan parses *meixi* as referring to the petals of the plum (*meiban*)—that is, Yingying's maidenhead. In Tang's borrowing, I feel that the referent for *meixi* is masculine (*xi* denotes the horn of the rhinoceros—more properly its tip) and have modified Birch accordingly. See Dong Jieyuan, *Dong Jieyuan Xixiang ji*, ed. and annot. Ling Jingyan (Beijing: Renmin wenxue chubanshe, 1962, 1978), 113; and Dong Jieyuan, *Master Tung's Western Chamber Romance*, trans. Li-li Ch'en (Cambridge: Cambridge University Press, 1976), 156.

[50] In her exhaustive study of plum motifs in Chinese painting, Bickford identifies a subtradition in which the plum is identified with elegant (feminine) sensuality, but when she discusses the plum's fragrance as an agent of rebirth, she does not dwell on the sexual dimension of this motif. See her *Ink Plum*, 135–138, 140, 154, and 163–64 (for red plum blossoms as sensual), but she notes (p. 164) that after the Yuan dynasty, the erotic and sensual aspects of plum imagery were largely foreclosed. For the plum's "soul-returning fragrance" (*fanhun xiang*) and regeneration, see pp. 25 and 60 of *Ink Plum*. Bickford's study of ink plum paintings emphasizes qualities associated with the plum's fragile white blossoms and cool fragrance (chaste elegance in women, moral integrity and endurance in men); see pp. 46, 51, 71, and 148.

[51] Zeng Yongyi, *Zhongguo gudian xiju lunji* (Taibei: Lianjing chuban shiye gongsi, 1975), 4; Stephen H. West, "Drama," in *The Indiana Companion to Traditional Chinese Literature*, ed. and comp. William H. Nienhauser (Bloomington: Indiana University Press, 1986), 20.

[52] E.g., the story of Zhenzhen, discussed below. In a Yuan play, *Liangshi yinyuan* (A marital affinity across two lifetimes), the courtesan Yuxiao paints a self-portrait, which after her death functions as her surrogate; in "Meifei zhuan," the emperor Xuanzong is given a portrait of the imperial consort Taizhen after she dies, but once her corpse is found at the foot of a flowering plum tree, it cannot be reanimated.

[53] For a brilliant discussion of Tang's use of portraits in the play, see Lu, *Persons, Roles, and Minds*, 28–62 ("The Girl's Portrait").

[54] For Liniang's self-portrait as a representation of her dream self, see Richard Vinograd, *Boundaries of the Self: Chinese Portraits, 1600–1900* (Cambridge: Cambridge University Press, 1992), 17; also Judith Zeitlin, "Shared Dreams: The Story of the Three Wives' Commentary on *The Peony Pavilion*," *Harvard Journal of Asiatic Studies* 54, no. 1 (1994): 158.

[55] *MDT*, 14.291; *PP*, 72. "Clouds and rain" is a euphemism for lovemaking.

[56] *MDT*, 14.287; *PP*, 67.

[57] *MDT*, 14. 290; *PP*, 71–72 (modified).

[58] "But that to take her portrait in my hands could soil its hues [*pa wode danqing ya*] / I long to embrace her image as I lie." (*MDT*, 28.356; *PP*, 157). The reference to semen is at the beginning of scene 24, as Liu inspects his stained bedclothes. Xu Shuofang and Yang Xiaomei suggest that *yunwo* refers to rain that has dampened Liu's quilt (*Mudan ting*, 137n),

but Birch translates faithfully: "the cloud stains of a passionate dream" (*MDT*, 24.338 [*Erfan wutong shu*]; *PP*, 135). Other sexually tinged references to staining and defilement are: scene 16 ("The Invalid"), where Liniang's mother fears that by venturing into the garden her daughter's limbs were "sullied by willow spirit [*pa yaoshen chuwuliao liu jingling*]," and scene 30 (discussed above), where *dian* and *dianwu* describes the "sullying" of the plantain's petals (Liniang's maidenhead). Feng removes all these passages, excepting the mother's verse in scene 16.

[59] *MDT*, 14.289; *PP*, 68–69. "Autumn's waves" refers to a woman's eyes, "Spring hills" to eyebrows that were brushed in after the natural brow had been shaved off.

[60] *MDT*, 20.313; *PP*, 102. Birch translates *zhizhong* as "to understand;" I follow him, but note that *Hanyu da cidian* (vol. 7, 1531) gives "to appreciate" (*shangshi*), "to value greatly" (*kanzhong*).

[61] For portrait as effigy of a deceased person and "stand-in or vehicle for harboring the spirit of the subject," see Vinograd, *Boundaries of the Self*, 10. Judith Zeitlin has taken the somatic dimensions of Liniang's portrait much farther than I have here, in "Making the Invisible Visible: Images of Desire and Constructions of the Female Body in Chinese Literature, Medicine, and Art," in *Crossing Boundaries: Attending to Early Modern Women*, ed. Jane Donawerth and Adele F. Seeff (Newark: University of Delaware Press, 2001), 48–79.

[62] *FLM*, 1.15.37a.

[63] *Jingling* appears several times in *Fengliu meng* (only once in *Mudan ting*) in more than one sense. In Feng's rewrite of scene 14 ("The Portrait"), he modifies difficult language in which Liniang expresses concern for her portrait and fear that there will be "none to call the living Zhenzhen from the painted scroll"; she then tearfully laments the "Sad death of one so young / Whose spirit [*jingshen*] having gone forth / Must stay hid for one who comes later to appreciate [*zuo Zhenzhen wu ren huanjiao / kanchou yao / jingshen chuxian liu yu houren biao*]." Feng simplifies: "Were my spirit [*jingling*] to appear from within the portrait / May it be conveyed into a good lad's keeping [*tang jingling huazhong chuxian / yuan chuan yu haoercao*]." *MDT*, 14.290; *FLM*, 1.11.27a; *PP*, 71 (modified). In Feng's next scene, however, which reworks scene 16 of *Mudan ting*, he preserves original language by Madam Du about her daughter's dream: "I only fear her limbs sullied by willow sprite [*pa yaoshen chuwuliao liu jingling*]"; here *jingling* clearly refers to the dream lover. *MDT*, 16.297; *FLM*, 1.12.28b; *PP*, 77.

[64] *MDT*, 20.314; *PP*, 105 (modified).

[65] *FLM*, 1.16.38b.

[66] "There, just beyond the enclosed bed of peonies / Against the mound of weathered Taihu rocks [*zhuanguo zhe shaoyao lanqian / jinkaozhe hushanshi bian*]"; *MDT*, 10.270 (*Shantao hong*); *PP*, 48.

[67] Birch takes *fenxiao* as referring to the hues of the portrait that will fade with time. *Ba* suggests (for me) agency in this process, though who the agent might be is unclear, syntactically speaking—is it waiting that will make the portrait's colors "fade," or a garden-strolling youth?

[68] Discussing constructions of the female body in connection with portraits and ghosts, Zeitlin notes that in stories about "beautiful woman paintings" (*meirentu*), the making of such portraits invariably proves fatal to their subjects, and the portraits themselves often perish. In these accounts, the portrait's destruction is sometimes described using euphemisms also used of the dead woman, who is "a sunken pearl," "shattered jade," "faded powder," or "perfume melted away." When Liniang speaks of her self-portrait as having faded, might she unconsciously be using *fenxiao* in this somatic sense? See "Making the Invisible Visible."

[69] *MDT*, 26.345; *PP*, 143.

[70] *MDT*, 26.345 (*Ying ti xu*); *PP*, 144.

[71] "Brush's tip" has phallic overtones, and the reference to Green Calyx suggests birth from the womb, especially when understood in conjunction with Liniang's earlier description of her ghost's emergence from her tomb: "Thrusting its way past plum's roots in fissured earth / My shade emerges forth." Ghosts and portraits, as we have seen, were often associated with each other. For the brush as an artistic alternative to political prowess, see Bickford, *Ink Plum*, 137.

[72] *FLM*, 1.11.25b. See Tang's version of this aria, translated above (p. 86–87). Feng incorporates several fanciful references: to an inkstone manufactured from tile taken from Tongquetai (Bronze Bird Tower) built by Cao Cao (A.D. 155–220). *Longxiang* (dragon's fragrance) and *tuhao* (rabbit's hair) refer to ink and brush. "Dotting the eyes" refers to filling in the pupils, an act by which a portraitist conveys his subject's spirit into the portrait. For eyes and "transmission of the spirit" (*chuan shen*) in portraiture, see Susan Bush and Hsio-yen Shih, comps., *Early Chinese Texts on Painting* (Cambridge: Harvard University Press, 1985), 13–14, and Anne Burkus-Chasson, "Disquieting Doubles: The Body in the Portrait and the Illusory Shape of the Self in *The Peony Pavilion*," in *Images in Exchange: Cultural Transactions in Chinese Pictorial Arts*, ed. Richard Vinograd (Berkeley: University of California Press, forthcoming).

[73] *FLM*, 2.19.2b.

[74] *FLM*, 2.19.2b.

[75] Feng's emphasis on eye-dotting anticipates the moment, in scene 33 of *Mudan ting*, when Liu Mengmei inscribes a dot on Liniang's spirit tablet at her shrine—a gesture of masculine prowess in the original play (see below).

[76] For one hundred days and nights, a young scholar calls out the name of a beauty depicted in a painting. When she then answers him, he pours wine on the painting, whereupon the lady descends and becomes his wife. Liniang alludes to this story after completing her portrait in scene 14, and so does Liu Mengmei when he calls to the portrait in scene 26. For the tale, see Li Fang (925–996) et al., comps. *Taiping guangji* (Beijing: Zhonghua shuju, 1981), 2283.

[77] *MDT*, 26.347; *PP*, 145–46 (modified).

[78] Not only is wine the instrument of revival in both story and play, but Tang also borrows playfully from Tang dynasty tale when he describes the life-restoring potion as wine mixed with the ashes of the burnt crotch section of a virile man's trousers (*wei nan'er shen kudang*). The recipe is given to Sister Stone by Chen Zuiliang in scene 34: "Magic potion

from lands across the sea / This trouser patch of a potent male. . . / Just cut a square inch and burn it / Mix the ashes in sweet wine / Wedge the teeth apart and pour it down." *MDT*, 34.388; *PP*, 198–99. In the tale, the infusion used is a preparation of wine mixed with ashes obtained from burning motley garments (*baijiacao huijiu*), so the intimate nature of the garment in *Mudan ting* is Tang's invention.

[79] For the erotic connotations of plantains in "beautiful woman paintings," especially their "leaves, like hearts / That open and close in an excess of love," see Ellen Johnston Laing, "Chinese Palace-Style Poetry and the Depiction of *A Palace Beauty*," *The Art Bulletin* 72.2 (1990): 291–95.

[80] For the plum's fragrance as a soul restoring agent (*fanhun xiang*), see Iwaki Hideo, "Baika to Hankon," 135–49; the essentials of this article are given in Bickford, *Ink Plum*, 24–26.

[81] *FLM*, 2.22.14a–b (*Chenzui dongfeng*).

[82] As Liu performs the gesture, he sings: "My brush turns stone to living person / As husband furnishes host [*kan an dian shi wei ren / kao fu zuo zhu*]." *MDT*, 33.385 (*Wu geng zhuan*); *PP*, 195. Feng supplies a subject for *kao*, underscoring the fact that Liniang relies on Liu, as husband, to perform the gesture: "See how my brush turns stone to living person / As she relies on husband to furnish the host [*ta kao fu zuo zhu*]." *FLM*, 2.24.21b (*Wu geng zhuan*).

[83] Liniang's aria in scene 14 (translated above) mentions "touching to life [*dianhuo*] the heart's tender shoots." When Liu dots (*dian*) the tablet, it moves, as if animated. These associations also come via Liniang's portrait. In theories of portraiture that emphasize conveying a subject's spirit (*chuanshen*), this process was completed by dotting the pupils of the eyes. See n. 72 above.

[84] *FLM*, 1.11.27a; 16.38a, 40a; 2.192b, 3a; and 22.13b. Most of these comments are reprinted in *MDTZL*, 64–65.

[85] Feng makes this observation twice: in a marginal comment to scene 22 and in his general remarks, where he describes how he has "made good Liu's flaws [*bu guo*]"; *MDTZL*, 63 and 65.

[86] See *FLM*, 2.19.3a (*Ji xianbin*). For the importance of recognition in Chinese thought and literature, see Eric Henry, "The Motif of Recognition in Early China," *Harvard Journal of Asiatic Studies* 47, no. 1 (1987): 5–30, especially 30, for its use in drama.

[87] Tang's improvisational methods are discussed in Zhang Xiulian, "Tang-Shen zhi zheng wailun," in *Tang Xianzu yanjiu lunwen ji*, comp. Jiangxi sheng wenxue yishu yanjiusuo (Beijing: Zhongguo xiju chubanshe, 1984), 480–99. See also Swatek, "Strategies of Containment," chapter 1.

[88] Swatek, "Strategies of Containment," 65–76. See also He Wei, "Tang Xianzu, Shen Jing, Ye Tang," in *Tang Xianzu yanjiu lunwen ji*, 463–79. The play that resisted adaptation was his early work, *Zichai ji*.

[89] In scene 9, which revises scene 12 of *Mudan ting*—specifically, Feng's substitution of the aria *Jin e shen* for *Erfan yao ling*; *FLM*, 1.9.21b–22a.

[90] Bickford, *Flowering Plum*, 25–26.

[91] Paintings of an ancient plum tree in flower (*gumei*) allude to endurance and strength in older men (and almost certainly also to sexual vigor) and were sometimes given as birthday gifts; James C. Cahill, *The Compelling Image* (Cambridge: Harvard University Press, 1982), 120–21; Bickford, *Ink Plum*, 60.

[92] In scene 2 Liu uses the canonical form of the plum image to declare his ambition: "Some day spring sun will touch in the dimness the willow to yellow gold [*You yi ri chunguang an du huangjin liu*] / And the snow's approach burst open the plum white as jade [*xueyi chongkailiao bai yumei*]." *MDT*, 2.237; *PP*, 5. Negeyama Tōru stresses the canonical aspects of plum imagery in *Mudan ting* and largely ignores the noncanonical aspects, particularly with respect to Liu Mengmei, whom he regards as the playwright's idealized self-image. See "*Kankon ki* ni okeru baika no keishō," *Kyūshū Chūgoku Gakkai hō* 29 (1991): 63–82; also his "*Kankon ki* ni okeru Ryu Mubai zo no settei," *Nippon Chūgoku Gakkai hō* 41 (1989): 167–82. For the association of plum with Confucian moral virtues, see Bickford, *Flowering Plum*, "The Plum Blossom Beauty" (pp. 18–22); and "The Flowering-Plum Recluse" (pp. 22–26); see also *Ink Plum*, 54–56.

[93] Li, *Enchantment and Disenchantment*, 52, observes of Liniang that "To fall in love with and die pining for a figure one dreams up is then to endow subjectivity with potential infinitude and willful autonomy." Liu Mengmei also exhibits willful autonomy in his response to Liniang's portrait. Both responses troubled Feng.

[94] This is the point of the following comment to scene 26, from the "Three Wives" edition: "People know that a dream is an illusory realm, but they don't know that the realm of a painting is even more illusory. Dreams are form without shadow; paintings are shadow without form. Liniang seeks love in a dream and the Spring Lord seeks a mate in a painting; in their obsession [*chi*] they are a pair for all time. That being so, by not considering [their experience] to be an illusion, the illusion becomes real"; *Wu Wushan sanfu heping Mudan ting*, 83a–b, reproduced in Liu Shiheng, *Nuanhongshi huike Linchuan simeng*, 159. I am grateful to Judith Zeitlin for sharing with me two copies of the "Three Wives'" edition in her possession. For very different readings of the portrait in *Mudan ting*, which problematize the figure as a representation of the self, see Burkus-Chasson, "Disquieting Doubles," and Lu, *Persons, Ideas, and Minds*, 28–62.

[95] Feng was careful to link together the disparate dream segments, so that Liniang and Liu Mengmei share one dream rather than experiencing separate ones. See his general critiques for *FLM*, reproduced in *MDTZL*, 63. In chapters 1 and 2 of my "Strategies of Containment," I examine in detail Feng's prosodic critique of *Mudan ting*, and conclude that he was very uncomfortable with Tang's playwriting because it made free with the arias' melodic patterns in order to accommodate the music to the text. See also Feng's preface to *Shuangxiong ji*, where he criticizes playwrights who improvise by constructing "live sequences" of arias (*huotao*).

[96] *SWJ*, 1077–78 "Heqi xu" (Preface to 'Agreeably amazing [accounts]'). I have for the most part followed Richard Lynn's translation of this preface, in "Alternate Routes to Self-Realization in Ming Theories of Poetry," in *Theories of the Arts in China*, eds. Susan Bush and Christian Murck (Princeton: Princeton University Press, 1983), 335. For Tang's aesthetic views see Zhou Yude, *Tang Xianzu lungao*, 87–105.

[97] As when he attacked an earlier revision of *Mudan ting* in a letter to Ling Mengchu (1580–1644), citing a painting in which Wang Wei (701–761) depicted a plantain as part of a winter scene. This unseasonal representation bothered innumerable critics, but Tang praised Wang's style for being "expansive and unrestrained" (*taidang yinyi*) and implied that *Mudan ting* was under attack for the same petty reasons; *SWJ*, 1345 ("Da Ling Chucheng").

[98] The importance of recurrent figurative language ("figural density") in Chinese narrative has been noted by Andrew Plaks and others. See Plaks' *Four Masterworks of the Ming Novel: Ssu ta ch'i shu* (Princeton: Princeton University Press, 1987) for detailed readings of the major novels based in part on this idea. A succinct discussion of similar techniques in Ming short stories can be found in Keith McMahon, *Causality and Containment in Seventeenth Century Chinese Fiction* (Leiden: E. J. Brill, 1988), 21–25.

[99] For Tang's privileging of feminine agency and irrational sexual energy in many of *Mudan ting*'s key scenes, see my "Strategies of Containment," 310–11.

[100] For Shen Jing and Feng's association of dramatic *qu* with the *yuefu* (Music Bureau poetry) of antiquity, see "Strategies of Containment," 7 and 27 n.

Notes to Chapter Four

[1] See Appendix C. With the exception of compendia in manuscript form, most of these collections are fairly accessible.

[2] For these two contexts, see Isabel Wong, "The Printed Collections of *K'un-ch'ü* Arias and their Sources," *Chinoperl Papers* 8 (1978): 100–1.

[3] Li Ping discusses *gundiao* and the miscellanies that reflect this style of performing in "Sanzhong wan Ming xiju," 9–30; see also Colin Mackerras, *The Rise of the Peking Opera, 1770–1870: Social Aspects of the Theatre in Manchu China* (Oxford: Clarendon Press, 1972), 6. Classic studies of the early Wanli miscellanies and *gundiao* are those of Fu Yunzi, *Baichuan ji* (Tokyo: Bunkyudō shoten, 1943), 77–116, 139–72, and Wang Gulu, *Mingdai Huidiao xiqu sanchu jiyi* (Shanghai: Shanghai gudian wenxue chubanshe, 1956).

[4] *Yuefu hongshan* (preface dated 1602), contains one extract from *Zixiao ji*; "Yang guan" ("Yang Pass"), which differs from both the scene of the same title in Tang's *Zichai ji* (probably completed in 1587) and from the comparable scene, "Songbie" ("Parting"), in his unfinished play *Zixiao ji*, written in 1577–1579. The extract is either from a different dramatic treatment of the Tang dynasty tale or a substantially altered version of one of Tang's scenes. If the latter, it is of uncertain date, since this edition of *Yuefu hongshan* is an 1800 reprint of the Ming edition.

[5] See "Fanli" (general rules) no. 4 for *Yue lu yin* and nos. 4 and 5 for *Shanshan ji*. These are reprinted in *XBHB*, 429, 437, respectively.

[6] These are in the last two *juan*; the first two contain song suites (*sanqu*). All appear to be the work of Ming authors.

[7] *Yue lu yin* contains 222 extracts from eighty-eight plays (including nine from unidentified works). Only three plays (*Tihong ji*, *Tanhua ji*, and *Zichai ji*) are represented with more extracts than *Mudan ting* (nine, nine, and ten, respectively).

[8] See "Fanli," no. 5, in *Yue lu yin*.

[9] Dramatic *qu* that retain dialogue or declaimed verse (ten extracts of forty-one) do so in small quantities, usually at the beginning or the end of a scene. In only two cases is dialogue found after any aria other then the opening or concluding one. It goes without saying that one does not find singing interspersed with dialogue, a style common in pre-Wanli era plays, extracts of which are preserved in the earliest extant miscellanies. The compiler of *Shanshan ji* retains dialogue only when it helps to contextualize the arias in terms of the plot and supplies "handles" for talking about the play (*tanbing*)—purposes reminiscent of headnotes often used for occasional poetry.

[10] Early Wanli miscellanies contain extracts from a variety of regional styles, including those that used *gundiao*. Other extracts that do not use *gundiao* make liberal use of dialogue and other features indicative of broad appeal. See, for example, Zhao Jingshen's comparison of extracts from the early Wanli miscellany *Hui Chi yadiao* with the equivalent scenes in editions of the complete play, in his *Yuan Ming nanxi kaolüe* (Beijing: Zuojia chubanshe, 1958), 128–33.

[11] This includes cuts to a sequence of "keening" arias that are a striking part of the original scene but disrupt its prevailing mood of pathos. See pp. 123–31 for more discussion of this extract.

[12] In *Yue lu yin* roles that sing are (by scene): 10 (*dan*, *sheng*, and *tie*), 12 (*dan*), 14 (*dan*, *tie*), 20 (*dan*, *tie*, *wai*, *laodan*), 26 (*sheng*), 27 (*dan*, *jing*), 28 (*sheng*, *dan*), and 53 (*sheng*, *wai*). There is no indication in the text of who sings; I have listed all roles that do, even when the number of arias assigned is one or at most two. For the prominence of *sheng* and *dan* roles in plays performed privately, see Guo Liang, "Ming Qing Kunshan qiang de biaoyan yishu," *Xiqu yanjiu* 1 (1980): 297–98, and Lu Eting, *Kunju yanchu shigao* (Shanghai: Shanghai wenyi chubanshe, 1980), 80 and 99, noting the preference in household performances for scenes that feature singing in pairs (*yi dui yi*).

[13] See Hanan, "The Nature and Contents of the *Yüeh-fu hung-shan*," *Bulletin of the School of Oriental and African Studies* 26 (1963): 348. Examples include "birthday congratulations," "husband and wife," "birth of a child," and "parting." *Yuefu hongshan* is reproduced in volumes 10 and 11 of *Shanben xiqu congkan*, comp. Wang Qiugui (Taibei: Xuesheng shuju, 1984–87; hereafter cited as *SBXQCK*).

[14] Hanan, "Nature and Contents," 348.

[15] Hanan, "Nature and Contents," 355.

[16] A miscellany that Zhao Jingshen dates to the same period as *Yichun jin* is *Zuiyu qing* (not to be confused with *Zuiyi qing*), which I have not seen. Another miscellany unavailable to me but mentioned in the literature is *Yuefu eyun bian* (listed in Appendix C), housed in the Nanjing Library. Extracts from *Huanhun ji* are included in it, but since this title refers to more than one play, the reference is ambiguous. See Zhou Miaozhong, "Jiangnan fangqu luyao," *Wenshi* 2 (1963): 245–46. Zhou feels that *Yuefu eyun bian* is post-Wanli and notes its fine illustrations and the fact that its extracts contain no dialogue. Both features increase

the likelihood that the extracts from *Huanhun ji* are in fact from our play. Wu Shuyin also mentions this miscellany in his "Ming chuanqi qumu gouchen," 157.

[17] See "Fanli," no. 4, which insists that dramatic *qu* (*juqu*) be kept separate from *qu* intended for singing only (*qingqu*). Collections that mingle the two "confuse the ear and eye" (*luan ermu*), *XBHB*, 454.

[18] *Xuanxuepu*, "Fanli," no. 3; *XBHB*, 453. According to Wang Jide, when it came to pure singing (*qingchang*), Shen Jing gave discretion in assigning beats. See "Lun banyan" ("On beats"), in Wang, *Wang Jide Qulü*, 108; also *ZGGD*, vol. 4, 118.

[19] For this notation, see "Fanli," no. 6. According to this scheme, scenes 2 and 12 from *Mudan ting* are rated as excellent in both diction and expression; in scenes 10 and 28 (both love scenes) expression outstrips diction, and in scene 53 (in which Du Bao beats Liu Mengmei), the reverse is the case. Presumably, scenes in which expression and diction are equally fine receive the highest rating.

[20] The full title, *Xinjuan xiuxiang pingdian Xuanxuepu* calls attention to these contributions. "*Dian*" can refer to a form of punctuation in which dots mark the end of lines, and also to evaluative marking in which dots and commas highlight especially fine passages of verse or dialogue. Both kinds are used in *Xuanxuepu*. For this terminology in fiction commentary, see David Rolston's essay "Sources of Traditional Fiction Criticism" in the volume he edited, *How to Read the Chinese Novel* (Princeton: Princeton University Press, 1990), 3–4. As is true for virtually all illustrated drama texts, *Xuanxuepu* has illustrations that make no visual reference to performance; some are barely recognizable as depictions of the scenes they accompany.

[21] "Portrayals of Secret Meetings" ("Youqi xiezhao"), "Solitary Strolling to Southern Sounds" ("Nanyin dubu"), "Plays by the Famous" ("Mingliu qingju"), and "Sounds for Strings" ("Xiansuo yuanyin"). I have read only the extracts in the first part; the basis for the other groupings remains elusive.

[22] There is a pronounced tendency for readers and viewers of *chuanqi* drama to compare scenes from different plays and for playwrights to imitate well-known scenes. For the tendency to write imitations, see Gao Yu, *Daoyanxue*, 41; Xu Fuming notes that *zhezixi* from different plays that share a common element (such as dreams or drunkenness) were often performed together; see "Zhezixi jianlun," *Xiqu yishu*, no. 2 (1989): 63.

[23] *Yichun jin*, vol. 1, 95a. The lost play is *Yimeng ji* (A different dream). Zhao Jingshen points out this reversal in *Ming Qing qutan* (Shanghai: Zhonghua shuju, 1959), 151.

[24] "Fanli," no. 4.

[25] "Fanli," no. 2; *XBHB*, 442. The selection of dramatic *qu* in *Cilin yixiang* is balanced between the great early Ming *chuanqi* and less exalted works, many of which were likely written for the Kun style of singing. Seventy-four extracts in the third volume are from eight early *chuanqi* (*Pipa ji* alone is allotted thirty-three extracts; the southern adaptation of *Xixiang ji*, fifteen). Sixty-seven extracts from thirty-six other plays are in the fourth and last volume, including two from *Mudan ting*. Volumes one and two are devoted to nondramatic *qu* (*shiqu*). All of the dramatic *qu* in *Cilin yixiang* feature arias only, a characteristic of most late Wanli miscellanies I have examined.

[26] For examples of both found in a Ming Wanli period miscellany, see Zhao Jingshen, *Qiuye yue*, in his *Yuan Ming nanxi kaolüe*, 133–35. This miscellany is included in *SBXQCK*, vol. 7, under the title *Hui Chi yadiao* (Elegant songs from Huizhou and Chizhou). See also note 10 above.

[27] Hanan observes that in *Yuefu hongshan*, extracts from Kun operas differ little from the "orthodox" versions; see "Nature and Contents," 348 n.

[28] Lin Fengxiong mentions four different editions of *Zuiyi qing*—the earliest dating from the Chongzhen (1628–1644) and the last from the Qianlong (1736–1795) eras. The editors of *SBXQCK* describe the edition reproduced in their series as early Qing. Working with catalogues of books imported to Japan between 1694 and 1754, Lin suggests that this work was reprinted in the 1690s; his description of the contents of that edition agrees well with the copy in volumes 54 and 55 of *SBXQCK*. See "Bozai shumu suolu *Zhui baiqiu quanji* shiyi," *Tenri Daigaku gakuhō* 140 (September 1983): 11. Wu Xinlei lists four distinct recensions of *Zhui baiqiu* and describes their contents: (1) a Wanli edition, *Baiqiu* (A cloak of white fur), not extant; (2) a Kangxi edition (dated 1689), *Zhui baiqiu hexuan* ('A patched cloak of white fur,' combined selections); (3) a new, "complete" edition, *Zhui baiqiu quanji* (A complete 'Patched cloak of white fur'), first published in 1694, with a preface dated 1740 and owned by the scholar Lu Gong; (4) a greatly expanded "popular edition" (*tongxingben*), *Zhui baiqiu xinji* (A new 'Patched cloak of white fur'), issued serially from 1764–1767, expanded and reprinted in 1770, then expanded again before achieving its fullest form in 1774. This "combined edition" was reprinted in 1777 under the title *Zhui baiqiu xinji hebian* (hereafter *ZBQXJ*) and went through numerous reprintings. See Wu Xinlei, "*Zhui baiqiu* de lailong qumo," *Nanjing daxue xuebao* 3 (August 1983): 36–43; see also Appendix C. Lin Heyi complicates the picture of the filiation of editions of *Zhui baiqiu* further by listing nineteen reprintings of the 1774 edition in "Ye tan *Zhui baiqiu* li de difang xi," *Taida zhongwen xuebao* 5 (June 1992): 246–50.

[29] Lin Fengxiong ("*Zhui baiqiu quanji* shiyi," 12–15) dates Kun opera's flourishing as a stage art from 1628 to 1736; Hu Ji and Liu Zhizhong push the dates later (1695–1801) and note that in the eighteenth century commercial theaters (*xiyuan*, also called *chayuan*) became important venues for drama; see their *Kunju fazhan shi*, 423–24. See also Lu Eting, *Yanchu shigao*, 204–5. Zhao Shanlin, *Guanzhongxue*, devotes a chapter to commercial theaters in the Ming and Qing, 86–97.

[30] A notice on the front page of *Zuiyi qing* advertises the collection as "enabling performers (*yanxizhe*) to fathom the fine points of *qu* and audiences (*pangguanzhe*) to hear the music and dance." A similar notice appears on the cover of *Zhui baiqiu xinji*: "Actors can refine their art; scholars can expand their appreciation." See Lin Fengxiong, "*Zhui baiqiu quanji* shiyi," 12–13; also Lin Heyi, "Ye tan *Zhui baiqiu*," 251, for *Zhui baiqiu*'s appeal to both audiences and actors. Lin Fengxiong likens the popularity of both miscellanies to that of Mao Jin's *Liushizhong qu*, an anthology published in the Chongzhen period that used theatrically based texts of complete plays. Lu Eting feels that collections such as *Zuiyi qing* were published to meet a new demand for extracts that could be used at social entertainments; see *Yanchu shigao*, 178.

[31] This translation incorporates portions of Tang's original text, based on the translation of Cyril Birch in *PP*, 49. In this chapter and the next, when more than one version of a

scene is reflected in the translation, as here, stage directions are not routinely italicized as in chapters 2 and 3. Instead, the typeface used for them, including aria titles, will conform to that designated for the version in which they are found. When only one version of a scene is translated, however, stage directions will be treated as they are in chapters 2 and 3.

[32] This line, found in the original version of the scene, is the inspiration for the change of title to "Ru meng." That change redirects attention from Liniang's unique experience and suggests that Liu Mengmei shares in the experience of the dream. Feng Menglong also reveals concern on this point in a marginal note to the Huashen's speech: "The Huashen says, 'Mistress Du being sick at heart, this has caused [the soul of] the young graduate Liu to enter her dream.' The dream must on no account be divided into two," *FLM*, 1.7.16b (text in brackets added by Feng). Here my translation is based on that of H. C. Chang, in *Chinese Literature: Popular Fiction and Drama* (Edinburgh: Edinburgh University Press, 1973), 298.

[33] I omit five illegible words spoken by the flower attendants. Huaxu refers to a paradisial land once visited by the Yellow Emperor in a dream. The reference here, immediately after the previous line, is contradictory, and in later versions of this aria these lines read "All because of a dream / In this pillow land of Huaxu / A joyful awakening for both." See the sequence from *Shenyin jiangu lu* in *SBXQCK*, vol. 73, 560.

[34] *SBXQCK*, vol. 54, 223–25.

[35] Wong, "Printed Collections," 107.

[36] Xu Fuming, *MDTZL*, 172–73; the scene is from the play *Yuanyang meng* (A mandarin duck dream). Hu Ji and Liu Zhizhong say that the "Heaped Blossoms" arias are taken over from regional opera, but name no source; see *Kunju fazhan shi*, 510–11.

[37] Lu Eting, *Yanchu shigao*, 201. A thorough investigation of the Huashen and of the "Heaped Blossoms" interlude appears in Chen Kaixin, "*Mudan ting*: 'Jingmeng' zhi Huashen yanchu kao," *Guoli bianyiguan guankan* 27, no. 2 (June 1998): 97–111.

[38] In an article on elegant (*ya*) and common (*su*) elements in Kun opera (specifically, *zhezixi*), Lu Eting discusses the addition of the Mengshen and "Heaped Blossoms" segments to "Wandering in the Garden, Startled by a Dream" as a classic instance of the interpenetration of styles; see "Tan Kunju de ya he su," *Xiqu yanjiu* 38 (1991): 28–29. I take up how these popular additions influence the viewer's understanding of the scene in the next chapter.

[39] See *Yanchu shigao*, 173, for renewal of both the content and aesthetic appearance of the plays, and 178 for popularizing tendencies in *Zuiyi qing*. For the enrichment of content, see 185–87.

[40] The 1694 edition of *Zhui baiqiu* lists in its contents a selection of *Mudan ting* extracts that is identical to that for the Kangxi edition of *Zuiyi qing* that I have just described, right down to the altered titles and the order in which the extracts are given: "Entering the Dream," "Pursuing the Dream," "The Portrait Recovered," and "Infernal Judgment." I have not seen this edition and cannot say whether the texts agree closely, but I suspect this is the case. The contents of these editions of the two collections are remarkably congruent: The titles of 97 of the 120 extracts listed for *Zhui baiqiu quanji* are identical to those found

in *Zuiyi qing* and the number and order in which they are presented is the same. The 1689 edition of *Zhui baiqiu* (*Zhui baiqiu hexuan*) does not contain any extracts from *Mudan ting*.

[41] When a *zhezixi* of "Jingmeng" consists only of the second half of the original scene (after Liniang's garden stroll), I rename it "Startled by a Dream" to indicate the change, and because in combination with "Youyuan" the resulting *zhezixi* is commonly translated as "Wandering in the Garden, Startled by a Dream."

[42] The entry of the Shuimoshen concludes "Wandering in the Garden," that of the Huashen and his entourage to perform "Heaped Blossoms" begins "Startled by a Dream."

[43] In *Zhui baiqiu xinji*, the *chou* plays the Mengshen, and enters holding a mirror.

[44] This tones down slightly Tang's stage directions: "The *dan* turns away, blushing. The *sheng* advances to take her in his arms, but she resists him." See *PP*, 48.

[45] *Zhui baiqiu xinji*, fourth collection, "Startled by a Dream" 366–76; facsimile of 1777 reprint by Hongwentang of 1774 combined edition, entitled *Zhui baiqiu xinji hebian*, in *SBXQCK*, vols. 58–71; *Shenyin jiangu lu*, *SBXQCK*, vol. 74, "Wandering in the Garden," 3a–b. Compare *MDT*, 10.270; *PP*, 48–49. The translation of added portions is mine.

[46] *FLM* 1.7.17b. Negeyama Tōru notes, and disparages, the tendency of Qing actors to borrow from the adaptations of both Feng and Zang Jinshu [Maoxun], in "Seidai ni okeru *Kankon ki* no enpen," *Nippon Chūgoku gakkai hō* 47 (1995): 174.

[47] *Shixing yadiao Zhui baiqiu xinji hebian* (A new 'Patched cloak of white fur,' containing currently popular elegant tunes). *Zhui baiqiu quanji* contains 120 extracts from thirty-six plays. The first four collections of *Zhui baiqiu xinji* contain 232 items from sixty-nine plays, and the twelve collections that make up the full edition contain 493 extracts, 429 of which were from eighty-six Kun operas. While thirty of the thirty-six plays in *Zhui baiqiu quanji* are also represented in *Zhui baiqiu xinji*, the number and selection of extracts for each play frequently differ. In the case of *Zhui baiqiu quanji* and *Zhui baiqiu hexuan* (1689) the disparity in contents is even greater. Only seven of the thirty-nine plays in the Kangxi edition are also represented in the 1740 edition, and only a few extracts are common to both collections.

[48] The preface claims that this collection emulates *Zhui baiqiu* in its selection of plays, Ye Tang's *Nashuying qupu* in its attention to the prosody of the arias, and Li Yu in its concern with dramaturgy; *XBHB*, 489. A check of titles shows correspondence with *Zhui baiqiu xinji* for forty-nine of sixty-five titles. Ye Changhai discusses *Shenyin jiangu lu* together with two other works (*Yangzhou huafang lu* and *Xiaohan xinyong*) that he feels reflect a shift of emphasis from singing (*quxue*) to performance (*wutai yishu*) in the eighteenth century; see his *Zhongguo xijuxue shigao* (Shanghai wenyi chubanshe, 1986), 409–23. Li Huimian describes it as a "performance register" (*shenduanpu*) and "model" (*guinie*) for actors and directors; see "Cong *Jingchai ji Pipa ji* taiben xitan *Shenyin jiangu lu* de biaoyan meixue," in Hua Wei and Wang Ailing, comps., *Ming Qing xiqu*, vol. 2, 669 and 673.

[49] Wu Xinlei feels that this edition of *Zhui baiqiu* preserves scripts for *zhezixi* that originated with troupes (*xiban de chuanyanben*), which were used as guidebooks (*shuomingshu*)—presumably by both actors and amateurs, though he does not say. Earlier collections that appeared under the title *Zhui baiqiu* were based on reader's texts (*wenxue juben*). See his "*Zhui baiqiu* de lailong qumo," 38.

[50] The twelve collections of this edition contain, in addition to the 429 extracts from Kun operas, sixty-four extracts from clapper operas and forty introductory pieces. This is by far the most comprehensive of the Qing collections. A reprint of this edition, dated Qianlong 42 (1778) is in *SBXQCK*. A supplementary volume 72 reprints the first collection of *Zhui baiqiu xinji*, published by Baorentang in 1764, but omits the other three collections that were published in 1765, 1766, and 1767 under this title.

[51] The advent of *zhezixi* put roles on a more equal footing; when southern dramas were enjoyed as wholes, roles other than the *sheng* and *dan* were considered secondary (*za*). See Lu Eting, *Yanchu shigao*, 192–93. Of eight extracts preserved in the late Ming miscellany *Yue lu yin*, for example, all but one ("Ying kao") feature only the *dan* or the *dan* and *sheng*.

[52] "Speed the Plough," "The School Hall" "Wandering in the Garden," "Startled by a Dream," "Pursuing the Dream," "The Soul's Departure," "Infernal Judgment," "Interrogation Upside-down," and "Reunion at Court."

[53] Lu Eting, *Yanchu shigao*, 184–92. Xu Fuming feels that *Shenyin jiangu lu* especially shows this shift to a performance-oriented taste (*ju de guannian*); see "Zhezixi jianlun," 65. Hu Ji and Liu Zhizhong (*Kunju fazhan shi*, 490–91) concur, noting that the work reflects performance standards for the period 1736–1820.

[54] See Hua Sheng, "Zhongguo xiju wenhua de yi dashanbian—cong juzuojia zhongxinzhi dao yanyuan zhongxinzhi," *Wenyi yanjiu*, no. 6 (1991): 85–92. Hua notes (p. 92) that the Kangxi emperor's imprisonment of Hong Sheng for showing disrespect to the dynasty in *Changsheng dian*—the last play by a literatus that became popular on the public stage—had a chilling effect on would-be literati playwrights.

[55] This discussion of actor-inspired revisions of texts is indebted to Lu Eting, *Yanchu shigao*, 184–202. See also Xu Fuming, "Zhezixi jianlun," 65–66.

[56] Revising dialogue while leaving the arias undisturbed is a hallmark of actor-inspired revision and is found in many of the extracts in *Zhui baiqiu xinji hebian*.

[57] Having the *jing* and *chou* roles speak a stylized form of Wu dialect in Kun operas was just becoming popular in the Wanli era. Tang's contemporary, Shen Jing, occasionally used it, but Tang did not. See Lu Eting, *Yanchu shigao*, 61 and 108 n. 1. An excellent study of Wu dialect's incursion into southern plays is Iwaki Hideo, "Nangi ni okeru Gogo no kinō," in *Chūgoku gikyoku engeki kenkyū* (Tokyo: Sōbunsha, 1972), 626–53. For "Asking the Way," see p. 633.

[58] *MDT*, 40.412–13; *PP*, 225.

[59] For these distinctions, see Iwaki Hideo, "Gogo no kinō," 632.

[60] *Zhui baiqiu xinji hebian*, twelfth collection, "Asking the Way," 1b–4a. In translating dialect I have consulted Xu Lingyun's version of this scene in *Kunju biaoyan yide* (Shanghai: Shanghai xinwenyi chubanshe, 1959), vol. 3, 78–81. Xu's version, which he appears to have learned orally, is based on the *Zhui baiqiu xinji hebian* text but renders dialogue in a stage dialect that he calls "old Suzhou speech" (*laoSubai*).

[61] This assessment is taken from Xu Lingyun's account, in *Kunju biaoyan yide*, vol. 3, 76, 81, 89. For Xu's lifelong interest in Kun opera, see Lindy Li Mark, "The Role of Avocational Performers in the Preservation of *Kunqu*," *Chinoperl Papers* 15 (1990): 106–7.

[62] Many an extract, thus augmented by actors, bears little resemblance to the scene in the play, whose meaning often is transformed in the process of becoming a *zhezixi*. Lu Eting cites as an example "Xia shan" ("Leaving the Mountain"), about a monk who wishes to return to lay life. In the play from which this scene is taken the monk is portrayed negatively, but "Xia shan" depicts his "beautiful and healthy" (*youmei jiankang*) struggle for freedom. See *Yanchu shigao*, 186.

[63] I here alter Birch's translation of "Shi hua" to reflect its new configuration as *zhezixi*. It and "Jiaohua" are usually printed sequentially. This is how they appear in *Zhui baiqiu xinji*, and in many musically annotated texts. In some, both extracts appear under one title: a *qupu* in the collection of the Shanghai Library (MS 485587) uses the elliptical title "Shi Jiao" ("Recovering [the Portrait] and Calling [to It]"). *Sulu qupu*, a popular collection of musically annotated *zhezixi*, uses "Shi hua" for the combined sequence.

[64] An uncut version of scene 26 (arias only) appears under its original title in the Ming collection *Yue lu yin*, and an abridged version of scene 24 is one of four extracts from *Mudan ting* published in *Zuiyi qing*.

[65] Yue Meiti, an actress in the Shanghai troupe, describes "Shi hua Jiao hua" this way. See *Wo—yige gudan de nüxiaosheng* (Shanghai: Wenhui chubanshe, 1994), 39–41. A handwritten pocket-sized text (*jingzhezhuang*) with musical notation (MS 994104 in the collection of Fudan University) puts "Shi hua Jiao hua" and "Xun meng" together, presumably on that basis.

[66] As just noted, they were rarely anthologized. Zang and Feng retain scenes 24 and 26 in consolidated form (and Feng featured this scene by having it begin the second part of *Fengliu meng*), but all cut Liu's solo segment from scene 28.

[67] This is Wai-yee Li's observation, *Enchantment and Disenchantment*, 52 n. Judith Zeitlin notes that "*wan*" of the scene's title "has the sense not only of appreciating or enjoying something, but can also mean to handle or fondle or dally with something," and associates these meanings with "tactile pleasure" that is part of Liu's response to the portrait. Her observations, made in a different context, support Li's. See "Making the Invisible Visible."

[68] See chapter 3, p. 96.

[69] Yue Meiti, "Nuli zhanxian renwu neixin de mei," *Shanxi xiju* no. 12 (December 1982): 11.

[70] Yue Meiti, "Renwu neixin de mei," 11.

[71] *MDT*, 26.345; *PP*, 144.

[72] Feng Menglong criticizes Liu's failure to notice the resemblance between the portrait and Liniang's ghost; see *FLM*, "*Fengliu meng* zongping," no. 4 and 2.22.13b.

[73] The extract "Shi hua" in *Zuiyi qing* contains cuts also found in the 1767 text in *Zhui baiqiu xinji*, but no revisions aimed at rehabilitating Liu's character.

[74] Negeyama Tōru compares "Shi hua Jiao hua" in *Zhui baiqiu* with scene 19 in *Fengliu meng* ("The Portrait Discovered"), discusses how the extract borrows from Feng's adaptation, and does the same for "The School Hall." See "*Kankon ki* no enpen," 165–66, 168–71.

[75] Feng Menglong's next aria, *Erlang shen man* (which replaces *Ying ti xu* in the original scene) is not used.

[76] The text returns to the sixth aria of the original scene (*Tiying xu*), but mislabels it *Ji xianbin*. The interpolated dialogue, however, is lacking in the original.

[77] Feng's aria revises only the first three lines of the original aria (the seventh aria and last before the coda), but interpolates more dialogue. The *zhezixi* uses Feng's revised aria and interpolates even more dialogue.

[78] *SBXQCK*, vol. 58, 182–88; *PP*, 144–47. I have not translated the abbreviated text of "Shi hua" that forms a continuous sequence with this extract.

[79] Yue Meiti, "Renwu neixin de mei," 11. These actions are organized around four arias, condensed from the original seven.

[80] At the comparable moment in Tang's version of this aria, Liu vaguely recalls a dream but fails to connect it with the portrait. *MDT*, 26.347; *PP*, 145.

[81] This can be seen in the videotape of her performance opposite Hua Wenyi in 1982, using a script based on the *Zhui baiqiu xinji* version of "Calling to the Portrait."

[82] The logical outcome of these actions is for the portrait to come to life, and in Yue Meiti's conception of the scene, this happens. A performance of "Calling to the Portrait" in the 1950s as a Jiangxi regional opera, in which the portrait "came alive," may have given Yue her idea (see chapter 5, n. 147). It is described in *TXZZL*, 1109–10.

[83] Zhao Jingsheng, "Tan *Mudan ting* de gaibian," in his *Xiqu bitan* (Shanghai: Shanghai guji chubanshe, 1962), 132–34; reprinted in *TXZZL*, 1102–4.

[84] In *chuanqi*, linkages occur between scenes, sometimes in proximity as here, at other times at a remove. Complexity results from the resonances created, in a manner similar to patterns of resonance between chapters in novels. See Plaks, *Four Masterworks*, 41–45.

[85] Bernard Beckerman's discussion of "act-schemes" (planned sequences of actions and forms used to effect the onstage representation), and his identification of two basic kinds—linked and autonomous—is useful conceptually for distinguishing *zhezixi* from corresponding scenes in *chuanqi*; see his *Theatrical Presentation*, chapter 7 (The act-scheme and the act-image), especially p. 106.

[86] For tragicomedy as the dominant method of presentation in *Mudan ting* and in this scene, see Lu Wei, "Xiabanbu *Mudan ting* qiantan," *Juying yuebao*, no. 9 (September 1992): 68–69. C. T. Hsia praises the play's "comic exuberance" in "Plays of Tang Hsien-tsu," 274–75; Wai-yee Li finds "comic reconciliation" achieved through the projection of other realms (in dreams, beyond death); see *Enchantment and Disenchantment*, 50–64.

[87] This is how Zang Maoxun treats it, but the grieving is by Madam Du and Du Bao only.

[88] *MDT*, 20.314–15; *PP*, 105–6.

[89] Tang assigns Sister Stone to the *jing* role. A grotesquely comic figure, one of her functions in this scene (and Tang's play) is as a foil to Chunxiang, whose presence is correspondingly reduced.

[90] Lu Wei observes that this denouement explodes the atmosphere of desolation at Liniang's death and continues, "moreover, the name of the scene is 'Nao shang' ['Disturbance at the

Deathbed']; it is evident that Tang Xianzu used '*nao*' deliberately, not wishing the death of the female lead to unfold as a tragedy," "Xiabanbu *Mudan ting* qiantan," 69. Wei Hua discusses Stone's "incongruous voice" in this sequence in "The Search for Great Harmony: A Study of Tang Xianzu's Dramatic Art" (Ph.D. diss., University of California at Berkeley, 1991), 243–48.

[91] *HHJ*, 1.11.40b–41a. Zang eliminates arias sung by Liniang and Chunxiang before Madam Du's entry (1–5) and has only Du Bao and Madam Du sing after Liniang's death, which takes place onstage. Hirose Reiko has so characterized Zang's changes to this scene in "*Kankon ki* no kaihen," 82–83.

[92] Feng's interest in the *dan/tie* pair is reflected in the enhanced role he gives to the character of Chunxiang here and elsewhere in *Fengliu meng*. Chapter 5 takes up the aesthetic effect of this pairing of roles in performance.

[93] In a marginal comment to his revised scene, "Plans for Burying the Deceased Daughter," Feng praises Chunxiang as a devoted servant (*yibi*) and takes credit for cutting through the tangle (*geteng*) of Tang's scene, *FLM*, 1.16.40a.

[94] *MDT*, 20.312; *PP*, 100–1.

[95] *SBXQCK*, vol. 71, 4965–77.

[96] In the first several lines of her aria, she is worried about lonely old age—a perfectly natural emotion, but one that takes her inside herself, rendering her momentarily unable to respond to her child.

[97] *MDT*, 312; *PP*, 101.

[98] As it is in every adaptation of the scene that I have consulted.

[99] In *Huanhun ji*, main arias (those other than brief introductions and codas) have been reduced from thirteen to six. For the supplanting of arias by dialogue, see Negeyama Tōru, "*Kankon ki* no enpen," 171, 175–76, and Iwaki Hideo, "Gogo no kinō," 639.

[100] This is especially true of Liniang's parents. Madam Du at times is preoccupied, and Du Bao, though affected by his daughter's death, does not yield to his grief and is soon distracted by other demands made of him. I suspect that the large number of arias sung solo in the scene (fourteen of seventeen main arias, if we except four short choral refrains) would reinforce this impression in a performance. These thoughts come from conversations with Professor Lu Shulun of Fudan University, with whom I read this play before his untimely death in 1984.

[101] An example of a comment about other performances of the scene incorporated into the stage directions, something not found in *Zhui baiqiu xinji hebian*.

[102] *SBXQCK*, vol. 74, 586–89.

[103] See Guo Liang, "Kunqu biaoyan yishu de yidai fanben—*Shenyin jiangu lu*," *Xiju bao*, nos. 19–20 (October 30, 1961): 54–59.

[104] Several times he criticizes interpretations by "vulgar actors" (*suling*) reflected in the *Zhui baiqiu* extracts, as in the following dialogue from this scene:

> *Liniang*: I have been so sunk in sickness, Chunxiang, tell me what night is this? (*Lowers her head*)

Chunxiang: It's the fifteenth of the eighth month, the Mid-autumn. (*The* xiaodan *makes a sharp, low sound; vulgar actors affect deafness; they are mistaken*)
Liniang: Aiya!—the Mid-autumn?
Interlinear comment: "Vulgar actors [have Liniang] repeat this question—hardly like one who is 'dying of longing for love'!"
Chunxiang: Yes.

Cf. *SBXQCK*, vol. 71, 4965; vol. 74, 584.

[105] Notably Ye Tang, whose musically annotated versions of Kun operas were published between 1789 and 1792 and were intended to be used for unstaged pure singing performances. Although familiar with Ye Tang's collections, the compiler of *Shenyin jiangu lu* did not choose to provide musical annotation for his selection of playtexts.

[106] Wu Xinlei, "*Zhui baiqiu* de lailong qumo," 38. Wu concludes that the Qianlong editions of *Zhui baiqiu* (the 1740 edition excepted) were compiled using performance scripts of professional troupes (*xiban de chuanyanben*) as the standard. Lin Heyi citing prefaces, feels that actors also were guided by the selections, "Ye tan *Zhui baiqiu*," 251. Guo Liang describes *Shenyin jiangu lu* as a collection of performance texts (*yanchu taiben*), "Kunqu biaoyan," 54.

[107] Gao Yu feels both Qing collections preserve working scripts (*changjiben*) that record information about actual performances and distinguishes them from Feng Menglong's "blueprints" for performance, *Daoyanxue*, 85.

[108] *Zhui baiqiu*'s influence with actors is demonstrable; the scripts of many *zhezixi* performed today are based on its versions. However, Guo Liang's claim that *Shenyin jiangu lu* was used to train actors ("Kunqu biaoyan," 54–55) strikes me as dubious, but it receives support from Hu Ji and Liu Zhizhong's discussion of manuscripts for *zhezixi* that date from the late eighteenth century and contain notes comparable in detail to those in *Shenyin jiangu lu*. Hu feels that actors consulted these manuscripts for ideas (sometimes even for application to a character in a different play), *Kunju fazhan shi*, 488–89. Lu Eting discusses the interaction between amateurs and professionals in *Yanchu shigao*, 82–86.

[109] The confrontation between Chunxiang and Chen Zuiliang ("The School Hall"), Du Bao's festive tour of the countryside ("Speed the Plough"), and the grand concluding scene ("Reunion at Court") were added to the 1764 collection; "The Soul's Departure," "Asking the Way," and the scene in which Liu Mengmei is beaten in Du Bao's court ("Interrogation Upside-down") were included in the augmented edition of 1774.

[110] By this time, tastes at court were also shifting to clapper and other popular styles of opera. See Hua Sheng, "Yi da shanbian," 89–92, and below.

[111] For the lack of continuity between editions of *Zhui baiqiu*, see n. 47. The first edition to include extracts of clapper and other popular styles of opera is the one produced between 1764 and 1767. Though the number is small (8 of 232), this is also the edition in which many "new" scenes from familiar Kun-style plays were added (including four from *Mudan ting*). Between 1767 and 1774 eight more collections were added, more than doubling the number of *zhezixi* and increasing the number of clapper operas from eight to sixty-four (of 493). The decisive shift to a more popularly oriented selection occurs between the

collection published in 1740 and the one published from 1764–1767. See Wu Xinlei, "*Zhui baiqiu* de lailong qumo," 38; and Lin Heyi, "Ye tan *Zhui baiqiu*."

[112] Jason Chia-sheng Wang makes the misleading claim that the popular edition of *Zhui baiqiu* "provides a good indicator of the range of the repertoire of early Ch'ing theatrical troupes." See his entry for *Zhui baiqiu* in Nienhauser, *The Indiana Companion*, 368.

[113] Guo Liang, "Kunqu biaoyan," 54–55. Guo takes "*gu*" in the title to refer to great actors dead and gone, whose art can be examined (*jian*) in the pages of this miscellany, which documents performances that reach back to the late Ming. Hu Ji and Liu Zhizhong understand "*gu*" as referring to performance standards for Kun opera in the Qianlong and Jiaqing eras only (1736–1820), *Kunju fazhan shi*, 490.

[114] Extracts from *Mudan ting* that appeared earlier in *Zhui baiqiu* are: from *Zhui baiqiu xinji*: "Speed the Plough" (scene 8, collection of 1766); "The School Hall" and "Reunion at Court" (scenes 7 and 55, collection of 1767); from *Zhui baiqiuxinji hebian*: "The Soul's Departure" and "Interrogation Upside-down" (scenes 20 and 53, collection of 1774). Four of the nine extracts from *Zhui baiqiu xinji hebian* that I have examined closely ("The School Hall," "Wandering in the Garden, Startled by a Dream," "The Soul's Departure" and "Asking the Way") have unique features not found in earlier printed versions of the scenes.

[115] Substantial differences between recensions titled *Zhui baiqiu* lead Zhou Miaozhong to conclude that the title was widely in use from the late Ming to the Qianlong period for collections of *zhezixi*. See her *Qingdai xiqu shi* (Zhengzhou: Zhongzhou guji chubanshe, 1987), 384.

[116] Dialect in 20 of 165 *zhezixi* indicates a popularizing trend that culminates in editions of *Zhui baiqiu* dated 1764 and after; Iwaki Hideo, "Gogo no kinō," 630.

[117] *Yanchu shigao*, 6–13; see also Lin Heyi's review of Lu's book in *Zhongguo wenxue yanjiu*, no. 3 (1989): 217–23.

[118] *Shenyin jiangu lu* was published in 1838, at a time when performances of Beijing operas by amateurs (*piaoyou*, friends of the box office) were becoming important. See Colin Mackerras, *Amateur Theatre in China, 1949–1966* (Canberra: Australian National University Press, 1973), 3–4, and *Rise of the Peking Opera*, 191, 187–88.

[119] "Wandering in the Garden, Startled by a Dream" and "Chunxiang Disrupts the Lesson" turn up in *Xi kao*, a collection of Beijing operas published in forty parts between 1913 and 1924. Lin Heyi discusses thirty-four extracts in *Zhui baiqiu* and the various popular forms of opera represented in them in "Ye tan *Zhui baiqiu*."

[120] *Gongpu* ("song registers" or "dramatic scores," also known as *qupu*) prescribe the textual and musical structures of Kun opera arias and include musical (*gongche*) notation heretofore lacking in prosodic manuals such as those compiled by Shen Jing and Feng Menglong. Those offered model arias for writers, distinguished regular from extrametrical syllables, specified the tonal category for each of the regular words (even or oblique), indicated which lines should rhyme, but did not provide musical notation. Nor did compendia of scenes such as *Zuiyi qing* and *Zhui baiqiu*. Richard Strassberg discusses *gongche* notation in "The Singing Techniques of *K'un-ch'ü* and their Musical Notation," *Chinoperl Papers* 6 (1976): 47–50.

[121] Ye Tang's methods resemble the evidentiary (*kaozheng*) research favored by Qing scholars. In the case of *Mudan ting*, he relied on the work of an earlier expert on Kun music, Niu Shaoya, who in 1651 had published a complete *Mudan ting* that accommodated Tang's text to the repertoire of Kun arias but lacked musical notation. Ye made additional corrections to Niu's blueprint of aria forms, then used his musical knowledge and old manuscript scores to provide each aria with *gongche* notation. See Wong, "Printed Collections," 108–110; Zhou Weipei, *Qupu yanjiu* (Nanjing: Jiangsu guji chubanshe, 1997), 246–48. Details of Ye's life and the features of his notation are described in Joseph S. C. Lam, "Notational Representation and Contextual Constraints: How and Why Did Ye Tang Notate His Kun Opera Arias?" In *Themes and Variations: Writings on Music in Honor of Rulan Chao Pian*, ed. Bell Yung and Joseph S. C. Lam (Hong Kong: The Chinese University of Hong Kong, 1994), 33–35. For "pure singing" in Ye Tang's lifetime, see Lu Eting, *Yanchu shigao*, 249–53. My thanks to David Rolston for making Lam's article known and available to me.

[122] Yu Zhenfei (1905–1994), the most influential molder of Kun opera in post-liberation China, learned it from his father, Yu Zonghai (1847–1930), a *qingchang* master who traced his training directly to Ye Tang. For this claim, see Richard Strassberg's translation of Yu Zonghai's manual, *Sulu qupu*, in "Singing Techniques of *K'un-ch'ü*," 52. Marjorie Bang-ray Liu gives a detailed description of techniques of ornamentation in the Yu style, as explained to her by Yu Zhenfei, in "Aesthetic Principles and Ornamental Style in Chinese Classical Opera—Kunqu." *Selected Reports in Ethnomusicology* 4 (1983): 44–61. Such ornamentation is an extreme refinement of Ye Tang's notation.

[123] Ye Tang's editions appeared in 1784, 1791, and 1792. A collection of fifty-one extracts from clapper operas, in an expanded edition of *Zhui baiqiu xinji*, had appeared in 1774 under the title *Zhui baiqiu bangziqiang shiyi ji, wai bian* (Outer edition of 'A patched cloak of white fur,' 11th collection, clapper operas).

[124] Wong, "Printed Collections," 109. The organization of Ye's collection is similar to that for *Zhui baiqiu*, but Ye's marginal comments reflect disapproval of the practices of contemporary singer-actors. See Lam, "Notational Representation," 35 and 39, also Zhou Weipei, *Qupu yanjiu*, 244.

[125] Isabel Wong discusses compilations commissioned by the Qianlong emperor in "Printed Collections," 102–8.

[126] Lam observes that the *gongche* notation used by singer-composers such as Ye Tang ("avocational singers") was not rigidly prescriptive and left many details about phrasing and the dynamics of tempo and rhythm for the user to work out. Ye's collections proved controversial, because his interpretations of the arias were idiosyncratic and differed from those of professional singer-actors. See "Notational Representation," 35, 36, and 38, and Zhou Weipei, *Qupu yanjiu*, 241.

[127] Followers of the pure singing tradition of Kun singing in the 1920s and 1930s considered themselves to be preservers of traditions going back to Ye Tang. Their motto was: "A good play is not performed; performance spoils a good play" (*haoquzi bu deng tai, deng tai bu shi haoquzi*). See Ch'ung-ho Chang Frankel, "The Practice of *K'un-ch'ü* Singing from the 1920s to the 1960s," *Chinoperl Papers* 6 (1976): 88. Lu Eting cites Gong Zizhen (1792–

1841), whose views epitomize the disdain of the Qing literatus for the theater: "[with] pure *qu* one makes an elegant repast; [with] plays one makes a brothel visit; in no sense do [the two activities] touch each other" (*qingqu wei yayan, ju wei xiayou, zhiyan bu xiangfan*), in *Kunju yanchu shigao*, 10. Lindy Mark considers the contributions of amateurs—both *piaoyou* (friends of the box office) and *qingke* (avocational performers)—in "Avocational Performers."

[128] For example, Ye appends "vulgar" versions of "The Portrait Examined" ("Su Wan zhen") and "Heaped Blossoms" ("Suzeng Duihua") to his complete text of *Mudan ting*. Lu Eting stresses Ye's receptivity to playtexts emanating from theaters (*juchang*) and feels that his collections register the impact of these popular practices and tastes in pure singing circles (*changtan*); but he also acknowledges that Ye's version of *Mudan ting* exerted little influence on actors, who learned their art orally from older artists. See "Ye Tang yu Suzhou jutan," in his *Qingdai xiqujia congkao* (Shanghai: Xuelin chubanshe, 1995), 252–58. Ye favored plays and scenes that exemplified "elegance" (*ya*), but two installments of his third collection contained scenes favored by the public (labeled "outer," *wai*) and scenes currently popular ("supplementary," *buyi*). See "Notational Representation," 36. Zhou Weipei feels that Ye tended to "elegantize" (*yahua*) the few *huabu* plays he chose to include, *Qupu yanjiu*, 248–49.

[129] *Yinxiangtang qupu* also provides musical notation for the complete *Mudan ting* (absent the prefatory scene), but I know of no study that discusses its relation to Ye's edition. Zhou Weipei discusses it, briefly, in *Qupu yanjiu*, 250–51; see also Yang Zhenliang, *Mudan ting yanjiu* (Taibei: Yiwen tushu gongsi, 1992).

[130] Scene 8 ("Quan nong") shows the greatest differences. For Wang's editing methods, see his preface to *Eyunge qupu*, cited in Yang Zhenliang, *Mudan ting yanjiu*, 142.

[131] Stage directions, other than indications of who sings, are omitted, consistent with this intermediate orientation. Wong, "Printed Collections," 110.

[132] Wong emphasizes reliance on both written and oral sources in "Printed Collections," 106.

[133] This brief survey of *gongpu* has not attempted to be comprehensive. Good discussions of other late Qing and Republican period *gongpu* appear in chapter 3 of Yang Zhenliang, *Mudan ting yanjiu*; Zhou Weipei, *Qupu yanjiu*, 240–59; and Wong, "Printed Collections."

[134] Notes on covers in this collection suggest an interest in the basics of musical interpretation: terms such as "general outline" (*zonggang*), "overview" (*zongjiang*), or "overview of general principles" (*zongjue zongjiang*) appear in parentheses beside the titles of some extracts. See Shanghai Library MSS 485585 –587, –589, –591, (also for "Yongxin xixue") –592; MS 485596 (dated 1878) contains the slip of paper addressed to "Master Shi Fengxiang" (Shi Fengxiang *laoxiansheng*), perhaps a teacher or singing master. The cover of MS 506275 reads *Sui zai wuxu zhongdong Julu shi Shouting rike* (Shouting's daily lesson, Julu [County] lineage [of Hebei province], midwinter, 1898). Calligraphy and notations suggest this collection may have belonged to professional artists; another volume (MS 506274) bears the motto "Able drumming, good dancing" ("Nenggu miaowu").

[135] MSS 506230, 506244, and 530616, respectively. "Gay with Joyous Cries" echoes a line in scene 10 of *Mudan ting*: "Where is the garden 'gay with joyous cries'?" It shows up in more than one collection. Such mottos appear on each of nine volumes in another

collection, among them: "Dust Dances on Painted Roofbeams" ("Huadong chen fei"), "Easy and Unburdened Feelings" ("Xianqing yizhi"), "Sufficient for Amusement" ("Yi zu yi le"), and "Shared Pleasures" ("Le zai qizhong"). See MSS 530613–21.

[136] *Zhipu* occurs in a handwritten collection of complete plays compiled by Zhaoqing shuwu, for which see entry 1226 in *Zhongguo yinyue shupuzhi*, comp. Zhongguo yishu yanjiusuo yinyue yanjiusuo ziliaoshi (Beijing: Renmin yinyue chubanshe, 1984), 33; see front covers of Shanghai MS 506230 (for *ding*, "to set") and 506244 (for *ding*, "to revise"). For comparable uses of *zhi* (to transcribe) and *zaizhi* (to retranscribe) see the inside covers of Shanghai MSS 500725–28. *Ji* (to record) is the term most frequently used by writers of these manuscripts.

[137] MSS 530613–621. The compiler notes that all but two of his sources (one being *Zhui baiqiu*) have the *gongche* notation.

[138] This is the last volume in the set (MS 530621). Other sources consulted and recorded on cover pages are listed in the section "Handwritten *gongpu*" in Appendix C.

[139] In one undated collection (MS 505310) dialogue is treated with great care. The correct tone is indicated for each character (with a red circle placed at one of its four corners). The compiler has drawn upon both *Zhui baiqiu* and the original playtext when copying dialogue, or else his source does, but dialect found in *Zhui baiqiu* is purged in favor of Tang's version. In a few places he or his source creates new dialogue, based on stage directions in Tang's text, which are omitted.

[140] I have not examined how *gongche* notation varies from text to text. Zhou Yibai finds diversity of interpretation even in printed *gongpu*; see his *Zhongguo xiju shi* (Shanghai: Zhonghua shuju, 1953), vol. 2, 396–97, with accompanying display of five musical interpretations of one aria from "The Interrupted Dream." Xin Qinghua, who scores scripts for the Shanghai Kun Opera Troupe, explained that since Ye Tang's time Kun singing technique has become more and more elaborate, especially among practitioners of pure singing. However, the elaborations do not necessarily show up in the *gongche* notation. For expressive singing technique, see Strassberg, "Singing Techniques of *K'un-ch'ü*," nos. 15b, 17, 18, 20, 22, and 23.

[141] MSS 781943–955, one of three handwritten *gongpu* for drama classified as a rare book. It contains the largest number of *Mudan ting* extracts (nine of sixty).

[142] MSS 484144–79 (earliest volume 1883, last volume 1957) show these features most strikingly. Assembled by members of the Jin lineage, the collection contains many extracts with large amounts of dialogue and interlinear notation about intonation and movements the performer should use. Some volumes contain pages with notation for gongs and drums only, or arias with musical notation only. Emended text almost always is dialogue. Given the collection's popular feel, it is not surprising that there are no *Mudan ting* extracts.

[143] One copyist for this collection also uses *xixue* (to practice) when referring to himself (MS 484148, dated 1947); another volume (MS 484167, dated 1929) bears the motto "With one glance, all becomes clear" ("Yi jian bian ming"). These are the only two instances of features that I identify with an amateur mode of compilation. Characters are blotted or crossed out, deleted, inserted, and occasionally miswritten.

[144] See Xu Chongjia et al., comps, *Kunshan xian xiqu ziliao huibian* (mimeographed copy, Kunshan, n. d.), vol. 1, 55–63. Nearly all of the several hundred manuscripts gathered in Kunshan district perished in the conflagration of the Cultural Revolution. However, many other manuscript collections of *zhezixi*—some perhaps from Kunshan—were gathered in the Shanghai Library at that time. I have examined only a fraction of them. Manuscripts owned by *tangming* contain many miswritten or wrong characters; a *tangming* artist might perform a *zhezixi* for years without knowing what it was about or the play from which it came. See Xu et al., *Kunshan xian xiqu ziliao*, vol. 1, 60. My thanks to Mr. Zhang Wanliang, former keeper of archives at the Shanghai Kun Opera Troupe, for sharing with me his copy of this work.

[145] Xu Chongjia and his collaborators point this out (vol. 1, 56). They suggest that the activities of *tangming* predate those of the *piaoyou* Lu Eting has written about in his history, for whom the *tangming* often were teachers and singing masters.

[146] Of three manuscripts of "Wandering in the Garden," only one gives the dialogue; all are written in fine calligraphy. Other extracts found in these collections include: "The School Hall" (one extract), "Pursuing the Dream" (two), "Infernal Judgment" (two), "Spirit Roaming" (one), "The Alarm" (one), "Asking the Way" (one), "Interrogation Upside-down" (one), and "Reunion at Court" (one). The predominance of "Speed the Plough" is explained by the fact that it was often the opening piece of a performance by *tangming*, which usually consisted of four extracts in one set. See Xu et al., vol. 1, 58.

[147] A partial list of performances at the Qing court from ca. 1820 to 1900 appears in Zhou Mingtai, *Qing Shenpingshu cundang shili manchao* (Taibei: Wenhai chubanshe, 1970). Several performances of "Speed the Plough" are noted as falling either on the first or the fifteenth day of the third month; these were part of the court's celebration of spring's arrival. Two performances of "Infernal Judgment" are also mentioned and one of "Wandering in the Garden, Startled by a Dream." A work that records court performances for the same period more selectively mentions three of "Speed the Plough," one of "Wandering in the Garden," one of "Wandering in the Garden, Startled by a Dream," and one each of "Reunion at Court" and "Sweeping the Garden" (a comic scene featuring the maid Chunxiang). See Wang Zhizhang, *Qing Shenpingshu zhilue* (Shanghai: Shangwu yinshuguan, 1937), vol. 1, 77, 79, and 109. "Shenpingshu" designated the department in charge of palace entertainments from 1827 onwards.

[148] The version of "Recovering the Portrait and Calling to It" I am using is from the edition of 1777 entitled *Zhui baiqiu xinji hebian*, which is reproduced in *SBXQCK*. It is a reprint of a combined and expanded edition of *Zhui baiqiu xinji* that was completed by Baorentang in 1774.

[149] In MS 506238 ("Recovering and Calling") miswritten characters crop up in arias, verse, and dialogue. Besides simplified forms or common variants (*dou* [all] for *duo* [many]), one finds phonetic substitutions that make no sense: *yan si tuo* (cheeks flush) becomes *yan zi tu* (cheeks smear). *Zhe shi xiaosheng de zhuozuo* (this is my clumsy verse) becomes *zhe shi xiaosheng de juezu* (this is my stupid foot). In MS 506275 ("Speed the Plough"), an allusion to the well-known story of Qiu Hu and his wife has Qiu He (river) instead of Qiu Hu (Tartar). In "Recovering and Calling" an unfamiliar aria title, *Bidizhai*, occurs in place of *Ji xianbin* from *Zhui baiqiu xinji* (itself a substitution for *Tiying xu* in *Mudan ting*).

[150] In printed playtexts, including Ming miscellanies, the text of dialogue is smaller and lighter, and usually printed in double columns. An exception is the 1777 printing of *Zhui baiqiu xinji hebian*, where the text of the dialogue approximates that for arias in size and darkness. But even in that edition text for dialogue is indented, hence set apart, from that for arias.

[151] Aria titles, however, are included, since they serve an obvious practical use for both the singer of the text and the musicians who accompany him or her. In manuscripts made by amateurs, the text is often embellished (as when titles are enclosed in cartouches or brackets and musical notation is written in colored ink).

[152] *MDT*, 24.339; *PP*, 137.

[153] Jin Shi discusses how these arias affect the depiction of Liu's character in "Wuxin, liuxin, zhixin: tan Zhang Fuguang zai Xiang Kun 'Shi hua jiao hua' zhong de biaoyan," *Hunan Xiju*, no. 4 (1984): 25.

[154] "Some time ago Sister Stone told me that there was a large garden in these precincts that is most suitable for strolling about; but it is only suitable for whiling away time, and one must avoid grieving. For this reason I have come forthwith, and am already arrived." In Tang's version of the scene, Sister Stone delivers her injunction to Liu in person.

[155] "What a desolate place!"

[156] A line of dialogue in *Zhui baiqiu xinji* ("Ya! I almost fell down!") is here omitted, which replaces a stage direction ("He stumbles") in Tang's text.

[157] Here the manuscript departs from *Zhui baiqiu xinji*, which preserves dialogue from the original scene (in which Liu wonders how the nuns who tend the Hongmeiguan could have built such a magnificent garden) and the more eerily evocative of two arias he sings as he enters the garden (*Jinchan dao*). It then takes up Liu's dialogue after *Jinchan dao*, omitting a stage direction that calls for offstage sounds that simulate the falling of rocks in the grotto.

[158] "Ai! It's a rosewood box, but I don't know what's inside it. Hmh! A small scroll, but what can be depicted on it? Hai! It's a painting of the Bodhisattva Guanyin." In an interesting case of orthographic change, our text has "Guanyin *xixiang*" (Guanyin's playful image) for Tang's "Guanyin *xixiang*" (Guanyin's smiling visage) and *Zhui baiqiu xinji*'s "Guanyin Dashi" (Teacher Guanyin).

[159] Here the copyist has substituted Tang's original wording (*ding li gongyang*) for *fen xiang gongyang* ("there to light incense and make formal obeisance to it") in *Zhui baiqiu xinji*. Insertion of fragments of original language here, and the similar case of MS 485587, where aria titles and phrases from *Fengliu meng* that are not in *Zhui baiqiu xinji* have found their way into "Shi Jiao," raise the question how these changes were introduced. It would seem that they were made by someone familiar with both written versions of the scene, but miswritten characters, in MS 506238 particularly, appear to have resulted from the writer's mistaken *hearing* of the text (for examples, see n. 149). This suggests that he was transcribing from memory. Such small, localized deviations from the version given in *Zhui baiqiu xinji* are numerous in these two manuscripts, and doubtless in others as well. This translation is based on that in *PP*, 135–38.

[160] *MDT*, 26.347; *PP*, 145 (modified).

[161] *Zhui baiqiu xinji*, first collection, "Calling to the Portrait," 2b, 3a.

[162] *FLM*, 2.19.3a–b.

[163] Zhao Jingshen has complained that Feng's rewritten aria turns Liu into a "lustful fellow" (*jise'er*); see "Tan *Mudan ting* de gaibian," 134; reprinted in *TXZZL*, 1104; Negeyama Tōru seconds this opinion in "*Kankon ki* no enpen," 169.

[164] *MDT*, 26.48; *PP*, 146. This line is kept unchanged in *Zhui baiqiu xinji*.

[165] In Song times a poet could be branded a libertine for using *ban'er* in a love poem. By the nineteenth century, the word likely no longer had powerfully vulgar connotations when used in *qu*. Nevertheless its presence here does inject a common (*su*) tone of familiarity into the line. For the case of the Song *ci* poet Liu Yong, see Kang-i Sun Chang, *The Evolution of Chinese Tz'u Poetry: From Late Tang to Southern Sung* (Princeton: Princeton University Press, 1980), 112–15.

[166] This manuscript from a different collection seems to be a slightly different version of the text found in MS 506238. The same arias are cut, but its many small changes to the dialogue often differ from that text.

[167] Cf. *Zhui baiqiu xinji: "Kan ni zheshuang qiaoyan zhiguan gupan xiaosheng."*

[168] Its arrangement more closely resembles a printed *gongpu*: each aria title is clearly framed, and each column of text contains seventeen characters, with *gongche* notation slanting to the right. MS 781946 departs from most texts for dramatic *qu* in its arrangement of *gongche* notation in a vertical column below each character.

[169] I.e., actions so theatrically exaggerated that they become comical.

[170] Both elegant manuscripts depart intriguingly, although differently, from the *Zhui baiqiu* text at another point. Where both falter is the line in which Liu Mengmei describes the portrait's mouth as a "tiny lotus bud, lips unparted." In MS 781946 "tiny lotus bud" (*yaohe*) becomes the nonsensical "*mohe*" ("grind lotus"); in MS 14689 *yaohe* is distorted even more, becoming "*mohu*" ("blur"). Both miswritings stem from taking *yao* in its alternative pronunciation *mo*, but it is fascinating that both writers stumble over erotically charged language.

[171] It does not include twenty-four *zhezixi* separately listed in *Zhongguo yinyue shupuzhi*, nor countless others that are part of larger collections also listed there.

[172] Compilers of several collections condemn vulgarities found in commercial editions (*fangben*); the compiler of *Xuanxuepu* has corrected mistakes and emendations made by actors that mar many texts.

[173] Use of illustrations in miscellanies has a similar effect. Many in *Yue lu yin* refer to the content of the scene obliquely, or at best generically. An illustration for "Interrogation Under the Rod," the scene in which Du Bao orders Liu Mengmei strung up and beaten, depicts the two men smiling and gesturing to each other. This could well be because it was made for another play, as is the case for an extract from *Lihua ji*, whose illustration has been borrowed from Zang Maoxun's adaptation of *Mudan ting* (where it illustrates scene 28, "Union in the Shades"). See *SBXQCK*, vol. 15, 261. The compiler might as well have saved it for that scene, which precedes it in the collection; instead he used another illustration, either borrowed from another play or taken from an edition of *Mudan ting*

now lost (*SBXQCK*, vol. 15, 211). In none of the miscellanies are the illustrations used to allude to performances. In this respect they fit Yao Dajuin's description of illustrations used in printed editions intended for desktop reading or amateur singing without acting; see "The Pleasure of Reading Drama: Illustrations to the Hongzhi Edition of *The Story of the Western Wing*," in West and Idema, *The Moon and the Zither*, 464.

[174] Although this was a time when several highlights from a play might be performed together, the miscellanies do not replicate that format. *Yue lu yin*, whose generous selection of scenes from *Mudan ting* (eight) favors those performed by the *dan* role, does not print sequentially. The compiler of *Cilin yixiang* does for several early Ming plays, but for recent popular plays he rarely selects more than two scenes. For the formats of late Ming performances see Wang Anqi, "Mingdai de siren jiayue yu jiazhai yanju," *Gugong wenwu yuekan* 7, no. 12 (March 1990): 74–76.

[175] See Wang Anqi, "Jiazhai yanjiu," 68–71 (for close supervision of performances by owners of household troupes). Hu Ji and Liu Zhizhong feel that most of the extant printed miscellanies catered to the taste for pure singing; see *Kunju fazhan shi*, 116–19. Lu Eting cites anecdotal evidence that even professional actors often had to perform a play as their hosts demanded, *Yanchu shigao*, 146–47.

[176] For the performance environment in the eighteenth century, see Hu Ji and Liu Zhizhong, *Kunju fazhan shi*, 423–28. These measures were strictest under the Yongzheng emperor, who was intensely suspicious of officials' passion for the theater.

[177] It would be interesting to investigate the situation for other Kun operas, since the contents of early Qing miscellanies are quite different from those for late Ming miscellanies (see n. 47 and 111). Iwaki Hideo singles out *Zuiyi qing* for the number of its extracts (20 of 165) that contain Wu dialect, an indicator of their popular provenance; see "Gogo no kinō," 627–30.

[178] The revisions in these extracts are similar in kind to (though less extreme than) those made in Mao Jin's popular anthology of complete *chuanqi* plays, *Liushizhong qu*, for which see n. 30 above. Iwaki Hideo, who examines uses of dialect in *Liuzhizhong qu*, *Zuiyi qing*, and *Zhui baiqiu*, feels that all three collections catered to a broad readership, increasingly so; see "Gogo no kinō," 626–30.

[179] The exception being the twenty extracts in *Zuiyi qing* in which Wu dialect, a new feature, is used (see the previous two notes).

[180] For prohibitions concerning private troupes and private theatricals in the Kangxi, Yongzheng, and Qianlong reigns, see Hu Ji and Liu Zhizhong, *Kunju fazhan shi*, 364–71; Hua Sheng, "Yi dashanbian," 86–88; Mackerras, *Rise of the Peking Opera*, 35–40. For the inattentiveness of audiences in wine and teahouses, see Lu Eting, *Yanchu shigao*, 204–5, and also the nineteenth-century novel *Pinhua baojian*, many of whose scenes are set in public theaters and winehouses associated with them.

[181] I have not seen the 1740 edition; reasons for believing this to be the case are given in n. 40.

[182] Hua Sheng states that the shift to actor control of playtexts took place in the Qianlong era; this evidence supports his contention. See his "Yi dashanbian," 89.

[183] Hu Ji and Liu Zhizhong situate the rejuvenation of the repertoire of *zhezixi* for Kun opera in the Qianlong and Jiaqing eras (1736–1820), *Kunju fazhan shi*, 402, but also date the beginning of Kun opera's decline in Beijing to the 1760s (p. 513); see also Mackerras, *Rise of the Peking Opera*, 106–112.

[184] See Hu Ji and Liu Zhizhong's discussion of Kun opera's amalgamation with popular styles in *Kunju fazhan shi*, 511–23 (518–21 for *Zhui baiqiu*). These developments, which began in the Qianlong era in Beijing and Yangzhou, were fully underway by 1780. See also Mackerras, *Rise of the Peking Opera*, 61, 106–8. Lu Eting discusses movement of actors between private and professional troupes at this time in *Yanchu shigao*, 139.

[185] Iwaki Hideo discusses the prominence of dialogue and varied uses of Wu dialect (associated with the *chou* and *jing* roles) in the popular edition of *Zhui baiqiu* in "Gogo no kinō." The greater importance of the *sheng* role in Beijing opera, compared to Kun opera, likely also accounts for the popularity of "Recovering the Portrait" and "Calling to the Portrait" from this time on; see Mackerras, *Rise of the Peking Opera*, 68.

[186] As noted earlier, "Speed the Plough" was often performed at the Qing court. It is also listed among plays performed by a specially assembled Yangzhou troupe for the Qianlong emperor during his second southern tour, as was "Heaped Blossoms," which was performed detached from "Startled by a Dream." A pocket-sized handwritten *gongpu* for "Heaped Blossoms" alone (undated), which enlarges the sequence with a sixth aria, lends support to the argument that court practices influenced tastes beyond the court (witness also the popularity of "Speed the Plough" in the manuscript collections). "Infernal Judgment," another scene performed at court that lends itself to spectacle, is among the repertoire of extracts performed by the Chuntai troupe from Anhui, a *huabu* troupe established in 1773; see Hu Ji and Liu Zhizhong, *Kunju fazhan shi*, 510–11.

[187] Hu Ji and Liu Zhizhong describe a few of them, including a manuscript for scene 14 from *Mudan ting* (renamed "Miao zhen," "Depicting the Portrait") and dated 1785 (*Kunju fazhan shi*, 487–88).

[188] Hu Ji and Liu Zhizhong single out one extract found in it, "Shang lu" (from *Jingchai ji*), which documents the interpretation of Sun Jiugao, a professional actor famous in Yangzhou (*Kunju fazhan shi*, 490–91).

[189] Concerning troupes formed by amateurs in Suzhou in the 1730s and 1740s, see Lu Eting, *Yanchu shigao*, 207; Lu there describes *chuanke* as "avocational lovers of drama" (*yeyu xiqu aihaozhe*) who enjoyed performing onstage (*chuan xi*). See also Hu Ji and Liu Zhizhong, *Kunju fazhan shi*, 435–36, 438, 457, and 485. Lu notes that both *chuanke* and practitioners of pure singing performed for high prices to limited audiences. Nevertheless their influence was felt in the professional troupes; by the 1760s the rosters of some professional troupes in Yangzhou include the names of well known *chuanke* (*Yanchu shigao*, 153–55 and 225–28). With the exception of the presence of *chuanke* in professional troupes, the situation in the late eighteenth century resembles another very fluid period for drama in the mid-to-late-sixteenth century. For *chuanke* in the late Ming theatrical world, see Wang Anqi, *Mingdai chuanqi zhi juchang ji qi yishu* (Taibei: Xuesheng shuju, 1985), 115–20.

[190] MSS 505310 ("Speed the Plough") and 505311 ("The Alarm"), both of which follow Tang Xianzu's text more closely than *Zhui baiqiu*'s.

[191] See p. 137.

[192] By the nineteenth century, use of texts was no longer a reliable indication of use by amateurs. *Mingxin jian* (A mirror of the actor's mind), a manuscript written by a *chuanke* based on information given orally by two actors from the troupe he managed, circulated among actors in the mid-Qing period; see Hu Ji and Liu Zhizhong, *Kunju fazhan shi*, 485. Zhou Yibai wrote notes and commentary for this text in *Xiqu yanchang lunzhu jishi* (Beijing: Zhongguo xiju chubanshe, 1962; 1980), 176–208.

[193] Zheng Zhenduo, "Zhongguo xiqu de xuanben," in *Zhongguo wenxue yanjiu* (Shanghai: Shanghai shudian, 1981), vol. 2, 5.

[194] Even "Wandering in the Garden, Startled by a Dream" the most celebrated extract from the play, was not enduringly popular. Performances of it are mentioned in the eighteenth-century novel *Honglou meng* and the nineteenth-century novel *Pinhua baojian*, but it was seldom performed at court after the Qianlong period and is represented in only three of seventeen manuscript collections surveyed. See Lindy Li Mark, "Kunju and Theatre in the Transvestite Novel *Pinhuan Baojian*," *Chinoperl Papers* 14 (1986): 37–59.

[195] There is little evidence that *zhezixi* from the same play were performed together by this time. Gu Duhuang reproduces a list of twenty-two extracts from *Mudan ting* that were part of the repertoire of court operas. If performed together they would plausibly replicate the plot of the whole play, but Gu indicates that by the end of the Qing dynasty the only scenes still performed were (with one exception) the twelve found in *Zhui baiqiu*; see his *Kunju shi bulun* (Nanjing: Jiangsu guji chubanshe, 1987), 184. The list favors popular scene titles such as appear in *Zhui baiqiu* (thirteen of twenty-two) and includes one or perhaps two extracts not derived from scenes in the original play. The popular orientation of Gu's list is clear when we compare it to a listing of handcopied *zhezixi* for *Mudan ting* in the collection of the Shengpingshu. *Yinyue shupuzhi* lists fifteen extracts distributed among thirteen scenes; five of these extracts use popular titles: "Wandering in the Garden, Startled by a Dream" (three); "Recovering the Portrait and Calling to it" (one); and "Interrogation Upside-down" (one). See Appendix C.

[196] For a recent study of European drama that considers these factors when assessing the meanings a play could assume, see chapter 1, pp. 16–17.

[197] Zhao Shanlin compares three playlists of varying origins, including one that mentions performances of *Mudan ting* in Jiangnan villages, in order to illustrate the different aesthetic tastes of Ming audiences; see *Guanzhongxue*, 237–50. In an example closer to home, some manuscript collections described in this chapter appear to intermingle Kun opera texts with those of other styles. MSS 506229–275 name approximately thirty-one plays, half a dozen of which do not seem to belong to the mainstream Kun opera repertoire.

[198] Lu Eting takes expanded dialogue as a prime indicator of popular orientation in play-texts, *Yanchu shigao*, 106–8. So does Iwaki Hideo, whose analysis of uses of Wu dialect in dialogue stresses the feeling of freedom that flowed between the actors and audience as a result, "Gogo no kinō," 642–43.

[199] See *Yanchu shigao*, 6–13; for the abyss of class, see 9–10. Negeyama Tōru covers much of the same ground in his analysis of extracts in *Zhui baiqiu* and *Shenyin jiangu lu* in "*Kankon ki* no enpen," especially 174–76.

[200] See Jonas Barish, *The Anti-theatrical Prejudice* (Berkeley: University of California Press, 1981), chapters 1 and 5 especially.

[201] *Yue lu yin* is a case in point: seven of its eight extracts are from scenes that feature the heroine and show Tang's brilliant use of language to maximum effect. A description of one such performance in a late Ming source is translated in chapter 1, p. 6.

Notes to Chapter Five

[1] Lu Eting, "Tan Kunju de ya he su," 19–33. Depending on the context, "common" is sometimes translated as "vulgar."

[2] Theatrical dance in Ming times was judged by its form more than by its expressive relation to sung lyrics. See Guangren Grant Shen, "Theatre Performance During the Ming Dynasty" (Ph.D. diss., University of Hawaii, 1994), 192–200; also Grant Shen, "Acting in the Private Theatre of the Ming Dynasty," *Asian Theatre Journal* 15, no. 1 (spring 1998): 69–72.

[3] Lu Eting, "Kunju de ya he su," 26–27. Lu suggests that the cultural gap between playwright, troupe owner, and performer was relatively narrow at this time because of the intimate contact between them. See also Shen's chapter on "communication," which uses the example of one actress's performance of "Wandering in the Garden," in "Theatre Performance During the Ming Dynasty," 210–25.

[4] Lu Eting, "Kunju de ya he su," 24–27. Lu astutely observes that in the first, "elite" phase of Kun's history, it was felt to be "*ya*" while other styles were "*su*." However, *within* the Kun style, pure singing was "*ya*," while fully staged performances were "*su*." Pushing the *ya/su* dichotomy further still, Lu suggests that performances by amateurs (*quyou*), no matter how amateurish, were felt to be "*ya*," while performances by professional actors, no matter how refined artistically, were regarded as "*su*." A strict dichotomizing of *ya* from *su*, which Lu contends has never accurately captured the reality of Kun opera even during this early phase, broke down completely in the subsequent, much longer phase of its dissemination in performance (p. 21). For *ya* and *su* as paired in the language of Ming connoisseurship, see Craig Clunas, *Superfluous Things: Material Culture and Social Status in Early Modern China* (Urbana and Chicago: University of Illinois Press, 1991), 82–83.

[5] *Liyuan chuanben mo shei xiu, yi shi fenghua yi dai chou*, cited in Lu Eting, "Kunju de ya he su," 30.

[6] "Kunju de ya he su," 28–29. For Ye Tang, see chapter 4, p. 134–35.

[7] "Kunju de ya he su," 29–31, which analyzes a *zhezixi* I discuss below in n. 81.

[8] "If you want to use the single word 'elegant' to characterize Kun opera, this cannot be gainsaid, but this is elegance that comes from a synthesis of elegance and commonness into a whole [*jingguo ya su rongwei yiti yihou de ya*], an all-encompassing elegance." Lu Eting, "Kunju de ya he su," 29.

[9] Actors often burned texts pertaining to their roles to preserve the secrets of their art. See Mackerras, *Rise of the Peking Opera*, 246.

[10] *Shenyin jiangu lu*, a *shenduanpu* published in 1834, contains several *zhezixi* from *Mudan ting* and is reproduced in *SBXQCK*, vols. 73–74. Other *shenduanpu* for *Mudan ting* are Xu Lingyun's detailed descriptions of "The School Hall" and "Asking the Way" in *Kunju biaoyan yide*, 316–55, and Zhang Yuanhe's line-by-line notes for "The School Hall" and "Wandering in the Garden" in *Kunqu shenduan shipu* (N.p., 1972). Manuscript *shenduanpu* from the collection of the Shengpingshu, which date from the 1780s, include one for scene 14 from *Mudan ting* titled "Miao zhen" ("Depicting the Portrait"). For these see Jiang Xingyu, "Zhou Mingtai zhi zhushu yu shoucang," in *Zhongguo xiqu shi gouchen* (Henan: Zhongzhou shuhuashe, 1982), 289–97.

[11] Prominent among them are those of Mei Lanfang (1894–1961), who performed in the Kun as well as the Beijing opera style; Bai Yunsheng (1902–1972), a professional actor of the northern tradition of Kun opera (*beiKun*), and Xu Lingyun (1885–1965), a celebrated *piaoyou* who was active in Shanghai.

[12] In 1995 I was often told that the number of Kun opera actors had so dwindled that interpretations were increasingly a matter of personal style and of choices unfettered by the prescriptions of a particular school. Wang Anqi cautions against assuming that modern interpretations of *zhezixi* reflect earlier practices in "Zailun Mingdai zhezixi" in *Mingdai xiqu wulun* (Taibei: Da'an chubanshe, 1990), 2. For *Mudan ting* in the "whole play" format, see n. 134 below; for linked sequences of extracts, see chapter 1, n. 49.

[13] One class was being trained in Shaoxing opera (*Yueju*), the other in Beijing opera. Each group spent approximately thirty hours learning the arias, with accompanying dialogue and verse. Their teacher was Zhang Xunpeng, an actress trained in both the *guimendan* and *huadan* roles. Singing classes were presided over by Wu Chongji, a flautist. I am grateful to both for their willingness to let me attend several sessions.

[14] I will say little about musical interpretation because I am not competent in this area and have had little opportunity to discuss Kun singing with those who are. Nor does the information reflect the practice of a particular school, because distinct schools no longer exist.

[15] Zhao Jingshen, scholar and *piaoyou*, echoed the views of many when he wrote, "The entire spirit of *Peony Pavilion* can be found in this scene." "Du Tang Xianzu ju suibi," *Xiqu bitan* (Shanghai: Shanghai guji chubanshe, 1962), 115.

[16] By the time that the practice of performing *zhezixi* had matured, a sequence of six (no more than eight) arias was considered an ideal; anything longer was liable to undergo cutting, and playwrights such as Hong Sheng and Kong Shangren (among the last of the literati playwrights whose works were successful theatrically) took this constraint seriously. The fifth of Kong's general rules for *Taohua shan* states that if playwrights wish to forestall wanton cutting by actors, they must write no more than eight arias for long scenes or four to six arias for short scenes; see *XBHB*, 1605.

[17] Based on articles documented in *Zhongguo gudian xiqu xiaoshuo yanjiu suoyin*, Yu Manling, comp. (Guangzhou: Guangdong gaodeng jiaoyu chubanshe, 1992), 167–71; other materials were gathered at the library of the Shanghai Theatre Academy (Shanghai xiju xueyuan).

[18] The *xiaosheng* actor Yue Meiti acknowledges that "Startled by a Dream" is not a primary vehicle for this role type, "Renwu neixin de mei," 11; see also Jin Zhiren, "Kunju ermeng," *Nanjing daxue xuebao*, no. 1 (1982): 38.

[19] See Elizabeth Wichmann, *Listening to Theater*, 20–23. Wichmann's observations about "emotional progression" structure in Beijing opera hold for Kun opera as well.

[20] "Actress" because the training of male *dan* actors has been discontinued.

[21] A vivid account of the *dan*'s performance by a *xiaosheng* actor is Yu Zhenfei's description of Mei Lanfang in "Wuxian shenqing Du Liniang," in *Yu Zhenfei yishu lunji* (Shanghai: Shanghai wenyi chubanshe, 1985), 197–202. Yu dwells on Mei's eyes: "Every time I performed 'Startled by a Dream' with him, no sooner did I feel the touch of those eyes, bright as autumn pools, than I would feel a big shock, as if a great warm current had engulfed my whole body" (*Meici wo yu ta hezuo yan 'Jingmeng,' yi jiechu ta nei ming ru qiushui de shuangtong, zhengge shenxin dou hui gandao hen da de zhendong, haoxiang yigu juda de nuanliu guanchuan quanshen*).

[22] A much longer soliloquy is Liniang's long solo scene "Pursuing the Dream," considered to be one of the most challenging scenes for the *guimendan* actress and rarely performed.

[23] Using Wichmann's analysis of lyric types in Beijing opera, *Shanpo yang* is emotive (*shuqing*), since its lyrics "are introspective, direct statements of a character's feelings." The four main arias of "Wandering in the Garden" are of the descriptive (*xingrong*) type, "metaphorical, indirect statements of a character's feelings, expressed through the description of physical surroundings"; see *Listening to Theater*, 27–33. Her six types are all found in Kun opera as well.

[24] Zeng Yongyi, "Juese gaishuo," 63.

[25] For the evolution of *sheng* and *dan* roles in *chuanqi*, see Zeng Yongyi, "Juese gaishuo," 261–74. Guo Liang discusses how the system of roles for Kun opera evolved from the seven basic types inherited from *nanxi* to a much more differentiated system, in which the concept of "character types" (*renwu leixing*) influenced the division of labor and associated acting skills within each category, "Kunshan qiang de biaoyan yishu," 314–15.

[26] Wang Jilie, *Xin yuefu renwuzhi* (Record of dramatis personae for new *yuefu*), quoted in Zeng Yongyi, "Juese gaishuo," 271. Wang finds chasteness (*jing*) to be the quintessential quality associated with the *guimendan* role and cites Du Liniang as an example of this. The terms *guimendan* and *fengyuedan* first appear in Li Dou, *Yangzhou huafang lu* (1797 edition, published by Ziran'an), vol. 5, 18b–19a.

[27] Zeng Yongyi, "Juese gaishuo," 289–90; Guo Liang, "Kunshan qiang de biaoyan yishu," 319.

[28] Excellent discussions of the two characters can be found in West and Idema, *The Moon and the Zither*, 98–109 (for Yingying) and 124–41 (for Hongniang).

[29] For difference within similarity with respect to Chunxiang and Liniang, see Yu Pingbo, "Zatan *Mudan ting* 'Jingmeng,'" *Xiju luncong*, no. 3 (1957): 82; Bai Yunsheng (performer of both *guimendan* and *xiaosheng* roles), "'Youyuan Jingmeng' de biaoyan yishu," in his *Sheng dan jing chou mo de biaoyan yishu* (Beijing: Zhongguo xiju chubanshe, 1957), 170–71; Mei Lanfang, "Wo yan 'Youyuan Jingmeng,'" *Mei Lanfang wenji* (Beijing: Zhongguo xiju chubanshe, 1962), 61.

[30] Zhang Xunpeng often spoke of this dialectic of similarity and difference and for this reason taught her students both roles, contrary to the usual practice.

[31] *MDT*, 10.267; *PP*, 42.

[32] Wang Anqi touches on uses of costume to depict age, temperament, and status and emphasizes how the symbolism of the costume helps the audience to apprehend immediately the character depicted; see *Mingdai chuanqi zhi juchang*, 258, 260, 268. Mei Lanfang discusses the color symbolism of the *doupeng* in "'Youyuan Jingmeng' cong wutai dao yinmu," reprinted from two 1961 issues of *Xiju bao*; in *TXZZL*, 1127–28.

[33] Actors speak of the need to fix a clear impression of character (*liangxiang*) at first entry. For the importance of entrances, see Chen Youhan, "Shilun Zhongguo xiqu wutai yishu de biaoyan chengshi," in *Zhongguo xiqu wutai yishu de biaoyan chengshi* (Xi'an: Shanxi renmin chubanshe, 1958), 53–55. Discussing Chunxiang's entrance in "Wandering in the Garden," Chen cites Mei Lanfang: " . . . from the dialogue, movements, and expression of the two characters at their entrance, their personalities are distinguished. The audience can immediately see that one is dignified [*duanzhuang*] the other lively [*huopo*]; clearly they are of different social status. This is one aspect of Kun opera's superiority when it comes to movement and stage direction." Wang Jide was the first to praise Tang's introductory arias in "Lun yinzi" (On introductory arias); see Wang Jide, *Wang Jide Qulü*, 157; also see *ZGGD*, vol. 4, 138.

[34] For Liniang's enchantment with her beauty, a mixture of bashfulness, longing, and "tender emotions towards the self" (*zilian*), see Li, *Enchantment and Disenchantment*, 53–54; also Shen, "Private Theatre," 75.

[35] *Bu xianggui zen bian ba quanshen xian*. Cyril Birch's translation ("Walking here in my chamber / how should I dare let others see my form?") suggests shyness about exposing one's beauty to the lover's gaze; H. C. Chang's ("Yet can I conceal myself when I walk?") better captures Liniang's uncertainty. See *MDT*, 10.267; *PP*, 43; Chang, *Popular Fiction and Drama*, 294. Lu Shulun of Fudan University found that Liniang's mirror makes her bashful (*jingzi jiao xiu*), a reading consistent with the decorum of the *guimendan* role.

[36] For this aria, see my discussion on pp. 167–70.

[37] Li, *Enchantment and Disenchantment*, 51–53. Li describes this self-consciousness as "a kind of narcissistic self-observation" and suggests that the intensity of Liniang's subjective projections is subversive in its representation of the desiring self (p. 76). She finds support for this reading of Liniang's character in an interest in dreams and "celebration of the human capacity to produce them" that was widespread when Tang wrote *Mudan ting* (p. 49).

[38] As the aria begins, Liniang is still seated at stage rear; Chunxiang stands beside a table at stage left, on which she has placed a mirror. My explanation of *Bubu jiao* is the one given by Zhang Xunpeng.

[39] Yu Pingbo, *piaoyou* and drama scholar, notes that these changes by actors are of longstanding, but condemns them; see his "Zatan *Mudan ting* 'Jingmeng,'" 87. He was unhappy with them because Liniang's garments are described in *Zui fu gui* and thus some action of changing garments is called for to support the sung lines—an important aspect of Kun performance aesthetics. On this point, see Jin Zhiren, "Kunju ermeng," 39–40. Mei Lanfang gives the actor's rationale for the changes in "Wo yan 'Youyuan Jingmeng,'" 64.

[40] *MDT*, 10.267; Chang, *Popular Fiction and Drama*, 294 (modified). Mei Lanfang says this action comes as Liniang sings "A long while I pause," a line to which dance movements

cannot easily be set, "Wo yan 'Youyuan Jingmeng,'" 63. However, Zhang Yuanhe indicates that for this line "[Liniang] places both hands on the make-up table and scrutinizes herself [in the mirror]. Chunxiang, hand resting on the back of the chair, scrutinizes Liniang's image in the mirror. Both heads move slightly—Liniang's to the left and Chunxiang's to the right, then Liniang's to the right and Chunxiang's to the left." Liniang then rises and removes the *doupeng* while singing the *next* line; *Kunqu shenduan shipu*, 92.

[41] I have observed this variation in a taped performance by the Nanjing troupe and in classes at the Shanghai school.

[42] *MDT*, 10.267; Chang, *Popular Fiction and Drama*, 294.

[43] These lines were sung as a duet in recent performances by the Shanghai troupe; the Nanjing troupe favors using an offstage chorus.

[44] Shen Yifu reviews dissatisfaction with these lines, commencing with the Qing dramatist Yang Enshou (fl. 1870) and his friend Cheng Yucang and finds that Liniang's boastfulness about her beauty detracts from her character; see "*Mudan ting* 'Jingmeng' xiaoyi," *Jiangxi xiju*, no. 4 (1982): 17. Feng Menglong removed them when revising *Zui fu gui*.

[45] Cyril Birch renders *ai hao* as "love of fine things"; William Dolby has "love for beauteous adornment." Both translations suggest, more than does Chang's, that there is no contradiction between the artificial beauty of Liniang's adornment, described in the first two lines, and the beauty of the garden, with which she intensely identifies. See *PP*, 44; William Dolby, *A History of Chinese Drama* (London: Paul Elek, 1976), 95. Xu Shuofang and Yang Xiaomei gloss *ai hao* as *ai mei*, in *Mudan ting*, 54n.

[46] Mei Lanfang, "Wo yan 'Youyuan Jingmeng,'" 65. This movement is described in "Danjue zheshan jiben jiaocai." This mimeographed pamphlet describes twenty-one movements for this kind of fan and some of the resulting effects. The movement in question, "blocking with the fan" (*dangshan*), is commonly used to express bashfulness (*hanxiu*), or to mime warding off wind and rain. The latter use is instanced twice for "Wandering in the Garden" in this pamphlet (in the arias *Zaoluopao* and *Mian daxu*), but not the former.

[47] For Yu's reluctance to tamper with long-established actor's practices, see "Zatan *Mudan ting* 'Jingmeng,'" 84; *TXZZL*, 1007.

[48] Beckerman, Bernard, *Theatrical Presentation*, 53–55, for the iconic mode of presentation; 134–35, for actor pairings.

[49] On the concentrated depiction of character in "Wandering in the Garden," see Jin Zhiren, "Kunju ermeng," 38. This tendency, likely present in early Kun opera performances, was taken further in *zhezixi*, many of which showcase a particular role.

[50] Mei Lanfang, "Wo yan 'Youyuan Jingmeng,'" 66.

[51] Mei Lanfang, "Cong wutai dao yinmu," 1149. Hua Wenyi emphasizes the use of the eyes to convey Liniang's happiness and excitement and emotions in which delight (*xiyue*) and frustration (*aiyuan*) comingle; see "Wo yan Du Liniang," *Shanxi xiju*, no. 12 (December 1982): 8.

[52] This description is based on videotaped performances of "Wandering in the Garden, Startled by a Dream" by Zhang Jiqing of the Nanjing troupe and Hua Wenyi of the Shanghai troupe. Mei Lanfang's comments on how to perform these arias agree remarkably

with the taped performances, although there are variations attributable to the styles of the artists and the teachers with whom they studied.

[53] *MDT*, 10.268; Chang, *Popular Fiction and Drama*, 295.

[54] See Luo Zheng, "Tang Xianzu de xiangxiang yu Mei Lanfang de maodun biaoyan: Kunju 'Youyuan' de xinli fenxi," *Xiju*, no. 2 (1993): 85.

[55] Lu Eting, "Tan Kunju de ya he su," 23. For this reason Zhang Xunpeng did not teach *Zaoluopao* to her young students at the drama school.

[56] *MDT*, 10.268; Chang, *Popular Fiction and Drama*, 295.

[57] *Zhui baiqiu* diminishes the contrast even more:

> *Chunxiang:* Mistress, why not save some of our excitement and come again tomorrow to play?
> *Liniang:* A good suggestion.
> *Chunxiang:* One can never see enough of this garden!

[58] Yu Pingbo, "Zatan *Mudan ting* 'Jingmeng,'" 85; *TXZZL*, 1007–8. In a "complete" version of *Mudan ting* that Yu helped to script for the Beijing Kun opera troupe in 1953, these revisions are kept. See *Mudan ting*, comp. Hua Cuishen et al (Beijing: Beifang kunju yuanben, 1953; mimeographed reprint, 1980).

[59] Yu Pingbo borrows a term from poetry criticism and describes the dance-acting of "Wandering in the Garden" as *hepan shenduan*. *Hepan* refers to lines in a parallel couplet whose meaning repeats. Yu uses it to suggest that the formalized movements that Liniang and Chunxiang perform together evoke "difference in similarity, similarity in difference" through effects of parallelism. "Zatan *Mudan ting* "Jingmeng,'" 82; *TXZZL*, 1003–4.

[60] Innumerable articles praise the obscurity of the arias that lead up to the *Shanpo yang* coda. Obscure language is *ya*, accessible to highly literate viewers who imaginatively participate in the performance. See, for example, Luo Zheng, "Tang Xianzu de mohu yuyan he xiangxiang tiandi: 'Youyuan' zhong de xinli fenxi," *Xiqu yishu*, no. 3 (1994): 14–19; also his "'Youyuan' de xinli fenxi," 80. I take up overly explicit acting later.

[61] *MDT*, 10.270; *PP*, 47.

[62] Mei Lanfang, "Yige zhongyao de guanjian: 'Youyuan Jingmeng,'" in his *Wutai shenghuo sishinian* (Beijing: Zhongguo xiju chubanshe, 1961, 1980), vol. 1, 175–76.

[63] Bai Yunsheng, "Tan Liu Mengmei," in *TXZZL*, 1242.

[64] Mei acknowledges ("Yige zhongyao de guanjian," 177) that young actors may prefer to perform *Shanpo yang* in the old way, but counsels them first to "be clear about Du Liniang's status [*shenfen*], and on all accounts avoid going overboard, making her into a 'licentious girl longing for love' [*dangfu si chun*]."

[65] For Bai Yunsheng, performances of *Shanpo yang* express only grief: "'Lingering' [*yanjian*] is a long phrase that meanders and lingers; as she sings, Du [Liniang] leans against the table and turns her body, her right hand pressed down on the table, her back close up against its side, her left hand on her breast. Leaning to her left, she slowly sinks down, the eyes staring slightly. For the forceful expression of inner feelings, this movement is very important.

At this point, Du [Liniang]'s grief at spring's passing has reached its peak." See "Tan Liu Mengmei," 75.

[66] Hua Wenyi remarks that "[w]hen depicting the character of Du Liniang, I want to manifest her qualities of reserve [*hanxu*] and refinement [*qingya*] and the waves of feeling agitating deep within her heart [*neixin shenchu jidangzhe de ganqing de bolan*]. If one of these two is lacking, then it isn't Du Liniang"; see "Wo yan Du Liniang," 7 and, for the use of the eyes to express excitement when singing *Zaoluopao*, 8.

[67] I have not seen Zhang Jiqing (head of the Nanking Kun Opera troupe) perform live, but her style has been described to me in these terms. Yao Chuanxiang was one of the last generation of male specialists in the *guimendan* role.

[68] "High intrinsic dignity" is from Wichmann, *Listening to Theater*, 9. Han Shichang, a *dan* actor who often performed opposite Bai Yunsheng, emphasizes Liniang's melancholy in this scene: "her heart is empty, she laments in secret, thinking of spring and grieving over spring the whole day, her spirits completely weighed down"; "Tan 'Youyuan' de biaoyan," *Beifang Kunqu juyuan jianyuan jinian tekan* (N.p., June 22, 1957), 33. Zhang Jiqing's interpretation of Du Liniang is akin to that of Bai Yunsheng.

[69] Kun opera purists find Zhang's style more "*ya*" because of her singing technique, Hua's more "*su*" because of her stage magnetism.

[70] Some find it too "sharp" (*jian*) for the *guimendan* role. Voiceover singing was used for *Shanpo yang*, which heightened the sharpness.

[71] One dismissed the performance as "high class porn" (*gaodeng huangse*).

[72] This is Yu Pingbo's position in "Zatan *Mudan ting* 'Jingmeng,'" 84.

[73] Indira Suh Satyendra, "Toward A Poetics of the Chinese Novel: A Study of the Prefatory Poems in the 'Chin P'ing Mei Tz'u-hua'" (Ph.D. diss., University of Chicago, 1989), also David Tod Roy, trans., *The Plum in the Golden Vase, or Chin P'ing Mei*, Volume One: *The Gathering* (Princeton: Princeton University Press, 1993), xliii–xlv.

[74] In the passage cited above, Lu remarks on the Mengshen's antiquity; "Heaped Blossoms" is cited as an example of the absorption of popular dance elements into Kun opera, in Hu Ji and Liu Zhizhong, *Kunju fazhan shi*, 510–11.

[75] Bai Yunsheng, "Tan Liu Mengmei," 79; *TXZZL*, 1239–40.

[76] Distrust of ornate diction was longstanding and not limited to actors. He Liangjun (fl. 1522–1566) singled out gorgeous (*nong*) and overwritten (*wu*) diction for criticism in *Qulun* (On *qu*), 8, 9 and 11; *ZGGD*, vol. 4, 7–8. His views, and those of other late Ming critics of drama who objected to the use of ornate diction, are discussed in Du Wei, "Ya su jiehe de gudian xiqu meixue sichao," *Qiushi xuekan*, no. 2 (1992): 85.

[77] Li, *Enchantment and Disenchantment*, 57. The lines quoted are from Liu's and Du's duet (*Shantao hong*) and the Huashen's aria (*Bao lao cui*), *MDT*, 270–71; *PP*, 48–49.

[78] Li, *Enchantment and Disenchantment*, 58. She does not discuss this in terms of a *ya/su* dichotomy, but in terms of different levels of language, which I feel can be formulated in *ya/su* terms. For a different view of the Buddhist language put in the mouth of the Huashen, see Lin Shuen-fu, "Chia Pao-yu's First Visit to the Land of Illusion: An Analysis

of a Literary Dream in Interdisciplinary Perspective," *Chinese Literature: Essays, Articles, Reviews* 14 (1992): 97.

[79] Various configurations of "Heaped Blossoms" are discussed in chapter 4. "Heaped Blossoms" is sometimes detached from "Startled by a Dream" and performed as a *zhezixi* in its own right. A handwritten, musically annotated copy appears in the collection of Zhang Wanliang, who manages the scripts of the Shanghai Kun Opera Troupe. This version introduces a new aria into the sequence, *Dajianglong,* and the whole is designated as "in praise of flowers" (*yong hua*). The aria *Shuangshengzi,* which concludes "Heaped Blossoms" in many late Qing *qupu,* is absent. The reconfigured sequence is: *Chu duizi, Dajianglong, Hua mei xu, Diliuzi, Bao lao cui, Wuban yi.*

[80] Tang was known for violating conventional genre boundaries when writing *qu.* Here he mingles philosophic language with the elevated diction of *shi* poetry and the concrete, explicit language found in *qu.*

[81] Lu Eting speaks of the "common appreciation" of the two (*ya su gong shang*). Thus his view of the relationship of *ya* and *su* language is in line with traditional aesthetics for *qu,* as articulated by Wang Jide and other late Ming and early Qing critics (see below). Discussing "Huozhuo," a *zhezixi* extracted from the late Ming *chuanqi Shuihu ji,* in which the ghost of Yan Poxi returns to plead with her lover to help her return to life, Lu remarks that as originally written, the pathos of Poxi's plight is evoked in arias written in allusive classical Chinese, but in the *zhezixi* that atmosphere of pathos is broken at the entrance of the lover Zhang Wenyuan, played by the *chou,* whose speech mingles Wu dialect with standard vernacular, and whose terrified responses to Poxi's ghost are the highlight of the scene. A scene featuring two low (*su*) characters was adapted by actors so as to preserve the allusive (*ya*) language in the original text while enhancing the role of the *chou* with dialect and comic business, both *su* elements that provide relief from the fear and pathos expressed in the original arias. See Lu Eting, "Tan Kunju de ya he su," 26 and 31. A description of this opera as performed in the tradition of Sichuan opera, with accompanying illustrations, can be found in *Chinese Opera: Images and Stories,* comp. Siu Wang-Ngai and Peter Lovrick (Vancouver: University of British Columbia Press, 1997), 195–97.

[82] Richard Hornby, *Script into Performance: A Structuralist Approach* (New York: Applause Books, 1977, 1995), chapters 1 and 5, passim. Hornby argues for the importance of the playtext and takes issue with theorists such as Richard Schechner, who downplay its importance in theatrical production.

[83] Zhao Jingshen finds ambiguity, even in the written text, about when the dream begins ("Tan *Mudan ting* de gaibian," *Xiqu bitan,* 132). Yu Pingbo is confused about when it ends and concludes that Tang himself was confused, since as he wrote the scene, Liniang dreams twice; "Zatan *Mudan ting* 'Jingmeng,'" 82–83; *TXZZL,* 1004–5.

[84] Bai Yunsheng, "Tan Liu Mengmei," 76; *TXZZL,* 1234.

[85] Li, *Enchantment and Disenchantment,* 50 and 53.

[86] Tina Lu addresses Li's reading of Liniang's dream and proposes that "the same two dreams [Liniang's and Liu Mengmei's] in *Mudan ting* that promise that kind of subjectivity [where things exist only insofar as they affect the subject] paradoxically also allow each dreamer to give life to the other." In her chapter on "The Lover's Dream," she gives

more attention to Liu Mengmei's dream than do most critics. See *Persons, Roles, and Minds*, 67, also 64 and 71.

[87] For Liniang's "willful autonomy," see Li, *Enchantment and Disenchantment*, 52.

[88] Bai Yunsheng, "Tan Liu Mengmei," 76; *TXZZL*, 1234.

[89] Zhao Jingshen, however, finds this adaptation to be a comparatively minor one, "Tan *Mudan ting* de gaibian," 132.

[90] Hornby, *Script into Performance*, 98–99 and 104.

[91] Lu Eting, "Kunju de ya he su," 26–27, attributes the split between playwright and actor to tensions between the design of original plays and both staging requirements and audience tastes; for tensions between stage and some segments of the Qing audience, see p. 30.

[92] Hornby, *Script into Performance*, 100–1; see also p. 54 for criticism of "piecemeal alterations." A chapter on "Current Performance Theories" reviews theorists who do not accord the same importance to the text that Hornby does.

[93] Chen Duo, "Du *Mudan ting* zhaji," in *TXZZL*, 265–67. Chen notes that critics often contrast Liniang, who is isolated in her struggle, with Yingying, heroine of *Xixiang ji*, who often relies on the good offices of her maid Hongniang: "When it comes to understanding *Mudan ting*, the difference in temperament between Du Liniang and Chunxiang is even more important than is the difference between Du Liniang and Yingying." A condensed version of this article incorporates observations on scene 10 as well; see Chen Duo, "Xiqu heyi xu bian?" in *Xishi bian*, ed. Hu Ji (Beijing: Zhongguo xiju chubanshe, 1999), 23–27.

[94] Chang, *Popular Fiction and Drama*, 280 (modified).

[95] Chen Duo, "Du *Mudan ting* zhaji," 263. The last two lines are from the mid-scene coda in scene 10, sung by Liniang after the two garden-strolling arias.

[96] "Chunxiang's stroll in the garden is just for fun; as for everything else, she just 'lets it be' and doesn't give it a thought. Du Liniang, however, must ponder and consider even such a small thing as this and is incapable of a careless act. This is precisely one of the important points of this scene." Chen Duo, "Du *Mudan ting* zhaji," 264.

[97] *Zhui baiqiu xinji*, fourth collection, "The School Hall," 8a–b. This is the earliest printed *zhezixi*, published in 1767. A more detailed version of "The School Hall" is in *Shenyin jiangu lu*; discussions of it can be found in Xu Lingyun, *Kunju biaoyan yide*, vol. 3, 53–75, and Bai Yunshen, *Sheng dan jing chou mo de biaoyan yishu*, 149–64.

[98] Chen Duo, "Du *Mudan ting* zhaji," 265.

[99] Chen ("Du *Mudan ting* zhaji," 265) feels this idea is especially important in three scenes (7, 9, and 10) that culminate in "The Interrupted Dream"; other scenes mentioned in this regard are "Pursuing the Dream," "The Portrait," and "Diagnosis." I would add "Keening" as well.

[100] "Du *Mudan ting* zhaji," 261. "Living prop" (*huodaoju*) is from Chen.

[101] "The School Hall," 4b–6a. My translation is based on Chang, *Popular Fiction and Drama*, 277–79.

[102] In the original text, Chunxiang exits immediately after this remark.

[103] Chang, *Popular Fiction and Drama,* 277 n, cites the tutor's quotation of Mencius as "the very ecstasy of pedantry" and gives James Legge's translation of the original passage: " . . . the scholar Lung said, 'If a man make hempen sandals without knowing the size of people's feet, yet I know that he will not make them like baskets.'"

[104] In the original, "Why isn't Chunxiang back?" is spoken by Liniang.

[105] Omitting a curse (directed at the tutor): "A pox on you!"

[106] Omitting Chunxiang's remark (to Liniang): "I had to pee," a line that has inspired actions performed with semi-ostentation for the tutor's benefit.

[107] Revising the simpler original: "Aha! Neglecting your books and wandering into the garden! Let me fetch the thornstick."

[108] Introduction here of *chenzi* (*Wo shi ge,* "I am") changes the sense of the opening line of the song from "Your young ladies" (Liniang included) to Chunxiang only.

[109] In some versions of her legend, the moon goddess Chang E transforms into a toad.

[110] A rare example of rewritten lyrics. The original lines express mock fear—stage directions instruct Chunxiang to dodge the tutor's stick as she sings them:

> Strike? Strike this poor child,
> One of your very own disciples?
> The culprit is scared indeed!

[111] Xu Lingyun, "The School Hall," *Kunju biaoyan yide,* vol. 3, 69–70.

[112] See Xu, "The School Hall," 70 and 64 (for the more "*hua*" treatment in Beijing opera).

[113] Bai Yunsheng, "'Chunxiang nao xue' de biaoyan yishu," in *Sheng dan jing chou mo de biaoyan yishu,* 158–59. "Nao xue" comes via Beijing opera; see Yang Baihua, "Shilun *Mudan ting* 'Guishu,'" *Jianghai xuekan,* no. 5 (1962): 41.

[114] This comment is from *Xiaohan xinyong,* a late nineteenth-century compilation of observations about actors and the theater of Beijing. See Zhou Yude, ed. and annot., *Xiaohan xinyong,* comp. Tieqiao shanren et al. (Beijing: Zhongguo xiqu yishu zhongxin, 1986), 63–64. My thanks to Andrea Goldman for sharing with me her copy of this inaccessible work. Zhou Yude cites this comment in "*Xiaohan xinyong* zhaji," *Xiqu yanjiu* 5 (1982): 250. Its author, Tieqiao shanren, refers to the *zhezixi* as "Xuetang," which suggests that he saw a performance of it in the Kun style. Jiang Xingyu criticizes distorted interpretations made of "Chunxiang nao xue" during the Cultural Revolution in "Tang Xianzu yanjiu de fansi," *Shanghai xiju* no. 1 (1987): 31. For a negative response to a humorous depiction of Chen Zuiliang in a current production of *Mudan ting,* see n. 14 of chapter 7.

[115] On the need for Liniang to use facial expressions to avoid becoming little more than a bystander to the action, see Bai Yunsheng, "'Chunxiang nao xue' de biaoyan yishu," 159, 163; for use of eyes, see Xu Lingyun, *Kunju biaoyan yide,* vol. 3, 62. For the emphasis on performances that have proportion (*hedu*) in *Xiaohan xinyong,* see Zhou Yude, "*Xiaohan xinyong* zhaji," 249–50.

[116] Zhao Jingshen notes that her role became such a minor one in popular versions of the scene that it could be played by another actor, to give the lead actor a rest, "Tan *Mudan ting* de gaibian," 130–31; *TXZZL,* 1101–2.

[117] "The School Hall," 6a–7a; Chang, *Popular Fiction and Drama*, 279, with changes and additions in italics.

[118] Replaces: "Wretched girl! You have offended the Tutor. Kneel down at once [Maid kneels]."

[119] Replaces: "May I look on?" and cuts Liniang's reply "Will you retort?"

[120] Omits direction in text: "Pulling at maid's hair."

[121] In the original, there is no indication that Liniang beats Chunxiang, and the tutor intercedes without Chunxiang's asking him to.

[122] Bai Yunsheng, "'Chunxiang nao xue' de biaoyan yishu," 160–61.

[123] "Textually, "Chunxiang nao xue" and "Xuetang" are nearly identical, but Beijing opera performances took the insurgency of Chunxiang's character farther than Kun-style performances did, though there was considerable cross-fertilization between the two styles, *ya* and *hua*, for this *zhezixi*.

[124] Levine, *Highbrow/Lowbrow*, 21–24, 31.

[125] Levine, *Highbrow/Lowbrow*, 36.

[126] Du Wei discusses this aesthetic bias in late Ming drama criticism, especially in Wang Jide's *Qulü*, in "Ya su jiehe," 114–19.

[127] For mixed entertainments and scenes performed from different plays, see Levine, *Highbrow/Lowbrow*, 21–23. For the similar situation for opera, see Levine's second chapter, "The Sacralization of Culture," 85–104.

[128] Levine, *Highbrow/Lowbrow*, 42.

[129] Levine, *Highbrow/Lowbrow*, 56, for theaters as places that brought together people from different classes in a focused gathering, there to relate to each other in a common activity. The mid-nineteenth century novel *Pinhua baojian* depicts, negatively, mixed audiences in Beijing commercial theaters, but I suggest below that outside a few urban centers the public for opera was fragmented and compartmentalized.

[130] Beckerman distinguishes two main forms of theatrical presentation: iconic (ritualized display) and dialectic (in which resistance, either psychological or social, is enacted between two or more actors). Although he associates the latter form with modern realistic theater and the former with theater in "traditional societies," the distinction is useful for contrasting Tang's presentation of Liniang's death, with its resistances between the various actors onstage, and forms her death takes in performance, which stress iconic display. See *Theatrical Presentation*, chapters 3 and 4.

[131] Du Wei ("Ya su jiehe," 87–88) presents Wang Jide as spokesman for what became the mainstream view among literati playwrights of how to incorporate *su* elements into dramatic *qu*. See also my discussion on pp. 199–202.

[132] All *zhezixi* for "Infernal Judgment" that I have seen, including the late Ming adaptations, either eliminate or tone down the punning sequence.

[133] Zhang Jing sees a different dynamic to the pairing of Stone and Chunxiang when she suggests that Stone's clumsy and simple (*zhuopu*) nature sets off Chunxiang's clever (*lingqiao*) one. See "Chuanqi juese zhi peida," 102.

[134] See, however, chapter 1, n. 35 for recent claims that the entire play has on occasion been performed. Performances of entire *chuanqi* died out in the Qing period, and for *zhezixi* a program of scenes drawn from different plays came to be favored over performances of several scenes from one play. See Xu Fuming, "Zhezixi jianlun," 62–63; Wang Anqi, *Mingdai chuanqi zhi juchang*, 210–12. In the twentieth century, performances of "complete" operas revived, probably modeled on dialect operas. These consist of various combinations of linked scenes, most taken from the Qing repertoire of *zhezixi*, some revived from the original play.

[135] See Mei Lanfang, "Yige zhongyao de guanjian," 173. Few of the actors at the Shanghai Kun Opera Troupe have consulted the original version of *Mudan ting*. They are more likely to consult adaptations of it made for other styles of opera (see below n. 147).

[136] For large public performances of Kun operas in late Ming times, see Lu Eting, *Yanchu shigao*, 3–4, 48ff. Wang Anqi, *Mingdai chuanqi zhi juchang*, chapter 3, contains an excellent discussion of the different venues for performances, their audiences, and the kinds of plays favored in each setting.

[137] Characters in *Pinhua baojian* often remark that Kun operas are too highbrow for their taste.

[138] Wang Jide, *Wang Jide Qulü*, "Zalun," no. 73, 225–26; *ZGGD*, vol. 4, 165. "*Bense*" here refers to language appropriate to drama, which Wang defined as language comprehensible even to the illiterate ("Zalun," no. 44, in *Wang Jide Qulü*, 200; *ZGGD*, vol. 4, 154). For the origins of this term and its use in late Ming drama criticism, see Chen and Ye's note for "Zalun," no. 36, 196; *ZGGD*, vol. 4, 152.

[139] See *Wang Jide Qulü*, "Zalun," no. 74, 227; *ZGGD*, vol. 4, 165.

[140] See "Lun jiashu" (On schools) in *Wang Jide Qulü*, 118; *ZGGD*, vol. 4, 121–22. This item is translated in Fei, *Chinese Theories of Theater and Performance*, 61–62. Wang's views about the proper mix of languages in drama were influenced by those of Xu Wei, who had stated in a preface he wrote to *Xixiang ji* that language for dramatic *qu* should fall between extremes of shallowness and depth, richness and blandness, elegance and plainness. Xu deplored the use of language and forms from *shi* and even *baguwen* in *chuanqi* and insisted that dramatic language err on the side of crudeness and comprehensibility rather than elegance and obscurity. See item 13 in his *Nanci xulu*, in *ZGGD*, vol. 3, 243, translated in Leung, *Hsu Wei as Dramatic Critic*, 71–72. Wang Jide expresses similar views in *Wang Jide Qulü*, "Zalun," no. 90, 243; *ZGGD*, vol. 4, 170. What is new is Wang's insistence that plain and elegant language be segregated according to the aria type: short and musically simple, or long and musically more complex. Xu's comments in his preface to *Xixiang ji* are quoted by Chen and Ye in a note to item 90; Wang repeated them in a preface he wrote for *Xixiang ji*, also reproduced in this note.

[141] See "Lun guoqu" (On main arias) in *Wang Jide Qulü*, 158; *ZGGD*, vol. 4, 138–39. The arias are from scene 25. The embellished lines, which refer to a tear-streaked letter that Cai Bojie sends to Zhao Wuniang, are in adjacent arias sung by Cai and the steward to whom he entrusts the letter. Here is Jean Mulligan's translation of the steward's aria, from *The Lute, Kao Ming's P'i-p'a chi* (New York: Columbia University Press, 1980), 192:

Thoughts of his distant hometown—
His lady there stares out with frozen gaze.
She sees the geese again and again fly by,
But his returning boat never comes in sight,
And still from high balcony she leans.
When she sees the silver strokes flying across rainbow-cloud paper,
Then tears will fall in streams, her makeup ruined.

[142] "Lun chake" (On comic routines) in *Wang Jide Qulü*, 165; *ZGGD*, vol. 4, 141.

[143] "Lun paixie" (On humor) in *Wang Jide Qulü*, 148–49; *ZGGD*, vol. 4, 135.

[144] "Lun qiangdiao" (On regional styles) in *Wang Jide Qulü*, 103–4; *ZGGD*, vol. 4, 117–18. Wang brands regional operas "renegade" forms (*daya zuiren*).

[145] "In the Yuan dynasty, customs above and below were unified [*shang xia chengfeng*], and everyone admired *ci*, such that some [among the elite] took it [playwriting] as their profession. Nowadays, men of our generation ply their brushes in writing eight-legged essays and have no time to dabble in drama. Until they become high officials, they can think of nothing but merit and fame; when they quit office and retire, they can think of nothing but their estates and descendants. Is it any wonder that we cannot compare with the Yuan masters?" See Wang Jide, *Wang Jide Qulü*, "Zalun," no. 6, 176–77; *ZGGD*, vol. 4, 147.

[146] Andrew Plaks discusses the sophisticated incorporation of popular elements in the literati novel in *Four Masterworks*, 71, and makes a case for "ironic discrepancies between the original import of the borrowed passages and the uses they are put to in their new contexts." I associate incongruities generated by *ya* and *su* juxtapositions in *Mudan ting* with parody and travesty, but also agree with Wai-yee Li that at times these force one to disengage and view the action from a different perspective, a technique conducive to irony. What differs from the strategy Plaks and others have outlined for the literati novel is that Tang's manner of incorporating *su* elements often compels reassessment of the elegant ones. For the philosophic implications of multiple registers of language in *Mudan ting*, see Lu, *Persons, Roles, and Minds*, 85.

[147] Xu Fuming lists sources for several *zidishu* based on scenes from *Mudan ting* (scenes 7, 10, 12, 20, and 35) and gives a text for "Chunxiang nao xue" in *MDTZL*, 270–78; he then gives brief segments from several *tanci* drawn from scenes 7, 8, 10, 12, 14, 23, 24, 28, 53, and 55 (pp. 278–88). *Zidishu* for "Youyuan xun meng" and "Li hun" are included in *Zidishu xuan*, comp. Zhongguo quyi gongzuozhe xiehui Liaoning fenhui (N.p., 1979), 216–27. For these two narrative genres performed to musical accompaniment, see entries in *The Indiana Companion*, 747–49, 844–46. References to *Mudan ting* in regional opera, most of recent date, are scarce and published texts even scarcer. Professor Kate Stevens has called my attention to a Cantonese opera published in Ye Shaode, ed., *Tang Disheng xiqu xinshang* (Hong Kong: Xianggang zhoukan chubanshe, 1986), 118–218. A Hua opera (*Huaju*), *Fengliu meng* was adapted from *Mudan ting*, but I have been unable to locate the text of it in the source mentioned in Zhao Junjie, "You shi yiqu *Fengliu meng*—guanyu *Mudan ting* ji qi Huaju gaibian," *Dangdai xiju*, no. 4 (July 1994): 9–12. Other references to (presumably unpublished) operas are Feng Yuzheng, "*Mudan ting Huanhun ji* daoyan zaji," *Juying yuebao*, no. 2 (February 1988): 9; see also Yue Meiti (*Nüxiaosheng*, 100) for regional

operas she consulted when undertaking a new adaptation of the "whole" play for the Shanghai Kun Opera Troupe in 1982.

Notes to Chapter Six

[1] A notice on the internet ("The Interrupted Dream: Re-Awakening Chinese Classical Drama") announced a performance-demonstration by Hua Wenyi of scene 10 from *Mudan ting* and a "conversation" moderated by Sellars. The free event was held at Berkeley in April of 1997. In this chapter I use *Peony Pavilion*, consistent with the translation in stagebills, for this production.

[2] For this information I am indebted to Susan Pertel Jain, translator for this production and a specialist in Sichuan opera. Much of it circulated by email when problems with the Lincoln Center production *Peony Pavilion* were first reported. Sellars tells me that he first saw *Mudan ting* when he wandered into a theater in Shanghai in 1982. What he likely saw was a new production by the Shanghai Kun Opera Troupe that starred Hua Wenyi and Yue Meiti.

[3] "It [*Mudan ting*] is written during the Ming dynasty, but looks forward to Tiananmen Square. . . . The Chinese piece I'm doing in London offers a vivid political image of a younger generation pursuing a dream." From an interview by Michael Billington, "East Side Story," *Guardian* (London), September 8, 1998. Sellars described Liu Mengmei to cast members as "someone who makes things happen in his own time," a "survivor" who is "trying to endure and get through the winter." Symbolically linked to the apricot tree in Liniang's garden, he is "total summer . . . huge, ripe, full of sap, fruit ready to fall, . . . [whose] juice runs down your [Liniang's] face."

[4] A performance by Liang Guyin, *huadan* specialist and star of the Shanghai troupe, suggested to Sellars the dark side of Liniang's character—an example of how crossing over to perform a character in another role category (*fanchuan*) can lead to fresh interpretations.

[5] The exceptions are scene 53 ("Interrogation Under the Rod"), in which Liu Mengmei is strung up and beaten in Du Bao's court, and scene 55 ("Reunion at Court"). Tang's comical depiction of drunk and lecherous Jurchens in some late scenes offended Manchu sensibilities, and those scenes were cut, even from editions of the whole play published for reading enjoyment.

[6] For this production, see chapter 7.

[7] Ye Tang's musically notated edition of 1791, discussed in chapter 4.

[8] So described by Mark Swed, a music critic, in his enthusiastic review of the Vienna premiere, "Traditions Converge in 'Peony Pavilion,'" *Los Angeles Times*, May 15, 1998, sec. F.

[9] Numbers in parentheses refer to the scene number in Tang's text. "Opera" refers to Western-style opera, sung in English. The script incorporated only portions of each scene. This was true especially for Part One, for which only the "Wandering in the Garden" portion of scene 10 was preserved intact; otherwise only small portions of the other scenes were used. In Part Two, segments taken from each scene were longer.

[10] I discuss containment of Tang's robust humor in Qing dynasty performance scripts in chapters 4 and 5.

[11] Takayo Fischer's kvetching portrayal of Madam Du supplied some light moments but did not survive the eleventh-hour cuts to Part One.

[12] Paul Taylor, "A long meditation about love: Double Take," *Independent* (London), September 12, 1998. Mark Pappenheim also felt that *Peony Pavilion* is Sellars's least political work to date, but made an observation that Sellars often makes: "But what, ironically, could be more 'political', in anyone's book, than this coming together of Mme Hua and Tan Dun, two generations of Chinese artists—the one establishment, the other anti-establishment—who simply would never have met each other on Chinese soil?" See "Helping to Mend Broken China," The Monday Review, *Independent* (London), September 7, 1998. Miryam Sas discusses how Sellars's work has responded to the ideologies of globalization and mass media in "Le palimpseste des cultures, la transparence des souvenirs: l'Asie du Japon à Java," in *Peter Sellars*, ed. Frédéric Maurin (Paris: CNRS Éditions / Les Voies de la création théâtricale, forthcoming). I thank Professor Sas for sharing with me an English draft of her article.

[13] Richard Trousdell, "Peter Sellars Rehearses *Figaro*," *The Drama Review* 35, no. 1 (1991): 71.

[14] Sellars could not find a suitable *xiaosheng* actor to partner Hua Wenyi and stressed movement and mime in her performances opposite Jason Ma and Michael Schumacher. He has said that his interpretation is intensely movement-based and Tim Pfaff, a Bay Area critic, agreed: "*Peony Pavilion* is a miracle of movement, . . . which speaks in many tongues, none more eloquent than another, all mesmerizing in synch." "His finest flower," *Bay Area Reporter*, March 11, 1999, 35. For Sellars's comment, see Janice Berman, "Exploring Far-Out Places and Far-Off Times," Arts and Leisure, *New York Times*, February 21, 1999, p. 1. Marcia J. Citron discusses movement in Sellars's earlier work in *Opera on Screen* (New Haven: Yale University Press, 2000), 237–43.

[15] Citron finds dualisms of many kinds in Sellars's staging of three Mozart operas. See her chapter on him in *Opera on Screen*, especially 213–19.

[16] For Part One, Tan retained the traditional *Kunqu* melodies but rescored them to feature the *pipa* performer Min Xiao-fen in a small ensemble. Portions of his score, performed by Ying Huang and members of the original ensemble, have been issued by Sony on a CD titled "Bitter Love: A Song Cycle (derived from the opera *Peony Pavilion*)."

[17] From a conversation between Tan and Sellars that was printed in the stagebill for the Berkeley performances. Subsequent citations of Tan's views are from this conversation.

[18] At the symposium in Berkeley, Steve Osgood, Sellars's conductor, discussed how Tan's score left gaps in which his musicians could improvise. Recurring melodic motifs were "Spring," "Floating," "Watered," "Moistening," "Blowing."

[19] Nancy Allen Lundy, who alternated with Ying Huang in performances in London, Rome, and Paris, told me that range rather than pitch made the greatest demand on her voice.

[20] For the characteristics of Kun opera music, see Liu, "Aesthetic Principles and Ornamental Style in Chinese Classical Opera." At the "Critics Circle" panel in Berkeley, Lindy Li

Mark, a scholar and performer of Kun opera, commented that Tan's music displays some basic features of its musical style.

[21] After Vienna she told me that at times she was at a loss how to perform to Tan's music ("What does it have to do with *Mudan ting*?"). But by London, she had begun on her own (in Sellars's words) to "get up and start acting."

[22] "If you go backwards, you feel things more avant garde and much deeper. . . . That is why I said, look at Monteverdi or [K]un opera, and how avant garde that is."

[23] "There are basic qualities of spirit in common among all kinds of music; it doesn't matter if you are from east or west, north or south." Tan feels that art music in the last century has had too much personality (too particular a geographic and cultural point of view).

[24] For similar views of Chen Shi-Zheng, Tan's compatriot and friend, see chapter 7.

[25] An assembly of clear perspex panels replaced the table, and Hua performed the movements both frontally and with her back to the audience. For performances of *Shanpo yang* in the *Kunqu* style, see chapter 4.

[26] Swed, "Traditions Converge in 'Peony Pavilion.'"

[27] Nick Kimberley, "A long meditation about love: Double Take," *Independent* (London), September 12, 1998.

[28] Richard Trousdell finds that "[Sellars's] eclectic style is built on an interplay of independent ideas, each holding its own on equal terms without being fused or transformed." "Peter Sellars Rehearses *Figaro*," 75. Miryam Sas feels that Sellars retains differences while making connections between disparate elements, through operations she compares to bricolage; see "Le palimpseste des cultures." I feel Sellars responds to his collaborators. Part One respected the particularities of Hua Wenyi's artistry; Part Two, more eclectic, complemented Tan's vision.

[29] *MDT*, 14.289; *PP*, 68.

[30] The more technical sense of dialogic used earlier is from Mikhail Bakhtin's discussion of the European novel, which finds that hitherto exclusive genres and languages coexist and "talk" to one another in a new linguistic environment. See "Discourse in the Novel," in *The Dialogic Imagination: Four Essays by M. M. Bakhtin*, ed. Michael Holquist (Austin: University of Texas Press, 1990).

[31] The young Hangzhou concubine Feng Xiaoqing is the best-known example; Ko's book contains an illustration that depicts her reading *Mudan ting* by her lamp, from a play about her first published in 1627, *Teachers of the Inner Chambers: Women and Culture in Seventeenth Century China* (Stanford: Stanford University Press, 1994), 94.

[32] "[R]eading was also an inventive act in the fundamental sense of the word. Women who read created not only their self images but also a multiplicity of meanings with which to construct their world as they pleased," in *Teachers of the Inner Chambers*, 69. *Mudan ting*'s reception among women is the subject of Jingmei Chen, "The Dream World of Love-Sick Maidens: A Study of Womens' Responses to *Peony Pavilion*" (Ph.D. diss., University of California at Los Angeles, 1996). Articles by Ellen Widmer and Judith Zeitlin listed in

the bibliography discuss the cult of female readers of *Mudan ting* and male anxieties aroused by that cult.

[33] Monitors in assorted sizes numbered three for each panel and two for the platform; other monitors framed the stage. I counted twenty-six in Vienna, twenty in London.

[34] For the portrait in Tang's play, see chapter 3. Only Lauren Tom's video snapshot was taken, except in the underworld scene at the beginning of Part Two, when all three Liniangs appeared onscreen in negative. Joel de la Fuente's image also sometimes appeared.

[35] See the comment of Francie Lin in "A Symposium on *Peony Pavilion*," ed. Wendy Lesser, *The Threepenny Review* 78 (summer 1999), 34.

[36] Trousdell, "Peter Sellars Rehearses *Figaro*," 83. At rehearsals in Berkeley, Lindy Mark told Sellars that she was having trouble taking in all that was happening on the stage. While she was looking at one thing, she was aware of other things going on in her peripheral field of vision. Sellars told her that he does this deliberately, "so that you have to talk to more than one person to put together what is happening." Nonetheless, after watching the rest of the rehearsal from the balcony he moved things closer together on the stage. Sas discusses this deliberate strategy of overload in "Le palimpseste des cultures."

[37] Fiona Maddox, "Chants would be a fine thing," *Observer Review* (London), September 13, 1998; Taylor, "Double Take."

[38] As noted in chapter 3.

[39] Wu Hung, *The Double Screen: Medium and Representation in Chinese Painting* (Chicago: The University of Chicago Press, 1996), 235–36. Sellars's other "bible" was Bickford, *Ink Plum*.

[40] Judith Zeitlin, in a talk at the Berkeley symposium, found that the video portrait enhanced Liniang's self-reflexivity but sacrificed somatic properties of scroll portraits that Tang likely exploited. On "Video Culture" and "Screen Dreams" in this production, see Sas, "Le palimpseste des cultures."

[41] For London, glass globes containing butterflies, branches, and other garden flora had been inserted between the panels of the screens. Warm activities, such as Liniang recalling lovemaking in "Pursuing the Dream," took place in the vicinity of screens with yellow or orange globes; cool activities, such as nocturnal visits by Liniang's ghost, were often situated in the vicinity of the green or blue ones.

[42] This portion of the aria can be found in chapter 3.

[43] This description is Jenny Gilbert's in "For Confucian, read confusion," The Independent on Sunday Culture, *Independent* (London), September 13, 1998, p. 6. At the Berkeley symposium, Gu Yi'an of the Shanghai Theatre Academy wondered why Tan used a worksong (*laodong haozi*), the most "*su*" of forms, to express the most sublime of things. Liao Ben, deputy secretary-general of the Chinese Dramatists Association, also saw the Berkeley performances and was struck by the emphasis in them on sexual thirst and fulfillment, and the use of naturalistic techniques to express Du Liniang's powerful experience of sexuality. In a critique submitted to *Wenyi bao*, he wrote that Tan Dun's use of the rhythms of a work song to express the moans and pleasures of orgasm made him feel a "naked sexual stimulus" (*chiluoluo de xing ciji*). Neither man felt that such techniques could be used in

China—for Kun opera at least. However, Gu was more amused by them than Liao was (or Hua Wenyi for that matter).

[44] *MDT*, 30.369; *PP*, 172.

[45] In Vienna, the exterior shot was not used, and it seems likely that it was later added to help make the desired association. Hua Wenyi was mystified by some of Sellars's visual imagery and asked me about it when I saw her in Los Angeles in August, after the Vienna premiere.

[46] *MDT*, 30.369; *PP*, 172–73.

[47] Objects onscreen often were submerged in or floating on water, and trickling was heard as Hua Wenyi trailed a hand in water that had been piped inside the perspex tomb for Part Two. Water is a feminine (*yin*) element in Chinese cosmology, correlated with earth, cold, tombs, and ghosts. Hand play between Michael Schumacher and Hua Wenyi at tombside accompanied Ying Huang and Lin Qiang Xu's energetic vocalizing. "High erotic" was Hua Wenyi's characterization of this sequence as Tang has written it; respecting the constraints of Kun opera conventions, Sellars never asked Hua to perform such sequences in an explicit manner.

[48] Citron, *Opera on Screen*, 216, 213–19. For Sellars's highly imagistic theater, see Trousdell, "Peter Sellars Rehearses *Figaro*," 72.

[49] For soap operas as one model for operas by Mozart that Sellars filmed for television, see *Opera on Screen*, 224. I find Citron's analysis of these productions relevant to his live staging of *Peony Pavilion*; she also suggests that this kind of digital aesthetic empowers viewers to create their own visual collage. For other techniques Sellars has used both to alienate and involve his viewer, see 213–19. Trousdell suggests that opera attracts Sellars because it offers a double perspective: "strong, immediate emotion and the distancing power of structured thought." See "Peter Sellars Rehearses *Figaro*," 67.

[50] Andrew Clements, "Sellars' market," Art News, *Guardian* (London), September 12, 1998, p. 11.

[51] Maddox, "Chants would be a fine thing."

[52] Taylor, "Double Take."

[53] Costumes were also color-coded: buttercup yellow for the dream scenes, gray for the death scene, purple for the scenes of ghostly lovemaking.

[54] An example, perhaps, of how Sellars creates gaps that the viewer must fill, so that a "secret world" unfolds for the viewer onstage. See Trousdell, "Peter Sellars Rehearses *Figaro*," 67, and Citron, *Opera on Screen*, 222.

[55] For an example, see my discussion in chapter 5 of how the fan is used in "The Interrupted Dream" (e.g., "Wandering in the Garden").

[56] "With video monitors on stage, when they turn yellow, green, or red, you feel the color energy of living beings: that green you feel in the woods which is full of life enters the theater. Normally in the theater what you can never do is a nature scene." This comment from Sellars is cited in Sas, "Le palimpseste des cultures."

[57] For the association of plum (apricot) with Liu Mengmei, see chapter 3.

[58] Sellars explained to his actors that a peony branch will take root if planted in the ground; for Chinese, the peony symbolizes female sexuality.

[59] In London Sellars described Liu as "this Jack Kerouac type, hitch-hiking around China and camping out at [Liniang's] shrine" (Billington, "East Side Story"). For these performances Joel de la Fuente sported a bandana and carried a knapsack and sleeping bag on his travels—details still in place at Berkeley.

[60] *MDT*, 12.280–81; *PP*, 60. I discuss this aria in chapter 3.

[61] Hua Wenyi's performance of this moment was conceived along similar lines. Initially, Jason Ma as tree was sandwiched between two large panels at stage rear, but in London Sellars had him and Joel stand behind the mirror assembly at the front of the stage. This enabled Hua, like Lauren, to nestle up to Jason as she recalls her dream ("So like to life was this young scholar / who took my life into his arms"). Sellars pronounced her performance, as amended, "much sexier." However, at Berkeley the staging had changed again.

[62] *Yijiangfeng* and *Jin luosuo*, from scene 18 ("The Invalid"). After Vienna Sellars abandoned a good deal of this staging.

[63] *MDT*, 14.289; *PP*, 68–69, quoted in chapter 3, pp. 86–87.

[64] Schumaker's movements (Fig. 6.11) called to mind Chinese ink paintings that depict the *mei* tree with twisted and gnarled limbs.

[65] "While I was obsessed with the Shakespearean connections, Tan Dun said: 'No, it's Monteverdi,' which of course was the moment opera was being invented in the West. So he's composed the next Monteverdi opera, treating the *pipa*, the Chinese lute, as Monteverdi's *chittarone*—there are these long melismatic vocal lines, open ariosos with giant melodies sweeping through with *chittarone* underneath." Rodney Milnes, "East meets West in song," *Times* (London), September 9, 1998. For simultaneity in Sellars's productions of Western opera, see Citron, *Opera on Screen*, 208 and 213.

[66] "Du Liniang meets Liu Mengmei first in her dream, then as a ghost and again as a mortal girl after being reborn by *Peony Pavilion*, on the Road of Three Lifetimes."

[67] Thus redeployed, the panels delimited Liniang's second breaking out, the first having occurred when she goes out from her rooms into the garden in Part One.

[68] In the conversation printed in the stagebill, Tan identified one melodic line of his music as "the haunting sound of Tibetan monks"; "dharma wheel" was Sellars's name for the choral segments.

[69] Sellars devised this ending on the day the show had its world premiere in Vienna. It seems to have been the genesis of the dharma wheel.

[70] The exit verse for scene 36 ("Elopement"); *MDT*, 36.399; *PP*, 214.

[71] "As far as I know, it's the longest female role in dramatic literature. It also inspired the first critical writing by Chinese women. They read the play, wrote in the margins, eventually began publishing commentaries and talking about the status of women in China." See Billington, "East Side Story." As Tang conceives her, Liniang is quite alone until Liu revives and marries her, isolated even from mother and maid.

[72] "Like Meyerhold, Sellars establishes significant gestures that capture the moral center of an action, and then he scores these gestures throughout the production, like themes." See Trousdell, "Peter Sellars Rehearses *Figaro*," 78.

[73] These remarks at a rehearsal in Vienna express Sellars's idea that "[opera's] form gives you permission to do what is not allowed in theater, which is explore a secret world." See also n. 54.

[74] In "Double Take" Paul Taylor complained of "a dreaded lack of spontaneity," but also found that "despite all the gadgetry, the production offers a beautifully limpid vision of the sensuality and romantic lyricism of this myth."

[75] I discuss the impact of the role system for Kun opera on the depiction of Du Liniang in chapter 5.

[76] Swed, "Traditions Converge."

[77] Sellars cut Part One to one and a quarter hours, the better to accommodate Part Two. Its plot was malnourished as a result.

[78] Liao Ben, "Meiguo Sai shi *Mudan ting*: Guannian nuoyi yu wenhua chanshi cuowei" (American [Peter] Sellars's 'Peony pavilion': Misappropriation of ideas and misplacement of cultural critique), *Wenyi bao*, April 8, 1999, p. 3.

[79] Sellars attributes this idealism to Tan Dun's music, and urged his actors to "create qualities of an ideal love" in unselfish performances, so that "one feeling runs through all, even when you are not the center of attention." In my conclusion I suggest, to the contrary, that Tang Xianzu's individuation of Du Liniang is without precedent in *chuanqi* drama.

[80] Hua's remark became clearer to me after Gu Yi'an pointed out Tan's highly unusual appropriation of a worker's song (see n. 43).

[81] Just before she reveals that she is a ghost in scene 4 of Part Two, Lauren ran from Joel and struggled to free herself from his embraces. Just after she did so, he wrestled her, screaming and struggling, into her water-filled tomb, as Tan Dun's music reached a crashing, dissonant crescendo. For Liniang's ghost as a "sensual attraction of the moment" in Tang Xianzu's play, see chapter 3.

[82] Hsia, "Plays of T'ang Hsien-tsu," 275.

[83] Billington, "East Side Story."

[84] Billington, "East Side Story."

Notes to Chapter Seven

[1] For the first comment of Chen's, see Tang Sifu and Ze Ping, "Yan 'chuanqi,' zai chuangzao yige chuanqi," *Henan xiju*, no. 5 (1998): 9; for the second, see Cai Ying, "Lianyan santian sanye fang neng yanwan quanben *Mudan ting* banshang wutai" (Only after three days and three nights can a complete 'Peony pavilion' be performed onstage), *Yangzi wanbao*, April 2, 1998. My thanks to Sheila Melvin, a freelance journalist based in Shanghai who covered rehearsals in Shanghai for the *New York Times* and *Wall Street Journal*, for making available some of the Shanghai press coverage referred to in these notes. Other friends in Shanghai also shared with me media coverage they had gathered as

well as opinions about the production.

[2] *Pingtan* ("narrate and pluck") refers to a form of storytelling popular in a region centered on Suzhou since late Ming times, especially with women. The number of performers can vary from one to two to several. Verbalization is elaborate, ranging from formal exchanges in standard Mandarin to comic passages in dialect. The lead performer plays musical accompaniment on the *sanxian* (three-stringed lute), and the supporting performer plays the *pipa*.

[3] The play was performed in six three-hour episodes: "Jingmeng" ("The Interrupted Dream," scenes 1–10); "Xunmeng" ("Pursuing the Dream," 11–20); "Yougou" ("Making Love with a Ghost," 21–28); "Hui sheng" ("Resurrection," 24–39); "Zhe kou" ("War Against the Bandits," 40–48); "Yuan jia" ("Reunion," 49–55).

[4] Qian Yi as Du Liniang, and Zhou Ming, who accompanied her on the horizontal flute and conducted the musical ensemble. Chen Shi-Zheng, who gave me two hours of his time in New York, told me that with these two members of the original cast he felt he could successfully revive the show. This production originally had four co-sponsors (The Lincoln Center Festival, The Festival d'Automne in Paris, The Sydney Festival, and The Hong Kong Arts Festival); once resurrected, its co-sponsors were The Lincoln Center Festival (with substantial help from Bloomberg News) and The Festival d'Automne.

[5] Chen Yunfa, "Jingdian fan pu de kegui changshi" (A valuable attempt to return a classic to simplicity), *Xinwen bao*, June 12, 1998. This is the only positive published response to the dress rehearsal that I have read in the Shanghai press, although another positive review, by Lou Jing, appeared in *Renmin ribao* on June 11. A harsh critique by Cheng Ji, published on June 20 in *Wenhui bao*, attacked both the show and the director and established the line that was followed in most of the subsequent Shanghai press coverage. Cheng's critique subsequently led off a ten-page section devoted to the production in *Henan xiju*, no 5 (1998): 4–13.

[6] Cheng Ji, "*Mudan ting* yiqu jing tianxia?" (Did 'The peony pavilion' amaze the world?), *Henan xiju*, no. 5 (1998): 4. Cheng's title makes sarcastic reference to the title of an article by Mo Tao ('The peony pavilion' will amaze the world) that enthusiastically previewed the dress rehearsals in Shanghai, which were held from June 2–7 and again from June 9–11. Mo's preview appeared in *Wenxue bao*, no 60 (no date indicated).

[7] "*Mudan ting* paiyan gousi" (Staging concept for 'The peony pavilion' [main points]). My thanks to Rachel Cooper of Asia Society in New York for making a copy of this statement available to me.

[8] Tang Sifu, "Yan 'chuanqi,'" 9.

[9] I discuss both historical developments in chapter 4.

[10] So does John Rockwell, the former director of the Lincoln Center Festival who appointed Chen as director. He was reported to say that an art form in decline, as Kun opera is, often becomes submerged in tradition and fiercely resistant to change. See Lin Qianxiu, "*Mudan ting* juran yaozhe; 'cuishengren' anran shenshang" ('The peony pavilion' dies premature; "expectant father" depressed), *Shijie ribao*, June 25, 1998.

[11] Zhai Qing, "Quanben *Mudan ting* qiyue zai Mei shangyan" (A complete 'Peony pavil-

ion' to go to America in July), *Zhongguo wenhua bao*, February 6, 1998; also an unsigned article, "Meiguo jiang xian *Mudanting* re" (America will enthuse over 'The peony pavilion'), in *Wenyi bao*, February 19, 1998.

[12] The enumeration of social groups was repeated in several press notices that appeared in April. Lou Jing mentioned the scroll in a review of the first of two dress rehearsals, "Hao yifu *Qingming shanghe tu*" (A handsome 'Qingming festival on the river'), *Renmin ribao*, June 11, 1998; an article in the April 1 edition of *Qingnian bao* also mentioned the scroll.

[13] Tang Sifu, "Yan 'chuanqi,'" 9.

[14] A *piaoyou* who attended the dress rehearsals in Shanghai told me that she felt that the tutor was too clownish.

[15] For Yue Meiti's comment, see Cai Ying, "Lianyan santian," for Zhang Jun's remark about the Liu Mengmei he discovered after reading the complete play, see chapter 1, n. 46. In his statement Chen Shi-Zheng writes that Liu's attitude towards love is rooted in his pursuit of fame and profit; to bring this side of him out it is necessary to resort to nontraditional staging methods.

[16] For Sister Stone's lovely side, see discussion of scene 48 ("Mother and Daughter Reunited") in chapter 2. Here, too, a Shanghai friend's response exemplifies the *piaoyou*'s reaction to some of Chen Shi-Zheng's innovations. She objected to the decision to perform Stone's solo scene in dialect, since the crudeness of the character was no longer covered by elegant language. According to Sheila Melvin, this decision became a practical necessity when Liu Yilong, who created the character for this production, found it impossible to memorize Tang's elaborate parody of the *Qianziwen* (Thousand-character text) in standard Mandarin.

[17] For this claim, see Liu Minjun, "Quanben Kunqu *Mudan ting* jiang liangxiang guoji wutai" (A complete Kun opera 'Peony pavilion' will make its entrance on the world stage), *Renmin ribao*, April 9, 1998.

[18] One account had it that "the reporters saw that all kinds of elements were intermingled in the performances onstage: disco and break dancing [*piliwu*] appeared from time to time; even *pingtan* will have a major presence." See Jian Hua, "Lü Mei daoyan duanshang 'dazahui'" (American-based director serves up a "big hodgepodge"), *Laodong bao*, April 1, 1998. None of the coverage names the scenes the press saw.

[19] See Cai Ying, "Shijimo de langman juechang" (An outstanding romance at the end of an era), *Qingnian bao*, April 1, 1998.

[20] Cai Zhengren, head of the Shanghai troupe, worked closely with Chen on the production and told reporters that Qian Yi and Zhang Jun had to do something that neither he, nor his teacher, nor his teacher's teacher had ever done. See Liu Minjun, "Quanben Kunqu *Mudan ting*." Qian Yi elaborated: "The director's concept is completely new. In a fifty-five scene play, one cannot [perform] each word and each beat, each stop and each pause, each glance of the eye and angle of the body, polishing and carving finely, not to mention the fact that there is no guide, no one who knows how to do it. For this reason, the opening for my creative method is the molding of character. Of course, I still use the formalized *xiqu* movements as the foundation because in many cases they are beautiful, but more than before I focus on the evolution of the character's inner feelings [*renwu neixin licheng de zhuanbian*]." This method of realizing her character came easily, Qian Yi added,

and was especially precious for that reason. See Liu Hua, "Qian Yi tan yici gudian aiqing gei ni kan," *Shanghai xiju*, no. 6 (1998): 26.

[21] Huang Haiwei's design combined both kinds of setting into one. David Rolston found this combination of private troupe traditions and commercial marketplace theater settings improbable and ahistorical. See his "Tradition and Innovation," 138. Sheila Melvin described the set design and rationale for it in "The Long March: Chinese Opera Nears New York," *Wall Street Journal*, February 12, 1998.

[22] Chen told me that paper troupes are used in funerals in the north of China. A peasant artist from Shandong made the ones for this production.

[23] See the long interview recorded in Tang Sifu, "Yan 'chuanqi.'" Items among the more than 1,000 props ranged from a large frame for stringing up prisoners to a small knife used to prepare medicine.

[24] See n. 6.

[25] The most infamous touch being the wooden chamber pots used in "The Search for the Candidate." Set in a brothel, this scene raised doubts in some quarters about the wisdom of staging *Mudan ting* complete. Chen replied to criticism of this scene by observing that it is one of several, never performed, that exemplify Tang Xianzu's humor. See Tian Dan, "*Mudan ting* banbudao Niuyue qu" ('The peony pavilion' can't go to New York), *Huanqiu shibao*, June 18, 2000. Jia Fang's piece appeared in *Jiefang ribao* under the heading "Gudian mingzhu neng zheyang gaibian banshang wutai ma" (Can a famous classic be adapted like this for the stage?). Another account of reaction to the dress rehearsals is Luo Bin, "Shi zaota mingzhu haishi zhongyu yuanzhu?" *Henan xiju*, no. 5 (1998): 5–7.

[26] Ben Wang's comment is cited in Ken Smith, "Now the Epic Tale Can Be Told," Calendar, *Los Angeles Times*, July 4, 1999. For the comment about the post-Liberation stage, see Chen Yunfa, "Kegui changshi."

[27] For example, a senior actress who consulted on the production explained to me that for audiences in Shanghai chamber pots are painful reminders of a recent past that they don't want to confront.

[28] "The director . . . had the prostitutes perform naturalistically the morning emptying of chamber pots. Facing the audience, they scrubbed out the pots, and facing it they emptied them into the pond. They even put water in them, and when [the pots were] emptied, it splashed out. Many in the audience said angrily of the coarse acting, 'This kind of performance is going too far.'" See Jia Fang, "Gudian mingzhu."

[29] Jin Tao, "Kunqu shouchuang 'waixiangxing' yanchu moshi" (Kun opera inaugurates a 'foreign model' of performance), *Wenhui bao*, March 26, 1998. Friends in Shanghai used "*chukouban*" (export edition).

[30] Yang Haipeng, "Chen Shi-Zheng qianzhe Du Liniang shang Bailaohui" (Chen Shi-Zheng takes Du Liniang to Broadway), *Shenjiang fuwu daobao*, April 1, 1998.

[31] Tang Sifu, "Yan 'chuanqi,'" 9.

[32] "Love, Death and Resurrection," 13–15.

[33] Cai Ying, "Lianyan santian." Chen's goal of recreating an "original" *Mudan ting* at times has given ground to his goal of recreating a pre-Kun opera performance style. For the

latter aim, see Zhou Yiqian, "Santian sanye zhanshi quanben *Mudan ting*" (A complete 'Peony pavilion' to unfold in three days and three nights), *Wenhui bao*, October 18, 1997.

[34] After the show was revived, Chen did not refer to any particular tradition, saying only that the production is his interpretation of Tang Xianzu's work. See James R. Oestreich, "Lincoln Center to Revive Opera Thwarted by China," *New York Times*, March 16, 1999, B3.

[35] Rolston, "Tradition and Innovation," 140. Like Rolston, I feel that Chen's interest in showcasing a variety of traditional performing arts at times dwarfed the concerns of the play that Tang Xianzu wrote. Judith Zeitlin found his reconstruction of the whole play imaginative, but also frequently "messy and unworked out," particularly when compared to Sellars's production, which she saw first. See "My Year of Peonies," *Asian Theatre Journal* 19, no. 1 (spring 2002): 128.

Notes to the Conclusion

[1] *HHJ*; 2.19.5b; reproduced in *TXZZL*, 128.

[2] For the cult of *qing* and *Mudan ting*'s importance in it, see Dorothy Ko, *Teachers of the Inner Chambers*, 68–112. I use Chunfang Fei's translation of *qingchi*, in *Chinese Theories of the Theater and Performance*, 58.

[3] In *Mudan ting*, Judge Hu, having authorized Liniang's return to the world of the living as ghost, orders his attendants to issue her a "passport for the wandering soul" (*youhun luyin*), but no mention is made of a *huisheng tie*.

[4] Zhang Jing has praised Tang's aria sequences and criticized those who have revised them character by character, line by line. See "Peitao zhi fenxi," 9.

[5] "Individualism and Humanitarianism in Late Ming Thought," in *Self and Society in Ming Thought*, 150–54. De Bary distinguishes Chinese from Western individualism, 145–50; see also Hegel, *Reading Illustrated Fiction*, 58, 160, 317. Wai-yee Li discusses "the autonomy of the dreaming, imagining or remembering self," in *Enchantment and Disenchantment*, 47–50.

[6] Feng Menglong's *sanqu*, on the other hand, are intensely personal, in a manner that I think Tang would have found too naked for any medium.

[7] Bourdieu, *The Field of Cultural Production*, 40 (for "an interest in disinterestedness" and "heretical breaks with tradition"), 101–02, 106–10 (heresy and "being different"), 63, 114 (artist as "pure" genius), 120–25 (consecration).

[8] *SWJ*, 1299 ("Da Sun Siju"). *Qu* and *ci* are used interchangeably to refer to verse written to existing melodies, in this case arias. Tang elaborated to another friend, "In writing *qu*, thought, flavor, spirit and color are the most important considerations. Whenever these four things come, the writer may hit upon pretty turns of phrase or fine passages of verbal music. How can he at the same time be worrying about modes and tones?" *SWJ*, 1337 ("Da Lü Jiangshan").

[9] *SWJ*, 1345 ("Da Ling Chucheng").

[10] Chapter 5, 199. For the amateur ideal see Joseph R. Levenson, "The Amateur Ideal in Ming and Early Ch'ing Society: Evidence from Painting," in *Confucian China and Its Modern Fate: A Trilogy* (Berkeley: The University of California Press, 1968), 15–43. For amateurization of painting and dematerializing of art, see James Cahill, *The Painter's Practice:*

How Artists Lived and Worked in Traditional China (New York: Columbia University Press, 1994), 5–11.

[11] Bourdieu, *The Field of Cultural Production,* 137 (legitimate symbolic violence), 140 (arbitrary formalism of strictly formal interpretations).

[12] A forthcoming dissertation will address these issues. It is by Andrea S. Goldman of the University of California at Berkeley, entitled "Opera Performance and Urbanite Aesthetics in Eighteenth- and Nineteenth-century Beijing."

[13] Bourdieu, *The Field of Cultural Production,* 117.

[14] Chen Shi-Zheng may have had Sellars in mind when he told an interviewer that Chinese audiences can recognize the people onstage "[w]ithout putting any modern technology or contemporary clothes on." I think he means that Chinese viewers, at least, see the resemblance between characters in the play and their contemporary counterparts without any need for modern touches. See Mary Campbell, "Smooth opera-tor," *Bangkok Post,* June 9, 1999.

[15] Mark Swed, "'Peony Pavilion's' Heroic Marathon," *Los Angeles Times,* July 20, 1999. John Rockwell had the re-creations of the Early Music Movement in mind when he decided to explore the feasibility of staging the complete play.

[16] This production had its dress rehearsal, by invitation only, in Shanghai on three successive evenings (August 21–23, 1999). Guo Xiaonan, the director, told me in May 1999 that officials in the Bureau of Culture told him to stage a production that was faithful to the original work but used some modern staging techniques. Like Chen Shi-Zheng, Guo lacks training in Kun opera; his reputation rests largely on his work in *Huaiju,* a relatively new style of regional (Subei) opera popular in Shanghai. As this book goes to press, the South China Morning Post reported on September 10, 2001, that China is drawing up a ten-year plan to save Kun opera. Cai Zhongren, head of the Shanghai Kun Opera Troupe, was cited as saying that international recognition helped highlight Kun opera as part of China's intangible cultural heritage.

[17] In Bourdieu's terms, however, both Sellars and Chen operate within a restricted subfield of modern opera, consisting of a consecrated avant-garde and an avant-garde of newcomers. But it is difficult to decide which of them occupies which niche. See *The Field of Cultural Production,* 53.

[18] Ma Bomin expressed feelings of betrayal to Isabel Wong, who interviewed her in June of 1999. She had thought that Chen was "one of us" when "he has become a foreigner." Sellars planned to recover the political dimension of Tang's play, but abandoned this plan because of time limitations.

[19] Yan Changke notes recent opinion that *Zuiyi qing* is the earliest extant collection of *zhezixi,* then pushes the popularity of this kind of performance earlier still, to the Jiajing–Longqing periods (1522–1572, hence prior to Kun opera's emergence). See "Tantan zhezixi," 243.

[20] *The Field of Cultural Production,* 140.

[21] *The Field of Cultural Production,* 52–55, 96.

[22] So, too, Zang Maoxun. Richard Schechner, in his preface to Faye Chunfang Fei's volume of translations of Chinese works on theater and performance, is struck by how the writers represented welcome theater as an important participant in and contributor to a well-ordered society, and by how much they are concerned with reception, what the spectator sees and hears. See *Chinese Theories of Theater and Performance,* ix–x.

[23] Experimentation is tolerated in spoken drama (introduced from the West) and in regional operas, which rank lower in the hierarchy of artistic forms.

[24] See Bourdieu, *The Field of Cultural Production*, 93, for such "connivance."

[25] Hegel, *Reading Illustrated Fiction*, 256–57, 272.

[26] *Reading Illustrated Fiction*, 272. Like the performance of an outstanding actor, art was "distinguished by the degree of polish with which familiar elements were executed and manipulated; the emphasis was on perfection rather than innovation." See 313.

[27] *Reading Illustrated Fiction*, 275–76. Hegel further divides the professionals into commercial artists and educated professionals, but notes that the practices of both differed from that of literati amateurs, in the subjects painted and the relative degree of conformity to convention. In landscape painting conventionalization came via professional painters who combined type-forms in familiar patterns. The type-forms, printed in manuals and albums, were widely available (p. 266).

[28] Birch finds the aria Tang wrote for the Huashen in scene 10 one of the most puzzling in the play, and as we have seen adapters and actors either cut it or else muffled it in the gauzy lyrics of "Heaped Blossoms." See *Scenes for Mandarins*, 141–42. Other examples include Tang's unusual treatment of the lovers' dreams, Sister Stone's presence at key moments of the action, and the iconoclastic staging of ritually important scenes: cacophony at the moment of death in scene 20, burlesque during the spring planting rituals in scene 8 (sources indicate that scene 8 was enjoyed "straight" when performed, whether at court or in the countryside). Generally speaking, Tang's incongruous juxtapositions of lyrically high and humorously crude moments often elicited quite radical changes by actors.

[29] This may account for the small amount of tampering with the texts of *zhezixi* preserved in late Ming and early Qing miscellanies—for example, *Zuiyi qing*, the earliest miscellany of *zhezixi* from favorite Kun operas (see n. 19).

[30] During a visit to Shanghai in May of 1999, I found that few people were willing to discuss what led to the decision to cancel the production, especially those who had been directly involved. Isabel Wong, however, has been able to interview Ma Bomin at length, and she has told me that Ma said that she became concerned about the production only in the final weeks of rehearsals, when complaints were made to her by some members of the local press and unnamed persons in the Chinese department at Fudan University. However, final authority for the decision to kill the show rested with political higher-ups (the Party Secretary [*dangwei shuji*] for Shanghai, according to Ma). This decision came after several days spent discussing reports (*qingbao*) that were circulated after the dress rehearsals were over. Kun opera "experts" were active participants in these discussions, and, I suspect, earlier as well.

[31] The most important of the *qushe* are described in *Shanghai kunju zhi* (Shanghai Kunju opera), comp. Shanghai wenhua yishu zhi bianzuan weiyuanhui (Shanghai: Xinhua shudian, 1998), 46–58. For brief biographies of "Chuan" generation actors, see 308–18, 321. Members of the Shanghai troupe perform with *piaoyou* both in China and abroad. Some *piaoyou* also make substantial donations to the troupe.

[32] Chen expressed these views to me in an interview that took place during the performances of *The Peony Pavilion* in New York. My thanks to him for giving me this opportunity at a very busy time.

[33] Performances of "Wandering in the Garden, Startled by a Dream" described in *Pinhua baojian* are erotically charged transactions between boy actors and male audience members.

[34] The description of a performance of "Chunxiang Disrupts the Lesson" from *Xiaohan xinyong*, mentioned in chapter 5, is an example. Sellars's description of Liang Guyin's portrayal of Du Liniang (see chapter 6, n. 4) is another.

[35] An article by Andrea S. Goldman discusses the dynamics of commercial theatrical culture in the Qing dynasty, using performance-based versions of "Si fan" ("Longing for the Secular Life"), a story popular both as a Kun opera and as a *zidishu*. Goldman reads "Si fan" within its performance contexts and explores the transgressive potential in its narrative of a young nun longing for mundane pleasures. She finds that over time, in the performance-based texts she has uncovered, "artful" eroticism replaces desire expressed through language. She sees this artfulness as reflecting the relationships that obtained between audience and performers in the aforementioned two genres. See "The Nun Who Wouldn't Be: Representations of Female Desire in Two Performance Genres of 'Si fan,'" *Late Imperial China* 22, no. 1 (June 2001): 71–76 and 121.

[36] Tang Baoxiang, *Yu Zhenfei zhuan*, 115. After his return Yu devoted most of his time to teaching. For "Duanqiao," see Chen Weiyu, *Kunju zhezixi chutan* (Zhengzhou: Zhongzhou guji chubanshe, 1991), 261–64.

[37] Her discussion of "Calling to the Portrait," cited in chapter 4, is one example of her style as a *xiaosheng* specialist; an analysis of Pan Bizheng (in *The jade hairpin*) is another, for which see *Nüxiaosheng*, 110–15.

[38] An account of Yu's performance of "Finding the Portrait and Calling to It" by the *dan* actor Nantiesheng hints at such provocative sensuality: "When the high point in 'Calling to the Portrait' was reached, with a precise flick of the wrist he controlled the water sleeves, soft as billowing clouds, so that they lightly brushed the Du Liniang [depicted] in the portrait, and she really seemed about to descend at his call." This description, from a reminiscence that appeared in *Wenhui bao*, April 14, 1980, is cited in Tang Baoxiang, *Yu Zhenfei zhuan*, 84. Mei Lanfang remarked that Yu's stage portrayals reflected his offstage temperament, in *Wutai shenghuo sishinian*, vol. 3, 27, also cited in *Yu Zhenfei zhuan*, 96.

[39] *Forms and Meanings*, 86. Chartier is here resisting theories that stress either popular culture's dependencies and deficiencies with respect to the dominant culture, or its complete autonomy and otherness.

[40] He cites David D. Hall's review of *High/Lowbrow* (*Reviews in American History* 18 [1990]), which faults Levine for not adequately considering tensions of class, gender, and race in antebellum America, or the impact of religion (Puritanism) and economic forces of capitalism in his analytical structure.

[41] This was the production that Sellars saw on his 1982 visit to China.

Notes to Appendix A

[1] My source for this appendix is Zeng Yongyi, "Juese gaishuo," *Shuosu wensue*, 233–95; another helpful survey of roles from Ming to Qing appears in Wang Anqi, *Mingdai chuanqi zhi juchang*, chapter 4. Zeng's analysis of roles for *chuanqi* surveys plays up to ca. 1550; for Kun opera, it covers plays written thereafter, though there is no fixed boundary. The list of role designations in this appendix is not exhaustive; if a particular role discussed by Zeng under the four major categories does not occur in any of the texts under discussion, then I do not include it. An exception is the *xiaodan* role listed under *chuanqi*. This

designation does not occur in the late Ming complete versions of the play but does appear in the Qing dynasty *zhezixi*, and I have included it as a point of reference.

[2] Characters in the late Ming complete versions have been grouped under *chuanqi* (*pace* Zeng), under the role category designated in the text. With one exception noted below, characters in the Qing *zhezixi* are grouped under Kun opera. For these I have checked only *Zhui baiqiu* (*ZBQ*) and *Shenyin jiangu lu* (*SYJGL*). I have not accounted for all minor characters (sentries, messengers, tea pickers, village elders, underworld demons), especially for the *zhezixi*.

[3] In "Reunion at Court."

[4] In "The School Hall" (Xuetang).

[5] In "The School Hall."

[6] *Zhui baiqiu* does not use the *xiaodan* that Zeng associates with Kun operas written after 1550, and so I have grouped it with the Ming versions in this case.

[7] In "Reunion at Court."

Notes to Appendix B

[1] The opening is unnumbered in *HHJ*.

[2] At first mention of a character, I give the role category assigned in *MDT*. If *HHJ* or *FLM* assigns a different category, I give it.

[3] He uses her entrance aria and dialogue from scene 9 of *MDT* for this purpose.

[4] Feng portrays Stone more negatively, as charlatan and practitioner of heterodox arts. Her visit to Liniang in scene 18 of *MDT* undercuts Du Bao's "rectitude" (*zhengqi*). He cuts her from that scene, and like Zang omits Tang's parody of the *Qianziwen*.

[5] Feng finds Liu's neglect of the portrait in scene 30 of *MDT* callous.

[6] Wearing the *mo*, the *dan* emerges from under the table. Liu assists her and removes the headcloth. In *MDT* the resurrection is offstage.

[7] Feng, who also moves the resurrection onstage, explains in a marginal note that the *dan* emerges from beneath a table "dressed for burial in flowered skirt and embroidered jacket."

[8] Scabby asks for the mercury Liniang has vomited and her grave clothes "for the Missus." His request for Liniang's skirt and jacket are Feng's touch.

[9] Feng chastises vulgar actors who omit this scene and compares it to the reunion between husband and wife in scene 36 of *Pipa ji*.

[10] Tang assigns the privy councilor to the *wai* actor; Feng follows Zang.

[11] Feng explicitly links corruption of the recruitment system in the Song dynasty to the problem of barbarian incursions. These are pet themes of his.

[12] "One need only mention that [Du Bao's] family members have been sent back to Hangzhou. The original text devotes a scene to it, which I have cut."

[13] Zang criticizes Tang's tendency to write several scenes in succession that feature singing by the *sheng* or the *dan*.

[14] E.g., not-so-subtle attempts to get a reward for bringing news. But Feng notes in the margin that Tang's portrayal of Chen's pedantry is very funny.

[15] Dialogue denouncing Li Quan becomes song combined with dialogue.

[16] In a note, Zang explains that he has rewritten Chen's aria to reflect less fear: he has letters from Du Bao and knows that warring parties don't kill envoys.

[17] Tang gives Li Quan and Yang Po a swan song after Chen has left the stage.

[18] In *MDT* they arrive like beggars, having journeyed by land on foot.

[19] I discuss this scene and these sequences in chapter 2.

[20] One of several instances where Feng uses details from *HHJ*.

[21] Zang usually favors more stage directions, not fewer. Here he may have found such staging of corporal punishment too demeaning for one of Liu's status.

[22] Zang cites prosodic reasons; saving Du Bao's face may be another factor.

[23] Family negotiations should not take place beyond the Wumen (Meridian Gate), as in *MDT*.

Notes to Appendix C

[1] For a chart that represents much of the following information, see Negeyama Tōru, "*Kankon ki* no enpen," 176 n.

[2] Negeyama Tōru, "*Kankon ki* no enpen," 179 n.

[3] Per Zhou Miaozhong, "Jiangnan fanqu luyao," 245–46.

[4] Zhao Jingshen, *Ming Qing qutan*, 149–53. See also Yang Zhenliang, *Mudan ting yanjiu*, 197–99; Zheng Zhenduo, "Zhongguo xiqu de xuanben," 2.

[5] Negeyama Tōru, "*Kankon ki* no enpen," 176–77 n; a list of contents, including plays represented (fifty-one) and extracts selected (seventy-six) is in Aoki Masaru, *Zhongguo jinshi xiqu shi*, 745.

[6] Fu Yunzi, *Baichuan ji*, 97–100.

[7] Hu Shi, "*Zhui bai* xu " (Preface to 'A patched cloak of white fur'), in *Hu Shi gudian wenxue yanjiu lunji* (Shanghai: Shanghai guji chubanshe, 1988), 654; see also Negeyama Tōru, "*Kankon ki* no enpen," 177 n, 179 n; *MDTZL*, 169.

[8] For a chart that compares the contents of this miscellany with those of various editions of *Zhui baiqiu*, see Lin Fengxiong, "*Zhui baiqiu quanji* shiyi," 3–11; for use of Wu dialect, see Iwaki Hideo, "Gogo no kinō," 628–30.

[9] For list of contents, see Wu Xinlei, "*Zhui baiqiu* de lailong qumo," 36–37; described in Zhou Miaozhong, *Qingdai xiqu shi*, 384–85.

[10] See Zhou Miaozhong, *Qingdai xiqu shi*, 384–85.

[11] See Wu Xinlei, "*Zhui baiqiu* de lailong qumo," 37, where this edition is dated as Qianlong 3 (1740), based on its preface. For the earlier date, see Lin Heyi, "Ye tan *Zhui baiqiu*," 247.

[12] For a list of contents, see Du Yingtao, "Tan *Zhui baiqiu*," 3–7, and Wu Xinlei, "*Zhui baiqiu* de lailong qumo," 40–42 (1764–1767 collections). *SBXQCK*, vol. 72 gives a facsimile of a reprint of the first collection of 1764 that may reflect original contents.

[13] For a list of contents, see Du Yingtao, "Tan *Zhui baiqiu*," 7–11; for discussion of clapper operas, Lin Heyi, "Ye tan *Zhui baiqiu*." Titles agree closely, but not exactly, with those for the first six collections of the next edition listed in this appendix. Du Yingtao regards the contents of this edition as distinct from all previous editions of *Zhui baiqiu*, including the Baorentang edition of 1764–1767. In his "*Zhui baiqiu* de lailong qumo," however, Wu Xinlei treats it as a continuation of that edition (pp. 39–40).

[14] See Wu Xinlei, "*Zhui baiqiu* de lailong qumo," 39–40.

[15] Negeyama Tōru, "*Kankon ki* no enpen," 177 n; "*Kankon ki* no hampon," 160, 164 n; also Ye Changhai, *Zhongguo xijuxue shigao*, 417–24 and Li Huimian, "*Shenyin jiangu lu* de biaoyan meixue," 671–77.

[16] This list does not include two earlier collections that provide *gongche* notation for the entire play: *Yinxiangtang qupu* (Fragrance-humming Hall's drama manual, 1789) and *Nashuying qupu* (A collection of arias for the bookshelf, 1791). For *Nashuying qupu*, see Wong, "Printed Collections," 108–11.

[17] See Negeyama Tōru, "*Kankon ki* no enpen," 179 n; see also Wong, "Printed Collections," 110.

[18] The Suzhou singing societies were the Purification Society (Xiji) and the Harmony Society (Xieji). For this and *Chunxuege qupu sanji*, the official score of another Suzhou singing society, Purple Cloud (Ziyun), see Wong, "Printed Collections," 111 and 126 n.

[19] See Wong, "Printed Collections," 111.

[20] See Wong, "Printed Collections," 111.

[21] For this collection, see *MDTZL*, 169–70.

[22] For this collection and its compiler, see Wong, "Printed Collections," 112–13.

[23] Reference supplied by David Rolston.

[24] For this collection, see Andrea Goldman, "The Nun Who Wouldn't Be," 76–80. Because I came to this collection as this book was going to press, I have given brief comments for each extract from *Mudan ting*.

[25] Original scene numbers are given in parentheses. Gu Duhuang, *Kunju shi bulun*, 176–77. Six of these are mentioned in Wang Zhizhang, *Qing Shengpingshu zhilüe*, and Zhou Mingtai, *Qing Shengpingshu cundang shili manchao*: "Quan nong," "Su yuan," "You yuan," "Youyuan jingmeng," "Ming pan," "Yuan jia."

[26] See *Zhongguo yinyue shupuzhi*, item 581 (p. 19), item 972 (p. 27), items 996–1003 (p. 28). All are Qing manuscripts, but few precise dates are given. This list does not include extracts from *Mudan ting* that are part of manuscript collections listed in this catalogue. The scene number from *Mudan ting* is given in parentheses after each item.

[27] See *Zhongguo yinyue shupuzhi*, item 454 (p. 17), items 494–498 (p. 18) and items 581 and 586 (p. 19).

[28] Full title: "Jinpen lao yue, Shihua Jiaohua, Yuqiao deng qupu." Late Qing manuscript compiled by Sizhitang. See *Zhongguo yinyue shupuzhi*, item 586 (p. 19).

[29] Designated as for "Liu Mengmei only." The copyist is Zhang Yaoxian. See *Zhongguo yinyue shupuzhi*, item 498 (p. 18).

[30] See *Zhongguo yinyue shupuzhi*, items 769–773 (p. 23).

[31] Copyist "Dechun." Manuscript dated 1881.

[32] Full title: "Shangxin leshi qupu 'Youyuan Jingmeng.'" In the collection of the Chinese Academy of Music (Zhongguo yinyue yanjiusuo). See *Zhongguo yinyue shupuzhi*, item 588 (p. 19).

Glossary

This glossary is arranged alphabetically by letter-order, syllable by Chinese syllable. Thus all words romanized as "chen" precede those romanized as "cheng," and "banyanjia" comes before "Bangxia," even though the latter would precede the former if alphabetized in strict letter-order sequence.

ai hao 愛好
ai mei 愛美
aiyuan 哀怨
antouju 案頭劇
ba 把
baguwen 八股文
bai 白
baijiacai huijiu 百家綵灰酒
baijing 白淨
Bailian xu 白練序
Baiyue ting 拜月亭
ban'er 伴兒
banlü'er 伴侶兒
banshi 板式
banyanjia 搬演家
"Bangxia" 榜下
bangzi qiang 梆子腔
Bao lao cui 鮑老催
"Baosi ganye" 寶寺干謁
beiKun 北崑
bense 本色
beng 迸
Bidizhai 筆涕齋
Bi Wei 畢魏
"Biaomu" 標目
"Biao you mei" 摽有梅
"Bingke yi an" 病客依菴
Bingsiguan 冰絲館
bolan 波瀾
Boxiao ji 博笑記
boxing 薄倖
Bubu jiao 步步嬌
bu guo 補過
bu nao 不鬧
bu seqing 不色情
bu shang yadao 不傷雅道
Bu shi lu 不是路
bu xianggui zen bian ba quanshen xian 步香閨怎便把全身現
bu xiang zuo ai, xiang laodong 不像做愛像勞動
buyi 補遺

Cai Bojie 蔡伯喈
cai hua 猜畫
Cai Ying 蔡穎
Cai Zhengren 蔡正仁
Cao Cao 曹操
caochuang 草創
caotai banzi 草台班子
chayuan 茶園
changong 蟾宮
changong zhegui 蟾宮折桂
chanmian bu liao, ci shi zuofa 纏綿不了此是做法
chang 唱
Chang E 嫦娥
changjiben 場記本

Changle jushi 常樂居士
Chang Ru 昌孺
Changsheng dian 長生殿
changtan 唱壇
"Chang tiao" 悵眺
Chen Shangzhi 陳上枝
Chen Shi-Zheng 陳士爭
"Chen Shi-Zheng qianzhe Du Liniang shang Bailaohui" 陳士爭牽著杜麗娘上百老匯
Chen Yunfa 陳雲發
chenzi 襯字
Chenzui dongfeng 沉醉東風
Chen Zuiliang 陳最良
chengshi 程式
Cheng Yucang 程雨蒼
chi 癡
chidai 癡呆
chihuan shenzhi tingzhi 遲緩甚至停滯
chiluoluo de xing ciji 赤裸裸的性刺激
chiqing 癡情
Chonghe jushi 沖和居士
chou 丑
Chu duizi 出隊子
Chujiang qing 楚江情
chukouban 出口版
"Chu shi zhenrong" 初拾真容
chuxuezhe 初學者
Chuan bo zhao 川撥棹
"Chuanjing xizi" 傳經習字
chuanke 串客
chuanqi 傳奇
chuan shen 傳神
chuan xi 串戲
"Chuan" *zi bei* 傳字輩
chuanggao 創稿
chun 春
Chunqing 春卿
Chuntai (troupe) 春台
Chunxiang 春香
"Chunxiang nao xue" 春香鬧學
"Chunxiang su yuan" 春香肅苑
Chunxuege qupu sanji 春雪閣曲譜三記
ci 詞
"Cijie" 慈戒
"Cimu qi fu" 慈母祈福
ciqu 詞曲
ciren danghang, geke shouqiang 詞人當行歌客守腔
Cu yulin 簇御林

Dajianglong 大江龍
da meishu yizhu, meizi leilei ke'ai 大梅樹一株梅子磊磊可愛
da'nao 大鬧
"Da Ling Chucheng" 答凌初成
"Da Sun Siju" 答孫俟居
"Da Tang Yireng" 答唐義仍
dasu daya bu ji 大俗大雅不及
"Daya" 大雅
daya zuiren 大雅罪人
dan 旦
danjuexi 旦腳戲
"Dan shi" 耽試
danxingben 單行本
dang 蕩
dangfu si chun 蕩婦思春
danghang 當行
dangshan 擋扇
dangwei shuji 黨委書記
"Dao shang" 悼殤
"Daoxi" 道覡
daoyan juben 導演劇本
Dechun 得春
Deng xiaolou 登小樓
Deng Xiaoping 鄧小平
Diliuzi 滴溜子
dishi 笛師
dizi 笛子
dian 點
dianban 點板
dianhuo 點活

dian jin cheng tie 點金成鐵
"Dian nü" 奠女
dianwu 點污
"Diao da" 吊打
"Diao da dongchuang" 刁打東床
Diao jiao'er 掉角兒
ding 定
ding 訂
dingli gongyang 頂禮供養
dou 都
Dou E yuan 竇娥冤
doupeng 斗篷
Dou shuangji 鬥雙雞
Douye huang 豆葉黃
Du Bao 杜寶
"Du Bao xun nü" 杜寶訓女
"Du Bao yi zhen" 杜寶移鎮
"Du Gong xun nü" 杜公訓女
Du Liniang 杜麗娘
"Du Liniang muse huanhun" 杜麗娘慕色還魂
"Du nü huisheng" 杜女回生
"Duanqiao" 斷橋
duanzhuang 端庄
duida 對答
"Duihua" 堆花
duo 多

ehun 惡諢
ezhu 惡竹
Erfan wutong shu 二犯梧桐樹
Erfan yao ling 二犯么令
Erlang shen 二郎神
Erlang shen man 二郎神慢
"Eryou yanhuai" 二友言懷

fanchuan 反串
fanhun xiang 返魂香
fanli 凡例
Fanshan hu 番山虎
fangben 坊本
fangke 坊刻
fei 肥
fei dangchang zhi pu 非當場之譜
fei dangjia zhi zuo 非當家之作
fen 憤
fen kulou 粉骷髏
fenjingtou juben 分鏡頭劇本
fenqi 分歧
fenxiang gongyang 焚香供養
Fenxiang ji 焚香記
fenxiao 粉銷
fengliu 風流
Feng ru song 風入松
Feng Xiaoqing 馮小青
fengyuedan 風月旦
fujing 副淨
"Fuqi he meng" 夫妻合夢
"Futan" 腐歎
fuza de yishu gongcheng 複雜的藝術工程

gankai 感慨
Gan Yilu 甘義麓
gao 稿
gaodeng huangse 高等黃色
"Gaokao xuancai" 告考選才
gelü 格律
geteng 葛藤
gezhongren 箇中人
gezhongren quan zai qiubo miao 箇中人全在秋波妙
gongche 工尺
gongpu 宮譜
Gong Zizhen 龔自珍
"Gudian mingzhu neng zheyang gaibian banshang wutai ma" 古典明珠能這樣改編搬上舞台嗎
Gugong bowuyuan tushuguan 故宮博物院圖書館
gumei 古梅
Gu Yi'an 谷亦安
guailü 乖律

Guan Hanqing 關漢卿
guanmu jincou 關目緊湊
"Guanshe yan shi" 官舍延師
guansheng 官生
Guanyin 觀音
Guanyin Dashi 觀音大士
Guanyin *xixiang* 觀音戲像
Guanyin *xixiang* 觀音喜相
Guanyuan ji 灌園記
guang 光
guanggun 光棍
guifanhua 規範化
guimendan 閨門旦
guinie 圭臬
"Guishu" 閨塾
gun 棍
gundiao 滾調
guntu 棍徒
guohuo 過火
guoqu 過曲
Guo Tuo 郭駝
guoxi 國戲
Guo Xiaonan 郭小男

"Hai bian" 駭變
Haiyan 海鹽
Handan ji 邯鄲記
hanxiu 含羞
hanxu 含蓄
Han Zicai 韓子才
hangjia 行家
haohan 好漢
Haojiejie 好姐姐
haoquzi bu deng tai, deng tai bu shi haoquzi 好曲子不登台,登台不是好曲子
haoshi 好事
Haoshi jin 好事近
"Hao yi fu *Qingming shanghe tu*" 好一幅清明上河圖
hedu 合度
He Liangjun 何良俊
"He meng" 合夢
hepan shenduan 合盤身段
"Heqi xu" 合奇序
Hongfu ji 紅拂記
honggou 鴻溝
Hongmeiguan 紅梅觀
Hong na'ao 紅衲襖
Hongniang 紅娘
Hong Sheng 洪昇
hongyu 紅雨
hong zhan yufei tian 紅綻雨肥天
Houting hua 後庭花
Houting hua gun 後庭花滾
Hu Panguan 胡判官
hua 花
huabu 花部
huadan 花旦
"Huadong chen fei" 畫棟塵飛
huaguxi 花鼓戲
Huaju 華劇
Hualang 花郎
Hua mei xu 畫眉序
Huashen 花神
Hua Wenyi 華文漪
huaxian 花仙
Huaxu 華胥
"Huai bo" 淮泊
"Huai jing" 淮警
Huaiju 淮劇
huan 幻
"Huan nao" 歡撓
Huanqiu shibao 環球時報
Huansha ji 浣紗記
Huansha xi 浣紗溪
huanxiang 幻想
"Huang'en ci qing" 黃恩賜慶
Huang Haiwei 黃海威
huanghu 慌惚
Huang ying'er 黃鶯兒
Huang Zhen 黃振
Hui Chi yadiao 徽池雅調

"Hui sheng" 回生
huisheng tie 回生帖
hundan 魂旦
Hunjiang long 混江龍
"Hunyou" 魂遊
"Hunyou qinggan" 魂遊情感
"Hunzou" 婚走
huodaoju 活道俱
huopo 活潑
huotao 活套
"Huozhuo" 活捉

ji 記
ji 集
Jiban ling 急板令
jiji yinsu 積極因素
jiluben 記錄本
"Ji nan" 急難
jiqu 集曲
jise'er 急色兒
Ji xianbin 集賢賓
jiadingxing 假定性
Jia Fang 賈方
jiagong 加工
jialing 家伶
"Jiamen dayi" 家門大意
jian 尖
Jian Hua 劍華
Jiang'er shui 江兒水
Jiang Ru 江孺
Jiangtou jingui 江頭金桂
Jiang Zemin 江澤民
"Jiao hua" 叫畫
"Jie bing" 詰病
Jiefang ribao 解放日報
jin 近
Jin 金
Jinchan dao 錦纏道
Jin'e shen 金娥神
Jin Tao 金濤
Jingu yuan 金谷園
jinhe 金荷
Jin luosuo 金落索
"Jinpen lao yue, Shi hua Jiao hua, Yuqiao deng qupu" 金盆撈月, 拾畫叫畫, 漁樵等曲譜
Jinqian hua 金錢花
"Jinse" 錦瑟
jinsheng 巾生
jing 淨
jing 靜
Jingchai ji 荊釵記
jingcui 精萃
jingdian 經典
"Jingdian fan pu de kegui changshi" 經典返朴的可貴嘗試
jinghua 精華
jingguo ya su rongwei yiti yihou de ya 經過雅俗融為一體以後的雅
jingling 精靈
"Jingmeng" 驚夢
jingshen 精神
"Jingxin xuexi" 靜心學習
jingya 驚訝
jingzhezhuang 經摺裝
Jingzhong qi 精忠旗
jingzi jiao xiu 鏡子教羞
Jiuhui chang 九迴腸
Jiujia yong 酒家傭
juchang 劇場
juchang yanchu 劇場演出
juchangzhong renshou yibian de shuomingshu 劇場中人手一編的說明書
jude guannian 劇的觀念
ju jinghua er tu zaopo, qu chenfu er geng xinying 咀精華而吐糟粕, 去陳腐而更新穎
juqu 劇曲
"Jue ye" 訣謁

kaibian 開遍
"Kaichang" 開場

kan an dian shi wei ren, kao fu zuo zhu 看俺點石為人, 靠夫做主
kan ni zheshuang qiaoyan zhiguan gupan xiaosheng 看你這雙俏眼只管顧盼小生
kan ta zheshuang qiaokeyan zhi ai gupan xiaosheng a 看他這雙俏渴眼只愛顧盼小生呵
kan yishu xue chuichui ru xiao 看一樹雪垂垂如笑
kanzhong 看重
kao 靠
"Kao Chun" 拷春
kaozheng 考正
"Ke bing yi an" 客病依庵
kehuade zui jianrui de yige shenduan 刻畫得最尖銳的一個身段
keyan 可厭
komono 小物
kong 空
kongke 空殼
Kong Shangren 孔尚任
"Koujian" 寇間
kuren 苦仁
kuang 狂
Kunqu 崑曲
"Kunqu shouchuang 'waixiangxing' yanchu moshi" 崑曲首創外向型演出模式
Kunshan *qiang* 崑山腔
Kunwei 崑味

Lali 蠟梨
Laitouyuan 癩頭黿
Lan hua mei 懶畫眉
lantu 藍圖
laodan 老旦
Laodong bao 勞動報
laodong haozi 勞動號子
laosheng 老生
laoSubai 老蘇白
le 樂
"Le zai qizhong" 樂在其中
Leifeng ta 雷峰塔
leishu 類書
lengchang 冷場
lengdan 冷淡
lengxiang 冷香
li 戾
li 俚
li 理
li 禮
lifu 俚腐
Lihua ji 梨花記
"Li hun" 離魂
Li Peng 李鵬
"Liniang xun meng" 麗娘尋夢
liqi 離奇
Li Quan 李全
"Li Quan qi bing" 李全起兵
Li Shangyin 李商隱
Li Xuanyu 李玄玉
Li Yu 李玉
Li Yu 李漁
liyu 麗語
Liyuan chuanben mo shui xiu, yi shi fenghua yi dai chou 梨園串本摹誰修, 亦是風花一代愁
"Lianyan santian sanye fang neng yanwan quanben *Mudan ting* banshang wutai" 連演三天三夜方能演完全本牡丹亭搬上舞台
liangchen meijing 良辰美景
Liang Guyin 梁谷音
lianghao de huanjing 良好的環境
Liangjiang ji 量江記
liangxiang 亮相
Liang xiuxiu 兩休休
Liao Ben 廖奔
"Liao yi zi yu" 聊以自娛
Linchuan 臨川
Lin Qianxiu 林潛修

Lin Qiang Xu 林強徐
Lin Sen 林森
linghuoxing 靈活性
Ling Mengchu 凌濛初
lingqiao 靈巧
liu 柳
"Liu Jin jie wei" 溜金解圍
Liu Mengmei 柳夢梅
Liu Minjun 劉敏君
liupai 流派
"Liu sheng nao yan" 柳生鬧宴
Liu Yilong 劉異龍
longxiang 龍香
Loujiang 婁江
Lou Jing 婁靖
lu 露
"Lu die" 虜諜
Lu Gong 路工
lugu 露骨
luxian 路線
lü emei 綠萼梅
"Lü ji" 旅寄
Lü Jiangshan 呂姜山
"Lü Mei daoyan duanshang 'dazahui'" 旅美導演端上大雜燴
Lü Tiancheng 呂天成
Luanxiao xiaopin 鸞嘯小品
luan ermu 亂耳目
"Lun banyan" 論板眼
"Lun chake" 論插科
"Lun guoqu" 論過曲
"Lun jiashu" 論家數
"Lun paixie" 論俳諧
"Lun qiangdiao" 論腔調
"Lun yinzi" 論引子
luoliao kong 落了空
Luo Rufang 羅汝芳
Luo Zhang'er 羅章二

Ma Bomin 馬博敏
maizang 埋葬
Manpai qian baochan 蠻牌嵌寶蟾
Manshan yi 蠻山憶
maodun 矛盾
Mao'er zhui 貓兒墜
Mao Ying 茅暎
Mao Yuanyi 茅元儀
mei 梅
"Mei'an yougou" 梅庵幽遘
meiban 梅瓣
Meici wo yu ta hezuo yan "Jingmeng," yi jiechu ta nei ming ru qiushui de shuangtong, zhengge shenxin dou hui gandao hen da de zhendong, haoxiang yigu juda de nuanliu guanchuan quanshen. 每次我與他合作演"驚夢,"一接觸他那明如秋水的雙瞳,整個身心都會感到很大的震動,好像一股巨大的暖流貫穿全身
"Meifei zhuan" 梅妃傳
"Meiguo jiang xian *Mudan ting* re" 美國將掀牡丹亭熱
"Meiguo Saishi *Mudan ting*: guannian nuoyi yu wenhua chanshi cuowei" 美國塞氏牡丹亭: 觀念挪移與文化闡釋錯位
Meihua anguan 梅花庵觀
Meihuaguan 梅花觀
meihua zhang 梅花帳
meipi 眉批
meirenjiao 美人蕉
meirentu 美人圖
meixi 梅犀
"Meng gan chunqing" 夢感春情
Menglei ji 夢磊記
Mengshen 夢神
"Meng yuan" 夢圓
"Mi yi" 秘議
Mian daxu 綿搭絮
mianmu quanfei 面目全非
Miao Shunbin 苗舜賓
"Miao zhen" 描真
mingjia 名家

"Mingliu qingju" 名流清劇
"Mingpan" 冥判
"Mingpan lianqing" 冥判憐情
"Mingshi" 冥誓
Mingxin jian 明心鑒
Mingzhu ji 明珠記
mo 末
mo 帕
mohe 磨荷
mohu 模糊
mohuan 魔幻
monoomoi 物思い
moriagari 盛り上ガり
Mo Tao 默濤
"Mou cuo shangnü" 謀厝殤女
"*Mudan ting* banbudao Niu Yue qu" 牡丹亭搬不到紐約去，
"*Mudan ting* juran yaozhe; 'cuishengren' anran shenshang" 牡丹亭遽然夭折; 催生人黯然神傷
"*Mudan ting* paiyan gousi" 牡丹亭排演構思

naihe tian 奈何天
Nan'an 南安
Nanke ji 南柯記
Nanlou 南樓
Nantiesheng 南鐵生
nanxi 南戲
"Nanyin dubu" 南音獨步
"Nao sang" 鬧喪
"Nao shang" 鬧殤
"Nao xue" 鬧學
"Nao yan" 鬧宴
neihan 內涵
neixiang 內向
neixiangxing 內向性
neixin shenchu jidangzhe de ganqing de bolan 內心深處激蕩著的感情的波瀾
"Nenggu miaowu" 能鼓妙舞
nian qingmei 撚青梅
nong 穠
nuoxi 儺戲

pa wode danqing ya 怕涴的丹青亞
pa yaoshen chuwuliao liu jingling 怕腰身觸污了柳精靈
paishou 拍手
Pan Bizheng 潘必正
pangguanzhe 傍觀者
pangmen waidao 旁門外道
"Pang yi" 旁疑
pengzhuang 碰撞
piliwu 霹靂舞
pipa 琵琶
Pipa ji 琵琶記
pianyue yingguang sheng haomo 片月影光生豪末
piaoyou 票友
Pinhua baojian 品花寶鑑
Pin ling 品令
"Pinzei" 牝賊
pingtan 評彈
Pingyao zhuan 平妖傳
Putian le 普天樂
"Pu zhen" 僕偵

qi shi dangjia zhi zuo 豈是當家之作
qianhou huying 前後呼應
Qiannü 倩女
Qiannü li hun 倩女離婚
Qian Yi 錢熠
Qianziwen 千字文
qiang 腔
qiaokeyan 俏渴眼
qiaoyan 俏眼
Qin Gui 秦檜
Qin *qiang* 秦腔
qing 情
qing 清
qingbao 情報
Qingbei xu 頃杯序

qingchang 清唱
qingchi 情癡
"Qing chi" 情癡
qingci wenchen 情詞穩稱
qinggong 清宮
qingke 清客
"Qinglang yin meng" 情郎印夢
Qingle 清樂
Qingming shanghe tu 清明上河圖
Qingnian bao 青年報
qingqu 清曲
qingqu wei yayan, ju wei xiayou, zhiyan bu xiangfan 清曲為雅宴, 劇為狎游, 至嚴不相犯
Qingyang 青陽
Qingyuan Shi 清源師
qingya 清雅
Qiu He 秋河
Qiu Hu 秋胡
Qiuye yue 秋夜月
qu 曲
qupai 曲牌
qupu 曲譜
qushe 曲社
quxue 曲學
quyi 曲意
quyou 曲友
"Quanben Kunqu *Mudan ting* jiang liangxiang guoji wutai" 全本崑曲牡丹亭將亮相國際舞台
"Quanben *Mudan ting* qiyue zai Mei shangyan" 全本牡丹亭七月在美上演
"Quan nong" 勸農

Raochi you 遶池遊
re'nao 熱鬧
ren 仁
ren 人
Renmin ribao 人民日報
Renshou guan 人獸關
renwu leixing 人物類型
renwu neixin licheng de zhuanbian 人物內心歷程的轉變
rouxiang xin zhang 肉香新長
"Ru Hang" 如杭
"Ru meng" 入夢
runhong 潤紅
Runyue huashen 閏月花神

Saxue tang 灑雪堂
Sanbao en 三報恩
San duanzi 三段子
sanqu 散曲
"Santian sanye zhanshi quanben *Mudan ting*" 三天三夜展示全本牡丹亭
sanxian 三絃
sanxiu 三羞
sao 騷
Shagou ji 殺狗記
shamaosheng 紗帽生
"Shan bei" 繕備
Shanpo yang 山坡羊
Shantao hong 山桃紅
shanzisheng 扇子生
shanggan 傷感
Shanghai xiju xueyuan 上海戲劇學院
Shanghai shi xiqu xuexiao 上海市戲曲學校
"Shang Kun xiaozibei jiqing tiao daliang" 上崑小字輩激情挑大梁
"Shang lu" 上路
shangshi 賞識
shang xia chengfeng 上下成風
"Shangxin leshi" 賞心樂事
"Shangxin leshi qupu 'Youyuan Jingmeng'" 賞心樂事曲譜遊園驚夢
she 社
"Sheshi mingxin" 設誓明心
Shen Bin 沈彬
shenduan 身段
shenduanpu 身段譜
shenfen 身分

Shen Huazhong 沈化仲

Shenjiang fuwu daobao 申江服務導報

Shen Jifei 沈際飛

Shen Jing 沈璟

sheng 生

Shengpingshu 升平署

shi 詩

Shi Daogu 石道姑

Shi Fengxiang *laoxiansheng* 史鳳翔老先生

"Shi gu zu huan" 史姑阻歡

"Shi hua" 拾畫

"Shi Jiao" 拾叫

Shi Jiehua 史潔華

"Shijiemo de langman juechang" 世界末的浪漫絕唱

Shijie ribao 世界日報

Shijing 詩經

shiqu 時曲

Shoudu tushuguan 首都圖書館

shujuanqi 書卷氣

shuqing 抒情

Shua Bao lao 耍鮑老

Shuazi xu fan 刷子序犯

Shuangshengzi 雙聲字

Shuangtian xiaojiao 霜天曉角

Shuangxiong ji 雙雄記

Shuihu ji 水滸記

Shuimoshen 睡魔神

shuixiu 水袖

shuomingshu 說明書

Shuoyuan shanding Mudan ting 碩園刪定牡丹亭

si 思

"Si fan" 思凡

Simengtai 四夢臺

Sizhitang 四知堂

"Songbie" 送別

su 俗

Subei 蘇北

su'er 俗耳

suling 俗伶

suren 俗人

Su Shi 蘇軾

"Su Wan zhen" 俗玩真

"Su yuan" 肅園

"Suzeng Duihua" 俗僧堆花

suan 酸

Sui zai wuxu zhongdong Julu shi Shouting rike 歲在戊戌仲冬鉅鹿氏壽亭日課

Sun Jiugao 孫九皋

"Suo yuan" 索元

ta kao fu zuo zhu 他靠夫作主

Taicang 太倉

taidang yinyi 駘蕩淫夷

taidang yinyi zhuan zai bimo zhi wai 駘蕩淫夷轉在筆墨之外

Taiping ling 太平令

Taixia xinzou 太霞新奏

tanbing 談柄

tanci 彈詞

Tan Dun 譚盾

Tanhua ji 曇花記

tang jingling huazhong chuxian, yuan chuan yu haoercao 儻精靈畫中出現, 願傳於好兒曹

tangming 堂名

Taohua shan 桃花扇

Tete ling 忒忒令

Tihong ji 題紅記

Tiying xu 啼鶯序

tian 天

Tian'anmen 天安門

Tian Dan 天丹

tie 貼

tiedan 貼旦

Tongmeng ji 同夢記

Tongquetai 銅雀臺

tongxingben 通行本

touming 透明

tuhao 兔毫

Tu Long 屠隆
tuanyuan 團圓

wai 外
waixiangxing 外向型
"Wan zhen" 玩真
Wang Jide 王驥德
Wang Jilie 王季烈
Wang Wei 王維
Wang Wenzhi 王文治
Wang Xichun 王錫純
Wang Xijue 王錫爵
"Wei cheng qian jian" 圍城遣間
Wei Liangfu 魏良輔
weinan'er shen kudang 偉男兒深褲襠
wei qu jiu zhi 委曲就之
Weisheng 尾聲
"Wei shi" 圍釋
weiwan 委婉
wei zhi yixin 為之一新
wenda 問答
Wenhui bao 文匯報
"Wen lu" 問路
"Wen xi" 聞喜
Wenxue bao 文學報
wenxue juben 文學劇本
Wenyi bao 文藝報
Wen Yiduo 聞一多
Wen Yuhang 溫宇航
wenzao 文藻
wenzhong 穩重
wo 涴
woliao 涴了
Wo shi ge 我是個
wu 物
wu 蕪
Wuban yi 五般宜
Wuchang 武閶
Wu Chongji 吳崇机
Wu geng zhuan 五更轉
Wu Mei 吳梅
Wumen 吳門
Wumen 午門
wu qi zhi, xi weiwan 惡其直, 喜委婉
Wushan 巫山
wutai de chuanben 舞台的串本
wutai yishu 舞臺藝術
wuwei 無謂
Wu Wushan 吳吳山
wuxing 無形
Wu Yueshi 吳越石

xiban de chuanyanben 戲班的串演本
xiban yong de yanchu taiben 戲班用的演出台本
xigong 戲宮
Xiji 禊集
xijie 細節
Xilou Chujiang qing 西樓楚江情
Xilou ji 西樓記
Xilou meng 西樓夢
xiqu 戲曲
Xixiang ji 西廂記
xiyuan 戲園
xiyue 喜悅
"Xia shan" 下山
Xia shan hu 下山虎
Xianqing ouji 閒情偶寄
"Xianqing yizhi" 閒情遺致
"Xiansuo yuanyin" 絃索元音
xian tingyuan 閒庭院
xiang 香
xiang hua 詳畫
xiangjian 相見
xiangnei cheng 想內成
xiaochou 小丑
xiaodan 小旦
xiaogugu 小姑姑
Xiaohualang 小花郎
xiaojing 小淨
xiao li zai chuichui huashu bian 小立在垂垂花樹邊

Xiao nan ge 孝南哥
xiaosheng 小生
xiaotie 小貼
Xieji 諧集
xielü 協律
"Xie mou fa mu" 協謀發墓
xieshu 邪術
xieyi 寫意
"Xie zhen" 寫真
xinling 心靈
Xin Qinghua 辛清華
Xinwen bao 新聞報
Xin yuefu renwuzhi 新樂府人物志
"Xing fang zhuangyuan" 行訪狀元
xingrong 行容
"Xiong yao" 詗藥
"Xiucai shuo" 秀才說
"Xiuge chuan zhen" 繡閣傳真
Xu Rixi 徐日曦
xuanben 選本
Xuancheng 宣城
xueshuxing 學術性
"Xuetang" 學堂
xueyi chongkailiao bai yumei 雪意衝開了白玉梅
xun 壎
"Xun meng" 尋夢
"Xun nü" 訓女

ya 雅
yabu 雅部
ya dongzuo 啞動作
yahua 雅化
ya su gong shang 雅俗共賞
ya su jian shou, chuanhe wuhen 雅俗兼收，串合無痕
yazhongsu 雅中俗
yanchu taiben 演出台本
Yan'er luo dai Desheng ling 雁兒落帶得勝令
Yan guo sheng 雁過聲
yanhong 嫣紅
"Yanhuai" 言懷
yanjian 淹煎
yanjian, pocansheng 淹煎，潑殘生
yanmu 眼目
Yan Poxi 閻婆惜
"Yan shi" 延師
yan si tuo 顏似酡
yanxi 演習
yanxizhe 演習者
yanzhuang 艷妝
Yanzi le 顏子樂
yan zi tu 顏自塗
Yang Enshou 楊恩壽
"Yang guan" 陽關
Yang Haipeng 楊海鵬
Yang Po 楊婆
Yangzi wanbao 揚子晚報
Yao Chuanxiang 姚傳薌
yaohe 么荷
Ye Jinmen 謁金門
Ye Tang 葉堂
Ye you gong 夜遊宮
"Ye yu" 謁遇
yeyu xiqu aihaozhe 業餘戲曲愛好者
yi 義
yibi 義婢
Yi bujin 意不盡
Yicuo zhao 一撮棹
yi dui yi 一對一
Yihuang 宜黃
"Yi jian bian ming" 一見便明
Yijiangfeng 一江風
"Yi meng" 憶夢
Yimeng ji 異夢記
"Yi nü" 憶女
Yipen hua 一盆花
Yipeng xue 一捧雪
yipian sahuaxin de hongying'er 一片撒花心的紅影兒
yi qing xie qing 以情寫情

yi shou zhiyin 以授知音
yi wo yuanben 依我原本
Yiyang 弋陽
"Yi zhen" 移鎮
"Yi zu yi le" 亦足以樂
yin 陰
Yin ling 尹令
yinlü xiexie 音律諧協
Yinxiangtang qupu 吟香堂曲譜
ying 影
Ying Huang 鶯黃
"Ying kao" 硬拷
Ying ti xu 鶯啼序
yingxiang 影響
Yingying 鶯鶯
yonggong 庸工
yong hua 詠花
Yong tuanyuan 永團圓
"Yongxin xixue" 用心習學
you 油
you 幽
you chicun 有尺寸
"Yougou" 幽媾
yougun 遊棍
"Youhuan" 幽歡
"Youhui" 幽會
youhun luyin 遊魂路引
youmei jiankang 優美健康
youpai 優俳
"Youqi xiezhao" 幽期寫照
you yi ri chunguang an du huangjin liu 有一日春光暗度黃金柳
"Youyuan" 遊園
"Youyuan Jingmeng" 遊園驚夢
youzuo 有做
"Yu Huai" 禦淮
Yu jiao zhi 玉交枝
Yujie 玉界
yukuo 迂闊
yulexing 娛樂性
"Yumingtang chuanqi yin" 玉茗堂傳奇引
"Yu mu" 遇母
"Yu Yi ling Luo Zhang'er" 與宜伶羅章二
Yu ying'er 玉鶯兒
Yu Zhenfei 俞振飛
Yu Zonghai 俞宗海
yuangao 原稿
"Yuan jia" 圓駕
"Yuan jin" 原近
yuanmao 元貌
Yuanyang meng 鴛鴦夢
Yuan Yuling 袁于令
yue 月
Yue'er gao 月兒高
yuefu 樂府
Yuefu hongshan 樂府紅珊
Yueju 越劇
Yue Meiti 岳美緹
yunwo 雲涴

za 雜
zahui 雜燴
zaju 雜劇
"Zalun" 雜論
zaidu chuangzao 再度創造
zaizhi 再識
zan nong mei xinshi 咱弄梅心事
Zaoluopao 皂羅袍
zaopo 糟粕
ze liu san men, buxu shang xin 則留散悶，不許傷心
Zhai Qing 翟青
zhan 綻
zhan ezhu 斬惡竹
Zhanhua kui 占花魁
zhangben 張本
Zhang Boqi 張伯起
Zhang Fengyi 張鳳翼
Zhang Jiqing 張繼青

Zhang Jun 張軍
Zhang Wanliang 張萬良
Zhang Wei 張位
Zhang Wenyuan 張文遠
Zhang Xunpeng 張洵澎
Zhang Yaoxian 張瑤仙
Zhao Wuniang 趙五娘
zhe ba meixi dianwu 輒把梅犀玷污
"Zhe kou" 折寇
Zhe shi xiaosheng de juezu 這是小生的掘足
Zhe shi xiaosheng de zhuozuo 這是小生的拙作
zhezixi 折子戲
"Zhen sui" 診祟
Zhenzhen 真真
zhenzheng 真正
zhengdan 正旦
zhengjing 正淨
zhengpai 正派
zhengqi 正氣
zhengsheng 正生
zhengti 整體
zhengtixing 整體性
zhi 識
zhili 支離
zhipu 製譜
zhi shao kou qi'er 只少口氣兒
zhiweisheng 雉尾生
zhiyinzhe 知音者
zhizhong 知重
zhong 衆
Zhongguo wenhua bao 中國文化報
Zhongguo xiju yanjiuyuan tushuguan 中國戲曲研究院圖書館
Zhongguo yinyue yanjiusuo 中國音樂研究所
"Zhongqiu qi ye" 中秋泣夜
Zhou Ming 周鳴
Zhou Mingxing 周明行
Zhou Yiqian 周怡倩
zhu 主
Zhuma'er zhuan 竹馬兒賺
zhumoben 朱墨本
Zhuan 賺
zhuanguo zhe shaoyao lanqian / jinkaozhe hushanshi bian 轉過這芍藥欄前/緊靠著湖山石邊
Zhuanlin ying 囀林鶯
zhuang 莊
zhuangyuan 狀元
Zhui baiqiu 綴白裘
Zhuo mu fan 啄木犯
zhuopu 拙樸
Zichai ji 紫釵記
"*Zichai ji* zongpi" 紫釵記總批
zidishu 子弟書
zilian 自憐
"Zimu xiangfeng" 子母相逢
ziran 自然
ziran lingqi, huanghu er lai, bu si er zhi 自然靈氣, 恍惚而來, 不思而至
zishang 自賞
Zixiao ji 紫簫記
Ziyun 紫雲
"Zixu er" 自序二
zonggang 揔綱
zongji 總集
zongjiang 揔講
zongjue zongjiang 揔訣揔講
zongping 總評
Zou Diguang 鄒迪光
Zui fu gui 醉扶歸
"Zuiliang xing mu" 最良省墓
"Zuiliang yu kou" 最良遇寇
"Zuiliang zhen bing" 最良診病
Zui taiping 醉太平
zui youzuo 最有做
zuo Zhenzhen wu ren huanjiao / kanchou yao, jingshen chuxian liu yu houren biao 做真真無人喚叫/堪愁夭, 精神出現留與後人標

Works Cited

Works in Chinese and Japanese

Aoki Masaru 青木正兒. *Zhongguo jinshi xiqu shi* 中國近世戲曲史 (History of latter-day Chinese drama). 2 vols. Translated by Wang Gulu 王古魯. Hong Kong: Zhonghua shuju, 1975. Originally published as *Shina kinsei gikyoku shi* 支那近世戲曲史, vol. 3 of *Aoki Masaru zensho* 青木正兒全書 (Complete works of Aoki Masaru). Tokyo: Shunjūsha, 1969.

Bai Yunsheng 白雲生 (1902-1972). *Sheng dan jing chou mo de biaoyan yishu* 生旦淨丑末的表演藝術 (Art of performance for the *sheng, dan, jing, chou* and *mo* roles). Beijing: Zhongguo xiju chubanshe, 1957.

——. "Tan Liu Mengmei" 談柳夢梅 (On Liu Mengmei). In *Tang Xianzu yanjiu ziliao huibian* 湯顯祖研究資料匯編, compiled by Mao Xiaotong 毛效同, 1232–42. Shanghai: Shanghai guji chubanshe, 1986. Originally published in *Xiju luncong* 戲劇論叢, no. 3 (1957): 74–80.

Cai Yi 蔡毅, comp. *Zhongguo gudian xiqu xuba huibian* 中國古典戲曲序跋匯編 (Comprehensive edition of prefaces and colophons from classical Chinese dramas). [*XBHB*]. 4 vols. Beijing: Qi Lu shushe, 1989.

Chen Duo 陳多. "Xiqu heyi xu bian?" 戲曲何以需辨 (How must drama evolve?). In *Xishi bian* 戲史辨 (Evolution in the history of drama), edited by Hu Ji 胡忌, 1–45. Beijing: Zhongguo xiju chubanshe, 1999.

——. "Du *Mudan ting* zhaji" 讀牡丹亭札記 (Notes from reading 'Peony pavilion'). In *Tang Xianzu yanjiu lunwen ji* 湯顯祖研究論文集, edited by Jiangxi sheng wenxue yishu yanjiusuo, 255–73. Beijing: Zhongguo xiju chubanshe, 1984. Originally published in *Jiangxi xiju* 江西戲劇, no. 3 (1982): 5–13.

Chen Kaixin 陳凱莘. "*Mudan ting* 'Jingmeng' zhi huashen yanchu kao" 牡丹亭驚夢之花神演出考 (The genesis and transformation of "Flower Spirit Dancing" in 'Peony pavilion'). *Guoli bianyiguan guankan* 國立編譯館館刊 27, no. 2 (June 1998): 97–111.

Chen Sen 陳森 (ca. 1796–ca. 1870). *Pinhua baojian* 品花寶鑑 (A precious mirror of ranked flowers). 2 vols. Taibei: Guangya chuban youxian gongsi, 1984.

Chen Youhan 陳幼韓. "Shilun Zhongguo xiqu wutai yishu de biaoyan chengshi" 試論 中國戲曲舞台藝術的表演程式 (Preliminary discussion of performance conventions of Chinese stage art). In *Zhongguo xiqu wutai yishu de biaoyan chengshi* 中國戲曲舞台 藝術的表演程式, 22–28. Xi'an: Shanxi renmin chubanshe, 1958.

Cheng Ji 程驥. "*Mudan ting* yiqu jing tianxia?" 牡丹亭一曲驚天下 (Did 'The peony pavilion' amaze the world?). *Henan xiju* 河南戲劇 no. 5 (1998): 4. Originally published in *Wenhui bao* 文匯報, June 20, 1998.

Cilin yixiang 詞林逸響 (Unconstrained music from a forest of verse). 4 vols. Preface dated 1623. Compiled by Xu Yu 許宇. Reprinted in *Shanben xiqu congkan* 善本戲曲 叢刊, compiled by Wang Qiugui 王秋桂, vols. 15–16. Taibei: Xuesheng shuju, 1984–1987.

Cunxin shuwu qupu 寸心書屋曲譜 (Dramatic scores from Inch of Heart Library). 2 vols. Compiled by Zhou Qin 周秦 et al. Suzhou: Suzhou University, 1993.

"Danjue zheshan jiben jiaocai" 旦腳摺扇基本教材. (Basic teaching materials on the folding fan for the *dan* role). 12 pages. Mimeographed pamphlet: n.p., n.d.

Dong Jieyuan 董解元 (fl. 1190–1208). *Dong Jieyuan Xixiang ji* 董解元西廂記 ('The western wing' of Dong Jieyuan). Edited and annotated by Ling Jingyan 凌景埏. Beijing: Renmin wenxue chubanshe, 1962, 1978.

Du Fu 杜甫 (712–770). *Du shi xiangzhu* 杜詩詳注 (Detailed annotations of the poetry of Du Fu). 2 vols. Compiled by Qiu Zhao'ao 仇兆鰲. Beijing: Zhonghua shuju, 1979.

Du Wei 杜衛. "Ya su jiehe de gudian xiqu meixue sichao" 雅俗結合的古典戲曲美學 思潮 (The aesthetic trend in traditional opera towards the combining of elegant and common). *Qiushi xuekan* 求是學刊, no. 2 (March 1992): 84–88.

[Du] Yingtao [杜] 穎陶. "Tan *Zhui baiqiu*" 談綴白裘 (On 'A patched cloak of white fur'). *Juxue yuekan* 劇學月刊 3, no. 7 (1934): 1–11.

Eyunge qupu. See Wang Xichun.

Feng Menglong 馮夢龍 (1574–1646). *Mohanzhai dingben chuanqi* 墨憨齋定本傳奇 (Ink-Crazy Studio's southern dramas). 1792 (reprint of late Ming edition). 3 vols. Beijing: Xinhua shudian, 1960. Reprint and supplement in *Feng Menglong quanji* 馮夢龍全集 (Complete works of Feng Menglong), 22 vols, edited by Wei Tongxian 魏同賢. Shanghai: Shanghai guji chubanshe, 1993.

——. *Fengliu meng* 風流夢 (A romantic dream). [*FLM*]. Post-1623. Reprinted in Feng Menglong, *Mohanzhai dingben chuanqi*, vol. 3.

Feng Yuzheng 馮玉錚. "*Mudan ting Huanhun ji* daoyan zaji 牡丹亭還魂記導演札記 (Random notes on directing 'Peony pavilion' or 'The soul's return'). *Juying yuebao* 劇影月報, no. 2 (February 1988): 8–10.

Fu Xueyi 傅雪漪. "Yi, qu, shen, se: zhengli *Mudan ting* qianshi, jian tan Zang Jinshu gaiben" 意, 趣, 神, 色: 整理牡丹亭淺識兼談臧晉叔改本 (Thought, flavor, spirit, color: brief thoughts on arranging 'Peony pavilion' and a discussion of Zang Jinshu [Maoxun]'s adaptation). *Xiju xuexi* 戲劇學習, no. 2 (1982): 19–23.

Fu Yunzi 傅芸子. *Baichuan ji* 白川集 (White Stream's collected works). Tokyo: Bunkyudō shoten, 1943.

Gao Yu 高宇. *Gudian xiqu daoyanxue lunji* 古典戲曲導演學論集 (Collected essays on directorial practice in traditional drama). Beijing: Zhongguo xiju chubanshe, 1985.

Guben xiqu congkan 古本戲曲叢刊 (Collectanea of rare editions of traditional drama). [*GBXQ*]. First series. Shanghai: Shangwu yinshuguan, 1954; second series, 1955.

Gu Duhuang 顧篤璜. *Kunju shi bulun* 崑劇史補論 (Supplementary essays on the history of Kun opera). Huaiyang: Jiangsu guji chubanshe, 1987.

Guo Liang 郭亮. "Ming Qing Kunshan qiang de biaoyan yishu" 明清崑山腔的表演藝術 (Performance art for the Kunshan style in the Ming and Qing dynasties). *Xiqu yanjiu* 戲曲研究 1 (1980): 296–323.

——. "Kunqu biaoyan yishu de yidai fanben—*Shenyin jiangu lu*" 崑曲表演藝術的一代範本—審音鑑古錄 (One era's models for Kun opera performance art—'A record for parsing notes and mirroring great performances'). *Xiju bao* 戲劇報, nos. 19–20 (October 30, 1961): 54–59.

Han Shichang 韓世昌 (1898–1977). "Tan 'Youyuan' de biaoyan" 談遊園的表演 (Performing "Wandering in the Garden"). In *Beifang Kunqu juyuan jianyuan jinian tekan* 北方崑曲劇院建院紀念特刊 (Commemorative issue celebrating the reestablishment of the Northern Kun Opera Troupe), 33–34. N. p., June 22, 1957.

He Wei 何為. "Tang Xianzu, Shen Jing, Ye Tang" 湯顯祖, 沈璟, 葉堂. In *Tang Xianzu yanjiu lunwen ji* 湯顯祖研究論文集, edited by Jiangxi sheng wenxue yishu yanjiusuo, 463–79. Beijing: Zhongguo xiju chubanshe, 1984.

Hirose Reiko 廣瀬玲子. "Zō Mojun ni yoru *Botan tei Kankon ki* no kaihen ni tsuite" 臧懋循による牡丹亭還魂記の改編について (Zang Maoxun's adaptation of 'Peony pavilion' or 'The soul's return'). *Tōhōgaku* 東方學 81 (1991): 71–86.

——. "Mindai denki no bungaku: Tō Kenso no gikyoku ni okeru shinri hyōgen o chushin to shite" 明代傳奇の文學: 湯顯祖の戲曲における心理表現を中心として (Ming dynasty *chuanqi* drama: The centrality of the representation of mental states in the plays of Tang Xianzu). *Tōyō Bunka* 東洋文化 71 (December 1990): 55–90.

Hou Yushan Kunqupu 侯玉山崑曲譜 (Hou Yushang's dramatic scores for Kun opera). Edited by Guan Dequan 關德權 and Hou Ju 侯菊. Beijing: Zhongguo xiju chubanshe, 1994.

Hu Ji 胡忌, and Liu Zhizhong 劉致中. *Kunju fazhan shi* 崑劇發展史 (History of the development of Kun opera). Beijing: Zhongguo xiju chubanshe, 1989.

Hu Shanyuan 胡山源. "Xiannishe zhi qianhou" 仙霓社之前後 (The Rainbow of Immortals Society, from first to last). *Zhongguo Kunju yanjiuhui huikan* 中國崑劇 研究會會刊 3 (October 1987): 30–39.

Hu Shi 胡適. *Hu Shi gudian wenxue yanjiu lunji* 胡適古典文學研究論集 (Collected essays by Hu Shi on research of traditional literature). Shanghai: Shanghai guji chubanshe, 1988.

Hua Sheng 華生. "Zhongguo xiju wenhua de yi dashanbian—cong juzuojia zhongxinzhi dao yanyuan zhongxinzhi" 中國戲劇文化的一大嬗變—從劇作家中心制到演員中心制 (A big transition in the culture of Chinese drama: From a playwright-centered system to an actor-centered system). *Wenyi yanjiu* 文藝研究, no. 6 (1991): 85–92.

Hua Wenyi 華文漪. "Wo yan Du Liniang" 我演杜麗娘 (My performance of Du Liniang). *Shanxi xiju* 陝西戲劇, no. 12 (December 1982): 7–8.

Huang Derong 黃德榮. "*Mudan ting* zhong Shi Daogu xingxiang lüebian" 牡丹亭中 石道姑形象略辨 (A brief analysis of the character Sister Stone in 'Peony pavilion'). *Jiangxi shehui kexue* 江西社會科學, nos. 5–6 (1981): 135, 146.

Huang Zhigang 黃芝岡. *Tang Xianzu biannian pingzhuan* 湯顯祖編年評傳 (A critical chronological biography of Tang Xianzu). Beijing: Zhongguo xiju chubanshe, 1992.

Iwaki Hideo 岩城秀夫. "Baika to hankon: Soshoku ni okeru saiki no higan" 梅花と返魂: 蘇軾における再起の悲願 (Plum blossoms and the return of the soul: on Su Shi's prayer for recovery). *Nippon Chūgoku Gakkai hō* 日本中國學會報 30 (1979): 135–49.

——. "Nangi ni okeru Gogo no kinō" 南戲における呉語の機能 (Functions of Wu dialect in southern plays). In *Chūgoku gikyoku engeki kenkyū* 中國戲劇演劇研究 (Researches on Chinese drama and performance), 626–53. Tokyo: Sōbunsha, 1972.

Jicheng qupu. See Wang Jilie, and Liu Fuliang.

Jiang Jurong 江巨榮, "*Mudan ting* yanchu xiaoshi" 牡丹亭演出小史 (A short performance history of 'Peony pavilion'). *Shanghai xiju* 上海戲劇, no. 6 (June 1998): 1–15.

Jiang Xingyu 蔣星煜. "Tang Xianzu yanjiu de fansi" 湯顯祖研究的反思 (Reflections on research on Tang Xianzu). *Shanghai xiju* 上海戲劇, no. 1 (1987): 29–31.

——. "Zhou Mingtai zhi zhushu yu shoucang" 周明泰之著述與收藏 (The writings and collection of Zhou Mingtai). In *Zhongguo xiqu shi gouchen* 中國戲曲史鉤沉 (Lost items recovered pertaining to the history of Chinese opera), 289–97. Henan: Zhongzhou shuhuashe, 1982.

Jiao Chengyun 焦承允. *Renzi qupu* 壬子曲譜 (Master Ren's collection of dramatic scores). Taibei: Zhonghua shuju, 1972, 1980.

Jin Shi 金式. "Wuxin, liuxin, zhixin: tan Zhang Fuguang zai Xiang Kun 'Shi hua Jiao hua' zhong de biaoyan" 無心，留心，知心：談張富光在湘崑'拾畫叫畫'中的表演 (Unintending, attending, loving: Zhang Fuguang's performance of the Hunan Kun opera 'Recovering the Portrait and Calling to It'). *Hunan xiju* 湖南戲劇, no. 4 (1984): 25–26.

Jin Zhiren 金志仁. "Kunju ermeng" 崑劇二夢 (Kun opera's two dreams). *Nanjing daxue xuebao* 南京大學學報, no. 1 (1982): 35–40.

Kunqu daquan 崑曲大全 (A compendium of Kun operas). 4 vols. Compiled by Yi'an zhuren 怡庵主人. Shanghai: Shijie shuju, 1925.

Kunqu jijing 崑曲集淨 (Kun operas for the *jing* role). 2 vols. N. p., n. d. Copy in the Fudan University Library.

Kunqupu 崑曲譜 (Dramatic scores for Kun opera). N. p., n. d. Copy in the Fudan University Library.

Kunqu xindao 崑曲新導 (New guidance for Kun opera). 2 vols. Compiled by Liu Zhenxiu 劉振修. Shanghai: Zhonghua shuju, 1928.

Kunqu xinpu 崑曲新譜 (New scores for Kun opera). Preface dated 1927. Compiled by Lü Mengzhou 呂夢周. Shanghai: Huadong shuju, 1930.

Kunqu zhuijin 崑曲綴錦 (A patched brocade of Kun operas). Preface dated 1881. Compiled by Yang Yinliu 楊蔭瀏. Wuxi lithograph edition, 1926.

Li Dou 李斗 (fl. 1764-1795). *Yangzhou huafang lu* 揚州畫舫錄 (A record of the painted boats at Yangzhou). 18 vols. Preface dated 1796. Facsimile reprint of an edition published in 1797 by Ziran'an 自然盦. Taibei: Xuehai chubanshe, 1969.

Li Fang 李昉 (925–996) et al., comps. *Taiping guangji* 太平廣記 (Extensive gleanings of the reign of Great Tranquility). Jiajing (1522–1566) edition. 10 vols. Beijing: Zhonghua shuju, 1961. Reprint 1981.

Li Huimian 李惠綿. "Cong *Jingchai ji*, *Pipa ji* taiben xitan *Shenyin jiangu lu* de biaoyan meixue" 從荊釵記琵琶記臺本析探審音鑑古錄的表演美學 (Analysis of the aesthetics of performance in 'A record for parsing notes and mirroring great performances,' based on 'Thorn hairpin' and 'The lute'). In *Ming Qing xiqu guoji yantaohui lunwen ji* 明清戲曲國際研討會論文集, edited by Hua Wei 華瑋 and Wang Ailing 王瑷玲, vol. 2, 669–714. Taibei: Zhongyang yanjiuyuan Zhongguo wenzhe yanjiusuo choubeibu, 1998.

Li Ping 李平. "Liuluo Ouzhou de sanzhong wan Ming xiju sanchu xuanji de faxian" 流落歐洲的三種晚明戲劇散齣選集的發現 (Discovery of three late-Ming drama miscellanies lost in Europe). In *Haiwai guben wan Ming xiju xuanji sanzhong* 海外孤本晚明戲劇散齣選集三種 (Three unique editions of late Ming drama miscellanies from overseas), edited by Li Fuqing 李福清 (Boris Riftin) and Li Ping, 9–30. Shanghai: Shanghai guji chubanshe, 1993. Originally published in *Fudan xuebao* 復旦學報, no. 4 (1991): 79–90.

Li Ping, Jiang Jurong 江巨榮, and Huang Qiang 黃強, annots. "Pidian *Mudan ting ji* xu" 批點牡丹亭記序 (Preface to 'The punctuated peony pavilion, with evaluative commenatry'). *Yitan* 藝譚, no. 3 (December 1980): 32–33.

Li Yu 李漁 (1611–1680). *Li Liweng quhua* 李笠翁曲話 (Li Liweng's drama criticism). Edited by Chen Duo 陳多. Changsha: Hunan renmin chubanshe, 1980.

Lin Fengxiong 林鋒雄. "Bozai shumu suolu *Zhui baiqiu quanji* shiyi" 舶載書目所錄 綴白裘全集釋義 (A study of editions of 'A complete patched cloak of white fur' listed in catalogues of books imported [from China]). *Tenri daigaku gakuhō* 天理大學 學報 140 (September 1983): 9–21.

Lin Heyi 林鶴宜. "Ye tan *Zhui baiqiu* li de difang xi" 也談綴白裘裡的地方戲 (Regional operas in 'A patched cloak of white fur'). *Taida zhongwen xuebao* 臺大中文學報 5 (June 1992): 245–79.

——. "Wan Ming xiqu kanxing gaikuang" 晚明戲曲刊行概況 (An overview of late Ming publishers of drama). *Hanxue yanjiu* 漢學研究 9, no. 1 (June 1991): 287–328.

——. "Lu Eting Kunju yanchu shigao duhou" 陸蕚庭崑劇演出史稿讀後 (After reading Lu Eting's 'Draft history of Kun opera performance'). *Zhongguo wenxue yanjiu* 中國文學研究, no. 3 (May, 1989): 217–23.

Liu Hua 劉驊. "Qian Yi tan yici gudian aiqing gei ni kan" 錢熠談一次古典愛情給你看 (Qian Yi talks about presenting an ancient love for you to see). *Shanghai xiju* 上海戲劇, no. 6 (June 1998): 24–26.

Liu Hui 劉輝. "Lun Wu Shufu" 論吳舒鳧 (On Wu Shufu [Wushan]). *Xiju yishu* 戲劇藝術 37, no. 1 (1987): 108–17.

Lu Eting 陸蕚庭. "Qingdai quanbenxi yanchu shulun" 清代全本戲演出述論 (Discussion of performances of whole plays in the Qing dynasty). In *Ming Qing xiqu guoji yantaohui lunwen ji* 明清戲曲國際研討會論文集, edited by Hua Wei 華瑋 and

Wang Ailing 王瑷玲, vol. 1, 327–61. Taibei: Zhongyang yanjiuyuan Zhongguo wenzhe yanjiusuo choubeibu, 1998.

——. "Ye Tang yu Suzhou jutan" 葉堂與蘇州劇壇 (Ye Tang and Suzhou theater circles). In *Qingdai xiqujia congkao* 清代戲曲家叢考 (Collected research on Qing playwrights), 245–58. Shanghai: Xuelin chubanshe, 1995.

——. "Tan Kunju de ya he su" 談崑劇的雅和俗 (Elegant and popular in Kun opera), *Xiqu yanjiu* 戲曲研究 38 (1991): 19–33.

——. *Kunju yanchu shigao* 崑劇演出史稿 (Draft history of Kun opera performance). Shanghai: Shanghai wenyi chubanshe, 1980.

Lu Shulun 陸樹崙. "Xiqu bixu antou changshang liang shan qi mei" 戲曲必須案頭場上兩擅其美 (The play must have beauty on both desktop and stage). In his *Feng Menglong sanlun* 馮夢龍散論 (Essays on Feng Menglong), 23–46. Shanghai: Shanghai guji chubanshe, 1993. Originally published in *Wenxue yichan* 文學遺産, no. 3 (1980): 74–88.

——. *Feng Menglong yanjiu* 馮夢龍研究 (Research on Feng Menglong). Shanghai: Fudan daxue chubanshe, 1987.

Lu Shulun, and Li Ping 李平. "Feng Menglong lun xiqu biaoyan yishu" 馮夢龍論戲曲表演藝術 (Feng Menglong on the art of dramatic performance). *Xiju bao* 戲劇報, no. 13 (July 15, 1961): 32–35.

Lu Wei 陸煒. "Xiabanbu *Mudan ting* qiantan" 下半部牡丹亭淺談 (Preliminary thoughts on the final portion of 'Peony pavilion'). *Juying yuebao* 劇影月報, no. 9 (September 1992): 67–69.

Luo Bin 羅賓. "Shi zaota mingzhu haishi zhongyu yuanzhu?" 是糟蹋名著還是忠於原著 (Is it ruining a famous work or being faithful to the original?). *Henan xiju* 河南戲劇, no. 5 (1998): 5–7.

Luo Di 洛地. *Xiqu yu Zhejiang* 戲曲與浙江 (Drama and Zhejiang). Hangzhou: Zhejiang renmin chubanshe, 1991.

Luo Jintang 羅錦堂. *Zhongguo xiqu zongmu huibian* 中國戲曲總目彙編 (Comprehensive catalogue of Chinese drama). Hong Kong: Wanyou tushu gongsi, 1966.

Luo Zheng 駱正. "Tang Xianzu de mohu yuyan he xiangxiang tiandi: 'Youyuan' zhong de xinli fenxi" 湯顯祖的模糊語言和想像天地: 游園中的心理分析 (Tang Xianzu's obscure language and the realm of the imagination: psychological delineation in 'Wandering in the Garden'). *Xiqu yishu* 戲曲藝術, no. 3 (1994): 14–19.

——. "Tang Xianzu de xiangxiang yu Mei Lanfang de maodun biaoyan: Kunju 'Youyuan' de xinli fenxi" 湯顯祖的想像與梅蘭芳的矛盾表演: 崑劇游園的心理分析 (Tang Xianzu's imagination and the complex acting of Mei Lanfang: psychological delineation in the Kun opera 'Wandering in the garden'). *Xiju* 戲劇, no. 2 (1993): 79–85.

Mao Jin 毛晉 (1599–1659), comp. *Liushizhong qu* 六十種曲 (Sixty southern dramas). 12 vols. Taibei: Kaiming shudian, 1970.

Mei Dingzuo 梅鼎祚□(1549-1615). *Luqiu shishi ji* 鹿裘石室集 (Collected works from Deerpelt Stone Studio). 65 vols. Original prefaces dated 1574–1583. 1623 Chunxuanbaitang 春玄白堂 edition in the Library of Congress.

Mei Lanfang 梅蘭芳 (1894–1961). "Wo yan 'Youyuan Jingmeng'" 我演游園驚夢 (My performance of "Wandering in the Garden, Startled by a Dream"). In *Mei Lanfang wenji* 梅蘭芳文集 (Collected writings of Mei Lanfang), 60–79. Beijing: Zhongguo xiju chubanshe, 1962.

——. "Yige zhongyao de guanjian: 'Youyuan Jingmeng'" 一個重要的關鍵: 遊園驚夢 (A critical juncture: "Wandering in the Garden, Startled by a Dream"). In *Wutai shenghuo sishinian* 舞台生活四十年 (Forty years of life on the stage), edited by Xu Jichuan 許姬傳, vol. 1, 160–78. Beijing: Zhongguo xiju chubanshe, 1961, 1980. Reprinted in *Tang Xianzu yanjiu ziliao huibian* 湯顯祖研究資料匯編, compiled by Mao Xiaotong 毛效同, 1197–1219. Shanghai: Shanghai guji chubanshe, 1986.

——. "'Youyuan Jingmeng' cong wutai dao yinmu" 遊園驚夢從舞台到銀幕 ('Wandering in the Garden, Startled by a Dream': from the stage to the silver screen). In *Tang Xianzu yanjiu ziliao huibian* 湯顯祖研究資料匯編, compiled by Mao Xiaotong 毛效同, 1122–57. Shanghai: Shanghai guji chubanshe, 1986. Originally published in 1961 in four parts: *Xiju bao* 戲劇報, no. 4 (February 28): 36–38; no. 5 (March 17): 36–39; no. 6 (March 30): 36–39; nos. 7–8 (April 30): 67–71.

Ming Qing xiqu guoji yantaohui lunwen ji 明清戲曲國際研討會論文集 (Collected essays from the International Seminar on Ming Qing Drama). 2 vols. Edited by Hua Wei 華瑋, and Wang Ailing 王璦玲. Taibei: Zhongyang yanjiuyuan Zhongguo wenshe yanjiusuo choubeibu, 1998.

Mudan ting 牡丹亭 (Peony pavilion). Compiled by Hua Cuishen 華粹深, Yu Pingbo 俞平伯, and Zhu Chuanming 朱傳茗 et al. Beijing: Beifang kunju yuanben, 1953. Reprint (mimeographed copy), 1980. Copy in the script collection of the Shanghai Kun Opera Troupe.

Mudan ting qupu 牡丹亭曲譜 (Dramatic score for 'Peony pavilion'). 4 vols. Compiled by Yin Guishen 殷桂深 (fl. 1880–1908). Shanghai: Chaoji shuzhuang, 1921.

Murakami Tetsumi 村上哲見. "Gazoku kō" 雅俗考 (Elegant and common). In *Chūkoku ni okeru ningensei no tankyū* 中國における人間性の探究 (Researches on the problem of human existence in China), edited by Osamu Kanaya 金谷治, 455–77. Tokyo: Sōbunsha, 1983.

Negeyama Tōru 根ケ山徹. "*Kankon ki* hampon shitan" 還魂記板本試探 (Exploration of editions of 'The soul's return'), *Nippon Chūgoku Gakkai hō* 日本中國學會報 49 (1997): 149–64.

——. "Seidai ni okeru *Kankon ki* no enpen" 清代における還魂記の演變 (Evolution of performances of 'The soul's return' in the Qing dynasty). *Nippon Chūgoku Gakkai hō* 日本中國學會報 47 (1995): 164–179.

——. "*Kankon ki* ni okeru baika no keishō" 還魂記における梅花の形象 (The symbolic meaning of the plum blossom in 'The soul's return'). *Kyūshū Chūgoku Gakkai hō* 九州中國學會報 29 (1991): 63–82.

——. "*Kankon ki* ni okeru To shi no juyō" 還魂記における杜詩の受容 (Reception of Du [Fu's] poetry in 'The soul's return'). *Chūkoku bungaku ronshū* 中國文學論集 20, no. 12 (1991): 45–65.

——. "*Kankon ki* ni okeru Ryū Mubai zō no settei" 還魂記における柳夢梅像の設訂 (Creation of the character of Liu Mengmei in 'The soul's return'). *Nippon Chūgoku Gakkai hō* 日本中國學會報 41 (1989): 167–82.

Niu Shaoya 鈕少雅 (ca. 1560–ca. 1650), comp. *Gezheng Mudan ting Huanhun ji cidiao* 格正牡丹亭還魂記詞調 (Rectification of aria forms in 'Peony pavilion' or 'The soul's return'). 1694. Reprinted in *Nuanhongshi huike Linchuan simeng* 暖紅室彙刻臨川四夢, compiled by Liu Shiheng 劉世珩. 1919. Reprint, Yangzhou: Jiangsu Guangling guji keyinshe, 1990.

Nuanhongshi huike Linchuan simeng 暖紅室彙刻臨川四夢 (Combined edition of 'Linchuan's four dreams' from Warm Red Studio). 5 vols. Compiled by Liu Shiheng 劉世珩. 1919. Reprint, Yangzhou: Jiangsu Guangling guji keyinshe, 1990.

Pan Zhiheng 潘之恆 (1556–1622). *Pan Zhiheng quhua* 潘之恆曲話 (Pan Zhiheng's notes on theater). Compiled by Wang Xiaoyi 汪效倚. Beijing: Zhongguo xiju chubanshe, 1988.

Pengying qupu 蓬瀛曲譜 (Dramatic scores from the Faery Isles). Compiled by Taiwan xueshuyuan Kunqu yanjiusuo 台灣學術院崑曲研究所. Taibei: Zhonghua shuju, 1972.

Shanben xiqu congkan 善本戲曲叢刊 (Collectanea of rare editions of works on dramatic prosody). [*SBXQCK*]. Compiled by Wang Qiugui 王秋桂. 104 vols. Taibei: Xuesheng shuju, 1984–1987.

Shanshan ji. See *Xinke chuxiang dianban zengding Yuefu shanshan ji*.

Shanghai Kunju zhi 上海崑劇志 (Shanghai Kunju opera). Compiled by Shanghai wenhua yishu zhi bianzuan weiyuanhui 上海文化藝術志編纂委員會. Shanghai: Xinhua shudian, 1998.

Shen Jing 沈璟 (1553–1610). *Shen Jing ji* 沈璟集 (Collected works of Shen Jing). Compiled by Xu Shuofang 徐朔方. Shanghai: Shanghai guji chubanshe, 1991.

Shen Min 沈敏. "*Mudan ting* Shi Daogu xingxiang jianlun" 牡丹亭石道姑形象簡論 (A brief discussion of the appearance of Sister Stone in 'Peony pavilion'). Paper presented at a conference commemorating the 450th anniversary of Tang Xianzu's birth. Dalian, Heilongjiang. August 2000.

Shen Yifu 沈義芙. "*Mudan ting* 'Jingmeng' xiaoyi" 牡丹亭驚夢小議 (Minor elucidation of "The Interrupted Dream" in 'Peony pavilion'). *Jiangxi xiju* 江西戲劇, no. 4 (1982): 17–19.

Shenyin jiangu lu 審音鑑古錄 (A record for parsing notes and mirroring great performances). 1834. Compiled by Qinyinweng 琴隱翁. Reprinted in *Shanben xiqu congkan* 善本戲曲叢刊, compiled by Wang Qiugui 王秋桂, vols. 73–74. Taibei: Xuesheng shuju, 1984–1987.

Shixing yadiao Zhui baiqiu xinji hebian 時興雅調綴白裘新集合編 (New combined edition of 'A patched cloak of white fur,' currently popular Kun operas). [*ZBQXJ*]. 48 vols. Compiled by Wanhua zhuren 玩花主人 and Qian Decang 錢德蒼. 1777 reprint by Horgwentang 鴻文堂 of Baorentang 寶仁堂 edition. Reprinted in *Shanben xiqu congkan* 善本戲曲叢刊, compiled by Wang Qiugui 王秋桂, vols. 58–71. Taibei: Xuesheng shuju, 1984–1987.

Sulu qupu 粟廬曲譜 (Sulu's manual of dramatic scores). Compiled by Yu Zonghai 俞宗海 (1874–1930) and Yu Zhenfei 俞振飛 (1902–1993). Hong Kong: n. p., 1953.

Tang Baoxiang 唐葆祥. *Yu Zhenfei zhuan* 俞振飛傳 (Biography of Yu Zhenfei). Shanghai: Shanghai wenyi chubanshe, 1997.

Tang Sifu 唐斯復, and Ze Ping 仄平. "Yan 'chuanqi,' zai chuangzao yige chuanqi" 演傳奇再創造一個傳奇 (To perform '*chuanqi*' we will recreate a *chuanqi*). *Henan xiju* 河南戲劇, no. 5 (1998): 8–9. Originally published in *Wenxue bao* 文學報, April 16, 1998.

Tang Xianzu 湯顯祖 (1550–1617). *Tang Xianzu quanji* 湯顯祖全集 (Complete works of Tang Xianzu). 4 vols. Compiled by Xu Shuofang 徐朔方. Beijing: Beijing guji chubanshe, 1999.

——. *Mudan ting* 牡丹亭 (Peony pavilion). Annotated by Xu Shuofang 徐朔方 and Yang Xiaomei 楊笑梅. Beijing: Renmin wenxue chubanshe, 1982.

——. *Tang Xianzu shiwen ji* 湯顯祖詩文集 (Collected poetry and prose of Tang Xianzu). [*SWJ*]. 2 vols. Compiled by Xu Shuofang 徐朔方. Shanghai: Shanghai guji chubanshe, 1982.

——. *Tang Xianzu xiqu ji* 湯顯祖戲曲集 (Collected plays of Tang Xianzu). [*MDT*]. 2 vols. Edited by Qian Nanyang 錢南揚. Beijing: Zhonghua shuju, 1962. Reprint, Shanghai: Shanghai guji chubanshe, 1978.

Tang Xianzu yanjiu lunwen ji 湯顯祖研究論文集 (Collected essays on research on Tang Xianzu). Compiled by Jiangxi sheng wenxue yishu yanjiusuo 江西省文學藝術 研究所. Beijing: Zhongguo xiju chubanshe, 1984.

Tang Xianzu yanjiu ziliao huibian 湯顯祖研究資料匯編 (Sources for research on Tang Xianzu). [*TXZZL*]. 2 vols. Compiled by Mao Xiaotong 毛效同. Shanghai: Shanghai guji chubanshe, 1986.

Wanhuo qingyin. See *Xinjuan chuxiang dianban beidiao Wanhuo qingyin*.

Wang Anqi 王安祈. "Zailun Mingdai zhezixi" 再論明代折子戲 (Another look at Ming dynasty highlights). In *Mingdai xiqu wulun* 明代戲曲五論 (Five essays on Ming dynasty opera), 1–47. Taibei: Da'an chubanshe, 1990.

——. "Mingdai de siren jiayue yu jiazhai yanju" 明代的私人家樂與家宅演劇 (Private troupes and household performers in the Ming dynasty). *Gugong wenwu yuekan* 故宮文物月刊 7, no. 12 (March 1990): 64–77.

——. *Mingdai chuanqi zhi juchang ji qi yishu* 明代傳奇之劇場及其藝術 (The theater and its art in Ming dynasty southern drama). Taibei: Xuesheng shuju, 1985.

Wang Gulu 王古魯. *Mingdai Huidiao xiqu sanchu jiyi* 明代徽調戲曲散齣輯佚 (Collected fragments of detached scenes from Anhui operas of the Ming dynasty). Shanghai: Shanghai gudian wenxue chubanshe, 1956.

Wang Jide 王驥德 (d. ca. 1623). *Wang Jide Qulü* 王驥德曲律 (Wang Jide's 'Rules for *qu*'). Annotated by Chen Duo 陳多 and Ye Changhai 葉長海. Changsha: Hunan renmin chubanshe, 1983. *Qulü* also reprinted in *Zhongguo gudian xiqu lunzhu jicheng* 中國古典戲曲論著集成, compiled by Zhongguo xiqu yanjiuyuan 中國戲曲研究院, vol. 4, 43–191. Beijing: Zhongguo xiju chubanshe, 1959.

Wang Jilie 王季烈, comp. *Yuzhong qupu* 與衆曲譜 (Dramatic scores for the masses). 8 vols. Shanghai: Shanghai yinshuguan, 1947. Reprint, Taibei: Shangwu yinshuguan, 1977.

Wang Jilie 王季烈, and Liu Fuliang 劉富樑, comps. *Jicheng qupu* 集成曲譜 (Assembled dramatic scores). 32 vols. Preface dated 1923. Shanghai: Shangwu yinshuguan, 1947.

Wang Shifu 王實甫 (fl. 13th century). *Xixiang ji* 西廂記 (The western wing). Annotated by Wang Jisi 王季思. Shanghai: Shanghai guji chubanshe, 1963, 1978.

Wang Shoutai 王守泰, ed. *Kunqu qupai ji taoshu fanli ji* 崑曲曲牌及套數範例集 (Collected models of aria patterns and sequences for Kun opera). 2 vols. Shanghai: Shanghai guji chubanshe, 1994.

Wang Xichun 王錫純 (fl. late Qing). *Eyunge qupu* 遏雲閣曲譜 (Cloud-stopping Pavilion's dramatic scores). 12 vols. Preface dated 1870. Shanghai: Shanghai Zhaoyitang shuju, 1893.

Wang Zhizhang 王芝章. *Qing Shengpingshu zhilüe* 清昇平署志略 (Record of the Shengpingshu of the Qing dynasty). 2 vols. Shanghai: Shangwu yinshuguan, 1937.

Wu Mei 吳梅 (1884–1939). *Guqu zhutan* 顧曲麈談 (Leisurely talks about reading drama). In *Wu Mei xiqu lunwen ji* 吳梅戲曲論文集 (Wu Mei's collected works on drama), edited by Wang Weimin 王衛民, 1–114. Beijing: Zhonghua xiju chubanshe, 1983.

Wu Shuyin 吳書蔭. "Ming chuanqi qumu gouchen" 明傳奇曲目鉤沉 (Recovered items from the Ming repertoire of southern dramas). *Xiqu yanjiu* 戲曲研究 40 (1992): 157–74.

Wu Wushan sanfu heping Mudan ting Huanhun ji 吳吳山三婦合評牡丹亭還魂記 (Wu Wushan's three wives' combined commentary to 'Peony pavilion' or 'The soul's return'). 1694. Copy in Tōyō Bunka Kenkyūjo 東洋文化研究所. Reprinted in *Nuanhongshi huike Linchuan simeng* 暖紅室彙刻臨川四夢. Compiled by Liu Shiheng 劉世珩. 1919. Reprint, Yangzhou: Jiangsu Guangling guji keyinshe, 1990.

Wu Xinlei 吳新雷. "*Zhui baiqiu* de lailong qumo" 綴白裘的來龍去脈 (The background of 'A patched cloak of white fur'). *Nanjing daxue xuebao* 南京大學學報, no. 3 (August 1983): 36–43.

Xi kao 戲考 (A selection of Beijing opera texts). 10 vols. Edited by Wang Dacuo 王大錯. Shanghai: Zhonghua tushuguan, 1913–1924. Reprint, Taibei: Liren shuju, 1980.

Xinjuan chuxiang dianban beidiao Wanhuo qingyin 新鐫出像點板北調萬壑清音 (Newly engraved, illustrated northern plays, 'Clear notes from ten thousand valleys,' with rhythmic notation). 1624. Compiled by Zhiyun jushi 止雲居士. Reprinted in *Shanben xiqu congkan* 善本戲曲叢刊, compiled by Wang Qiugui 王秋桂, vols. 48–49. Taibei: Xuesheng shuju, 1984–1987.

Xinjuan chuxiang dianban Yichun jin 新鐫出像點板怡春錦 (Newly engraved, illustrated 'Brocade of spring delights,' with rhythmic notation). 6 vols. Chongzhen (1628–1644) edition. Compiled by Chonghe jushi 沖和居士. Reprinted in *Shanben xiqu congkan* 善本戲曲叢刊, compiled by Wang Qiugui 王秋桂, vols. 19–20. Taibei: Xuesheng shuju, 1984–1987.

Xinjuan xiuxiang pingdian Xuanxuepu 新鐫繡像評點玄雪譜 (Newly engraved, illustrated 'Dark snow collection,' with punctuation and evaluative commentary). 4 vols.

Chongzhen (1628–1644) edition. Compiled by Chulan renren 鋤蘭忍人. Reprinted in *Shanben xiqu congkan* 善本戲曲叢刊, compiled by Wang Qiugui 王秋桂, vols. 50–51. Taibei: Xuesheng shuju, 1984–1987.

Xinkan fenlei chuxiang taozhen xuancui Yuefu hongshan 新刊分類出像陶真選粹樂府紅珊 (Newly printed, classified, and illustrated selected highlights of *taozhen*, 'Red corals from the Music Bureau'). Preface dated 1602. Compiled by Qin Huai moke 琴淮墨客. Reprinted in *Shanben xiqu congkan* 善本戲曲叢刊, compiled by Wang Qiugui 王秋桂, vols. 10–11. Taibei: Xuesheng shuju, 1984–1987.

Xinke chuxiang dianban shishang Kunqiang zaqu Zuiyi qing 新刻出像點板時尚崑腔雜曲 醉怡情 (Newly carved, illustrated assortment of *qu* in the currently popular Kun style, 'Feelings of drunken delight,' with rhythmic notation). 8 vols. Qianlong (1736–1795) reprint of Ming edition by Zhihetang 致和堂, Suzhou. Compiled by Qingxi gulu diaosou 青溪菰蘆釣叟. Reprinted in *Shanben xiqu congkan* 善本戲曲叢刊, compiled by Wang Qiugui 王秋桂, vols. 54–55. Taibei: Xuesheng shuju, 1984–1987.

Xinke chuxiang dianban zengding Yuefu shanshan ji 新刻出像點板增訂樂府珊珊集 (Newly carved, illustrated and expanded 'Collocation of corals from the Music Bureau,' with rhythmic notation). 4 vols. Late Ming edition. Compiled by Zhou Zhibiao 周芝標. Reprinted in *Shanben xiqu congkan* 善本戲曲叢刊, compiled by Wang Qiugui 王秋桂, vol. 14. Taibei: Xuesheng shuju, 1984–1987.

Xu Chongjia 徐崇嘉 et al., comps. *Kunshan xian xiqu ziliao huibian* 崑山縣戲曲資料匯編 (Sources for opera in Kunshan district). 2 vols. Mimeographed copy. Kunshan, n. d.

Xu Fuming 徐扶明. "Zhezixi jianlun" 折子戲簡論 (A brief discussion of highlights), *Xiqu yishu* 戲曲藝術, no. 2 (1989): 62–68.

——. *Mudan ting yanjiu ziliao kaoshi* 牡丹亭研究資料考釋 (An investigation and elucidation of sources for research on 'Peony pavilion'). [*MDTZL*]. Shanghai: Shanghai guji chubanshe, 1987.

Xu Lingyun 徐凌雲 (1885–1965). *Kunju biaoyan yide* 崑劇表演一得 (My minor success in Kun opera performance). Edited by Guan Ji'an 管際安 and Lu Jianzhi 陸兼之. Suzhou: Suzhou daxue chubanshe, 1993. Originally published in 3 vols. Shanghai: Shanghai xinwenyi chubanshe, 1959.

Xu Shipi 徐世丕. "Feng Menglong xiqu chuangzuo lilun jianlun" 馮夢龍戲曲創作 理論簡論 (A brief discussion of Feng Menglong's theory of dramatic creation). *Xiqu yanjiu* 戲曲研究 31 (1989): 32–61.

Xu Shuofang 徐朔方. comp. *Wan Ming qujia nianpu* 晚明曲家年譜 (Chronological biographies of late Ming playwrights). 3 vols. Hangzhou: Zhejiang guji chubanshe, 1993.

——. *Yuanqu xuanjia Zang Maoxun* 元曲選家臧懋循 (Zang Maoxun: collector of Yuan dramas). Beijing: Zhongguo xiju chubanshe, 1985.

——. *Lun Tang Xianzu ji qita* 論湯顯祖及其他 (On Tang Xianzu and other subjects). Shanghai: Shanghai guji chubanshe, 1983.

Xu Wei 徐渭. (1521–1593). *Nanci xulu* 南詞敘錄 (Account of the southern style of drama). Preface dated 1559. In *Zhongguo gudian xiqu lunzhu jicheng* 中國古典戲曲論

著集成, compiled by Zhongguo xiqu yanjiuyuan 中國戲曲研究院, vol. 3, 233–56. Beijing: Zhongguo xiju chubanshe, 1959.

Xuanxuepu. See *Xinjuan xiuxiang pingdian Xuanxuepu*.

Yagisawa Hajime 八木澤元. "Zang Maoxun de xiqu yanjiu" 臧懋循的戲曲研究 (On Zang Maoxun's plays). In *Mingdai juzuojia kaolüe* 明代劇作家考略, translated by Luo Jintang 羅錦堂, 449–74. Hong Kong: Longmen, 1977. Originally published as "Zō Mojun no gikyoku kaitei" 臧懋循の戯曲改訂 (Zang Maoxun's revisions of dramas) in *Mindai gekisakka kenkyū* 明代劇作家研究 (Researches on Ming dynasty playwrights). Tokyo: Kōdansha, 1959.

——. "*Botan tei* no hampon ni kansuru ikkōsatsu: Zō Mojun kaiteihon to Bō shi shubokuhon to no kankei ni tsuite" 牡丹亭の版本に關する一考察: 臧懋循改訂本と茅氏朱墨本との關係に就いて (An investigation concerning woodblock editions of 'Peony pavilion': On the relationship of the Mao brother's red ink edition to Zang Maoxun's adaptation). *Shibun* 斯文19, no. 11 (1937): 61–65.

Yan Changke 顏長柯. "Tantan zhezixi" 談談折子戲 (On highlights). *Zhonghua xiqu* 中華戲曲, no. 6 (August 1988): 242–55.

Yang Baihua 楊白華. "Shilun *Mudan ting* 'Guishu'" 試論牡丹亭閨塾 (On "The Schoolroom" in 'Peony pavilion'). *Jianghai xuekan* 江海學刊, no. 5 (1962): 35, 41–42.

Yang Yinliu 楊蔭瀏, comp. *Kunqu zhuijin* 崑曲綴錦 (Patched brocades of Kun arias). Preface dated 1881. Wuxi lithograph edition, 1926.

Yang Zhenliang 楊振良. *Mudan ting yanjiu* 牡丹亭研究 (Researches on 'Peony pavilion'). Taibei: Yiwen tushu gongsi, 1992.

Ye Changhai 葉長海. *Zhongguo xijuxue shigao* 中國戲劇學史稿 (Draft history of Chinese dramaturgy). Shanghai: Shanghai wenyi chubanshe, 1986.

Ye Shaode 葉紹德, ed. *Tang Disheng xiqu xinshang* 唐滌生戲曲欣賞 (An appreciation of dramas by Tang Disheng). Hong Kong: Xianggang zhoukan chubanshe, 1986.

Ye Tang 葉堂. (ca. 1722–ca. 1795), comp. *Nashuying qupu Linchuan simeng chuanji* 納書楹曲譜臨川四夢全集 (Complete dramatic scores of 'Linchuan's four dreams' for the bookshelf). 5 vols. 1791 woodblock edition. Reprint, Yangzhou: Jiangsu Guangling guji keyinshe, 1990.

Yichun jin. See *Xinjuan chuxiang dianban Yichun jin*.

Yoshikawa Kōjirō 吉川幸郎. *Yuan zaju yanjiu* 元雜劇研究 (Researches on Yuan drama). Translated by Zheng Qingmao 鄭清茂 (Taibei: Yiwen yinshuguan, 1960). Originally published as *Gen zatsugeki kenkyū* 元雜劇研究. Tokyo: Iwanami shoten, 1948.

Yu Pingbo 俞平伯. "Zatan *Mudan ting* 'Jingmeng'" 雜談牡丹亭驚夢 (Random remarks on "The Interrupted Dream" in 'Peony pavilion'). *Xiju luncong* 戲劇論叢, no. 3 (1957): 81–89. Reprinted in *Tang Xianzu yanjiu ziliao huibian* 湯顯祖研究資料匯編, compiled by Mao Xiaotong 毛效同, 1002–15. Shanghai: Shanghai guji chubanshe, 1986.

Yu Zhenfei 俞振飛 (1902–1992). "Wuxian shenqing Du Liniang" 無限深情杜麗娘 (Du Liniang: passion without limit). In *Yu Zhenfei yishu lunji* 俞振飛藝術論集 (Collected essays on the art of Yu Zhenfei), edited by Wang Jiazhao 王家照 et al., 197–202. Shanghai: Shanghai wenyi chubanshe, 1985.

Yuzhong qupu. See Wang Jilie.

Yuefu hongshan. See *Xinkan fenlei chuxiang taozhen xuancui Yuefu hongshan*.

Yuefu shanshan ji. See *Xinke chuxiang dianban zengding Yuefu shanshan ji*.

Yue lu yin 月露音 (Sounds drenched in moonlight). Wanli (1573–1620) edition. 4 vols. Compiled by Lingxuzi 凌虛子. Reprinted in *Shanben xiqu congkan* 善本戲曲叢刊, compiled by Wang Qiugui 王秋桂, vols. 15–16. Taibei: Xuesheng shuju, 1984–1987.

Yue Meiti 岳美緹. *Wo—yige gudan de nüxiaosheng* 我—一個孤單的女小生 (Me—a solitary female *xiaosheng*). Shanghai: Wenhui chubanshe, 1994.

——. "Nuli zhanxian renwu neixin de mei" 努力展現人物內心的美 (Energetically depict the character's inner beauty). *Shanxi xiju* 陝西戲劇, no. 12 (December 1982): 9–12.

Zang Maoxun 臧懋循 [Jinshu 晉叔] (1550–1620), ed. *Huanhun ji* 還魂記 (The soul's return). [*HHJ*]. In *Yuming xinci, sizhong* 玉茗新詞四種 (White Camelia Hall's four new plays). 1618. Wanli woodblock edition in the National Central Library, Taiwan. Microfilm at University of Michigan.

——, ed. and comp. *Yuanqu xuan* 元曲選 (A selection of Yuan dramas). 4 vols. Beijing: Zhonghua shuju, 1958, 1979.

Zeng Yongyi 曾永義. "Zhongguo gudian xiju juese gaishuo" 中國古典戲劇腳色概說 (Overview of role categories in traditional Chinese drama). *Shuosu wenxue* 說俗文學 (Popular literature). Taibei: Lianjing chuban shiye gongsi, 1980, 233–95.

———. *Zhongguo gudian xiju lunji* 中國古典戲劇論集 (Collected essays on traditional Chinese drama). Taibei: Lianjing chunban shiye gongsi, 1975.

Zhang Jing 張敬. "Chuanqi juese zhi peida ji changmian zhi anpai 傳奇腳色之配搭及 場面之安排 (Role pairings and scene arrangement in southern dramas). *Hanxue yanjiu* 漢學研究 6, no. 1 (June 1988): 95–103.

——. "Tang Ruoshi *Mudan ting Huanhun ji* qingjie peitao zhi fenxi" 湯若士牡丹亭 還魂記情節配套之分析 (Analysis of aria sequences that accompany the plot of Tang Xianzu's 'Peony pavilion' or 'The soul's return'). *Dong Wu wenshi xuebao* 東吳文史學報 1 (March 1976): 1–21.

——. "Nanqu liantao shuli" 南曲聯套數例 (Explanatory examples for the linking of sequences in southern drama). *Wen shi zhe xuebao* 文史哲學報 14–15 (1965–66): 345–95.

——. *Ming Qing chuanqi daolun* 明清傳奇導論 (Introduction to southern drama in the Ming and Qing dynasties). Taibei: Dongfang shudian, 1964.

Zhang Xiulian 張秀蓮, "Tang-Shen zhi zheng wailun" 湯沈之爭外論 (An outside perspective on the Tang-Shen debate). In *Tang Xianzu yanjiu lunwen ji* 湯顯祖研究論文集, compiled by Jiangxi sheng wenxue yishu yanjiusuo, 480–99. Beijing: Zhongguo xiju chubanshe, 1984.

Zhang Yuanhe 張元和, *Kunqu shenduan shipu* 崑曲身段試譜 (A manual of movements for Kun opera). N. p., 1972.

Zhao Jingshen 趙景深. *Xiqu bitan* 戲曲筆談 (Notes penned on drama). Shanghai: Shanghai guji chubanshe, 1962.

——. *Ming Qing qutan* 明清曲談 (Talks on Ming and Qing drama). Shanghai: Zhonghua shuju, 1959.

——. *Yuan Ming nanxi kaolüe* 元明南戲考略 (Notes on southern drama in the Yuan and Ming). Beijing: Zuojia chubanshe, 1958.

Zhao Junjie 趙俊玠. "You shi yiqu *Fengliu meng*—guanyu *Mudan ting* ji qi Huaju gaibian" 又是一曲風流夢—關於牡丹亭及其華劇改編 (Another 'Romantic dream': 'Peony pavilion' and its adaptation as Hua opera). *Dangdai xiju* 當代戲劇, no. 4 (July 1994): 9–12.

Zhao Shanlin 趙山林. *Zhongguo xiqu guanzhongxue* 中國戲曲觀衆學 (The audience for Chinese opera). Shanghai: Huadong shifan daxue, 1990.

Zhenfei qupu 振飛曲譜 ([Yu] Zhenfei's dramatic scores). Compiled by Yu Zhenfei 俞振飛 . Shanghai: Shanghai wenyi chubanshe, 1982.

Zheng Zhenduo 鄭振鐸. "Zhongguo xiqu de xuanben" 中國戲曲的選本 (Chinese drama miscellanies). In *Zhongguo wenxue yanjiu* 中國文學研究 (Research on Chinese literature), vol. 2, 1–32. Shanghai: Shanghai shudian, 1981.

Zhongguo gudian xiqu lunzhu jichen 中國古典戲曲論著集成 (A corpus of critical writings on classical Chinese drama). [*ZGGD*]. 10 vols. Compiled by Zhongguo xiqu yanjiuyuan 中國戲曲研究院. Beijing: Zhongguo xiju chubanshe, 1959.

Zhongguo gudian xiqu xiaoshuo yanjiu suoyin 中國古典戲曲小說研究索引 (Index of research on Chinese traditional drama and fiction). Compiled by Yu Manling 于曼玲. Guangzhou: Guangdong gaodeng jiaoyu chubanshe, 1992.

Zhongguo yinyue shupuzhi 中國音樂書譜志 (Catalogue of books and notated sources on Chinese music). Compiled by Zhongguo yishu yanjiuyuan yinyue yanjiusuo ziliaoshi 中國藝術研究院音樂研究所資料室. Beijing: Renmin yinyue chubanshe, 1984.

Zhongyang yanjiuyuan lishi yuyansuo suocang suqu 中央研究院歷史語言研究所所藏俗曲 (Popular songs stored at the National Research Institute of History and Philology [Academia Sinica]). Ca. 10,000 vols. Compiled by Liu Fu 劉復. Microfilm in Harvard-Yenching Library.

Zhou Miaozhong 周妙中. *Qingdai xiqu shi* 清代戲曲史 (History of drama in the Qing dynasty). Zhengzhou: Zhongzhou guji chubanshe, 1987.

——. "Jiangnan fangqu luyao" 江南訪曲錄要 (Investigations of drama in Jiangnan). *Wenshi* 文史 2 (1963): 209–53; 12 (1981): 246–59.

Zhou Mingtai 周明泰. *Qing Shengpingshu cundang shili manchao* 清昇平署存檔事例漫抄 (Random notes from the archives of the Shengpingshu). Taibei: Wenhai chubanshe, 1970.

Zhou Weipei 周維培. *Qupu yanjiu* 曲譜研究 (Researches on song registers). Nanjing: Jiangsu guji chubanshe, 1997.

Zhou Yibai 周貽白. *Xiqu yanchang lunzhu jishi* 戲曲演唱論著輯釋 (Interpretive notes for critical writings on Chinese drama). Beijing: Zhongguo xiju chubanshe, 1962, 1980.

——. *Zhongguo xiju shi* 中國戲劇史 (A history of Chinese drama). 3 vols. Shanghai: Zhonghua shuju, 1953).

Zhou Yude 周育德. *Tang Xianzu lungao* 湯顯祖論稿 (Draft essays on Tang Xianzu). Beijing: Wenhua yishu chubanshe, 1991.

——. "Tang Xianzu juzuo de Ming Qing gaiben" 湯顯祖劇作的明清改本 (Ming and Qing adaptations of Tang Xianzu's plays). *Wenxian* 文獻 15 (1983): 21–41.

——. "*Xiaohan xinyong* zhaji" 消寒新□劄□(Notes on 'New odes to disperse the cold'). *Xiqu yanjiu* 戲曲研究 5 (1982): 245–52.

——. "Hua shuo Zang Jinshu gaiben 'Simeng'" 話說臧晉叔改本四夢 (Remarks on Zang Jinshu's [Maoxun's] revised texts of the 'Four dreams'). *Jiangxi xiju* 江西戲劇, no. 3 (1982): 14–18.

Zhou Yude, ed. and annot. *Xiaohan xinyong* 消寒新□(New odes to disperse the cold). 4 vols. 1795 Hongwenge 宏文閣 edition. Compiled by Tieqiao shanren 鐵橋山人 et al. Beijing: Zhongguo xiqu yishu zhongxin, 1986.

Zhu Wanshu 朱萬曙. "Changshang zhi qu de changdaozhe yu shijianzhe—chongping Shen Jing de xiqu lilun ji chuangzuo" 場上之曲的倡導者與實踐者—重評沈璟的戲曲理論及創作 (Advocate and practitioner of "drama for the stage": a reappraisal of Shen Jing's dramatic criticism and oeuvre). *Xiqu yanjiu* 戲曲研究 27, no. 9 (1988): 185–207.

Zhui baiqiu 綴白裘 (A patched cloak of white fur). 12 vols. Edited by Wang Xieru 汪協如. Shanghai: Zhonghua shuju, 1955.

Zhui baiqiu xinji hebian. See *Shixing yadiao Zhui baiqiu xinji hebian*.

Zidishu xuan 子弟書選 (Selection of scions' tales). Compiled by Zhongguo quyi gongzuozhe xiehui Liaoning fenhui 中國曲藝工作者協會遼寧分會. N.p., 1979.

Zuiyi qing. See *Xinke chuxiang dianban shishang Kunqiang zaqu Zuiyi qing*.

Works in European Languages

"A Symposium on *Peony Pavilion*," *The Threepenny Review* 78 (summer 1999): 31–34.

Bakhtin, M.M. *The Dialogic Imagination: Four Essays by M. M. Bakhtin*. Edited by Michael Holquist. Austin: University of Texas Press, 1990.

Barish, Jonas. *The Anti-theatrical Prejudice*. Berkeley: University of California Press, 1981.

Beckerman, Bernard. *Theatrical Presentation*. New York: Routledge, 1990.

Besio, Kimberly. "Gender, Loyalty, and the Reproduction of the Wang Zhaozhun Legend: Some Social Ramifications of Drama in the Late Ming," *Journal of the Economic and Social History of the Orient* 40, no. 2 (1997): 251–82.

——. "From Stage to Page: Moments in the Textual Reproduction of Two Yuan Plays." Paper presented at the annual meeting of the Association for Asian Studies, Chicago, Illinois, March 1997.

Bickford, Maggie. *Ink Plum: The Making of a Chinese Scholar Painting Genre*. Cambridge and New York: Cambridge University Press, 1996.

——, ed. *Bones of Jade, Soul of Ice: The Flowering Plum in Chinese Art*. New Haven: Yale University Art Gallery, 1985.

Birch, Cyril. *Scenes for Mandarins: The Elite Theater of the Ming*. New York: Columbia University Press, 1995.

——. trans. *The Peony Pavilion*. [*PP*]. Bloomington: Indiana University Press, 1980.

Bourdieu, Pierre. *The Field of Cultural Production: Essays on Art and Literature*. Edited and with an introduction by Randal Johnson. New York: Columbia University Press, 1993.

Burkus-Chasson, Anne. "Disquieting Doubles: The Body in the Portrait and the Illusory Shape of the Self in *The Peony Pavilion*." In *Images in Exchange: Cultural Transactions in Chinese Pictorial Arts*, edited by Richard Vinograd. Berkeley: University of California Press, forthcoming.

Bush, Susan, and Hsio-yen Shih, comps. *Early Chinese Texts on Painting*. Cambridge: Harvard University Press, 1985.

Cahill, James C. *The Painter's Practice: How Artists Lived and Worked in Traditional China*. New York: Columbia University Press, 1994.

——. *The Compelling Image*. Cambridge: Harvard University Press, 1982.

Chang, H. C. *Chinese Literature: Popular Fiction and Drama*. Edinburgh: Edinburgh University Press, 1973.

Chang, Kang-i Sun. *The Evolution of Chinese Tz'u Poetry*. Princeton: Princeton University Press, 1980.

Chartier, Roger. *Forms and Meanings: Texts, Performances, and Audiences from Codex to Computer*. Philadelphia: University of Pennsylvania Press, 1995.

——. *The Order of Books: Readers, Authors, and Libraries in Europe between the Fourteenth and Eighteenth Centuries*. Trans. Lydia G. Cochrane. Stanford: Stanford University Press, 1994.

Chen, Jingmei. "The Dream World of Love-Sick Maidens: A Study of Womens' Responses to *Peony Pavilion*." Ph.D. diss., University of California at Los Angeles, 1996.

Ch'en Li-li, trans. *Master Tung's Western Chamber Romance*. Cambridge: Cambridge University Press, 1976. Reprint, New York: Columbia University Press. 1994.

Cheng Pei-kai. "Reality and Imagination: Li Chih and T'ang Hsien-tsu in Search of Authenticity." Ph.D. diss., Yale University, 1980.

Citron, Marcia J. *Opera on Screen*. New Haven: Yale University Press, 2000.

Clément, Catherine. *Opera, or the Undoing of Women*. Translated by Betsy Wing. Minneapolis: University of Minnesota Press, 1988.

Clunas, Craig. *Superfluous Things: Material Culture and Social Status in Early Modern China*. Urbana and Chicago: University of Illinois Press, 1991.

Crump, J. I. "Giants in the Earth: Yüan Drama as Seen by Ming Critics." In *Chinese and Japanese Music Dramas*, edited by J. I. Crump and William P. Malm, 1–63. Ann Arbor: Center for Chinese Studies, 1975.

de Bary, Wm. Theodore. "Individualism and Humanitarianism in Late Ming Thought." In *Self and Society in Ming Thought*, edited by Wm. Theodore de Bary, 145–247. New York: Columbia University Press, 1970.

——, ed. *Self and Society in Ming Thought*. New York: Columbia University Press, 1970.

de Certeau, Michel. *The Practice of Everyday Life*. Trans. Steven Rendall. Berkeley: University of California Press, 1988.

Dolby, William. *A History of Chinese Drama*. London: Paul Elek, 1976.

Fei, Faye Chunfang, ed. and trans. *Chinese Theories of Theater and Performance from Confucius to the Present*. Ann Arbor: The University of Michigan Press, 1999.

Frankel, Ch'ung-ho Chang. "The Practice of *K'un-ch'ü* Singing from the 1920s to the 1960s." *Chinoperl Papers* 6 (1976): 82–92.

Frankel, Hans H. "The Plum Tree in Chinese Poetry." *Asiatische Studien* 6 (1952): 88–115.

Goldman, Andrea S. "The Nun Who Wouldn't Be: Representations of Female Desire in Two Performance Genres of 'Si fan.'" *Late Imperial China* 22, no. 1 (June 2001): 71–138.

Hall, David D. Review of *Highbrow/Lowbrow: The Emergence of Cultural Hierarchy in America*, by Lawrence W. Levine. *Reviews in American History* 18 (1990): 10–14.

Hanan, Patrick. *The Chinese Vernacular Story*. Cambridge: Harvard University Press, 1981.

——. "The Nature and Contents of the *Yüeh-fu hung-shan*," *Bulletin of the School of Oriental and African Studies* 26 (1963): 346–61. Translated by Wang Qiugui in *Zhongwai wenxue* 4, no. 9 (1976): 116–42.

Hegel, Robert E. *Reading Illustrated Fiction in Late Imperial China*. Stanford: Stanford University Press, 1998.

Henry, Eric. "The Motif of Recognition in Early China." *Harvard Journal of Asiatic Studies* 47, no. 1 (1987): 5–30.

Hornby, Richard. *Script into Performance: A Structuralist Approach*. New York: Applause Books, 1977, 1995.

Hsia, C. T. "Time and the Human Condition in the Plays of Tang Hsien-tsu." In *Self and Society in Ming Thought*, edited by Wm. Theodore de Bary, 249–90. New York: Columbia University Press, 1970.

Hua Wei. "The Search for Great Harmony: A Study of Tang Xianzu's Dramatic Art." Ph.D. diss., University of California at Berkeley, 1991.

Idema, Wilt, and Stephen H. West. *Chinese Theater 1100–1450: A Source Book*. Wiesbaden: Franz Steiner Verlag, 1982.

Iopollo, Grace. *Revising Shakespeare*. Cambridge: Harvard University Press, 1991.

Ko, Dorothy. *Teachers of the Inner Chambers: Women and Culture in Seventeenth Century China*. Stanford: Stanford University Press, 1994.

Laing, Ellen Johnston. "Chinese Palace-Style Poetry and the Depiction of *A Palace Beauty*." *The Art Bulletin* 72, no. 2 (1990): 284–95.

Lam, Joseph S. C. "Notational Representation and Contextual Constraints: How and Why Did Ye Tang Notate His Kun Opera Arias?" In *Themes and Variations: Writings on Music in Honor of Rulan Chao Pian*, edited by Bell Yung and Joseph S. C. Lam, 31–44. Cambridge, Mass.: Harvard University Press, 1994.

Leung, K. C., trans. *Hsu Wei as Drama Critic: An Annotated Translation of the Nan-tz'u hsü-lu*. Eugene: University of Oregon Press, 1988.

Levenson, Joseph R. "The Amateur Ideal in Ming and Early Ch'ing Society: Evidence from Painting." In *Confucian China and Its Modern Fate: A Trilogy*, 15–43. Berkeley: The University of California Press, 1968.

Levine, Lawrence W. *Highbrow/Lowbrow: The Emergence of Cultural Hierarchy in America*. Cambridge: Harvard University Press, 1994.

Levy, Howard S. *Harem Favorites of an Illustrious Celestial*. Taichung: Chungtai Printing Co., Ltd, 1958.

Li, Wai-yee. *Enchantment and Disenchantment: Love and Illusion in Chinese Literature*. Princeton: Princeton University Press, 1993.

Lin, Shuen-fu. "Chia Pao-yu's First Visit to the Land of Illusion: An Analysis of a Literary Dream in Interdisciplinary Perspective." *Chinese Literature: Essays, Articles, Reviews* 14 (1992): 77–106.

Liu, Marjorie Bang-ray. "Aesthetic Principles and Ornamental Style in Chinese Classical Opera—Kunqu." *Selected Reports in Enthnomusicology* 4 (1983): 29–61.

——. "Tradition and Change in Kunqu Opera." Ph.D diss., University of California at Los Angeles, 1976.

Lu, Tina. *Persons, Roles, and Minds: Identity in Peony Pavilion and Peach Blossom Fan*. Stanford: Stanford University Press, 2001.

Lynn, Richard. "Alternate Routes to Self-Realization in Ming Theories of Poetry." In *Theories of the Arts in China*, edited by Susan Bush and Christian Murck, 17–40. Princeton: Princeton University Press, 1983.

Mackerras, Colin. *Amateur Theatre in China, 1949–1966*. Canberra: Australian National University Press, 1973.

——. *The Rise of the Peking Opera, 1770–1870: Social Aspects of the Theatre in Manchu China*. Oxford: Clarendon Press, 1972.

McKenzie, D. F. *Bibliography and the Sociology of Texts*. London: The British Library, 1986.

McMahon, Keith. *Causality and Containment in Seventeenth Century Chinese Fiction*. Leiden: E. J. Brill, 1988.

Mark, Lindy Li. "The Role of Avocational Performers in the Preservation of Kunqu," *Chinoperl Papers* 15 (1990): 95–114.

——. "Kunju and Theatre in the Transvestite Novel, *Pinhua Baojian*," *Chinoperl Papers* 14 (1986): 37–59.

Mulligan, Jean. *The Lute, Kao Ming's P'i-p'a chi*. New York: Columbia University Press, 1980.

Nienhauser, William H. Jr., ed. and comp. *The Indiana Companion to Traditional Chinese Literature*. Bloomington, Indiana University Press, 1986.

Orgel, Stephen. "The Authentic Shakespeare," *Representations* 21 (1988): 1–25.

——. "What is a Text?" *Research Opportunities in Renaissance Drama* 24 (1981): 3–6.

Plaks, Andrew H. *Four Masterworks of the Ming Novel: Ssu ta ch'i shu*. Princeton: Princeton University Press, 1987.

Rockwell, John. "Love, Death and Resurrection, in and of *The Peony Pavilion*." *Kaikodo Journal* 15 (spring 2000):10–24.

Rolston, David. "Tradition and Innovation in Chen Shi-Zheng's *Peony Pavilion*." *Asian Theatre Journal* 19, no. 1 (spring 2002).

——. *Traditional Chinese Fiction and Fiction Commentary: Reading and Writing Between the Lines*. Stanford: Stanford University Press, 1997.

——, ed. *How to Read the Chinese Novel*. Princeton: Princeton University Press, 1990.

Roy, David Tod, trans. *The Plum in the Golden Vase, or Chin P'ing Mei*, Volume One: *The Gathering*. Princeton: Princeton University Press, 1993.

Sas, Miryam, "Le palimpseste des cultures, la transparence des souvenirs: l'Asie du Japon à Java." In *Peter Sellars*, edited by Frédéric Maurin. Paris: CNRS Éditions / Les Voies de la création théâtricale, forthcoming.

Satyendra, Indira Suh. "Toward A Poetics of the Chinese Novel: A Study of the Prefatory Poems in the 'Chin P'ing Mei Tz'u-hua.'" Ph.D. diss., University of Chicago, 1989.

Scott, A. C. *The Classical Theatre of China*. London: George Allen and Unwin Ltd., 1957.

Shen, Guangren Grant. "Acting in the Private Theatre of the Ming Dynasty." *Asian Theatre Journal* 15, no. 1 (spring 1998): 64–86.

——. "Theatre Performance During the Ming Dynasty." Ph.D. diss., University of Hawaii, 1994.

Sieber, Patricia. "Rhetoric, Romance, and Intertextuality: The Making and Remaking of Guan Hanqing in Yuan and Ming China." Ph.D. diss., University of California at Berkeley, 1994.

Siu Wang-Ngai and Peter Lovrick, comps. *Chinese Opera: Images and Stories*. Vancouver: University of British Columbia Press, 1997.

Stein, Rolf. *The World in Miniature: Container Gardens and Dwellings in Far Eastern Religious Thought*. Stanford: Stanford University Press, 1990.

Steinberg, Leo. "The Line of Fate in Michelangelo's Painting." In *The Language of Images*, edited by W. T. J. Mitchell, 85–128. Chicago: University of Chicago Press, 1980.

——. "The Metaphors of Love and Birth in Michelangelo's Pietas." In *Studies in Erotic Art*, edited by Theodore Bowie and Cornelia V. Christenson, 231–335. New York and London: Basic Books, 1970.

Strassberg, Richard."The Singing Techniques of *K'un-ch'ü* and their Musical Notation." *Chinoperl Papers* 6 (1976): 45–81.

Swatek, Catherine Crutchfield. "Plum and Portrait: Feng Menglong's Revision of *The Peony Pavilion*." *Asia Major*, 3d ser., 6, no. 1 (1993): 127–60.

——. "Feng Menglong's *Romantic Dream*: Strategies of Containment in his Revision of *The Peony Pavilion*." Ph.D. diss., Columbia University, 1990.

Trousdell, Richard. "Peter Sellars Rehearses *Figaro*." *The Drama Review* 35, no. 1 (1991): 66–89.

Vinograd, Richard. *Boundaries of the Self: Chinese Portraits, 1600–1900*. Cambridge: Cambridge University Press, 1992.

West, Stephen H. "A Study in Appropriation: Zang Maoxun's Injustice to Dou E." *Journal of the American Oriental Society* 111, no. 2 (1991): 283–302.

——. "Drama." In *The Indiana Companion to Traditional Chinese Literature*, edited by William H. Nienhauser Jr., 13–30. Bloomington: Indiana University Press, 1986.

West, Stephen H., and Wilt L. Idema, trans. *The Moon and the Zither: The Story of the Western Wing*. Berkeley: University of California Press, 1991.

Wichmann, Elizabeth. *Listening to Theater*. Honolulu: University of Hawaii Press, 1991.

Widmer, Ellen. "Xiaoqing's Literary Legacy and the Place of the Woman Writer in Late Imperial China." *Late Imperial China* 13.1 (June 1992): 111–55.

Wong, Isabel. "The Printed Collections of *K'un-ch'ü* Arias and their Sources." *Chinoperl Papers* 8 (1978): 100–29.

Wu Hung. *The Double Screen: Medium and Representation in Chinese Painting*. Chicago: University of Chicago Press, 1996.

Yao Dajuin. "The Pleasure of Reading Drama: Illustrations to the Hongzhi Edition of *The Story of the Western Wing*." In *The Moon and the Zither: The Story of the Western Wing*, translated by Stephen H. West and Wilt L. Idema, 437–68. Berkeley: University of California Press, 1991.

Yung, Sai-shing. "A Critical Study of *Han-tan chi*." Ph.D. diss., Princeton University, 1992.

Zeitlin, Judith, T. "My Year of Peonies." *Asian Theatre Journal* 19, no. 1 (spring 2002).

——. "Making the Invisible Visible: Images of Desire and Constructions of the Female Body in Chinese Literature, Medicine, and Art." In *Crossing Boundaries: Attending to Early Modern Women*, edited by Jane Donawerth and Adele F. Seeff, 48–79. Newark: University of Delaware Press, 2001.

——. "Shared Dreams: The Story of the Three Wives' Commentary on *The Peony Pavilion*." *Harvard Journal of Asiatic Studies* 54, no. 1 (1994): 127–79.

Index

1. Scenes from *Mudan ting* and the adaptations by Zang Maoxun and Feng Menglong are indexed by their translated titles. Scenes from the adaptations are listed as subentries under the heading of the original scene from *Mudan ting*. Extracts (*zhezixi*) of the scene then follow, and are arranged chronologically according to the date of the source in which they can be found, if one can be identified.

2. Scenes from the international productions of the play are listed as separate entries, by their translated titles.

3. With a few exceptions (e.g., *Thousand-character text*), Chinese works are indexed by their romanized titles.